W9-ATM-434

CONSUMER ADVISER

READER'S DIGEST

CONSUMER ADVISER

An Action Guide to Your Rights

The Reader's Digest Association, Inc.
Pleasantville, New York • Montreal

CONSUMER ADVISER

Edited by Maxwell Associates
with the editors of The Reader's Digest Association, Inc.

Editor James A. Maxwell

Senior Staff Editor Nancy E. Gross

Senior Editors Peter M. Chaitin
Lynne Rogers

Research Editors Rosemarie Conefrey
Harriet Heck
Rosanne M. Morey
Estelle Steinberg

Copy Editors Elaine P. Adam
Charlotte Mosenthal

Editorial Assistants Francine Caroll
Caryl Ehrlich

Designer Perri DeFino

Chief Consultant Edward B. Cohen
of the law offices of Davis,
Wright, Todd, Reise & Jones

CAUTION: The editors have used the most up-to-date information in preparing this volume. However, laws and regulations change, and consumer programs described in this book may be discontinued or expanded. Before using this information, be sure to check its validity with the offices or agencies listed in the various chapters.

Library of Congress Cataloging in Publication Data
Main entry under title:

Consumer Adviser.

Includes index.
1. Consumer education. I. Reader's Digest Association.
II. Reader's digest.
TX335.C638 1984 640.73 84-2044
ISBN 0-89577-180-2

Printed in the United States of America

About This Book

For generations, American consumers were in the same helpless position in the marketplace as Charles Atlas' "97-pound weakling" was on the beach. When they were the victims of shady businessmen or charlatans, there was little to be done but shrug and resolve to be more careful in the future. *Caveat emptor*, "Let the buyer beware," more or less ruled all commercial transactions.

Starting in the late 19th century, laws were passed to guard the public from the worst offenders. But it was not until the last several decades that consumers have gained the legal and economic muscles to fight back effectively when basic rights are abused or ignored.

New and strengthened federal and state laws, militant consumer movements, help from the communications media, even enlightened self-interest measures by a number of businesses have given buyers a power they never had before. Obviously, the situation is still not Utopian; some sellers of goods and services continue to kick sand in the faces of their customers. But now retaliation is far more likely than ever before. Consumers who receive shoddy merchandise or pay for work poorly done, or not done at all, can counterattack, often with the assistance of strong governmental and civilian allies. And each buyer who enters the fray in a just cause strengthens the consumer movement.

But this capacity for retribution does not — and probably never will — deter everyone who wants to part you from your money. There will always be advertisers who will promise you almost anything during a sales pitch; conmen who view consumers as game that never goes out of season; merchants who refuse to honor warranties; and a host of others who bilk the public in various ways.

In short, there are two requirements for your being an effective, get-your-money's-worth consumer in today's market: first, to be a careful, informed, questioning buyer who accepts little or nothing on faith; second, to be a determined activist who uses fully the economic and legal muscle you now have to fight back when your rights are violated.

This book deals with both components. *Consumer Adviser* is designed to do just what the title implies — to offer guidance in almost every area in which you spend your money. You will find hundreds of ways to cut costs. You will learn to be a sophisticated shopper whether you are visiting a supermarket, buying a household appliance, seeking a loan, considering investments, purchasing insurance, selecting a doctor, lawyer or other professional, dickering for a house or renting an apartment, bargaining for an automobile, planning a vacation or utilizing credit. You will find how misleading advertising can tempt you to make wrong decisions. Pitfalls in numerous fields are clearly mapped.

But if, despite precautions, you do become the victim of unethical or fraudulent practice, *Consumer Adviser* will show you how to retaliate with maximum effect. Civil courts were once about the only avenue of redress for the buyer, but following this route often cost more than the amount in question. Consumers can now take action in numerous other ways with minimal, or no outlay of money. Step-by-step procedures are clearly outlined.

Here is a sampling of how this book will help you:

- if you want to return an item to the store, see page 332
- if you want to write an effective letter of complaint, see page 333
- if a computer repeatedly bills you for something you never ordered, see page 334
- if you want to cancel a door-to-door purchase, see page 336
- if a brand-new major appliance keeps breaking down but the dealer refuses to take responsibility for repairs , see page 339
- if you cannot resolve new car problems with the dealer, see page 339
- if a manufacturer won't make good on a piece of damaged furniture, see page 341
- if you have a problem with a funeral director, see page 341
- if you have a complaint against a moving company, see page 341
- if a mail-order company refuses to honor its policies, see page 342
- if you have a problem with your home computer or any other piece of electronic equipment, see page 343
- if your new house develops a major structural defect, see page 343
- if you sign up for a magazine subscription but it never arrives, see page 344
- if you have a complaint against a doctor, dentist, or lawyer that you have not resolved by direct discussion, see pages 345, 346, 347
- if you have been denied payment on a medical claim, see page 346
- if your complaint — whatever it's about — falls on deaf ears, see pages 348-352

President Theodore Roosevelt was speaking of foreign policy when he advised the nation to "speak softly but carry a big stick." *Consumer Adviser* offers somewhat the same counsel to buyers of goods and services: "Shop wisely but don't forget you *have* a big stick."

The Editors

Contents

Chapter 1

"Let the Buyer Beware" Versus "The Customer Is Always Right"

"Let the buyer beware" — the English translation of the Latin phrase *caveat emptor* — is a time-honored legal doctrine that for centuries governed most transactions in the marketplace. If you bought a defective pair of shoes and could not persuade the cobbler to repair or exchange them, or return your money, you had no option but to accept the situation. After all, you had your chance to examine the shoes carefully before buying them.

The doctrine — in reality less harsh than it sounds — first came into force in ancient times, when trade was a relatively minor aspect of the economy and often involved no more than barter. Moreover, because communities were small, buyers and sellers were friends and neighbors who often exchanged roles. The cobbler who sold you a pair of shoes might be the same person who bought your cloth. So when you showed up at the cobbler's door with a defective shoe in your hand, you could be reasonably confident that he'd quickly take some remedial action to set things right.

Still, even in ancient times, there doubtless were some merchants who had no scruples about cheating their customers. We have no legal records about them, but we do have evidence that, by the Middle Ages, cheating by tradesmen had become a fairly serious problem. Bakers in England, for example, were so notorious for shortweighting the bread they sold and for using inferior flour that the *caveat emptor* doctrine was modified somewhat by the passage in 1202 of a law regulating the price of a loaf both in relation to its weight and to the quality of the flour from which it was made. Those convicted of violating this statute were subjected to penalties that were demeaning, at the very least. The court sentenced one London baker to be carried in a special prisoner's wagon "from the Guildhall to his own house, through the great streets, where there may be most people assembled and through the great streets that are most dirty, with the faulty loaf hanging from his neck."

As the economic system became more complex and barter played a lesser role, buyer-seller relationships took on a greater importance. Although the *caveat emptor* doctrine did not disappear entirely, the nature of the new economic system gave buyers an advantage they had not had before. After all, the marketplace is the single most important part of a competitive, free-enterprise system, and that marketplace has only one objective: to sell goods and services to consumers. In such a situation, the consumer becomes the final authority in all transactions. By voting with his or her pocketbook, the buyer determines the success or failure of those with goods or services to sell. It is, therefore, in the seller's self-interest to please the consumer — to deliver the best possible goods or services at the best possible prices. Those who fail to do so can be pretty sure of losing customers.

This concept of consumer sovereignty finds popular expression in the old business slogan, "The customer is always right," and it explains, as well, the rule laid down by Adam Smith, the father of free-enterprise capitalism, whose great work, *An Inquiry into the Nature and Causes of the Wealth of Nations*, was published in the same year the Declaration of Independence was signed. "The interest of the producer," Smith wrote, "ought to be attended to only so far as it may be necessary for promoting that of the consumer."

But if in theory the customer was always right, in the real world, he often got the short end of the stick. Enlightened self-interest may have been an adequate motive for the honest merchant to remain honest and, in general, customers could fairly well rely on those with whom they dealt. But the law was still largely based on *caveat emptor* and, with no strong legal deterrents, cheats felt quite free to continue cheating.

Cons, Frauds and Robber Barons

In this country, the middle and late years of the 19th century were the heyday of consumer fraud. Clever con men — and there were plenty of them — would, for example, place advertisements in local newspapers offering "complete sewing machines" and steel engraved portraits of General Ulysses S. Grant for 25 cents each. Even in those bygone days, when $5 was a more than respectable weekly salary, such offers seemed genuine bargains, and thousands of people sent in their quarters by mail. All of them got something in return: those who had ordered sewing machines got penny packets of ordinary needles and those who had ordered the steel engraving got penny stamps — the postage denomination that was graced with the portrait of the former President.

Such frauds were not the only ones regularly perpetrated on a gullible public. Medicines were an especially lucrative field. Americans pursued good health as avidly as they pursued bargains, and no laws restrained the traveling medicine show or other dispensers of patent medicines and miracle cures. *Dr. Williams' Pink Pills for Pale People; Piso's Cure for Consumption; Seroco Specific for the Tobacco Habit* — these and hundreds of other fake remedies with equally misleading and mellifluous names made rich men of those who sold them and did their purchasers no good whatever. The best of such products were merely useless; the worst — which often contained liberal quantities of alcohol or opium — were downright dangerous.

Equally dangerous were the activities of some of the nation's most powerful captains of industry. The United States was still a young country, with great tracts of virgin land and apparently limitless natural resources. The country cried out for development, and enterprising businessmen of all stripes were quick to answer the call. But in their rush to take advantage of the opportunities presented to them, some — the so-called robber barons — engaged in practices harmful both to the economic health of the nation and of its citizens. By combining and controlling virtually all aspects of certain basic industries — oil and cattle feed, for example — the great trusts that were formed towards the end of the 19th century put a stranglehold on major sections of the economy and made a mockery of the free-enterprise system on which the nation was founded. The trusts destroyed competition, monopolized entire industries, and fixed the price consumers had to pay for vital commodities.

Moreover, as the novelist Upton Sinclair documented in his book *The Jungle*, published in 1906, the country's huge meat packing industry was jeopardizing the very lives of consumers. Conditions in the main slaughterhouses and meat-processing plants were often appalling. The rules of hygiene and sanitation were ignored completely; sick cattle were slaughtered along with the healthy, and even sick animals that died without slaughtering were processed for human consumption and placed on the market.

The Birth of Consumer Protection

Public outrage gradually forced the federal government to take action against some of these practices. In 1872, Congress passed the nation's first consumer protection law empowering the postmaster general to investigate and prosecute mail-order frauds. In 1890, the Sherman Antitrust Law outlawed "every contract, combination in the form of trust or otherwise, or conspiracy in restraint of trade or commerce," and an antitrust division was subsequently established in the Department of Justice to enforce this law. The year 1906 saw the passage of the Pure Food and Drug Law, initially designed to ban the sale of adulterated and fraudulently labeled foods, later amended to provide government inspection of slaughterhouses and meat-processing plants and, still later, amended to ban patent medicines carrying exaggerated claims.

Principal Federal Consumer Protection Agencies and What They Do

Consumer Product Safety Commission
Mandate: To establish and enforce safety standards and oversee safety-related product recalls for common household products.
Jurisdiction: Appliances, home furnishings, toys and other household products; flammability standards for carpets, children's sleepwear and other clothing; and packaging of medicines and hazardous household products.

Environmental Protection Agency
Mandate: To protect and enhance the environment by controlling pollution in the air and water.
Jurisdiction: Pesticides and herbicides; the disposal of toxic wastes; automobile and factory emissions; noise reduction standards.

Federal Reserve System
Mandate: To establish regulations governing equal credit opportunity, home mortgage disclosure, fair credit billing.
Jurisdiction: All Federal Reserve Banks and member banks.

Federal Trade Commission
Mandate: To protect the free-enterprise system against any encroachments by monopolies, restraints of trade and unfair and deceptive trade practices.
Jurisdiction: Prevention of general trade restraints in interstate commerce (such as price fixing, boycotts or illegal mergers); warranties for all kinds of consumer products; unfair or deceptive advertising, marketing or credit practices; truthful packaging and labeling of products; trademarks; labeling of wool, fur and textile products.

Food and Drug Administration
Mandate: To protect the nation's health against impure and unsafe drugs, foods, and cosmetics, medical devices, and radiation-producing products.
Jurisdiction: Approval of the safety, effectiveness and labeling of prescription and non-prescription drugs; approval of the safety of certain foods, food additives and colors, and cosmetics; regulation of biological products; approval of certain medical and radiological devices.

Food Safety and Quality Service
Mandate: To assure the safety of all meat, poultry and related products.
Jurisdiction: Inspection of poultry and livestock at slaughterhouses; inspection of meat-processing plants and their products; grading standards for foods and food products; National School Lunch Program.

National Highway Traffic Safety Administration
Mandate: To assure the safety and fuel economy performance of motor vehicles and motor vehicle equipment and to oversee safety-related motor vehicle recalls.
Jurisdiction: Establish standards for fuel economy, safety and damageability (bumper) for all domestic and imported motor vehicles.

United States Postal Inspection Service
Mandate: To enforce mail fraud laws.
Jurisdiction: All offers of merchandise, services etc., made through the mail.

United States Attorney General's Office
Mandate: To enforce antitrust legislation, act as legal representative of U.S. government agencies.

In time, these early laws were amended to broaden their scope, and new laws were passed that strengthened existing protections and provided new ones. In addition, regulatory agencies were established within the federal government to carry out the provisions of the laws and to assure their enforcement by the courts.

The Sherman Antitrust Law, for example, had proved less than effective in dealing with some of the abuses it was designed to correct. It contained no provisions to guard against such monopolistic practices as price fixing, and it made no provision for adequate enforcement. In an attempt to close these loopholes, Congress in 1914 passed the Clayton Antitrust Act, and in 1915, the Federal Trade Commission was established as an independent agency to keep U.S. business competition free and fair.

Similarly, the Food and Drug Administration was established in 1931 to carry out the government's obligations under the Pure Food and Drug Law, which itself had been amended and strengthened several times. (Even so, these statutes were weak by current standards.)

The disastrous stock market crash of 1929 and the numerous bank failures that followed led to government recognition that federal regulations and programs were also required to protect Americans' savings and investments. The collapse of great fortunes may have been the most dramatic effect of the crash, but ordinary citizens, as well as millionaires, had invested in the stock market and they, too, were wiped out. In addition, many of those who had deposited their money in the presumably safe banks were also destroyed financially.

During the Great Depression, a third of the banks failed and millions of depositors suffered severe losses.

After the crash, one-third of all these banking institutions failed, partly because panic had sent depositors running to retrieve their money and partly because the banks themselves had lent enormous sums on dubious securities during the boom that came before the crash.

In 1933, the Federal Deposit Insurance Corporation (FDIC) was established to insure savings in all banks belonging to the Federal Reserve System; in 1934, the Federal Savings and Loan Insurance Corporation (FSLIC) was formed to protect deposits in savings and loan institutions. In the same year, the Securities and Exchange Commission (SEC) was formed, to supervise all stocks and bonds offered for public sale.

Consumer Protection Comes of Age

If one were to assign a date to the birth of the modern consumer protection movement, it would have to be March 15, 1962, when President John F. Kennedy sent a message to Congress. The years since World War II, the President pointed out, had seen dramatic changes in American society: "The march of technology — affecting, for example, the foods we eat, the medicines we take, and the many appliances we use in our homes — has increased the difficulties of the consumer along with his opportunities. . . . The typical supermarket before World War II stocked about 1,500 separate food items — an impressive figure by any standard. But today it carries over 6,000. Ninety percent of the prescriptions written today are for drugs that were unknown 20 years ago. Many of the new products used every day in the home are highly complex. The housewife is called upon to be an amateur electrician, mechanic, chemist, toxicologist, dietitian and mathematician — but she is rarely furnished the information she needs to perform these tasks proficiently.

"Marketing is increasingly impersonal. Consumer choice is influenced by mass advertising utilizing highly developed arts of persuasion. The consumer typically cannot know whether drug preparations meet minimum standards of safety, quality and efficacy. He usually does not know how much he pays for consumer credit; whether one prepared food has more nutritional value than another; whether the performance of a product will in fact meet his needs; or whether the 'large economy size' is really a bargain. . . ."

No president had ever before devoted such detailed attention to the problems of consumers — or put forth such detailed goals for Congress to meet in dealing with them. The very uniqueness of his message gave it powerful significance. By the simple act of focusing on the importance of consumer protection, President Kennedy placed the issue squarely on the national agenda and elevated it to a matter of national concern.

His proposals led, in time, to the passage of a number of important new federal consumer protection measures that broadened the scope of the FDA, regulated credit practices, established content labeling for a variety of products, and set safety standards for all kinds of products, from medicine containers to auto-

CONSUMER ALERT

The U.S. Office of Consumer Affairs

One of the first federal agencies established in 1964 to help achieve the provisions of the Consumer Bill of Rights was the President's Committee on Consumer Interests. It was later renamed U.S. Office of Consumer Affairs (OCA). The OCA is designed to ensure the consumers' right to be heard and to make certain that consumers' interests are taken into account when government policy is formulated and carried out.

Mandated specifically to "encourage and assist in the development and implementation of consumer programs, coordinate and review them, seek resolution of conflicts and advise agencies on the effectiveness of their consumer programs," the OCA is part of the executive branch of government and is headed by a special assistant to the president. It acts to:

- Improve and coordinate the consumer education programs of federal, state and local governments.
- Encourage the development of voluntary consumer protection and information programs by business and industry.
- Provide federal agencies with consumer perspectives.
- Provide consumer information to the public. (Currently available, at no cost, is the *Consumers' Resource Handbook*, which explains how to complain effectively and where to find help in resolving complaints. To receive a copy, write to "Handbook," Consumer Information Center, Pueblo, CO 81009.

  Also available is a free bimonthly consumer newsletter, *Consumer News*. You can ask to be put on the mailing list by writing to the Office of Consumer Affairs, Washington, DC 20201.)
- Provide technical assistance to state and local consumer offices, congressional staffs and businesses on the most effective ways to resolve consumer complaints. (Note that the federal OCA does not itself deal with individual complaints; these are handled by state and local consumer affairs offices — or, in cases where no such offices exist, by consumer affairs divisions within the offices of the attorneys general. On page 16 you will find a state-by-state directory of such offices.)
- Coordinate the Federal Consumer Affairs Council, a committee made up of high-level representatives of all the major federal agencies, which is responsible for assuring that consumers' needs and interests are taken into consideration in all the agencies' activities.

mobiles. In addition, the force of presidential leadership served to encourage the states to enact consumer protection measures of their own and further inspired them to establish their own enforcement agencies. (These will be discussed in the chapters devoted to the specific products, services and practices to which the legislation applies.)

But the Kennedy message did more. It stimulated the development of more effective self-policing systems by businesses and professions, and awakened the mass media — radio, television and the press — to their responsibility for serving consumers' needs.

Perhaps most important of all was the effect of the message on consumers themselves. It gave them a stronger sense of their power, an increased awareness of their rights and a strengthened determination to act on their own behalf. And it brought home forcefully their need to prepare and educate themselves to deal more effectively with today's complex marketplace.

The Consumer Bill of Rights

The heart of the Kennedy message lay in the four goals he outlined, which have become known as the Consumer Bill of Rights:

1) The right to safety — to be protected against the marketing of goods that are hazardous to health or life.

2) The right to be informed — to be protected against fraudulent, deceitful or grossly misleading information, advertising, labeling or other practices, and to be given the facts the consumer needs to make an informed choice.

3) The right to choose — to be assured, wherever possible, of access to a variety of products and services at competitive prices; and in those industries in which competition is not workable and government regulation is substituted, an assurance of satisfactory quality and service at fair prices.

4) The right to be heard — to be assured that consumer interests will receive full and sympathetic consideration in the formulation of government policy, and fair and expeditious treatment in its administrative tribunals.

The federal agencies that guard these rights are shown in the chart on page 11, which indicates the specific jurisdiction of each agency and the specific laws it is designed to implement and enforce.

Non-governmental Guardians of Consumers' Rights

The government and its agencies are not the only guardians of consumers' rights. Indeed, the government sometimes takes action only after it has been sharply prodded by crusading individuals and organizations. Just as Sinclair's *The Jungle* sparked passage of the Food and Drug Law, so Ralph Nader's book *Unsafe at Any Speed*, published in 1965, played a major role in the passage of The National Traffic and Motor Vehicle Safety Law in 1966.

But the mere existence of a consumer protection law or agency does not automatically guarantee that the law will be enforced or the agency mandate carried out. If only for this reason, such groups as the Consumer Federation of America and Consumers Union perform vital functions: they serve as watchdogs and lobbyists for consumer interests.

Increasingly, these functions are also being served by the consumer reporter-advocates of the mass media, whose ability to reach into millions of homes and thus mold public opinion gives them a power exceeded only by that of the government itself. The year 1979 provided a heartwarming example of the positive results this power can achieve.

At that time, the consumer reporter for a Washington, D.C. television station joined forces with two young mothers, both of whose babies had been made ill by a particular formula. At the time, the FDA had no authority over infant formulas, and although this one had been recalled by its maker, it was still available in many stores and there was every reason to be concerned that it would make other babies ill, too. The story was documented and exposed on the air, and the resultant publicity was a major factor in the passage of the Infant Formula Act of 1980, which regulates the manufacture and marketing of infant formulas.

Reputable businessmen and manufacturers also have strong motives for protecting consumers. Manufacturers who need product liability insurance, for example, can only obtain it if their merchandise lives up to the safety specifications established by insurers. For instance, the cords of many common electric appliances — irons, toasters, blenders — bear a tag which says "UL Tested" on it: this signifies that the manufacturer has voluntarily had the product checked for safety by the Underwriters' Laboratory, an independent testing agency. Enlightened owners of retail businesses usually recognize that it is in their real interest to satisfy their customers and to live up to consumer protection standards, since the effort pays off in increased good will.

Such motives of self-interest are not the only ones that keep business in line. Professional and trade organizations and the local chambers of commerce are, by their nature, eager to protect the good names of those they represent. They are usually alert to their members' practices, and can and do exert pressure to see that standards are maintained. The Better Business Bureau (BBB), for example, was originally founded shortly after the turn of the century by reputable advertising men who were concerned about the deceptive and dishonest advertising that was common at the time and were determined to combat it. It was, as a matter of fact, largely through their efforts that a series of so-called "Printer's Ink" statutes were passed in most states outlawing dishonest advertising. Even today, the BBB monitors advertising carefully. In every city in which it has an office, the staff regularly checks local advertisements for honesty, and sends shoppers to investigate those that are suspect. When a shopper finds the facts in a situation to be at variance with the advertising claims, the owner of the establishment is asked to alter or withdraw the offensive material.

Local BBB offices perform other functions for consumers, as well. They keep extensive files on business firms in their areas and can provide basic information on how long they have been in operation; what their record is in handling complaints; and how often complaints have been made about them. In addition, the Bureau acts for consumers in complaints involving misrepresentation or faulty service, interceding with businesses that have not been responsive to the problems of the buyer.

But the Better Business Bureau is not the only guardian of consumer interests in the business community. The automobile, furniture and major appliance industries, all of which produce goods that represent significant investments for buyers, have organized voluntary Consumer Action Panels, as have the nation's funeral directors. These CAPs, as they are called, are made up of consumer representatives and members of the industries involved, and their function is to deal with complaints consumers have not been able to resolve on their own. The CAPs' decisions are not legally binding, but industry members generally abide by them, even when they are in the consumers' favor.

BBB checks the ads for honesty, and "shoppers" visit advertisers whose claims seem too good to be true.

Other industry organizations and trade associations also take an active role in resolving consumer complaints. In Minneapolis, for example, the dry cleaning industry has volunteered the services of experts to the local small claims court, where they act as expert witnesses. On regularly scheduled "Dry Cleaning Days," the experts appear in court to examine the goods consumers have complained about and to testify as to whether the work is up to industry standards. Similarly, the automobile repair industry in Philadelphia has formed an Automotive Technical Assistance Panel; for a nominal fee, AUTO-TAP, as it is called, will examine repair work consumers have called into question, and testify about it.

The Educated Consumer

A large East Coast retail clothing chain has a slogan: "An educated consumer is our best customer." That slogan should hold true for every honest merchant, manufacturer and purveyor of services. Slightly rewritten, it holds true for every consumer: "An educated consumer is his or her own best friend."

True, *caveat emptor* no longer dominates the marketplace. Over the years, courts and legislatures have steadily chipped away at it. But the motto still serves to protect sellers from frivolous complaints. However, courts today also uphold the doctrine of "implied warranty of merchantability," which gives customers the right to expect that the goods they buy will satisfactorily perform the functions for which they were designed, even without a written warranty. A knife must cut; an electric bulb must light; a camera must take pictures. If the item does not perform its basic function, the buyer has an inherent right to satisfaction.

Moreover, as we have seen, a large number of federal laws and regulations — and state and municipal laws and regulations as well — guard consumers in their daily dealings, and act as deterrents to merchants or businessmen who might otherwise be tempted to take advantage of their customers. And if the deterrents do not work, the law is always available to consumers who have been ill-used. Small claims courts, in which consumers can appear without lawyers, handle suits involving relatively small amounts of money (the specific amounts permitted vary from jurisdiction to jurisdiction); civil courts provide a forum for complaints in which larger sums are involved; and a number of other legal and quasi-legal procedures have also been established to provide redress for injured consumers. We will be discussing all these in detail later in the book.

Still, valuable as all these mechanisms are, the consumer's best protection is knowledge of his or her rights. At the least, it is frustrating and time-consuming to have to go to court; if you have to have a lawyer, it will be expensive, as well. Knowledge of your rights will not protect you against the minor irritations that have become an almost inevitable part of our lives as consumers — your new refrigerator may arrive chipped; your credit card company may accuse you of not paying a bill for

(continued on page 18)

State Offices of Consumer Affairs

Alabama
Consumer Protection Division
Office of Attorney General
560 South McDonough Street
Montgomery, AL 36104

Alaska
Consumer Protection Center
Office of Attorney General
1049 West Fifth Avenue
Anchorage, AK 99501

Arizona
Financial Fraud Division
Office of Attorney General
207 State Capitol Building
Phoenix, AZ 85007

Arkansas
Consumer Protection Division
Office of Attorney General
Justice Building
Little Rock, AR 72201

California
California Department of Consumer Affairs
1020 N Street
Sacramento, CA 95814

Colorado
Antitrust and Consumer Protection Enforcement Section
Office of Attorney General
1525 Sherman Street, 2nd Floor
Denver, CO 80203

Connecticut
Department of Consumer Protection
State Office Building
165 Capitol Avenue
Hartford, CT 06115

Delaware
Delaware Division of Consumer Affairs
820 N. French Street, 4th Floor
Wilmington, DE 19801

District of Columbia
Office of Consumer Protection
1424 K Street, N.W., 2nd Floor
Washington, DC 20005

Florida
Division of Consumer Services
110 Mayo Building
Tallahassee, FL 32304

Georgia
Governor's Office of Consumer Affairs
205 Butler Street, S.E., Suite 356
Atlanta, GA 30334

Hawaii
Governor's Office of Consumer Protection
250 South King Street
P.O. Box 3707
Honolulu, HI 96812

Idaho
Business Regulation Division
Office of Attorney General
State Capitol
Boise, ID 83720

Illinois
Consumer Protection Division
Office of Attorney General
500 South Second Street
Springfield, IL 62706

Indiana
Consumer Protection Division
Office of Attorney General
219 State House
Indianapolis, IN 46204

Iowa
Consumer Protection Division
Office of Attorney General
1300 East Walnut, 2nd Floor
Des Moines, IA 50319

Kansas
Office of Attorney General
Kansas Judicial Center, 2nd Floor
Topeka, KS 66612

Kentucky
Consumer Protection Division
Office of Attorney General
209 St. Clair Street
Frankfort, KY 40601

Louisiana
State Office of Consumer Protection
2610A Woodale Boulevard
P.O. Box 44091, Capitol Station
Baton Rouge, LA 70804

Maine
Bureau of Consumer Protection
Department of Business Regulation
State House Station No. 35
Augusta, ME 04333

Maryland
Consumer Protection Division
Office of Attorney General
26 South Calvert Street
Baltimore, MD 21202

Massachusetts
Executive Office of Consumer Affairs
John W. McCormack Building
One Ashburton Place, Room 1411
Boston, MA 02108

Michigan
Consumer Protection Division
Office of Attorney General
690 Law Building
Lansing, MI 48913

Minnesota
Minnesota Office of Consumer Services
128 Metro Square Building
Seventh and Roberts Streets
St. Paul, MN 55101

Mississippi
Consumer Protection Division
Office of Attorney General
P.O. Box 220
Jackson, MS 39205

Missouri
Missouri Department of Consumer Affairs, Regulation, and Licensing
P.O. Box 1157
Jefferson City, MO 65102

Montana
Consumer Affairs Unit
Department of Commerce
1424 Ninth Avenue
Helena, MT 59620

Nebraska
Consumer Protection Division
Department of Justice
605 South 14th Street
Lincoln, NE 68509

Nevada
Consumer Affairs Division
Department of Commerce
2501 East Sahara Avenue
Las Vegas, NV 89158

New Hampshire
Consumer Protection and Antitrust Division
Office of Attorney General
State House Annex
Concord, NH 03301

New Jersey
New Jersey Office of Consumer Protection
1100 Raymond Boulevard, Room 405
Newark, NJ 07102

New Mexico
Consumer and Economic Crime Division
Office of Attorney General
P.O. Box 1508
Santa Fe, NM 87503

New York
New York State Consumer Protection Board
99 Washington Avenue
Albany, NY 12210

North Carolina
Consumer Protection Division
Department of Justice Building
P.O. Box 629
Raleigh, NC 27602

Ohio
Office of Attorney General
30 East Broad Street
Columbus, OH 43215

Oklahoma
Office of Attorney General
112 State Capitol Building
Oklahoma City, OK 73105

Oregon
Consumer Protection and Services Division
Department of Justice
500 Pacific Building
520 SW Yamhill Street
Portland, OR 97204

Pennsylvania
Bureau of Consumer Protection
Office of Attorney General
Strawberry Square, 15th Floor
Harrisburg, PA 17120

Rhode Island
Department of Attorney General
72 Pine Street
Providence, RI 02903

South Carolina
Department of Consumer Affairs
2221 Devine Street,
P.O. Box 5757
Columbia, SC 29250

South Dakota
Division of Consumer Protection
Office of Attorney General
Insurance Building
Pierre, SD 57501

Tennessee
Antitrust and Consumer Protection Division
Office of Attorney General
450 James Robertson Parkway
Nashville, TN 37219

Texas
Consumer Protection and Antitrust Division
Office of Attorney General
P.O. Box 12548, Capitol Station
Austin, TX 78711

Utah
Office of Attorney General
419 Boston Building
Salt Lake City, UT 84111

Vermont
Consumer Protection Division
Office of Attorney General
109 State Street
Montpelier, VT 05602

Virginia
State Office of Consumer Affairs
Department of Agriculture and Consumer Services
Box 1163, Washington Boulevard
Richmond, VA 23209

Washington
Consumer Protection and Antitrust Division
Office of Attorney General
1366 Dexter Horton Building
Seattle, WA 98104

West Virginia
Consumer Protection Division
Office of Attorney General
3412 Staunton Avenue, SE
Charleston, WV 25304

Wisconsin
Assistant Attorney General
Office of Consumer Protection
Department of Justice
P.O. Box 7856
Madison, WI 53707

Wyoming
Assistant Attorney General
Office of Attorney General
123 Capitol Building
Cheyenne, WY 82002

Puerto Rico
Department of Consumer Affairs
Minillas Governmental Center
Torre Norte Building
De Diego Avenue, Stop 22
P.O. Box 41059
Santurce, PR 00940

U.S. Virgin Islands
Consumer Services Administration
Golden Rock
Christiansted, St. Croix
U.S. VI 00820

which you already have a canceled check; the utility company may read your meter incorrectly and bill you for an outrageous sum. But even in these cases, the more you know, the more efficiently you can deal with the problem. For example, you can probably get a price break on the refrigerator — and one that's large enough to make up for the chip. You can save yourself the expense and bother of a fruitless telephone call by mailing a photocopy of your canceled check to the credit card company. You can deal with the overcharge in your utility bill by paying the usual amount and noting on your payment the reason you have not paid the amount of the bill. The mistake will probably be corrected the next time the meter is read.

But knowledge of your rights is not always an effective protection in cases of outright consumer fraud. The law may not be able to find the con men whose mail order schemes bilk the unwary. For example, the advertisement that promises a fantastic sum of money for work-at-home arrangements — such as selling books or greeting cards or addressing envelopes — may never bring a cent. Operators of such schemes are usually agile escape artists, expert at evading the law by simply going into bankruptcy or temporarily folding up their businesses. And if they are arrested, your only satisfaction may lie in seeing that justice is done. The courts may send the miscreants to jail for mail fraud, but that will neither get you back your money nor restore the time you have wasted.

But if knowledge of your rights cannot protect you from the honest mistakes that honest businesses make (or from the "computer errors" that bedevil all of us today) and cannot assure you of recompense if you have fallen victim to a scam, knowledge *can* provide you with enormously valuable tools. It can help you distinguish between a scam and an error, between high-pressure salesmanship and get-rich-quick schemes on the one hand and honest merchandising on the other. Knowledge can guide you in all your buying, whether of large or small items; help you take advantage of bargains; teach you what to look for before you make a purchase; show you how to complain effectively and how to resolve complaints in the quickest, least expensive and least frustrating way.

And even if knowledge cannot save you from small annoyances, it *can* save you from making major mistakes. It can, in short, make you an educated consumer — not just your own best friend, but the best friend of every honest merchant.

Conveying consumer knowledge is the purpose of this book, for your sake and for the sake of that vast majority of American businessmen and professionals who are both reputable and responsible.

Chapter 2

Look Before You Leap

As the title of this chapter suggests, a consumer's life does have its perils. In the American economy, the most varied and complex the world has ever known, producers of goods from toys to limousines and sellers of services from car washes to Caribbean cruises are all busy contending for your money. They want you to buy — and from them, not their competitors — and toward that end they use every form of persuasion at their command: clever advertising, attractive packaging, free offers, premiums, discounts, layaway plans, "as-is" sales and rebates, to say nothing of skillful personal salesmanship.

Competition, of course, is an essential element of the free-enterprise system. In vying for the consumer's dollar, manufacturers and merchants are forced to keep on their toes, and consumers often reap the benefit in improved goods and services and lower prices. But competition also carries hazards for the unwary consumer. American business has made a high art of marketing — of dazzling and beguiling the buying public. "Sell the sizzle, not the steak" is an old maxim that marketing professionals still follow. But no sizzle, however tantalizing and attractive, can supply any nutritive value. For that, we need the steak. So it is important that we learn to distinguish between them. If we are to get what we want for our money, we must have at least a nodding acquaintance with modern marketing and advertising techniques. In this chapter, we offer you that acquaintanceship, so that you do not find yourself manipulated by slick and calculated blandishments.

Advertising

Advertising is a $60-billion-a-year business in this country — $60 billion spent solely for the purpose of getting you to buy. It grew to that gargantuan size from very small beginnings. If, as Webster's dictionary says, advertising is "the action of calling something to the attention of the public, especially by paid announcements," it is an ancient practice. Archeologists have discovered ads that date back as far as 1000 B.C. — commercial messages painted on prominent rocks along the shipping lanes used by the Phoenicians, prosperous seafaring traders of the eastern Mediterranean. Shops in ancient Pompeii had signs advertising their wares. Advertising even played a role in the settlement of the American colonies. Many a Briton set sail across the Atlantic after reading handbills describing opportunities in the New World.

For nearly 300 years thereafter, print remained the major medium through which those with goods to advertise got their messages across. But then, in the early 1920's, a communications medium came into being that was to have a profound effect on advertising and on the consumer. The medium, of course, was radio, and throughout that decade and the next two, millions of Americans gathered around their sets to hear their favorite programs — and to hear, as well, the commercial messages through which the sponsors advertised their products. Television, which began full-scale operation in the late 1940's, made advertising virtually all-pervasive in the United States. Everywhere we turn, we Americans are bombarded with messages urging us to buy — not only on television and radio and in newspapers and magazines, but on outdoor billboards and posters in buses, subways and commuter trains; on matchbooks, calendars and theater programs; in sky writing and messages carried by blimps; and at the "point of sales" — in store windows, display racks and on the counters and shelves of supermarkets and other retail stores from pharmacies to boutiques.

How Advertising Helps Consumers

What good do all these messages do us? A very great deal, according to the Better Business Bureau. (See box below.) Advertising tells us about new or relatively unknown products or services, thereby informing us of possible improvements; it keeps us up-to-date on established products, particularly those that have been changed; it gives us daily price information, including details on legitimate money-saving sales; it tells us the location of specific sellers and where to find specific products and services.

But we can make use of the help that advertisements offer only if we know how to separate the wheat from the chaff. One major piece of consumer protection legislation gives us considerable help in that direction: it is the Wheeler-Lea Amendment, which was passed in 1938 as a supplement to the act that originally established the Federal Trade Commission (FTC). This law, which deals with truth in advertising, makes false and deceptive advertising illegal and empowers the FTC both to establish certain kinds of regulations governing advertising content and to take action against advertisers whose messages it deems harmful to the public. For example, the FTC forbids advertisers to use illustrations implying that a product has components, parts or characteristics that it does not have. A toy train that must be pulled by hand, for example, cannot be pictured in an advertisement in such a way that it appears to move under its own power. Similarly, it forbids advertisers from showing pictures of high-priced models of particular products in conjunction with the prices of less expensive ones, thus leading people to expect more for their money than they actually get. In addition, it forbids advertisers to misrepresent a product's price in advertising. But although the FTC *can* control those aspects of advertising that relate to its truth or falsity, other aspects of the art are outside its jurisdiction. There is nothing in the Wheeler-Lea Amendment to prevent advertisers from putting their very best foot forward, as long as they do not deceive us in the process, or from using the colorful words, sounds and images — sizzle — that whet our appetites for their products.

The Better Business Bureau Advertising Code

The Council of Better Business Bureaus has devised a Code of Advertising all advertisers, advertising agencies and the media. Although the code has no legal force, every member of the BBB is expected to live up to it.

- The primary responsibility for truthful and nondeceptive advertising rests with the advertiser. The advertiser must be prepared to substantiate any and all claims or offers made *before publication or broadcast* and, upon request, to present such substantiation promptly to the advertising medium or to the Better Business Bureau.
- Advertisements that are misleading, deceptive, untrue, fraudulent or falsely disparaging of competitors shall not be used.
- An advertisement as a whole may be misleading even though every sentence separately considered is literally true. Misrepresentation may result not only from direct statements but by omitting or obscuring a material fact. This kind of advertising must not be used.

How Advertising Plays on Us

The admen are expert at the art of tempting us. They have studied us to a fare-thee-well, and there is virtually nothing they do not know about the kinds of people we are, the kinds of things that interest us and the kinds of appeals to which we respond. No national advertising campaign is ever undertaken until research investigators have drawn up a so-called "buyer profile" — a description of the consumers who already own or buy a given product or one like it. What are their ages? How many are men? How many are women? What is their financial status? What are their ethnic backgrounds, their occupations, the size of their families? With this basic demographic information, the admen can begin to plan an effective campaign — one that will give prospective consumers necessary information about a given product in the way best calculated to arouse their appetite for it.

The appeal to glamour, for example, often

helps sell a product that in itself is primarily utilitarian. Automobiles are sold as much for their good looks as for their good engineering. A little-known shirt manufacturer became nationally famous as a result of an advertising campaign that featured an aristocratic-looking man wearing a dashing black eyepatch. Somehow, the look of the gentleman imparted a sense of quality and panache to the shirt he was wearing, and the product quickly acquired a large market. Nor is this surprising. Who among us — despite the warnings of our critical minds — does not harbor a sneaking suspicion that if a particular brand of coffee is good enough to satisfy the discriminating taste buds of the celebrity promoting it on television, it is more than good enough to satisfy our palates? All of us hope to have the good things in life — health, happiness, success, good looks, loving families, charming and accomplished children — and a great deal of the advertising we are exposed to in print and on radio and television commercials, is directed toward assuring us we can have them — if only we buy whatever product is being sold.

Educated consumers are aware of this manipulative use of advertising and guard themselves against it. But sometimes the manipulation is very difficult to detect. Motivation research, a special branch of the advertising art, uses the insights of psychiatry and depth psychology to explore our hidden feelings so that advertisers can appeal to them. Why, for example, do you think that many cake mixes require the addition of eggs and milk or water and advertise that their users can also add "creative touches" of their own? Cake mixes can easily be made that contain powdered milk and eggs and need no "creative touches" — and, in fact, a few are made in precisely that way. To prepare a cake from such a mix, all that is needed is to add water.

But, as the motivation researchers discovered, the mere addition of water is not satisfactory to most women who want to bake cakes for their families. According to these researchers, many women subconsciously equate the baking of a cake with "making a gift of themselves" to their families. But giving a gift of oneself implies making an effort. A mix that requires only water makes the giving too easy — it deprives the baker of any role of her own.

Indirect Advertising

Within the last few decades, a new, highly effective form of advertising has evolved into a multi-million dollar business. In most instances the consumer is not consciously aware that a product is being touted; the unconscious mind is another matter.

The media used are motion pictures and TV drama. You go to a movie and in one scene, the hero settles down to drink a bottle of beer; the label of a nationally advertised brand is clearly visible. In a television sitcom, the heroine boards a plane which bears the name of a well known airline. The star roars down a driveway in a readily identifiable sports car. A he-man in a supporting role pulls a cigarette from a pack everyone recognizes. (Normally, only sympathetic characters use the product. An advertiser would probably not enjoy seeing his candy bar being savored by a mass murderer.)

A number of advertising agencies specialize in placing clients' products or services before the camera. Their success is evident in a large number of the productions we see.

Although most such indirect advertising is done at low key, there are instances when matter is handled with all the subtlety of a siren. In a recent film, one long scene was played in the living room of a young couple's new home. Dominating the set were a dozen or so huge packing cases, each bearing in large print the name of a nationally advertised moving company. A viewer would be more likely to remember that name than the import of the scene.

Some movie and TV buffs now keep notes of the number of times such puffery occurs in a given drama. "It's an amusing form of detective work, especially when the film is dull," one of them explained.

How to Analyze Advertisements

In this section, we've outlined no more than a few of the many techniques advertisers use to get us to spend our money. But even this brief overview should be enough to indicate how clever the admen are in plying their art, how vulnerable we can be to their appeals, and how important it is for us to learn to examine advertisements with an appraising eye.

Such products as washing machines and refrigerators can be — and frequently are — described in advertisements in reasonably

Testing Consumer Response to Ads and Commercials

If the men and women who create ads and commercials are to do their work effectively, they need to know how we respond. For this reason, it has long been industry practice to check consumers' reactions to advertisements before they reach the print or broadcast media.

The simplest way to do this is to ask us what we think — and, in one form or another, this procedure is widely used. Consumers push YES or NO buttons while watching commercials at special "preview" theaters; they fill out questionnaires in writing and answer them verbally. But these methods have their limitations. It may be difficult to construct a questionnaire that pinpoints the specific factors the experts want to know our reactions to. To be polite, we may give answers that are more positive and enthusiastic than our actual feelings.

The ad experts have learned to deal with these difficulties. "Psychophysiological technologies" — as they are known in the jargon of the trade — measure automatic body responses that the individual cannot falsify, which occur in connection with specific aspects of the ad or commercial being tested.

It is known that the pupils of our eyes dilate when we see something that interests us. The pupillometer is a machine that measures this eye response. If our pupils widen when we look at an ad, they know it has won our attention.

Similarly, they use a special camera that traces the movement of the eyes as we examine a visual stimulus. Our eyes linger longest over those parts of an ad that are consequently described as having "stopping power."

The testers check our vocal reactions, too. They record our voices on tape — first during ordinary conversation and then when we are describing our responses to the ad or commercial they are testing. Computer analysis of differences between the two tapes then tells the testers whether or not we were candid in describing our reactions.

The electroencephalograph (EEG) — an instrument that measures the electrical activity in the brain — is another tool the ad testers use. When we are interested in something we are watching, the EEG shows a pattern — a beta wave — which moves quite rapidly; when we are indifferent, it shows an alpha wave, which moves slowly.

Still other psychophysiological technologies are used to measure response to television commercials. Sometimes, the seats in the theaters where they are shown are wired to record the movements of the viewers' buttocks. If the recordings show that a high percentage of the viewers was squirming during a commercial, you can bet that commercial will not make it to the television screen. Sometimes the seats are equipped with electrodes that are attached to viewers' bodies to measure perspiration. The less perspiration, the better the commercial.

In their search for positive consumer reactions, the experts have developed new ways of manipulating the commercials themselves. Listeners appear to like speed in radio and television commercials, and to retain the messages contained in fast commercials longer than those contained in slower ones. But when sound is speeded up by the usual methods, it becomes distorted and incomprehensible, just as images speeded up by the usual methods tend to look peculiar. Recently, however, the electronics wizards have developed ways of overcoming these difficulties. They have learned to speed up sound as much as 40 percent without distorting it. They have also learned to speed up television commercials by as much as 25 percent without distorting them. And advertisers who have used these speeded-up messages report that viewers find them more interesting than those run at the normal rate.

concrete terms that give the consumer the information he or she needs to decide whether or not to purchase them. But — as the Better Business Bureau points out — there are countless other products, of a less practical nature, that are often described in empty words that provide no real information at all. Perfumes are "exotic" or even "forbidden;" after-shave lotions are "crisp" or "masculine." Facial cream becomes *crème*; soap lathers "luxuriously." Words like these are designed to appeal to our vanity and should be read with a coolly skeptical eye.

Obviously, no one automatically becomes "stylish" or "fashionable" by buying a garment advertised in those words. No one enters the charmed circle of the elite by buying products described as "trend-setting" or "exclusive." Such words are pure puffery, matters of opinion expressed by copywriters paid for their skill with words by an advertising agency.

Just as the advertising business uses words to bedazzle us, so it uses images to suggest that the products it is selling can change our lives for the better in a multitude of ways. Like empty words and puffery, the images are pure sizzle. Driving a particular model of car or drinking a particular brand of wine is, after all, highly unlikely to enhance anyone's sex appeal, no matter what the commercial suggests. Serving a particular brand of cheese or crackers at a party is unlikely to turn an ordinary gathering into the unforgettable social event of the season.

Because advertising is so all-pervasive in our culture, it is particularly important that we learn to examine it with a critical eye. If we are to be wise consumers, we have to learn to pay attention not only to the explicit messages that advertising conveys ("Buy this product; it's good and you'll like it") but to the implicit messages as well — the messages about us, and about ways to fulfill our dreams and fantasies. In looking at ads and commercials, it is up to us to learn to:

- Separate fact from opinion and be on guard against puffery of all kinds.
- Recognize "no-promise promises" — statements, for example, that a particular product *may* clear the skin of blemishes or *could*, under certain circumstances, relieve a bad pain in the back.
- Watch out for appeals to guilt as, for example, in snack food ads that caution against skimping on children's diets.
- Look skeptically at ads that offer goods for "less than cost" or "below original wholesale price." Except in very rare and unusual circumstances, sellers do not sell at prices that produce no profit for them.
- Look equally skeptically at ads that offer merchandise for "25 (or some other figure) percent off." "Off what?" is the question to ask here. (The FTC has issued a set of guidelines for businessmen that specifically covers the advertising of sale and bargain items; these guidelines are discussed in detail in Chapter 7. Here, we want only to point out that in the words of the FTC, "Truthful price advertising, offering real bargains, is a benefit to all. But the advertiser must shun sales 'gimmicks' which lure consumers into a mistaken belief that they are getting more for their money than is the fact.")
- Keep a sharp eye out for misplaced emphasis. The lending institution that advertises the availability of credit by stressing its friendliness and cooperation while at the same time, ignoring any discussion of specific credit terms is engaging in precisely this kind of practice. (The FTC has issued guidelines on this subject, too; they will be discussed in Chapters 7 and 9.)
- Be alert to the fact that some advertised prices do not necessarily include the extras, such as installation or delivery charges, that might be added to the cost of the purchase.
- Most important, wise consumers should be alert to the impact that television advertising has on children. To the admen, children are "allies" or "assistant salesmen," who can strongly influence their parents' buying habits. One estimate is that the average American child is exposed to about 20,000 television commercials a year, and many children can sing fast food commercials long before they have learned "The Star-Spangled Banner." It is up to parents to recognize these facts and to start their children's education as consumers at an early age, if only by resisting the youngsters' often persistent demands to buy heavily advertised products.

Marketing

Advertisements and commercials are not the only techniques that merchants and manufacturers use to try to get us to buy their products.

The art of marketing also plays an important role. The way a given article is packaged and displayed can have a significant influence on your desire to buy it; the strategic methods by which a new product is called to your attention can definitely make the difference between its acceptance or its failure in the marketplace. Like advertising, marketing is a big business in the United States: packaging alone is a $52-million-a-year industry.

Packaging As a Sales Tool

Like advertising, packaging developed from humble origins in ancient times. Ceramic jars of wine and olive oil were shipped throughout the western world when Greece and Rome were supreme. But packaging, as we understand the term, was unknown until the early 19th century, when the Frenchman Nicholas Appert perfected a means of preserving and storing food in glass jars for Napoleon's armies.

Still, packaging remained only a minor facet of merchandising until well into the 20th century. Some products were sold in brand-labeled cans and cartons, but the greatest number of items were displayed by stores in bins, barrels or kegs and sold by the pound, the dozen or the yard. When our great-grandmothers bought milk, the grocer dipped a ladle into a large metal container and poured its contents into the small can great-grandmother had brought with her.

Even after the milk can was replaced — first by the bottle, then by the carton — personal service remained the rule. Many of us can still remember the time when the normal shopping procedure involved a trip to the grocery store with a list of things to buy, which we read off item by item to the clerk behind the counter, who fetched the product from the shelves.

Then, after World War II, when many Americans moved to the suburbs and the supermarket replaced the corner grocery, packaging came into its own. By its very nature, the supermarket encourages impulse buying — the purchase of items we have no intention of getting when we walk into the store, but which happen to catch our eye as we push our shopping carts down the supermarket aisle. Moreover, the average supermarket stocks a staggering number of items — generally about 15,000. If a given manufacturer is to be able to persuade consumers to buy the particular one he makes, he has to find distinctive ways of calling it to their attention. And, as manufacturers quickly realized, the look of a package can be a major influence on the buying decisions consumers make as they wander through the market and look along the shelves. Effective packaging — bright colors, attractive shapes, catchy brand names and labels — all of these assumed an importance which they had never had before.

From the manufacturer's point of view, a successful package produces what the jargon of the professionals calls "brand identity." The consumer immediately knows and recognizes the product when he or she sees it on the shelves. The red and white soup can with its brand name written in script is immediately identifiable. So are the cleaning liquid whose label shows a powerful looking man with one earring and the one that comes in a package shaped like a no-nonsense industrial drum. And there are many other examples. Some widely advertised products have such strong brand identities that even small children, who have not yet learned to read, can distinguish them. When the brand identity of a product is particularly strong, manufacturers of less well-known competitive items — house brands, for example — often try to take advantage of it, packaging their own goods in such a way that they are easily mistaken for the better-known brand. This practice is known as "passing off," and can easily lead unwary consumers to purchase brands they do not want.

Nor is brand identity the only factor in a consumer's decision on whether or not to buy. Marketing studies indicate that color strongly influences the consumer's choice and that certain colors are particularly effective in selling certain products, not only because the colors are intrinsically attractive but because of the qualities with which they are associated in our minds. Yellow is a well-known eye-catcher, particularly for foods. Green, symbol of freshness and health, is commonly used on mentholated cigarettes; red, say the psychologists, has a strong appeal to men, and it is used on products aimed chiefly at the male market.

Increasingly, goods are packaged to satisfy the consumer demand for convenience. New

CONSUMER ALERT

Generics on the March

The cans, cartons and bottles in the generics section of a supermarket look very different from those in the other aisles — no greens and reds and yellows; no eye-catching labels and designs. But these packages are not there to beguile you. They are strictly functional, and usually black and white. But cost-conscious consumers are not interested in frills, and no frills is what they get when they buy generic products.

Generics — meaning products without brand names — were first introduced in 1976 by the French supermarket chain of Carrefour. The merchandise was contained in plain white packages and labeled with nothing more than the name of the product inside. These unbranded products were priced much below the brand-name items on nearby shelves, and within months they accounted for nearly half the sales of items available both in brand-name and no-brand form.

Other French stores soon jumped on the bandwagon, and in the fall of 1977 the idea of generic products crossed the Atlantic to a Chicago supermarket. In the months that followed, generics were introduced by supermarket chains from Boston to Los Angeles, and by the fall of 1978, well over 8,000 stores were carrying the no-names. By 1979, generic food products had achieved a 10 percent share of the market.

The rapid spread of no-name products was, of course, related to their price. At one Chicago supermarket, the total cost of 30 frequently used national brands was $32.09; the total for the same basket in the store brand was $24.42; and the total cost of the same items in generics was $19.52. The generics were, in other words, about 40 percent cheaper than the name brands.

Manufacturers of generics can offer their goods at such low prices because they spend next to nothing on advertising and very little on packaging. Their cans have no pull-tabs; their containers have no pouring spouts. A generic dish-washing detergent may not have the pleasant perfume the brand-name detergent has. Canned fruits and vegetables are usually "standard" grade rather than "choice" or "fancy." But this difference has to do with esthetics rather than nutritional quality: for example, generic sliced peaches are usually cut less regularly than brand-name peaches. And if the paper towels are less absorbent, this may not matter to consumers who do not expect to use them for heavy-duty jobs.

Generic drugs are yet another success story. For many years, the spread of no-name pharmaceuticals was hampered by restrictive legislation, the opposition of huge multinational drug companies, and, just as important, lack of public awareness. By 1982, however, generic drug firms held 20 percent of the approximately $6-billion-a-year prescription drug business.

Part of the increase in their use was due to changes in state laws, many of which had prohibited the substitution by pharmacists of generic drugs for brand-name drugs unless specifically directed by the prescribing physician. After many long struggles in the courts and in state legislatures, these restrictive statutes were eliminated until, by 1982, Indiana was the only state that still had this kind of legislation on the books.

The generic drug manufacturers have also gained from a growing public awareness that quality is in no way sacrificed for the lower price of generic drugs. In fact, U.S. government regulations require that generic drugs have precisely the same formulation and medical effectiveness as the original, costlier brand-name products.

And so, in the drugstore as well as in the supermarket, generics have been increasingly on the march. Those black and white packages with no brand names and no frills are likely to be around for a long time to come.

materials and new technologies have led to innovations in convenience packaging — pull-tab cans, unbreakable shampoo bottles, vacuum-sealed plastic lids, boil-in-the-bag frozen meats and vegetables. The introduction of the spray can has provided new ways of packaging products from shaving creams and hair sprays to room fresheners and dessert toppings. The products inside these packages remain pretty much the same as they always were, but the packages themselves offer consumers advantages that were not previously available. At a price, of course: the new forms of packaging almost invariably cost the manufacturer money, and that cost is passed on to the consumer.

If a product is to gain consumers' attention in the supermarket, it must also get adequate shelf or display space. Indeed, the product's visibility is so important to its sale that manufacturers and their distributors engage in strenuous competition with one another for the most advantageous shelf position. That competition also has its effect on packaging: the product must be housed in a container that encourages the retailer to give it adequate space, and the right space as well. Numerous studies have shown that consumers buy 60 percent more of a product when it is moved from a floor-level shelf to a position that is waist high; when the same item is moved from floor level to eye level, sales shoot up by nearly 80 percent.

Consumer Protection in Packaging

Although packaging and labeling are sellers' tools — ways of making products more attractive to prospective buyers — government action, spurred by the consumer movement, has forced manufacturers to use these devices to serve buyers' needs as well. During the 1960's, packaging and labeling became the subjects of hot contention. Consumer groups and individual consumers cited case after case in which manufacturers were far from accurate in describing the contents of their packages. One woman bought a can of peaches labeled "6-7 average servings." On opening it, she found that it contained five peach halves swimming in syrupy juice. Another consumer told of buying a writing tablet labeled "300 pages;" it turned out to contain 150 sheets. The manufacturer had counted both sides of each page. A man bought a large box of cereal to discover that it was only a bit more than half full. Infuriated, he fired off a letter to the president of the cereal company. "Why not include a jack-in-the-box in the package?" he asked. "Then, when it is opened, Jack can spring up holding a sign that reads 'Sucker!' "

Thousands of such cases were brought to the attention of Congress, and in 1966, despite the opposition of many manufacturers, the Fair Packaging and Labeling Act was passed. It did not remove all abuses; manufacturers can still put small amounts in deceptively large packages. But the law *does* require that the principal display panel of the container must hold a statement of the net quantity of the contents; and if the number of servings is mentioned on the panel, the size or quantity of each serving must also be mentioned. So it is possible for the consumer to figure out how much of a product the package actually contains.

In addition, the Food and Drug Administration established guidelines for food manufacturers who wish to disclose the nutritional content of their products, and most major manufacturers of processed foods do follow them. If you look at a mayonnaise or peanut butter jar, for example, you will probably find that it lists the amounts of fat, protein, carbohydrates and calories and expresses vitamin and mineral content as a percentage of the recommended daily allowance (RDA). And the ingredients that go into making up the product (in the case of mayonnaise, for example, soybean oil, eggs, salt, vinegar, etc.) will be listed in the order — most to least — in which they are contained in the product. This information is usually carried on the label.

Sales Promotion Devices

Sales promotion is another seller's tool for encouraging consumers to buy. Unlike advertising, sales promotion does not necessarily rely on the public media. Instead, it tries to spur us into making purchases with such incentives as coupons, contests, free samples, premiums, rebates and money-back guarantees. A look through your own medicine cabinet and your kitchen cupboards will show you how popular these promotional schemes are: a high percentage of the products carry some kind of sales promotion on their containers.

In launching a new product, manufacturers

often distribute free samples. Pretty girls hand out packets of cigarettes in shopping malls and on the street; a bar of soap or a plastic bottle of shampoo appears in your mailbox. These giveaways are not acts of altruism. Manufacturers know that most of us tend to buy the same brand of certain kinds of products time after time, and in fact they spend a good deal of advertising money trying to build this brand loyalty in us. The free sample is an effort to wean us away from our old love and marry us to the new. If we like it well enough, we may switch from the old, accustomed brand.

The money-back guarantee is another promotional technique used to get new products off the ground. The guarantee costs the manufacturer far less than the free sample and is less of a gamble than it might appear. Even those of us who dislike the product after we have bought it seldom take the trouble to send for a refund.

As a stimulus to sales for long-established products, manufacturers will sometimes make special "cents-off" offers. But, unfortunately for consumers, companies are wary of dependence on this technique, both because it can cheapen the image of the brand involved and because it can lead buyers to believe that the cents-off price should be the normal one.

When the "cents-off" offer graduates to dollars off, it is known as a rebate. Rebates are often made in connection with purchases far more expensive than those made in the supermarket or drug store, and the technique can be very successful in increasing the sales of items from major kitchen appliances to automobiles. But even a substantial rebate can fail to attract consumers if they do not want the product with which it is associated. In 1980, as the time for new models approached, Detroit's auto makers were faced with enormous inventories of unsold cars. In an effort to move them, they offered rebates that ranged from $400 to $1,000. But the cars on which the rebates were offered were large ones, which were well-known gas guzzlers, and the public was interested in fuel efficiency. Not surprisingly, the rebate program did not succeed.

Still another promotional device is the combination offer that brings together two or more products at a price a little higher than the usual price for one of them. Toothpaste

CONSUMER ALERT

Cashing in on Coupons

The American consumer once looked down on the use of "cents-off" coupons. Was it worth it, after all, to go to the trouble of clipping and saving the coupons and then presenting them at the checkout counter of the supermarket just for a few cents off on breakfast food, detergent or cleaning tissues? But, beginning in the 1970's, huge numbers of Americans, seeking ways to cope with high prices, embraced the coupon as a convenient way to cut rising shopping costs. In the early 1980's, the American Coupon Club estimated that the judicious use of coupons and supermarket specials could save the average family as much as $1,000 a year in food bills.

Inevitably, the growing popularity of coupons has led to large-scale fraud by counterfeiters and by "gang-clippers." Counterfeiters can produce bogus coupons which are indistinguishable from the originals.

"Gang-clippers" are persons who usually have access to large numbers of coupons through associates in newspapers or printing establishments, and literally stack up dozens of sheets of coupons and "gang-cut" dozens of them at a time. Then, representing themselves as agents of fictitious retailers, they redeem the coupons for cash at the clearing houses. If these establishments do not have facilities for checking credentials, the con artists can easily walk out with thousands of dollars.

In 1977, in an effort to put an end to this fraudulent practice, federal authorities, working with manufacturers, invented a bogus coupon for a nonexistent detergent named Breen at 25 cents off the supposed price, and placed it in an advertisement that appeared in three newspapers in the New York City area. Within a few weeks more than 70,000 of the fake coupons had been presented at the clearing house; not long thereafter, more than 100 criminal indictments were returned against the thieves.

makers combine their product with toothbrushes; razor manufacturers offer blades and shaving foam along with the razors. Sometimes a new, unknown product is paired with a widely-sold item as an inducement to consumers to try the new arrival. Combination offers are always ways of saving money. But whether or not they are bargains depends on whether or not you like, or need, all the products involved.

The use of discount coupons as a selling tool dates back to 1898, but they never were more popular than they are today. Consumers get packets of them in the mail, offering reduced prices on everything from pet food to panty hose and from film developing to magazine subscriptions. Manufacturers of supermarket goods regularly run discount coupon ads in newspapers and service magazines. In 1981, the total number of such coupons distributed in the United States reached 102.4 billion! (See box, page 27.)

Then there are the premiums — the manufacturer's way of selling his product by satisfying our desire to get something for nothing. Probably the best-known premium of all time is the prize that can be found in the bottom of a package of well-known snack food. But there are hundreds of others. Cereal manufacturers have given away toys in exchange for box tops; potato chip manufacturers have given away recipe booklets, flower seeds, plastic roses and miniature dinosaurs.

Sometimes premiums are not offered free, but are sold at a minimal price. One year, a cigarette manufacturer offered a sailboat for $88 plus 10 empty cigarette packages. The response was phenomenal: over 20,000 sailboats were redeemed. And, lest you were worried, the manufacturer did not lose money on the offer. Because he bought the boats in such huge quantities, they cost him something under $88 each.

For decades, sellers have used contests as a means of gaining consumer attention. Sometimes, a contest will require skill: the contestant has to write an essay about the product or compose a limerick or a slogan. But the best known of these contests involves the oven rather than the typewriter. Yearly, a major flour company conducts a national baking contest that attracts a large number of entrants and brings a considerable amount of publicity to the company.

More often, however, promotional contests are based on chance rather than skill. All the contestants have to do is fill out the entry blank and mail it in. They are not required to buy the product involved. In fact, the law that regulates such contests expressly forbids any purchase requirement, and its provisions are strict enough to guarantee that the contests are both honest and legitimate. Everyone who enters has an equal chance to win. But the more successful the contest is from the promoter's point of view, the less mathematical chance does any contestant have of winning a prize. One large soap company, for example, received more than 10 million contest entries — which means that every contestant stood a one in 10 million chance of winning the first prize. The types and numbers of prizes offered in various contests differ considerably. Some give away as many as 65,000 prizes, none worth very much; others offer such valuable prizes as trips abroad, automobiles or homes.

Spending Your Money

Consumers shop in all kinds of establishments — huge department stores and supermarkets; small convenience stores and spartan warehouses; neighborhood groceries as well as elegant boutiques and specialty shops. They buy at shopping malls and from vending machines; through direct mail and at sales parties in their neighbors' homes. No matter where they buy, they must keep their wits about them. This is where the long process of advertising, packaging and sales promotion comes to its climax — the place where consumers actually part with their cash. And the merchants from whom they make their purchases are no different from any other sellers. They have perfected techniques to get people to buy — from them, and not their competitors.

How Retailers Get Consumers to Buy

Like manufacturers, merchants use advertising — in daily newspapers, on local radio and television, in circulars. They offer special prices on selected items, print "snip and save" coupons in their newspaper ads and run regular sales. Even when they make little profit on the items being sold at reduced rates, these projects are worthwhile. Merchants can usually count on impulse buying to get consumers to purchase more than the items they originally set out to buy. It is not unusual for supermarket shoppers to get so carried away by all those dazzling products they see up and down the aisles that when they get to the checkout counter, they find they haven't enough money to pay for what they bought. Nor is impulse buying the only thing merchants look for when they advertise special promotions or sales. Any device that gets consumers into a store for the first time carries with it the possibility of turning those first-time buyers into steady customers. And steady customers are the backbone of most legitimate retail establishments.

One of the most effective selling tools in such large retail stores as supermarkets and department stores is the physical arrangement of the store itself. As a rule, department stores place their impulse-buying merchandise — those spur-of-the-moment eye-catchers — on the ground floor or, if there is only one floor, near the entrance. This is where off-the-street browsers, perhaps on lunch hours, will pick up stockings or gloves or neckwear.

Many stores artfully arrange certain kinds of merchandise to attract the attention of impulse buyers.

The street floor may also contain bargain tables, particularly for advertised products. It is the place for relatively inexpensive merchandise and for quick shopping. The more expensive goods, whether rugs, furniture, television sets or major articles of clothing, are on the upper floors, where the atmosphere is less hectic and the customer can deliberate.

The smart supermarket operator also arranges his store very carefully, with an eye to maximizing sales. The meat department is usually located along the back wall and dairy products are often placed toward the rear of an aisle. Such an arrangement assures that a quick trip to the store, planned only to pick up some hamburger and a container of milk, will take the consumer through aisles teeming with attractive products. It is a strong-minded individual who is not tempted to buy a few extra things: studies of consumer habits show that roughly seven out of 10 purchases are decided on in the store.

A clever supermarket operator in New Canaan, Connecticut used a variant of this technique to increase his Sunday sales considerably. His bait was neither meat nor milk, but *The New York Times*. Its Sunday edition sells widely outside the city, and many people in his area regularly drove to his store on Sundays for the sole purpose of buying the newspaper. By placing stacks of the paper in the far recesses of the store — instead of at the front, near the checkout counter — he compelled buyers to travel through the aisles of merchandise, and a good many left the store with purchases they had never intended to make.

Children are even more prone to impulse buying than adults, and the retailers know it. This is why they place highly advertised candies and pastries on shelves and racks that tots can easily see and reach. One supermarket operator in Indiana stocked his store with a dozen child-sized shopping carts that the kids pushed happily around the store in the wake of the adults with whom they had come. Predictably, the children piled candy, cookies, ice cream, and other favorites into their carts. At the checkout counter, the parent usually insisted that the child return some of the items. But, much to the storekeeper's satisfaction, the youngster generally managed to keep a fair number of them.

Like manufacturers, retailers also offer samples, premiums and contests. Department stores bring in authors to autograph books; they conduct cooking classes to show customers how to use new utensils or stoves; they demonstrate new types of washing machines or food blenders; they stage fashion shows for business women or prospective vacationers. They provide group instruction in sewing, home decoration, baby care and beauty culture — all, of course, in the hope of turning the casual visitor into a regular patron of the store.

Some sponsor events designed to generate long-term good will. A few large department stores stage mammoth Thanksgiving or pre-Christmas parades. Others sponsor art exhibits and concerts or support baseball or basketball teams. All these tactics are honest and aboveboard. But this does not mean that consumers can let down their guard. The retailer is naturally out to coax dollars out of your pocket. It is up to you to see that those dollars are well spent.

Wooing the Working Woman

One of the major events of our time has been the change that has occurred as millions of women moved out of the kitchen and into the job market. Not only do American women now have more money to spend on their own, they also have values, tastes and requirements they did not have before. And this has meant that manufacturers and advertisers have had to learn new ways of appealing to the "women's market."

In the past, both print and broadcast advertising pictured women almost exclusively as homemakers; if they *were* shown as workers, the roles they were awarded were those of secretaries or stewardesses.

The picture was false even when it was popular. In 1965, approximately 39 percent of all women 16 and over were working, and by 1983, that figure had climbed to 48 percent. Working women were no longer the exception in the United States. They were the rule.

These new working women were a varied lot. Some were career women; some worked because they had to; some were married; some were not; some were part time workers; a few held two jobs. Given these differences, it was not easy for the advertising experts to put together a single picture that would represent all of them. But studies showed that some generalizations could safely be made.

As a group, women who worked were younger, better educated and in better financial position than women who did not. They thought of themselves as independent and intelligent. They were more style-conscious than those who stayed at home and therefore more interested in clothes. They owned more electric hair dryers and more microwave ovens; they bought more fast foods; they traveled more. Working women were more likely than nonworkers to have drivers' licenses and more likely to have bought their own automobiles. Far more of them had their own checking accounts, savings accounts and a variety of credit cards.

But with all this information at hand, the initial response of the advertisers was slow and clumsy. For the most part, they continued to portray the average American woman as a housewife, and many women — housewives included — deeply resented the image that advertising presented of them. Where were the women professionals, the executives, scientists and athletes in the plethora of ads that tried to persuade them to buy products the advertisers were so anxious to sell?

Slowly, advertisers came to realize that women had to be approached intelligently if they were ever going to be persuaded to buy the products being presented. Commercials began to show women as pilots, jockeys, newscasters, surgeons, veterinarians, and the ads began to suggest that women played many roles in their lives — they could be achieving employees and professionals as well as wives and mothers.

Moreover, as manufacturers became aware that women had substantial purchasing power, the ads and commercials that had previously been primarily addressed to men began to be addressed to women. In the past, only men were in the driver's seat in ads and commercials for automobiles. Now, some ads show women in the lead role — not only driving the car with superior skill, but holding forth with great authority on everything from radial tires to motor oil.

A great many women still feel that advertising has a long way to go in giving an accurate portrayal of their role in American life. The old stereotypes die hard, and there is no doubt that some of them will stay with us for a long time to come. As the purchasing power of the working woman continues to expand, it is certainly predictable that the purveyors of goods — and their representatives in the advertising world — will continue to woo her.

A Guide to Wise Shopping
Just as wise consumers guard themselves against advertising blandishments, so they guard themselves against the marketing experts' arts. They are alert to dubious selling practices; they prepare themselves before they go shopping; they watch themselves when they are in the store and they check up on themselves when they return home. Here are some hints, culled from business and consumer studies, on how the intelligent buyer copes.

Sellers' Tactics to Anticipate
Sales that are not really sales. There are, of course, many genuine sales and bargains, and wise buyers always watch for them. But be alert for retailers who regularly run sales on some particular item. This practice strongly suggests that they are violating FTC guidelines, and that the so-called sale price is what the regular price should be. Even more unscrupulous are the retailers who actually raise prices so that when they reduce them, they can announce a sale.
The dubious bargain. The low-priced product may *not* be the best buy. Wise shoppers always look for quality as well as price. As the Better Business Bureau points out, a bargain is a bargain only if it is an item you need or want, sells at a price you are willing to pay, and is sold by a reliable merchant.
Something-for-nothing offers. Retailers sometimes offer "free" merchandise or service with the purchase of a given item. The "free" product or service may not be free at all. If you do not want it and the retailer is willing to reduce the price of the item you *do* want, he was clearly charging for the free one in the first place. Or his "free" item may not be worth anything. The store that offers "free" developing with the purchase of a roll of film is usually offering you the negatives only and charging you for the prints — which are the actual pictures.
Bait-and-switch sales. Stores sometimes offer fantastic bargains as "bait." Then, when you get to the store, the salesman will tell you the item is out of stock or that it really isn't very good. He may even show it to you to indicate its deficiencies, after which he will guide you to a more expensive version of the item and tout its high quality. That is the "switch." Bait-and-switch is illegal — forbidden by Federal Trade Commission regulations. Unfortunately, however, it is still widely used by unscrupulous merchants, and it still works on unwary consumers.

Preparations Before You Shop
- If you plan to make a major purchase — an automobile, for example, or an appliance — ask yourself whether you really need it. Too many people replace things that are working entirely satisfactorily only because they are a few years old or because friends and neighbors own newer models.
- Once you are certain that you want to buy, do your homework. Information about many products is available from a variety of sources and discussed in later chapters of this book under the products concerned. Make it your business to consult these sources when you know precisely what you want. Shop around. If you don't have the necessary time, phone the stores that carry the item and compare prices. And be sure you understand the terms of the sale: credit arrangements, if any; delivery date; warranty.
- If you have been attracted by an ad for a sale on a given item, or for an item carried only by one particular store, study that ad closely to be sure it gives you all the information you need. Then phone the store in advance to make certain the item is in stock and to get any additional facts you want.
- A shopping expedition to the supermarket also takes some planning. Many people are too busy to sit down and plan in advance for a week's worth of meals. But it *does* help to make a list of products you know you will need and want in the foreseeable future.
- Clip discount coupons on a regular basis. You can make substantial savings if you use them wisely.
- Check your store's advertised specials.
- Protect yourself against the temptation to buy what you do not need by removing any extra money you may have from your pocket or pocketbook before you go out to shop.

While You Shop
- Use your list as much as possible. Resist impulse buying.
- Use "cents-off" coupons only for items you want. And do not let the fact that you have them lull you into thinking you can afford to spend more money because of the savings

(continued on page 34)

State Directory of Better Business Bureaus

Alabama
2026 Second Avenue North
Birmingham, AL 35203

Central Bank Building, Suite 410
West Side Square
P.O. Box 383 (35804)
Huntsville, AL 35801

60 Commerce Street, Suite 810
Montgomery, AL 36104

Arizona
4428 North 12th Street
Phoenix, AZ 85013

Arkansas
1216 South University
Little Rock, AR 72204

California
639 South New Hampshire
Avenue, 3rd Floor
Los Angeles, CA 90005

1401 21st Street, Suite 305
Sacramento, CA 95814

4310 Orange Avenue
San Diego, CA 92105

2740 Van Ness Avenue, #210
San Francisco, CA 94109

1111 North Center Street
Stockton, CA 95202

Colorado
841 Delaware Street
Denver, CO 80204

Connecticut
250 Constitution Plaza
Hartford, CT 06103

35 Elm Street
P.O. Box 2015
New Haven, CT 06506

Delaware
1901-B West Eleventh Street,
P.O. Box 4085
Wilmington, DE 19807

District of Columbia
1334 G Street, NW,
Prudential Building, 6th Floor
Washington, DC 20005

Florida
8600 NE-2nd Avenue
Miami, FL 33138

3015 Exchange Court
West Palm Beach, FL 33409

Georgia
212 Healey Building
57 Forsyth Street, NW
Atlanta, GA 30335

P.O. Box 13956
Savannnah, GA 31406

Hawaii
677 Ala Moana Boulevard,
Suite 602
Honolulu, HI 96813

Idaho
Idaho Building, Suite 324
Boise, ID 83702

Illinois
35 East Wacker Drive
Chicago, IL 60601

109 SW Jefferson Street,
Suite 305
Peoria, IL 61602

Indiana
1203 Webster Street
Fort Wayne, IN 46802

15 East Market Street
Indianapolis, IN 46204

230 West Jefferson Boulevard
South Bend, IN 46601

105 South Third Street
Terre Haute, IN 476801

Iowa
234 Insurance Exchange
Building
Des Moines, IA 50309

Benson Building, Suite 645
7th & Douglas Streets
Sioux City, IA 51101

Kansas
501 Jefferson, Suite 24
Topeka, KS 66607

Kentucky
844 South Fourth Street
Louisville, KY 40202

Louisiana
301 Camp Street, Suite 403
New Orleans, LA 70130

320 Milam Street
Shreveport, LA 71101

Maryland
401 North Howard Street
Baltimore, MD 21201

Massachusetts
8 Winter Street
Boston, MA 02108

293 Bridge Street, Suite 324
Springfield, MA 01103

32 Franklin Street
P.O. Box 379
Worcester, MA 01601

Michigan
150 Michigan Avenue
Detroit, MI 48226

1 Peoples Building
Grand Rapids, MI 49503

Minnesota
1745 University Avenue
St. Paul, MN 55104

Mississippi
P.O. Box 2090
Jackson, MS 39205

Missouri
P.O. Box 4331, GS 319 65806
Hollard Building, Park Central
Springfield, MO

Mansion House Center
440 North Fourth Street
St. Louis, MO 63101

Nebraska
719 North 48th Street
Lincoln, NE 68504

Nevada
1829 East Charleston Boulevard, Suite 103
Las Vegas, NV 89104

New Hampshire
One Pillsbury Street
Concord, NH 03301

New Jersey
836 Haddon Avenue
P.O. Box 303
Collingswood, NJ 08108

34 Park Place
Newark, NJ 07102

2 Forest Avenue
Paramus, NJ 07652

New Mexico
Sante Fe Division
227 East Palace Avenue, Suite C
Sante Fe, NM 87501

New York
775 Main Street
Buffalo, NY 14203

257 Park Avenue South
New York, NY 10010

1122 Sibley Tower
Rochester, NY 14604

209 Elizabeth Street
Utica, NY 13501

435 Old Country Road
Westbury, NY 11590

158 Westchester Avenue
White Plains, NY 10601

North Carolina
Commerce Center, Suite 1300
Charlotte, NC 28202

100 Park Drive Building, Suite 203
P.O. Box 12033
Research Triangle Park, NC 27709

Ohio
P.O. Box F 596
Akron, OH 44308

26 East Sixth Street
Cincinnati, OH 45202

527 South High Street
Columbus, OH 43215

903 Mahoning Bank Building
P.O. Box 1495 44501
Youngstown, OH 44503

Oklahoma
606 North Dewey
Oklahoma City, OK 73102

4833 South Sheridan, Suite 412
Tulsa, OK 74145

Oregon
623 Corbett Building
Portland, OR 97204

Pennsylvania
1218 Chestnut Street
Philadelphia, PA 19107

610 Smithfield Street
Pittsburgh, PA 15222

Puerto Rico
P.O. Box BBB, Fernandez Juncos Station
San Juan, PR 00910

Rhode Island
248 Weybosset Street
Providence, RI 02903

Tennessee
1835 Union, Suite 202
Box 41406
Memphis, TN 38104

506 Nashville City Bank Building
Nashville, TN 37201

Texas
American Bank Tower, Suite 720
Austin, TX 78701

1511 Bryan Street
Dallas, TX 75201

2501 North Mesa Street, Suite 301
El Paso, TX 79902

P.O. Box 7499
Houston, TX 77008

400 West Market Street, Suite 301
San Antonio, TX 78205

First National Bank Building, Suite 600
Wichita Falls, TX 76301

Utah
1588 South Main
Salt Lake City, UT 84115

Virginia
First & Merchants Building
300 Main Street, East
P.O. Box 3548
Norfolk, VA 23514

4020 West Broad Street
Richmond, VA 23230

Washington
2332 Sixth Avenue
Seattle, WA 98121

North 214 Wall
Spokane, WA 99201

Wisconsin
740 North Plankinton Avenue
Milwaukee, WI 53203

they will produce. A recent study showed that coupon users spend more on shopping trips than non-users and that heavy coupon users make more unplanned purchases — particularly of "treat" foods — than other shoppers.
• Buy less expensive items — chicken, for example, instead of steak.
• Buy less expensive brands. Pay attention to no-name (generic) brands and private (store) brands. They are often substantially lower in price than nationally advertised brands and in many cases just as good in quality — or close enough to make little difference. (See box, page 25.)
• Do not buy only on the basis of price. Weigh the merits of competitive products against the difference in price. The more costly one may be better for you. If a heavily advertised brand of cosmetics or toiletries gives you some psychic pleasure you do not get from cheaper versions of the same product, you may want to splurge a little. Just be sure you know what you are doing.
• Exercise second judgment. If you arrive at the checkout area of the supermarket with more in your cart than you want, do not hesitate to put some of the merchandise back.
• Take your time if shopping for an expensive item. This is especially important if the purchase requires a credit arrangement. Do not sign anything you do not fully understand.

Back Home

• Cut down on your throwaways. Learn to be imaginative with leftovers.
• Freeze or preserve fresh food items that cannot survive long storage.
• Educate all the members of your family to be intelligent consumers. This is particularly important for children, who are exposed to a good deal of persuasion by commercials on television.
• Check with neighbors about experiences in various stores in your vicinity. We are all creatures of habit, but habit does not always serve us well, and we should always be on the alert for shopping tips that can be of advantage to us.

Chapter 3

Frauds, Scams and Rip-offs

Like the poor, swindlers will always be with us. No business or profession is fraud-proof, and no amount of consumer protection legislation, however skillfully written and strictly enforced, can frighten off all the swindlers or put them all in jail. The law can deter and the law can punish, but as long as there is money to be made by cheating people, there will always be those who are willing to take their chances on being caught.

We do not know precisely how many Americans are victimized yearly by consumer fraud, or how much money is lost. Despite their best efforts, law enforcement agencies cannot track down all the crooks and crooked operations. And all too often, consumers who have been victimized will fail to complain to the authorities. Still, we know that consumer fraud is a big business. Estimates number the victims in the millions every year and the amount they lose at well over a billion dollars. Some scams rob people of their entire life savings.

Because one of the major purposes of this book is to help you protect yourself against consumer fraud, some space in every chapter is devoted to the specific swindles and shady practices you should be aware of. But certain aspects of the problem deserve special attention. There are, for example, the work-at-home schemes — a whole group of businesses, usually run by mail order, many of which are in fact nothing but frauds. There are the pyramid schemes — chain letters, clubs, and certain forms of business distributorships that not only victimize consumers but can make criminals of them. There are investment schemes designed to steal from their investors: these scams are run by the most dangerous of all the con artists — men and women who charm their victims into genuine financial catastrophe.

And there are the more subtle forms of cheating engaged in by presumably respectable businessmen — the use of marketing methods that have been declared out of bounds by the law because they rob consumers of their rights in the marketplace. In the examples we will give here, you will see how greedy firms use these illegal methods of pressuring customers in order to make a quick profit for themselves.

Consumers who have been caught by any of these frauds are in serious trouble. These are not honest errors made by honest businessmen. They are blatant violations of the law, and those people who engage in them are quite aware of what they are doing and are entirely unmoved by their victims' complaints. Obviously, the best course is to avoid them utterly. But if by any chance you are entrapped by any of them, it is important to report this fact to the appropriate authorities — your local Consumer Affairs Office or the Consumer Frauds Division of your state's attorney general's office or, if the use of the mails is involved, the Consumer Protection Program of the U.S. Postal Inspection Service. (A directory of Consumer Affairs Offices will be found on page 16; of Attorney General's Offices on page 48; and of Postal Inspection Offices on page 175.)

Frauds That Masquerade As Businesses

Of all frauds, probably the most attractive to swindlers are the ones that masquerade as legitimate ways for consumers to make some money. Few of us are as well off as we would like to be, and the promise of extra cash is, therefore, always tempting. Con men who dangle that temptation in front of us know that if they spread their nets widely enough, they are bound to catch a good number of innocents.

Work-at-Home Schemes

"Earn $400 to $600 a month in your own home for a few hours of pleasant, easy work. No experience necessary. You can choose your hours." Ads like this appear with regularity in newspapers and magazines all over the country. And, with equal regularity, gullible consumers rise to the bait and answer them. Most often, the respondents are older, retired persons living on fixed incomes; or disabled workers who cannot hold down regular employment; or mothers of very young children who cannot leave home to work; or jobless workers whose unemployment benefits are running out. They are, in other words, people of modest means, who live in straitened circumstances and cannot afford to lose even small sums of money.

Unfortunately, they often do. If any single group of businesses can be marked as "dangerous to your financial health," it is work-at-home schemes. Whatever promises the work-at-home promoter makes and whatever project he proposes, the consumer should be extremely cautious.

Work-at-home schemes come in a variety of guises. Among the most popular is the one that advertises the chance to make money by hand-addressing envelopes. It often costs as much as $30 to register for this work by answering the ad. But the fee can seem quite reasonable to anyone who needs money and has time and a ballpoint pen. However, in return for the $30, the only thing the consumer usually gets is an impressive looking certificate designating him or her an authorized representative of the promoter's envelope-addressing company. The promoter does not provide work for participants; they have to go out and find it themselves. At the turn of the century, there may have been large numbers of businesses that sent out envelopes to be addressed by hand. Today, however, there are virtually none. Those firms that do not handle their mailings by machine on their own premises, send them to one or another of the large companies devoted exclusively to performing this service. Even in the unlikely event that an individual should discover a firm that wants hand-addressed envelopes for its mailings, he or she would hardly need a certificate of authorization from some unknown promoter's so-called company in order to land the job!

Work-at-home and Run Your Own Business Schemes

Caution is the watchword in dealing with companies that promise to help you earn money by working out of your own home. Be especially suspicious if the deal requires you to:

- Pay any sum in advance to join or get the details of the plan;
- Buy *any* materials from the company sponsoring the plan;
- Recruit new participants into the plan;
- Supply your own leads and prospect list, if the plan involves selling.

Not all work-at-home schemes require such a large initial outlay. Some promoters lead up to their demands more gradually. They do not ask consumers to send in any money when answering the ad or, if they *do* ask for money, they ask only for small sums — from $1 to $5 — for registration and detailed instructions on how the project works. Frequently, respondents who send in these payments never hear from the promoter again. And if they write a letter of complaint, it either goes unanswered or comes back marked "Moved; left no forwarding address." Work-at-home promoters are often little more than agile escape artists, who carry their scams in their hats and run like rabbits at the faintest hint that the law may be catching up with them.

Not that the situation is improved if the instructions do arrive. In most instances, it costs money to carry them out. And although this money is represented as an investment that will quickly earn the consumer a substantial profit, it is often nothing more than a contribution to the promoter's scam.

In one recent case, the Postal Inspection Service successfully tracked down and prosecuted the promoter of a work-at-home scheme involving a baby-shoe bronzing service for which participants were to act as salesmen on a commission basis. According to the glowing testimonials they were sent from others who had, presumably, enlisted in the scheme, it was an ideal way to make some extra cash. It was not. To sell the service, participants had to buy order forms from the promoter and mail them at their own expense to a list of prospects they themselves had to supply. Once he or she had paid off this investment in time and materials, the Postal Inspection Service figured, the average participant would be lucky to clear the princely sum of 45 cents a week. The promoter of the scheme did considerably better — and not by bronzing the occasional pair of baby shoes. He made his substantial profit by selling instructions and order forms.

Other work-at-home schemes involve the sale of such small and inexpensive items as name plates or key rings, which participants are most unlikely to be able to sell profitably. Still others offer participants the opportunity to sew or knit some product — usually baby booties or caps or mittens — that the promoter says he will then buy back for subsequent sale to individuals and stores. In this scheme, the participant — usually an older woman with a lifetime's experience in knitting or sewing behind her — is required to purchase patterns and the necessary yarn or fabric from the promoter. But after she has spent hours working, and has sent in her finished work, the promoter will refuse to buy it from her on the grounds that it does not meet his "high standards." In most instances, he's not really in the business of selling booties at all. He's in the business of selling yarn — or fabric — and patterns to the victims he has entrapped.

...The average work-at-home scheme requires an investment by you, but the likelihood of earning money is slight.

Sometimes, as recently happened in a work-at-home knitting scam that robbed nearly 60,000 persons, a few individuals *are* paid for their efforts. But this is not a compliment to the professional quality of the work they do. Indeed, their work is not likely to be any better than that of any other participant. The payment is an insurance policy for the promoter. Mail fraud is a criminal offense, for which conviction can be obtained only if the prosecution can prove beyond a reasonable doubt that the accused deliberately set out to commit the fraudulent act. If the promoter pays even a few participants, he can offer the payments as evidence of the honesty of his intentions, and the case against him is likely to collapse.

Not all the promoters of work-at-home schemes take this precaution. Some, indeed, are so brazen that they do not even hesitate to make accomplices of their victims by offering them a commission for every new participant they bring into the project. But the moment the victims mail out recruitment invitations, or place ads in a local newspaper or tack notices on a community bulletin board, they have enlisted in a pyramid scheme. And pyramid schemes, which are discussed in detail on page 38, are frauds. Participants can be fined or imprisoned, or both. Victim participants in pyramids like this are seldom prosecuted, and even more seldom punished. But the possibility, however remote, is not pleasant to contemplate. Nor is it pleasant to discover that, albeit unwittingly, one has engaged in a scheme to defraud!

Start Your Own Business

Closely allied to the work-at-home scheme is the one that sells the possibility of starting your own business. (This scheme should be distinguished from the legitimate franchise or distributorship offers that will be further detailed in Chapter 10.) The start-your-own-business offers, whose ads extol the joys of individual entrepreneurship and promise tens of thousands in yearly earnings from an enterprise you can set up in your own garage, are often no more than sophisticated versions of the work-at-home scheme, designed to appeal to a more skilled and affluent audience — people who are dissatisfied with their jobs or tired of working for others and willing to back their hopes with a fair amount of money.

Often, these schemes are promoted as "clubs" that, for a membership fee of $100 or more, promise a kit describing a number of different kinds of businesses — from repairing small appliances to building electric cars — that a reasonably skilled person can run from his or her home. When the kit arrives, you may decide that none of the proposed businesses are right for you, and your initial investment may be lost. The ads for these clubs frequently promise refunds to those who decide to cancel their memberships, but that promise is not always kept. If, on the other hand, you decide that you would like to try one of the club's suggestions, you may find that the next step involves an additional financial outlay for the purchase of detailed instructions on establishing the business you have chosen.

Sometimes, the instructions are of little or no value. They may be inadequate or incomplete. They may call for more capital or space than you have available. They may require the hiring of additional help. They may have some other defect that makes them equally useless.

Pyramid Schemes

Of all the frauds designed to part people from their money, the pyramid scheme is one of the most persistent and difficult to stamp out. It comes in varying guises — sometimes as a guaranteed get-rich-quick scheme, a way of making a great deal of money on a small investment; sometimes as a harmless gamble; sometimes as a legitimate business distributorship, offering money in return for work. And it costs its victims varying amounts — sometimes only $1, sometimes $1,000 or more. Whatever form the pyramid scheme takes, and however much money it bilks its victims of, it is virtually indestructible. No sooner do law enforcement officials knock down one kind of pyramid scheme in one area of the country than another springs up in a different area.

Perhaps the best-known form of the pyramid scheme is the chain letter that asks for money — the "promotional letter" as it often calls itself in an attempt to sound both enterprising and legitimate and to justify the two false claims it cheerfully makes: that it is entirely legal and that it is guaranteed to bring its participants a substantial return on a minimal investment.

"This promotional letter was started from Nashville, Tenn., by Jill Nelson for the purpose of acquiring investment capital . . . ." says one chain letter that makes the rounds every few years. "Please note: this is not an illegal letter . . . ." And it explains in detail how the chain works: "Send one dollar wrapped in a blank sheet of paper to the first person on the list of four names and addresses below. Then omit that name from the list and add your name in the fourth position. Send the new letter bearing your name to 20 new prospects . . . . When your name reaches the first position, it will be your turn to collect. One dollar will be sent to you by 8,000 people like yourself. Please do not break the chain. It really works. In fact, if the chain is not broken, there is no way it cannot work."

In fact, there is no way it can work for all its participants. If everyone followed the instructions, no one broke the chain, and the circulation of the letter was confined to the United States, it would be a bonanza for the Postal Service, which would sell an endless number of stamps. For if the chain were to continue indefinitely, everyone in the country would be mailing out a dollar for every dollar he or she received.

So far, that has never happened. And it's doubtful it ever will, if only because someone always breaks the chain. But even if a chain letter were to continue until the moment it became the circular exercise in futility we described above, it would not pay off for most of its participants, and more people would lose their dollars than gain any. If at each link of a chain letter each recipient mailed a copy to 20 people, at each link the number of recipients would be 20 times greater than it was at the preceding one, and by the time the sixth link was reached, there would be serious trouble, as a little simple arithmetic will show:

Link Number	Number of People in Chain
1	1 × 20 = 20
2	20 × 20 = 400
3	400 × 20 = 8,000
4	8,000 × 20 = 160,000
5	160,000 × 20 = 3,200,000
6	3,200,000 × 20 = 64,000,000

To whom shall each of these 64,000,000 people mail their 20 copies of the letter? Simple mathematics should provide a totally convincing answer. There are only about 230,000,000 people in all of the United States, and 1,280,000,000 — about one third the population of the entire world — are required to continue the chain without duplication!

And what about all the money that each of these 64,000,000 persons is supposed to get? Even if everyone in the chain up to this point — a total of 3,368,420 persons — collects handsomely, virtually no one at this sixth link is going to get a single penny, and virtually every one of them is going to lose the dollar he or she has mailed off.

It is for this reason that pyramid schemes — whatever form they take — are against the law. They are inherently fraudulent. It is in the very nature of a pyramid scheme to take money from the many so that a few can profit.

"Pyramid schemes are not victimless criminal activity, as some argue is true of gambling, for example," wrote Robert Abrams, the Attorney General of New York State. "The pyramid schemes are founded on promises that ultimately cannot be fulfilled. People rely on those promises, and they get hurt. That they may have been motivated by the desire to turn a large profit, or even that they planned to do so at others' expense by getting them to join the pyramid, is no reason for the law not to protect them against the consequences of their own gullibility and not to protect those they solicit against exploitation and loss."

Mr. Abrams wrote those words as a warning to New Yorkers in July 1980, when an epidemic of so-called pyramid clubs was sweeping the country from coast to coast. Despite successful prosecutions of dozens of pyramid club promoters in a number of different states, the clubs continued to proliferate — at least in part because law enforcement agencies were never able to discover precisely how or where the scam started, or whether there was any organized criminal conspiracy behind it. In Minnesota, where the clubs had by then been flourishing for a long time, the attorney general's office believed they had first come from New Jersey or Pennsylvania and later from California; in California, the attorney general's office suspected that they came from Alaska; and in Alaska, the Consumer Protection Agency "always assumed [they] came from the lower 48 somewhere." Whatever their origins, the clubs — which generally cost $500 or $1,000 to join — were a bonanza for the con men who promoted them and for a small number of early investors, who made considerable money. But they were a tragedy for thousands of others, all of whom lost at least half the money they paid for their memberships.

The clubs functioned on the basis of a chart — a pyramid-shaped diagram with six rows of boxes: the top row, or apex, contained one box, the second two, the third four, and so on until the sixth, which contained 32 boxes. Each member progressed from the last box on the bottom row of the pyramid to the apex by bringing in new members. As each new member joined, the recruiter moved one step farther along the way, and the new recruit's investment was divided equally between the person whose name occupied the first box on the chart and the person whose name was in the box directly ahead of the new investor's. At a $500-membership fee, the person at the apex would have received $15,500 ($250 from each of 62 people) by the time all the boxes of an initially empty chart were filled; and everyone, except the last member to join, would have got back $250 of his or her initial investment — a fact that in itself helped persuade some participants they would eventually make money.

At this point the pyramid would split, and a new chart would begin with each of the two individuals on the second row rising to the top of his or her own chart. These two would make less money on the scheme than the original promoter, since only the 32 boxes on the bottom row of their chart would remain to be filled. But an $8,000-return on a $500-investment is not to be sneezed at.

The promise of a fantastic profit is, of course, a lie. The pyramid club is not a sure thing, in which everyone is guaranteed to win. It is not even a gamble, in which winning or losing are related to calculable odds. The

Chains and Pyramids Guaranteed Ways to Lose

Chain letters and other pyramid schemes can make money for a few people. But those few make it at the expense of many others. Most participants in chains or pyramids are guaranteed to lose. Get-rich-quick schemes such as these are inherently fraudulent and are to be avoided — not only for the sake of your pocketbook, but because they are against the law.

If you receive a chain letter that requires you to mail money, or anything else of value, report it to the Postal Inspection Service in your state. If you are approached about any kind of pyramid scheme, report it to your state's Attorney General's office.

only person on any given pyramid chart who makes money is the person at the apex. Everyone else loses. Nor is it possible for everyone on the chart to reach the top spot. Like a chain letter, a pyramid club must keep constantly increasing the number of its participants. In time, it is bound to run out of recruits and there are bound to be many more losers than there are winners.

Still, tens of thousands of people joined the clubs, lured not only by the false assurance that they were both harmless and legal and by the promise of easy money, but also by the slick techniques that the promoters used. They rented elegant hotel suites in which to hold the meetings; they hinted broadly that local and national celebrities belonged to the clubs and would show up for the gatherings (in a few cases, this was even true); they imbued the meetings with a spirit that combined the fervor of an old-fashioned revival with the glamour of a Las Vegas gambling casino.

"I was attracted [to the pyramid club] by a celebrity whose name would be instantly recognizable . . .if I mentioned it," one club member told a reporter during the 1980 craze. "When I attended the meetings, he was there, and he was actively involved in the pyramid . . . . I enjoy the social aspects. I have always been interested in anything new . . ."

In an effort to track down the promoters of the pyramid clubs, law enforcement agencies sent undercover operatives to infiltrate the meetings. One operative told a reporter about the contagion the meetings seemed to spread. Even he, who knew precisely how dishonest the enterprise was, found himself caught up in its atmosphere. "They all sing and clap hands. . . and have a good time," he said. "The organizers whip up the audience and then you have to ask yourself if you're not crazy by not joining and taking advantage of a really good deal."

Don't let a celebrity's endorsement draw you into a pyramid rip-off.

Thanks in large measure to vigorous law enforcement and prosecution in a number of states, the pyramid club craze of 1980 finally came to an end, and it has not so far surfaced again. But the quiet may be only temporary. Pyramid promoters are a special breed of con men who combine the skills of a circus barker with those of a TV game show host, and who are always looking to put those skills to work. Masters of the arts of fast-talk and drama, they know how to appeal to our longings for glamour and excitement. The next time around, if there is one, they'll undoubtedly find a slightly different way to entrap their victims and to mask their fraud. But the principle that underlies the fraud will be the same. Whether it is represented as a harmless gamble or a guaranteed get-rich-quick scheme, it will in fact be a scheme to separate gullible people from their hard-earned money.

Chain Distributorships

Most deceptive of all the pyramid schemes are the so-called chain distributorships. It may not be easy for a participant in a pyramid club or a chain letter to recognize that the scheme is not a gamble but fraud. Still, no participant in either is likely to think of the project as a straightforward business proposition, in which one exchanges time, hard work, and investment money for a source of continuing income. This, however, is precisely the basis on which dishonest promoters regularly, and quite successfully, sell chain distributorships. They represent the deal as a way to earn one's living as an independent entrepreneur in the American tradition of individual initiative.

It all sounds quite attractive. The prospective entrepreneur agrees to buy the promoter's product in some specified quantity so that he can sell it to an eagerly waiting market. Nor does his income depend exclusively on the sale of the product; the promoter also promises to pay him for every new sub-distributor he recruits (on the same basis, of course, as the one on which he himself was recruited).

Such a deal is, obviously, a pyramid scheme and therefore inherently fraudulent. Like all chains and pyramids, it requires an infinitely expanding pool of participants — and no such pool exists.

As we have already mentioned, some work-at-home schemes are nothing more than chain distributorships. But this fraud is also found in connection with the sale of goods or services far more expensive than those associated with the typical work-at-home scheme.

Not too long ago, for example, virtually all

the residents of one small suburban community found themselves victimized by a chain distributorship that had them frantically trying to sell one another memberships in a shop-at-home food service. All of them had laid out considerable capital, paying the promoter in advance for food he was presumably keeping in a warehouse for them to sell. But, as the first few investors quickly discovered, prospective customers would buy it only if they, too, were given distributorship rights.

Since the scheme did not provide territorial exclusivity to any distributor and did not offer any distributor a list of potential customers, it turned into a nightmare only a few months after it began. Every new participant now became a competitor of the person who enrolled him, rather than a customer. The promoter who owned the service had made a fortune by the time the law caught up with him, and the first few participants had also made tidy sums. But, as could have been predicted from the nature of the plan, everyone else lost money.

Boiler-room Operations

Just as there is a special breed of con men and women who promote pyramid schemes, there is another breed that specializes in various types of investment fraud. The so-called boiler-room operation, for example, involves the fraudulent sale of investments exclusively through solicitation by telephone.

The con artists who work in this field have perfected the art of dealing with people whom they know only as voices over the telephone, and they are expert at winning the trust of their intended victims. Indeed, the con man gets his name from his ability to inspire confidence. Some boiler-room salesmen have actually had training or experience as actors. They spout statistics, confide "inside information" paint rosy pictures of the profits investors are practically guaranteed to make when they decide to sell the investment the con artist has let them in on.

They are masters of the technique known as the "take-away" — the art of building a potential customer's desire for whatever they are selling. They describe it as so scarce — and valuable — that even they, with all their connections, cannot get their hands on it. They repeat this claim over several days, in several phone calls, until they have so whetted their victim's appetite that when they finally announce they've managed to procure it, the victim cannot wait to send off his money. (It goes without saying, of course, that on the very day they're telling victim A that the material is unavailable, they're telling victim B that by their diligence, hard work and concern for his financial well-being they have at last turned up some.) Anyone who has been worked over by a really top-flight boiler-room salesman will agree with Orestes Mihaly, head of the New York Attorney General's Bureau of Investor Protection and Securities: "By the time the call is over, you think they're doing you a favor."

...Boiler-room salesmen have often bankrupted families with promises of enormous yields on bad investments.

Moreover, dedicated boiler-room salesmen do not give up. As long as they see any chance of hooking a prospect, they continue their pursuit, no matter what kind of disaster may be in store for the victim. People on whom boiler-room salesmen have set their sights can become so mesmerized that they put themselves deep in debt to buy the investment the salesman is touting. They borrow from their families, mortgage their homes, and drive themselves into bankruptcy.

Even when they are defeated, boiler-room salesmen continue to play their cons. If they are brought to trial, they do not hesitate to perjure themselves on the witness stand and to use whatever tricks they can think of to obstruct justice — whether by winning sympathy for themselves or by trying to confuse the issue and postpone the day of reckoning.

In one boiler-room prosecution that recently made headlines in New York City, 15 defendants — the president of the operation and 14 members of his sales staff — were convicted of fraud. The case was noteworthy not only because so many con artists were caught in one net, but because of the conduct of one defendant, the lone female in the group. She was young — in her early twenties — and extremely pretty, and no sooner had the jury been selected than she began flirting with one of its younger male members, "making eyes at him and ogling him and smiling," as a spectator reported, "until he mouthed the words 'your phone number' and she mouthed her phone number back." The trick did not work. The judge dismissed the juror and replaced him. Nothing daunted, our heroine tried again. She telephoned the prosecutor at his home during the evening, to whisper sweet nothings softly into his ear and to tell him, seductively, that she had "a mad crush" on him. When this was reported to the judge, he sent her off to jail for a few days of reflection, which apparently persuaded her that in this case her charm would be unavailing, and she would be better off leaving her defense in her lawyer's hands. He tried his best, but was no more successful than she was. Like the other 14 defendants, she was convicted.

Precisely what do boiler-room salesmen sell, and to whom do they sell it? They sell any kind of investment that sounds attractive, whether or not they actually have it to sell. The firm for which our young woman worked described itself as selling warehoused stocks of tantalum, a strategic metal which the U.S. government stockpiles for use by the defense

...Boiler-room salesmen will very often tie their scams to materials that are currently in the news.

industry. In fact, unlike boiler-rooms that make their money by inflating the price of an investment they actually own, this company was selling scrap metal as tantalum at $300 a pound — the going price for tantalum because that metal was in the news. Boiler-rooms build their scams around investments that sound particularly desirable because of their association with the political and economic headlines of the day.

In the 1950s, the beginning of the nuclear age, boiler-rooms were selling stocks in uranium mines; in the 1970s, with the oil embargo, they shifted to oil wells and coal mines; in the early 1980s, when the government embarked on a program of increased military spending, strategic metals became the favorite vehicle — with tantalum occupying a special place. It is extremely rare; it is seldom found in the United States; and the largest deposits are in Africa. This made it sound like an investment bound to skyrocket in value.

And to whom do boiler-rooms sell these investments? To affluent people all over the country. Some of them are small-town merchants and farmers, whom one would expect to be innocents in matters of high finance. But doctors, scientists and prosperous businessmen also fall for boiler-room scams, and the business managers of high-priced entertainers have even been known to invest their clients' money in them. The boiler-rooms find their victims on prospect lists they are able to purchase from reputable direct mail list houses that will supply names and addresses according to virtually any set of criteria the promoters may choose. Is the boiler-room interested in people who live in the Midwest, own at least three cars and have excellent credit ratings? The list house can supply such names. And the boiler-room salesmen know that if they make enough calls to the people on the list, they are bound to catch at least a few of them. Over a period of four months, for example, our scrap metal-tantalum salesmen made a total of 48,000 phone calls — more than 500 every business day — in order to hook the 140 people who eventually invested with them. Some of those calls, of course, were second, third and fourth tries to land the same prospect, and some were part of the "take-away" described above. But this proportion of calls to successes is typical. High telephone bills are a large part of the promoters' operating costs.

Printing costs are also a factor in their expenses. The operators set forth fictional information on their so-called investments in dignified and expensive-looking prospectuses, printed in several colors on heavy, glossy stock; the prospectuses themselves seem a testimonial both to the companies' bank balances and their integrity.

And often, the promoters have high rents to pay. In actual fact, a boiler-room could operate out of Oklahoma City or Sioux Falls, since it needs only telephones, desks and chairs to do its work. But most boiler-rooms prefer to operate out of New York City. Long distance phone calls from this city and an address near Wall Street lend a special touch of credibility that helps to lull the suspicions of potential victims. Because New York City exercises such an attraction for boiler-room operators, the state legislature has passed strict laws that augment the federal statutes regulating in-

CONSUMER ALERT

The Classic Pocketbook Drop

For generations, the pocketbook drop — that old chestnut of a scam — has repeatedly succeeded in parting people from their money. From Maine to California, thousands fall for it every year.

This ancient scam requires con men and women who are particularly well cast in their roles. Don't expect the smooth talking, high-pressure individuals we know from the movies and television. For this scheme, the "actors" must seem as ordinary and guileless as your next-door neighbors. They must be capable of gaining the victim's confidence in a very short time, and therefore make any suspicion of their motives unworthy.

The pocketbook drop begins when a pleasant person — generally a woman — approaches you on the street and strikes up a conversation. As you're standing and talking amiably, a second woman then comes up, carrying an envelope she says she has just found and which — as she shows you — contains a large roll of bills.

"I don't know what to do with it," she says. "It has no identification, so it wouldn't do the owner any good if I were to turn it over to the police. Maybe I ought to talk to my boss. He's a lawyer. He would know. His office is just around the corner. Wait here for me."

So you and your new friend wait, and in a few minutes the second woman returns. "He says that it probably came from gambling, and that whoever lost it kept it in cash in order to avoid paying taxes. He says we're entitled to split it among us, and he'll hold onto it and give us each our share if we put up some money to show our own good faith."

"I can do that right now," says the woman who first stopped to talk to you. "I happen just to have collected an insurance award, and I have the money with me." She marches off, presumably to the lawyer's office, and comes back announcing she's made the exchange. You, meanwhile, have been sent to your bank to get your good-faith money, a substantial amount of cash which the lawyer's employee is kind enough to volunteer to take to his office for you. She returns — but without your share of the found money. "He didn't want to give it to me. You have to sign for it in person. We'll wait here until you come back." She tells you where the lawyer's office is, and you start out for it.

Is there any lawyer at that address? Of course not. Are the two women waiting when you get back to them? No, indeed. They're far away, gloating over the money you were kind enough to hand them.

Who falls for the pocketbook drop — or any of the variations that are played on this same theme? Usually, these victims are older women who feel reasonably secure on the street during the daylight hours, and have the time and inclination to engage in relatively long conversations with strangers. Mothers with young children are not likely to be willing to stop for any length of time. Men and other younger women are also generally in a rush. Most of them have jobs to get to or errands to run, and this makes them poor prospects.

But the pocketbook drop also robs the relatively sophisticated who pride themselves on their "street smarts" and their imperviousness to efforts to put anything over on them. The innocent victim may fall for the pocketbook drop because she really believes the tale the con artists tell. The sophisticate, on the other hand, is generally victimized by his or her own ego and greed.

For in this case, the con artist pretends to be a naive "pigeon" ready to be plucked, and this appeals to the victim's self-confidence. Con artists are much more adept at sizing up their victims than their victims are at sizing them up; they know precisely how to play upon the victims' weaknesses, whatever they may be.

vestment sales, and the state's attorney general's office vigorously searches out and prosecutes investment fraud. In consequence, a number of boiler-rooms have fled to the neighboring states of Connecticut and New Jersey — or even farther, to Florida and Texas. But there are always some whose operators, mindful of the advantages of a New York address and of the huge profit that can be made, are prepared to accept the higher risk.

Almost anyone who makes an investment of any kind purely on the basis of a few telephone calls from a total stranger is guaranteed to lose. If the law is aware of the scam early enough, and moves with considerable speed, it may be able to impound whatever cash assets the boiler-room has. But those assets never equal the amounts that gullible investors have paid out. Moreover, conviction for investment fraud does not automatically carry with it an order for restitution. Often, while boiler-room salesmen and operators are languishing in prison, the funds they have stolen are earning interest in a bank — waiting to be picked up when the thieves are released.

The Ponzi Scheme

A few years ago, after a nation-wide manhunt, a 36-year-old prescription drug salesman was arrested on charges of having swindled more than 100 people out of $10 million over a period of six years. Many of these people were so convinced of the profitability of the "investment" he had sold them that they gave him additional money in increasingly large amounts. Some had turned over their entire life savings; others had mortgaged homes or businesses. All investors were convinced of the salesman's honesty and decency, and most were more than simply business associates. They were friends and neighbors, who were extremely fond of him and trusted him implicitly, remaining loyal to him even when it began to be evident that something was seriously wrong. "Nobody has knocked him — even if they invested money," said one neighbor who had escaped the swindle. "They just can't believe it."

At last, however, they had to believe it. One summer evening the salesman simply vanished, taking his wife and two sons with him — and his investors' money as well.

The salesman had been engaged in a Ponzi scheme — a kind of fraud that takes its name from Charles A. Ponzi, a swindler who became notorious for this practice in the 1920s. In essence, the Ponzi scheme is a pyramid in which a con man repeatedly takes money from a group of Peters in order to pay a group of Pauls. He gets the first Paul to give him money on the grounds that he has access to some extraordinarily attractive form of business investment, and then pockets the money for his private benefit. Next, using the same argument, he persuades the first Peter to turn over money to him. He keeps most of it, but gives a portion to Paul, representing it as profit from the business.

Now, in order to give at least some money to Peter — and to get more for himself — he has to find more Pauls and more Peters. And so the scheme progresses, entrapping more and more victims. In the end, a Ponzi scheme must collapse — either because the swindler runs out of Pauls and Peters or because one of the investors has to pull out of the business and asks for the money that is due him.

Like other investment frauds, the Ponzi scheme depends for its success upon the con artist's ability to win and keep the trust of his victims and on the timeliness of the vehicle chosen for the scam. The drug salesman's fraud lived up to both of these criteria. His first victim had been a friend for years, and the fraud developed out of an event that was very much in the news at the time — the impending passage of a state law governing the sale of generic (or non-trade name) prescription drugs. The law, designed to enable consumers to save money, gave doctors and patients the right to choose between generics and the more expensive medications manufactured by the companies whose research had initially developed the drug in question. It thus presaged an increased demand for the generics and — because the mark-up on all drugs is extremely high—a generous profit for any firm selling them to retail pharmacies.

This was the business for which the drug salesman said his investors' money was going. He would use his contacts in the industry to buy generic drugs at very low prices and would then sell them to pharmacies. At first, things seemed to work out handsomely. His investors were earning 40 percent a year on their money and, as the business presumably expanded, this profit increased to 33 percent every six months. And, during this period, it is

You Really Can't Believe Everything You Read in the Papers!

A common misconception among consumers is that the appearance of an advertisement in a newspaper or magazine, on the radio or television, constitutes some kind of implicit endorsement of the product or service involved. From this misconception, many people draw a dangerously erroneous conclusion: that if the medium carrying the ad is trustworthy, the ad must be equally trustworthy.

In fact, the media generally have no legal obligation to stand behind their advertisers' claims, or to check those claims for legitimacy. If the media had to test every product or service they accepted for advertising, the cost would be prohibitive.

On the other hand, if the media carry an ad they *know* to be fake or deceptive, they might be found guilty of false advertising. For this reason most publishers and most radio and television stations have advertising codes that set standards for the acceptance of advertising copy. These standards vary considerably, however, from one publication or station to another. A very small number of publications are so cautious that they refuse ads from any firm whose activities are under investigation by a government agency. This policy may save consumers from possible difficulty, but it can be extremely unfair to the business involved. Not every investigation ends in an accusation of wrongdoing. But such high standards are the exception rather than the rule, and in many cases, the code is so lenient that misleading and even dishonest advertising can easily slip through.

One of the major functions of the Better Business Bureau is to police advertising and persuade advertisers to keep it honest. But persuasion seldom influences unscrupulous operators, who go right on making their dishonest claims. It is really up to the consumer to provide his or her own protection against the lure of false advertising.

The rule of thumb to follow is really quite simple. If an ad makes a promise that seems too good to be true, it probably is. Ignore the promise and don't buy what the ad is selling. Or, if you think you really *must* have it, don't lay out a penny until you've checked with some reputable agency — the Better Business Bureau or the U.S. Postal Inspection Service, if mail order is involved. Neither will tell you directly whether or not to buy the product. But both will tell you whether or not complaints have been made about it.

entirely possible that the drug salesman was in fact operating completely honestly. But then, apparently overcome by greed and ambition, he began to speak of expanding the operation. Given his record up to then, his backers were entirely willing to reinvest the money they had already earned, and even to add new capital.

It was probably at this point that the salesman started siphoning off money for his own use and turning his business into a Ponzi scheme. For six years, he managed to keep the juggling act going, accumulating a tidy nest egg for himself while paying his investors with regularity. Then, one evening, a group of his backers — doctors, lawyers and businessmen among them — gathered at the restaurant where they traditionally met to collect their dividends and enjoy a pleasant meal. When the salesman was a few minutes late, they did not worry. But as time passed and he still did not arrive, they began to be concerned. Was he ill? Had there been an accident? They called his home, but there was no answer. A call to the vacation house where his wife and sons were staying produced no answer, either. Now they were alarmed. In a group, they hurried to his home where they found the front door unlocked, the closets bare and no one at home. The pyramid had toppled. The salesman had no money to pay his backers. So he packed up and ran.

Marketing Scams and Frauds

Until now, we have been discussing outright swindles — illegal schemes and tricks deliberately used by promoters to bilk consumers. But for every victim who has lost money in a work-at-home scheme or an investment fraud, there are thousands of others who have been taken by more subtle violations of the law — by covert forms of deception and coercion. By high-pressuring consumers, telling them half-truths, and failing to convey information they are entitled to have, the unscrupulous businessman regularly manipulates the unwary into actions contrary to their best interests. Unlike the swindles we have discussed, whose success is largely dependent on consumer gullibility, these frauds succeed because consumers are ignorant of their rights and do not know of the many state and federal laws and regulations that can be invoked to protect them.

We will be discussing these laws, rights and regulations in specific detail in subsequent chapters. Here we want to give you one example of the ways greedy businessmen can violate both the spirit and the letter of consumer protection laws and how aggressive action by consumers and the law enforcement agencies that represent them can bring these businessmen to account. We've changed the name of the company involved, and omitted the name of the state in which the events occurred. Everything else is factual.

The story had its beginning in May 1981, when more than 130,000 residents of a particular state started receiving copies of the following letter:

"Dear Selectee:

"Recently a direct mail advertising program was completed to over 2,000,000 people for a firm representing a resort travel club. As a result of that program some major awards were unclaimed. A drawing has been scheduled to give away all of the remaining unclaimed awards. This is your official and only notification that you have been randomly selected to receive one of the awards listed below in accordance with both state and federal laws governing awards programs. One of the awards listed below definitely must be given to you.

211122 Two hundred dollars ($200.00) cash
212112 Microwave oven, 650 watts
221122 25" color console television
211121 AM/FM receiver and headset system
221222 Five hundred dollars ($500.00) cash
212221 Video recorder, 6 hr. capability
211212 One thousand dollars ($1,000.00) cash

"All awards that were advertised must be given away. To receive your award, you must visit Steeltrap Camping Club before the expiration date shown above your name. Steeltrap is open 7 days a week from 9:00 a.m. to 3:30 p.m.

"You must bring this notification along on your visit. Failure to respond by the time allotted will cause forfeiture of your award and reissue. This is your only notification. When you arrive you will be taken on a courteous tour of the beautiful Steeltrap Camping Club and then you can pick up your award. Dress according to the weather.

"While at Steeltrap Camping Club this letter will entitle you to a very special opportunity limited only to guests like yourself. There is absolutely no obligation to purchase anything. For your convenience, a map is provided on the reverse side of this notification."

The letter enticed a substantial number of people to Steeltrap, a large campsite in another state that was operated as a vacation facility by a private club. Some had to travel 60 or more miles, but the time and expense seemed eminently worthwhile. If the letter was to be believed — and reference to state and federal laws made it seem trustworthy — everyone was guaranteed a substantial gift.

But when the visitors got to Steeltrap, they found the situation quite different from what they had been led to expect. The letter had told them they would be taken on a "courteous tour" of the camp and could then pick up their gifts. It had not told them that the gift was merely a device to lure them to the camp, and that they could not even find out what they were getting until they first took the tour — which was used by the guide as an occasion to extol Steeltrap's beauty and its charm as a vacation spot. Following the tour, they were herded into the recreation room where, still in the dark as to the gifts in store for them, they were subjected to a long, high-pressure sales pitch, complete with color movies and background music. Steeltrap's virtues were again dinned into them and they were urged to sign up for membership immediately, at the "one-time only special bargain rate" then in force. For $5,000 — payable over time at interest rates that turned it into $10,000 or more — plus an annual maintenance fee of $120, they would be guaranteed the use of Steeltrap's facilities for 18 years. But they had to sign up then and there. The special fee held only for the duration of a first visit and they were told that they would never be able to take advantage of it again.

All this was hammered home by smooth-talking salesmen, expert at weakening the visitors' resistance, arguing down their objections and deflecting any embarrassing questions they might ask.

Not until the last visitor to agree to purchase had signed the official contract form were any members of the group permitted to find out what their gifts were and to pick them up. The gifts turned out to be a stunning disappointment. Without exception, everyone got the same thing: the "AM/FM receiver and headset system" — a small, battery operated radio worth no more than $15.

By the time they arrived home, most of the visitors were extremely upset. Those who had not signed up for membership were angry at the waste of their time and money. Many of those who *had* signed up had permitted themselves to be manipulated into a costly, long-term commitment to something they were now far from sure they wanted or even needed.

Still, the greatest number of them saw no solution to their problem. To those who had not invested in Steeltrap memberships, it seemed that they had taken a gamble and lost. After all, no one had guaranteed that they would win one of the valuable gifts. And those who *had* signed the contract — well, they were adults, and legally empowered to sign such documents, and no one had threatened or coerced them in any way. They had gotten themselves into this mess, and they would have to take the consequences.

Fortunately, however, a handful of the Steeltrap visitors did not share this sense of helplessness. They did not know precisely what could be done, but perhaps the state attorney general's office had some ideas.

That office had ideas aplenty. The first was to determine whether the complaints were

(continued on page 50)

Health and Diet Rip-offs

How would you like to lose weight the easy way? With no diet, no exercise, no change in your eating habits. Just buy our "magic liquid," add it to the water in your bathtub and take off "60 pounds of ugly fat while relaxing" in that tub. Or would you prefer to lose the weight by swallowing our "amazing powder?" It "burns away more fat in each 24 hours than if you ran 14 miles a day!"

Such claims are so preposterous it's difficult to believe anyone would have the nerve to make them. But the quotes above are from actual ads that appeared only recently in leading publications. And they managed to persuade a substantial number of gullible people. Every year, at least $1,500,000 is spent on phony diet products and other items — "waistline reducers," "hair growers" and "bust developers" are only a few among them — that purport to make their users more attractive.

Even worse than the scams that promise beauty are those that promise health. Despite the efforts of the FDA and the Postal Inspection Service, quack medicines of all sorts continue to be manufactured and sold — sometimes across the counter, but primarily through the mail. And these so-called remedies can be extremely dangerous. A "Personal Home Treatment Kit," designed for the "solution and prevention of as many as 40 different diseases and illnesses" and sold for $29.95, contained equipment for "colonic irrigation" — in other words, an enema bag. But enema is a useless treatment for most diseases and a dangerous treatment for some.

The moral is clear. Claims that are made for health, diet and related products are often exaggerated, in some cases downright false. At the very least, consumers should take them with the proverbial grain of salt. There are no instant ways to beauty of face and form and there are no panaceas for illness, and any promise of either is a rip-off and a fraud.

State Offices of Attorneys General

Alabama
Attorney General Of Alabama
State Administration Building
Montgomery, AL 36130

Alaska
Attorney General of Alaska
Pouch K, State Capitol
Juneau, AK 99811

Arizona
Attorney General of Arizona
1700 W. Washington
Phoenix, AZ 85007

Arkansas
Attorney General of Arkansas
Justice Building
Little Rock, AR 72201

California
Attorney General of California
3580 Wilshire Boulevard
800 Tishman Building
Los Angeles, CA 90010

Colorado
Attorney General of Colorado
1525 Sherman Street
Denver, CO 80203

Connecticut
Attorney General of Connecticut
Capitol Annex, 30 Trinity Street
Hartford, CT 06115

Delaware
Attorney General of Delaware
Department of Justice
Wilmington Tower Building
Wilmington, DE 19801

District of Columbia
Director
Office of Consumer Protection
1424 K Street, N.W.
Washington, DC 20005

Florida
Attorney General of Florida
Department of Legal Affairs
Tallahassee, FL 32304

Georgia
Attorney General of Georgia
132 State Judicial Building
Atlanta, GA 30334

Hawaii
Attorney General of Hawaii
405 State Capitol
Honolulu, HI 96813

Idaho
Attorney General of Idaho
State House
Boise, ID 83720

Illinois
Attorney General of Illinois
500 S. Second Street
Springfield, IL 62701

Indiana
Attorney General of Indiana
219 State House
Indianapolis, IN 46204

Iowa
Attorney General of Iowa
State Capitol
Des Moines, IA 50319

Kansas
Attorney General of Kansas
Kansas Judicial Center
Topeka, KS 66612

Kentucky
Attorney General of Kentucky
State Capitol
Frankfort, KY 40601

Louisiana
Attorney General of Louisiana
2-3-4 Loyola Avenue
New Orleans, LA 70112

Maine
Attorney General of Maine
State House
Augusta, ME 04330

Maryland
Attorney General of Maryland
Department of Law
One S. Calvert Building
Baltimore, MD 21209

Massachusetts
Attorney General of
Massachusetts
One Ashburton Place
State House
Boston, MA 02108

Michigan
Attorney General of Michigan
Law Building
Lansing, MI 48913

Minnesota
Attorney General of Minnesota
102 State Capitol
St. Paul, MN 55155

Mississippi
Attorney General of Mississippi
Carroll Gartin Justice Building
State Capitol
Box 220
Jackson, MS 39205

Missouri
Attorney General of Missouri
Box 899
Jefferson City, MO 65102

Montana
Attorney General of Montana
Department of Justice
State Capitol
Helena, MT 59601

Nebraska
Attorney General of Nebraska
State Capitol
Lincoln, NE 68509

Nevada
Attorney General of Nevada
Heroes Memorial Building
Carson City, NV 89710

New Hampshire
Attorney General of New Hampshire
208 State House Annex
Concord, NH 03301

New Jersey
Attorney General of New Jersey
State House Annex
Trenton, NJ 08625

New Mexico
Attorney General of New Mexico
Bataan Building, Box 1508
Sante Fe, NM 87501

New York
Attorney General of New York
Two World Trade Center
New York, NY 10047

North Carolina
Attorney General of North Carolina
Justice Building
Box 629
Raleigh, NC 27602

North Dakota
Attorney General of North Dakota
State Capitol
Bismarck, ND 58505

Ohio
Attorney General of Ohio
State Office Tower
30 E. Broad Street
Columbus, OH 43215

Oklahoma
Attorney General of Oklahoma
112 State Capitol
Oklahoma City, OK 73105

Oregon
Attorney General of Oregon
100 State Office Building
Salem, OR 97310

Pennsylvania
Attorney General of Pennsylvania
Strawberry Square
Harrisburg, PA 17120

Rhode Island
Attorney General of Rhode Island
Providence County Court House
Providence, RI 02903

South Carolina
Attorney General of South Carolina
Hampton Office Building
Columbia, SC 29211

South Dakota
Attorney General of South Dakota
State Capitol
Pierre, SD 57501

Tennessee
Attorney General of Tennessee
450 James Robertson Parkway
Nashville, TN 37219

Texas
Attorney General of Texas
Capitol Station
Box 12548
Austin, TX 78711

Utah
Attorney General of Utah
236 State Capitol
Salt Lake City, UT 84114

Vermont
Attorney General of Vermont
Pavilion Office Building
Montpelier, VT 05602

Virginia
Attorney General of Virginia
Supreme Court Building
Richmond, VA 23219

Washington
Attorney General of Washington
Temple of Justice
Olympia, WA 98504

West Virginia
Attorney General of West Virginia
E-26 State Capitol
Charleston, WV 25305

Wisconsin
Attorney General of Wisconsin
Box 7857
State Capitol
Madison, WI 53707

Wyoming
Attorney General of Wyoming
123 State Capitol Building
Cheyenne, WY 82002

accurate. Once this was done, through interviews with other visitors to the camp, it was clear that Steeltrap was in serious trouble. Its conduct was not merely unethical, it was illegal. The camp had violated state laws expressly passed to save consumers from entrapment by unscrupulous merchandising methods.

By failing to tell the recipients of its letter that the only way to win a prize was to submit to a sales presentation for membership in Steeltrap at the then-going rate; by failing to tell them the cash value of the merchandise prizes; and by failing to tell them their chance of winning each prize (the chance of winning something other than the radio, for example, turned out to be approximately one in 10,000), the camp had violated specific provisions of the state's lottery laws, which governed such merchandising promotions as this.

It had violated the state's general business law as well. Under the provisions of this act, consumers have a grace period of five business days within which to cancel any contract they may sign. But the camp had neither informed its visitors verbally that they had this right nor had it been disclosed in writing on the contract form.

Given these facts, it was evident that there were strong grounds for legal action against Steeltrap, and the attorney general's office informed the camp's owners of its intention to institute court proceedings. Confronted with the possibility of a trial which it was almost sure to lose, Steeltrap signed a document known as an Assurance of Discontinuance — the equivalent at the state level of a federal Consent Decree. Such documents are commonly used for out-of-court settlement of government charges of unfair practices against business establishments. They are not admissions of guilt on the part of the business involved, but they *are* promises that the business will never engage in the practices of which the government has complained and they are in addition legally binding statements of the practices the company will, in the future, employ.

In the case of Steeltrap, those future practices focused primarily on disclosure. In its conduct of prize promotions, the company promised to give consumers all the information they would need in order to decide whether to visit the camp. What were their chances of winning a given prize and what were the prizes worth? Were they willing to sit through a sales talk for the sake of winning any of the prizes offered? It was up to the consumer to decide whether the game was worth the candle. But to make that decision, the consumer had to be told the facts.

The company also promised to make full disclosure about the laws governing contracts, both by informing purchasers orally that they had the right to cancel their contracts within five business days, and by printing this information in bold-face type right next to the section of the contract where the purchaser put his or her signature. It further promised to hold each purchaser's down payment in a special escrow account until the expiration of the grace period, so that anyone who canceled would be guaranteed return of any money already paid.

...Courts often come down on shady promoters with considerable force.

These provisions protected consumers who might in the future become involved with Steeltrap. But what about those who had already suffered as a result of the company's practices? The Assurance of Discontinuance did not neglect them. Among the people who had originally complained to the attorney general were several who had signed contracts at Steeltrap and had subsequently tried, unsuccessfully, to cancel them. The Assurance guaranteed that anyone who had requested cancellation within five days of signing could get his money back by writing to Steeltrap. It even guaranteed that the early visitors who so requested would be paid a travel allowance, according to a schedule fixed by the distance between the camp and their homes.

So the story had a happy ending. Consumers who knew they had been badly used stood up for their rights and a conscientious attorney general's office acted to protect them. And that is the major moral of our tale. For consumers to deal effectively with businesses who try to defraud them, they must be willing to take action. They must be willing to complain — both to the offending merchants and to the authorities — so that the appropriate resources can be used to solve their problems.

Chapter 4

The Roof Over Your Head

The largest single item in the budget of most Americans is housing and the myriad expenses — from utilities to insurance (Chapter 10) — connected with it. Moreover, that cost is steadily rising. Only two decades ago, it amounted to less than a quarter of the average family's income; today it amounts to roughly a third. Under such budgetary pressures, housing decisions obviously have to be made with extraordinary care and thorough examination.

The first of these decisions is a fundamental one: whether to buy or rent. For those who have not accumulated enough capital for a down payment on a home, there may be little choice. But renting has positive virtues, as well. Renters are often able to live closer to their jobs and to the cultural attractions a city has to offer. They do not have to tie up their savings in a house when those savings might be more profitably invested elsewhere. They can leave the worries of mortgages, taxes and repairs to the landlord. In addition, they don't have to go through the time-consuming (and possibly difficult) process of finding a qualified buyer if a time should come when they want to sell.

On the other hand, renters have to learn to live with their landlords, who may be less interested in spending money on repairs and services than in raising the rent. Fewer rental units are being built these days and in some cities apartment vacancy rates have dwindled to as low as 1 or 2 percent — which means that tenants have little choice of where to live and equally little mobility. Moreover, the income of renters has generally failed to keep up with rising rents.

In this chapter we begin by examining various ways of securing the best rental housing for your money: how to look for a place to live — on your own or through agents; how to spot illegal practices and what to do about them; how to check out rental space and scrutinize a lease; how to live with your landlord, register complaints and safeguard your rights if the landlord succeeds in a plan to convert your building to a condominium or cooperative.

Owning a home, too, has its pros and cons. Although two-thirds of the dwelling units in the United States are occupied by people who have managed to achieve the American dream of home ownership, that dream has become increasingly expensive in the last decade or so. Land prices have soared; so have the costs of materials, labor, taxes and mortgage interest. The construction of new housing units has slumped far behind the need. The effort to cut costs and make housing more affordable for a greater number of families has made the condominium principle of shared ownership more and more popular and has also produced the housing equivalent of the compact car — the "down-sized" single family house.

The joys and benefits of home ownership, however, are still there: the pride in having a place you can call your own; the puttering around on weekends; the income tax deductions for mortgage interest payments and property taxes; and of course, the comforting thought that your investment, if well chosen and maintained, will almost certainly bring you a substantial profit when the time comes to sell.

In the second section of this chapter we explore the intricacies of buying a home: sizing up new and old homes; dealing with real estate brokers and attorneys; arranging for home appraisals and inspections; shopping for mortgages; negotiating with sellers and drawing up a contract of sale; looking for savings in the long list of closing costs. We

CONSUMER ALERT

Buying or Renting — Which Makes More Financial Sense for You?

Which is the wiser step from a purely economic point of view — to buy a place to live in or to rent one? Millions of Americans ask themselves this question every year. To help them answer it, the Cooperative Extension Service of Cornell University has prepared a detailed eight-page questionnaire that covers the information necessary to make an informed choice. The questionnaire includes such factors as taxes, anticipated length of residence, projected changes in housing values, repair costs, maintenance expenses, interest rates and a multitude of others.

Consumers can make their own estimates of the proper course to follow on the basis of the information the questionnaire gives them. Such estimates are also available in the form of a computer print-out from the University, which you can order by returning the filled-out questionnaire to Cornell. The print-out includes projections on the basis of high, low and average anticipated changes in costs and interest rates and on the basis of varying lengths of residence. There is a modest fee — under $20 — for the service. The information supplied is confidential and all data relating to your questionnaire is erased from the computer's memory three weeks after it is received.

If you would like a copy of the questionnaire, write to the Department of Consumer Economics & Housing, 108 Martha Van Rensselaer Hall, Cornell University, Ithaca, NY 14853.

look, as well, at the mirror image of this process: selling a home when it is time to move on. Also examined are those increasingly popular and economical forms of housing — condominiums and mobile homes; how to deal with architects and building contractors; and with real estate tax assessments, utilities and movers.

Renting a Place to Live

Good rental housing at a decent price has become increasingly scarce in many parts of the country, but it can be found. Finding it, however, is only part of the battle. The wise tenant must know how to negotiate a proper lease, how to live with his landlord, what his rights and obligations are, and how to deal with problems when things go wrong. The general rules that govern these questions are much the same for tenants all over the country. But the specifics of landlord-tenant law vary widely from state to state and even among municipalities in the same state. Moreover, although in some places the laws of the free market prevail, in others where rental housing is in particularly short supply, stringent controls have been placed on rents and other aspects of the landlord-tenant relationship. On page 99 you will find a directory that tells you the office to check with in order to discover the specific laws, if any, that regulate landlord-tenant relationships in your area. It is especially important that you know about them if you have any dispute with your landlord — not only because of the variations from one locality to the next, but because the law in any given locality can change literally from year to year.

Finding the Space You Want. In the old days one could often find satisfactory quarters — a room, an apartment, even a whole house — by walking down the street and looking for signs saying "For Rent." In today's market it may not be that easy, though that shouldn't discourage you from strolling around an area that interests you and making inquiries here and there. Let friends, relatives and acquaintances know what you're looking for. If you hear of a possible opening in an apartment building where you might like to live, talk directly to the management. If you cannot get your name on a list, make it your business to keep calling or dropping in to see if a vacancy has developed.

One of the best sources for leads is the classified advertising section of the local newspaper under "Apartments for Rent" or

"Houses for Rent." Some will be listed directly by the owner or landlord. Others will involve a broker, for whose services you will have to pay a fee that may range from the equivalent of a month's rent or less to as high as three months' rent, depending on the local market and the broker involved. (A reputable real estate broker will not expect to be paid his fee until the client signs a lease.)

Illegal Practices and How to Deal With Them. Because of the scarcity of rental housing, situations frequently arise in which people attempt to line their pockets at your expense. You may, for example, learn of an available apartment on your own and when you go to see it, be "steered" — by the doorman, superintendent or landlord — to a specific broker in order to get it. In this situation, you are not obliged to pay a broker's fee. If you really want the apartment, however, it may be wise to register with the broker, pay the fee, and then take action to get your money back. One way is to file a complaint with your state department of licensing, which licenses real estate brokers and other professionals to do business in the state. (See Chapter 12 for a further discussion of licensing.) In some states and cities, the law prohibits an unlicensed person from sharing in a commission. If the broker has paid those who steer clients to him, you may be able to sue in civil court. In New York State, for example, you can sue for as much as four times the fee.

Sometimes applicants for apartments are asked for money which is described as a "broker's fee," but in fact is a bribe. This so-called "key money" never makes its way to a broker at all. It remains in the hands of the building employee who extorted it. Here again, the practical course may be to pay the bribe, sign the lease, then report the incident to the local district attorney's office and sue to recover the amount.

Practices for which a broker may be fined or have his license suspended include:

- Keeping your fee even when a landlord refuses to rent you an apartment.
- Misrepresenting apartments in any of the advertising.
- Baiting renters with "bargains" that do not exist, then switching them to more expensive deals.
- Charging a higher brokerage fee than was originally quoted to you for an especially desirable find.

Apartment Referral Services

The tight market in rental housing in various metropolitan centers has encouraged the emergence of a number of so-called Apartment Referral Services and Apartment Finders. For a fee, these establishments supply prospective tenants with lists containing the addresses and rents of apartments that are presumably available. You should not pay that fee, however, until you have found out from the service whether or not it is operated by a licensed real estate broker and what sources it uses in compiling its lists. Services that are not agents for landlords sometimes use a source readily available to anyone — the "for rent" ads in local newspapers — and have no way of knowing whether the apartments they list are available or have already been rented. If you deal with such a service, you are likely to be wasting both money and time.

It is also wise to check any apartment referral service you are considering with your local Better Business Bureau, which will tell you whether any complaints have been received about it, and with your local Office of Consumer Affairs, which may also have information. In some states, the attorney general has taken action against one or more of these services. Check with the Consumer Frauds Division of the attorney general's office.

If you suspect wrongdoing, talk to your local consumer affairs office (see directory on page 16).

Discrimination in Rentals. Federal law prohibits landlords, brokers and their agents from discriminating against prospective or current tenants because of race, color, religion, national origin or sex, and in a few states and municipalities the law also forbids discrimination because of age, disability or marital status. Exceptions are made in the case of rooming houses or apartment buildings of four or fewer units in which the owner lives;

Friends and Lovers

Leases often specify that the only occupants of an apartment shall be "the tenant and members of his immediate family." Where does that leave you if you want to have a friend or relative over for the night?

If your guest visits only occasionally, few landlords are likely to object. And if the landlord *does* object, and you and he wind up in court, few judges will rule that this technical violation is serious enough to warrant eviction.

But suppose you make a more permanent arrangement. According to *New York* magazine, which periodically reports on the guerilla warfare between landlords and tenants in that city of serious housing shortages, legal decisions on this question can go either way. In one case in which a tenant shared his apartment with his fiancée, and the landlord sought an eviction, the trial court refused to grant it on the grounds that the close, loving relationship already qualified the fiancée as part of the tenant's immediate family. But when the landlord appealed to a higher court, the tenant was given 60 days to marry the woman, or get her out.

In another case, involving a woman named Joyce and her companion Charlie, a judge posed the issue as "Full-time live-in or part-time love-in?" Three nights a week, Charlie stayed at Joyce's place; another three, she stayed at his. When Joyce's landlord objected, the issue was brought to court. The judge decided in Joyce's favor. Charlie, he ruled, had not occupied her apartment enough to constitute a serious violation. "The fact that tenant's life-style may not meet with landlord or court's approval cannot restrict her use of the apartment," he ruled. "There is no contention that tenant's relationship with Charlie resulted in legal nuisance, disorder, increased expenses or any damages to landlord's property."

In a still more recent case a New York landlord tried to evict a woman from the apartment she had lived in for more than 40 years on the ground that her live-in lover was not authorized in her lease. She fought back, won her case in trial court, lost it on appeal, and won it again in the state's highest court. The decision appeared to confirm the state's human rights law, which bars discrimination on the basis of marital status — not to mention the maxim that love conquers all.

and for private clubs or associations that rent rooms exclusively to persons of one sex. The box on page 57 describes specific acts forbidden under Federal Fair Housing legislation and outlines the steps to take if you believe your rights have been violated.

In some states a landlord may place limits on the number of people allowed to live in a given rental unit. In some, he may be permitted to set aside a specified percentage of the units in a building for the exclusive use of childless tenants. The law is not always as explicit in the case of unmarried couples sharing an apartment. Courts have decided in a number of different ways, sometimes depending on how much of the time the apartment is jointly occupied, sometimes on whether the couple has created a public nuisance (see box above). Probably the safest course is to get the landlord's written permission to share the apartment with anyone not a member of your immediate family.

Keeping Pets. Courts generally agree that it is legal for a lease to prohibit a tenant from keeping a pet. A landlord can enforce this prohibition by obtaining an eviction order, and can do so even if other tenants in the building have pets. If such a clause appears in the lease you are to sign and you have a pet you can't bear to part with, try to get the landlord to delete it and give written permission. As an inducement you might offer to pay a deposit to cover possible damage or produce a letter of reference from your previous landlord, testifying that the pet created no trouble.

Applying for an Apartment. Most landlords ask a prospective tenant to fill out a rental application and agree to hold the unit while the application is being checked with employers, credit agencies or other references. Some landlords charge an application fee. Before paying it, find out whether it will be applied against the first month's rent if you are accepted, and whether you will get it back in the event that you are rejected or change your mind. Also ask how long you will have to wait to find out if the apartment is yours.

Inspecting the Premises. Before entering into any agreement to rent, make a thorough inspection of the unit itself, the building and the grounds, if there are any. Make sure all the plumbing fixtures, electrical fixtures and outlets, telephone jacks, kitchen appliances, exhaust fans and air conditioners are in good working order; that adequate heat and hot water are supplied; that doors — and windows if necessary — can be securely locked. Note the condition of walls, ceilings, floors, windows and screens, as well as carpeting, draperies or any other furnishings. Are there signs of insects, rats or mice? Is the apartment reasonably soundproof, or will your neighbors' arguments and musical tastes become a part of your life? Are the building lobby, hallways and elevators clean and well lighted? Are there fire exits and a fire alarm system? Is refuse disposal convenient, and is the surrounding area well kept and clean?

Check out such facilities as tenant storage space, parking, a master TV antenna, and such tenant recreation areas as play yards, pools or tennis courts. Are they extra or included in the rent? What maintenance and repair jobs are you responsible for, and which are the responsibility of the landlord? How good is the maintenance? How is emergency service handled if something goes wrong? Talk to other tenants to find out how well the building is run and whether the landlord responds to tenant complaints.

On your inspection tour, make a written list of any defects or damages you note and any questions you have. Try to get the landlord to correct the major ones before you move in, and make an inventory of those that remain, describing the problems clearly. If possible, have a third person look at the problems with you and sign the inventory. If you can, get the landlord to sign it also; if he will not do this, give him a copy and ask him to attach it to his copy of your lease. Keep a copy yourself and file it in a safe place along with your lease, security deposit receipt, monthly rent receipts or canceled checks, and any correspondence you have with the landlord, including complaints. All of this material can come in handy in case of a dispute.

Signing the Lease. Agreements between landlord and tenant can take several forms. A verbal agreement is the simplest, but it holds the greatest possibility of misunderstandings and gives the tenant least protection should the landlord fail to live up to his promises. Even a short, informal document specifying the terms and duration of the rental is better than spoken words, and is sometimes used for month-to-month rentals.

For most rentals, however, particularly those of a year or more, the best assurance for both parties concerned (and often required by law) is a lease: a detailed, written document that constitutes a legal contract between owner and renter. At minimum it should contain:

- The date, names and signatures of both parties.
- A brief description of the premises to be rented.
- The dates and times of day the lease begins and ends.
- The amount and due date of rent payments and any penalties for late payments.
- The tenant's duties and obligations.
- The landlord's duties and obligations; who pays the utility bills.
- The amount and terms of the security deposit (see below).
- The tenant's right to sublet.
- The conditions under which the lease can be terminated or renewed.

When a lease is presented to you for signing, *make sure you read all of it first;* if you don't understand any parts of it, ask for clarification. An increasing number of states and municipalities now require that leases be written in clear, everyday language and printed in at least 8-point type. "Plain English" lease forms are widely available through legal printers and local real estate boards, and you are entitled to ask for one before you sign. You may not get it, if the law where you live does not require it. But it is at least worth a try.

Illegal Clauses. Since leases are written by landlords, it is understandable that they are designed to protect the landlords' interests. However, there are legal limits to the requirements a landlord can place in a lease. A lease cannot:

- Force you to accept the landlord's assertion that you are wrong in any dispute between you. You are always entitled to a legal hearing. Nor can the lease compel you to pay the landlord's court costs if such a legal hearing rules in your favor.
- Allow the landlord to keep your security deposit or prepaid rent when you move if you have not damaged the apartment or breached the lease by moving when it is still in force.
- Allow the landlord to take possession of your personal property if you do not pay your rent.
- Free the landlord from responsibility for negligence on his part that causes you or your guests injury.

Also illegal in most states is any retaliation by the landlord against a tenant — locking him out, shutting off his heat or water, refusing to renew his lease — if the tenant complains to government authorities about violations of housing codes, performs necessary "do-it-yourself" repairs the landlord won't, joins a tenants' organization or withholds rent in protest against insufferable living conditions in his apartment.

The Landlord's Obligations. In most, although not all states, rental leases carry an "implied warranty of habitability" that requires landlords to provide "rental units and common areas that are fit for human habitation and free of conditions detrimental to the life, health or safety of the occupants." But the phrase means different things in different states. In some, courts have declared the landlord in violation of the warranty if he does not provide proper air conditioning or elevator service, fix noisy building pumps and fans, or keep party-throwing tenants from disturbing their neighbors. In others, he need only provide the bare essentials — heat, light and water — and, if the tenants inform him of any problems, maintain the corridors, stairs and elevators in safe condition. And in still others, the courts have rejected the concept of implied habitability, holding that the landlord is bound only by the actual terms of the lease.

But all this is a rapidly changing area of the law. You would be wise to check with the attorney general's office in your state (see directory on page 48) to see what obligations — beyond those spelled out in the lease — your landlord has to you.

Most leases contain a clause giving the landlord the right to enter an apartment for purposes connected with carrying on his business and meeting his obligations: to inspect the premises, make repairs, perform agreed-on services, or show the unit to prospective tenants, purchasers, lenders, workmen or contractors. But this clause should also provide that he will come at reasonable hours and give you reasonable notice, except in an emergency or when it is impracticable for him to get in touch with you.

Security Deposits. The lease will almost certainly require you to give the landlord a deposit before you move into the apartment. This may be a month's rent in advance, to be credited to the first or last month of the lease. You may also be asked for a security deposit — an amount the landlord holds as security for the full performance of your obligations under the lease. Make sure you understand the exact purposes for which the deposit will be used and under what conditions it will be returned to you. Security deposits generally cover damages to the apartment by the tenant beyond normal wear and tear. A worn carpet or chipped paint on the edge of a cupboard door would be considered normal wear and tear, while broken windows, gaping holes in the wall, and indelible crayon marks would not. In addition, the lease may specifically ask for a cleaning deposit, which the landlord can use to clean or repaint the unit after you move out (and which may not be refundable) and/or a damage deposit to take care of repairs necessitated by damage you have caused during your tenancy.

Security deposits are generally regulated by laws that provide varying degrees of protection to the tenants. At best, this protection includes the following: The deposit cannot exceed an amount equal to two months' rent, it must be placed by the landlord in an escrow account (in some states bearing a minimum amount of interest) and, unless the landlord finds damage, it must be returned in full with interest within a specified period — 30 or 60 days, for example — after the tenant moves out. If the landlord does find damage, trash or abandoned property he must dispose of, he can deduct the cost of returning the apartment to a habitable condition from the deposit, but he must provide the tenant with a written statement itemizing the charges. If he fails to return all or part of the deposit within a specified period, the tenant can pursue the matter in court (see Chapter 14).

Subletting Your Apartment. Most leases contain a clause forbidding a tenant to sublet his or her quarters without the landlord's written approval, which cannot be "unreasonably withheld." It is both to your advantage and the landlord's to assure that the subtenant is an acceptable, financially responsible person. Unless you have made some specific written arrangement to the contrary with the landlord, you still retain legal responsibility for the apartment when you sublease it.

If you want to sublet, the best procedure is to notify the landlord by registered or certified mail, providing him with the name, business and home address of the proposed subtenant, and any other information that indicates he or she is the kind of tenant the landlord would want. Depending on local law, the landlord may be entitled to ask you for additional information. If he does not notify you of his consent, or reasons for not consenting, within a specified period, you may be free to sublet on your own.

Registering a Complaint. A tenant's best assurance that the landlord will keep a rental unit in liveable condition lies in the terms spelled out in the lease. The implied warranty of habitability, where it exists, may cover only the bare essentials. But the lease *can* detail a landlord's obligations with respect to repair and maintenance and it is therefore important that a tenant press to have these obligations spelled out in the document.

If the landlord fails to live up to them — if, say, the heat is inadequate or the plumbing doesn't work — the first step is to notify him. If he doesn't correct the problem within a reasonable period, notify him in writing that you will file an official complaint. If he still doesn't correct the condition, you can report him to the local housing code enforcement authorities and/or take him to court.

CONSUMER ALERT

Your Fair Housing Rights

The Fair Housing Section of the Civil Rights Act of 1968 prohibits discrimination based on race, color, religion, sex or national origin in either the rental or sale of housing, and specifically prohibits the following acts:

- Refusing to sell or rent or otherwise deal with a person on the basis of such discrimination.
- Discriminating in the conditions or terms of sale, rental or occupancy.
- Falsely denying that there is housing available.
- Advertising in such a way as to indicate preference, limitation or discrimination.
- "Blockbusting" — causing persons to sell or rent by telling them members of a minority group are moving to the area.
- Discriminating in financing for the purchase, construction, improvement, repair or maintenance of a home — whether by a bank, savings and loan association or other lending institution.
- Denial of membership or participation in or access to brokerage, multiple listing or other real estate services.

If you believe that you have been, or are about to be, discriminated against in any of these ways, you have the right to complain within 180 days to the U.S. Department of Housing and Urban Development (HUD), whose regional offices are listed at the end of this chapter (see directory, page 101).

If HUD finds your complaint justified, it will attempt to end the discrimination by conciliation or, if your state or municipality has a Fair Housing Act, HUD will ask a state or local agency to try to resolve the problem.

You can also go directly to court and, in certain cases, an attorney will be appointed for you without cost. Court action may sometimes provide quicker, more effective relief than conciliation and, if you are successful, may entitle you to collect actual damages, punitive damages up to $1,000, court costs and attorney's fees.

In some states the law recognizes a tenant's right to withhold part or all of the rent until the landlord lives up to his obligations, or allows the tenant to repair certain dangerous conditions and deduct the cost from the next month's rent. Check with your state attorney general's office (see directory, page 48) to see if the law in your area gives you this right, and be sure to find out the requirements it places on you. You may have to notify the landlord in writing of your intent, giving him an opportunity to do the work himself within a specified period. You may have to hire a licensed professional to work on any problem involving heating, plumbing or electricity. The cost of fixing the condition may be limited to a relatively small amount — perhaps $100 or half the monthly rent — and you may have to give the landlord an itemized statement, with copies of receipts, on any work that has been done.

The Tenant's Obligations. Naturally you, too, must live up to your responsibilities as stated in the lease. You must use the premises only for the purposes agreed on (that is, as a residence, not a place of business), avoid disturbing your neighbors, pay the rent on time, keep your apartment clean, undamaged and in compliance with local codes, use the plumbing, wiring and other systems prudently and abide by any other agreements you and the landlord may have made.

Eviction. The first step in an eviction proceeding is for the landlord to send you a "notice to quit." Such a notice is *not* an eviction order and does not require you to move. But it is a signal that he intends to take action, and if you have not already sought legal advice, either from your attorney or from a tenants' organization, you should do so immediately so that you will be able to present your side of the case properly at the eviction hearing. The hearing will be scheduled after the landlord has taken the second step — serving you with a summons to appear in court. If the landlord wants to get rid of you, he cannot simply throw you out, lock your door or cut off your electricity or heat. Nor can he evict you for reporting a code violation, for receiving welfare payments, or because of your race, your religion, or your sex.

He can, however, evict you if you fail to pay rent within the specified period after it is due, if you violate any other agreement in the lease, if your lease contains a cancellation clause that he has invoked and you have ignored, or if state law otherwise allows him to terminate the lease by proper notice. Usually, the presence of a cancellation clause means that the owner intends to convert the building to a condominium or cooperative. (See page 59 for a discussion of your rights under such circumstances.)

Breaking a Lease. If you break a lease yourself and vacate the unit before the specified term is up, the landlord can sue you for the balance of the rent unless he fails to make a reasonable effort to find another tenant or you can prove either that he has deprived you of the full use and enjoyment of your apartment or has unreasonably refused to permit you to sublet under a right-to-sublet law. In either case you will need legal help.

Tenants' Organizations. In some, usually larger apartment buildings, the residents have formed tenants' organizations in order to maintain or improve their living conditions and to assure their rights. Such organizations can help establish clear working relationships between tenants and landlord, can improve the care and appearance of the building and grounds, can arrange for group recreation, social or child-care facilities and can influence the landlord to install such necessary equipment as fire extinguishers or new garbage cans. Building owners like the proprietors of other businesses are likely to pay more attention to a group tenants than to individual "complainers;" if you take the trouble to organize, your landlord will understand that you are serious, too.

If the law in your state protects the right of tenants to organize, a landlord cannot legally interfere with or harass a tenant who wants to join or form a tenants' group, nor can he stop tenants from distributing leaflets under apartment doors or using the building lobby or other common areas for meetings.

If a landlord refuses to correct flagrant violations of the building code, a tenants' group can organize a rent strike to withold payments until the correction is made. However, such an action should not be attempted without first consulting a city or statewide tenants' organization or an attorney. Information on how to start and run a tenants' organization can be obtained from existing tenants' groups in your neighborhood, from social service agencies or regional conferences of churches in your area, or from such tenant groups as Shelter Force, 380 Main Street, East Orange, New Jersey, 07018; Metropolitan Tenants Organization, 109 North Dearborn, Chicago, Illinois, 60602; and California Housing Action and Information Network, 2004 Foothill, Oakland, California, 94601.

Conversions to Condos or Co-ops

In the last few years many rental apartment buildings have been converted to the forms of occupant ownership known as condominiums or cooperatives. (See page 71 for a detailed description of these two types of ownership.) In theory, both building owners who sell, and individuals who buy, stand to profit from conversions. But the process can be long, complex and trying, and benefits are not assured to everyone. Recognizing the problem, a growing number of states and municipalities have passed conversion laws designed to protect tenants by giving them the right to buy their apartments — often at a lower price — before they are offered for public sale. Such laws enable tenants who do not want, or cannot afford, to buy to stay on as renters for a specified period of time, during which the landlord must help them find another place to live. Senior citizens and the handicapped often receive special protection under these conversion laws.

In New York State, where urban dwellers have traditionally lived in rental units, and where the housing shortage is acute, strict conversion laws have been passed that provide a model for tenants all over the country. In New York, any plan must be fully described in a preliminary prospectus (sometimes called the "red herring" after the bold red letters of conversion on its face), and submitted to each tenant and to the state attorney general's office. Tenants and their lawyers can file objections with the attorney general to any statements they believe to be distortions or omissions of fact, and can ask for corrections. When the review is completed and the plan is judged legal — no endorsement of prices, terms, or the building itself is implied — it is accepted for filing and copies of the final version (the "black book") are distributed to tenants.

In many areas that have adopted conversion laws, a building owner or sponsor can choose an "eviction" or a "non-eviction" plan. Under the former, which becomes effective only if a certain proportion of the tenants (35 percent, for example) agree to buy their apartments within a specified time, non-buyers can be evicted only after a certain period and only by outside purchasers of their apartments. Under the "non-eviction" plan, which becomes effective when a lower number of the units (15 percent, for example) is sold either to tenants or outsiders, non-buying tenants may not be evicted. Their apartments may, however, be sold to outside purchasers, to whom they must pay rent.

The provisions of conversion laws vary widely from place to place and are generally quite complicated. Moreover, the tenants in buildings for which conversion is planned do not all necessarily want the same thing. Some may wish to purchase, others to stay on as renters, and still others may want to move. It is therefore important, if you have not already formed a tenants' organization, to form one at this time so that you can hire a lawyer who knows how to achieve as satisfactory a solution as possible. Literature may be obtained from the attorney general's office in your state (see directory, page 48) and from other tenants' associations.

Buying a Home

If there was only one rule to follow in purchasing a home, it could be stated very simply: Take your time. Rushing will almost certainly cost you both money and trouble, and you may well wind up with unforeseen expenses and with a house that really doesn't suit your needs. It is estimated that, on the average, people who buy previously occupied houses take at least two months and visit five different properties before making up their minds, and shoppers for new houses visit up to 10 houses over a period of approximately three months.

Even before looking at houses, there are several preliminary points to consider. First, narrow your choices to the communities that appeal to you. Second, examine your finances to determine what area you can afford to live in. Finally, try to come up with an estimated down payment you can reasonably afford, the kind of mortgage loan you may be able to get, and the size of the monthly payments you will be able to swing.

Looking for a House. The material that follows is aimed primarily at the would-be buyer of a single-family, detached house, but it applies almost equally well to purchasers of condominiums and mobile homes, both of whose special aspects and potential problems are examined in later sections.

Houses that are for sale can be found in a number of ways — through classified listings and display ads in local newspapers, through word of mouth and through real estate brokers who maintain lists. Perhaps a quarter of all home sales are direct transactions between owners and buyers at savings to the seller of a 6 to 7 percent broker's commission. If this saving is passed along to the buyer, he in turn reaps a financial benefit, though it deprives him of professional advice on such important matters as market values, appraisals, negotiations and financing.

Choosing a Broker. Most buyers work through real estate brokers for good reasons. In the first place, most sellers place their homes on the market through brokers, and a good broker knows not only what houses are for sale in various price brackets but also, in many cases, those that are about to go on the market. And the broker who belongs to a multiple listing service (MLS) has access to virtually all houses that are for sale through his or her particular MLS. A broker can give you information on neighborhood trends, schools, shopping, community facilities, zoning and building laws, property taxes and plans that may be afoot for new town improvements and assessments. He can often help clarify your ideas on your real needs and what you can afford, explain architectural styles, construction and financing, suggest mortgage lenders, and even help get quick action on a loan.

He can save you time by showing you photographs and detailed descriptions of available houses right in his office, and can drive you to see those you like. He can advise you on asking prices, resale value, counteroffers and what the seller is willing to accept. In short, he may be able to get you a better deal than you could get on your own.

However, keep firmly in mind that the broker is paid by the seller, either directly or by splitting the commission with the broker who originally listed the house, and that it is in his interest to make a sale. He is not your employee, and although the courts in some states have ruled that brokers have a professional responsibility to verify the information sellers give them and to disclose the true facts about a property to the buyer, not all states have issued such rulings. The wisest course is to investigate a broker carefully before deciding whether or not to work with him. Ask friends about a broker you are considering; talk to mortgage officers at a couple of local banks. If their responses and your instincts agree, you are probably safe in using him.

State laws require that brokers and their salesmen be licensed to do business. The specifics of the laws vary from state to state, but in general they require prospective brokers to take an approved course of study and pass a licensing examination. In addition, some states require the completion of a certain number of hours of continuing professional education every few years for license renewal. Many brokers and their associates belong to the 600,000-member National Association of Realtors (NAR). Membership is based on a favorable business reputation, the completion of an indoctrination course, and the observance of the code of ethics of the NAR, realtors' state associations and local real estate boards. NAR members in good standing are entitled to use the registered trademark "Realtor" and to display the emblem of the association.

Spotting an Unethical Broker. It is not difficult to spot a broker whom you should best avoid. The language of real estate is designed to attract attention to the best features of a house and to skip over its defects. But the broker's advertisement that promises the moon has gone too far, and the broker who placed it is probably untrustworthy. Be wary of:

- The high-pressure salesman who tries to sell you what happens to be on hand, without considering your stated needs.
- The one who tries to sell you a house he knows you are already considering with another broker.
- The one who does not hesitate to "knock" a competing broker and his listings.

• The one who tells you something you know to be untrue and sticks to the untruth even when you correct him.
• The one who puts pressure on you so that you will place a mortgage with a specific lender. He may be looking for a finder's fee from that lender.

If you come across such sharp practices, you can file charges against the offender either through the local board of realtors or the state real estate board. If the charges are proved, the broker can lose his license or be subjected to other penalties.

Looking at Houses. Two out of three buyers purchase older houses, which usually offer more space for the money, a more convenient location, established landscaping and a comfortable, lived-in look. But these advantages always have to be balanced against possible problems, and before you buy that sweet little colonial, there are several things you must do. Ask your broker if a recent appraisal has been made and at what prices similar houses in the neighborhood have sold. If this information is unavailable and you yourself are unsure of neighborhood property values, you may want to have your own appraisal made. You can find a reliable appraiser by asking the broker, your lawyer, the local building inspector, tax assessor or an officer of a local bank for recommendations. Or you can consult the yellow pages of the telephone book under "Real Estate Appraisers" or "Appraisers — Real Estate." Look for listings that indicate membership in the Society of Real Estate Appraisers, the American Institute of Real Estate Appraisers, or some other recognized professional group. And, of course, check out the fee in advance and do some comparison shopping if you choose.

An appraisal provides useful information about location, liveability, the chances of appreciation, quality of construction, equipment and fair market price. It can also reveal any major faults which require careful inspection by a contractor, engineer, plumber, electrician or other specialist.

Inspecting a House. Whether or not you have an appraisal made in advance, you must check out the physical condition of the house, both on your own and with the expert help of a building contractor or licensed building engineer, who can go over the place with a fine tooth comb.

Problems encountered in older houses include settlement — often evidenced in cracks, doors or windows out of line; wet basements, leaky roofs and rot or decay — especially in the roof or along the eaves. Old electrical systems can be inadequate for the loads imposed by modern appliances.

Furnace boilers may need replacement, especially if they are made of steel rather than cast iron (fuel companies often provide free inspection and replacement or repair estimates). Check overall water pressure by turning on several faucets at the same time. The main water supply may have slowed to a trickle, especially when the galvanized pipes used in older houses have caused mineral deposit build-up.

Waste disposal, too, can be a problem. Older septic systems, installed when codes were less stringent, may not adequately meet the demands of a large family with its shower and laundry needs.

Insulation and weatherstripping, commensurate with today's need for energy conservation, are also apt to be lacking. Houses built 30 or more years ago, when fuel was cheap, may have only a layer of batting on the attic floor and very little, if any, protection in the roof or walls.

Make sure the equipment in the house — hot water heater, range, refrigerator, washer, dryer, air-conditioning units — is in good working order, and that all windows, storm windows, screens, doors, locks, fireplaces, thermostats and so forth, are in good condition. If repairs or replacements are needed, get estimates of the cost and, if possible, get the seller to pay for them or deduct their cost from his asking price.

Many lenders will not issue mortgages unless the house has been inspected for termites. Even if the lender does not make this demand, you should not buy a house in areas where this problem is serious until you are certain that it is termite-free. If you cannot get the seller or lender to provide you with a certificate attesting to that fact, you would be wise to hire a professional exterminator to make an inspection.

Checking Out a New House. New homes may not provide as much space for the money as older ones, but their floor plans are often better adapted to modern living. Moreover, the heating/cooling, electrical and plumbing systems, the built-in appliances and conveniences, and the various energy-conserving factors — insulation and thermal glass, for example — are usually more up-to-date. Before buying a new house, it is imperative that you check the reputation of the builder, whether he is an individual contractor or the developer of an entire community. Find out what other homes he has built and talk with their owners to learn how satisfied they are and what problems they may have had. If the neighborhood itself is new, find out whether you will be assessed for street paving, sidewalks, water and sewer lines, or whether the builder will assume these costs. If you are considering a purchase on the basis of a model home, make sure exactly which features — built-in furniture and appliances, lighting fixtures, carpeting, alarm systems, intercoms — are included in the price and which ones you will have to pay for. If you *do* have to pay for them, how much will they cost? Your contract should describe any extras or changes you want in your house and also specify a completion date.

Check on the house from time to time while it is under construction. On the day before you take title, make a thorough inspection or take a "walk-through" with the builder or his representative, checking all equipment, appliances, finishes, windows and doors.

Homeowner Warranties. According to a federal government survey, 62 percent of new home buyers sampled report that they have had at least one problem that cost them $100 or more to repair because the builder had not taken care of it. Some builders expect buyers to correct problems themselves. Others promise to fix anything that goes wrong during the first year, but then renege by blaming the buyer for the difficulty. And unfortunately, there are always the fly-by-night operators who disappear and cannot be tracked down. Even reputable builders can sometimes create problems for buyers because the written warranties they offer against certain basic structural or mechanical defects rarely run for more than a year and on some items for much less time.

New houses carry an "implied warranty of habitability," which requires builders to make good on major construction defects — for example, if a three- to four-inch-wide crack opens between the chimney and the house, or if filled ground subsides, cracking open the foundation and leaving the house in danger of collapse. This warranty is an indispensable protection against disaster. But it does not cover such relatively minor problems as, say, the settling of a wall, which makes doors crooked and can be expensive to repair. It would be practical then, to ask for an insured warranty — a form of protection that has lately come into increasing use. The Homeowners' Warranty (HOW) program, the most popular of these warranties, was initiated by the National Association of Home Builders in 1974, has already insured almost a million new homes and covers some 42 percent of the new units built each year.

The builder — but not the owner — gives up the right to sue when a dispute is submitted to an arbitrator.

Under this plan, HOW stands behind new-home warranties for up to 10 years. The builder pays a one-time premium, the amount of which is determined by the selling price of the house, and passes this cost on to the buyer. During the first year, the builder warrants the home to be free from major structural defects and specified deficiencies in the plumbing, heating, cooling and electrical systems, and from defects in workmanship and materials. During the second year, the builder warrants *only* against major structural defects and problems in the wiring, piping and duct work. During the third through tenth years, HOW insurance covers major structural defects alone.

If the builder fails to live up to his obligations, HOW assumes repair costs above a $250 deductible amount. The warranty covers single-family homes, town houses and condominiums (a newer five-year plan covering remodelings is discussed elsewhere), and is also transferable to a new owner in the event the house is sold.

Disputes between builders and owners are submitted to an arbitrator whose decision is binding on the builder, but not on the owner who still retains the right to sue. So far, over

20,000 disputes have been settled out of court. (See Chapter 13 for a full discussion of the arbitration proceedings.)

Warranties on Older Homes. It is also possible to purchase warranty coverage on an older house from a number of warranty firms. There are two basic forms. One, the *inspection warranty*, is generally paid for by the buyer, but is increasingly purchased by the seller as well. It is often offered in connection with a professional inspection of the house, and covers only the items inspected, provided they are or can be put in satisfactory condition. If a problem develops, the homeowner contacts the warranty company, which pays for the repairs above a deductible amount.

The second, the *non-inspection warranty*, usually taken out by the seller as an inducement to prospective buyers, can also be purchased by the buyer. Typically, a non-inspection warranty protects the buyer for a year after the house changes hands. Since it does not involve inspection, coverage rarely extends to the structural soundness of foundations, walls and roofs, and is limited even with respect to plumbing, heating and electrical systems. Repairs are generally subject to deductibles and may be limited to certain maximum amounts. From a buyer's viewpoint, a non-inspection warranty is no substitute for a professional house inspection, and it should not be relied on to cover major repairs.

Home-warranty firms are not always adequately capitalized. More than one has gone out of business in the past because of insufficient reserves to meet claims. If you are interested in a warranty plan, check to see whether it is backed up by an insurance company that will pay your claims if the warranty firm cannot.

Agreeing to Buy. When you have found the house you want, and whose asking price seems reasonable, you are ready to begin negotiating the sale. Don't forget that the asking price is just the first move in the negotiating process. Most homes are sold for less — sometimes considerably less — than the asking price. After one or more offers and counter-offers, made in writing and relayed through the broker, you may reach a middle figure on which both of you agree.

At this point, you will be asked to put up a cash deposit or "earnest money" as evidence that you intend to go through with the deal. In some places, this may take the form of a preliminary, tentative agreement variously called a "binder," "bid" or "offer to buy," and is accompanied by a token payment ranging from a small sum up to several hundred dollars or more, depending on local custom and the price of the house. A binder commits the buyer to a price. Once it is signed, the seller is expected to take the house off the market for a specified period until details can be worked out and a more complete, formal contract can be drawn up. But more often, the binder is bypassed and the offer takes the form of a "purchase agreement," "sales agreement" or "contract of sale," accompanied by a larger down payment, often 10 percent of the purchase price.

Don't accept any binder or contract simply because the broker or seller says it is a "standard form" or "can't be changed"; it can.

What the Contract Should Include. Any contract should contain an accurate description of the property in question, and designate who will pay for a professional survey if one is needed. It should specify purchase price and amount of deposit. In many states, the broker must place this money in a trust account until the transaction is closed or canceled in a written agreement between buyer and seller. In such states, the disposition of the deposit is not mentioned in the contract. But where there is no such requirement, the contract should state that the deposit is to be held in escrow by the broker, the seller's lawyer or another third party until the sale is actually made. Also, the contract should spell out the conditions and terms under which you can cancel your offer and get your deposit back. These conditions are normally based on:

- Satisfactory evidence by the seller that he has clear title to the property (see "Title Search," later in this chapter).
- A final inspection — to be paid for either by buyer or seller — to certify that the house is free from termites and/or termite damage, and that the plumbing, heating and electrical systems, and appliances are in working order and the house is structurally sound.
- Your ability to obtain satisfactory financing at a stated rate of interest within a stated period of time.

The contract should specify the "closing" date — the time when you sign papers and take possession of the house. It should also contain an itemized list of any and all fixtures, equipment, appliances, furniture, carpeting and draperies that are to be included in the purchase price. In addition, it should specify who is responsible for insurance and loss on the house until the closing (see "Closing," later in this chapter.)

Most important, the contract must indicate the type of deed the seller will convey and the fact that it may be subject to "encumbrances"; a statement that he will convey to you a "marketable" title whose defects do not pose a serious question as to the ownership of the property and thus to your right to use, mortgage or sell it later on. The contract will not specify the nature of these "encumbrances." That surfaces later, through the title insurance policy. But generally they are such things as regulations or covenants limiting what can be done or built on the land; easements that allow a utility company to run pipes or wires through the property or permit a neighbor to use the driveway in order to reach his house; outstanding mortgage payments, taxes or assessments; and mechanic's liens or other claims against the owner for unpaid bills. You may have to accept some normal restrictions, of course, but the contract should specify the evidence the seller will provide about the reasonable marketability of his title and his responsibility for correcting any defects in his power before turning the property over to you.

The Title Search. The marketability of any title is determined by a title search, a detailed examination of the seller's title and often of all public records on the property as far back as 60 or more years. The purpose of the search is to assure the buyer that no one other than the seller has a valid claim to or against the property, and that it has been legally transferred from owner to owner in years gone by — for example, it precludes any possible claims that the house still belongs to a former owner's spouse because it was sold without his or her signature.

Title searches may be conducted by qualified lawyers but more often they are turned over to title or abstract companies that specialize in this work. Even if the company certifies that a title is apparently clear, it is customary to take out title insurance against "hidden defects" that may have been overlooked, or errors that the searcher himself may have made. This is normally done at the closing and is discussed further below.

Types of Deeds. After the title has been searched, the seller's lawyer will draw up the deed — the formal document by which the property will be transferred from seller to buyer on closing day. The sales contract will already have specified which of three types of deeds it will be. A *general warranty deed,* or full covenant and warranty deed, is the best. It guarantees that the property is free of major encumbrances and that the seller will defend you against all claims arising at any time before you take title to the property. Desirable as it is, however, the warranty is only as good as the person who signs it, and provides no assurances as to his future whereabouts or financial ability to defend you should any problems arise.

A *special warranty deed,* often called simply a warranty deed, offers more limited protection. In it the seller assumes responsibility only for claims arising from his period of ownership.

A *quitclaim deed* is the least desirable from a buyer's point of view. This deed merely conveys the seller's interests or rights in the property, but does not assure title to the property itself. (There's a saying in real estate that you can't pass on a better title to a house than the one you already have.) In the case of a quitclaim deed, the title search is of major importance in assuring that the seller has a better claim to the property than anyone else.

If all this sounds complicated, it is — often considerably more complicated than the above summary might indicate. Ask your lawyer to explain the ins and outs of titles and deeds and to recommend the best course for you to follow. After all, that's the sort of advice you're paying for.

Forms of Ownership. Another matter to discuss with your attorney is the form the title to, or ownership of, your new property should take. The most common, and generally regarded as the clearest and best, is a *fee simple estate* or *fee simple absolute,* in which the owner or owners have total rights to the property and can lease, sell or otherwise dispose of all or part of those rights either during their lifetime or by will. A *life estate*, by contrast, is limited to the life of the owner.

If title is taken in the names of two (or more) persons, such as husband and wife, it constitutes a co-ownership or *concurrent estate*. In the eight states that have community property laws — Arizona, California, Idaho, Louisiana, Nevada, New Mexico, Texas and Washington — both spouses are presumed to be owners, even if only one name appears on the documents. However, that presumption is what the law calls "rebuttable": it can be argued in court, should a problem arise.

Shopping for Mortgages. One of the most critical, and often most difficult, steps in home-buying is finding financing on terms you can afford. In the days when mortgage money was plentiful and most loans carried a low, fixed rate of interest with monthly payments remaining at the same level for 20 or 30 years, things were relatively simple. But current inflation and high interest rates have produced competitive pressures which themselves have spawned a bewildering variety of different mortgage schemes.

There is only one way to find the plan that is best for you. Shop around. Talk to your real estate agent, your lawyer, your friends; to the lending officers of local banks, savings and loan associations, credit unions, mortgage or life insurance companies; to the builder or seller of your house, who may be able to help close the deal with financing of his own. If a particular mortgage plan appeals to you, make sure you understand all its ramifications so there will be no unforeseen and unpleasant surprises down the road.

Any lender will want to know details about your income, assets, employment and credit rating as well as the location, construction and condition of the house you want to buy. Expect him to make a certain number of demands. Have the pertinent figures and documents ready and be frank with him. He may, for example, require you to include property taxes and home insurance premiums in your monthly payments, or to pay for a mortgage insurance policy that covers payments in the event of your default.

Under the Equal Credit Opportunity Act, lenders may not discriminate against an applicant for a mortgage loan on the basis of race, color, religion, national origin, sex, marital status or age, provided the applicant meets the legal requirements for entering into a binding contract. Nor can credit be denied because an applicant derives part or all of his income from a public assistance program, or has in good faith exercised any right under the Consumer Credit Protection Act. (See Chapter 9 for a full discussion of the act and for directories of agencies to complain to if you believe that you have been discriminated against.)

Obviously, the longer the repayment period of a loan, the lower the monthly payments will be and the greater the amount of the interest. Indeed, over the long term, the interest can substantially exceed the amount of the loan itself. It is thus important to compare lenders' offers carefully. Even if the difference in interest rates offered by two lenders is only a fraction of a percent, it can add up to a healthy sum over a period of years. Also compare the basis on which different lenders add "points" to mortgage charges to make up for regulated interest rates. If a lender charges three points, for example, this could mean a deduction of 3 percent from the face value of the loan, or the payment of an equivalent amount as a closing cost (see "Don't Forget Closing Costs!," below). Find out how long a grace period a lender will allow after each payment is due, and what the late payment penalty is. If at all possible, try to get a prepayment clause that will allow you to repay the entire balance of the loan at no penalty, or a minimum penalty, should you discover that you have the money or the opportunity to refinance your home at a more advantageous interest rate.

Following are some of the types of mortgage plans that may be available to you, including many the industry likes to call "creative" or "alternative" financing. Not all of them are available everywhere, but it can be guaranteed that more than one will be available to you. Because their terms vary and can change with market conditions, lenders' whims and government regulations, it is wise to scrutinize them in detail, and to consult a lawyer who is up-to-date in real estate mortgages and contracts.

• **Government-insured Mortgages.** One of the first things you should do in shopping for a

The Deed of Trust: An Alternative Device for Home Financing

Almost any agency that provides financing for your home will want to be sure that the loan is secured. This can be done either with a mortgage or a deed of trust. Both are devices by which real property is put up as collateral for the loan. A mortgage involves two parties: the first, the homeowner-borrower, who conveys a lien interest in the property, and the second, the lender, to whom it is conveyed. A deed of trust, on the other hand, involves three parties: the homeowner-borrower, the lender and the so-called "trustee." The homeowner conveys title to the property to the trustee, who holds it in trust for the lender. Just as in the case of a mortgage, there can be more than one deed of trust on a piece of property. Like a second or third mortgage, a second or third deed of trust simply reflects the priority of the particular loan involved relative to the other loans secured by the property.

When deeds of trust were first introduced they had an important practical advantage for the lender. If a borrower defaulted on his payments, the foreclosure procedure was considerably simpler than in the case of a mortgage, and took less time. In some states, this difference continues to exist, but in most, state law and court decisions have virtually wiped it out. In these states, the procedures for foreclosure under the two devices may vary in minor respects, but otherwise the use of one rather than the other is essentially a matter of form rather than substance.

mortgage is to find out if you can get one insured by the U.S. government, which over the years has helped some 25 million people buy homes. The government does not make housing loans directly, but insures loans made by lending institutions to encourage them to accept low — or no — down payments, long terms and lower interest rates.

For the ex-serviceman or ex-servicewoman, the so-called G.I. loan is probably the best form of government-insured loan, whether for buying a house, a condominium or a mobile home, for building a new house or for making improvements on an existing one. Look up the nearest office of the Veterans Administration for details. If you are not an ex-G.I., you may qualify for a loan insured by the Federal Housing Administration of the Department of Housing and Urban Development. For current information and literature, get in touch with your local or regional HUD office. (See directory, page 101.)

FHA and VA loans involve some red tape and delays, so be patient. Moreover, some banks won't bother handling them, or charge extra "points" if they do. If you look around long enough, however, you may be able to find a government-insured loan that suits your needs. In addition to insuring fixed-rate, long-term mortgages, FHA and VA back graduated-payment mortgages and are moving into other areas of the alternative financing described below.

• **Assumable Mortgages.** The most popular form of home financing is for the buyer to take over, or assume, the seller's existing mortgage on a house. This is simpler for everyone concerned, and often has the additional advantage of offering lower interest rates than those demanded currently. On the other hand, if a fair amount of the loan has already been paid off, a larger down payment or additional financing will doubtless be necessary. Moreover, the lender may not always cooperate. Many conventional (not FHA or VA) mortgage contracts contain a "due-on-sale" clause, which allows the lender to demand full payment of the outstanding loan when the house is sold. The Garn-St. German Banking Act, signed into law in October 1982, makes "due-on-sale" clauses generally enforceable. Still, some lenders do not enforce this clause and do permit assumption. At the same time, however, they may raise the interest rate, although the amount of the raise may be limited by state law.

• **Seller Mortgages.** Also known as "take-back" or "purchase money" mortgages, these are arranged directly between a buyer and a seller in order to close a deal and may be negotiated in addition to the assumed mortgage or other financing the buyer has obtained. The mortgage note, which is held by the seller, generally covers the amount of the purchase price that the buyer cannot pay in cash. If the owner is eager to sell, he may agree to a take-back mortgage at a favorable rate of interest.

• **Installment Contracts.** If no other form of financing is readily available, an owner might agree to sell you the house on an installment contract, which you must fulfill in regular payments. Such a contract may give you the right to pay off the entire amount when you do obtain regular financing, or give you title to the house in return for a mortgage when the balance has been reduced to a previously agreed-on sum. Like any other agreement, an installment contract should be written with the help of a lawyer. If you don't keep up your payments, you might find your money in the owner's pocket — and yourself out on the street.

• **Wrap-around Mortgages (WAMs).** These "all-inclusive" mortgages combine the balance due on an existing mortgage with an additional amount "wrapped around" it and provided by the seller or the lending institution, whichever holds the wrap-around. Each month the buyer makes one lump-sum payment. If the seller holds the wrap-around, he in turn makes payments to the holder of the original mortgage.

Although wrap-arounds can be used with assumable mortgages, they are usually associated with non-assumable ones. These mortgages are advantageous to both sides: the buyer obtains a lower overall interest rate than the market average allows for an all-new loan, while the seller has an opportunity to accomplish a sale in a difficult market.

• **Fixed-rate Mortgages (FRMs).** The old-fashioned, long-term, fixed-rate mortgage has picked up a new acronym, pronounced FIRM — an ironic reflection on the uncertainties of today's mortgage market. Although one prominent economist predicts the return of the 4 percent traditional mortgage by 1998, some real estate experts are less optimistic on this score. If you *can* find a brand-new FRM, it will probably carry a stiff interest rate. Many lenders prefer floating-rate loans (see below) that offer protection against inflation.

• **Adjustable-rate Mortgages (ARMs).** Also known as Adjustable Mortgage Loans (AMLs), Variable Rate Mortgages (VRMs) and Renegotiable Rate Mortgages (RRMs), all these are mortgages whose interest rates rise and fall with an index reflecting the rates lenders must pay their depositors or investors. Interest rate adjustments occur at intervals that must be specified in the mortgage contract, and generally range from six months to five years. If the chosen index decreases, the lender must lower the rate; if it increases, the lender has the option of raising it. Most such mortgages have a limit, or "cap," on the amount of the rise at any one adjustment date (2 percentage points for example) and some have limits on the total amount of the increase over the life of the loan. All these limits (or caps) are imposed by federal law.

Interest rates may be pegged to any one of a number of indexes used to chart the cost of money: the interest rates on three- or six-month treasury bills, the yield on one- to five-year treasury securities, the average cost of funds to savings and loan associations, the Federal Home Loan Bank Board's national average of contract mortgage rates. Variations on ARMs, called inflation-indexed or adjustable-balance loans, link interest rates with the consumer price index. Some indexes are more volatile than others. They can go down from time to time, but can also shoot up dramatically. In deciding which index is most advantageous to you, you should take into account both the worst-case scenario proposed for the money market and the length of time you expect to stay in your house. Real estate experts generally warn against any mortgage tied only to the actual cost of funds to the individual lender, since such an index allows him to pass on to borrowers any reverses he may suffer.

• **Graduated-payment Mortgages (GPMs).** Young, first-time buyers, and others whose incomes are low but can be expected to increase, should be especially interested in GPMs. In the early years of the loan, monthly payments are smaller than usual, although they increase by a set amount each year for the first five or ten years. Then they level off at a constant, fixed rate for the balance of the loan. Since payments during the early years

(continued on page 71)

Mortgages: Pro and Con

This chart describes some of the major advantages and disadvantages for the *buyer* of various types of financing devices discussed in the text. A particular financing device may be better suited for some home buyers than for others. To determine which is the best for you, you should take into account a number of factors including your age, income, likelihood of increased income in the future and tax needs; how much money you have for a down payment and settlement costs, other financial commitments you have or may have and interest rates. Note that not all types of mortgages will be available at a particular time or in a particular area and that these financing devices might have different names in your area.

Mortgage Type	Advantages	Disadvantages
Government-insured Mortgage	Provides rate of interest below current rate, amortized over life of loan (*i.e.*, no balloon payment), fixed monthly payments, and assumable. Lenders require lower down payment than with conventional loan.	Seller may be discouraged from selling since he must pay additional loan discount points.
Assumable Mortgages	Rate of interest may be lower than the prevailing rate. Buyer may be able to avoid or save on loan placement fees.	None, although they have become increasingly more difficult to obtain.
Seller Mortgages — Purchase Money Mortgage	Seller will often provide more favorable interest rate than the prevailing rate. No loan placement fees.	Seller may demand balloon payment provision, requiring buyer to refinance perhaps at higher interest rate.
Installment Contract	Allows buyer to purchase without obtaining commercial loan. Rate of interest may be lower than prevailing rates, there are no loan placement fees, and monthly payments are fixed.	Seller retains legal title to property, and death of seller during pendency of contract may complicate buyer's getting clear title to the property. In many states this may be a risky financing device while alternative devices may offer many of same advantages.
Wrap-around Mortgage (WAM)	Buyer obtains a rate of interest below prevailing rate and can reduce loan placement fees.	Underlying lender who had not authorized WAM may be able to invoke any existing due-on-sale clause, necessitating refinancing of property or, if unavailable, foreclosure.
Fixed-rate Mortgage (FRM)	Monthly mortgage payment remains fixed despite rising interest rates.	Monthly mortgage payment remains fixed even if interest rates decline.

Mortgage Type	Advantages	Disadvantages
Adjustable-rate Mortgage (ARM)	Interest rate may be lower than rates for fixed rate mortgage (assuming such mortgages are available). Monthly payment decreases if interest rates decline.	The amount of the monthly mortgage payment or the number of monthly payments will increase if interest rates rise.
Graduated-payment Mortgage (GPM)	Requires smaller monthly payments in the early years of the loan. Thus, if buyer's income is expected to increase in time, the burden of higher mortgage payments is shifted to coincide with those increases. A GPM makes it easier for such a buyer to qualify for a loan.	Monthly payments will be higher than for a fixed-rate mortgage in the latter years of a loan. Also since payments in the early years do not cover the principal and accrued interest, the principal balance on the loan may *increase*.
Graduated-payment Adjustable-rate Mortgage (GPARM)	Same as for GPM's. In addition, monthly payments may decrease from what they would have been under a fixed-rate GPM if interest rates decline. Initial interest rate may be lower than rates for a fixed-rate GPM.	Same as for GPM's. In addition, monthly payments may increase from what they would have been under a fixed-rate GPM if interest rates increase.
Balloon Mortgage	Lower rate of interest than for a fully amortized loan (assuming one is available).	Buyer must repay balance after a specific number of years, risking higher interest rates, paying new loan placement and settlement costs. If no financing of the balloon is available buyer may face foreclosure.
Interest Rate Buy-downs	Rate of interest below market rates for a specified period.	If buy-down rate applies for only a specified period, interest rate (and monthly payment) will subsequently increase.
Zero-interest Mortgage (ZIM)	No interest on the outstanding principal of the loan. Accelerated schedule for full ownership of home.	High down payment required. High purchase price for home, without resulting increase in value. Loss of some home-ownership tax benefits deductibility of interest payments.
Land Leases and Lease with Option to Buy	Reduces the purchase price, making it easier for a purchaser to qualify for a mortgage and reducing monthly	Loss of partial tax benefits (that is, interest deductions), since rental payments rather than payments are made on the land. Buyer may subsequently

Mortgage Type	Advantages	Disadvantages
	payments. Allows buyer to accumulate a down payment while he lives in the house. May be able to apply rental payments to purchase price.	have to purchase land at its appreciated value if contract so requires. Option money to preserve right to purchase could be lost if option is not exercised.
Shared-equity Mortgage (SEM)	An investor shares in down payment and/or mortgage payment, thereby reducing the financial burden for home buyer.	Buyer must share appreciation in value of property. Agreement between investor and buyer may require buyer to buy out investor's share, possibly necessitating refinancing of property, or if financing is not available, foreclosure.
Shared-appreciation Mortgage (SAM)	Purchaser obtains a rate of interest below prevailing rates (and thereby lower monthly payments).	Buyer shares appreciation in value of property with an investor or lender. Property may have to be sold or refinanced (at possibly a higher rate of interest and with loan placement and settlement fees) after a specified period.
Growing-equity Mortgage	Allows buyer to accumulate equity in his property on an accelerated basis, thereby paying off mortgage more quickly. Shorter term mortgage results in a lower rate of interest than prevailing fixed-rate, fully amortized mortgages. Buyer pays a lower total amount of interest than would be paid in conventional financing arrangements.	Reduced tax benefits, since interest rate payments (and thereby interest deductions) are lower than they would be under a conventional mortgage. Monthly payments will be higher than with a conventional loan.
Home Equity Conversion Plans (for example, Reverse-annuity Mortgage (RAM)	Provides source of income to elderly homeowners who have no outstanding mortgage.	Once payments cease, a homeowner who wants to keep home may have to repay all payments made, plus interest, plus a portion of the appreciated value of the property. If property has appreciated to a sufficient extent, the owner can refinance with another RAM. If owner dies, does not want or cannot keep the property, lender assumes title. If owner cannot repay loan, he may lose the home.

do not cover all the interest due, the interest is deferred and added to the loan principal. In consequence, the overall cost of the loan is somewhat higher than it would be under a conventional loan.

• **Graduated-payment Adjustable-rate Mortgages (GPARMs).** As you might suspect, these combine features of the GPM and ARM. As in the GPM, payments increase each year until they reach the fixed level required to pay off the loan in the specified term. At the same time payments are adjusted on the basis of an index, which is generally set at longer intervals than in a simple ARM, to save the borrower from having to cope with two kinds of adjustments at once.

• **Balloon Mortgages.** Sometimes known as roll-over mortgages, these loans fix monthly payments similar to those of conventional, long-term, fixed-rate mortgages. But they run for a much shorter period — generally from two to ten years. At the end of this period, the borrower must pay off the balance in a large lump sum — the "balloon" — unless he has been able to sell the home or refinance — "roll over" — his mortgage before the balloon was due. Such mortgages hold down monthly payments, and are therefore attractive to young couples and borrowers who believe they will be able to refinance later at favorable rates. On the other hand, when the time comes to pay off the balloon, a borrower may have to refinance at a higher rate or take out another balloon.

If you are considering a balloon loan, find one in which the lender guarantees to refinance at the end of the term. If a lender wants his money in three years and you feel safer with seven, you may be able to convince him to compromise on five and to throw in a "safety valve" clause to protect you if you cannot pay him at that time. Even if he imposes a financial penalty in return for this concession — such as increasing your interest every quarter until full payment is made — the arrangement may be advantageous.

• **Interest Rate Buy-downs.** Builders sometimes offer below-market interest rates on new mortgages in order to sell their homes. These are the result of "buy-downs" in which a builder pays the lender a lump sum in exchange for a lower interest rate, or places money in an escrow or pledged account that can be drawn on by the lender to supplement the buyer's monthly payments. The low-interest feature can run for any period up to the life of the loan, but in practice it rarely exceeds three years. At that point, interest rises — either to the market level or some predetermined rate. Builders often pass on the cost of a buy-down to the buyer in the form of a higher selling price for the home.

• **Zero-interest Mortgages (ZIMs).** To move unsold houses, some builders and developers, acting as their own bankers, offer loans that enable the buyer to make the large down payment — typically one-third or more of the purchase price — which can sometimes be partly financed by a second mortgage. The remainder is paid off in interest-free monthly installments over five to seven years. If the builder-seller makes the loan, he may cover his financing costs by raising the price of the home by 10 percent or more, or by adding on a loan fee of about 5 percent. Normally, such a loan would give the buyer no tax deduction. But if the house is seller-financed, he should be able to take advantage of the "imputed" interest rate (generally 10 percent) associated with the financed portion of the house.

• **Land Leases.** To make housing more affordable, some sellers, in a sale-rental combination, will sell the house proper and lease the lot it is sitting on, giving the buyer the option of buying the land later. For the buyer, this means a lower down payment and, in many cases, lower monthly payments, since house mortgage and land rental are financed separately. On the other hand, because no interest is paid on the land, the buyer loses some tax benefits.

• **Lease with Option to Buy.** Under this agreement, a buyer without sufficient capital can move into a home, pay rent to the owner and hope to accumulate enough money for the required down payment by the time — generally a year or two — that he must exercise his option to buy. The purchase price, or a formula to determine it, is written into the contract along with the terms of the lease and the buyer also pays a certain amount of "option money" that may be applied to the down payment. This money is not usually refunded if he decides against buying.

• **Shared-equity Mortgages (SEMs).** These plans, also known as "rich uncle loans," bring a lender or investor together with a buyer who cannot quite afford to swing the purchase of a home on his own. The investor pays part or all of the down payment, a portion of the monthly payments, or both, in return for a proportionate share in the ownership of the property, including any appreciation in its worth. The buyer/occupant pays a fair market rent on the investor's share. At the end of the agreement, which usually runs for three to five years, the buyer can, if he chooses, buy out the investor's share or use his share of the proceeds from selling the house as a down payment on another home. A shared-equity mortgage may hold special appeal for first-time buyers and for parents who want to help their children buy a home. Since tax laws are complex and misunderstandings can arise, it is best to consult a lawyer and tax expert to be sure that all the arrangements are strictly businesslike.

• **Shared-appreciation Mortgages (SAMs).** Another new scheme, the SAM, brings together a buyer and a lender or investor who offers a lower mortgage interest rate in return for a share in the profit earned on the appreciated price of the home, either when it is sold or at some specified time — five or 10 years, for example — during the life of the loan, whichever comes first. As yet relatively few of these loans have been made. Most lenders are reluctant to forego interest income and assume the problems which are associated with joint ownership.

• **Growing-equity Mortgages (GEMs).** A recent variation on the graduated-payment loan is the growing-equity or early-ownership mortgage, in which monthly payments increase either in accordance with an index or an agreed-on schedule — 3 or 4 percent a year, for example. Since the interest does not change, the increased payments enable the borrower to accumulate equity in his home at an accelerated rate and to pay off his mortgage earlier than he normally would — in 14 to 16 years, for example, on a 30-year mortgage. GEMs appeal mainly to buyers with rising incomes who want, and can afford, to pay off loans as fast as possible.

• **Home Equity Conversion Plans.** Several different kinds of plans have been designed to permit older people to remain in their homes despite the effects of inflation on their pensions and Social Security checks. The so-called Reverse-Annuity Mortgage (RAM) enables a homeowner to take out a loan on his house and have it paid to him in the form of a monthly check for a specified period — 10 years, for example — after which he must pay it back. Variations on the RAM include open-ended and lifetime-income plans, in which the loan is paid off either upon sale of the house or the borrower's death. Under other schemes, older residents actually give up ownership but continue to live in their homes. In a sale-leaseback, for example, the house is sold to an investor who rents it to the previous owner for life at a controlled rate and who pays for home insurance, taxes and repairs. Similar lifetime-residency arrangements can be worked out with nonprofit community organizations that pay housing expenses and, in some cases, an additional monthly stipend in return for title to the house when the owner or surviving spouse dies. Further information on these plans can be obtained from the National Center for Home Equity Conversion, 110 East Main St., Madison, Wisconsin 53703.

Don't Forget Closing Costs!

As many first-time home buyers have discovered, to their chagrin, buying a home involves many more expenses than the purchase price. There are attorneys' fees, lenders' fees, title examination and insurance, state and local transfer taxes, to mention only a few. These "closing costs" or "settlement costs" must be paid at the time the deed to the property is transferred. According to an old rule of thumb, they run about 5 percent of the purchase price. But they can run higher. It is therefore wise to calculate them in advance in order to be sure that you have enough cash in the bank at closing time.

With a few exceptions, such as mortgage assumptions and refinancing, the loans that finance the purchase of houses, condominiums, cooperative units and building lots are regulated by a federal statute called the Real Estate Settlement Procedures Act (RESPA), passed by Congress in 1974 to protect consumers against unfair practices and help reduce settlement costs.

RESPA requires that within three business days after the lender receives your formal application for a loan, he either give or mail you two documents: a booklet on settlement costs and procedures, prepared according to Department of Housing and Urban Development guidelines; and an itemized, good-faith estimate of your settlement costs, together with a list of names, addresses and telephone numbers of persons or firms that provide the specific services associated with the settlement. The list is required to indicate any business relationship these firms or individuals have with the lender, and can therefore alert you to any possible conflicts of interest. Between the time you receive this material and the day of closing, you will have ample chance to look it over and, if you desire, get in touch with other firms or individuals to see whether you can get a better price.

Local custom generally determines who does what in the settlement process and whether the buyer or seller pays the various fees. There are no fixed rules, however, and you may be able to negotiate individual items with the seller. You may also be able to negotiate the choice and services of the settlement agent, who conducts the actual closing and who — again depending on local custom — may be a representative of a lending institution, title insurance or escrow company, real estate broker or attorney for either buyer or seller. If you compare practices and rates, you may find that you can satisfy everyone's needs and at the same time save money by using a different agent from the one originally proposed.

How to Analyze Costs

Use the work sheet provided in the HUD/RESPA booklet to compare settlement costs. A copy of this form, or one with similar terminology and numbering of items, must also be filled out with actual (rather than comparative) costs by the person conducting the settlement. Combined with summaries of the amounts due the buyer and the seller at closing time, these items make up the Uniform Settlement Statement. One business day before the closing or settlement, the settlement agent must allow you to see the statement, filled in with whatever final figures are available at that time, if you request it. At the end of the settlement on closing day, you will receive a copy of the completed statement.

Loan Charges. In looking over line items on the work sheet, you should keep a few things in mind. The *loan origination fee* — normally 1 percent or more of the face value of the loan and often amounting to several hundred dollars — covers the lender's administrative costs in processing the loan. In addition, it may include the costs of an appraisal of the property and a check on your credit standing. The *loan discount,* or "points," is a charge used to offset constraints placed on the lender's yield by state or federal regulations, adjusting it more closely to the actual demands of the market. Each "point" is equal to 1 percent of the mortgage amount. Thus three points on a $100,000 mortgage would come to $3,000 — a hefty share of total closing costs.

In comparing overall costs among different lenders, the rough rule of thumb is that any "points" — or other one-time settlement charges such as origination fees, application fees or lender's attorney fees — that equal 1 percent of the loan amount, increase the loan's effective interest rate by 1/8 of 1 percent for a payback period of about 15 years. If you expect to sell the property and pay off the loan in five years, the factor should be increased to 1/4 of 1 percent. Translating all of a lender's one-time charges to percentages of your loan amount and adding them to the quoted or "contract" interest rate enables you to compare his total with other lenders.

At the time the loan is actually made, the law requires the lender to give you a Truth-in-Lending statement that discloses his effective interest rate or annual percentage rate, including discount points, fees and other charges levied on top of the stated interest rate. It is wise to ask for this statement at the time you apply for the loan so that you can compare rates among lenders.

The *appraisal fee,* listed next on the form, covers an assessment of the value of the property by an independent appraiser or a member of the lender's staff. It may be paid for either by the buyer or the seller, as agreed upon in the sales contract, and in some cases it is included in the mortgage insurance application fee (see below). The appraisal report may contain information of value, so don't hesitate to ask the lender for a copy.

The *credit report fee* covers the cost of investigating your credit standing. Under the Fair Credit Reporting Act (see Chapter 9), you do not have the right to see a copy of the report, but you are entitled to receive a summary of the nature and sources of the information it contains. The *lender's inspection fee* pays for any inspection of the home the lender may wish to conduct for his own purposes. The *mortgage insurance application fee* covers the cost of processing the application for the private mortgage insurance that may be required on certain loans and may also include an appraisal fee. The *assumption fee* is charged for processing papers when a buyer takes over the seller's existing mortgage loan.

Items Paid in Advance

The lender may require you to prepay certain items at the time of settlement. You may have to pay *interest* that accrues on the mortgage from the settlement date to the date of your first regular monthly payment. The lender may request that you take out mortgage insurance, particularly if his loan exceeds 80 percent of the value of the property, in order to protect him from loss in case you default on your payments. He may also require you to make an advance payment, covering several months or a full year, on your first *mortgage insurance premium.* Mortgage insurance should not be confused with mortgage life or disability insurance designed to pay off your mortgage in the event of your disability or death (see Chapter 10, Investments and Insurance). The lender may also require you to prepay your first year's *hazard insurance premium* on a policy that insures both of you against loss from fire or natural hazards like windstorms. This coverage may be included in a homeowner's policy that also insures against personal liability and theft. If you live in an area where floods are common, federal law may require you to carry special flood insurance.

Under "reserves deposited with lender," you may have to pay an initial amount into a reserve or escrow account that covers such items as the next premiums due on hazard and mortgage insurance, your first regular monthly payments for *city property taxes, county property taxes,* and *annual assessments* for any local improvements such as sidewalks and sewers or homeowners' association fees.

Title Charges

"Title charges" embrace a variety of services connected with the closing, including the *settlement* or *closing fee* paid to the settlement agent, *the abstract* or *title search* and *title examination* of previous ownership records (see "Title Search," above), any *title insurance binder,* separate charges for mortgage, deed and other *document preparation* not covered by other service fees and *notary fees* to a licensed notary public to authenticate executed papers.

You may also have to pay, or share with the seller, the *attorney's fee* for legal services provided to the lender for examining the sales contract, title binder and other documents, or for handling the closing as settlement agent. Do *not* forget to allow for your own lawyer's fee, which is billed separately from the closing and can range from several hundred to several thousand dollars. Some lawyers still follow the old practice of charging 1 percent of the purchase price. Others charge an hourly rate ranging from $50 in some rural areas to several hundred dollars in city and suburban locations.

Many lenders also insist on *title insurance* to protect against errors in the title search. Depending on the arrangements you have made, you may be required to pay all, part or none of these costs. *Lender's coverage* specifies a one-time premium paid at closing for a title insurance policy that protects only the lender. It is usually written for the amount of the mortgage loan and unless the seller agrees in the sales contract to pick up part or all of the tab, it is customarily paid for by the buyer. *Owner's coverage,* in contrast, protects your equity in the house against defects in the title. In some areas, it is traditional for the seller to provide, and pay for, the owner's policy while in other areas the buyer who wants such coverage must pay for it himself. An owner's policy is usually much less expensive when purchased simultaneously with a lender's policy, so it may be to your advantage to talk to your lender about his plans.

Lenders often require title insurance — protection against errors in the title search — before making loans.

Since title insurance can vary widely in price, it usually pays to shop around. You may also be able to save money if the house you are buying has changed hands within the last several years. Under these circumstances, you may not need a full title search and a brand-new policy. Ask the seller for his title insurance policy and take it to the title insurer or to the lawyer who is conducting your search. You may be able to simplify the process and get the policy transferred to you at a "reissue rate," which can be as much as 40 percent below the rate charged for a new policy (reissue rates are not generally publicized, so you will have to ask). On any title policy, look for exceptions to insurance coverage that appear on Schedule B and ask your lawyer about them. Some may not be in your best interests — or may even be totally unnecessary — and the title company may be willing to remove them. Rates for title insurance are regulated by the insurance department of each state and vary with the selling price of the house. Although the premium is paid only once, it can amount to several hundred dollars or more.

Closing the Deal

The recording charge imposed by state and local governments is customarily paid by the buyer. However, it is usually no more than a nominal sum. The excise transfer tax — and surtax, if one exists in the locality — is generally a percentage of the selling price of the house. Some states have statutes requiring the buyer to pay these taxes within a specified number of days of the closing. In other states, it is a matter of negotiation who pays them. The lender or title insurance company may also require a *survey* to determine the exact location of the house and lot lines as well as any easements or rights of way. Because a survey is of value to the buyer, he generally pays the fee. On the other hand, if the seller has an old survey and will sign an affidavit that no changes have been made, or if the original surveyor brings the survey up to date, a new survey may not be necessary. A *pest inspection* for termites, carpenter ants or rodents may be paid for by either seller or buyer. All these fees, and fees for structural, plumbing or other inspections (discussed in a previous section), are entered on the blank lines on the work sheet.

The long-awaited day of closing, if properly planned for, can be a day of relief, even rejoicing, for all concerned. "Just bring your checkbook," the real estate agent may cheerfully remind you. But it wouldn't be a bad idea to bring a pocket calculator too, to check on the settlement agent's line-by-line review. When the whole sheet of adjustments has been completed and money has changed hands, you'll finally get your title, your mortgage, and the keys to your new home. And, who knows, someone may even offer to pay you for the ordeal by taking you out to lunch!

Selling Your Home

In many ways, the processes involved in selling a home are mirror-images of the ones involved in buying it. If the time has come for you to move on, you would do well to read the sections on aspects of home-buying concerning brokers, lawyers, mortgages, contracts, closing procedures and costs. This material, while directed to the buyer, contains information equally useful to the seller.

"For Sale By Owner." As noted previously, about a quarter of the homes that change hands each year are sold directly by owner to buyer. The seller who uses a real estate broker normally pays the broker's commission out of the proceeds of the sale; you therefore stand to save a substantial sum of money if no broker is involved. If you believe you have the right home, the right price, the right financing and the skill to negotiate with the right buyer, you may want to try this route. On the other hand, if the market is weak, or you have neither the time nor the talent or are simultaneously concentrating on moving to another home or another job, you may want to leave the headaches to a pro.

Before deciding which route to take, talk to any friends you may have in banking or real estate or to people who have sold their homes without brokers; ask them to point out the pitfalls they encountered and the devices they found effective. Whatever you do, don't rely on your own judgment of what your home is worth. Surveys show that many people have no idea of the true value of their homes. Some fail to take account of inflated prices and housing shortages and therefore undervalue them, particularly if they have lived in them for a long time. Others, who take personal pride in the care and the improvements they have lavished on their homes, have a highly overblown picture of what those homes might be worth to someone else.

Getting an Appraisal. Before deciding to sell your home — whether on your own or through a broker — obtain a professional appraisal of its actual, current market value. You can get the names of reputable appraisers through the mortgage officers of local banks, through local lawyers experienced in real estate matters, and through acquaintances you may have in real estate firms. Many real estate brokers themselves specialize in appraisals, and will provide one for a fee. Some firms offer free appraisals, in hopes that you will list your property with them. You are not obligated to do so, however, and you may be able to get one, or even several, appraisals of this kind without committing yourself. Make sure any appraisal is thorough, not just a quick, off-the-top-of-the-head opinion. Remember, too, that although it is more accurate than your own assessment, even a professional appraisal is not much more than an educated guess as to what a given buyer might actually pay for your home.

Getting Buyers Interested. Depending on the character of your neighborhood and your own strategy, you may want to use that oldest and simplest of announcements: a for-sale sign. Although you can buy one at a hardware store, you would probably be wiser to invest in a tastefully lettered sign by a professional sign painter. (But before making that investment, check to make sure that local law permits such signs.) You can save yourself from annoyance by the merely curious if you get one reading: "For Sale By Owner, By Appointment Only" with your telephone number underneath.

Sign or not, you will have to get the word around that your home is for sale. Besides telling friends and acquaintances, plan at least a modest advertising campaign in the real estate columns of the local newspaper and possibly those of a nearby big-city paper as well. The ads needn't be large — a few lines may be sufficient — but they should run on a regular basis and contain a brief description of the type of home, number of bedrooms and baths, any special features, the location, and the important fact that it is FOR SALE BY OWNER — which often attracts buyers who, like you, hope to save money by eliminating the middleman. Don't be surprised if the phone starts ringing immediately — or if most of the callers are not eager buyers but real estate brokers trying to talk you out of the folly of not listing your home with them.

Tax Breaks for Sellers

If you are unfortunate enough to sell your home for less than you paid for it, you cannot take a tax deduction for your loss. However, if you sell it at a profit, it is possible that you may be able to reduce, defer or even eliminate payment of the federal income tax on capital gains.

By adding to the original price you paid for your home the attorney's fees, survey and appraisal fees, title insurance premium and mortgage origination fees that you incurred in the sale of it, you can, in effect, reduce your profit for tax purposes. You can also take into account the cost of any capital improvements — remodeling, major repairs, a new kitchen or heating system — any alterations designed to make the place more saleable — even painting or minor repairs — as long as they were initiated no more than 90 days before you signed the contract of sale. In addition, you are permitted to deduct the costs of the sale itself, including the real estate broker's commission, attorney's fee and other closing costs paid by you.

If within 24 months you buy or build another, more expensive, home you can postpone taxes on any gain realized in selling your old one.

Or, you may be able to spread taxes on your gain by arranging to receive payments on your old house in installments which are spread over two or more years.

Finally, if you are 55 years of age or older on the date of the sale and have lived in your home for at least three of the five previous years, the government allows you to take a special, once-in-a-lifetime exclusion of up to $125,000. Unless your profit is greater than that amount, you pay no tax at all.

For more detailed provisions of the law, and ways of calculating the most advantageous tax breaks for your situation, ask your local office of the Internal Revenue Service for its latest pamphlets on home ownership and selling and buying homes.

Handling Prospective Buyers

Make your home neat and attractive, and fix whatever has to be fixed. When promising-sounding prospects stop in, use common sense in showing them around. Don't oversell features dear to your heart, keep up a constant chatter, or make them feel rushed. Be prepared to answer detailed questions about the heating system, the fuel bills, water supply, taxes, schools or whatever else they are interested in. Don't misrepresent any material facts; you can be sued for damages caused by the misrepresentation and lose the sale even after title to the house has changed hands. It is, therefore, particularly important for you to make clear which appliances, furnishings and fixtures go with the house and which you intend to take with you when you move.

Even before you start showing your home, it is prudent to have a purchase agreement drawn up by a lawyer and ready for discussion. Beside the items standard in such contracts, make certain it contains clauses that uphold your interest as a seller, including a binder or down payment sufficiently large to make it worthwhile for you to take your home off the market. Remember to include a "time-is-of-the-essence" clause that allows you to start looking for other prospects if the buyer can't meet your deadlines or get the financing he wants.

In a tight mortgage market, you as seller may have to be ready to help with financing if the buyer is unable to get what he needs at the bank. You may be able to work out a deal with your lender so that the buyer can assume your present mortgage, or a new "wrap-around mortgage" at a compromise interest rate. You may have to become a lender yourself, taking back a second mortgage or agreeing to an installment contract, lease-purchase deal or some other form of "creative financing" (see "Shopping for Mortgages").

Selling Through a Broker. If you decide to enlist the assistance of a real estate broker, you must then agree on his services in a "listing" agreement. There are basically four types of listings. The ones you will find available will depend upon real estate custom in your community.

- Open listing. The seller agrees to pay a stated commission at a specified time — settlement, for example, or when a satisfactory purchaser signs a purchase contract. It does not preclude the seller from making the sale himself, or from entering into a contract with other brokers. Many brokers, with some reason, are not too interested in open listings, which put them in competition with other brokers and with the seller. A broker who signs on this basis may not have the incentive to prepare fancy advertising or actively promote the sale of your home.
- Net listing. The seller sets a base price below which the property may not be sold and normally the broker adds his commission to the price. Though net listings assure sellers of a certain amount, some brokers take a dim view of them and may not be willing to sign.
- Exclusive listing. One broker alone acts as the seller's agent for a specified period of time such as one or two months, or until the broker sells the home, whichever comes first. Since this arrangement gives the broker a full commission, he is likely to be quite energetic in finding a buyer and arranging a sale.
- Exclusive right to sell. The broker receives a commission if the property is sold at any time during the term of the contract, even if the owner arranges the sale himself. Because owners sometimes turn out to have found potential buyers directly before listing their homes, it is common to modify this agreement so that the broker does not receive a commission if a sale is concluded with that buyer prior to the listing.

In addition to the four basic types of listing contracts, many areas offer a *multiple listing service*, an increasingly common and popular method under which a number of participating brokers go about finding buyers for the same home at the same time. The broker with whom the home was originally listed places it on multiple listing and if he does not sell it himself, splits the commission with the broker who actually makes the sale. A multiple listing generally offers a seller the widest audience for his house and for that reason may also bring the quickest results. On the other hand, multiple listings have their drawbacks. The broker who actually makes the sale may not communicate directly with the seller, and seller and buyer may not meet until the closing, if at all. Under these circumstances, serious misunderstandings can arise. If you plan to use a multiple listing service, therefore, it is important to insist that all offers be presented to you through the listing broker, and that you check regularly with him or her as to contacts with the buyer, information communicated and questions the buyer asks.

Closing the Sale. Dealing with brokers, buyers and lenders can be a complex and time-consuming business. If you're not up to it, your best bet is to find one broker you trust — and make sure he or she earns the commission. Check to see that the broker advertises your home sufficiently and well, carefully screens prospects before bringing them around for a first-hand look, negotiates fairly between you and a buyer on an agreeable price and that he or she follows through to help with financing and settlement costs.

When you have finally closed the deal and turned over the title to your home, you can get on with the business of living somewhere else — assuming, of course, that in the meantime you have succeeded in the whole exasperating, if ultimately rewarding, business of finding another place to live.

Buying a Condominium

High housing prices and changing lifestyles — not to mention the lure of a profitable investment — have attracted all sorts of buyers to America's newest, fastest growing form of home ownership: condominiums. Statistics indicate that condominiums already account for some 30 percent of all for-sale housing units started annually, and the figure is going up each year. According to housing economists, within two decades half the population will live in housing that involves shared facilities — not only condominiums, but cooperatives and planned unit developments as well. The material that follows applies to these forms of ownership, too. (Co-op conversion is discussed earlier in this chapter.)

"Condos," as they have been nicknamed, conjure up a variety of images, from swinging singles lounging on high-rise city balconies to suburban families splashing in Olympic-size swimming pools. But in fact condominiums are not limited either with respect to the types of building or social group. Basically, in a condominium arrangement each resident owns his or her own living unit and shares with other residents an undivided interest in the property's common facilities — hallways, lobbies and social rooms; electrical, mechanical, heating and air-conditioning systems; grounds, access roads and parking areas; and any recreational amenities such as play yards, tennis courts, club houses and swimming pools.

In planned unit developments and planned subdivisions, the dwellings, and sometimes the lots they sit on, are owned by individual residents, who also have a membership interest in a separate common property owned by the homeowners' association. By contrast, cooperative residents do not have direct title to any property. Instead, they own shares of stock in a corporation that holds title to the entire project, elects a board of directors and issues proprietary leases to buyers of individual living units.

The Advantages. Condominiums offer many advantages. Because individual living units are generally efficient and compact, share common walls and mechanical systems, and occupy less land than single-family homes, they are often less expensive and therefore more affordable by young couples, single persons, retired couples and any other would-be homeowners who might have difficulty handling the expense of more traditional housing. The newer units often have modern floor plans, airy rooms, the latest conveniences, and are thus relatively easy to maintain. Moreover, a paid maintenance staff does the dreary chores of shoveling snow, raking leaves, mowing lawns, pruning trees and making repairs. If you own a condo, you do not need a landlord's permission to install built-in bookcases or paint walls any color you like. You may take deductions for mortgage interest and property taxes, like any other homeowner. You also have the option to rent your unit or sell it — often at a profit. And, if they are part of your condo, you can enjoy those tennis courts, boat docks, swimming pool, health clubs or other features you couldn't afford to build for yourself.

. . . and Disadvantages. On the other hand, condos have drawbacks, too. Like any other apartment dweller, you may have to live with the every-day irritations of togetherness: other people's Doberman pinschers, messy teenagers or noisy rock-and-roll parties next door. As a condo owner, you automatically become a member of the homeowners' or community association. Unlike voluntary social or athletic clubs, these associations are mandatory mini-governments charged with operating, maintaining and protecting the value of the property.

As a member of such an association, you will have to pay a regular assessment to cover your portion of the ongoing costs, including garbage collection, snow removal, lawnmowing, security, repairs to roofs and exterior walls. You will have to help toward the upkeep of the pool and tennis courts, even if you never use them. Your assessment is almost bound to increase periodically to cover rising costs. Should some residents fail to pay their assessments, the association will either have to force them to do so or cut back on services. This can easily lead to a deteriorating situation throughout the community, and more and more "For Sale" signs may begin to appear.

You may find you have to attend regular meetings of the association and perhaps serve as a member or officer of any of several committees if you want to get things done as you see fit. For example, the architectural committee may or may not permit you to add a room, put up your own outside TV antenna or patio awning, or paint your front door a nice bright red. You may even have to walk your harmless dachshund on a leash.

Looking at Condos. In many respects, finding and buying (or leasing) a condominium is just like finding and buying (or leasing) any other home. This means you must first check the building or development for location, convenience, attractiveness and amenities in relation to price, and thoroughly investigate the developer, particularly if the complex is new or only a few units have been built. Is he reputable, well financed, experienced in the field? Talk to real estate brokers, bankers, the local Better Business Bureau, people who live in other condos he has built. Carefully inspect the model unit or units and talk to owners already in residence to find out how well satisfied they are.

Although the laws governing condominiums differ in their specifics in the various states and U.S. territories, most of them require disclosure of all pertinent information about a given development. Before signing any subscription or purchase agreement, read all the organizational documents — the declaration or offering statement, the bylaws, the operating budget and the management agreement. If you are considering a unit in an older building that is being converted to condominium ownership, ask to see the engineer's report. It will indicate the condition of the building and what repairs and replacements may be necessary for structural, electrical and mechanical components.

Find out the association's assessment on the unit, how often it is collected (monthly, quarterly, annually), how it is determined (by size or value of the unit or by valuing all units at the same amount) and what exactly it includes (maintenance of common spaces and the exterior of your unit, services like snowplowing and trash collection). Be wary if the assessment rate seems too low. Sometimes, in order to get the development started, a developer will "low ball" assessments by absorbing the losses himself. Then, when he turns the place over to the homeowners' association, the assessments may have to be increased, perhaps dramatically, to cover maintenance and other costs.

Also examine the budget to see if it provides sufficient reserves for major repairs or replacements, and if the regular assessments include contributions to those reserves. If not, you may be confronted with special assessments every time a new roof is needed or some other emergency occurs. Check the declaration to see whether the master hazard insurance policy adequately covers the development against fire and other perils. Also make sure there is sufficient liability coverage and that it applies not only to the association officers but to each unit owner.

Finally, do not accept verbal promises that amenities not yet installed — pools, tennis courts, parking facilities, for example — will be built "soon." They should either already exist or be specifically written into the contract and be large enough for the planned number of residents in the development.

The Developer and You. In the initial stage of a condominium development, while it is still largely unoccupied, the developer holds the major investment in the property. He determines the budget, the assessments, the management procedures and pretty much everything else. But by the time half or three quarters of the units have been sold, the whole operation should be running sufficiently smoothly so that he can turn over control to the residents.

At this point, however, he may decide to retain ownership of the land underneath the buildings, or the parking garage, or the recreational facilities (or all three) and lease them to the residents for additional annual fees. Although such arrangements are legal and, of course, profitable for the owner, they may mean additional annual payments for the privilege of living on someone else's land, parking your car in his garage, or cooling off in his swimming pool on a hot summer day. Moreover, the VA will not back mortgages with five-year "recreational leases."

Other Considerations. Look closely at the bylaws, master regulations and house rules to see whether they suit your lifestyle. They may include restrictions on pets, visiting grandchildren, exterior alterations, or limitations on the right to sell or rent your unit. Take a good look at the other units in the development, particularly if they have been there for a while. What kind of shape are they in? Has there been much turnover in ownership? If so, that may indicate basic instability or poor management. How many of the units are owned by people who bought them for investment purposes and are renting them out? Tenants are not always as concerned as owner-occupants with keeping up a unit or shared buildings and grounds, and high turnover in renters or transients can lower long-term property values. To find out if values in the development have been going up or down, check title transfer records at the county or town hall. You will be able to compare what earlier buyers paid for their units with current asking prices for similar ones.

The Contract of Sale. Before signing the contract for a condo that has not yet been completed, make sure that the developer has enough capital to finish the entire project without using your down payment, and that your deposit will be returned if a specified number of units remains unsold by a specified date. Don't allow your deposit to be commingled with the developer's other funds. It should be placed in an escrow account and earning interest until the development is substantially completed. This is in fact required by law in some states and in all cases where the mortgage money is federally insured.

Obtaining a mortgage for a condominium is much the same as obtaining one for a single-family home (see section above). If the unit is to be used year-round, it will probably qualify for standard long-term financing. If, however, it is to be used primarily as a vacation home, the interest rate may be higher and the loan may run for a shorter period of time. Your contract should specify that your down payment will be refunded if you are unable to get a particular kind of mortgage or certain terms within a specified period. Have your lawyer review the contract to make sure it includes this provision as well as all the others that are outlined above.

For further information about condominiums, write to your regional office of the U.S. Department of Housing and Urban Development for the booklet, "Questions About Condominiums" and other relevant literature. (A directory of HUD offices will be found on page 101.) The catalog put out by Community Associations Institute at 3000 South Eads St., Arlington, Virginia 22202, lists a wide selection of publications on condominium operations and management.

Buying a Mobile Home

Not too many years ago "mobile home" was virtually synonymous with "trailer" — a sort of cabin-on-wheels that you towed behind a car and lived in overnight wherever you stopped. Today, however, although people still take to the open road in campers, trailers and self-propelled land yachts, the term mobile home is used to describe a highly popular form of full-time housing — nearly a quarter-million mobile homes were sold in the U.S. in a recent year — that is inexpensive, increasingly spacious and doesn't go anywhere at all. According to the Manufactured Housing Institute, whose members produce three quarters of all mobile homes, fully 97 percent remain on the first plot of land to which they were taken, and a growing number are installed on permanent foundations or basements. Bureau of Census figures indicate that 46 percent are located in mobile-home parks or communities and 54 percent are placed by their owners on individual lots.

The biggest single appeal of mobile homes is price, particularly for younger and older couples and single people who have been locked out of the housing market because of the cost. Efficient factory production, which cuts normal labor time in half, has typically kept price tags on mobile homes within a range 25 to 40 percent lower than comparable site-built houses. This price normally includes not only complete plumbing, heating and electrical systems and such major appliances as ranges and refrigerators; it also covers furniture, lamps, draperies and carpeting, and the cost of transporting the home from the factory to the site and setting it in place. Moreover, a strict code of construction and safety standards laid down by the U.S. Department of Housing and Urban Development governs all units manufactured since mid-1976. This code specifies permissible heat losses and gains for energy conservation, requires smoke detectors, pop-out windows in every bedroom and fire-retardant materials near cooking and heating facilities.

Mobile homes often provide the solution for couples who cannot afford conventional housing.

Mobile homes — MHI prefers the term "manufactured house" — come in a variety of forms. The most common type is towed to its destination on its own permanent chassis and detachable wheels. Another type, a "modular" version, is carried in one or more sections on flat-bed trucks. About 70 percent of all mobile homes are "single" models, with dimensions limited to the highway clearance regulations of 12 to 14 feet wide, 11 feet high and 70 or more feet long. These units provide between 600 and 1,000 square feet of living space — about the same as a small two-bedroom apartment or condominium. The remaining 30 percent are multiple-section models trucked separately and joined on a foundation. These models, usually two "mirror-image" halves, contain three or four bedrooms and two baths, and provide 1,400 to 1,800 square feet of living space. Optional sections — attached garages, porches, bedroom wings — can be used to expand the total area to 2,500 square feet or more. Choices of architectural styles range from contemporary to traditional and even include "cathedral" ceilings, wood siding and peaked or shingled roofs. Prices of homes have ranged recently from under $15,000 to more than $50,000, with an overall average of around $20,000, plus the cost of purchasing or renting a site.

Shopping for a Mobile Home. Most mobile homes are bought from mobile-home retail dealers, of whom there are an estimated 10,000 throughout the U.S. Most are listed in local telephone yellow pages under "Mobile Homes." In considering any dealer, check his reputation in the community and his record of service. Make sure that he offers a written warranty on the home and a guarantee of after-sale service, and that he has a service crew that can respond promptly if your furnace breaks down in the middle of a winter night. Make sure also that any after-sale service is written into your contract. A reputable dealer is usually happy to give you the names and addresses of some of his customers to check on the quality of his homes and the services he provides.

When you see a model that interests you, be sure to find out precisely what the price covers, including appliances and furnishings, and the choices available to you. If you want to use some or all of your belongings, ask to have the home delivered unfurnished. This will reduce the price somewhat, but not, perhaps, as much as you would expect, since dealers buy furnishings and appliances at wholesale prices. Check the price list for available options — air conditioning, washer and dryer, dishwasher, microwave oven, trash compactor, central vacuum cleaning system — against the prices charged by local dealers. Find out what extras, if any, are required by local codes or mobile home parks: foundations, skirting to conceal the wheels, steps with handrails for each outside door, an anchoring system to tie the home down against high winds. Be sure the contract includes delivery and set-up, otherwise your total outlay can rise by as much as several thousand dollars.

Finding a Site. Don't sign any sales contract for a mobile home until you have secured a specific site for it and have obtained written approval to locate it there. If you are thinking

Some Common Remodeling Rip-offs

Unfortunately, the remodeling business often attracts shady characters. They realize that the profits are high and that the risks are usually minimal. Government officials and legitimate builders spend considerable amounts of time and energy trying to keep charlatans under control, but consumers must also be on the alert, particularly for such age-old schemes as the following:

The Scare Tactic. This game, which has infinite variations, is sometimes played by an contractor whom you have asked to look over your house. (You, of course, don't know he has a questionable reputation because you failed to make adequate inquiries.) More often, however, a stranger shows up one day at your front door, describes himself as the "furnace inspector," "termite inspector" or "electrical inspector," and offers to inspect your home's heating system, structure or wiring without charge. Or he may offer a bargain in cleaning out your furnace or chimney or giving you a free estimate on a new roof.

After poking around mysteriously and taking things apart, he announces gravely that he came in the nick of time: your furnace (chimney, wiring, structure, roof, etc.) is in a highly dangerous condition; in fact, you're lucky the whole place hasn't fallen down or gone up in flames. Naturally, since he knows about such matters, he can arrange to fix the problem, bring your house "up to code" and make it safe and secure to live in again. When the work is completed, you may discover that it was either totally unnecessary or that it could have been done better and far more cheaply by someone else.

The Itinerant Gyp. Similar tactics may be used by other characters who show up at your house in a truck, tell you they "just happened to be in the area" and point out something that needs to be done. Some describe themselves as "tree surgeons" and suggest that your favorite old maple is about to fall on your house and should be pruned back or cut down immediately, or that many of your trees are infested with insects or fungus and must be sprayed if they are not to be lost. Others announce that your driveway needs resurfacing — a job they can do at a "bargain" price since they just happen to have some materials in the truck left over from the project they just completed. The "resurfacing" material may turn out to be nothing more than used crankcase oil, the "insect spray" simply colored water — and the so-called "bargain" quite worthless at any price.

The Bait-and-Switch. Another scheme used to lure customers into paying for overpriced home improvements is the illegal "bait-and-switch" routine. You see an advertisement, or get a telephone call, offering new home siding, replacement windows, floor

of buying a private lot, check local zoning ordinances for restrictions on mobile homes, or on additions to them after they have been set up. If such restrictions exist, find out if you can obtain a variance. Also look into requirements for foundations, tie-downs, connections to electric, gas and telephone lines, and to water and sewer mains (you may have to provide your own septic system and well). Until recently, zoning laws and high land costs have kept mobile homes out of many residential areas. In California and Michigan, communities may not prohibit mobile homes on lots zoned for single-family dwellings if the grounds for this prohibition are no more substantial than they are mobile homes.

If you want to locate your unit in a mobile-home park or development, check it out carefully. If your dealer operates his own park, you can make arrangements directly with him, or you can ask him to recommend other parks that accept your type of mobile home.

Look beyond the park's appearance, lot sizes and rental fees. Do the fees include utilities, garbage and snow removal, laundry facilities, and such amenities as a swimming pool or tennis court? Are there limitations on age, children, additional occupants, pets, tile, even a swimming pool, at an unbelievably low price. You respond with great interest. When the company's representative arrives, he tells you in confidence that the advertised materials would not really suit a person as discriminating as yourself. For example, the siding is all right — if it doesn't blow off in a high wind; the windows are acceptable, but they generally rust and have to be repainted at least once a year. Fortunately, however, he always happens to carry a better grade or model on which he can guarantee your satisfaction, and he will, of course, be more than happy to install it — at a much higher price.

The "Referral" or "Model Home" Pitch. A salesman for a company offering a new "miracle" siding, a burglar-proof alarm system or some other product plays to your vanity by telling you that you have a "model home," are "obviously a community leader" or "have many friends who will follow your lead." He then offers his product or service at "a greatly reduced price" if you will agree to recommend it to others or to allow your home to be used as a before-and-after model. As an added inducement he promises to pay you a commission for each resulting sale. All you have to do is sign a piece of paper and make a "modest down payment" on the deal. If you do, you are likely to find that 1) the commissions are never paid, 2) the paper you signed puts you under legal obligation to pay the full amount stated in the contract and/or 3) the "special bargain price" is much higher than any reputable contractor would have charged.

Other Scams. Be skeptical of any home-improvement salesman who indulges in high-pressure techniques or tells you his price is "good only for today."

Don't agree in writing to pay for a substantial portion of any job before it is actually finished. The files of consumer complaint agencies are crammed with stories of trusting homeowners who agreed to pay half the amount of a renovation on delivery of materials to the site, only to have the contractor pick up a load of scrap lumber, dump it in their driveway, demand — and receive — payment, and promptly disappear.

Never tell a salesman or contractor how much money you think you can afford to spend on a job. His estimate may turn out to match that amount exactly, whether or not it is a fair price.

Don't fall for suggestions that you can save money by somehow getting around the law. If you do not obtain a building permit for a job that requires one, you may find yourself paying a stiff fine, not to mention having to do a shoddy piece of work all over again. Also, be leery if a contractor proposes not to give you a written receipt of payment "so you won't have to pay sales tax." You may need the receipt for tax purposes. And you will certainly need it if you have any subsequent dispute with the contractor.

parking, home additions, fencing, landscaping? Are there "entrance" and "exit" fees? How long a lease can you get; is it transferable if you want to sell your home? Are there limits on rent increases? (Beware that when parks fill up, owners sometimes sell to management companies that substantially increase rents.) A few parks are set up as condominiums where residents own their living units and an interest in the common facilities and management (see "Condominiums," above).

Financing Your Purchase. Dealers commonly arrange financing for buyers, often including insurance on their unit. But you may be able to do better by shopping around among lenders and insurance companies yourself. Remember, as a borrower, you are protected by the federal Truth in Lending Law (see Chapter 9), which requires the lender to supply written disclosure of the terms of the loan.

Most homes are financed through chattel (or personal property) loans similar to those used to finance automobile purchases, although home loans run for a considerably longer period. Today the average down payment is just under 20 percent, the interest rate a few points higher than that associated with conventional mortgages, and the payoff period from 10 to 15 years.

In some areas, where mobile-home owners commonly purchase their lots and occupy multi-section units, the homes are accorded real estate or real property status, making them eligible for regular home mortgages with their lower rates and longer payoff periods. If you can find a lender willing to participate probably the best deal is a VA- or FHA-backed loan offering low (or no) down payments and terms of up to 20 or 25 years.

Traditionally, mobile homes, like the wheeled vehicles from which they evolved, have depreciated in value over time. But there is evidence that this too is changing, particularly in areas where they are widely accepted alternatives to conventionally-built single-family homes. Many new units placed on permanent foundations have retained their original value and, according to some studies, have been appreciating in value by as much as 10 to 15 percent a year.

Taking Delivery of Your Home. When your new mobile home arrives, look it over carefully. See that the features it contains are precisely the ones described in the sales contract, and that everything is in good repair. Look for such defects in workmanship as poorly operating drawers or doors, snags in carpeting or scratched linoleum floors, and damaged roofs, walls or windows. Check the homeowner's manual and the warranty papers which by law must be provided with the home. (See Chapter 7 for a discussion of the Magnuson-Moss Warranty Act.) Look also for the label plate indicating that the unit has been built to HUD standards and for the diagram showing the required positions of placement piers and anchoring devices. There should be a posted certificate covering the expected performance of the heating system during varying outside temperatures and wind velocities as well as a map indicating the weather zone for which the home was constructed and whether it requires tie-downs against high winds.

If there are any problems, speak to your dealer promptly. Any unresolved complaints should be directed to the manufacturer, your state consumer agency, or the nearest HUD office (see directory, page 101). Irregularities regarding sales practices, warranties and service should be reported to the same groups.

Inquiries and requests for literature on mobile homes can be directed to HUD, your local Better Business Bureau, or to the Manufactured Housing Institute, 1745 Jefferson Davis Highway, Suite 511, Arlington, Virginia 22202. A helpful booklet, "Tips on Buying a Mobile Home," is published by the Council of Better Business Bureaus, 1515 Wilson Boulevard, Arlington, Virginia 22209.

Building and Remodeling

Rather than buying and moving into a home "as is," some people prefer a more creative approach: designing and building their own house, buying an older home and renovating it, or simply staying put and improving the house they already own. Bookstores and libraries abound in books offering advice on do-it-yourself architecture, construction and home improvement, and many government publications are available through county extension offices and regional branches of the U.S. Department of Housing and Urban Development (see directory, page 101). But for any major building or remodeling job, you would also do well to seek the first-hand counsel of knowledgeable residential architects and contractors.

Your Own New House

Building a home tailored to your own special taste and style of living can be a rewarding experience. But be prepared to pay for it. It will almost surely take a good deal more of your time and patience, not to mention money, than buying a house someone else has built. The more individual its design and special features, moreover, the less likely it is to appeal to a wide range of buyers, and the greater the risk that you will not be able to recoup your full investment if you subsequently decide to sell.

Buying the Land. In looking for land, check the local zoning regulations governing what can and cannot be built on a given lot and how close any structure can come to property lines. If your plans do not conform to the zoning laws, you must apply to the zoning board for a variance. Before buying, make sure that you have an accurate survey to avoid drainage or bedrock problems, and to ascertain that access and utilities are readily available or can be provided. Also, a professional title search will assure you that there are no liens or other defects that could cloud your ownership of the land. Finally, it is useful to talk to local lenders about the availability of loans to finance the purchase of the land and/or the construction of your home.

Choosing an Architect. You may be tempted to sketch up ideas for the house yourself, perhaps with the help of a contractor who offers planning services. But you will probably get a better product, with fewer headaches, if you consult a licensed architect experienced in house design. He can advise you on your building site, match your needs to your budget, provide preliminary sketches for discussion, and prepare final working drawings and specifications. He can also arrange for competitive bids from several suitable contractors, help choose the best among them, and supervise construction of the house. Interview one or more candidates (most established professionals are members of the American Institute of Architects), look at other houses they have designed, and talk with the owners if possible. If you are undecided at first, the architect may agree to an hourly consultation fee. Once you have decided to retain him on contract, he may propose a commission based on a fixed fee plus expenses, or on a multiple of his expenses, or on a percentage of total building costs. Since his total fee will depend on the size of the job and the precise nature and extent of his services, it is important to spell out these factors clearly in your contract with him.

Remodeling an Older House. If you are contemplating extensive remodeling of an older home, either your own or one you are thinking of buying, the services of an architect can also be a good investment — as can a thorough inspection by an architect, a contractor or a building engineer. After such an inspection, decide first what must be done, and second, what would be nice but not vital. An old rule in real estate says that the actual cost of an improvement is rarely reflected, dollar for dollar, in the resale value of a house. If you put in a new roof or furnace, or remodel your kitchen because the work is necessary, you will be making your property more liveable, and hence more desirable, when and if the time comes to sell. But a $20,000 investment in a fancy deck, a sauna, a hot tub, a greenhouse, a swimming pool or a tennis court will not automatically make your $100,000 house worth $120,000. It may even discourage buyers who are not interested in these amenities. Another rule of thumb regarding resale value is that improvements should not total more than 30 percent of the market value of a home, and should be geared to overall values in the immediate neighborhood. If you sink $50,000 into a $100,000 home in an area of $100,000 houses, don't expect to get it back.

Certain improvements, however, can add value as well as practicality and convenience. Surveys of the $50-billion-a-year upkeep and remodeling market in the U.S. show that the most popular items are kitchen modernization, bathroom remodeling and the installation of energy-saving features such as efficient heating systems, insulation, double-paned windows and storm doors.

Some expensive improvements can make a home more comfortable for you but add little to its resale value.

Federal law allows an income tax credit of 15 percent on the first $2,000 ($300 maximum) spent for installing such energy savers as insulation, thermal windows and doors, weatherstripping, replacement and modifications of furnace burners, clock thermostats and energy meters. A 40 percent tax credit is allowed on the first $10,000 ($4,000 maximum) for installing such renewable energy sources as solar energy collectors, windmills and geothermal wells. (For further information, ask the local Internal Revenue Service office for IRS pamphlet 903.) Some states also exempt certain energy-saving materials and equipment from sales taxes, allow towns to exempt part of the value of alternate energy systems from local property taxes, or offer state-backed low interest loans for renewable-energy improvements. Ask your state tax department if such regulations apply to you.

Before starting any remodeling or major repair, visit your town hall or county office to check on local zoning regulations and building codes. You may be limited in how close to your neighbor's property line you can erect an addition, or you may be required to build a child-proof fence around a new swimming pool. Building codes can be quite rigid in matters of safety and health, especially with respect to electrical, heating and plumbing systems. Your plans will have to pass muster before a building permit can be issued.

You should also find out whether local regulations require all work to be performed by licensed professionals — such as electricians and plumbers — or whether you may hire unlicensed persons or, if you consider yourself capable, you may elect to do the work yourself.

Working with a Contractor. You may want to do the home improvement job yourself, or hire a contractor, or share the work with him. The decision depends on your own skills and enthusiasm and on the amount of work involved. But be wary. This is a field in which rip-offs and fly-by-night operators are all too common (see box, page 82, and Chapter 8). The checklist below will help you.

• Investigate candidates thoroughly. A good contractor with an experienced crew can complete a major building or remodeling job faster and better than you can do it yourself. He can also be helpful in getting more favorable financing, obtaining the necessary permits and inspections, dealing with subcontractors, and getting a lower price on materials. Check the reputation of any contractor you are considering. Ask people he has done work for; your architect, if you have one; local bankers, real estate brokers, lumber yard dealers and others who have supplied him with materials. It is a good idea to ask the local Better Business Bureau or Chamber of Commerce if any complaints have been filed against him and how they were resolved. You might visit his place of business to see if it has the feel of a well-established shop.

Some other questions for you to consider are: Is the contractor experienced in the specific type of building or remodeling that you have in mind? Does he have good financial references? Is he a licensed professional, if local regulations so require? Is he a member of a recognized trade association with a code of ethics, such as a local builders' group, the National Association of Home Builders, or the National Association of the Remodeling Industry?

• Get several estimates on the job. Determine exactly what work you want done and write it down in detail, attaching any manufacturers' brochures, magazine clippings or your own sketches to show what you have in mind. If a particular brand of materials or equipment is important to you, make a note of it. Ask several contractors to give you estimates, and let each one know you are asking for a number of estimates. If they are aware of the competition, they are more likely to sharpen their pencils and give you their lowest price. Ask each for a list of his subcontractors and suppliers, his starting and completion dates, and his schedule of payments.

Ask each contractor if he will stand behind his work with a warranty, either full or limited; ask also what items the warranty covers, and how long it lasts. In addition to the established Home Owner's Warranty (HOW) program for new houses, described earlier in this chapter, HOW has launched a new program through which qualified remodeling contractors can offer their clients an insured protection plan that covers their work completely for the first two years, and covers major structural defects for the next three.

Compare the bids carefully, with the help of your architect if you have one. You are not obliged to accept the lowest one — or any, for that matter — and you may be able to negotiate price reductions, including substitutions or changes to fit your budget, before choosing the bid you want.

• Get everything in writing. To avoid future misunderstandings and disputes, you and the contractor should sign a written contract that specifies everything you have agreed on:

— Working drawings or diagrams.

— Names or detailed descriptions of materials to be used (including their quality or grade, manufacturers' brand names, colors and model numbers).

— A provision that any substitutions, changes or additions must be agreed to in writing before they are made.

— The contractor's warranty to cover materials and workmanship.

— Starting and completion dates for the work, including penalties for days late.

— If the job is sizeable, a progressive schedule of payments based on percentages of the total work finished, with the final payment due only after completion of the work and

securing of any necessary inspections and certificates.
— The amount of the down payment agreed on (10 to 15 percent is customary for many jobs), and under what conditions it is to be returned.
— A provision that unless all work is done in accordance with local building codes, the contractor must bring it up to code at no added cost to you, should the official inspection uncover any irregularities.
— A requirement that all materials and appliances be applied or installed according to manufacturers' instructions so that warranties can be fully effective.

The contractor should be required to obtain the necessary zoning and building permits, as well as progress inspections and approvals. He should carry adequate liability insurance, and the name of the carrier should be written in the contract. A certificate of coverage should be issued before the work starts, providing coverage for workers on the building site, the property of neighbors, accidental damage to your property by the contractor's workmen, and proper cleanup after the job is done. Before the contract is signed, examine it again with care. If it was with a door-to-door salesman who solicited you, federal law allows a three-day "cooling off" period in which to cancel it and get back your deposit. But you have no such federal protection if you yourself went out to hire the contractor. So you must be sure before you sign.

• Follow the job to completion. Before work is substantially underway, talk to the broker handling your home insurance to make sure your coverage is increased as the job progresses so that you are fully covered at all times against accident, fire or theft. Show an interest in the work and keep track of how it's coming along. The contractor won't appreciate your getting in the way or making suggestions directly to his workmen, but he will probably toe the line a little more closely on matters of schedule and workmanship if he knows you're watching. He may also be able to point out ways to save money or to get better results. And of course, if you are around, you can help resolve the problems and choices that always seem to come up in any building job.

When the work is finally complete, make sure you have all the official inspection certificates and that you thoroughly inspect everything yourself. If there is anything wrong, even if it's only a loose molding or a light switch that doesn't work, see that it is corrected before you make your final payment. It is also a good idea before paying to ask the contractor for receipts and waivers from his subcontractors and suppliers in order to make sure they have all been paid and are not about to file a mechanic's lien on your home.

Municipal Services

Water supply, a sewage system, trash disposal, police and fire protection, schools for children — all these are necessities of life in 20th century America. In nearly all cities and a great many suburbs these services are supplied by the community and paid for by local taxes. Small towns and rural areas may supply only a few of them, relying on volunteer fire departments and requiring residents to provide their own water and waste disposal via wells and septic tanks. But whether a community offers many services or few, those services cost money, and it is the residents of the community who pay for them.

In many communities, these services are financed entirely by real estate taxes. In others, real estate taxes may cover only a few — schools and police protection, for example — while others are financed through separate taxes or fees. Water is often metered, and householders are required to pay monthly or quarterly for the water they use, just as they pay for natural gas or electricity. Indeed, in some areas, water is not a municipal service at all, but is provided by a private company which has been granted a monopoly by the municipality. But the bulk of municipal services are generally paid for through real estate taxes, which can run to several hundred dollars each month for a family and which are, therefore, matters of great concern to every homeowner.

How Real Estate Taxes Are Set. In most areas, two factors determine the amount that each householder pays annually in real estate taxes. The first is the assessed valuation of the property, which, in a few areas, is based on its actual market value but in most is based on some percentage of that value. However the value is established, you can be sure that if the local taxing authorities (often called the

Board of Assessors) set the value of a house at $80,000, the real estate taxes on it will be higher than those on a neighboring house assessed at only $25,000. (There are exceptions to this rule. In California, for example, Proposition 13 holds down tax increases for current homeowners even if there is an increase in the assessed valuation of their homes, but permits taxes to rise precipitously when ownership changes hands.)

The second factor determining real estate taxes is the local tax rate. If the tax rate in your community is 5 percent, and your house is assessed at $100,000, your real estate tax will be $5,000 for the year. If you have a mortgage through a lending agency, you will probably be required to maintain an escrow account for the payment of these taxes. After making your initial contribution to this account — usually one-half the current yearly tax bill — you will be charged monthly at the rate of one twelfth the yearly tax bill. This assures that there will always be enough funds in your account to enable the lending agency to pay the taxes on your property.

Protesting Your Real Estate Taxes. If you feel that the real estate tax rate in your community is too high, there is — unfortunately — very little you can do about it as an individual except through political action. If enough people in your community feel as you do, you can "throw the rascals out" and elect officials more sympathetic to your views.

If, however, you feel that the assessment on your house — and, therefore, your real estate tax — is too high, there are several steps you can take. The first is derived from the fact that tax assessing is not a factual science but, at least in part, a subjective matter. Suppose, for example, the board of assessors has determined that the brick or stone facing on your house makes it very handsome and, therefore, adds to the value of your property. An equally good argument can be made for the opposite point of view. Brick and stone are poor insulators and it is extremely difficult to add insulation behind them. So whatever their esthetic merits, they present an economic problem for the householder — a problem that makes the house worth less than it would be were it faced with wood shingle. Under such circumstances, you have the right to protest the assessment.

Even if you have no such argument to present, you can still take action to get the assessment reduced if you suspect that your house has been over-assessed. The information you will need in pursuit of this action is a matter of public record, and is therefore available to you.

Begin by going to the local assessor's office and asking to see the work sheet that was used for your house. Check it carefully to see if it contains any errors of fact, such as lot size, house dimensions, or date of construction. If there are no such errors, the next step is to look around your own and comparable neighborhoods for houses that resemble yours in size, age and condition. Make a note of their addresses and check their assessments in the assessor's tax rolls. If your assessment exceeds the average by 10 percent or more, you may have a good case. You can also consult published listings of recent sale prices on homes similar to yours, comparing their average assessment with the assessment on your house. (Such listings are available through the assessor, or your public librarian, real estate broker or bank loan officer.) Lastly, you can pay an independent appraiser for an up-to-date appraisal of the market value of your home, and then compare that figure with the assessor's appraisal and with current prices of similar homes.

If any one of these tests shows that things are out of line, talk to your assessor about it. He may see things your way. If he does not, you can present your case to the local board of equalization or tax review. Don't fall for such comments as "Would you be willing to sell your home for that price?" or "What price would you sell your house for?" or "Do you want us to cut back on policemen, firemen and schools?" The question is not what price you would accept for your house, or whether you like teachers, firemen and police officers. The question is whether your property has been assessed fairly.

If the board will not budge, and you still think you are right, your next step is the court, where you can institute legal proceedings. (For information on your rights in court, see Chapter 14.) If you win, it can save you thousands of tax dollars over a period of years.

One cautionary note on this matter. Efforts to lower assessments sometimes backfire. The assessors may inspect your property to

Reading Your Electric Meter

It is a good idea to know how to read your electric meter, if only to be able to check the accuracy of your bills, the effectiveness of your energy conservation efforts and the functioning of the meter itself. Like any piece of equipment, it can go off course.

An electric meter consists of four clocks, two of which read clockwise and two counter-clockwise, as shown by the arrows on the accompanying illustration.

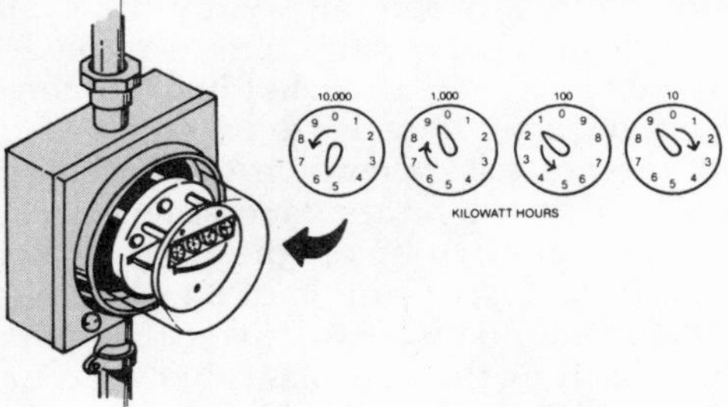

Added together, the readings on the clocks register your use of kilowatt hours (KWHs). (A kilowatt equals 1,000 watts — the amount of electricity a lighted 100-watt bulb uses in 10 hours.)

The first of the four clocks — the one at the far left — registers KWHs between 10,000 and 1,000; the second, KWHs between 1,000 and 100; the third, KWHs between 100 and 10; and the fourth, KWHs between 10 and one.

Read the clocks from left to right. If the pointer is between two numbers, the lower number applies. If it is directly on a number, look at the clock to its right. If the pointer on that one has not passed 0, the lower number on the first clock is the applicable one. If it *has* passed 0, the higher one applies.

In the example given here, the meter reads 5,919 KWHs. Although the pointer on the first clock has almost reached the 6, the one on the clock to the right has not yet passed 0. And that clock must be read as 9, since the hand lies between the 9 and the 0. The third clock reads 1 because its hand almost reached the 2, but the hand on the fourth has not yet reached 0. And the fourth clearly reads 9, since that is precisely where the pointer lies.

To translate this reading into dollars and cents, check the KWH reading on the last electric bill you received, and subtract that figure from the one your reading produces. If, in our example, the previous reading was 4,500 KWHs, you will have used 1,419 KWHs since your meter was last read. Then check your bill for the figure indicating what your utility company charges for electricity per kilowatt hour and multiply that figure by the number of kilowatt hours you have used. If, for example, the charge is seven cents per kilowatt hour, you will have used $99.33 worth of electricity during the period since your last reading.

Gas meters, which record your use of natural or manufactured gas, come in several varieties — some with as few as two clocks and some with five or six. If you want to check your own gas meter, ask your utility company for instructions on how to proceed. You are entitled to this information.

check out your argument. If they find improvements you have not reported to them, they may raise your assessment instead of lowering it.

Gas and Electric Service

Although some gas and electric services are municipally owned, most are owned by private companies. But these firms differ from others in the private sector in one important respect. They do not operate in a free enterprise market, where the costs and quality of goods and services are set at least in part by consumer preference and competition among suppliers. They are monopolies, which have been granted the right to be the sole suppliers of gas and electricity within a particular state or some part of it.

Because this right deprives consumers of the free choice they exercise in buying the other necessities of life, state governments have established boards — usually called the Public Utility Commission (PUC), but sometimes known as the Public Service Commission (PSC) — to regulate specific aspects of the utilities' operation in accordance with state law. In most states, the members of the board are appointed by the governor for a specified term of service; in a few, they are elected by the public. However they are chosen, their primary responsibility is to set the rates at which gas and electricity are supplied to utility customers — business and industry as well as private individuals — and to ensure that these customers receive the services for which they are paying.

Factors in Utility Regulation. In carrying out their franchises, Public Utility Commissions should not act as advocates either for consumers or for utilities. Their job is to be judges, deciding what is equitable and possible. All of them are, therefore, faced with the same continuing problem in setting rates: how to balance the public's need for affordable gas and electric service with the utilities' need to meet expenses and their right to provide stock holders with a fair return on their investment. This balance, always delicate, has become even more so in recent years.

Utilities have had to pay tremendous increases for oil, which fuels many of the electricity-producing turbines in America, and for natural gas, both domestic and imported. Rising almost as fast has been the cost of constructing the new power plants — both conventional and nuclear — which are needed to keep pace not only with the present demand, but with the needs both industry and householders may have in the future. And the utilities have had to raise their employees' salaries to keep pace with inflation. Such factors are ultimately represented in higher utility bills for the consumer.

On the other hand, many, if not most, consumers already feel pushed to the edge of financial distress by the large increases in utility bills during the past decade. The result has been a rise in consumer militance at the same time that the utilities press for higher rates to offset increased expenses. Even these demands by the utilities cost the consumer money, for they are often promoted with expensive lobbying campaigns, the costs of which are eventually passed along to utility users. Caught in the middle, trying to act as honest brokers between competing interests, are the Public Utility Commissions.

Take, for example, the problem of the financing of new facilities for the utilities. Gas and electric companies often press for rate increases to pay the costs of new plants under construction on the grounds that these facilities will improve service to customers, that delaying construction will only further increase costs and that the companies cannot afford this necessary expansion unless they are continually reimbursed by their clients. Most consumer groups are vigorously opposed to such rate rises, holding that they are, in effect, an enforced interest-free loan made by the current generation of consumers for the benefit of a future generation. Moreover, the consumer groups point out that such increases are especially hard on older people, who are unlikely ever to receive personal benefits from the new plants but are required to subsidize benefits for future customers out of their own, often meager, financial resources. In some states — New Hampshire and Oregon, for example — utilities have been forbidden by law to pass on the costs of current construction. But in others, the PUCs retain the right to decide if, when and how such costs can be transferred to consumers. Their rulings on this question vary.

One set of considerations the PUCs follow in setting electric rates are the guidelines established by the Public Utility Regulatory Policy Act (PURPA), which the Congress passed in 1978. It should be emphasized that the standards set by PURPA are not regulations. State PUCs are bound by law to take PURPA into consideration in the rate-making process, but they may bend or ignore its guidelines if they conclude that the guidelines are not appropriate to a particular situation. On the other hand, consumer groups that wish to challenge electric rates can look to PURPA guidelines as a support. The act *has* helped establish generally recognized rate-making standards on a nationwide basis. These guidelines cover:

- Service Costs: PURPA holds that the rates charged by an electric utility should reflect its actual costs in providing service. Before the

CONSUMER ALERT

Cutting the Energy Cost of Your Appliances

One of the most obvious ways of cutting the cost of electricity is to avoid using it wherever possible. You may, for example, be able to realize considerable savings by air-drying clothes instead of using an electric dryer and by turning off the drying cycle on your dishwasher.

In buying appliances it is important to keep their operating costs in mind. Models that have high energy-efficiency ratios (EERs) — that require relatively small amounts of electricity to perform their work efficiently — may cost more to buy than those with low EERs, but they are more economical to run. So the price difference may be worth paying.

Since 1975, federal law has required that the manufacturers of certain appliances — water heaters, refrigerators, refrigerator-freezers, freezers, dishwashers, clothes-washers, room and central air conditioners, television sets, kitchen ranges and ovens, humidifiers, dehu midifiers and furnaces — place labels on the products showing their estimated annual operating costs. When buying, compare various models and brands.

In the list below are some common appliances, the average number of kilowatt hours (KWHs) each uses in a year, and the typical cost of operation of each. (Depending on the EER, some will cost less, others more.) The costs are figured on the basis of 5.89 cents per kilowatt hour, the average price of electricity in the United States near the end of 1982.

	KWH per Year	Cost per year
Air conditioner room	1,398	$82.34
Broiler	100	5.89
Clock	17	1.00
Clothes washer[1]	103	6.07
Clothes dryer	993	58.49
Dishwasher[1]	363	21.38
Fan, attic	291	17.14
Hair dryer	14	.82
Heater, portable	176	10.37
Hot plate	90	5.30
Iron, hand	144	8.48
Mixer	13	.77
Oven, microwave	300	17.67
Oven, self-cleaning	1,146	67.50

	KWH per year	Cost per year
Stereo	66	3.89
Range	1,175	69.21
Refrigerator/ freezer 14 cu. ft.	1,137	66.97
Refrigerator/ freezer 14 cu. ft. frostfree	1,829	107.73
Sewing machine	11	.65
Toaster	39	2.30
Television, color	502	29.57
Water heater	4,219	248.50
Water heater (quick recovery)	4,811	283.37

[1] *Does not include cost of heating water.*

act was passed, electric utilities often charged residential customers more per unit of electricity than industrial customers. Under PURPA guidelines, no class of users is expected to subsidize the rates paid by another class, and if a utility wishes to continue the old practice, it is generally required to prove that the real cost of providing service to homes and apartments is higher than that of servicing such facilities as steel plants or appliance factories.

- Block Rates: Before the fuel shortage of the 1970's, electric utility companies frequently charged customers using large amounts of power less per kilowatt hour than customers using smaller amounts. Under PURPA guidelines a utility wishing to do this should be ready to prove that the cost of supplying power declines with increased use.
- Peak Period and Slack Period Rates: PURPA requires PUCs to consider setting different rates for electric service at different times of day and different seasons of the year, to reflect the changing costs of supplying

power. For example, demands for power are generally highest on weekday mornings and in the late afternoons; lowest on weekends, holidays and at night. Unless a utility company can prove that the cost of supplying power is substantially the same during all periods, these guidelines indicate that it should charge less per kilowatt-hour of service supplied during non-peak periods.

- Interruptible Rates and Load Management Techniques: Under PURPA, each PUC must consider the possibility of lowering costs to consumers by permitting those who agree to the procedure to have unneeded services turned off during peak hours.
- Master Metering: As a fuel conservation measure, PUCs are required by PURPA to consider banning the use of a single meter in newly constructed multiple dwellings or office complexes. If each tenant has a separate meter and pays his or her own electric bill, each will have a financial stake in conservation, and considerable savings may result.
- Consumer Awareness: Under PURPA guidelines, utility companies must provide consumers with information about how rates are set and what the rates actually are.
- Fuel Adjustment Charges: In most states, PUCs permit utility companies to pass along increased fuel costs to consumers — that figure appears on your utility bill under the heading "fuel adjustment." If, for example, there is an increase in the cost of the oil used to generate electricity, this increase is spread out among the utility's customers. Critics of the practice have long contended that this automatic pass-along gives the utilities no incentive to secure the lowest possible price for fuel, since they are not paying its cost. Under PURPA, PUCs are required to consider the establishment of guidelines for regulating fuel-adjustment charges. In Illinois, this requirement has resulted in the passage of legislation forcing the PUC to employ extremely rigorous accounting procedures in determining whether a utility will be permitted to pass along increased fuel costs.

Lifeline Rates. For several years, consumer groups around the country have been campaigning for state laws to establish so-called "lifeline" electric and gas rates: special low rates to cover the service necessary to meet the energy requirements of the average household. Energy use above the amount the lifeline rate covered would be billed at a higher rate. Lifeline rates would be particularly helpful to those on low, fixed incomes — among whom are a considerable number of the elderly. But despite this fact, only a few states — among them California — have as yet mandated them.

An alternative to the lifeline rate is the so-called "inverted rate" — a lower charge for the first units of service than for subsequent ones. Most utility companies strongly oppose both lifeline and inverted rates. They argue, and with some justification, that the cost per unit of providing minimum service is often higher than the cost per unit of providing greater service, and that legislative enactment of these pricing methods would force major utility customers — business and industry, for example — to subsidize householders with modest utility needs.

Utility Deposits. When you move into a new residence, you may find that the utility and telephone companies demand a deposit before hooking up service lines or installing phones. This is particularly likely to be the case if your new home is serviced by different utility and phone companies from your old one. The deposit required by the telephone company is usually small, but the gas and electric company may ask as much as $200 or $300 — the equivalent of two months' bills — in areas where energy costs are high.

In most cases, the demands for such deposits are legal. The courts have usually held that they represent security on the company's advance supply of its services. On the other hand, the courts have also held that a company may not be arbitrary in its demand for deposits and must hold them in escrow and pay customers the interest that the monies earn. State regulations regarding deposits vary greatly, as do requirements concerning the amount of interest they must pay. To discover your specific rights regarding deposits, write to the Consumer Regulations Department of your local utility company or to your state PUC (see page 99).

If a public utility feels that a customer has established a good credit rating, it may not demand a deposit at all or, if it has routinely asked for one, may withdraw the request when the householder objects. On the other hand, a utility may suddenly demand a deposit after years of providing service and receiving prompt and full payment. This is particularly likely to happen if the account is in the name of one member of a family and that person dies or leaves the home for some reason. Under those circumstances, the utility may claim that it is entitled to the money as a safeguard since it has no knowledge of the credit worthiness of the individual now paying the bills. In such cases, the company is likely to prevail in the courts. For this reason, it is advisable for husbands and wives — or roommates sharing the same residence — to open utility accounts in both their names.

Estimated Bills. Sometimes bills for gas and electricity bear notation as "Avg" or "A." This means that the meter reader was unable to secure entry to the house to determine the amount of electricity and gas actually used during the billing period, and that the company has therefore estimated the amount of the bill on the basis both of the customer's past pattern of energy use and of such other considerations as weather. Unusually cold weather, for example, will be reflected in an increased cost as will any rise in fuel costs to the company during the period in question. Such estimated bills are sometimes very wide of the mark, indeed. If you close up your house during the cold winter months to vacation in a warmer clime, you may on your return be greeted by an absolutely preposterous utilities bill, since the meter reader will have been unable to secure entry into the house and the utility company will therefore have sent you an averaged bill. An estimated bill is merely a conditional charge that most utility companies are willing to set aside if it appears excessive. The company may send a revised bill based on a meter reading by the householder, or it may permit the withholding of payment until the meter is read by a company employee.

Many utility companies put meter reading dates on their bills. If you cannot be home or arrange for the entry of a meter reader at the designated time, you have the right to ask for a reading at your convenience. If your utility company does not list the meter reading day, you can call the company to ascertain when the meter reader is due at your home so that you may make arrangements to be there.

Cutting off Utility Service. The enormous increase in utility costs over the past decade has made it extremely difficult for many low income and elderly householders to pay their energy bills. In some cases, utility companies have cut off service to delinquent customers in the middle of winter, and in a few of these situations, elderly persons have actually died from the cold. PURPA guidelines suggest that utilities either be forbidden to cut off service without giving several weeks' notice and instructing consumers on the proper way to dispute the intended termination, or that utilities be barred from cutting off service during the cold months if the customer can prove inability to pay or is willing to arrange for installment payments. Moreover, PURPA mandates that PUCs give particular attention to the elderly and handicapped in connection with this problem. But these guidelines do not have the force of law, and PUCs are not required to adopt them.

Some utility companies, acting on their own, have introduced procedures that go a long way towards satisfying PURPA guidelines, and some states have adopted regulations that satisfy them. In Georgia, for example, a regulation forbids public utilities to discontinue residential service in any 24 hour period when the temperature falls as low as 32° F, provided that the delinquent customer agrees to pay outstanding — as well as current — bills in installments during spring and summer when heating costs are down. Although in other states consumer groups are still battling for the adoption of similar or more far-reaching regulations or laws, you should check with local government officials if you have trouble paying your utility bills. There may be a federal or local program that can help you.

Consumer Action

Most consumer complaints about utility service concern money — either individual bills or rates in general. In the first category are such matters as faulty meter reading, meters that are operating improperly and sudden increases in bills — whether justified or not.

As a utility customer, you have an absolute right to ascertain that your meter is being read properly and is functioning as it should. If you have any doubts, call your local utility company, ask for the consumer-relations department and request a field survey. Most companies respond promptly and positively to such requests, sending a supervisor to your residence to read the meter and check out its functioning. If, however, the company denies your request, write or call your state Public Utility Commission (see page 99) and ask for help. Some PUCs respond to telephoned requests; others require a letter and will tell you so when you call. In either event, the Commission will forward your complaint to the utility for action.

If you feel that you are being charged electric or gas rates higher than PUC regulations allow, get in touch with that body. If your complaint is justified, action will be taken.

If your complaint is with the rates that the PUC has mandated, you will have to make use of the procedures established in your state. Details of these procedures vary from one state to the next, but in all states the PUC *must* hold public hearings when a utility requests an increase in rates. The utility will appear at the hearing with its expert witnesses, all of whom will testify in favor of a rate increase. But consumers also have the right to testify, either as individuals or as representatives of organized groups, as do representatives of state consumer agencies, who can and do exert significant influence on behalf of utility customers. If these consumer advocates — both governmental and non-governmental — come to the hearings well prepared, and with facts and figures that counter those presented by the utilities, they can be successful in convincing the PUC to reduce — if not deny — a proposed rate increase.

More than 30 states have so-called utility consumer advocates — public officials who deal solely with consumer problems concerning utilities. These officials represent consumers at rate hearings before the PUCs and will intervene on behalf of the public where there are complaints against the utilities. You can find out if your state has a consumer utility advocate by writing: National Association of State Utility Consumer Advocates, c/o Florida Public Counsel, Room 4, Holland Building, Tallahassee, Florida 32304.

Telephone Service

Dramatic changes have recently taken place in the organization of telephone service in the United States. In the past, the instruments themselves were available only on a rental basis and were manufactured by a wholly-owned subsidiary of the American Telephone and Telegraph Company (AT&T). In addition, although local telephone service in some parts of the country was handled by an independent company rather than by AT&T subsidiaries, all long distance service was handled by AT&T. Today, as a result of decisions by the courts and the Federal Communications Commission (FCC), which regulates interstate lines, phone subscribers are no longer required to use only the instruments manufactured by the company and are permitted to own, rather than rent, the equipment. Moreover, as the result of an out-of-court settlement of an anti-trust suit brought by the federal goverment, AT&T was required to divest itself of its local subsidiaries, which now function as independent organizations. And finally, new companies now compete with AT&T's long distance service.

Owning Your Own Telephone. The right of telephone subscribers to own their own telephones and to carry them from one residence to another has already brought considerable financial benefit to consumers. Instruments can be purchased both at telephone company and independent stores all over the country and in some places a simple but workable telephone can be purchased for as little as $10.00. A customer paying 75 cents a month in telephone rental would pay off this cost in a little over a year.

But the right has also brought with it some complications and difficulties. For example, not all types of phones work on all types of systems. In a home that is wired for rotary dial phones, it may be necessary to have changes made in order to add a "touch tone" system — one with push buttons.

Repair service presents a more complex problem. In the past, the phone company was responsible for the maintenance and repair of rented phones. Since January 1, 1984, the situation has changed. If you continue to lease a phone you had before then, its maintenance and repair will be handled by your local telephone company in areas where service is provided by an independent firm, and by AT&T in areas serviced by a Bell company. If you leased your phone after that date, the company from which you leased it will

CONSUMER ALERT

Dealing With Erroneous Long Distance Telephone Bills

One of the most common problems of telephone subscribers is that they are occasionally billed for long distance calls they did not make. The Washington, DC office of AT&T, for example, receives approximately 82,000 complaints on this subject every year — and, on checking, discovers that about 85 percent are valid.

If you think you have been wrongly billed for a long distance call, do not hesitate to complain, no matter which long line service you use. Call the company's service representative and ask for an investigation. While it is going on, you do not have to pay for the disputed calls.

In 92 percent of all cases, AT&T has been able to track down the calls made on its lines. Most commonly, the calls have been made, but were billed to the wrong person. Less often, the billing is correct. Someone in the household — perhaps a guest or a child — made the call without informing anyone.

Consumers who use the newer long line companies may have a different problem. Billing for these calls begins shortly after the caller finishes dialing and virtually at the moment the phone at the other end has begun to ring. The result is that subscribers are sometimes charged for calls that are never completed because no one answers. Users of these lines should, therefore, be careful not to let the phone ring too long when they make calls. If three rings produce no answer, hang up and try again, later.

No matter what long line company you are doing business with, there is a further step to take if you cannot get a satisfactory solution to a problem about long distance calls. Get in touch with your state's Public Utilities Commission (see directory, page 99). It may appoint a mediator to help settle the matter.

handle necessary maintenance and repairs. But check to see whether you must bring the phone to the company; there may be a charge for a service call to your home.

If you own your own phone, however, you will have to find someone to service it, and if your warranty has run out and you have no service contract, you will have to pay for the work done. But bear in mind that if your phone is not working, the problem may be in the wiring or in the company's switch. If you have more than one phone, you can find out where the problem is by checking whether the other phones work. If they are not in operation, the problem is somewhere in the line. Call your local company — *not* AT&T. The local company will probably make the repair at no cost.

All this means that consumers must now think of their telephones in the same way they think of other appliances. When you buy a dishwasher, refrigerator, television set — or even such a small item as a toaster or electric razor — you check its warranty with care, and you look for the best servicing arrangements available. When you buy — or lease — a telephone, you must exercise precisely these same precautions.

Local Telephone Service. Most local telephone companies offer several different types of service, and the law requires that the company inform you of the various options available. The following types of local service are among those that may be available:

- Budget or Lifeline Service. This option offers the lowest base rate: a modest monthly fee that enables the consumer to receive an unlimited number of phone calls but charges the user for every local call he or she makes.
- Message Unit Service. With this option, the consumer can receive an unlimited number of incoming calls, but pays a somewhat higher monthly fee to cover a certain number of outgoing calls within the local area. Any calls beyond this area are charged at a per minute rate based on the distance of the call.
- Unlimited Local Service or Flat Rate Service. This service, which also permits unlimited incoming calls, carries the highest monthly fee, since it allows the consumer an unlimited number of outgoing local calls.

The service that is best for you depends entirely on your situation. Single individuals who make only a few local calls a week are likely to be best off with the budget or lifeline service. Families with teen-age children who are constantly calling their friends may want unlimited local service. Message unit service may best serve the needs of families with no teenagers and of individuals who make a substantial number of local phone calls. But you can always change from one kind of service to another, and before making a final decision, check the phone usage in your home for a couple of weeks. You may be surprised at what you find. According to one official of a local company, nearly half the customers in his area who buy unlimited service would save money by using one of the plans with a cheaper base rate, even though it carries a charge for local calls.

Check with your local telephone company about rates for intrastate phone calls — those made to phone numbers within the state but outside the local area code. Normally, these are charged as toll calls, but in some areas discount plans exist that reduce their costs considerably. These plans are not always publicized, but you can find out about them by calling your telephone company. Remember, however, these special rates are subject to change.

Long Distance Services

A major result of the revolution in telephone service is the emergence of companies that have broken AT&T's monopoly on long distance telephone calls. These firms offer alternatives to AT&T's long lines service, although some of them limit their service to metropolitan areas.

By September, 1986, telephone users in most areas served by Bell companies will have a choice of the long distance service through which they want their calls automatically routed. But they will also have access to the other lines. If you select Company A as your automatic long distance line and Company B charges less for calls to a given city, you will be able to route your calls there through the second firm. Consider the following when choosing the line to use as your automatic hook-up:

- At what hours of the day do you make the greatest number of your long distance calls? All long distance services charge different rates at different times of day and some charge much less at night and over the weekends than do their competitors. But all charge their highest rate during the so-called peak-use period — from 8 a.m. to 5 p.m. on weekdays — and there are fewer differences among their rates at these times than at others.
- How often do you make long distance calls? Some alternative services may charge an initial fee; others charge a minimum amount that must be paid each month whether or not the service is used during the billing period. Customers pay for AT&T's long lines only when using them. So the number of long distance calls you make is a significant factor in determining which service is most economical for you. Most alternative services offer consumers a "rule of thumb" figure to help them decide whether the service is worthwhile for them. Ask for this rule when talking to these firms.
- What towns and cities do you telephone most often? Check to make sure that the alternative service you are considering reaches the places you call.

Moving

In any one year, 20 percent of America's households pull up roots and move. Some of these moves are from one coast to another, some from state to state, and some no more than a few miles across town. However long the move and however many possessions it involves, the experience is always difficult and can be traumatic. Every one of us has heard at least one horror story about a nightmare move — the lost sofa, the barrels of broken dishes, the extra hours to get from here to there. If you don't want to be an actor in this melancholy drama, it is urgent that you shop around before deciding on a mover and that you get recommendations from friends, colleagues and neighbors. It is equally urgent that you plan precisely in advance and that you acquaint yourself with your rights in dealing with moving companies.

Interstate Moves. All moving companies that operate across state lines come under the authority of the Interstate Commerce Commission (ICC). The legislation regulating moving practices is the Household Goods Transportation Act of 1980, which in considerable measure eased the rules under which moving companies operate. Until recently, the ICC regulated the fee that an interstate mover could charge on the basis of a formula involving the weight of the materials to be moved and the distance to be covered. Rates are still calculated on this basis, but it is up to the individual moving company to set its own fees, which can, therefore, vary from one company to another. All interstate moving companies must register their fees with the ICC, and must charge the rates they have listed with the agency. They may charge lower rates during certain periods of the year than at others, but these lower rates and the specific periods must also be listed with the ICC. Some companies may charge 10 or 15 percent less during off-peak periods (usually autumn, winter and spring) than during their busiest season, summer.

The ICC requires that all of the approximately 2,500 moving companies carrying goods across state lines present prospective customers with a statement of their performance record. This statement must include such information as the number of late pickups or deliveries; the percentage of customers who protested inaccurate estimates; and the number who complained about lost or damaged goods. If the moving company you are considering does not voluntarily offer you a copy of its performance record, be sure to ask for it. If the company declines to provide it, find another to deal with. And be sure, also, to complain to the nearest field office of the ICC (see directory, page 100).

If you wish to compare the records of several moving companies, you can get a computer read-out on the performance records of all the nation's movers at the ICC field offices in San Francisco, Los Angeles, Fort Worth, Chicago, Miami, Atlanta, Philadelphia, New York City and Boston.

In addition to comparing the records of various moving companies, it is wise to compare their estimates. Most movers are happy to send a representative to your home to determine the size of the job to be done and to provide a written estimate of its cost. Any mover who asks you to accept a spoken estimate should be crossed off your list. What you want is a written estimate — either binding or non-binding.

A binding estimate is a contract in which both the fees involved and the responsibilities of the contracting parties are clearly spelled out. It describes in great detail all the services for which the moving company is responsible, and obligates the company to do what it says it is going to do for the price that is stipulated. On the other hand, it does not obligate the company to perform any service not included in it. If you want additional services and the company is willing to perform them, you will have to pay an extra fee. If, for example, the binding estimate stipulates that you will do all the packing and will provide your own cartons and wardrobes, the moving company has the right to demand extra payment if you ask for cartons or packing assistance at the time of the move.

Because a binding estimate requires considerable time and effort on the part of the mover's representative, the firm may charge for this service. But the practice is not universal and companies often offer free binding estimates. Binding estimates have an important advantage for consumers by letting them know in advance exactly what the cost of a move will be. A mover who underestimates his expenses is still required to provide the services contracted for at the fee already set. On the other hand, since consumers who accept a binding estimate are committed to pay its cost, it is important to shop around for several before making a decision.

A non-binding estimate does not bind the mover to a predetermined price and must, under the law, be given without charging a fee. A non-binding estimate requires that the mover transport your goods at a fixed per pound price that accords with the tariff he has filed with the ICC. However, a mover giving a non-binding estimate may overestimate or underestimate the actual weight of your possessions, and thus your final bill may be quite different from the amount listed in the estimate. Like the binding estimate, the non-binding estimate must be given in writing and must describe in clear, understandable terms all the services to be provided.

Estimated charges must appear on what is called an "order for service" — the paper you receive from the mover before the move — as well as on the bill of lading, which you receive at the time your possessions are packed into the moving van. Unlike the bill of lading, an order for service is not contractually binding on the customer. If the move is cancelled for any reason, or if the customer decides to use a different mover, he or she may cancel the order for service without charge.

For your own protection, it is essential in any interstate move that you verify the weight of your shipment. It is not difficult to do. When the movers arrive at your door, they are required to give you a weight ticket, which lists the "tare" weight of their truck — its weight when it is empty. After your possessions have been loaded, the truck is taken to a weighing station where the gross weight is recorded. If you are on hand for this weigh-in, you can make sure that the weight of your goods — the difference between the gross weight and the tare weight — is properly recorded. It is legal for necessary moving equipment, such as dollies, to be aboard the truck during the weigh-in, but neither the driver nor the crew should be in the vehicle when its gross weight is being determined. Be aware that the law provides severe penalties — a fine of up to $10,000, and imprisonment for up to two years, or both — for any mover found guilty of defrauding a consumer in the weighing process.

The Inventory. As the movers pick up your possessions they prepare an inventory, listing each separate item and carton of items, noting the condition of each. The notation BU next to the listing for a bureau means that it has burn marks; CH next to the listing for a boxful of plates indicates that the china is chipped. You will be asked to sign this inventory. Unless you agree that the notations describe the actual condition of the items involved, make your own counter-notations next to the disputed listings before you sign. Your ability to claim damages may depend on this.

All movers use a code to describe the condition of furnishings they are going to handle. Listed below are the ones most commonly employed:

BE — bent
BU — burned
CU — contents and condition unknown
F — faded
L — loose
MI — mildew
PBC — packed by carrier
BR — broken
CH — chipped
D — dented
Z — cracked
G — gouged
M — marred
MO — moth-eaten
PBO — packed by owner
R — rubbed
SC — scratched
T — torn
RU — rusted
SO — soiled
W — badly worn

Moving companies are automatically liable for 60 cents per pound for damages sustained when they ship goods. You can increase this liability to $1.25 per pound by paying a modest fee, but even this amount is unlikely to cover the actual worth of your possessions if they are damaged.

It is also possible to make a contract with your mover that insures your possessions against loss or damage at full market rates. In some instances, the mover will repair a damaged item; in others the company will provide a replacement, or offer a payment to cover the item's monetary worth. Available plans differ in detail from company to company, as do their costs; it is a good idea to ask about them when comparing movers' fees.

Some homeowners' insurance policies cover goods in transit. If yours does not, you may be able to purchase a rider that provides this coverage. If you have no homeowner's policy or cannot purchase a rider, it may be worth your while to buy a short term policy that will protect your possessions while in transit.

Payment for interstate moves is customarily made by certified check, traveler's check, money order or cash. A mover has no obligation to accept a personal check for an interstate move, and in most instances will not do so unless such an arrangement has been written into the contract. But if the move is not covered by a binding estimate, or if the consumer is not present at the weigh-in, he or she has no way of knowing precisely what the cost will be. It is therefore advisable to have a certified or other acceptable check in the amount of the original estimate and enough cash to allow for 10 percent more. If the actual cost is more than 10 percent above the estimate, ICC regulations give you 30 days after the move to pay additional charges.

Try to get a clause in your contract with the mover that obligates the company to pay living expenses for your family in the event that your goods are not delivered within a specified range of dates. If you do not have such a clause and the delivery is late, you can take the mover to court to recover these expenses. Obviously, however, it is much simpler to have the matter clearly spelled out in your

(continued on page 102)

State Government Utility Regulatory Commissions

Alabama
Public Service Commission
P.O. Box 991
Montgomery, AL 36130

Alaska
Public Utilities Commission
338 Denali Street
Anchorage, AK 99501

Arizona
Corporation Commission
1688 West Adams
Phoenix, AZ 85007

Arkansas
Public Service Commission
Justice Building
Little Rock, AR 72201

California
Public Utilities Commission
350 McAllister Street
San Francisco, CA 94102

Colorado
Public Utilities Commission
1525 Sherman Street
Denver, CO 80203

Connecticut
Public Utilities Commission
545 State Office Building
Hartford, CT 06115

Delaware
Public Service Commission
820 North French Street
Wilmington, DE 19801

District of Columbia
Public Service Commission
1625 I Street, NW
Washington, DC 20006

Florida
Public Service Commission
700 South Adams Street
Tallahassee, FL 32304

Georgia
Public Service Commission
15 Peachtree Street
Atlanta, GA 30303

Hawaii
Public Service Commission
1164 Bishop Street
Honolulu, HI 96813

Idaho
Public Utilities Commission
State House
Boise, ID 83720

Illinois
Commerce Commission
527 East Capitol Avenue
Springfield, IL 62706

Indiana
Public Service Commission
807 State Office Building
Indianapolis, IN 46204

Iowa
State Commerce Commission
State Capitol
Des Moines, IA 50319

Kansas
State Corporation Commission
State Office Building
Topeka, KS 66612

Kentucky
Public Service Commission
P.O. Box 496
Frankfort, KY 40601

Louisiana
Public Service Commission
One American Place
Baton Rouge, LA 70825

Maine
Public Utilities Commission
State House
Augusta, ME 04333

Maryland
Public Service Commission
904 State Office Building
301 West Preston Street
Baltimore, MD 21201

Massachusetts
Department of Public Utilities
One Ashburton Place
Boston, MA 02108

Michigan
Public Service Commission
P.O. Box 30221
Lansing, MI 48909

Minnesota
Public Service Commission
Kellogg and Robert Streets
St. Paul, MN 55101

Mississippi
Public Service Commission
Walter Sillers State Office Building
P.O. Box 1174
Jackson, MI 39205

Missouri
Public Service Commission
Jefferson Building
Jefferson City, MO 65101

Montana
Public Service Commission
34 West 6th Avenue
Helena, Mt. 59601

Nebraska
Public Service Commission
1342 M Street
Lincoln, NE 68508

Nevada
Public Service Commission
505 East King Street
Carson City, NV 89710

New Hampshire
Public Utilities Commission
26 Pleasant Street
Concord, NH 03301

New Jersey
Public Utility Commission
1100 Raymond Boulevard
Newark, NJ 07102

New Mexico
Public Service Commission
State Capitol Building
Santa Fe, NM 87501

New York
Public Service Commission
Empire State Place
Albany, NY 12223

Two World Trade Center
New York, NY 10047

North Carolina
Utilities Commission
P.O. Box 991
Raleigh, NC 27602

North Dakota
Public Service Commission
State Capitol Building
Bismarck, ND 58505

Ohio
Public Utilities Commission
180 East Broad Street
Columbus, OH 43215

Oklahoma
Corporation Commission
Jim Thorpe Office Building
Oklahoma City, OK 73105

Oregon
Public Utility Commission
Labor and Industries Building
Salem, OR 97310

Pennsylvania
Public Utilities Commission
North Office Building
Harrisburg, PA 17120

Rhode Island
Public Utilities Commission
100 Orange Street
Providence, RI 02903

South Carolina
Public Service Commission
P.O. Box 11649
Columbia, SC 29211

South Dakota
Public Utilities Commission
Capitol Building
Pierre, SD 57501

Tennessee
Public Service Commission
C1-100 Cordell Hull Building
Nashville, TN 37219

Texas
Public Utility Commission
7800 Shoal Creek Boulevard
Austin, TX 78757

Utah
Public Service Commission
330 East 4th Street
Salt Lake City, UT 84111

Vermont
Public Service Board
120 State Street
Montpelier, VT 05602

Virginia
State Corporation Commission
P.O. Box 1197
Richmond, VA 23209

Washington
Utilities and Transportation Commission
Highways-Licenses Building
Olympia, WA 98504

West Virginia
Public Service Commission
E-217 State Capitol Building
Charleston, WV 25305

Wisconsin
Public Service Commission
432 Hill Farms State Office Building
Madison, WI 53702

Wyoming
Public Service Commission
Capitol Hill Building
320 West 25th Street
Cheyenne, WY 82002

Offices of the Interstate Commerce Commission

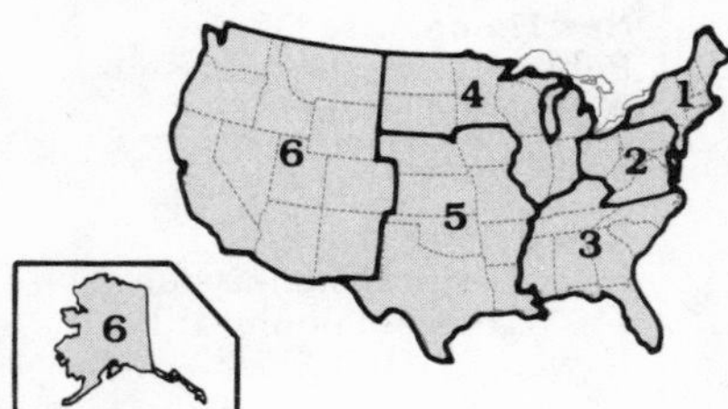

Region 1 **Connecticut, Maine, Massachusetts, New Hampshire, New Jersey, New York, Rhode Island, Vermont**
150 Causeway Street, Boston, MA 02114

Region 2 **Delaware, District of Columbia, Maryland, Ohio, Pennsylvania, Virginia, West Virginia**
101 North 7th Street, Philadelphia, PA 19106

Region 3 **Alabama, Florida, Georgia, Kentucky, Mississippi, North Carolina, South Carolina, Tennessee**
1776 Peachtree Street, NW, Atlanta, GA 30309

Region 4 **Illinois, Indiana, Michigan, Minnesota, North Dakota, South Dakota, Wisconsin**
219 Dearborn Street, Chicago, IL 60604

Region 5 **Arkansas, Iowa, Kansas, Louisiana, Missouri, Nebraska, Oklahoma, Texas**
411 West 7th Street, Fort Worth, TX 76102

Region 6 **Alaska, Arizona, California, Colorado, Hawaii, Idaho, Montana, Nevada, New Mexico, Oregon, Utah, Washington, Wyoming**
211 Main Street, San Francisco, CA 94105

Offices of the U.S. Department of Housing and Urban Development

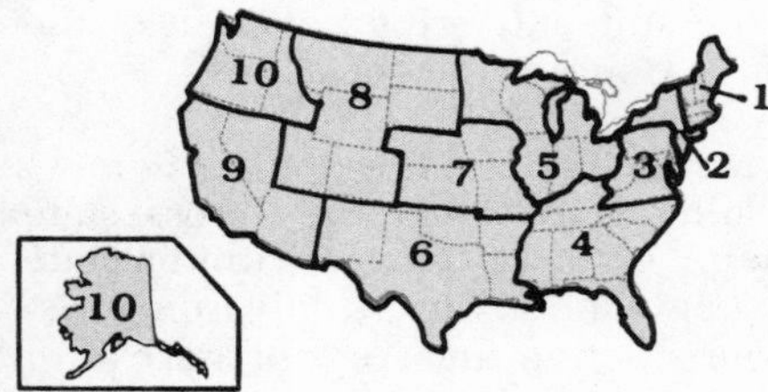

Main Office **U.S. Department of Housing and Urban Development, Washington, DC 20410**

Region 1 **Connecticut, Maine, Massachusetts, New Hampshire, Rhode Island, Vermont**
HUD, John F. Kennedy Building, Boston, MA 02203

Region 2 **New Jersey, New York, Puerto Rico, Virgin Islands**
HUD, 26 Federal Plaza, New York, NY 10007

Region 3 **Delaware, District of Columbia, Maryland, Pennsylvania, Virginia, West Virginia**
HUD, Curtis Building, 6th and Walnut Streets, Philadelphia, PA 19106

Region 4 **Alabama, Florida, Georgia, Kentucky, Mississippi, North Carolina, South Carolina, Tennessee**
HUD, 75 Spring Street, SW, Atlanta, GA 30303

Region 5 **Illinois, Indiana, Michigan, Minnesota, Ohio, Wisconsin**
HUD, 300 South Wacker Drive, Chicago, IL 60606

Region 6 **Arkansas, Louisiana, New Mexico, Oklahoma, Texas**
HUD, 221 West Lancaster Avenue, P.O. Box 2905, Fort Worth, TX 76113

Region 7 **Iowa, Kansas, Missouri, Nebraska**
HUD, Professional Building, Rm 1200, 1103 Grand Avenue, Kansas City, MO 64106

Region 8 **Colorado, Montana, North Dakota, South Dakota, Utah, Wyoming**
HUD, Executive Tower Building, 1405 Curtis Street, Denver, CO 80202

Region 9 **Arizona, California, Hawaii, Nevada, Guam, American Samoa**
HUD, 450 Golden Gate Avenue, P.O. Box 36003, San Francisco, CA 94102

Region 10 **Alaska, Idaho, Oregon, Washington**
HUD, Arcade Plaza Building, 1321 Second Avenue, Seattle, WA 98101

moving contract. If the van arrives at your new residence before the agreed-upon range of dates and no authorized person is present to accept delivery, the moving company is obligated to store your goods, re-deliver them during the agreed-on period and pay the storage costs. If, however, the van appears at the appointed time and you are not there within two hours, any expenses involved in storage and re-delivery are your responsibility.

Claims for Damages. After your possessions have been unloaded at your new residence, a member of the moving team will ask you to sign his copy of the inventory. Since your signature is, in effect, an acknowledgement that your goods were delivered in the same condition in which they were picked up, do not sign it until you have inspected your possessions. ICC regulations give you up to nine months after a move to file a claim against the mover. Even so, a notation on the inventory indicating that a particular item was broken, marred, scratched or lost in transit can be extremely useful to you in the event of a dispute.

When filing a claim with a moving company, send photocopies, not original documents. Buttress your claim for damaged goods with copies of any receipts you may have indicating their value, or with appraisal certificates. For expenses you have borne due to late or early delivery, send photocopies of hotel or motel bills and restaurant receipts.

The ICC requires an interstate mover to acknowledge receipt of your claim within 30 days and respond to it within 120 days either by denying it or making a settlement offer. If the mover refuses to acknowledge your claim or make satisfactory restitution, call or write the nearest field office of the ICC.

The Household Goods Dispute Settlement Program, an arbitration procedure which has been approved by the ICC and is administered by the American Arbitration Association, provides another mechanism through which to solve serious problems with movers. Not all moving companies subscribe to this program, nor can any consumer be required to do so. But if both parties voluntarily agree to make use of arbitration, they are legally bound by the arbitrator's findings. The moving companies most likely to accept arbitration are those that belong to the American Movers Conference or the Movers' and Warehousemen's Association of America, two trade associations discussed in Chapter 13.

If all other methods of resolving a disagreement with a mover fail, the consumer can bring a court suit, provided the claim is filed within the 120 days mentioned previously. Winning the suit will bring payment of the claim plus reasonable attorney's fees.

Intrastate Moves. Federal law applies to moving companies only when they cross state lines. When it comes to moves within a state or locality, regulations vary widely from jurisdiction to jurisdiction, and some of these offer consumers only a minimum of protection. For this reason, it is absolutely essential that you deal with a thoroughly trustworthy company. Check with friends, neighbors and business associates. Call your local Better Business Bureau (see directory, page 32). It can tell you which movers have been the subjects of the smallest numbers of complaints.

Unlike interstate movers, which charge on the basis of weight and distance, local and intrastate movers often charge entirely on the basis of the time it takes to complete a move. However your mover is billing you, make sure that you have a detailed contract, and that you exercise all the care recommended for interstate moves. Get an estimate; ask for an order for service as well as a contract; check the inventory.

Address complaints about intrastate and local movers to your state Public Utility Commission (see directory, page 99), state Consumer Protection Agency (see directory, page 16), state attorney general's office (see directory, page 48), local Better Business Bureau (see directory, page 32) or, if the mover belongs to the American Movers Conference, to that organization at the address above.

Chapter 5

Wheels

Next to housing, the biggest single expense for most Americans is transportation — specifically, the myriad costs associated with buying and operating an automobile. Those costs, which have gone up far faster than the general inflation rate, are taking a larger and larger bite out of the average budget every year. The problem is aggravated for many of us who own more than one car, or perhaps a pickup truck, camper or motor home.

Yet surveys indicate that a high percentage of car owners have only a vague idea of what all their costs actually add up to, or of the many ways they can be held down. Moreover, studies show that automobile maintenance and repairs are the number one consumer complaint in the United States. And all too many of the complaints, unfortunately, have to do with overcharging, shoddy practices and even outright fraud.

In this chapter we examine such techniques as how to shop for a car, new or used, how to finance a purchase, how to trade in or sell an older car and what to do when that shiny chariot you fell in love with at the dealer's showroom turns out to be a hopeless dud. We also look into common maintenance items and minor repairs that you can do yourself, as well as ways to choose and deal with garages and mechanics for larger jobs. We consider good practices aimed at economical driving: buying gasoline, tires and other supplies; and minimizing the risks of auto theft. Finally, we analyze the pros and cons of renting or leasing vehicles versus the advantages and disadvantages of owning them.

The High Cost of Driving

Because of the vast number of variables — purchase price, financing, insurance, annual mileage, costs of fuel, parts and repairs, inflation, to name a few — it is difficult to generalize about the overall cost of owning a car. But one thing is sure: it is much higher than most people realize. A U.S. Department of Transportation study pegged the total cost of a large $9,000-plus American car at $32,000 (not counting inflation) if it was driven an average of 10,000 miles a year and kept for 12 years — close to the limit of most cars' useful lives. Another study put the true cost of an $8,000 standard-size car, driven 10 years and 100,000 miles, at more than $33,000 — more than four times the original purchase price. And these figures are based on the most economical form of car ownership: keeping it until you get all the mileage out of it you possibly can rather than trading it in for a new one every few years.

If you buy a new automobile every year, the costs are far greater. According to the Department of Transportation, a series of large cars costs you nearly $30,000 in depreciation alone over a 12-year period. If you trade in your car every two years, the depreciation amounts to a little over $23,000 — this amount is in addition to all your other annual operating expenses.

Depreciation, in fact, is the hidden villain of car ownership — along with gasoline the largest single item in annual driving costs. With the exception of certain specialty and vintage automobiles dear to the collectors' market, cars generally lose value the moment they are bought and continue to lose it, though at a diminishing rate, until they are finally turned into junk. Depreciation varies widely from model to model and from year to year, but as a rough rule of thumb an average full-size car will lose a quarter of its value in its first year (more for some larger luxury models), about 15 percent in its second year and 13 percent in its third year, tapering off to about 6 percent a year in its sixth through tenth years. Smaller cars, and those with exceptionally good reputations for reliability, depreciate less dramatically and more evenly, about 12 percent in the first year, 11 percent in the second through fourth years and about 7 percent by the tenth. Nor is this general rate of depreciation the only one a car owner has to worry about. Other factors are involved in determining the depreciation rate of a specific vehicle: how popular the model is, the car's frequency-of-repair record, how many miles it has been driven and how well it has been maintained. If you trade in your car for a new one annually, depreciation can account for half of your total operating costs, compared with a quarter if you continue to use your car for a number of years.

Fixed Versus Variable Costs
Many drivers think of the expenses of operating a car only in terms of gasoline and oil and, in some cases, parking and tolls. The true costs of operating your car, however, also include repairs, maintenance, tires and replacement parts — all the variable expenses that depend on individual cars and owners. And in addition, they include not only the usual cost of depreciation, but such other fixed costs as insurance, loan interest, licenses, taxes and other fees. The bottom line of car ownership is not miles per gallon, but total cost per mile driven: the total of all these items divided by the number of miles you drive each year. This is the figure that tells you what it actually costs for each mile your automobile takes you from here to there.

This cost can vary broadly. A middle-aged rural couple who bought their small used car for cash, who don't have to commute to work and who plan to use the car until it breaks down for good, might find their total expenses as little as 20 cents a mile over the life of the car. A young, single, aspiring executive who lives in a metropolitan area, buys a flashy car every year on time and drives to his office, paying daily parking charges and tolls, might well pay five times as much.

A study by the American Automobile Association, the nation's largest federation of motor clubs, and Runzheimer & Company, a management consulting firm of Rochester, Wisconsin, indicates that the fixed costs of owning a typical late-model car driven 10,000 miles a year amount to some 76 percent of total annual costs, while the variable operating costs, including gasoline, oil, maintenance and tires, account for only about 24 percent.

Here is the breakdown, based on a 1983 domestic compact. (In this example, the car is a Chevette four-cylinder, four-door hatchback with standard accessories, automatic transmission, power steering, power disc brakes and radio, driven up to 15,000 miles per year, with gasoline at $1.297 a gallon; insurance is based on pleasure use — less than 10 miles driven to or from work per day — and no youthful driver in the family.)

Fixed Cost *(Annually)*	
Depreciation (based on trading in the car at end of four years or 60,000 miles, whichever comes first — the period during which the car is expected to deliver the greatest economy)	$1,121
Finance charge (20 percent down, four-year loan at 15 percent)	450
Liability ($100,000/$300,000) and property damage ($50,000) insurance	222
Collision insurance ($250 deductible)	169
Comprehensive (fire and theft) insurance ($100 deductible)	58
License, registration, taxes	85
Total fixed costs	$2,105 ($5.77 per day)

Variable cost *(Average per mile)*	
Gasoline (unleaded) and oil	5.14 cents
Maintenance	0.87 cents
Tires	0.61 cents
Total	6.62 cents

Based on these figures, a motorist driving 10,000 miles annually would be paying 27.67 cents a mile: $2,105 in fixed costs plus $662 in variable operating costs (10,000 miles x 6.62 cents) equals $2,767, which, divided by 10,000, gives us 27.67 cents a mile. A motorist driving 15,000 miles a year would pay $3,098, or 20.6 cents a mile. For mileage in excess of

Calculating Your Car Costs

Use this work sheet to figure the true annual cost of your present automobile, or to compare costs between two automobiles. For an explanation of individual items and comparative figures, see text.

Fixed Costs

Annual depreciation	________
Finance charges	________
Insurance	________
License, registration, taxes	________
Total Fixed Costs	________

Variable Costs

Gas and oil	________
Maintenance and repairs	________
Tires	________
Other costs	________
Total Variable Costs	________
Total Driving Costs (add fixed and variable totals)	________
Cost Per Mile (divide total by miles driven)	________

15,000 a year, add $51 depreciation per 1,000 miles. If the car is equipped with air conditioning, add 36 cents a day to fixed costs and 20 cents per mile in operating costs.

Figuring Your Own Costs

To compute your own annual driving costs, either on your present automobile or one you are thinking of buying, use the work sheet above. To figure the first item, your annual depreciation expense, subtract the trade-in value of your car from the purchase price and divide by the number of years you plan to keep the car. If you finance the car (see box, page 117), include annual interest charges in your finance cost. Under insurance, put in the annual premiums of all policies related to operating your automobile (see Chapter 10 for more information on automobile insurance). Add annual driver's license and auto registration fees plus any annual property tax on the car (not sales or excise taxes paid when it was bought, which are considered part of the purchase price).

To figure the variable costs, you will first have to make some observations. In determining the gas consumption of your present car, note the mileage on the odometer (it's a good idea to keep a notebook in the glove compartment to record all expenses) when the tank is full. Then each time you stop at a service station, note the number of gallons needed to fill the tank, the cost of the fill-up and the odometer reading. To figure your miles per gallon, periodically subtract the first mileage reading from the current one to get the number of miles you have driven, then divide this figure by the total number of gallons bought. For your cost of gas per mile, add the costs of the fill-ups and divide by the number of miles driven. Oil, though not a major expense for a car in good condition, should be figured the same way (don't forget to include the cost of complete oil changes as well). To determine maintenance costs keep a record of all tune-ups, repairs and other service items, and at the end of the year total these costs. Do the same if you buy any replacement tires during the year. (If the car you are planning to buy is a typical compact, you can use the figures given for gas and oil, maintenance and tires in the example above to produce a rough estimate; for a rough estimate of expected gasoline consumption on particular models, look at the EPA ratings on the window stickers of cars in dealers' showrooms or listed in consumer magazines.)

Under "other costs," include your total or estimate for any parking charges, bridge or highway tolls, car washes and accessories such as floor mats, seat covers and windshield-wiper blades. Add your totals for fixed costs and variable costs and divide by the number of miles you have driven, or expect to drive, during the year.

Your cost per mile will vary with a number of factors, including the type of car, how well you maintain it, where you live and the kind of driving you do.

Basic Decisions

Cost analyses such as the above can help reveal what you are really paying for your

Those Mileage Ratings or How EPA Rates MPG

The magic numbers these days in auto ads — and consumer buying decisions — are the fuel economy figures attributed to various cars. The small print warns that these ratings are "for comparison only" and that "actual mileage may vary." But a buyer cannot help feeling cheated on discovering that his new car, purchased on the basis of a "30 mpg" rating, gets a measly 20 miles to a gallon of gas. Where did that 30 figure come from?

Passage of the Energy Conservation Act in 1975 made fuel economy labeling mandatory on all passenger cars, vans and light trucks. The task of determining mileage ratings was assigned to the Environmental Protection Agency, which is also responsible for emissions testing to check compliance with the Clean Air Act. Each year some 900 new models are submitted to tests conducted or supervised by EPA.

Each vehicle is tested by a professional driver on a machine called a dynamometer, with the drive wheels touching its rolling drums and each vehicle going through exactly the same routine. Since some 55 percent of all driving is done in and around cities, the procedure simulates a typical 7.5-mile, stop-and-go trip, with speeds ranging from zero to 56 miles per hour and averaging 20 miles per hour. The "trip" takes 23 minutes and involves 18 stops, with 18 percent of the time spent idling — thus approximating city driving with traffic lights. Test conditions simulate warm weather (about 70° F) and dry, level roads. Engines are subjected to "cold starts," similar to those occurring the morning after a car has been parked all night, and "hot starts," similar to those occurring after the engine has warmed up in driving and then been stopped.

After the tests are completed and mathematically adjusted for typical road conditions, miles per gallon are measured and published as each vehicle's "estimated MPG." This is the number placed by law on each new car sticker, listed in comparative-rating booklets, and carried in automobile ads. Manufacturers are also permitted to advertise their models' estimated "highway average," a figure arrived at by a separate test that simulates, as nearly as possible, a 10.2-mile highway trip at a maximum speed of 60 miles per hour and an average speed of 48.2 miles per hour.

EPA points out that its figures are only estimates and not guaranteed guides, and are designed only to help buyers compare the *relative* fuel economy of each vehicle in a given model class. (Results of actual road tests for selected cars appear periodically in consumer and auto magazines.) The agency estimates that *average* fuel economy of cars in actual use

present car, as against what you would be paying for a new one. In the face of rising costs, more new-car buyers are keeping their cars for longer periods to save money — the average age of all passenger cars on the road is now more than seven years, versus four only four years ago, according to a study by America's largest rental car company. Most experts, including those in the U.S. Department of Transportation, agree that it is almost never cheaper to trade in a car every year or two than to keep it, and that it is a real economy to drive it for 100,000 miles or for 10 years or more.

True, older cars tend to use more fuel, and their maintenance and repair costs can also go up sharply as things start to wear out, usually between the fourth and sixth year. After that, however, repair and maintenance costs usually decline somewhat. Moreover, whatever increases there are in variable operating costs are more than offset by savings in fixed costs: depreciation dips below 10 percent annually; finance charges, if any, have been paid; rates for collision and comprehensive (fire and theft) insurance are much lower; and so are similar expenses.

It has been estimated that it costs the owner of a 10-year-old automobile 40 percent less to run his car than it would if he traded in for a new model each year. It has also been estimated that a long-term owner can realize a saving of 60 percent in costs per mile as compared with an annual trader if he buys a smaller, less expensive car and drives it for 10 is about 4 percent less — and about 30 percent less on the highway. Actual experience may vary even further from the estimate under certain circumstances.

For example, a car averaging 10 miles per hour instead of 20 on the same 7.5-mile trip in heavy traffic would lose 30 percent in fuel economy, while a car able to average 30 miles per hour on that trip would get a bonus of 16 percent. A car traveling only one mile instead of 7.5 would be 45 percent less fuel-efficient because of the gas-guzzling time required for the engine to warm up, whereas the same car would be 8 percent more efficient on a 15-mile trip.

Other enemies of fuel economy include:

- Cold weather (1 to 2 percent drop for each 10°F).
- Rain, powerful headwinds (10 percent or more).
- High altitudes, steep grades, winding roads (about 33 percent for a 3 percent grade).
- Rough surfaces (15 to 35 percent).
- Heavy loads (1 to 3 percent for each 100 pounds).
- Poor engine tuning (5 to 20 percent).
- High speeds (15 to 20 percent for a car going 70 miles per hour instead of 55).

Car weight and options also exact their toll. A 5,500-pound vehicle gets about half as many miles per gallon in city driving as does an automobile that weighs 2,500 pounds.

An increase of 10 percent in the size of the engine reduces fuel economy by 6 percent.

Air conditioning imposes an average penalty of 6 percent and can cost as much as 20 or 30 percent on a hot, humid day in slow-moving traffic.

Automatic transmissions are generally 2 to 6 percent less efficient than properly handled manual transmissions.

On the plus side, an axle ratio 10 percent lower than standard can increase fuel economy up to 5 percent in large cars and 10 percent in smaller ones because it allows the engine to run more slowly at a given vehicle speed.

Whatever car you buy, the EPA observes, you can improve your miles per gallon by:

- remaining current with recommended lubrication and filter changes;
- regularly checking the condition of your carburetor and ignition system;
- avoiding short trips or combining them into a single errand;
- driving smoothly — as little speeding up and slowing down as possible — and accelerating gradually;
- and, perhaps most important, slowing down your highway speed. Driving at 55 miles per hour may seem tame in an age of "aerodynamic" automobile bodies and "high performance" engines, but the relatively leisurely pace *does* help save gasoline — and lives as well.

years before getting another. If you do keep a car that long, of course, it becomes extremely important to maintain it in good and safe operating condition. You can try to anticipate problems by having a reliable mechanic check the automobile over at regular intervals. If he recommends major repairs and replacements that amount to more than half the current market value of the car and your finances permit it, you may want to consider the option of selling and starting over again.

By the same token, a new car may not automatically be the best buy, either as a first car, a second car or a replacement car, particularly if you cannot, or do not wish to, tie up a substantial amount of money in a purchase and if you intend to drive the car less than 10,000 miles a year. Under such conditions you might be better off buying a two- or three-year-old used car in relatively good condition, in which the lion's share of the depreciation has already been paid, and out of which you may expect to be able to get as much as 70,000 more miles.

Buying a New Car

People buy new cars for many reasons: because they offer comfort, convenience or good gas mileage; because they are fun to drive, promising jack-rabbit acceleration and blazing highway speeds; because they reflect well on the owner's status, or exquisite taste; because they are sleek metallic gray or glittering fire-engine red; or just because, as op-

Handling Salesmen's Tricks

"In combativeness and in pure, raw competition, the automobile business makes the forces of Attila the Hun look like a group of butterfly collectors running through the fields in their safari shorts...." So writes veteran car salesman and dealer Remar Sutton in his entertaining book *Don't Get Taken Every Time*. Among common tricks of the trade to beware of are these, which have been honed to perfection by such star salesmen as Sutton's "Killer Monsoon":

Lowballing. Quoting an extremely low price to get a customer "into the tent" and stop him from shopping elsewhere or, as a last-ditch effort, to get him to come back if he starts to leave. Unless you get immediate, written confirmation from the sales manager or dealer — *not* the salesman — you may find that "someone else just got the last one" or that the salesman made a "mistake." Of course, the dealer just happens to have a nicer car he'll be willing to part with — at a higher price.

Switching. Similar to the above. Often involves convincing a customer to buy not the car that was advertised, or the one he wants, but another with a larger profit margin for the dealer, or a hard-to-move model that carries a special bonus to the salesman who can get it off the lot.

Highballing. Quoting an unrealistically high price on your trade-in as a come-on — a figure that may drop dramatically by the time you actually sit down to sign the contract or bring in the old car to pick up your new one. Again, get the figure in writing, and make sure it is good until the delivery date.

Double-talking, Bumping. These can take any number of forms, the first designed to wear you down by confusing you, the second to raise the price you will eventually pay. If you don't understand what's going on, ask. If you do, and don't like it, leave.

The Turnover or "T.O.". You're mixed up, bushed and want to call it a day, but the salesman introduces you to another salesman who is specially trained in getting buyers' signatures, or to the sales manager or the dealer

posed to last year's models, they are new. Like children in a toy store, some adults rush from one showroom to another, unable to decide. Then, at a critical moment, a smiling salesman says something that strikes a nerve, and the sale is made. The car they buy may not be the best one for them. It may be one they cannot afford. It may turn out, when they get it home, to be a horrible mistake. The back seat may lack adequate leg room. The rearview mirror may fall off. And one day the engine may not start at all. There may be a great chasm between the car's advertised claims and its performance, and the dealer's service department may seem to be expert at giving customers the runaround when they seek redress. Suddenly the shiny apple has turned into a lemon. Automobile buyers by the thousands have thought darkly of suing their car dealer, along with the manufacturer and, if necessary, taking the case all the way to the Supreme Court. Such is America's love-hate relationship with the car.

Many of these frustrations can be avoided by doing a little homework *before* setting foot in the supercharged atmosphere of any automobile store. If you have made basic, well-researched decisions about the kind of car you really need and can afford, you will be more likely to get it at a reasonable price — and less likely to have a salesman "trade you up" to a fancier car or one loaded with an excess of optional equipment.

Think Finances First

Many new-car buyers pick a car that appeals to them and then try to shoehorn its costs into their budgets, sometimes with unfortunate results. If money is a major factor — two out of three new-car buyers finance their purchases on time — you would do well to approach the problem in reverse. Compare cars and prices himself. You are a lamb in a wolves' den, and outnumbered at that. Smile, make some excuse, and go home before you are eaten alive.

The Advance "Deposit". To keep you from leaving before the real horse-trading begins, a salesman may ask you for a deposit to hold a car, or may tell you that his manager requires a deposit before he will consider an offer "this low." Once you've parted with any money, even a modest amount, you're at a psychological disadvantage. The only deposit you are required to make is the one specified when you sign the contract. If the dealer wants your business, he'll have to settle for that.

Contests and Carnivals. Clowns, balloons and free color television sets may be lots of fun for the whole family, but they aren't going to get you a better car or a lower price ("Sorry, Mr. Jones, but we just gave away our last set," or "We just can't sell you a car at *that* price *and* give you a color TV!"). Nor should you fall for the nice young salesman who tells you that he's competing with the other salesmen for a trip to Hawaii and that your sale will put him "over the top." Dealers offer incentives for most cars sold, most add-ons, most rustproofing jobs, most financing packages — things you couldn't care less about. And, if you are really the one who's going to send the salesman to Hawaii, all expenses paid, he can surely afford to make a little less profit on you.

Honest dealers and salesmen do not play these games. But some in the business do engage in such tactics, especially in large dealerships that pit salespersons against one another, and in highly competitive areas where dealers conduct economic warfare for sales.

The vast majority of people who sell automobiles want to make money but not by being unscrupulous. Be aware of possible sharp tactics, but do not go into a showroom with a chip on your shoulder. If you enter with an antagonistic attitude, you can hardly expect to be treated with thoughtful consideration.

As Sutton suggests, be polite and reasonable when you shop, but have your homework done and your facts well in hand. Keep control of the conversation and insist on straight answers to your questions. Deal with only one person if at all possible; multiple sales pitches muddy the waters. Insist on following your agenda, not his. Remember, if your terms are reasonable, the dealer would rather sell you a car than have you walk out the door for good.

in what you think is your general range. To avoid paying heavy interest charges, plan on making the largest down payment possible, either in cash or in the form of a trade-in on your present car — 25 percent or more of the purchase price if you can. For the balance, figure out how much per month you are willing and able to spend, and for how many months. (In your overall budgeting, do not forget to estimate other major fixed expenses, such as depreciation and insurance, plus variable operating costs as outlined above.)

For an average buyer, monthly automobile payments should probably not exceed about 15 percent of net monthly income. Shop around among several lenders for the lowest annual percentage rate, and ask the lender offering it how much of a loan your maximum monthly payment will buy (see box, page 117). At the same time, figure the worth of your present car if you plan to use it as the down payment on the new one. You can look at various price books — Edmund's *Used Car Prices*, the Kelley *Blue Book* or the National Automobile Dealers Association's *Official Used Car Guide*, available at bookstores, libraries and bank lending offices. But for a more accurate reading of the value of your particular car in your particular area, the surest way is to clean it up and take it to three or more used-car dealers, asking each what he would pay for it in an outright sale. The best offer will give you an idea of your car's highest wholesale value: what a new-car dealer might also give you for it in trade. If you still owe money on your present car, subtract that amount from the wholesale value to find your equity in the car. Then add your equity to the amount you can borrow from your lender: this figure will give you the total price you can afford to pay for a car, including all extras, taxes and fees.

"Rustproofing": A Dubious Option

Because so much of an automobile's body and frame is made of steel, its natural enemy is rust, which costs car owners billions of dollars annually and sends thousands of otherwise useful vehicles to the junkyard before their time. Responding to understandable consumer concern about this problem, auto dealers and makers of rust-inhibiting products have promoted "rustproofing" into a multi-million dollar business, selling the option to millions of new-car buyers each year.

Are those buyers getting their money's worth? In a six-month field study prompted by consumer complaints, investigators of the New York State Attorney General's office found that 83 percent of the cars they inspected around the state failed to receive an adequate coating of rustproofing compound in critical areas called for by industry standards; only two autos scored over 90 on a scale of 100, and some were not coated at all, even though the owners had paid for the service. The average price charged customers was $150, while the dealer's cost was $45. Some buyers of hard-to-get foreign cars were required to accept rustproofing as part of a package of unwanted dealer-installed options in order to get delivery of their cars.

The investigators also found that the "warranties" furnished to buyers of rustproofing jobs were so full of loopholes as to be essentially worthless. Moreover, the study pointed out, virtually all domestic and foreign car manufacturers rustproof their cars at the factory and provide at least a 36-month anti-corrosion warranty. Indeed, some manufacturers expressly discourage additional rustproofing after manufacture because the drilling of holes and the possible clogging of drainage ducts by the compounds used can actually accelerate rather than retard rust.

Neverthless, the investigators found, new-car salesmen generally failed to make customers aware of the manufacturers' warranties, in direct violation of the federal Magnuson-Moss Warranty Act. The New York Attorney General's office — which pressured guilty dealers into redoing work on 3,600 cars and mending their ways in future — concluded that rust-proofing offers no benefit to buyers who intend to keep their new cars for three years or less, and that any benefit for more than three years depends largely on how well the rustproofing is done.

The best way to fight rust, automakers point out, is to wash a car frequently, hose down the underside and wheel wells at least twice a year — particularly if there is salt in the air or it is used to keep roads free of ice — and touch up any scratches in body paint before rust can reach the bare metal and spread.

What Kind of Car?

After you have some knowledge of what you can realistically afford, you can start to look at cars within your reach. However, don't rush immediately into the nearest showroom. First ask yourself how you will actually use the car, most of the time. How many passengers will there *usually* be in the car — one, two, three, four? How much cargo space do you really need? Is the car to be used primarily for long-distance commuting or for short shopping trips and errands around town? Are four doors and ample leg-room required for car-pooling, picking up hordes of children or taking the whole family on frequent weekend jaunts? Is it worth buying a full-size, expensive station wagon if you only need it for occasional vacations? Do you need a van if the only hauling you're going to do is to take a child's possessions to and from college twice a year? (A wagon, van or truck can be rented for only as long as you need it, at considerably less cost.) How much highway driving do you do, and are the extra comfort and conveniences of a large car worth the price?

Automobiles come in myriad models, sizes and body styles, all with advantages, disadvantages and prices to match. Small cars, which include "compacts," "subcompacts" and even a few "minicompacts," are generally the most economical to operate. They are, however, not necessarily the cheapest to buy, since they range from low-cost "econoboxes" to high-priced luxury cars. With four-cylinder or six-cylinder engines, they deliver high mileage per gallon, good maneuverability and ease of parking. In addition, they are ideally suited to manual transmissions, which can make them not only more economical but also more fun to drive. Depreciation and repair costs are usually lower than for larger cars. However, most small cars can seat only four at best, and on an extended trip the rear leg-room may be too cramped for anyone but a midget. Smaller cars are usually noisier and stiffer-riding than larger cars, and smaller engines often give only moderate performance in accelerating or climbing hills (they generally lack the power to pull any but the lightest trailers). Because of their lighter weight, small cars may come out second-best in accidents involving larger vehicles, though individual models vary widely in how well occupants are protected.

Medium or mid-size cars, also called intermediates, may be somewhat more expensive than the lowest priced small economy cars, but generally strike a useful balance between comfort and cost. They can usually seat five or six adults comfortably, have more cargo capacity and may run more smoothly and quietly at an acceptable per-gallon mileage.

Large, also known as standard or full-size, cars generally offer the roomiest interiors and smoothest rides, and thus are still the choice of some drivers who value power, comfort and a certain touch of class, particularly if they frequently take long highway trips or tow a live-in trailer. Big cars carry weight, and thus may be safer for the occupants in case of collision. But they get fewer miles to the gallon and are less maneuverable for in-town driving and curb parking. They also cost more, not only in initial outlay but in insurance premiums and repairs, and tend to depreciate much faster than their smaller kin.

Most cars, whatever their size group, come in different body styles. Two-door coupes and sedans may look sportier and may cost slightly less, but four-door models usually have more leg-room in the rear and are easier to get in and out of. So-called hatchbacks open up from the rear like station wagons and have fold-down rear seats to provide extra space for cargo. Some hatchback roofs, however, slope sharply enough to limit the storage space, and in certain models cargo cannot easily be hidden from sight and possible theft. Station wagons and vans may also expose their contents, but offer a versatile combination of maximum seating and maximum cargo space within a minimum body envelope, generally at a higher price. Convertibles, which waned in popularity in recent years, may be making a comeback, though buyers will have to weigh the joys of sun and breeze against higher price, noise, vulnerability to vandalism and theft and, in most cases, a lack of rollover protection in accidents.

What Price Options?

Virtually every car sold today is offered in a base model with standard features — the one on which claims of low price and high fuel economy are usually made. As additions to this standard model, the maker generally offers more expensive trim packages (fancier appointments, seat coverings and carpets, more chrome, or brightly colored "racing stripes") and a host of optional equipment from tinted windows to power seats.

There are four things to remember about options: 1) they often sound irresistible, 2) many of them yield the dealer a high profit — which is why he wants you to buy them, 3) some may cost more to operate and repair than they are worth and 4) you can do very well without many, if not most, of them.

It's a mistake to buy an overequipped or "loaded" car just because the dealer has it in stock and offers it to you at an unbelievably low cost. If you are willing to wait a month or more for delivery, you can have him order a car tailored to your exact specifications, including the body and interior colors that you want. Or he may be able to get what you want, or pretty close to it, by swapping cars with another dealer in the area.

In considering options, keep in mind not only your own basic needs but the more or less "standard" options that add to the resale value of a car in your area. These may include an automatic transmission, power steering and power disc brakes on medium-size and larger cars, an AM/FM radio and, in hot regions, air conditioning.

Engines. The engine on the base model generally has adequate power for highway driving and passing. Larger optional engines cost more to buy and operate, but may be necessary if you plan to tow a heavy trailer, or drive mostly in hilly terrain or load your car with power accessories. A diesel engine can improve fuel economy 25 to 35 percent or more, but generally its purchase price is considerably more than that of a comparable gasoline engine. In the past diesels have tended to be hard to start in cold weather, sluggish, noisy and smelly, though some newer designs seem to have overcome these problems. Diesels generally require more frequent routine servicing, and certain models have had more than their share of breakdowns. In some areas diesel fuel may be hard to find.

Transmissions. Manual transmissions are usually standard on smaller cars and may be offered as options on some intermediates. They provide higher fuel economy than automatic transmissions and a somewhat better feel for the car and the road; five-speed manuals with overdrive save still more fuel and engine wear in highway driving and can lessen interior noise. On some models, however, shifting may be sticky or awkward — an important reason to test drive a car before you buy. Automatic transmissions, standard on large cars and many mid-size ones, require little shifting but consume more fuel (though the gap is narrowing). On some cars, particularly certain smaller imports, automatics not only hike the price but may also shift erratically and increase noise.

Front-wheel drive. While a basic manufacturing feature and not an add-on option, front-wheel drive gives cars somewhat better handling and good traction on snow and ice because most of the weight of the car is over the driving wheels. It is most compatible with smaller cars and lower-powered engines without power steering, and gives such cars a little more needed footroom and luggage space. Some repair mechanics, however, still feel more comfortable working on the familiar rear-wheel drive, which also gives larger cars better traction for towing trailers.

Power brakes. Standard on large cars and many mid-size ones, these require less effort than regular brakes. They are not necessary, although they are sometimes offered as options, on smaller, lighter automobiles. On some models power brakes can be too efficient, resulting in a touchy, grabby feel and extremely abrupt stops.

Power steering. Again, standard on large cars and many intermediates. A power assist makes steering and parking easier and speeds up the response of a larger car, though it may reduce the "feel" of the front wheels on the road. As an extra-cost option, power steering is not needed on most small cars.

Adjustable steering wheel. Convenient if drivers of different sizes and preferences will be using the car. Can be tilted up to facilitate getting in and out.

Tires. Radial tires are standard on most models, and a sound investment as an option if they are not. Many cars now come with a small, space-saving spare tire designed only for emergency use to get you to the nearest service station in case of a flat. A regular-size spare tire is still offered as an optional extra on some models. Buy it if you like the old-fashioned feeling of having a tire you can rotate with your others.

Heavy-duty suspension. Needed only if you haul heavy loads, do considerable fast driving or often drive on rough roads.

Trailer-towing packages. These commonly include a trailer hitch and upgraded engine cooling, suspension and electrical systems. All are needed for heavy trailer towing — which usually also requires a larger engine, automatic transmission and power brakes.

Air conditioning. Nice for comfort and quiet on long trips in summer heat. However, air conditioning is expensive, cuts fuel mileage, can increase service costs if it breaks down and — according to some authorities — may require a larger engine. Automatic temperature control features are not always reliable. Factory-installed units are usually best.

Tinted glass. Reduces glare and air-conditioner load on sunny days, but also cuts visibility at night. Tall drivers may be bothered by the dark band at the top of the windshield. Sunglasses are cheaper.

Seats. Standard "bench" seats allow seating three abreast, split benches permit individual adjustments for two and "buckets" generally give the most comfort and support. Cloth upholstery is more comfortable to the touch in hot and cold weather, but vinyl is easier to clean. Most cars have manually adjustable front seats. Power-operated seats, sold as options, may give you a greater adjustment range, but they are expensive and complex, and can break down.

Power windows. Costly and often confusing to operate. Most important, they may be a safety hazard for children, and might cause injury to a hand or even a head.

Central locking system. Push a button and you lock all the doors at once when you are leaving the car — or when some unsavory character threatens to get in. This option should not, however, be confused with devices that discourage auto theft. A central locking system is not a high-priority item.

Cruise control. Allows you to maintain a preset speed, stay under the limit or improve gas mileage on long trips. Not recommended for heavy traffic or slippery roads or for drivers who are easily lulled to sleep at the wheel.

Visual aids. Anything that helps you see better in an automobile could conceivably save your life. The most important element is the proper automobile design — one that provides good visibility when you are sitting behind the wheel, with a minimum of blind spots, plus rear-view mirrors that can be easily adjusted to provide an unobstructed view of the road behind. Outside mirrors are highly desirable, including one on the passenger side; mirrors that can be adjusted electrically or mechanically from inside the car are the most convenient, although, like all gadgets, they can break down. A rear-window defogger or defroster is handy to clear condensation, and a rear-window wiper-washer or air deflector will help keep the view open through snow, rain or outside grime. Intermittent or interval wipers can be set for occasional sweeps, to keep windshields clear in light rain or mist.

Radios and tape players. These range from ordinary radios for news and weather to AM/FM cassette stereo sound systems costing a thousand dollars and more. The choice depends on what, if anything, you want to listen to while you drive. If you can find the device you want at a local audio store, you may be able to get better quality for less money, and if you can install it yourself, you can make even greater savings. The same is true of CB radios, if you feel you have to keep in touch with everyone else on the road, including the police. Radar detectors? They are illegal in many places, and not generally sold by dealers. If you want one, you're on your own.

Body add-ons. Roof racks are handy for extra luggage; if you really need one, get it factory-installed. Rubberlike vinyl side moldings reduce the chance of dents when someone opens his door next to yours in a parking lot. Bumper facings protect bumpers; bumper guards help stop the bumpers of other cars riding up over or under yours. Vinyl-covered roofs are questionable on both practical and esthetic grounds. In any case, they seem to be going the way of tailfins and the dinosaur. Sun roofs are expensive, unless you really want the feel of a convertible in a coupe or sedan.

Dealer extras. Sound-deadening, including undercoating and acoustical insulation applied at the factory, serves to reduce interior noise, as does undercoating applied by a dealer — if you feel the car is going to be noisy enough to need it. Your dealer may also offer paint sealers or "glazes" and upholstery preservatives, but they are usually expensive, add little to a good factory finish and do not last very long. Buy a good car wax or upholstery spray and do the job yourself for a fraction of the price.

Rustproofing. One of the most questionable of all options is the so-called rustproofing some dealers will try to get you to buy. All domestic cars and most imported models are now designed to resist corrosion and carry a three-year warranty against perforation from rust; indeed, many manufacturers discourage additional rustproofing as unnecessary. (See box, page 110.)

Since options can easily add a third or more to the price of a car, it is wise to total the cost of items you are considering ahead of time. On the other hand, it is important to bear in mind that you may be able to negotiate a better trade-in for your present car if the one you plan to buy has quite a few options. And remember also that you can always haggle on total price.

Useful guides to what a dealer actually pays the manufacturer for each base model and for each factory-installed option, as compared with the suggested list prices, can be found in Edmund's *New Car Prices,* published three times a year, and *Foreign Car Prices,* published twice a year. Along with *Used Car Prices,* which is published four times a year, they are available at bookstores and libraries or directly from Edmund Publications Corp., 515 Hempstead Turnpike, West Hempstead, New York 11552.

In a nationwide sampling of used-car buyers by the Hertz Corporation, car owners gave their opinions of options. Answers to the question "What options would you eliminate?" were: power windows, 91 percent; vinyl roof, 89 percent; appearance trim, 56 percent; air conditioning, 49 percent; tinted glass, 49 percent; rear-window defroster, 46 percent; automatic transmission, 40 percent; power brakes, 30 percent; power steering, 23 percent. (Almost 70 percent of these used-car buyers had also purchased new automobiles at some time.)

Consumer Tips

Much information is published about automobiles during any given year. The glossy promotion brochures, free for the taking in dealers' showrooms, contain useful data on specifications and options — along with a lot of breathless prose designed to sell. More objective, and illuminating, are the observations and comparisons derived from actual test driving of new cars by such organizations as Consumers Union (CU). It publishes its findings in *Consumer Reports* magazine, and includes an annual roundup each April, a Buying Guide issued in December and individual articles on new cars, accessories and other automotive subjects throughout the year. (Copies are obtainable at newsstands and libraries.)

CU, which accepts no advertising and buys its own cars for testing, evaluates such factors as handling, braking, comfort, fuel economy, reliability, list price of cars and options (with a percentage factor to convert them to actual dealer costs), as well as frequency-of-repair records for most models going back four or five years. Similar but more limited judgments are made by the monthly magazine *Consumers' Research,* P.O. Box 168, Washington, New Jersey 07882.

Performance evaluations of selected models are also published by automobile journals, among them *Motor Trend, Car and Driver* and *Road and Track.* Members of the American Automobile Association's affiliated motor clubs can read monthly summaries of "Autograph Reports" on popular new models in their club magazines or request free copies of the full evaluations, conducted by AAA's engineering staff, from local club offices or from AAA headquarters at 8111 Gatehouse Road, Falls Church, Virginia 22047. Articles on new cars and related subjects also appear in such general magazines as *Popular Mechanics, Money* and *Changing Times.*

Publications of independent testing organizations can often be helpful to the prospective car buyer.

Since 1968 the U.S. Department of Transportation has been crash-testing various new cars, using a concrete barrier and electronically monitored dummies in the driver's and passenger's seats. Test results comparing cars in the same weight class for occupant protection, windshield retention and intrusion, and fuel leakage can be requested from the department. Write to the Department of Transportation, 400 Seventh Street, SW, Washington, D.C. 20590. The results are also published in consumer magazines and in *The Car Book,* a federal best seller whose 1981 edition is available free from the Consumer Information Center, Pueblo, Colorado 81009. Editions from 1982 on, privately published following cuts in government spending, can be purchased through the Center for Auto Safety, 1223 Dupont Circle Building, Washington, D.C. 20036. In addition to safety information, *The Car Book* contains valuable tips on car buying, fuel economy, maintenance and warranties, auto insurance, tires, used cars and resolving complaints.

Visiting Dealers' Showrooms

Once you have narrowed your choices to the kinds of cars and options that make sense for you, start shopping around. Don't be lured by such dealer advertising claims as "never undersold," "wholesale prices," "at cost," "below cost," "below invoice" or "factory to you." All dealers have to make a profit or they would soon be out of business. Don't bite on "factory fresh": according to voluntary standards developed by Better Business Bureaus and the automotive industry, the term cannot be used unless the car is one that has never been sold, titled or registered — one that is, in fact, new. "Demonstrators," "executive" or "official" cars may not have been sold or registered, but they have been used by the dealer for sales or personal purposes and must be offered for sale as used cars.

But keep in mind that you may be able to do better with one dealer than with another. Some dealers are willing to trade off lower markups for higher volume, and many will offer lower prices from time to time in order to reduce accumulated inventory. Remember that the "list" or "retail" price on the window sticker of the car or in a price guide is only the manufacturer's suggested figure; a dealer buys his cars from the manufacturer at wholesale prices and can sell the cars he owns at any price he wants.

And don't let price alone be your guide. Veterans of the automobile sales business observe that most people buy their cars the wrong way, concentrating on a single aspect of the "deal" — how much the dealer will cut his profit, how big a loan he will arrange, how much he will allow on a trade-in — and forgetting some other equally important aspects. There is usually room to negotiate (most cars in fact sell for less than suggested list although some unusually popular models in short supply may be priced higher) but you should consider other factors as well.

Check the Dealer's Service

One of the most vital considerations is service, both in quality and convenience. You may want to rely on the dealer who sells you your car to provide routine maintenance and repairs, at least during the period of the car warranty — a minimum of 12 months or 12,000 miles (see "Warranties," below). And if your relationship with one another is good, a dealer can be very useful not only with respect to continuing maintenance but with problems that arise after the warranty has expired, including emergencies, uncorrected defects and recalls.

As you visit each dealer, size up the service shop and, if possible, talk to the service manager. If you have to leave a car for service, can you get a "loaner" car for a day or two or have someone drive you to your office or commuter train? How convenient will it be for you to bring your car in for service — what, in other words, are the hours the shop is open and how far will you have to drive? It doesn't make much sense to buy a car from an out-of-the-way or out-of-town dealer because it saves a few dollars, if you then discover that you have to spend far more in mileage and time taking the car back repeatedly for repairs. Technically, you may be able to get warranty service from any authorized dealer who sells and services your make of automobile. As a practical matter, however, dealers understandably tend to favor their own customers, and you may not get quick service from a dealer who did not sell you your car.

Ask neighbors and friends who may have done business with the dealer about his or her reputation for reliability and responsiveness. If you can, make your visit to the showroom in the morning when customers are dropping off cars for service, and don't hesitate to ask a few of these clients how well they are satisfied. If you have doubts, find out from your local Better Business Bureau or consumer protection agency whether any complaints have been lodged against the dealer, either for service or sales.

Try the Car for Size

When you have zeroed in on one or more dealers, try on their cars for size and feel, just as you would a new coat or pair of shoes. Bring along your spouse or anyone else who will be using the car regularly to make sure that this person also fits in comfortably, has enough headroom, can adjust the seats and safety harnesses to his or her liking, can operate everything easily and can see clearly out the windshield and around the sides and rear.

One of the biggest mistakes car buyers

make is failing to test drive an automobile before signing on the dotted line. Ask to take out a dealer's demonstration model for a half-hour or more (make sure you're covered by insurance), and allow for the fact that the particular car you are driving may be a high-performance version with a more powerful engine and other options you don't necessarily want. Test the car in road conditions you will normally encounter. Does it have adequate acceleration for on-ramp highway merging and passing on the road? Does it handle well if you suddenly have to swerve or brake to a stop? How does it adapt to hilly or bumpy terrain, stop-and-go traffic, tight parking spaces? If you are undecided, ask the dealer if you can borrow the car for the weekend or on a day when the dealership is closed. If this is not possible, you can probably rent the same make and model from a local car-rental company for as long as you need to check things out. The cost is likely to be minuscule compared to the value of the first-hand information you get from driving the car.

Comparing Dealers' Prices

As you shop among dealers, look at the manufacturer's window sticker on each car that interests you and write down the price information in a notebook: base price of the car, the cost of factory-installed options, and freight and additional fees. Find out whether the dealer's preparation charges are included or will be billed separately, and don't forget to allow for any local sales taxes. The car may hold a second window sticker, pasted up by the dealer. Unlike the manufacturer's sticker, which is required by law, this one is unofficial and you do *not* have to take any of the dealer-added options it may list — undercoating, rust-proofing, paint sealers, fancy wheel covers, floor mats, a special service contract. If you do decide to take them, plan on offering about a quarter less than the asking price; this will be closer to their actual cost to the dealer.

Remember, too, that various divisions of major manufacturers make cars that differ mainly in name. Such corporate "twins" may be offered by the Ford and Mercury divisions of Ford or the Plymouth and Dodge divisions of Chrysler. If you like a particular model but don't care for its price, you may be able to solve the problem by selecting its twin at a better price.

Next, use a guide — Edmund's *New Car Prices* or *Foreign Car Prices*, for example — to look up the wholesale cost to the dealer for the car and for each option, as well as suggested list or retail prices. Then compare these figures with the prices on the sticker. Any number of factors go into determining the profit a dealer can expect to make — the car model, the options, the time of year, the part of the country. But on the average you can anticipate that the dealer will be looking for about 10 percent.

If you have an older car that you plan to trade in on the new one, subtract the rough wholesale value you have determined for it from what you plan to offer for the new car. Then ask the salesperson to quote you a price on the new car, including base price, options, delivery, dealer prep, taxes — and all in writing if possible. *Then* — and not until then — say that you are thinking of trading in your old car, and ask for an appraisal on it — not an "allowance," but the wholesale price. Compare this with the best offer you have received from a used-car dealer (and, if you like, what you think you might be able to get by selling directly to an individual — see page 124). If the salesperson's figure is low, say so, but do *not* say by how much. Let the salesperson raise the offer, and indicate by your behavior that you don't have all day, that there are other dealers and cars that interest you. If this produces a figure that matches or betters yours, make an offer on the new car, pegging it somewhat below your available cash (the total of your equity in the old car and any out-of-pocket cash you can afford plus what you can get on a loan). The salesperson may dicker some more to bring you up, but don't go above what you can afford.

When you agree on a price for the new car, subtract the salesperson's trade-in offer from it. If the difference is still acceptable, ask to have a buyer's order drawn up. The order may not be designed to show the new-car offer and the wholesale trade-in as such; it may instead show that you are buying at the regular sticker price and in return are receiving more than the wholesale trade-in price. That doesn't matter so long as the difference between the two figures is what you had in mind.

Don't let any hocus-pocus about financing or insurance throw your negotiating off the track. You don't have to finance your car

Shopping for a Car Loan

If you are financing the purchase of a car, do not immediately make arrangements with the car dealer, despite promises of "easy payments" and/or "no money down." Some dealers and manufacturers have been offering increasingly competitive rates in order to move cars — particularly the clearance-price, year-end models — and may even suggest that you will get a better price if you finance with them. (Because of dealer contributions, special year-end financing may actually increase the clearance price.)

But you are not obliged to accept these terms, and before you buy, you would be advised to compare the dealer's package with others you may be able to get.

First, shop around for the lowest true annual percentage rate (APR), which all lenders by law are required to disclose. Remember, the length of the repayment period is equally important in determining the total amount of interest you will have to pay over the period of the loan.

If you have a whole-life insurance policy that was bought some years ago, you may be able to borrow against its accrued cash value at the APR established the year you purchased the policy — which, in all probability, is quite a bit lower than current rates.

If you belong to a credit union or an auto club, check with them: either or both may be able to arrange particularly advantageous terms.

If you have a bank savings account that contains at least as much money as your proposed loan, plus interest and financing charges, you may be able to use it as collateral against a loan from the same bank. The effective interest rate on the money you borrow will be the difference between the interest you continue to receive from your savings and the interest you pay the bank for the loan. And, if you itemize deductions on your income tax return, you can deduct your interest payments. If you have no savings account but can put up stocks, bonds or other assets as collateral, rather than the car itself, you may also be able to get an attractive deal on a loan from your bank or some other bank in your area.

A finance or loan company should probably be your last resort; these firms assume high risks by making loans to people with poor credit ratings and therefore generally charge higher rates than banks.

If you need a relatively small amount of money for a limited period, and have a personal credit card with a sufficient line of credit, you may want to cover the balance that way, though credit card APRs are usually close to the limit allowed by law. You'll probably find this the most expensive way to meet the problem.

In considering any lender, make sure you know all the details of the terms — some of which may not come up until the moment before the papers are signed. (See "Truth in Lending," page 9.)

Does the lender insist that you purchase expensive credit insurance to pay off the balance of the loan in the event of your disability or death? State laws often prohibit lenders from requiring borrowers to purchase credit insurance (see Chapter 9). In any case, your regular life insurance, or a cheaper term policy, may be more than adequate to pay off any claims.

If the lender or dealer tries to sell you, or arrange for, collision and comprehensive insurance as part of the deal, are the terms as good as those you can get from another insurance company?

Find out also if you will have to pay a loan application fee or a credit investigation fee, whether there are any penalties for late payments or for paying off the loan before it is due.

Finally, make sure you know all your rights in the event you cannot fulfill your payment schedule and the lender starts re-possession proceedings to take back your car. (See Chapter 15.)

through the dealer if you can, or already have been able to, get a better deal elsewhere. Nor do you have to insure it through the dealer; if you need insurance, or your lender requires it, you can probably get it more cheaply through a regular insurance agent.

After the buyer's order has been approved and signed by the sales manager or dealer, check all the figures on it. It should spell out details of the make, model, or engine number, options, sale price, trade-in price, financing, if any, taxes and fees. Make sure the order specifies a date by which the car is to be delivered, that the sale price and trade-in price will be good until that date, that the deposit is part of the purchase price and will be returned if the sale is not completed or the car is not equipped as specified.

Everything that is written in the document is legally binding on you. So if you don't like any clauses, ask to have them struck out and be sure that the deletions are initialed both by you and the dealer. Also, make sure that all the blanks are filled in or marked "not applicable" and initialed.

Car-buying Services

If comparison shopping and horse-trading aren't your strong suits, you may want to make use of a car-buying service. These organizations, which run newspaper ads in areas where they operate, offer to take some of the footwork and figuring out of car buying in return for a modest fee. One service claims to save its customers an average of more than $800 off showroom prices on the cars they buy. The customer decides the make, model and body style of the car he or she wants, and sends the service this information — together with a check to cover the company's fee. In return, the company sends a computer printout of the lowest price available through a participating dealer in the customer's area, including the dealer's cost, suggested retail price of the car and each option, and the total markup the dealer is willing to settle for (often as little as $75 to $200).

The customer may then buy the car from the suggested dealer at this price, arranging any trade-in and financing (the dealer, of course, can pick up a little more profit by financing the car or offering less on the trade than other dealers might) or use the print-out to negotiate with other dealers. If the purchase is made through the specified dealer, or if the customer proves he or she has bought the same car for a lower price from another dealer in the area, the buying-service fee is refunded. If there is no dealer associated with the service in the customer's area, he or she can buy the car through the service's purchasing division and pay an additional fee of one or two percent to take delivery from a local dealer.

When to Buy a Car

A well-informed, patient buyer can get a fair price on a car at almost any time, but it is generally easier to negotiate with dealers when business is slow. This can be any time a dealer is feeling the effects of a slump in the economy, when car sales in general are down and competition is great; or it can be at more or less predictable times of the year, the month or even the week.

One such period is the weeks before Christmas. Many dealers find sales dropping precipitously at this time and may well be willing to take smaller profits in order to move autos off their lots. Don't refer to the car as a "Christmas present" for someone, however, and don't act as though you have to buy it before Christmas Eve. A salesperson who suspects you are in a gift-buying mood may well hold out for a higher price. The period after the holidays and on into February is also apt to be slow in many areas, particularly when the weather is bad and people stay home. (Some self-styled connoisseurs of the market try to buy on a dismal Monday afternoon in January after it has been snowing for three days and everything has come to a halt.)

The period from March through June may be the least advantageous time to buy, as spring prompts thoughts of the outdoors and summer vacations. You may regain a bargaining edge in midsummer, when all those buyers are driving their expensive new cars around on vacations. But late summer and fall are problematical. Before new-model introduction, known in the trade as "NMI" or "show time," the bargain hunters start to come out in force, and dealers may either make "deals" on older cars in inventory or, depending on the market, hold out for top dollar on everything. When show time officially arrives, manufacturers encourage their dealers to make room for the new cars by giving them an extra 4 or 5 percent profit for sales of those of the previous year's models that are still in stock. Many dealers are reluctant to share this bonanza. But if you inform the dealer that you know it exists (after all, 5 percent on a $9,000 car is $450), you may be able to make some savings. Remember, however, that if you buy a car late in the model year, it has already depreciated by a full year's value. If you are not to lose out in the future, you will have to stick to the same schedule when you buy your next car.

Most dealers set monthly quotas, putting pressure on the sales force to sell at lower prices toward the end of any month in which the quota is not being met. Even the last week of a good month may be the best time to buy. If you arrive at this time, you are the icing on the cake. But the opposite may also be true: most dealers like to start each month well, and shopping early may get you a good deal.

Days of the week may be significant. Mondays and rainy days tend to be slow; Saturdays and sunny days tend to be busier. To capitalize on Saturday volume, some dealers offer their salespeople cash bonuses — spiffs — for moving the most cars. A salesperson trying for a spiff may be willing to let you have a car at the price you are willing to pay.

Taking Delivery of Your Car

The day finally arrives when you're about to get your hands on the wheel of that new car you've worked so hard to decide on, to negotiate for and to finance. But you still can't just jump in the front seat and drive away. Whether you ordered the car from the factory, had the dealer find it for you at another dealer's on a swap, or are simply buying it from your dealer's lot, you must first make sure it is exactly what you thought you were buying. Check the window sticker, which by federal law must remain on the car until it is delivered to you. That sticker is required to identify the car by make, model and identification number; state its final assembly point, the name and address of the dealer to whom it was delivered and the method by which it was delivered; and list the manufacturer's suggested retail price — both for the car and for each accessory or option attached — as well as the amount (if any) charged to the dealer for transportation, and the total price of all these items.

Are the engine, options and accessories precisely what the bill of sale says they are, and are they actually on the car itself? If you requested the dealer to make some changes, it is possible that they were made but that the window sticker wasn't changed to reflect that fact. If this is the case, have the dealer write in any corrections and initial and sign them. If something was added or omitted without your authorization, have it removed or installed and make sure the sticker and bill of sale agree. Keep both documents so you will have an exact record of what you paid for.

Be patient while the dealer prepares the car for you. It may take a few days. All cars need checking of systems, fluid levels, adjustments and cleaning, and may require installation of accessories. Make sure this "dealer prep" or "make ready" is done to your satisfaction and that the service is noted on the bill of sale and marked either "paid in full" or "completed — no charge." If something crops up a few days later, such as loss of coolant fluid because someone failed to tighten the hose clamps, there will be no doubt about whose responsibility it is.

If any problems appear after you have taken possession of the car, don't put them off on the theory that they will "work themselves out." Don't let the dealer tell you "Oh, just wait for your next regular maintenance checkup, we'll fix the problem then." Problems usually get worse if they are neglected, and can result in a need for major repairs or even in an accident.

Finally, don't just throw the owner's manual and warranty in the glove compartment and forget about them until disaster strikes. *Read them,* understand them, and be sure you know what your and the dealer's responsibilities are. Whenever you bring your car in for repairs — whether or not they are covered by the warranty — insist on an itemized accounting of just what was done and what was charged, including parts, part numbers and labor performed on your car. Keep every itemized receipt. If the problem is a recurring one, you will have proof that you tried to have it fixed, not once but several times. Car owners often complain of repeated malfunctions during warranty, only to discover that the underlying problem required a major repair that was postponed during the warranty period and then done — at their cost — after the warranty expired. Your major goal is to reach the end of the warranty period with a car that is as free of problems as it possibly can be — even if you have to make it clear to the dealer that you will come back again and again until you get the service that is your warranteed right.

New-car Warranties

All new cars are sold with written warranties from their manufacturers, and carry implied warranties defined by law. The written warranties are covered by the Magnuson-Moss Act. It provides that all written warranties must be in clear language, in readable print and easy to understand (how successful some are in this regard is still open to question). They must also disclose which parts of the product are covered and which are not, what the seller's responsibilities are in remedying defects, and how, step-by-step, the buyer can require the manufacturer to meet his obligations, including any procedures for settling disputes. "Full warranties" cover anyone owning the car during the warranty period and provide the owner a choice of either a new replacement car or his money back if the car cannot be fixed after a reasonable number of attempts. Virtually all car warranties, however, are "limited," and must be so labeled under Magnuson-Moss. Limited warranties do not offer either replacements or refunds. But they *do* give owners definite legal rights. The specific details may vary but manufacturers typically offer the following limited written warranties:

Basic warranty. For a specified period — generally 12 months or 12,000 miles, whichever comes first — the manufacturer agrees, through the dealer, to make any needed repairs resulting from defects in materials and workmanship at no charge to the owner. The basic warranty does not cover damage to the car from accidents; environmental hazards — storms, road salt, tree sap, airborne chemicals; misuse of the car — overloading, racing, alterations, lack of proper maintenance as described in the owner's manual, use of the wrong fuel, oil or lubricants; or owner's expenses resulting from loss of use of the car. It does not cover normal maintenance services such as oil changes, lubrication, tune-ups, new filters, replacement of such parts as clutch linings, brake pads, wiper blades, light bulbs or fuses that have to be replaced because of normal wear. Nor does it cover tires, which are separately warranteed by the tire maker (see below). Auto manufacturers recommend that all warranty work be done by the selling dealer, although you can request service from the manufacturer's nearest authorized dealer in an emergency, on a long trip or in the event that you or the selling dealer moves. Under federal antitrust laws, manufacturers probably cannot prevent a motorist from having routine maintenance performed by any qualified service outlet. But if you do this, be sure to hold on to your receipts: if any warranty work becomes necessary, you will be able to prove the required maintenance was done on schedule.

Powertrain warranty. On expiration of the basic warranty, most manufacturers continue coverage on defects in the vehicle's powertrain — engine, transmission, front- or rear-wheel drive. The owner may, however, have to pay a deductible amount such as $75 or $100 for each repair visit. Periods of coverage vary, generally from 24 months or 24,000 miles to five years or 50,000 miles from the original delivery date. (In the latter case coverage may be limited to the first retail purchaser of the automobile.) Special powertrain warranties, such as 36 months or 50,000 miles, may be offered on diesel engines.

Emissions-system warranty. Under federal law, emissions-control systems are warranteed for five years or 50,000 miles, whichever comes first. During that period, repairs must be paid for by the manufacturer if the system fails to conform with applicable emission standards of the U.S. Environmental Protection Agency (EPA) and the owner is faced with a penalty, or is prohibited by local or state law from using his car. The warranty does not cover conditions that result from tampering with the system, from improper maintenance or from use of the wrong kind of fuel — leaded gas in a car designed for unleaded gas, for example. With an increasing number of states and localities requiring periodic vehicle inspections, owners are therefore encouraged to make sure their cars pass both emissions and safety tests.

Corrosion warranty. Manufacturers generally warrant for at least 36 months, regardless of mileage, that their dealers will repair or replace any body parts, except components of the exhaust system that have developed perforation (rust-through) because of corrosion in normal use. Not covered are corrosion due to damage or vehicle alteration, or surface corrosion caused by airborne chemicals, sand, salt, hail or stones. Some car makers extend coverage on rust-through of outer panels for periods up to five years or 50,000 miles. Rusting due to defects in materials or workmanship is generally covered by the basic warranty of 12 months or 24,000 miles.

Other warranties. Separate warranties are generally provided on a new car's tires by the tire manufacturer, and may also be provided on batteries and options such as stereo systems by the makers of this equipment. Make sure you get copies of any such warranties from the dealer when you accept your car. Tire warranties vary, but a manufacturer will usually replace a tire, and pay for mounting and balancing it, if it is found to be defective during the first year of operation or before a certain amount of the tread has worn down. After the free replacement period, makers offer credit toward the purchase of a new tire. The credit is based on the amount of tread depth remaining, with the owner paying the balance plus mounting costs. Not covered are irregular wear or damage resulting from improper mounting, alignment or inflation or abusive driving.

Extended-service plans. In addition to the manufacturers' warranties that come with the car, auto dealers offer various optional or "added-coverage" plans under which the buyer can choose to protect himself against major repair bills for as long as five years and 60,000 miles (up to 24 months and 24,000 miles on used cars). These extended-service contracts, many of which are backed by the auto manufacturers themselves, involve an initial fee that can amount to several hundred dollars and a deductible amount such as $25 or $50 each time you bring the car in for repair. They generally extend coverage on the powertrain and also on steering, front suspension, brakes, electrical system, cooling system, fuel system and factory-installed air conditioning but not on normal maintenance items and replacement of worn parts.

Whether you want an extended-service contract depends on the amount you are willing to pay for added peace of mind, the length of time for which the particular contract offers that peace, and the number of years you expect to keep the car. The warranties that you get without payment cover most items for the first year and major ones for longer periods. If your car is in good shape when these warranties run out, you may not have a major repair for quite some time, particularly if you take your car with some regularity to a mechanic you trust. And if the repair is necessitated by a major manufacturing defect that turns out to be shared by other cars of the same model, the manufacturer may rectify it even if the warranty has expired and you do not have an extended-service contract (see "Recalls," below).

Implied warranties. Many people believe that once the written warranty expires the car is their problem and they are stuck with it. This is not necessarily true. All products carry a so-called "implied warranty of merchantability" — an assurance that the product will do what it is meant to. In the case of a new car, this means that it must be fit for the purpose for which it is used — providing transportation. Less common, but no less valid, is an implied warranty of fitness for a particular purpose. If, for example, you buy a vehicle to haul a large trailer and the seller claims it is suitable for such a use, this warranty means that it must be capable of doing that job.

In most states the law allows the manufacturer not only to limit the period of time an implied warranty is in effect, but also to limit an implied warranty to the duration of the written one. However, some states — Maine, Vermont, Massachusetts, Maryland and Kansas among them — have modified their laws in such a way that implied warranties cannot be limited to a specific period. Moreover, the Magnuson-Moss Act specifies that the limitation of your implied warranty rights by a manufacturer cannot be "unconscionable." In other words, if through no fault of your own your car self-destructs after the written warranty is up, you may still have a claim against the manufacturer or dealer.

Handling Your Complaints

All auto manufacturers have systems for handling complaints. You should exhaust these, step by step, not only because they frequently work, but because you must prove that you have done everything within reason to make them work before resorting to other means.

First, give the dealer every chance to fix

your car. If a problem is not satisfactorily resolved, talk to the service manager. If this does not produce results, see the salesman who sold you the car; he may be able to put pressure on the service department because he wants to keep your good will for a possible future sale. If things continue to go awry, talk to the dealer himself.

Second, keep meticulous records. Note down each problem as it occurs, with the date and the mileage reading on the odometer. Describe the *symptoms* to the service department — stalling on starts, grinding noise when shifting, for example — rather than trying to tell them what to repair or how (see "Maintenance and Repairs,"). If you bring in the car with five or six different problems, make an itemized list of everything that is wrong and have it attached to the work order, then check the finished, signed work order to see that each repair was done, and keep both the list and work order in your files. Be just as meticulous about general maintenance, such as lubrications and oil changes. You must be able to prove that all needed maintenance was done, and on schedule as specified in the owner's manual. (More than one owner has lost in court for failing to comply with warranty requirements that all fluid levels be properly maintained.) Keep a record of any communication you have with the dealer or his employees, whether you handle the matter in person, by phone or by mail.

The regional representative of the car manufacturer can often settle disputes between dealer and buyer.

If repeated efforts with the dealer still fail to get the problem resolved, you may want to consider taking your car to a good independent mechanic for a second opinion. Pay him for a written statement analyzing the problem and how it might be fixed, then give a copy to the dealer and keep another for yourself. Do *not* allow the independent mechanic to make any repair covered by the warranty, or you may void it. (You can, however, ask him to perform any routine maintenance while the car is in his shop).

Third, contact the manufacturer's regional representative. The address of the zone or district office nearest you is generally given in the owner's manual or other literature, or can be obtained from the dealer. Write the representative describing the make, model and year of your car, the nature of your problem or problems, the name and address of the selling dealer and the attempts he has made at repairs. Include your address and phone number in the letter, and keep a copy in your files. The zone representative can arrange to inspect the car if necessary, at the dealer's or at another location convenient to you.

Fourth, if the outcome still does not satisfy you, contact the manager of customer relations at the manufacturer's headquarters, or the automobile complaint-handling panel in your area. Most major manufacturers have such panels, as does the Better Business Bureau, and all are described in detail in Chapter 13. Here we briefly describe only two. Chrysler Corporation gives its new-car buyers a pamphlet listing 55 "consumer satisfaction boards" around the country that they can appeal to on service-related disputes, along with a questionnaire form for submitting a dispute to arbitration. If the complaint does not qualify, the customer receives an explanation. If the complaint does qualify, it is submitted to a five-person board made up of three voting members — a local consumer advocate, an independent certified technician and a representative of the general public — and two nonvoting members — a Chrysler Corporation representative and Chrysler dealer. Neither the buyer nor the dealer is present, although both parties provide information about the history of the vehicle and the board may request to inspect it, giving the owner free use of a "loaner" car if necessary. The decision of the board is binding on the dealer and Chrysler Corporation, but the owner is free to pursue the matter in court, if he or she does not accept the decision. Under these circumstances, however, the decision is admissible as evidence. Some 350 to 375 cases a month are submitted to the system. Close to half of them do not qualify — most commonly because the car is no longer under warranty — but Chrysler feels that with the others the system is working well: at this writing, no cases have yet gone to court.

A similar complaint-handling system called AUTOCAP (Automotive Consumer Action Program) covers the cars of 17 foreign and smaller manufacturers — among them American Motors, Toyota, Honda, Subaru, Mazda, Volvo, Saab-Scandia, Jaguar-Rover, Triumph and Peugeot. It is sponsored by 15,000 local dealers and the National Automobile Dealers Association. Some 88 percent of the complaints brought to AUTOCAP are equitably settled by informal mediation, with the balance arbitrated by panels consisting of dealers and an equal or greater number of consumer representatives. Again, decisions are binding on dealers and manufacturers but not on individual car owners. (For more information, see Chapter 13.)

"Lemon Laws"

For the average car buyer the ultimate nightmare is getting stuck with a "lemon" — a hopeless clunker. Some buyers think a car is a lemon if a knob comes off the radio and they can't figure out how to get it back on, but most apply more rigid criteria — as, for example, a car that persists in making terrible noises no matter how many times it is repaired, and then suddenly lies down and dies on a cold, snowy evening 75 miles from home.

Every state gives some protection to owners of genuine lemons. But some states have recently taken the pains to define what a "lemon" is and specify the steps to be taken for redress.

Connecticut's new "lemon law," passed in late 1982, defines a lemon as any new motor vehicle — passenger car, van or truck — with a substantial defect that has not been repaired in four attempts during the warranty period or within a year of the delivery date, whichever is less, or any vehicle that has been out of service for repair for a total of 30 days during the same period. An owner who bought such a vehicle in Connecticut must first go through any mediation procedure established by the manufacturer. But if this does not work, the lemon law gives the owner the right to take the manufacturer to court to replace the vehicle or refund the purchase price, minus a reasonable allowance for the owner's use.

Other Strategies

Whether or not your state has a lemon law as such, there are other strategies you can pursue. One is to complain to your state or local Consumer Protection Office, Attorney General's office or Department of Motor Vehicles. (Some states have published helpful booklets, such as the New York State Consumer Protection Board's *Lemon Owner's Manual* and the Maine Bureau of Consumer Protection's *Down Easter's Lemon Guide.*) Another avenue is to seek advice from your local Better Business Bureau, your automobile club or a local consumer organization (such as the Automobile Owners Action Council, 1010 Vermont Avenue, NW, Washington, D.C. 20005, which serves some 6,000 members in the Washington-Maryland-Virginia region).

You can also contact the Center for Auto Safety, a consumer-oriented group that monitors the safety, economy and quality of motor vehicles, highways and mobile homes. The center's lawyers, researchers and engineers analyze more than 20,000 complaint letters a year, instigate legislation and automobile recalls, and publish reports on everything from passive safety restraints to automobile rust. The organization also supplies lawyers with "litigation packages" and consumers with the names of attorneys in their area who have handled automobile suits. Perhaps the center's best-known publication is *The Lemon Book,* a detailed manual of action for car buyers by Ralph Nader, Clarence Ditlow and Joyce Kinnard. The center has also helped publish *The Car Book,* a guide to new cars, safety, fuel economy, maintenance, warranties, insurance, tires, used cars and consumer complaints, written by two former employees of the Department of Transportation, Jack Gillis and Ivy Baer. Both books are available, along with a publications list and membership information, through the Center for Auto Safety, 1223 Dupont Circle Building, Washington, D.C. 20036.

Recalls

From time to time a particular car model makes news when a safety defect subjects it to recall. Recalls may be initiated voluntarily by a manufacturer when the company discovers a problem common to a group of vehicles of the same make, model and year. Or, if the National Highway Traffic Safety Administration (NHTSA) or a consumer body amasses enough reports, the NHTSA can order a recall, which requires the manufacturer to notify all owners so that they can bring their cars to authorized dealers for correction of the defect at no charge. (Two of the largest recalls

Selling Your Old Car

If you want to sell your car, chances are you will fare better in a private transaction with another individual than in a sale to a dealer. However, you are going to have to do some extra work that may be time-consuming and frustrating.

First, you must find out what the car is worth. Many people underestimate or overestimate the value of their car, which, in a private transaction, lies somewhere between the wholesale price — what a dealer pays in the current market — and the retail price — the amount he asks his customer for, which includes his overhead, the cost of getting the car in shape and his profit. By eliminating the dealer, you can offer your car at a price advantageous both to you and the buyer.

To get an idea of going prices, look up the car's make, model and year in the current NADA *Official Used Car Guide*, Edmund's *Used Car Prices* or other "blue book" available at newsstands, libraries or your bank. These publications will provide you with the average trade-in value of the model; its average retail price; the amounts to add or subtract for optional equipment; and the amounts to add or subtract for low or high mileage.

For a closer check on wholesale prices in your area, ask several used-car dealers how much they would pay for your car. For an idea of retail prices, look at those of similar cars on used-car lots and in classified ads. Bear in mind that actual selling prices will usually be lower than advertised prices. The dealer knows that bargaining is usually an intrinsic part of the sale.

Using this information, set two prices in your mind: the highest you think you can reasonably expect to get — at which you will advertise the car — and the lowest you are willing to accept. Be realistic about your asking price — our own possessions usually seem more valuable to us than to an outsider. Otherwise it may take you much more time and trouble to sell the car.

To inform as many people as possible, place classified ads in the weekend editions of newspapers and in local shoppers' or "Pennysaver" sheets. Keep the ad short. Specify the make, model and year, the major options the car has, a general note on condition and mileage and the fact that the sale is "by own-

of recent years involved the Ford Pinto gas tank and the Firestone 500 steel-belted radial tire. Action was ordered by NHTSA on the basis of studies by and pressure from the Center for Auto Safety.)

The Federal Trade Commission is also empowered to issue consent orders under which auto manufacturers agree to repair or replace parts that are defective even though they do not create a safety hazard. Such FTC orders have involved hundreds of thousands of cars whose fender designs have caused premature rusting, whose oil filters have caused engine damage or whose transmissions have failed, even if the defects appeared after the warranty period. Additionally, recalls can be ordered by the Environmental Protection Agency (EPA) for vehicles that do not comply with motor vehicle emissions standards.

If you get a recall notice on your vehicle, particularly for a safety hazard, don't try to judge the necessity for the repair or weigh it against whatever inconvenience it may cause you. Take the car to your dealer and have it fixed as soon as you can. If you move to a new neighborhood or another town, notify the manufacturer, not the dealer, by sending him the change-of-address card supplied with the owner's manual, or by writing him and giving your new address as well as the make, model, year and vehicle identification number (the number is on your bill of sale and visible on top of the dashboard through the windshield on the driver's side).

Should you have any difficulty with a recall, suspect your car is subject to a recall, or want to know if a used car you are buying has ever been subject to recall, contact the National Highway Traffic Safety Administration, Department of Transportation, Washington, D.C. 20590, or call the administration's 24-hour "hotline." You can get the er." Include the asking price. Put your telephone number at the end, but not your name and address, which might encourage unwanted visitors.

For greater exposure, pin notices on company, supermarket or church bulletin boards. Put a "For Sale" sign in the car window with the price and your telephone number and, of course, tell your friends, neighbors, and coworkers that you have a car for sale.

Before showing your automobile to any prospects, put it into presentable shape. Wash the car well, and wax it if necessary. Clean the inside, including the glove compartment, ashtrays and trunk. Be sure everything is working well — including all lights — and that the oil, coolant, battery water and other fluids are up to the proper levels. Have the tires properly inflated. If needed, clean the corrosion off the battery terminals and remove oily grime from the engine with a degreasing compound.

Next, assemble your certificate of title, registration and any warranties or transferable service contracts, as well as your service records so that a buyer can see proof of proper maintenance and repairs. Check with your motor vehicle department regarding the forms necessary for transfer of ownership, and ask whether the license plates are non-transferable or may remain on the car.

Draw up two copies of a bill of sale. It should state the make, model, year and vehicle identification number; the price; your name and address and the buyer's; and the fact that the car is being bought "as is, with no guarantees of any kind." Federal law requires you to include a statement of mileage on the odometer ("The mileage on this vehicle at the time of sale is. . . ."). If you still owe the bank money on the car, arrange to pay off the loan so that a clear title can be turned over to you for transfer to the buyer. He or she will not want any financial complications.

If the buyer asks for a test drive, by all means allow it, but be sure to go along to ensure that the vehicle will not be altered, abused or stolen. Bargaining on final price is, of course, up to you. When you agree on a figure, ask for payment, or a deposit, by certified check, money order or cash. An ordinary check may or may not be good.

Finally, remember that you must sign over title to the car to the new owner (who should make sure it is free and clear) and tell your insurance company that coverage on the car is cancelled.

number from the Directory Assistance operator. Give the hotline operator the make, model, year and vehicle identification number and a description of the part or equipment in question. You will get any recall information NHTSA has, either on the phone or by a printout mailed to your home. You can also use the hotline or write NHTSA to report any safety problem you believe your car has. The agency will send you a questionnaire asking for information needed by its technical staff. Copies of the completed questionnaire will be sent to NHTSA's investigators and to the manufacturer with a request for help. If the problem indeed poses a safety risk and is common to a number of vehicles, NHTSA may initiate a recall.

If you have other car-related problems, the NHTSA operator may be able to advise you or refer you to the federal, state or local agency equipped to deal with them. NHTSA establishes fuel economy standards for manufacturers, though it cannot guarantee actual gas mileage on individual cars.

If you suspect that the odometer mileage reading on your new car has been tampered with, report it to NHTSA, the Department of Justice, 10th Street, NW, Washington, D.C. 20530, and/or local or state law enforcement authorities. The Department of Justice also enforces the law requiring manufacturers to affix the sticker on each new vehicle that carries the suggested retail price and options.

The Environmental Protection Agency enforces pollution standards for motor vehicles, tests fuel mileage economy and issues the EPA mileage ratings put on new-car stickers for the purposes of comparison between cars (see "Those Mileage Ratings," page 106). Queries may be addressed to the EPA, 401 M Street, SW, Washington, D.C. 20460.

The Federal Trade Commission has general jurisdiction over marketing practices and has frequently negotiated consent settlements whereby manufacturers have recalled specific models for nonsafety defects. The FTC office is at Pennsylvania Avenue and Sixth Street, NW, Washington, D.C. 20580.

Last Resorts

If all else fails, there are three basic strategies to consider. All are drastic and require a lawyer's advice. Many lawyers are willing to discuss a problem for a modest initial fee; try to find one who has handled similar cases before. If you don't know such a lawyer, get help from the local bar association's referral service, and if you can't afford a lawyer, contact your local Legal Services or Legal Aid. In many cases when a car owner wins his suit, the court will order an auto dealer or manufacturer to pay the owner's attorney's fees.

Strategy No.1, as outlined by consumer affairs attorneys in the New York State *Lemon Owner's Manual,* is outright rejection of the car — but it has to be done soon after delivery and has to involve a serious defect. In one case, a new car burst into flames after 17 miles because of a faulty electrical system. The owner refused the dealer's offer to repair it and demanded his money back. When the dealer balked, the owner sued. The court ordered the dealer to return the money. In another case, a new car stalled repeatedly as the buyer drove it off the lot, and by the time the driver reached home the vehicle could barely make 10 miles per hour. The car was towed back to the dealer, who offered to replace a defective transmission, but the buyer declined. The court ruled that when someone's faith in the dependability of a new car had been that badly shaken, he or she had the right to return it and receive a refund.

If it is to be effective, the technique of rejection must be handled carefully. If the car has been financed through the dealer, you must notify him in writing that you are rejecting his car and explain why; you must return the car to his lot with a witness if possible; you must offer him the keys and the certificate of title; you must demand your money back, take off your license plates and return them with the registration to the motor vehicle bureau. You should not cancel your insurance, but ask your agent about reducing it to a minimum to protect you while the car is on the dealer's lot. If you made your payment — either full or partial — by check and it has not cleared, have the bank stop payment immediately; if the finance contract has been sold to a lender by the dealer, notify the lender in writing why you are refusing to pay.

If you financed the car yourself through a bank, credit union or other lending institution, the procedure is somewhat different. Keep possession of the car; advise the lender of what you are about to do and then tell the dealer that you are revoking your acceptance and you want a refund. If he gives it to you, pay off your loan and return the car to the dealer. If he does not, you will have to consult a lawyer.

Strategy No. 2, revoking acceptance, involves first giving the dealer a reasonable number of chances to correct defects, whether they show up immediately or later. If the car continues to be a problem, take it to a reputable independent repair shop and pay for a written statement of the problem and recommended solutions, as described in "Handling Complaints." If the dealer still fails to remedy the defect, go through the manufacturer's zone representative and any complaint-handling panel. Then, with your lawyer, make sure you can show that the defect substantially impairs the value of the car to you, that you are returning it within a reasonable time after discovering the defect and that, aside from the defect, you are returning it without substantial change. Then notify the dealer in writing that you are "revoking acceptance" and follow the rest of the steps under Strategy No. 1.

Strategy No. 3 is suing for damages. Give the dealer a reasonable number of chances to repair the car. Then turn it over to an independent mechanic and ask him for a written statement of the problem, the recommended solution and an estimate. If the statement seems reasonable, let the independent mechanic do the actual repairs and give you an itemized receipt. Show the receipt to the dealer and ask him for reimbursement. If the dealer refuses, have your lawyer sue. If the damages are less than the maximum permitted in small claims court (see Chapter 14), take the case there yourself. Some lawyers consider suing for damages the riskiest strategy, because it permits the dealer to claim that unauthorized repairs voided your warranty, both on the defect about which you complained and any other that may turn up. But it may be worth a try.

Buying a Used Car
A few people still attach a social stigma to buying a used car: it means that you can't afford a new one. But with the average price of new cars soaring past the $10,000 mark, even these status-conscious individuals are beginning to realize what most Americans have known all along — that a good used car can provide perfectly adequate transportation at a much lower overall cost.

Used cars, in fact, outsell new ones each year by an average of at least two to one. A nationwide survey by the Hertz Corporation indicates that in three out of four households where one or more cars is owned, a used car is the primary means of transportation. While average new-car prices rose 62 percent over a recent three-year period on a model-for-model basis, used-car prices rose only a third, reflecting in part an increase of some 50 percent in both their mileage and their age — used-car owners are holding onto their automobiles longer, too. The average used-car buyer pays 40 to 50 percent less than the new-car buyer to purchase, own and operate his automobile, saving roughly a quarter on the price of a year-old car and up to 85 or 90 percent on a six- or seven-year-old model.

The greatest saving in buying a used car is, of course, the saving in depreciation — as much as 30 percent for a new car in the first year and a total of 50 percent or more in the first two years. Savings are also produced by the lower purchase price itself. Loan payments and insurance premiums are lower and generally more than offset the higher operating and maintenance expenses associated with older cars. Indeed, maintenance costs have risen less than any other element of car ownership, amounting to only about 20 percent of total outlays even in a car's 10th year.

So it makes sense to consider buying a used car, whether as a second car for commuting to work or to a suburban train station, as a teenager's first car, or as a runabout for local shopping or car pooling to take children to school. Or you may want to turn in a car you already own for a one- or two-year-old model of a high-performance, "quality" car you have always wanted but cannot afford to buy new.

Whatever your reason, first decide what kind of car is really best for your purposes and what you can afford to spend. (Factors to consider in making this decision will be found under "Buying a New Car.") It is also a good idea to find out beforehand the kind of financing that may be available, if you need any; the insurance rates on various models you are considering; and the amount they will add to, or subtract from, your present rates.

According to the experts, the best buy in a used car is one that is three years old or less, is in relatively good condition and has been driven no more than 10,000 or 15,000 miles a year. The lion's share of the depreciation will already have occurred on such a car; any major "kinks" will probably have worked themselves out and been repaired; and with care the vehicle will still be good for at least another 50,000 miles.

Best buy in a used car: three years old or less; driven no more than 10,000 to 15,000 miles per year.

Several factors should be taken into account in deciding whether to buy a larger or smaller car. Small, fuel-efficient, popular models depreciate more slowly, so you will probably have to pay more for them initially, but you will save considerably in the long run on fuel, repairs and parts, including tires. A larger model will cost more to run and possibly to insure, but can be fine for occasional or short-trip use, and you may be able to buy it for quite a bit less than a small model. Unless you can't resist owning one, stay away from flashy types, such as sports cars, convertibles and luxury models — not only because they cost more, used as well as new, but because they deteriorate just as quickly as more modest cars and can prove expensive to maintain. Avoid any car loaded with power accessories, which are prone to breakdown and costly to repair.

Other things being equal, and unless the use you have in mind makes it impractical, probably the best buy as a practical, all-around used car is a mid-size sedan with a standard engine, the usual transmission for the model (whether it is manual or automatic), the least amount of fancy trim and accessories and no air conditioning, unless you live in an area where summers are really hot.

Whatever automobiles you are thinking of, check out their frequency-of-repair records, gathered in owner surveys and published in consumer magazines. Each year the April issue of *Consumer Reports* carries detailed five-year charts indicating whether the engines, transmissions and other components of the models rated were better or worse than average in their need for repairs. Its December Buying Guide reviews and ranks automobiles of the model year just finished; it also summarizes in a "trouble index" how problem-prone models of the previous five years have proved compared to their brethren, and in a "cost index" whether their maintenance and repairs have been relatively expensive or cheap.

If a particular component has been reported to be a special source of trouble in a car and model year you are considering, try to find out from the seller if it has proved troublesome in his car, and if it has been satisfactorily fixed. Remember, the true worth of any used car depends not so much on the repair history of its kin, or where you buy it, as on its actual condition. As you narrow your choices, it is also a good idea to check with local mechanics you trust, asking which makes and models have given the least trouble and, when problems arise, are easiest to repair.

Pricing Used Cars

Once you have closed in on two or three candidates, compare them on the basis of price. Dealers and others who sell or finance used cars as part of their business, generally rely on periodically updated price lists, those either distributed to them by large car wholesalers or published by other organizations. You can use those guides too. Among the best are the NADA *Official Used Car Guide*, the Kelley *Blue Book* and Edmund's *Used Car Prices*. All three are generally available at bookstores, newsstands, public libraries and the automobile-loan office of banks.

The NADA guide, for example, is published monthly in regional editions by the National Automobile Dealers Used Car Guide Company, 8400 Westpark Drive, McLean, Virginia 22101. It lists virtually all domestic and foreign cars, vans and trucks sold in the United States by manufacturer, year and model, going back seven or eight years, and giving the original suggested delivery price; the current average trade-in or wholesale value; the current average retail or "list" value, based on dealer reports; and the average loan that can be obtained on the car for each model. Below these are listed the amounts of money that the presence or absence of various options adds to or subtracts from the base trade-in, retail and loan figures. Also included are tables of amounts to be added for exceptionally low-mileage cars and amounts to be subtracted for high-mileage cars, by year, mileage and size of car. By looking up a car you are considering (see box, page 131), you can get a good general idea of its going price and the room you have to bargain. Most dealers will start out by asking for an amount closer to the retail price, while a private seller will probably settle for something between wholesale and retail price. Prices can also vary widely depending on the general condition of the car — whether it is "extra clean," "clean," "fair," "rough" or "reconditioned." A car that is in poor shape and has heavy mileage on it may be worth less than the listed wholesale value of that model, while one in spotless condition with very low mileage on it may be worth more than the listed retail price.

You can also get an idea of the asking prices for particular cars in the area where you live by looking in the classified section of newspapers under "Automobiles for Sale." There you will find listings both by dealers and by private owners who want to sell direct, thus saving both owner and buyer a healthy middleman's fee.

Shopping Around

When you begin to look at used cars, the first thing to bear in mind is just that — they are used. Every caution about buying a new car applies, only more so: the machinery of a used car is worn, and, therefore, closer to the point where it is likely to break down. However, don't assume that you are "buying someone else's headaches." While some used cars on the market are indeed clunkers, others are sound, well-maintained vehicles whose previous owners simply wanted other, newer automobiles. It is up to you to find out which category fits the car you are looking at. The process may be time-consuming, but if you are to get your money's worth, it must be carried out:

- Inspect the car carefully, inside and out.
- Take it for a thorough test drive.
- Talk to the last person to own and drive it, if at all possible.
- Have a mechanic check out the car for problems and estimates of repairs.
- Negotiate a fair price for what you buy.
- Make sure you have a proper, signed contract of sale, clear title to the car, and any warranties written out in detail.

The Odometer Law

Sellers of used cars may be tempted to conceal a car's true mileage by disconnecting the odometer or turning it back to show lower mileage. "Rolling back" or "spinning" the odometer on any motor vehicle is strictly prohibited by federal law. No one, not even the owner, is permitted to do it. Moreover, anyone selling a vehicle, whether a dealer or a private individual, must provide the buyer with a signed statement of the mileage registered on the odometer at the time of transfer. If the odometer is broken — or has been repaired or replaced so that it does not reflect the true mileage — it must be set at zero and a sticker must be attached to the left door frame indicating the true mileage and date at the time it stopped functioning. When the vehicle is sold, the statement given the buyer must also reflect the false reading.

Before buying any used car, ask for the mileage disclosure statement. Check the odometer for evidence of tampering, such as misaligned numbers or scratches. Compare the recorded mileage with the general condition of the car — with wear on the brake pedal or floor mats, for example — and with the figures on oil-change stickers, inspection stickers and other service records. If anything seems suspicious, ask to see the mileage statement given to the seller by the previous owner. Dealers are required to keep disclosure statements for four years, and any dealer who claims not to have one is probably violating the law. If you still have doubts, contact the former owner yourself. You can get the name and address either from the present seller or through your state department of motor vehicles. A victim of odometer tampering can sue the seller for up to $1,500 or three times the amount of damages, plus court costs and attorney's fees. Violations should also be reported to the state attorney general's office and to the National Highway Traffic Safety Administration (see directory, page 153) for possible civil or criminal action.

Other Buyer Protections

It is wise to be extremely cautious in buying any used car marked "as is." In some states, the law has modified that term to include a measure of protection for consumers. But in many, the term means precisely what it says: the car carries no warranty and may be defective, and although some courts have held used car dealers liable for injuries suffered by riders in such defective cars, this is not uniformly the case. Even if it were, it would be cold comfort indeed. In many places, used-car dealers must be licensed and must post their licenses prominently. But bear in mind that the license offers only minimal protection. It does not carry with it any government warranty that the licensee is honest, fair or even financially solvent. Some state laws, however, *do* offer used car buyers a measure of protection. New York, for example, requires dealers to provide a Certificate of Adequacy stating that a car is in satisfactory condition at the time of delivery and that brakes, steering, seat belts, lights, directional signals, windshield wipers, defroster, muffler, odometer, horn and rear-view mirror are in good working order. In many states, used cars sold by dealers must pass state inspections for safety and emissions standards.

Insist that a dealer repair a warranteed part in his own shop. Don't let him send you to another garage.

In some states, dealers are prohibited from selling a used car without giving the buyer a written warranty. Depending on the dealer and on the model year and condition of the car, you may be able to get a complete warranty covering repair, parts and labor for a period of 30 days or more. Or you may have to settle for more limited coverage — perhaps a 90-day warranty on parts only (you pay the labor); or a 50/50 warranty for 30 days or more under which you and the dealer split the costs. But be careful if you are offered this one. Dealers have been known to rig repair statements so that the buyer actually winds up paying more than his share — even the full amount. Some dealers prefer to sell their buyers "service contracts" for an extra fee; fees and terms vary as widely as warranties and are often subject to the same deficiencies.

Read any warranty carefully to see which components it covers and which it does not. Most are limited to the powertrain (engine, transmission and drive wheels) or to safety components required under state inspection laws. Don't accept any promises that are not put in writing, and if you have to bring the car in for repair of a warranteed part, don't let the dealer postpone the work or send you to someone else on the grounds that his service shop is jammed. By the time you get the car fixed, the warranty may have expired and you may find yourself paying for all repairs.

In the belief that all too many dealers mislead buyers of used cars, not only about the true mechanical condition of the vehicles but about what they will do if things go wrong, the Federal Trade Commission established regulations requiring dealers to post warning stickers on all used cars offered for sale, disclosing any known defects, giving full information about warranties and service contracts, and suggesting that buyers ask the dealer if the car can be inspected by an independent mechanic. This proposal was turned down by Congress on the grounds that it was confusing and would force dealers into costly inspections and repairs that would raise the price of used cars. When two consumer organizations brought suit against Congress in the U.S. Court of Appeals, the court struck down the legislative veto. The Federal Trade Commission decided to review the regulation rather than enforce it.

Buying from a New-car Dealer

New-car dealers have been more or less forced into the business of selling used cars by the trade-ins they accept, and they have learned how to make it increasingly profitable as new-car sales have slumped and the used-car business has become necessary to help them stay alive.

Because many of a new-car dealer's customers trade in their cars every two or three years, there is generally an assortment of late-model cars on the company lot. If the dealer has a good service department, the cars have probably been well maintained, and the necessary minor repairs and tune-ups have been performed before they were put on sale. A dealer usually keeps only the best and newest of the trade-ins, the ones that sell fastest at the highest prices. It is not worth the cost in time or room on the lot to put older or defective models into salable condition. It is more profitable for the dealer to get rid of them to wholesalers or used-car dealers or at auctions. So what you will see on the new-car dealer's lot is usually the cream of the crop, a selection limited to the most popular models and options, preferably with low mileage and good owner records.

If you are hoping to trade in an old jalopy for a newer used automobile, a new-car dealer probably won't want the ancient model on his hands and will suggest that you sell it yourself for a higher price. But if you are paying cash or financing a car, you may be able to get a favorable deal. Don't let a high asking price discourage you. As long as you offer more than the wholesale price you have discovered by consulting a used-car guide, the dealer may decide to keep you as a customer and accept only a modest profit. Buying from a new-car dealer plugs you into a service department, and this can come in very handy if problems develop later.

The dealer can also handle time-consuming details — title, licensing and registration, any car inspections required by the state — and can arrange for financing through contacts at a local bank. (You need not accept such an offer, of course, if you can get better terms somewhere else.) A new-car dealer should also be able to offer you a reasonably fair deal on a used-car warranty or service contract. As in buying a new car, make sure you are doing business with a dealer who is straightforward and has a good reputation to uphold in the community.

Used-car Dealers

Scattered among new-car dealers along every town's "automobile row," or located in lower-rent locations along the fringes, you will find the independent dealers who deal in nothing but used cars. They range in size and quality from large, well-established organizations with their own service shops to marginal, one-

Pricing a Used Car

Whether you are trading in an older car on a new one, selling it to a private individual, or buying a used car from its current owner or a dealer, you can get an idea of going prices by consulting one of the guidebooks available at public libraries, banks, some bookstores and newsstands.

The example below is from the National Automobile Dealers Association's *Official Used Car Guide*, which is published monthly in regional editions by the National Automobile Dealers Used Car Guide Company. The average trade-in or wholesale price at left is the amount you can expect to be offered for a 1979 Ford Mustang by a dealer, based on auction reports and dealer wholesale reports throughout the region for which the edition is designated. The insurance symbol next to it is the code used in determining fire, theft and collision insurance rates on the car. (Your insurance agent can supply further particulars.) Under *Body Type* are listed the various models: two- and four-door sedans with either four- or six-cylinder engines, along with the model numbers and range of vehicle identification numbers assigned to each. *Fact. ADP* refers to the original manufacturer's suggested *advertised delivered price* with standard equipment only (including provision for recovery of federal excise tax and suggested delivery handling but not transportation or state and local taxes). *Wgt.* is the established shipping weight of the car in pounds. *Av'g. Loan* represents the average amount of credit that may be obtained on cars sold at or near the average listed value. *Av'g. Retail* is the price at which the car can be expected to sell at a new- or used-car dealer once he has added his overhead, profit and cost of getting the car into selling condition.

Beneath are listed the amounts to be added to base model prices for various options with which a particular car is equipped, as well as amounts to be deducted for lack of desirable options. Each NADA guide also lists dollar amounts to be subtracted or added from the total for unusually high or low mileage.

These prices are from the September, 1983 Eastern edition and will doubtless decline as a given car gets older.

MUSTANG 1979

Av'g. Trd-in	Ins. Sym.	Body Type	Model	Fact. A.D.P.	Wgt.	Av'g. Loan	Av'g. Retail
MUSTANG-4 Cyl.		Veh. Ident.:9() (Model)() 100001 Up.					
3000	5	Sedan 2D	02	$4494	2431	2700	3675
3100	6	Sedan 3D	03	4828	2451	2800	3775
3150	6	Sedan 2D Ghia	04	5064	2539	2850	3825
3250	6	Sedan 3D Ghia	05	5216	2548	2925	3925
MUSTANG-V6		Veh. Ident.:9() (Model)() 100001 Up.					
3100	5	Sedan 2D	02	$4767	2511	2800	3775
3200	6	Sedan 3D	03	5101	2531	2900	3875
3250	6	Sedan 2D Ghia	04	5337	2619	2925	3925
3350	6	Sedan 3D Ghia	05	5489	2628	3025	4050
25		Add Vinyl Roof		$ 102		25	50
75		Add Flip-Up Roof		199		75	100
50		Add AM/FM Stereo		188		50	75
75		Add AM/FM Stereo W/Tape		255		75	100
350		Add Cobra Package		1173		325	125
50		Add Sport Option (Std. 3D Sedan)		175		50	75
25		Add Power Door Locks				25	50
25		Add Speed Control				25	50
25		Add Tilt Steering Wheel				25	50
25		Add Aluminum Wheels				25	50
25		Add Rear Window Defroster				25	50
50		Add 4 Cyl. (2.3L) Turbo Eng.		542		50	75
75		Deduct Manual Trans.				75	75
50		Deduct Conventional Steering				50	75
75		Deduct V8 Engine from 6 Cyl.				75	75
225		Deduct w/out Air Cond.				225	225

man operations that throw up a chain-link fence around a vacant lot, put up a shack for an office — and often vanish overnight. The stock at a used-car lot generally consists of leftover trade-ins from new car dealers; cars bought at auctions or from "road hogs" (wholesalers who travel from dealer to dealer peddling their wares); automobiles sold by individual owners for cash or as trade-ins on other used cars; and sometimes cast-offs from police or taxicab fleets.

Used-car dealers usually have a wide range of cars. Some are older models offered as "good, inexpensive transportation," which indeed they may be. But others may be "dogs" — vehicles with especially high mileage or hard use; cars that have been in accidents; even a few out-of-state cars whose legal ownership may be in question. Because such used-car dealers pick up many of their automobiles cheaply, and their overhead is lower than most new-car dealers', you may be able to strike a bargain — provided that you determine a car's true market worth versus the asking price, and that you put it through the rigorous examination and road test described elsewhere in this chapter.

Be especially wary of cars that have obviously been given new paint jobs, a new vinyl roof, new seat covers or floor mats. These cosmetic touches may be hiding rust or accident damage. Or the car may have been a taxicab or police squad car before its reincarnation — because of its long, rough life, probably the last car you want to buy — and these touches may be hiding holes drilled for mounting lights and other paraphernalia. Used-car dealers may not always be able to give you a service record on a car or put you in touch with the original owner, though you should ask. Depending on the firm and the car in question, you may or may not be able to get a written warranty, but you should try.

Rental and Leasing Companies

Among the most frequently overlooked sources for late-model used cars are companies that have large automobile fleets for business use. You may be able to get a bargain from the company you work for or from some other local company that is constantly replacing cars in its business fleet. For most people, however, the place to call is the toll-free number or local office of one of the national rent-a-car chains, which among them place hundreds of thousands of used automobiles, vans and trucks on the market each year to make room for new cars in their fleets.

As a rule, rental companies put up for retail sale only their best cars, disposing of the rest to wholesalers. (They usually do not sell any that have been in accidents or have a record of major mechanical problems.) On average, the cars are nine to 18 months old and have logged 12,000 to 25,000 miles, although some may have gone only 9,000 miles and others may have gone as much as 35,000 miles. Some people are hesitant about the condition of car-rental company automobiles — after all, each one has been driven by an average of 80 or 90 different drivers. But the companies point out that the bulk of their renters are businessmen and professionals, with the balance consisting mainly of family drivers. Moreover, the cars usually are meticulously cleaned after each use and are maintained at standards well above those followed by most car owners.

Rental companies are often good outlets to shop when buying a used car.

Rental companies are generally choosy about the models they pick. In addition, because they buy from manufacturers at bulk rates, they can pass along the savings when they sell and can even throw in such popular options as air conditioning, automatic transmission, larger engine and power steering. Prices can be as much as 10 to 15 percent below those offered by dealers.

But these prices are generally not negotiable and, except for some franchised outlets that accept trade-ins, must be paid for in cash, although help with financing may be arranged. Rental companies submit their cars to safety checks and tune-ups before selling, and stand behind them with substantial warranties ranging from 12 months or 12,000 miles on the powertrain to 24 months or 24,000 miles on most major components, not including mileage already on the cars. Test drives are generally encouraged, and you may be able to rent the car you are considering for a few days to try it out, with the rental cost applied to the price if you buy.

Some of the larger companies offer free booklets of consumer advice. "Used Cars:

Where to Shop, How to Buy" is available at National Car Rental offices or from National's Public Relations Department, 7700 France Avenue, South, Minneapolis, Minnesota 55435; "How to Sell Your Old Car" can be obtained at Avis Rent A Car outlets or from Majestic Direct Marketing, 135 North 12th Street, Kenilworth, New Jersey 07033.

If you are looking for a somewhat older automobile with higher mileage, check both the leasing division of car-rental companies and the major leasing companies that do business in your area. They generally advertise in the automobile sections of local newspapers and are listed in the yellow pages of telephone directories under "Automobile Renting and Leasing." You may be able to find what you want in a two- or three-year-old model leased to a single owner who has opted not to buy at the expiration of his lease.

Private Sales

Nearly all used-car sales are handled the old-fashioned way — by horse-trading between individuals. Because private transactions involve no middleman's profit, they can be a good deal for both buyer and seller. However, you will have to do all the paperwork. You will probably have to pay cash, or arrange your own loan if necessary, and unless you have a guarantee in writing or the seller has committed outright fraud, you will have little recourse if things go wrong with the car.

Would-be sellers advertise in various ways: by word of mouth among neighbors and friends, through notices on bulletin boards in offices and supermarkets, with "For Sale" signs on the cars themselves, and — most commonly — by classified ads in local newspapers and shopping sheets. Fridays and weekends are the favorite times for running ads, and if you make a point of buying the earliest editions as soon as they come out, your chance of getting first crack at a car that interests you is likely to be improved.

Understandably, sellers tend to stress the virtues rather than the shortcomings of their merchandise, and often use the curious shorthand of "automobilese." Study the ads to familiarize yourself with the language. If the ad lists a phone number and requires you to call, ask politely if the seller is a car dealer. If the answer is yes, and no such identification has appeared in the ad, you are talking to someone devious enough to be avoided. If the answer is no, make an appointment to see the car at the earliest convenient time.

A used car can usually be bought from an individual at less than the going retail price — sometimes well below if the seller is in a hurry to get cash, either for personal reasons or as a down payment on another car already on order. But he or she may be getting rid of the car because it is due for major repairs. You are entitled to ask why he or she is selling, whether the car has any problems, whether it has ever been in an accident, whether the seller is the clear owner (and has a certificate of title and registration to prove it), whether the bank is still owed any payments or whether there are any other liens on it. If you have doubts about the car's ownership, ask the state motor vehicle bureau or police department to make sure the car was not stolen somewhere along the line.

The owner should allow you to test drive the car and should allow your mechanic to inspect it. If all seems well, and you have agreed on a price, have the owner draw up a bill of sale listing the make, model, year and vehicle identification number, the date and amount paid, leaving room for both your signatures. Many states require a bill of sale and provide an official form, available through the nearest office of the state motor vehicle bureau. They also require the seller's signature on the certificate of ownership, which you will have to take to the motor vehicle bureau to have the title recorded in your name. Ask the seller for a signed statement of the mileage reading on the odometer. It should correspond to the actual mileage on the car. Most states also require that a sales tax be paid and may ask for evidence that the car is properly insured and has passed safety and emissions tests. If the car is still under any new-car warranty, ask to have the warranty transferred to your name.

Safety Defects and Recalls

Before buying a used car, be sure to find out if that particular model has been subject to recall for a safety defect (see "Recalls"). Only about two out of three owners of such cars actually bring in their autos to have recall problems corrected, but there is no time limit for fixing the defects, nor is it difficult to determine if the particular automobile you plan to buy suffers from the flaw that caused the recall.

First ask the dealer or owner who proposes to sell you the car if it has ever been recalled, what the flaw was, and whether it was repaired. A more certain procedure, particularly if you get an inconclusive answer, is to note down the vehicle identification number (VIN), which is listed on the registration and on most cars is readily visible through the windshield atop the dashboard on the driver's side. Give this number, along with the make, model and year, to the manufacturer's zone office or customer service division, or call the National Highway Traffic Safety Administration toll-free "hotline." Either should be able to tell you in short order if the car belongs to a group that was recalled, as well as when and why, although neither can tell you whether the defect was actually set right on the particular vehicle in question.

If the dealer sold the car new and subsequently serviced it, his records will probably show if the previous owner brought it in for the correction, and in any case he can fix it for you without charge. If there are no records available, as is the case with many vehicles on used-car dealers' lots, ask your own mechanic to examine the car. If he believes the repair was not made, and it is serious enough, arrange to have it done without charge at the manufacturer's nearest authorized dealer.

Checking Over the Car

The most critical step in buying a used car is a thorough inspection, particularly if the car is being sold by an individual or used-car dealer and there are relatively few guarantees of its history. Don't attempt to examine a car at night, when darkness can mask subtle signs of trouble, or in the rain, which can make even a bad repaint job sparkle. Wear clothes you don't mind getting a little soiled, and take a note pad and a flashlight. Plan on spending the better part of an hour to make the examination. If you don't know much about cars it helps to bring along a friend or mechanic who can do the job.

First check the exterior. Sight along each side of the body for ripples or poor panel alignments, and look all over for dull or mismatched paint. Any of these signs could indicate that the car has been in an accident and that, despite the cosmetic treatment, it may still have a frame bent out of alignment, a source of future trouble. If you are suspicious, ask how bad the accident was and how extensive the repairs.

Look for signs of rusting, particularly around the bottom of the doors and underneath the fenders. Bubbles or blisters under the paint indicate that the car is rusting from the inside out, and may soon rust right through. Tap the body panels with your fingers. Solid steel will have a metallic ring, but rusted panels will feel spongy and areas given quick repairs backed with plastic body putty will produce a dull clunk.

Open and close all the doors, the trunk and the hood. If they don't work easily and fit properly, the frame may be bent. Check the weather seal moldings to see if they are brittle or cracked; roll the windows up and down and lock and unlock the doors from both inside and out. A defect in any of these places could mean that expensive repairs are needed.

Check all tires for uneven wear. It often indicates poor wheel-alignment, a bent frame or a worn-out suspension.

Check the tires, including the spare. Uneven wear could indicate poor alignment, a bent frame or a worn-out suspension. Be suspicious if the odometer shows unusually low mileage but the tires have little tread left. Brand new tires on an old car could be a cover-up. Kicking the tires won't prove anything, except that you are an amateur. Instead, grab the top of each front wheel and pull it in and out. If it seems loose or makes a strange sound, the bearings and/or suspension will probably need work.

Push down hard on each corner of the car several times and then let go. If it bounces more than once or twice, you will probably need new shock absorbers.

Look under the car for fluid leaking on the ground from the oil pan, transmission or shock absorbers. Check the exhaust system from engine to tailpipe for rust, holes or patches, preferably with the engine running so you can pinpoint leaking fumes. Look for signs of fresh undercoating sprayed on the car to conceal whole areas of rust. Check for any cracks in the frame or signs of recent welding, and if there are any such defects, ask why.

While you're checking the trunk lid and spare tire, make sure the car comes with lug wrench and a jack in working order. Pull up any floor mats and look again for rust coming through. Look also for suspicious welding seams. Look under seat covers for battered upholstery, a sign of heavy use, and along the windows and doors for stains that indicate leaks. Check the horn and windshield wipers. If there are power windows or power seats, check the way they operate. Turn on the heater, defroster, rear-window defogger, air conditioning and any other gadgets to make sure they work. With the engine running, ask your friend to look from outside while you test the headlights (high and low beams), tail lights, turn signals, emergency flashers, brake and backup lights. Look at the dashboard to see that all the gauges operate.

Press down hard on the brake pedal and hold it for a good half-minute. If the pedal goes too low or continues right to the floor, there is a leakage in the hydraulic system that will have to be fixed.

A Used-car Road Test

After your inspection, take the car out for a road test. If the seller asks for a deposit to ensure the return of the car, give him a small one and ask for a receipt. Make sure you and the car are covered by insurance. If the seller will not permit a test drive, reject the car.

First, see how easily the engine starts and whether it idles smoothly without stalling. If the car has manual transmission, set the parking brake with the engine running, shift into first and let out the clutch while you gradually press on the accelerator; if the clutch is not worn, the engine should stall when the clutch pedal is about half to three-quarters of the way up because the hand brake is preventing movement. Test an automatic transmission by shifting from neutral to drive and neutral to reverse with your foot on the brake; if there is a clunking noise, the transmission will surely need work.

Drive slowly in a straight line while your friend watches from behind to check if the wheels line up or if any of them wobble (if you are alone, try to find a muddy stretch to drive through, then check that the front and rear wheel tracks are precisely atop each other). Turn the steering wheel back and forth, both while running and stopped, to make sure it doesn't vibrate or feel loose.

When the engine has warmed up, race it in neutral while you or your friend check the exhaust. A lot of blue smoke coming from the tailpipe can mean that the engine needs an overhaul. Black smoke indicates that the carburetor needs adjustment or replacing.

Take the car out on the highway to see how smoothly it accelerates through the gears and how it takes hills, noting any stumbling, hesitation or noises in the transmission. At a safe spot, check how well the car responds to sudden lane changes and sharp turns. Test the brakes by braking fairly hard two or three times, then again at a slower speed with your hands just off the steering wheel. If the brakes are either sloppy or grab hard, if they pulse rhythmically or if the car pulls to one side, you may have an expensive brake job in store. Set the parking brake on a hill to see if it holds. Check the car's road-holding ability on a bumpy stretch. Excessive bouncing, wallowing, swaying, rattles or squeaks may indicate that the suspension needs repair. While driving, turn on the headlights, radio, air conditioning and other accessories: all should be able to work at the same time without depressing the ammeter needle and draining the battery.

Toward the end of your drive, check the temperature gauge and warning light for overheating, and when you stop, look under the hood for any signs of steam coming from the radiator or of leaking coolant. Check all fluid levels and examine belts, hoses and battery for cracks or leaks. See how easily the engine restarts when it is hot. Let it idle for a few minutes, then move the car forward and check the ground for puddles indicating leaks (a reddish color is transmission fluid, black or dark brown are oil or rear axle fluid; gasoline and brake fluid are lighter in color).

If the car does reasonably well on its test drive, tell the seller you'd like to have a few things checked over by a professional before you buy. Take the car to a good local mechanic, or an automobile diagnostic center, with a list of your observations. Ask for a checkup of all systems, an opinion on the condition of the car and a written estimate of needed repairs. (The last may be useful in negotiating with the seller about price or who pays for the repairs.) Even if the estimate comes to several hundred dollars to fix certain components, the investment may be worth it if the car is otherwise in good shape.

Renting and Leasing

With the costs of car ownership rising steadily, drivers are increasingly finding it both convenient and economical to use vehicles owned by someone else. The rental and leasing market constitutes the fastest-growing segment of the automotive industry, and has more than doubled in volume in recent years. Nearly one in four passenger automobiles produced by U.S. manufacturers today is purchased by firms in the lease-rental business, and some industry executives predict the figure will be more than one in three by the end of the decade.

Business travelers and vacationers have long known the advantages of renting a car by the day, the week or even the month. But renting can also make sense for other drivers, particularly those who live in larger metropolitan areas. A surprising number of cars are used less than their owners realize; the rest of the time they stand at the curb or in the garage, costing money 24 hours a day, 365 days a year. Studies have shown that in many areas people who drive less than 12,000 miles a year can save substantially on total annual costs and costs-per-mile by renting a car when they need it rather than buying one.

A new compact car rented at budget rates and driven for 11,400 miles — 100 miles a day for 50 weekends and a two-week vacation — costs about three-quarters as much as it would if it was purchased and driven for 10,000 miles. Renting permits a driver to put the money a car would cost into more fruitful investments and eliminates garaging, maintenance and insurance costs. It also gives the driver a chance to pick the most appropriate kind of vehicle for particular trips, from an economical runabout to an expensive luxury car, sports car, truck, van or even camper.

Generally, anyone 18 or older (21 or 25 in some instances) who has a valid driver's license and a major credit card can rent a car from a nationwide rental company or from any one of the myriad local firms listed in the yellow pages of telephone directories. If you don't have a credit card, you may be asked to fill out a cash qualification form and to leave a cash deposit based on estimated charges.

Rental rates vary considerably, depending on the size of the car, the company, the location, availability of vehicles, peak season demands, discounts and promotions. Lower rates are often available on weekends and holidays, at popular vacation sites and through tour packages that include air fare or lodging. Most major companies feature rates that include unlimited free mileage when the car is returned to the renting location, though if you don't plan on traveling far you may be able to get a rate based on the number of days you keep the car plus a small charge for each mile you actually drive.

Most rates do not include the cost of gasoline; you start with a full tank, and if the tank is less than full when you return the car, you pay the cost of filling it up again. If you plan to return the car at another location, you may have to pay an additional "drop charge" or "one-way" rate.

To determine the best type of rental for your purposes, call several firms (all the larger ones have 24-hour toll-free numbers) and tell them the general type and size of car you want, the number of days you will need it and the approximate number of miles you expect to travel. Most reservations clerks will help you work out the most economical deal for your intended use.

Inquire about discounts. Virtually anyone nowadays is eligible for a discount card that offers savings of as much as 30 percent less than the quoted rate, particularly if he or she belongs to a credit union, driving club or other organization that has an arrangement with the rental firm or works for a company that has such an arrangement. But remember that discounts do not apply to most so-called "budget" rates.

If the places of rental and return are not the same, the fee may be higher.

If you are talking to a company that has several branches in your area, it is a good idea to check whether the rates are the same at all branches. In several cities, for example, rental rates from airport branches differ from rates in the business section. If you can find a way to get to the cheaper location at reasonable cost, the inconvenience may be worth your while.

Ask also if the quoted rates include insurance, and if they do, how much. Find out whether the discount depends on your taking out additional coverage from the company. Most reputable car-rental firms include basic liability and comprehensive insurance at no extra charge, with no-fault insurance provided where required by law. (A good standard package is $100,000/$300,000 liability and $25,000 property damage.) A "collision damage waiver" is available at additional charge. It relieves you of financial responsibility for damage to the car. Ask if this is mandatory and how much it will add to the daily rate, if you will be liable for a deductible amount if you take it, and if you will have to put up a cash or credit-card voucher deposit if you decline. Many companies also offer, at a small additional charge, personal life and medical insurance to cover the driver and passengers in the event of an accident; if you feel you need this coverage, inquire about the rates. If any others will also be driving the car, make sure the rental company's insurance or your own automobile insurance covers them as well.

If you are not sure you will be able to return the car by the agreed time, find out if there is a penalty for lateness, or whether lateness will change any weekend or other special rate you are getting.

Finally, if you plan on driving some distance or will be on the road a good deal, ask if the company offers around-the-clock emergency road service, how far away from the renting location it applies, and whether it is indeed available a full 24 hours a day.

When you have noted down information from several firms, compare total estimated costs with the kinds of cars and services you will get. The large nationwide rental companies generally have the newest cars, the most convenient locations at airports and in downtown areas, more offices open longer hours to offer travel assistance, "courtesy bus" service, road service and drop-off privileges in various cities. Smaller local firms, on the other hand, may offer lower rates and, therefore, considerable savings. Bear in mind, however, that their cars may be somewhat older and less convenient to pick up and drop off. Moreover, the precise car you want may not be available at the time you request it.

No matter what firm you rent from, make reservations well in advance to assure your choice, and give yourself enough time to check over the car and the contract before you drive away. See that the mileage written down matches the figure on the odometer, and that the gas gauge registers full. Look in the trunk to see that the spare tire and tools are there, and make sure everything else is in good working order. Inspect the vehicle for dents or scratches.

If anything is less than perfect, have the defects noted on the contract: this is your protection against unjust accusations that you damaged the car. Wherever you drive, lock the doors and trunk when you park. When you return the car, check its condition once more and make sure you leave it in the right place, either locked or in the custody of a rental firm employee. Note the mileage and gas you have used and look over the filled-out contract before you sign and pay.

Leasing a Car

Automotive leasing originally developed as a way for businesses to avoid buying and owning their own vehicles, and thus to free their capital for more productive ends. Today, it has become an increasingly attractive alternative to owning both for people whose car is used for business purposes (and therefore has value as a tax deduction) and for other individuals as well.

There are two basic kinds of leases, offered in varying forms by leasing companies, by the leasing division of car-rental firms and by franchised new-car dealers. One is the *closed-end lease* — also known as a net, fixed-cost or walk-away lease — under which you contract with the company for the use of an automobile, truck or van for some specified period of time and some maximum of mileage. In such a lease, your monthly fee is based on a prediction of the resale value of the vehicle at the end of the rental period. Because the leasing company assumes responsibility for disposing of the car thereafter and takes any profit or loss depending on the actual resale price it can get, most closed-end leases impose additional charges for mileage above the specified maximum and for damage to the car.

On the other hand, there may be an adjustment in your favor if the mileage is below the maximum. Some companies are willing to extend closed-end leases at a reduced rate, or to give you first choice if you are interested in purchasing the vehicle at its current wholesale value.

The *open-end lease* — sometimes called an equity or finance lease — also runs for a fixed term. Its monthly payments are also based on a calculated resale price. The rates, however, are generally lower than in a closed-end lease because you assume responsibility for keeping the car in shape and for making up any loss incurred if the car sells for less than its market value at the end of the lease, although you are not charged for damage or excessive mileage. Moreover, at the end of the lease you generally have several options: renegotiating the lease at a reduced rate; purchasing the car; selling it to a third party; having the leasing company sell it for you. If the company sells it for more than the predicted figure, you sometimes get the difference; if the sale brings in less, you take the loss.

Both closed- and open-end leases specify who is responsible for servicing and repairing the car and to what degree. Under a *no-maintenance contract,* you take care of all servicing costs. Monthly fees are higher in a *full maintenance contract,* but the company agrees to perform all scheduled servicing and repairs, short of those caused by accident or neglect. A full maintenance contract may also include new batteries and tires, emergency travel repairs, towing and the use of a replacement car.

Car leasing frees capital for other uses and may provide a tax deduction.

Leasing a car provides some important advantages, among them simplicity, convenience, freedom from detailed record-keeping and the use of a new car at a predictable cost. But there are so many variables in possible leasing arrangements that it is important to compare leasing packages closely.

- Check whether an advance payment or security deposit is required, and whether it will be refunded at the end of the lease.
- Find out exactly when payments begin and end, what penalties there are for late payments, and whether the charges include periodic fees for registration, taxes and insurance. Remember that you may be able to get insurance elsewhere for less.
- Be sure you understand all the limitations the lease places on you: mileage restrictions; payments for excess mileage; the persons in addition to yourself who are permitted to drive the car; conditions for terminating the lease before the time is up or renewing it on expiration.
- Get clear information on how to handle the problem if the car turns out to be a lemon or is damaged, disabled or wrecked during the course of the lease.
- Compare the costs of several different types of leasing arrangements with the cost of buying, financing, and operating the same car over the period of the lease.
- If you *do* decide to lease a particular car, inspect and test drive it (as described earlier) before accepting it to ensure that you will not wind up paying for problems that are not of your creation.

Fighting Auto Theft

According to the National Automobile Theft Bureau, well over a million motor vehicles are stolen in the United States each year, and an additional 2.5 million are robbed of their contents or accessories.

Despite efforts to stem the tide, the ratio of auto thefts to the national population has nearly doubled since 1970. Moreover, nearly half the vehicles that are stolen are never seen again by their owners. Some are disguised so that they are not recognizable; others are dismantled and "cannibalized" for replacement parts in secret "chop shops"; still others are re-registered with phony papers or sold abroad in countries desperate for automobiles at almost any price. Of those that are recovered, a good many are so stripped and vandalized that they are no longer of much use.

These facts and statistics add up to a warning. Your car could be next — unless you make things difficult enough to persuade a thief to look somewhere else. Don't think your automobile is an unlikely target just because it is not new or fancy. Even an older car can be attractive to a car-theft ring that has an order for a particular make and model, whether for the whole car or for the valuable replacement parts it contains. Nor is your car necessarily safe when parked in your own driveway. Half of all auto thefts occur in residential areas.

While there is no foolproof method of stopping a skilled professional, you can throw up enough obstacles to buy time — the one thing no thief can afford to spend. Most cars are stolen because they are easy to steal quickly. Some 80 percent of those that are stolen are unlocked and 40 percent actually have their keys in the ignition.

Crime prevention experts recommend these precautions:

1. Never leave your car running and unattended, no matter how short a time you expect to be away. Many thieves hang around convenience stores just waiting to spot such a car and make off with it.

2. Wherever you park, even in your own driveway, make a habit of removing the keys, rolling up the windows tight (a thief can "fish" for the inside locks through even a small crack) and locking all the doors. Keep any packages or valuables in the trunk and lock it. Use a detachable mounting for a CB radio or tape deck so you can take it with you or lock it temporarily in the trunk.

3. Never leave your driver's license or registration form in the car, and keep your certificate of title to the automobile in a safe place at home. These documents make it easy for thieves to sell a car fraudulently. Don't keep spare keys in the car. Professionals know all the hiding places.

4. Park with your front wheels turned sharply to the right or left or into a curb, making it difficult for a thief to tow your car away backward. (Yes, some thieves tow cars they want if they can't get them an easier way.) Set the emergency brake; put a manual transmission into first gear or reverse, an automatic transmission in "park." At night, park in well-lighted or heavily traveled areas, if possible. Two-thirds of all auto thefts take place under cover of darkness. If you have a garage, use it, locking both the car and the garage. If you park in a driveway, face the car toward the street so anyone tampering with the engine is more likely to be seen.

5. When leaving your car at a parking lot or parking garage, don't tell the attendant how long you will be gone unless you have to. Give him only the ignition key; take the trunk key and claim check with you. If you have doubts, write down your mileage reading on the claim check in full view of the attendant and check the reading when you come back. (Cars have been driven away to other locations where an accomplice can switch valuable parts).

6. Make a record of the serial numbers of such easily removed accessories as stereos, tape decks and CB radios so that they can be traced. Since the vehicle identification number (VIN) on a stolen car is usually altered, you can improve your chances of recovering it if you "brand" it by scratching it, or your license number and state, into the metal in several hard-to-find places on the body and engine, or by using an engraving tool that you can purchase or, in some instances, borrow from the police department under neighborhood crime prevention programs. Some owners who have been unable to positively identify altered cars, have nevertheless recovered them because, some time prior to the theft, they had slipped a business card down the slot between a window and door.

Anti-theft Devices

Beyond these precautions, there are many types of special devices you can install on your car to deter thieves. They may well thwart an amateur and even an expert who knows how to circumvent them but may not have the time to do so and, therefore, will pass up your car. In Illinois, Massachusetts and New York, insurance companies offer discounts on automobile theft premiums to cars so equipped, particularly in the high-crime areas of larger cities.

The devices, which are available through car dealers, auto stores, locksmiths and mail-order houses, range from modestly priced gadgets to expensive systems:

Alarms — loud sirens or piercing horns — are simply automotive adaptations of the old burglar-alarm system, and work on the theory that the thief will panic and run. The alarm may be activated by a pin switch when someone opens the hood, doors or trunk, or by other sensors that respond to tampering with a window, "hot wiring" the ignition without a key, or lifting the vehicle for towing. Alarms

Rip-offs on the Road

Although most service stations are honest, motorists are occasionally victimized by operators or attendants who are not above performing a shady trick or two, especially upon motorists whose license plates indicate they are a long way from home. The best protection against these charlatans is to inspect your car thoroughly before leaving on any protracted trip or to have your own service shop put it into top traveling condition. That way you can feel fairly certain no service problems will come up. The second line of defense is to watch the station attendant closely while your car is being serviced during your trip. Below is a list of tricks to be on guard against:

Short-sticking. Pushing the dipstick only part way down and then pulling it out will create the impression that you need more oil. Tell the attendant you've had trouble with that dipstick yourself and have him check it again.

Honking. While checking your air pressure, the attendant surreptitiously cuts or punctures a tire and says you need a new one. If you're unlucky enough to have this happen to you, *don't* buy the tire then and there. Put on your spare and take the damaged tire somewhere else.

Slashing. Cutting a belt on the fan, power steering or air conditioning so that it hangs by a thread is another typical rip-off. Carry spare belts in the trunk of your car, and tell the attendant to use one of them. A similar stunt is sometimes attempted by puncturing a hose.

Shock treatment. Squirting some ordinary lubricating oil on a shock absorber can give the impression that the seal is broken. Bounce the corner of the car over the shock and let go: if it does not continue bouncing more than once or twice, the shock is OK.

Battery boil. A little bit of soda or seltzer dropped into a battery cell reacts violently with the acid and makes it boil over. If the eruption soon subsides, your battery is probably all right.

Alternator burn. Dropping a pinch of a chemical, or even barbecue sauce, on a hot alternator (generator) makes it smoke and smell; pulling the alternator wires off turns the dashboard warning light on. If the wires themselves are intact and there is no sign of other burnt parts after the smoke has cleared, you don't need a new alternator. If a wire is detached, say it must have come loose accidentally. Tell the attendant to reattach it and drive off.

Wheel wobble. Still another ugly trick of the trade consists in shaking a free-hanging front wheel while your car is up on a lift for servicing, then warning that you need extensive repairs. Front wheels are supposed to have some play. If the car drives satisfactorily when you get it off the lift, you can always have the wheels checked later at a more reputable shop.

are generally expensive, and in an isolated area may not deter a professional who knows how to disconnect them. Even on a crowded city street a thief may try to silence the alarm and drive away, aware that most passersby won't risk a confrontation.

System interrupters, which operate automatically or when you push a hidden switch on leaving the car, disable one or more of the vehicle's vital systems so that it cannot be driven away. Some simply lock the ignition to prevent the car from starting, or stall it within a matter of seconds. Others cut off the fuel going to the engine. The small amount of fuel left in the fuel line and carburetor allows a thief to drive for a block or two, after which the engine dies. One expensive system electronically shuts off both fuel and ignition and locks the brakes on two wheels, thereby giving a thief three problems.

Other gadgets include locks for the hood or the steering wheel, armored collars that lock around the steering column to cover the ignition, and bars that lock the steering wheel to the brake pedal. An inexpensive set of four locking lugs, which come with a special wrench that must be used to unlock them, frustrates thieves who try to remove wheels and tires. Keyless entry systems work on code numbers that have to be punched before the doors and trunk will open. Others require the driver to enter a four-digit code on a dashboard panel before the car will start. Tapered or headless door-lock buttons can be substituted for the original mushroom-top plungers on the insides of doors, preventing a thief from "fishing" the locks through a window that is not completely closed.

For general tips on thwarting auto theft, get a copy of "The Car Crime Prevention Book," one of the free "answer" booklets on cars published by the Shell Oil Company and generally available at Shell service stations or through the company's regional offices. Analyses and ratings of auto anti-theft devices, as well as other car accessories, appear in the magazine, *Consumer Reports*.

Automobile Clubs

Some one-third of America's 150 million registered drivers belong to auto clubs, at annual fees of about $25 to $50. These clubs offer their members everything from maps and trip-planning services to bail bonds and legal fees. But the main reason people join them is that they provide assurance of speedy help when something goes wrong with a member's car. Ninety percent of the problems automobile clubs are called on to handle occur when drivers are 100 miles or less from their residences, and more than 40 percent occur when the car is in the owner's driveway or garage. In over half the cases, the problem is a car that won't start, and about half those times, the car has to be towed. More than 40 percent of the problems occur under winter conditions of freezing temperatures, snow and ice.

Of the dozen major clubs in this country, by far the largest is the American Automobile Association (AAA), a federation of 175 regional clubs serving 23 million members through about a thousand offices and branches in Canada as well as in the United States. AAA affiliates respond to some 17 million calls for emergency road service each year, an average of more than 45,000 a day. Nearly half these calls reflect battery or electrical failures, and in winter, a good many involve frozen gas lines. By calling a nationwide toll-free number, an AAA member can get the names and telephone numbers of the two AAA contract garages nearest the site of the disabled car. The responding garage bills the club for its basic services in getting the car operating again, and the member pays the garage directly for parts and any extensive repairs. If neither garage is able to send a repair truck at the time, the member is free to request service from another source and apply to AAA for reimbursement up to a specified amount.

AAA affiliates, whose fees and services vary somewhat from club to club, also maintain an extensive network of carefully screened AAA-approved auto repair shops where members can go for reliable, guaranteed work on their cars (see "Signs of Quality," page 147). In addition, the AAA offers trip-planning advice, maps and travel guides; the services of some 600 accredited travel agencies for domestic and foreign tours; personal and accident insurance; rewards in cases of car theft; discounts on car rentals and other travel services; credit cards and check-cashing privileges; help with automobile financing, insurance claims and attorney's fees. Most branches also publish a magazine or newspaper for their members, conduct programs aimed at better driver education and support lobbying efforts at local, state and national levels on motoring, highway and travel matters. Further information on membership can be obtained from any local AAA club or from the American Automobile Association, 8111 Gatehouse Road, Falls Church, Virginia 22042.

Many auto clubs offer discounts, travel advice, and access to a network of approved repair shops.

Other automobile clubs offering similar services include the ALA Auto & Travel Club, 888 Worcester Street, Wellesley, Massachusetts 02181; the Amoco Motor Club, P.O. Box 28281, Raleigh, North Carolina 27696; the National Automobile Club, 1 Market Plaza, San Francisco, California 94105;

and the National Retired Teachers Association/American Association of Retired Persons Motoring Plan, P.O. Box 28205, Raleigh, North Carolina 27696.

Some major auto clubs do not maintain their own networks of participating service stations but reimburse members up to a limit of $50 or $60 after they have made their own arrangements for road service. These include the Allstate Motor Club, 30 Allstate Plaza, Northbrook, Illinois 60066; the Exxon Travel Club, 4550 Dacoma Street, Houston, Texas 77092; the Gulf Auto Club, P.O. Box 4189, South Bend, Indiana 46634; and the Montgomery Ward Auto Club, 2020 West Dempster, Evanston, Illinois 60202.

Maintenance and Repairs

After making a major investment in an automobile, all too many motorists fail to protect that investment with proper maintenance. A car that is not well cared for is not only more expensive to run, but wears out sooner, contributes more than its share to harmful air pollution and is more likely to be in an accident caused by mechanical defects.

One national study revealed that the typical one-owner car less than four years old has never been put through six of the 14 basic maintenance jobs necessary for keeping the vehicle in good condition. According to the Car Care Council, an organization of companies in the automotive "aftermarket" industry, owners wait nearly half again as long as they should before servicing their cars. Many services are performed only after the equipment in question has failed. And this means, of course, greater expenditures.

Most of the guidelines necessary for good maintenance appear in the owner's manual that comes with the car. The manual specifies time or mileage intervals at which oil changes, filter changes, lubrication, spark plug replacement and many other services should be performed, and it generally gives other good advice on operating economies and keeping a car in shape. Unfortunately, as one industry professional wryly says, the manual is "one of the major unread documents in Western literature."

If you are reasonably handy, you can save money by doing some of the jobs described in the manual yourself, and you will not void your warranty by doing them if you keep records and can prove that the work was done as required. Among many helpful maintenance and repair books for do-it-yourselfers is the *Reader's Digest Complete Car Manual*, available through Reader's Digest, Pleasantville, New York 10570. For more advanced amateurs, step-by-step, illustrated procedures for specific cars, by manufacturer, model and year, are contained in professional compendia, such as *Motor Auto Repair Manual* published by *Motor*, 224 West 57th Street, New York, New York 10019.

Using Gasoline Wisely

Good auto maintenance as well as performance begins with the fuel you buy and the way you use it when you drive. Oil companies generally blend their gasolines for the temperature and altitude conditions in the regions where they are sold. While some brands may perform better in your car than others, the most important thing is to choose a grade with an octane rating just high enough to prevent engine "knock" — the pinging, rattling noise that is heard particularly during acceleration. Knocking indicates uneven combustion and decreases power and efficiency. If it is allowed to continue, it can damage an engine severely enough to require costly repairs.

The octane rating of a gasoline — a number like 87, 89 or 91.5 — by law must appear on a bright yellow sticker on all gasoline pumps. The rating is not a measure of the gasoline's quality or power but simply its resistance to engine knock. The most common number is an average of "research octane," determined in laboratory engines running at low speeds, and "motor octane," determined at higher speeds (this accounts for the notation on pump stickers of "R + M/2," or Research plus Motor divided by 2). The principal additives for controlling knock are tetraethyl and tetramethyl lead — hence, "leaded" gasoline.

In order to reduce levels of harmful lead emissions in the air, most automobiles built since 1975 require unleaded gas. Putting old-fashioned leaded gas in such cars will *not* improve their performance or fuel economy and can easily ruin the catalytic converter installed to control emissions. Morever, it is a violation of federal law and can carry a $10,000 fine. Altering or removing the emissions controls to permit the use of leaded gasoline will not make a car run any better, either, and in fact will throw an unleaded fuel system out of balance, fouling spark plugs and other parts. It is also against the law in most states. Under the Clean Air Act, the U.S. Environmental Protection Agency can, and has, levied stiff penalties against gasoline retailers and distributors for selling leaded gas misrepresented as unleaded, and against repair shops for removing the catalytic converters from cars.

True, unleaded gasolines with low octane ratings will "knock" more easily, particularly in high-compression engines, and may also contribute to the problem of "dieseling" or "run-on" — the annoying tendency of an engine to keep firing spontaneously and jerkily for a few moments after the ignition has been switched off but while the cylinders are still hot. In most cases, however, the remedy is simple. If your car knocks or runs on, try a slightly higher octane of the same brand, or another brand, the next time you fill up. If the problem persists, continue to increase the octane level by small amounts until the knock stops. (If it doesn't, have a mechanic check the car.) An engine's octane requirement usually increases with age as deposits build up, so a new car that runs well on 87 octane may need 89 or more a few years later.

Altering or removing emission controls is a violation of federal law and can result in a large fine.

On the other hand, many owners run their cars on "premium" gas when they do not need to. If your car is not knocking, try lowering the octane by small amounts until your engine starts to knock, then go back up to the next higher rating. Your car will run just as well, and you'll be saving money on gas.

When buying any gasoline, don't rely on labels like "regular," "premium" or "super." Standards for minimum octane ratings applied to such terms vary from state to state, and some states set no standards at all. Go by octane numbers instead. If you don't find the yellow sticker on a gas pump, ask the station owner why. If you don't get a satisfactory answer, write to Octane Posting, Federal Trade Commission, Washington, D.C. 20580. Violations can carry penalties of up to $10,000 per day.

Fuel-saving Tips

If your car persists in knocking or dieseling, or acts generally sluggish, you may need a tune-up — one of the things drivers frequently postpone on grounds of inconvenience or cost. A properly tuned car can save at least 10 percent, and as much as 20 percent, in fuel consumption over one badly out of tune.

Each time you stop for gas, check your oil level, fill it as soon as it is down a quart, and don't forget the periodic oil changes recommended in your owner's manual. A high-quality, multigrade oil may add slightly to the cost of an oil change but can save several times that in fuel economy until time for the next change. Steel-belted radial tires, inflated to the recommended pressure, can also save money (underinflated tires waste as much as a gallon out of every 20 gallons of gasoline).

One of the best ways of saving fuel, not to mention wear and tear on your car, is paying attention to the way you drive. First, simply don't drive when you don't have to. Use public transportation, a bicycle or your feet whenever you can, or car pool with others going in the same direction. Combine several short errands into one longer trip, so that you are driving as little as possible with a cold engine. (Until your car warms up, you may get as little as four or five miles to a gallon of gas.)

Don't waste gas by "warming up" the engine for several minutes, or by racing it; but start off as soon as the engine is running smoothly and proceed at a moderate speed. Avoid fast starts, accelerate gently and get your car into high gear as soon as you can. Don't brake and accelerate constantly; but anticipate traffic and lights ahead of you so that you can maintain a steady speed. With a manual transmission, downshift only when you have to in order to climb a hill or pass another car. If you have an automatic transmission, encourage it to shift into higher gear sooner by letting up slightly on the accelerator. Keep your speed to the posted limits — not only because it is required by law and is safer but because it saves considerably on gas. Most cars get optimum mileage at about 35 or 40 miles per hour, and much better mileage at 55 miles per hour than at 70. You can also save gas by turning off the engine whenever you stop for more than a minute. Never let your engine idle for long periods, especially if it is turning over at high speed, and never leave the car unattended with the engine running (engine overheating can cause damage, especially if you are not there to heed the temperature warning light).

At highway speeds, reduce air drag on the car by closing the windows and using the dashboard air vents instead. Limit your use of air conditioning, which consumes a significant portion of the engine's power, especially on less powerful cars. Unnecessary weight also reduces gas mileage, so keep snow tires, chains, bags of sand, baby carriages and other paraphernalia in the garage until you need them. The garage is also the best place for a removable luggage or ski rack, which creates wind resistance and lowers fuel economy by about 5 percent even when it is not loaded up. When you do load a roof luggage rack, minimize air drag by arranging the items in "steps" with the lowest at the front and back and cover them with a tarpaulin or heavy-duty plastic sheeting securely lashed to the rack.

Diesel engines offer the real possibility of producing fuel economy, but they have to be treated with special care. Use only diesel fuel made for cars and do not blend it with gasoline or fuel additives, particularly those containing alcohol. Alcohol can attack plastic parts in the fuel injection pump and cause the pump to fail. Diesel fuel tanks should be kept well above empty at all times. Water condensing in the tank can contaminate the fuel, causing rough engine operation and rapid wear. A diesel also requires special restarting procedures if it ever runs out of fuel.

Gas-saving Gimmicks

In recent years, close to a hundred different "gas-saving" devices have been touted in the marketplace as the answer to motorists' prayers. Some make gas mixtures leaner by delivering more air or less gas to the carburetor. Others recirculate exhaust gases or advance the ignition timing. Still others are pill or liquid fuel additives put in the gas tank in hopes of improving combustion, gizmos placed on the tank to "energize" fuel molecules into mysterious new configurations, synthetic compounds added to engine oil to further reduce friction and improve mileage.

But be careful, because some of these marvelous inventions don't work. Only a handful of products subjected to controlled, scientific tests by the Environmental Protection Agency (EPA) have shown signs of improving fuel economy to any measurable degree. One temporarily cuts off the compressor of the air-conditioning unit when the vehicle accelerates. This produces a fuel saving of as much as 4 percent for automobiles that labor under the load of an air conditioner. A second, which injects a water-alcohol solution into the carburetor air intake, produces increased exhaust emissions, although it can save an average of nearly 6 percent. A third permits an eight-cylinder vehicle to operate on four cylinders whenever possible, improving fuel economy on the highway up to 20 percent. On the other hand, it reduces the drivability of the car and raises emissions to a level above EPA standards, thus violating the anti-tampering provisions of the Clean Air Act.

EPA has found some fuel economy improvement with antifriction additives, but not as much as their makers proclaim. Devices that introduce more air into fuel make the mixture harder to ignite, and when it *does* ignite, it burns hotter, thus creating a risk of damage to cars whose carburetors have already been set to run as lean as possible to reduce pollutants released into the air. EPA warns that no one knows what effect most "gas-savers" may have and what harm they may cause when used over long periods.

For consumers who buy such devices and later feel cheated, the Federal Trade Commission advises contacting the manufacturer first and asking for a refund. ("Money-back guarantees" are offered on most such products.) If the buyer fails to get satisfaction, the next step is to contact a local or state consumer protection agency, sending copies of letters to the consumer agency in the state where the company is located and additional copies to the local Better Business Bureau and to the FTC, Washington, D.C. 20580. The FTC itself cannot handle individual complaints, but the information can help the agency identify patterns of abuse and pinpoint the worst offenders for regulatory action.

Basic Car Care

Over the years, cars have become more efficient. Unfortunately, however, this is not uniformly true of car owners. Not too many years ago, the oil had to be changed and the car lubricated every 1,000 miles, and owners followed this ritual religiously. But now oil change and lubrication are needed, on the average, only every 7,500 miles, and drivers tend to forget such infrequent requirements.

"Self-serve" gas station pumps contribute to the problem. Their convenience and economy cannot be denied, but there is no attendant on hand to remind the driver that a check may be needed. One oil company, which inspected the same items on 100 cars of self-serve customers, found that 56 were at least a quart low on oil, 34 were low on radiator coolant, 33 had at least one tire well below recommended inflation levels, 29 needed power-steering fluid, 28 needed brake fluid and 27 needed water in their batteries.

According to a panel of veteran mechanics assembled by this company, the basic maintenance checks most commonly neglected are the fluid levels of oil, radiator coolant, transmission, brakes, power-steering and battery water. Of these, the cooling system and the transmission get the least attention. The former should be drained, flushed and refilled at least once every year or two with a 50/50 mixture of antifreeze and water, and the transmission fluid and filter changed at the intervals recommended by the manufacturer.

To keep a car running smoothly and to head off repairs, most experts advise that it should be inspected regularly at least once a month. You can, of course, take your car to a service station. But you can also inspect it in your own driveway.

- Open the hood and check the coolant level. Many new cars have translucent overflow tanks with markings that make a visual check and fill-up simple. On older cars, you will have to remove the radiator cap. Be careful not to do this while the engine is hot: the pressurized coolant may spew out and scald you severely. Wait until the radiator is cool enough to rest your hand on, then remove the cap with a protective rag and fill with antifreeze and water to an inch below the bottom of the filler neck.
- Look closely at the belts that drive the alternator, radiator fan, air conditioner and power steering. If any are worn, frayed or glazed, or have more than a half-inch of slack when you push them with your thumb, they should be replaced.
- At the same time, check all the hoses connecting various components under the hood. Squeeze them to see if they are unusually brittle or soft. Look for cracks, leaks and signs of swelling, particularly near the clamps. Any of these symptoms can mean that the hose could cause a problem on the road and should be replaced.
- With the engine off, check the level of engine oil in the crankcase by removing the dipstick, wiping it dry, inserting it all the way and pulling it out again. If the level is down to the "add oil" mark or below, put in a quart or more to bring it above the mark. Check the oil filter too, and replace it at intervals recommended in your owner's manual.
- With the engine off, remove the dipstick and check the power-steering fluid in the same way. If the level is low, add the needed fluid or have it done the next time you visit a service station.
- With the engine warmed up and running and the brake on, shift into "drive" and then into "park." Leave the engine idling and check the transmission fluid by removing its dipstick as above. If it does not read "full' or near "full," add fluid. If you do it yourself, be careful not to overfill.
- Remove the big, round air filter atop the engine by unscrewing the lid. See if enough dirt has accumulated to clog the baffles and prevent proper air flow to the carburetor. If the filter needs to be changed, you can do it yourself with a replacement of the same size and type bought at an automotive store.
- Check the brake fluid level by wiping dirt from the lid of the master cylinder reservoir, prying off the retainer clip and removing the lid. Fill with fluid of the recommended type and check for any leaks.
- Make sure the windshield washer reservoir is full and the spray jets are unobstructed. While you are topping off the reservoir with the washer fluid and water, put some of it on a rag and clean off the windshield and the wiper blades.
- Check the battery to see that the cables are securely attached, and clean off any corrosion around the posts. (The light-colored powder can be removed by applying a paste of baking soda and water, waiting a few minutes, then washing it off.) If the battery is not of the permanent, sealed type, remove the caps and add water (preferably distilled water) as

needed until it touches each filler neck and "puckers" a little. Batteries can give off explosive hydrogen fumes. Never smoke or use a lighted match when working near them.

• Test the windshield wiper blades by squirting fluid on the glass and running the wipers. If they streak, miss portions of the glass or chatter, replace the blades.

• Check all lights, including high and low beams, parking lights, brake lights, backup lights, turn signals and emergency flashers to make sure they are working, and clean any dirt off the lenses. Replacement bulbs can be bought at an automotive store.

• Look at the tires for cuts, bulges, large cracks or imbedded nails, and pry out any small stones stuck in the treads. Inspect the treads for uneven wear, which could mean the wheels need alignment. The treads should not be worn down to less than 1/16th of an inch, the minimum required by most states' safety laws. You can easily check this by inserting an ordinary penny into the tire grooves upside down. If the top of Lincoln's head shows, you have less than 1/16th inch left. All new tires now made have bars of solid rubber imbedded in them as wear indicators; if they are showing in two or more adjacent grooves, it is time for a new tire.

• Check the pressure in each tire when it is "cold." A visual inspection is virtually worthless in radial tires, which have a characteristic "bulge," and air-pump gauges at service stations can be inaccurate. The best way to proceed is to buy a good pencil-size hand gauge. (You can get an inexpensive one — along with a tread-depth gauge, four spare valve caps and a glove-compartment guide to better tire mileage and safety — by sending $2.75 to the Tire Industry Safety Council, Box 1801, Washington, D.C. 20013.)

• Keep all your tires, including a regular spare, inflated to the correct pressures found in the owner's manual or noted on the door jamb on the driver's side, on the inside of the glove compartment or on the fender lid that conceals the gas cap. Underinflation not only wastes gas and causes excessive wear on outer treads, but results in flexing and heat build-up that can mean tire failure and a serious accident at high speed. Overinflation causes tires to ride hard and makes them more vulnerable to impact damage and weakening of the tire body.

• While you're down near the tires, look at the inside of the wheels to see if any brake fluid is leaking, and check the shock absorbers for oil seepage too. Test the shocks by bouncing each corner of the car; if the car keeps on bouncing when you release it, it has worn or leaking shocks. They should be replaced, always in pairs.

• Finally, look under the car for loose or broken clamps and supports on the exhaust system, and check for holes in the muffler and pipes. Rusted or damaged parts should be replaced.

Keep It Clean

A clean car not only looks better, it lasts longer. The best way to preserve the finish of an automobile and help avoid rust is to wash it frequently — hosing down the undersides as well as the top — and to wax it at least every six months.

An automatic car wash will get an automobile clean, but washing it yourself is less expensive — and easier on the car. Hand washing also forces you to inspect surfaces for scratches, chips and incipient rust spots you might otherwise overlook. Flood the car first with plenty of water in a broad stream to wash off grit, then use lukewarm water and a mild liquid soap or a good commercial car-wash brand (not a harsh kitchen detergent) applied with a sponge or soft rag. Soak particularly dirty areas with a stronger solution and let them stand for a few minutes. As each section is soaped, wash it clean with cold water from the hose. Avoid washing when the surfaces are hot from the sun; do it in the shade so that they won't dry out quickly or produce spotting. Dry off with a clean, damp cloth or chamois rather than a dry cloth.

While you're washing, get the hose down under the car as far as you can and direct a heavy stream up under the fender walls. Hose off the frame, floor pan, exhaust system, fuel lines and everything else you can reach. Use an old, cut-off broom or a brush to loosen caked mud, road salt, leaves and other debris that can retain moisture and promote rust, then spray again to rinse off the residue. This is especially important in areas where salt or sand is used on icy winter roads, and should be done at least once in midwinter and again in spring — preferably more often. If you can't reach all areas with a full spray, lay down

Signs of Quality

When looking for a repair shop, either for routine work or for emergencies, keep your eye out for garages, dealers and independent mechanics displaying one or both of the signs shown below.

The National Institute for Automotive Service Excellence, a voluntary, nonprofit organization founded by the automobile industry in 1972, has tested and certified a quarter of a million mechanics for competence in eight areas of expertise: engine repair, automatic transmission, manual transmission and rear axle, front end, brakes, electrical systems, heating and air conditioning, and engine tune-up. To earn a certificate in one or more of these categories, a mechanic must have at least two years of on-the-job experience or have spent three years in an apprenticeship program and must pass a difficult two-and-a-half hour examination which is administered by the American College Testing program.

The applicant who qualifies — only two out of three who apply pass the first time around — is entitled to display the certificate in the shop, carry a wallet card and, in addition, may wear the orange, blue and white shoulder patches and bars that signify the categories in which he or she is certified.

A mechanic who passes all the tests has earned the right to wear the special emblem of a General Automobile Mechanic.

To further reduce the motorist's gamble in auto repairs, the American Automobile Association, the nation's largest federation of motoring clubs, identifies those repair shops that have proven they can provide consistent, high-quality, guaranteed work. Started as a pilot program in 1977, AAA's network of "Approved Auto Repair Services" now includes several thousand facilities of all kinds and is growing apace.

To earn the right to display the red, white and blue AAA sign, a garage must submit to rigorous inspection by AAA investigators and must meet high standards in service facilities, mechanic training, appearance, community reputation and, most important, customer satisfaction. Before being approved, the shop must sign a contract with AAA which requires that it offer written estimates to all AAA members, make replaced parts available for inspection and guarantee its work for 90 days or 4,000 miles, whichever comes first. The shop must also agree to cooperate with the AAA in any dispute involving a member and to abide by the association's ruling.

Non-members, of course, are free to use an AAA-approved facility, and indeed may do so with the added assurance that the shop has been carefully screened. Such persons can call or write the local AAA affiliate or the national organization for names of approved shops in their area. However, in order to be eligible for mandatory guarantees and AAA assistance in handling disputes, drivers must be AAA members.

Other organizations that offer assurance of better-than-average repairs and servicing include the Automotive Service Councils, Inc., a nonprofit trade association of local repairmen's groups, which was established in 1955. Members of the association, who may display the ASC logo and code of ethics in their shops, pledge to provide itemized bills, inspection of replaced parts and good repair work at fair prices.

a sprinkler hose equipped with many small holes in a series of curves on the driveway and drive the car back and forth over it with the water on.

If you notice any chips or deep scratches on the exterior finish, catch them before they rust by treating them with matching touch-up paint available at a car dealer or auto supply store. Larger rust spots should be sanded down to bare metal with emery paper, treated with primer and, after that is dry, given one or more coats of touch-up paint. Surfaces caked with grime or stubborn road tar, or where the paint has turned dull, should be gone over with a good liquid cleaning and polishing compound. Finally, give the whole car a thorough waxing with a silicone glazing product or a good old-fashioned hard car wax. For more information on maintaining an automobile's appearance, and thus its resale value, see your owner's manual or get a copy of Shell's "Car Fix-Up Book."

Professional Repairs

In his book *Mr. Badwrench,* Arthur Glickman tells the story of a college professor who stopped at a service station in Colorado because the generator in his car wasn't charging. He asked the station owner to recharge the battery so that he could get to a dealer for the needed repairs. Instead, the owner removed the generator and forced the professor to wait for a replacement — while he stayed at the owner's motel, the only lodging in town. Four long, frustrating days later, the professor had to pay not only a steep motel bill but an exorbitant $175 for another generator, which unhappily soon burned out.

Such horror stories are all too commonplace. U.S. Department of Transportation surveys have indicated that more than 50 cents of every auto repair dollar is wasted. In one undercover test, cars needing only minor repairs or none at all were taken to 62 repair shops in six states. Half of the shops either fixed something that didn't need fixing or failed to fix something that did. Consumer groups and government agencies report that complaints about auto service and repairs outnumber all other consumer protests. Motorists complain of faulty work, outrageous bills, long delays and, in a number of cases, deliberate fraud.

The problem is complex. Garage personnel certainly play their part in it — but so do drivers and the cars they drive. Drivers are keeping their cars longer, so there is a greater need for major repairs — some of which could have been avoided if the drivers themselves had performed some simple preventive maintenance. Moreover, new cars are becoming increasingly sophisticated with smaller, harder-working engines, and are crammed with complicated equipment that makes them more difficult to fix when something goes wrong. Also, it is easier and more profitable to replace components than to take the time for careful diagnosis and repair.

Why Repairs Cost So Much

After leaving his or her car for service in the morning, many a driver has returned to a repair shop to experience what is commonly known as "five-o'clock shock." All the driver asked for was a simple tune-up. Instead, a team of automotive surgeons performed six or seven intricate operations on the vehicle, and replaced several components with new ones. The total bill for parts and labor comes to an astronomical figure.

In this typical tale both car owner and service shop probably bear a part of the blame. But the system is probably the real villain of the piece. Most customers believe they are going to be charged for *repairs* and not a lot of shiny new parts, and that they will be billed for the actual number of hours worked on their cars.

In fact, many repair shops base their labor charges on so-called flat-rate manuals, compilations of average times required to perform common auto repair and maintenance jobs — engine tune-up, replacement of a fuel pump and so on. Originally, flat rates were devised to average out the differences between fast and slow workers, to protect customers from being billed for excessive time and to make it easy for garages to give customers an accurate advance estimate on a given job. Depending on the shop, the mechanic and the manual used, however, they can result in overcharges to the customer.

One study of flat rates showed that mechanics could beat flat-rate times on three-quarters of all jobs, sometimes by considerable amounts. In another study, the New York State Attorney General's office found that 56 percent of automobile repair invoices over-

Seat Belts and Other Safety Devices

Each year, more than 40,000 Americans are killed and between 4 and 5 million are injured in auto accidents. According to the National Highway Traffic Safety Administration, 90 out of every 100 persons killed were not wearing safety belts; at least 57 of those people would have been saved from serious harm had they been using them. Despite this evidence, only one out of 10 motorists regularly uses the belts that have been mandated as standard equipment on all vehicles for almost 20 years —equipment that they pay for when they buy a car.

Safety experts and consumer advocates have long pleaded for changes in car design that would lead to greater safety in accidents, particularly in view of the popularity of smaller cars, which offer less protection than larger ones against injury and death in the case of collisions. To make up for motorists' indifference to their own safety, the activists have also pushed for the adoption of mandatory "passive restraints": lap-and-shoulder belts that automatically encircle occupants as they enter cars; air bags that instantly inflate to cushion bodies thrown forward in a crash. Some progress has been made in safer car design, certain car models are available with airbags and some have lap-and-shoulder belts. But for the millions of drivers whose cars predate these changes, there is only one solution: they — and their passengers — must remember to buckle up.

Even more shocking than the overall statistics of carnage on the road are those that relate to children. The number 1 killer and crippler of our kids is the automobile accident. In recognition of this fact, a growing number of states has enacted laws requiring parents to use restraints — if not for themselves, at least for their youngsters. In most cases, the laws cover children up to the age of four or five, and mandate that the child must ride in a specially designed safety seat meeting federal standards. (All safety seats made since January 1, 1981 must adhere to these standards and be so labeled.) Violations are punished by fines of about $25; however these may be waived if parents show proof that they have purchased an approved seat and are using it.

Before buying a safety seat for your child, try it out to make sure it fits the youngster and can be securely attached within the car. If you choose the one that is most comfortable for your child, you may find that he or she is not only safer, but happier and better behaved in the car.

If cost is a problem for you, check with the hospitals, public service groups and motor clubs in your area. Some of these organizations supply child safety seats for nothing — or at manufacturer's cost. That safety seats work is evidenced by the experience of one insurance company in Michigan, which has actually saved money by giving each customer who has a child a safety seat free of charge.

charged customers for the time mechanics put in by an average of nearly three-quarters of an hour. When the study was done, the average hourly labor rate was $25.26; the overcharge therefore added $18.19 to a typical bill for repairs. Only 30 percent of the customers got a break as a result of the flat-rate system, saving an average of 36 minutes, or $15.15, on their bills. The remaining 14 percent were properly charged, since bill time was essentially the same as clock time worked. On the basis of the conservative assumption that only half the state's 25,000 repair shops used flat-rate manuals, the attorney general's office estimated that New York residents were being overcharged for their automobile service by nearly $75 million a year.

Critics of the flat-rate system contend that the manuals generally exaggerate the times required for an average mechanic to do various jobs, and that most mechanics can beat those times, often by as much as 50 percent.

Since mechanics are usually paid half the hourly labor rate the repair shop charges — and may work for a commission on replacement parts sold — they have a strong incentive to "beat the book" and pocket their share of the profit so that they can get on to another job. In other words, the system encourages speed and the mistakes that often go with it. It also favors the "shotgun" approach — replacing one part after another, faulty or not, until by trial and error the problem is finally corrected. Performing more painstaking diagnostic tests, isolating the problem to one or two parts and repairing or replacing them alone obviously require more time. The customer, of course, is the one who winds up paying, both for unperformed labor and for unneccessary parts. Nor does the system allow much time for a mechanic to road-test a car after repairing it. The customer gets that chore too.

Choosing a Mechanic

Some state and local laws offer consumers adequate protection with respect to auto repair practices. But even if your state or locality offers you only minimal protection, there are some things you can do to increase your chances of getting satisfactory service at a decent price:

• Start looking for a reliable repair shop *before* you are faced with an emergency. If you wait until there is a crisis, you may have to settle for anything you can get. Ask friends and neighbors whom they use and are particularly satisfied with, including the names of the mechanics they trust in any given shop.

• Don't let little problems mushroom into big ones. If you suspect trouble, have it checked immediately. A good way to evaluate garages and mechanics is to try them out on a routine tune-up or a minor repair. If they do the job well, promptly and at reasonable cost, you can go back to them later with bigger jobs.

• Look around the shop and talk to the people. A neat, orderly place doesn't necessarily guarantee spotless work, but it *does* indicate that the work will probably be done in an organized way. And it certainly doesn't hurt if the firm has courteous employees.

• Find out precisely what kinds of work the shop is qualified to do. Ask if individual mechanics are certified in programs conducted by auto manufacturers, oil companies or other industry organizations, and in what areas of automotive repair. Two of the best assurances of a shop's competence are certification of mechanics by the National Institute for Automotive Service Excellence (NIASE) and of the shop itself by the Approved Auto Repair Service program of the American Automobile Association (see box, "Signs of Quality," page 147).

• Will the shop give you a written estimate of repairs beforehand, advise you on additional needed work for your approval, provide a written guarantee on parts and labor, and show you any old parts that have been replaced? Is the shop convenient to where you live or work, and are its prices for typical jobs competitive with others in the area? On major work particularly, you can always get a second or third estimate somewhere else.

• When you have decided on a repair shop and need service, always call ahead for an appointment, allowing several days to a week if the problem is not urgent. Bear in mind that Monday morning is generally the busiest time: not only is the shop dealing with repairs that have just come in, it also has to handle those that are left over from the previous week. Fridays and Saturdays are also apt to be jammed with people trying to get their cars ready for weekend travel. Chances are far better for an appointment — and for good, unhurried service — if you aim for the middle of the week. Describe the problem on the phone. If your automobile has to remain in the shop for a day or two, inquire about obtaining a "loaner" car.

If possible, have repairs done in midweek when shops are usually not crowded and work is less hurried.

• Make a duplicate list of the car's symptoms and of other things you would like to have checked, so that you can leave a copy with the work order and keep a copy for yourself. This is especially important if you do not deal with the mechanic directly when you bring the car in, but have to talk to someone who writes up service orders and relays your communications to the mechanic.

• Don't say that you want "a front-end alignment" or "a new fuel pump" or any other specific repair. You may wind up with just that, while the real problem is something else and remains unrepaired. At the other extreme, don't make a vague request like "put the car in working order." You and the mechanic may have vastly different ideas of what this entails, and you could wind up paying for more than you bargained for. Instead, explain *why* you brought in the car for service. Perhaps the engine is hard to start, or the car hesitates when accelerating, or the steering feels wobbly, or there is a strange smell when you brake, or whatever else you have noticed when you are using the car. A good mechanic, like a good doctor, never wants to be *told* what to do. He wants to know what the problems are so that he can determine a cure based on his training and experience. If you have difficulty putting a problem into words, don't hesitate to ask if a mechanic can go with you for a short demonstration drive.

• Bring in your maintenance and service log, and your warranty if the repairs still come under it. Ask for a written estimate. If the shop needs time to prepare it, leave a telephone number where you can be reached to approve it or any additional needed work discovered by the mechanics as they go over your car. You can request a diagnosis only, with any recommended work and estimated costs submitted for your approval. Don't leave a list of 20 items to be done and expect to have your car back by closing time. If you need your car by a certain hour, list the items in order of priority and discuss with the service writer what can reasonably be accomplished in the allotted time. Don't be offended if you're told you can't go into the back of the shop to talk to the mechanics or watch the work being done. Insurance requirements may forbid your presence in repair areas where you could stumble over something and get hurt.

• If you want to see just how bad your old fuel pump or muffler was, tell the shop manager, in writing, if possible, that you would like to look at any replaced parts when you return. In many states you have the right to keep replaced parts unless they must be returned to the manufacturer or distributor under a warranty agreement. In any case, you may inspect them before they are shipped out.

• Don't sign anything unless you fully understand it. If you are asked to put your name on any authorizations, bills or forms, read the small print first, on both sides of the paper. You surely don't want to sign a blank order for repairs.

• When you pick up the car, make sure you get an itemized bill, check it over and inquire about anything that puzzles you. Ask for a receipt, and keep both bill and receipt in your records. If the repair has not solved the problem, you will need proof of the work that was done and the date. If the shop's warranty on parts and labor is not printed on the bill, ask for it in writing. And allow enough time for a quick test drive to make sure the car is running properly before you take it home.

Notify the shop manager in advance if you want to examine old parts after replacements have been made.

• Try to have your car serviced by the same mechanic each time if at all possible, and get to know him on a personal basis. If he becomes familiar with your car's idiosyncracies and its service record, you will be more likely to get better advice and better work. When he does a particularly good, prompt job, tell him you appreciate it, and consider giving him a bonus if shop policy permits it.

• If you have any complaint, discuss it with the service manager on a friendly, businesslike basis. Many problems are caused by a simple lack of communication and can be rectified easily enough. If you feel you have been overcharged for parts or labor, ask to see the supplier's price list and any flat-rate manual used by the shop.

• If you get into a dispute over a major repair, be sure to check local laws before refusing to pay your bill. Under what is called a mechanic's lien, most states allow a repair shop to seize an owner's automobile and even sell it to satisfy an unpaid bill, no matter how outrageous the charges may seem or how valuable the car. Although some states void such a lien if the shop has not complied with regulations requiring written estimates and authorizations for repairs, it is not wise to take a chance. If a lien could be used in your case, you probably would be wiser to pay the bill and then take the garage owner to small claims court, or a higher court if necessary, to recover your costs.

(continued on page 154)

Offices of the Environmental Protection Agency

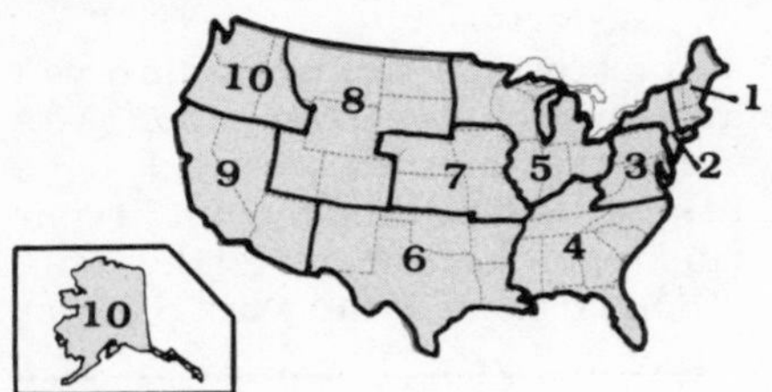

Main Office **401 M Street, SW, Washington, DC 20460**

Region 1 **Connecticut, Maine, Massachusetts, New Hampshire, Rhode Island, Vermont**
John F. Kennedy Federal Building, Boston, MA 02203

Region 2 **New Jersey, New York, Puerto Rico, Virgin Islands**
26 Federal Plaza, New York, NY 10007

Region 3 **Delaware, District of Columbia, Maryland, Pennsylvania, Virginia, West Virginia**
Curtis Building, 6th and Walnut Streets, Philadelphia, PA 19106

Region 4 **Alabama, Florida, Georgia, Kentucky, Mississippi, North Carolina, South Carolina, Tennessee**
345 Courtland Street, NE, Atlanta, GA 30308

Region 5 **Illinois, Indiana, Michigan, Minnesota, Ohio, Wisconsin**
230 S. Dearborn Street, Chicago, IL 60604

Region 6 **Arkansas, Louisiana, New Mexico, Oklahoma, Texas**
First International Building, 1201 Elm Street, Dallas, TX 75270

Region 7 **Iowa, Kansas, Missouri, Nebraska**
324 East 11th Street, Kansas City, MO 64106

Region 8 **Colorado, Montana, North Dakota, South Dakota, Utah, Wyoming**
1860 Lincoln Street, Denver, CO 80295

Region 9 **Arizona, California, Hawaii, Nevada,**
215 Fremont Street, San Francisco, CA 94105

Region 10 **Alaska, Idaho, Oregon, Washington**
1200 6th Avenue, Seattle, WA 98101

Offices of the National Highway Traffic Safety Administration

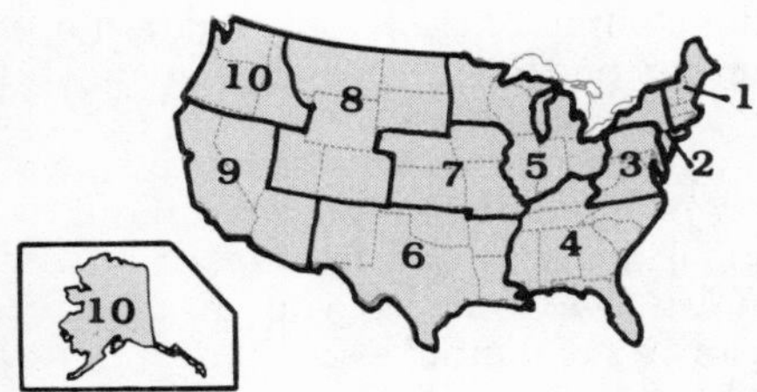

Main Office	**400 Seventh Street, SW, Washington, DC 20590**
Region 1	**Connecticut, Maine, Massachusetts, New Hampshire, Rhode Island, Vermont** 55 Broadway, Cambridge, MA 02142
Region 2	**New Jersey, New York, Puerto Rico, Virgin Islands** 222 Mamaroneck Avenue, White Plains, NY 10605
Region 3	**Delaware, District of Columbia, Maryland, Pennsylvania, Virginia, West Virginia** 793 Elkridge Landing Road, Linthicum, MD 21090
Region 4	**Alabama, Florida, Georgia, Kentucky, Mississippi, North Carolina, South Carolina, Tennessee** 1720 Peachtree Road, NW, Atlanta, GA 30309
Region 5	**Illinois, Indiana, Michigan, Minnesota, Ohio, Wisconsin** 1010 Dixie Highway, Chicago Heights, IL 60411
Region 6	**Arkansas, Louisiana, New Mexico, Oklahoma, Texas** 819 Taylor Street, Fort Worth, TX 76102
Region 7	**Iowa, Kansas, Missouri, Nebraska** P.O. Box 19515, Kansas City, MO 64141
Region 8	**Colorado, Montana, North Dakota, South Dakota, Utah, Wyoming** 555 Zang Street, 1st Floor, Denver, CO 80228
Region 9	**Arizona, California, Hawaii, Nevada** 2 Embarcadero Center, Suite 610, San Francisco, CA 94111
Region 10	**Alaska, Idaho, Oregon, Washington** 3140 Federal Building, 915 2nd Avenue, Seattle, WA 98174

Before going to court, however, check with your state attorney general's office, motor vehicle department, consumer protection agency or local Better Business Bureau about the best course to pursue. If your problem is with the service department of a new-car dealer, you may be able to settle the dispute through the manufacturer's complaint handling system or an AUTOCAP panel in your area (see Chapters 13 and 14).

One protection against shoddy repairs by an authorized service station is to pay your repair bills by a credit card of the oil company affiliated with the station. If you are dissatisfied, you can write the company a letter describing the situation and giving your reasons for not paying their bill. The company may bounce the complaint back to the station operator, thereby putting the pressure on him to make things satisfactory for you.

Never forget the large investment you have in your car or the amount you have spent or will spend in maintaining it properly. Anything you can save — and if you are careful, the total can be substantial — is literally money in the bank.

Chapter 6

In the Mail and at Your Door

In the past, mail-order purchases were precisely what you would expect them to be: purchases you ordered, paid for and received through the mail. Today, the term is much less descriptive. Now, mail-order purchases are often ordered over the telephone (sometimes even by push buttons connected with a television set), paid for by credit card and delivered by private parcel shipping services. For this reason, professionals in the field refer to their work as "direct response marketing." It is a sales area of growing importance: according to its trade organization, the Direct Marketing Association (DMA), by 1990 this way of doing business will account for a full 20 percent of all consumer goods sold in the United States.

Although laws and regulations protect consumers who purchase through direct response, they may face problems, too — not only because honest businessmen in the field make mistakes, as do their counterparts who deal with customers directly — but because the mail order business has a special attraction for fly-by-night operators and other cheats. In this chapter, we will discuss both the legitimate problems you may run up against when you buy through direct response and the frauds you may, unwittingly, fall victim to.

The chapter will also discuss door-to-door selling, a form of merchandising similar to direct response in many respects. More than 35 million Americans buy $6 billion worth of products from door-to-door salespersons every year — not only the vacuum cleaners and encyclopedias which we have traditionally associated with the field, but costume jewelry, cosmetics and vitamins as well.

In addition, the chapter will give attention to two other kinds of big business in the United States that frequently make use of the techniques of direct response marketing and door-to-door sales. One is charity. Make no mistake about it, charity is truly a big business in this country. In the single year of 1981, Americans gave more than $50 billion to charitable causes — and of that sum, more than $40 billion was contributed not by corporations, foundations or other organizations, but by individuals. Most of the money goes to bona fide agencies that channel the greatest portion of the funds they collect into vitally needed services. But some do not spend their money wisely. There are even a few that are downright frauds. This chapter will give you the information you need to be able to distinguish among them.

Finally, the chapter will discuss those offers all of us get — often in the mail — that hold out the hope of bringing money to us, rather than taking it away. Lotteries and sweepstakes contests serve as a means of sales promotion for many companies and as a means of raising funds for state and local governments. Most such lotteries and sweepstakes are entirely legitimate. At the same time that they pay off handsomely for their sponsors, they put millions of dollars into the hands of lucky winners. Unfortunately, neither this book nor any other can give you any inside tips on how to win these gambles if you choose to participate in them. There are no such tips: honest sweepstakes and lotteries are truly matters of chance. On the other hand, they are governed by laws and regulations you should know about so that you can distinguish between the honest and dishonest enterprises.

Direct Mail Marketing

The variety of items sold through direct response marketing is truly astonishing — not only magazines, books and book club sub-

Negative Option Plans

One popular form of mail order buying is through so-called "clubs" — services that, at regular intervals, supply subscribers with specific products, such as fruits, cheeses, records, tapes or books. Most such clubs are direct descendants of a project that originated in the 1920's, when two enterprising advertising men, Maxwell Sackheim and Harry Scherman, thought up an unusual way of selling books by mail. They called it the Book-of-the-Month Club. Soon after the first ad appeared, the club had 40,000 members.

When it began, the Book-of-the-Month Club automatically sent members a book each month at a special price, permitting them to return any unwanted selection within a given period.

The Club soon ran into difficulties. One selection, *The Heart of Emerson's Journals*, did not appeal to many members and, as Harry Scherman put it, "That book came back by the carload."

This calamity led the founders to develop the device now known as the negative option plan. Instead of automatically mailing out selections, each month the club sent subscribers an advance notice, naming the upcoming book, reviewing it, and telling them the selection would be mailed to them unless, within two weeks, they returned a form instructing the club not to send it, or requesting an alternate also described in the advance notice.

From a merchant's point of view, the negative option plan works very well. Sending an advance notice costs far less than absorbing the enormous loss attendant on a flood of returned merchandise. For this reason, the plan was adopted by many mail order clubs established after the Book-of-the-Month Club.

The original negative option plan had drawbacks for consumers, however. To reject an offer, they had to find and address an envelope, and mail it to the company within a certain period of time. If they did not, they automatically received the selection and were billed for it. Given the human tendency to procrastinate, this often happened.

In an effort to protect consumers from receiving and having to pay for goods they did not want, the FTC in 1974 adopted a rule covering negative option plans. The rule is a compromise between the FTC's original proposal — to ban all negative option selling — and the industry's desire to keep things as they were. Consumers still must inform any mail order club to which they belong that they do not want a particular selection, but the rule assures them adequate time and information on which to act. Specifically, it requires that all advertising and other promotional material for any negative option plan must clearly state:

- The nature of the plan.
- Exactly how many items the subscriber has to buy over how long a period of time.
- How often the company sends offers.
- How the subscriber can tell the company that a selection is not wanted.
- Whether billing charges include shipping and handling.
- That the subscriber has a right to cancel membership once the obligation has been fulfilled.

Most important, the negative option rule guarantees subscribers at least 10 days to decide whether they want a given selection and, if they do not have that much time — whether because of late delivery or late mailing by the club — the seller must give them full credit and pay the shipping cost for items they return.

Like magazine subscriptions, negative option plans are exempt from the 30-day Rule discussed in this chapter. The rule *does* apply, however, to any introductory merchandise or bonus goods offered. The seller must ship these items within 30 days of receiving the order; if for any reason he cannot, he must notify subscribers of the delay and give them the option of canceling the subscription.

scriptions; shoes and clothing; records, tapes and cassettes; seeds, plants and garden supplies; film and film-developing services; hobby and craft equipment; housewares and foods; but even college courses and diamonds. Indeed, virtually every product the inventive American mind can think of is available through direct response. And almost every communication medium is used to bring these products to the attention of the American public — radio and television, newspapers and magazines, even matchbook covers. And, of course, the famous mail-order catalogs, through which a major part of all direct response buying is done.

The pioneer in catalog selling was Aaron Montgomery Ward, who began his business in 1872 with $1,600 in capital and a catalog made up of a single letter-size sheet of paper listing his wares and prices and telling how to order them. Within two years, the single sheet had grown to an eight-page booklet and by the early 1890's, Ward's completely illustrated catalog ran 540 pages and listed 24,000 items; his original 12- by 14-foot shipping room had grown into a building with an area of 120,000 square feet and his company — Montgomery Ward — was doing more than a million dollars worth of business a year.

Ward did not enjoy a monopoly in the mail-order field for long. In 1874 R. H. Macy published its first catalog, and in 1886 Richard W. Sears began a mail-order business with a case of $12 watches, some 50-cent chairs and cheap kitchen tables. Sears saw his mail-order receipts increase from $5,000 in his first six months to more than $40 million a year in less than a generation. Since then, the field has continued to grow. Today, all kinds of businesses sell by catalog — retail stores as well as mail-order companies; specialty firms as well as those that carry a variety of merchandise; firms that sell luxury items as well as those that stock only routine goods. Millions of catalogs are mailed out yearly: according to the DMA the average American household receives 40 every year.

The Pluses and Minuses of Direct Response Buying

The principal advantage of direct response buying is obvious: it is extremely convenient. The cost and trouble of shopping, the effort of fighting one's way through department store crowds only to wait in line for a cashier — all of these make buying from home a very appealing idea. In addition, since women do most of the shopping in the United States and more and more of them are working, convenience is especially important. About half of the country's working women have young children at home, so their time is at a premium. Buying merchandise through direct response saves precious hours.

Direct response buying has other advantages. Some specialty items — exotic foods and hobby supplies, for example — are often more easily available through direct response than in any other way. Some items are less expensive. For example, it is cheaper to buy magazines by subscription than to purchase individual issues at the newsstand. Book clubs usually sell their selections for less than those same volumes cost in most bookstores. Other merchandise, too, may be less expensive even when you add the cost of shipping and handling: it is advisable to do some comparison shopping before you buy. Certainly prices are not always lower. Direct response marketers may spend less on rent and sales personnel than do retail merchants, but they spend more on advertising — which serves as their only sales force — and on filling orders. On the whole, products bought through direct response cost about the same as they do at retail stores.

On the other hand, direct response buying has its disadvantages. Because, by its nature, the mail-order business keeps consumers from direct, personal contact with merchants, it holds a particular attraction for unscrupulous and fly-by-night operators — both those who specialize in shoddy or fraudulent goods and those who do not even bother to fill their customers' orders. Direct mail fraud is a serious problem for consumers, which we will discuss in detail later in this chapter.

Like all other merchants, mail-order firms are bound by the Wheeler-Lea Amendment, which prohibits unfair and deceptive advertising, and are subject to Federal Trade Commission guides relating to advertising practices. (See Chapter 2.) But even the most ethical advertisement can be an insufficient guide. A product that looks good in a photograph may not look equally good when it arrives. Clothing may not fit properly, even if the size is correct, or it may be unbecoming.

Pots and pans may have more — or less — heft than you expected. Nor is there any salesperson of whom you can ask the questions that may occur to you. The only information you have is what the seller chooses to give you in the advertisement or catalog.

Another disadvantage of direct response buying is the wait for delivery and, if you have a problem with the merchandise, the wait for satisfaction either by replacement or refund. Federal protections, discussed in the following section, cover you in some cases of unusual delay, but they cannot prevent slow delivery from occurring. When you order a product by mail or telephone, the date on which you will actually receive it can seldom be predicted exactly. It may be weeks before you get your goods — especially if, as sometimes happens, a computer jumbles the zip code and the package is sent to the wrong city or state. What is more, when the package arrives, the goods may be damaged or otherwise unacceptable, and then the process of waiting begins again. Reputable mail-order companies work hard — and usually successfully — to give their customers good service, to see that deliveries are made promptly to the correct addresses, and to handle complaints quickly and expeditiously.

The 30-day Rule

To deal with the problem of delays, the Federal Trade Commission (FTC) has established the 30-day Rule, which guides the practices of merchants who sell by mail, and offers protection to consumers against unreasonable delay — both in receiving merchandise they have ordered and in getting refunds to which they are entitled.

The rule does not apply to direct response orders that do not involve the mail in any way — as, for example, orders placed by telephone and either charged (also by telephone) to a credit card or paid for on delivery. Nor does it cover situations in which the seller clearly states in his advertisement or order form that delivery will take more than 30 days, in such a phrase as "Allow six to eight weeks for delivery." If you order anything described in this manner, you have then accepted the seller's terms and he has nearly two months in which to send your merchandise. On the other hand, once he has your order, he has accepted the obligation of delivering it within the period he promised.

But if the seller does not specifically state that the waiting period will exceed 30 days, the rule gives him only that much time to make delivery. He cannot escape it by such vague statements as "Shipment will be made as soon as possible." He still has 30 days, and no more.

The 30-day period covered by the rule begins when the seller receives your properly completed order or — if you are buying on credit — when he enters the charge against your account. If you have not received your order by 30 days after that, the rule gives you the right to cancel it and get your money back. (See Chapter 13 for procedure to follow.)

Merchants who sell products by mail must notify purchasers when an item can't be delivered in 30 days.

In addition, the rule requires a company that discovers it will be unable to deliver your merchandise within 30 days (or some longer period, if it has so stipulated) to send you a first-class letter before that period has elapsed, notifying you of the delay, informing you of the revised shipping date and giving you the option of canceling your order and getting your money back. The rule also requires that the company supply you with a means of doing so at no cost to you, by sending you a postage-paid card, for example.

If the letter informs you that the shipping delay will be 30 days or less, you have a choice of canceling your order or accepting the new date. If you want to cancel, be sure to mail the prepaid form that was sent you. If you do not, the 30-day Rule interprets that as consenting to the delay.

If, on the other hand, the letter informs you that the delay will be more than 30 days, the opposite holds true. Your order will be automatically canceled *unless* you return the company's prepaid form within 30 days.

In the event the company discovers it cannot meet its revised shipping date, it must again send you a notice, enclosing a postage-paid form and offering you the same options as before. In this case, too, the order is automatically canceled unless you reply within 30 days — or unless the shipment is already on its way by the time that your reply arrives.

If you want to cancel in either of these situations, you will get your refund much more quickly if you expressly inform the company of that fact. Under those circumstances, the firm has seven working days after receipt of your request to give you a refund in full or, if you've charged your purchase on a credit card, one billing cycle to remove the charge. If you cancel by default — by simply not replying to the company's announcement of a delay longer than 30 days or a second delay after you've accepted that one — the firm has seven days beyond the implied date of cancellation in which to make a refund or, if you've charged your purchase, one billing cycle beyond the implied date.

The 30-day Rule gives you an even broader right to cancel if the company's letter to you does not specify the length of the delay. Under these circumstances, you can cancel your order at any time before you receive it, even if you have previously agreed to take the merchandise.

Certain kinds of direct response businesses are exempt from the 30-day Rule. It does not cover photo-finishing services or firms that sell seeds and growing plants. Gardeners usually order several months in advance for delivery at a later planting date, and nurseries are among the oldest and most reputable mail-order companies in existence; complaints are seldom received about this category of mail order.

The first delivery on a magazine subscription is covered by the 30-day Rule, but the rule does not apply to the delivery of subsequent issues. The FTC has found that delivery problems having to do with subscriptions to magazines tend to cluster around the first issue, and there are usually few complaints after that. Nor does the rule apply to the so-called "negative option" plans that are used by most book clubs and other mail-order clubs. (See box, page 156.)

The 30-day Rule is a useful protection for consumers dealing with reputable direct response merchants. But if you become involved with one who is less than honest, you may find that the protection itself presents a problem. For obvious reasons, no consumer protection agency — federal, state or local, public or private — will help you with a complaint about mail-order purchases until you have waited the full 30 days that the rule allows. This creates a large loophole for unscrupulous merchants to slip through. The guiding principle of just about every fraudulent direct response company can be summed up in five short words: "Get the money and run." A company may successfully bilk the public of hundreds of thousands of dollars, close up shop and disappear long before a law enforcement agency can close in on it. Therefore, before placing an order, it is particularly important to check the credentials of any direct response firm with which you are not already familiar.

Placing a Direct Response Order

The best way to prevent difficulty with direct response orders is to take the proper precautions before placing them. The first step is to make sure that the company you are dealing with is honest. Try to do business with firms you know or have heard of, or firms your friends do business with. Ask around — in these times, direct response buying is so common that it shouldn't be difficult to find someone who has had experience with the company in which you are interested. Another way to find out is to get in touch with your local Better Business Bureau (see directory, page 32). Bureaus nationwide maintain a list of problem companies and, if you ask about a specific firm, will tell you whether complaints have been received about it.

Once you are satisfied that the company is reliable, you are ready to go ahead. If you are thinking of buying something you have learned about through a print medium, read the catalog copy or advertisement and order form carefully. If an ad appears in a newspaper or magazine, do not assume, simply because you like and trust the publication, that the advertisement is equally trustworthy. Most media have guidelines for advertising acceptance, but these do not automatically guarantee either the accuracy or the legitimacy of the ads. Some guidelines are less than rigid, and even the most stringent guidelines are not proof against human error and the consequent appearance of an unethical or dishonest ad.

Make sure the descriptive copy spells out everything you need to know about the merchandise involved: size, weight, color, contents and any other relevant product informa-

CONSUMER ALERT

Getting on and off Mailing Lists

If you subscribe to a magazine, own a credit card, have ever bought anything through direct response or contributed to any kind of organization in response to a mail appeal — if, in other words, your name has ever appeared on any mailing list anywhere — you can be fairly sure of hearing from a variety of companies and groups with which you have never dealt directly. Not only is the rental of their mailing lists a source of additional revenue to many firms and agencies, there is an entire industry of companies whose only business is renting out mailing lists.

Many of us have no objection to receiving this unrequested material, but others are annoyed to discover their mail boxes crammed with it every day. Even the U.S. Privacy Protection Study Commission, while rejecting the concept that unsolicited mail is a trespass on personal privacy, agrees that it can be a nuisance and has recommended that mail-list users remove from their lists the names of those who do not want to be included on them.

Some companies inform customers that they rent out their mailing lists, and include in their catalogs instructions for those who want their names deleted from such rental lists. This may lessen the amount of mail, but will not eliminate it.

The most effective way to get your name off mailing lists is to write to DMA Mail Preference Service, 6 East 43rd Street, New York, New York 10017 and request a name-removal form. You will receive material to complete and return, and when you have done so, your name and address will be sent to all the companies affiliated with the DMA — there are more than 2,000 — and you will no longer receive mail from them.

This does not mean, however, that you will eliminate all unwanted mail. You will still get material from groups that are not affiliated with the DMA. To get your name off their lists, you will have to write directly to the companies.

Consumers who want to get *on* mailing lists, rather than off them, should write to the address above and ask for the "More Mail" form. On it you may designate the kinds of mailings you are interested in receiving. The service, however, cannot guarantee that you will get exactly what you have asked for.

tion. Do not rely on photographs or so-called "puff" copy — copy that depends on a writer's skillful use of language rather than on straightforward information to persuade you to buy. Read the details.

If the company gives a post office box as its address, make sure it has a street address also. In some states, the law requires that a street address be listed, but even if there is no such requirement where you live, the information is important. A street address is not an automatic assurance that the company is honest, but it does suggest that it is stable and not fly-by-night. If you can find no street address, write or phone the company to learn it before placing your order.

Check the ad or catalog for mention of a warranty — or, as it is sometimes called, a guarantee. Federal guidelines, established under the Magnuson-Moss Warranty Act, which is described in detail in Chapter 7, cover all warranties or guarantees on merchandise, whether sold in a store or through direct response. These guidelines require that the seller of direct response merchandise either provide a copy of the warranty in the catalog, sales brochure or ad, or make one available to any prospective customer who requests it in writing.

You will probably feel more comfortable if you do business with a company that offers an across-the-board guarantee. Most reputable direct response firms make this offer. Their guarantees cover the entire product and assure you of your choice of adjustment if, within the period of the guarantee, you return the product for any reason whatever — except, of course, if you yourself have damaged it. The guarantee may be phrased as "Satisfaction guaranteed or your money back in 30 days" or "Ten days' free trial" or some similar statement, as long as the words make the meaning perfectly clear — that the buyer has the right to change his or her mind, and return an item, in perfect condition, within the time period stated. Moreover, if you *do* return it under the terms of this guarantee, the company cannot compel you to accept a merchandise credit if you do not want one. The company must refund your money or exchange the product, whichever you prefer.

If a company offers an unqualified "lifetime" guarantee, FTC regulations construe this as a guarantee for *your* lifetime — unless the company specifically states that it means some other lifetime. A company that sells car batteries with a "lifetime" guarantee, for example, cannot refuse your claim against it in the event the battery fails to perform by saying that the guarantee referred to the lifetime of the car.

Once you have checked the ad or catalog copy in detail, you are ready to fill out the order blank. And here it is important for you to take just as much care as you did in examining the ad. Incomplete or improperly filled-out order forms are a major cause of shipping delays. Print legibly — neatness really counts. The order form may ask you to indicate a second choice — of color or fabric, for example. If you have a second choice, mark it in the appropriate place. However, if you want only your first choice and nothing else, then write "no substitute" on the order form. Even if the form does not ask for your second choice, write "no substitute" if you do not want one. Some companies automatically substitute a comparable item if the one you ordered happens to be unavailable.

Finally, make a copy of your filled-out order form on a copying machine or, if that is inconvenient, by writing down the name, address and phone number of the company, the specifics of your order and the date on which it was placed. If you have the ad from which you placed the order, keep that also. And keep a copy of the guarantee. File all these papers in a place you will remember if you have need of them.

Make your payment by check, money order or credit card, being sure — in the first two cases — to include any shipping and handling charges and the sales tax where required. (See box, page 162.) Despite warnings, people still tend to send cash through the mail, especially when the amount is a nice round figure, like $1 or $5. But it is an extremely poor idea. Aside from the obvious risk of theft, there is the fact that you have no record of payment, should any problem arise.

If the company turns out to be dishonest, the difficulties will be compounded. Many fraudulent mail-order businesses make their profit by doing a large volume of business in small sums — all too often sent in cash. When and if the law catches up with them, consumers who have paid in cash will have much more difficulty in getting their money back, since they have no proof of payment. Those who pay by check, credit card or money order *do* have proof of payment and are in a much better position.

The precautions we have just discussed also apply to purchases made on the basis of television or radio commercials. Here, too, bear in mind that the commercial may not be entirely trustworthy, no matter how large and prestigious the broadcasting station may be. You may find it somewhat difficult to determine the exact nature of the warranty or the company's return policy, or to get all the other necessary information in the brief period that the commercial lasts. Still, it is important for you to know these things before you place your order. A second exposure to the commercial may help. If you do not know when you will see or hear it again, write to the advertiser or telephone the 800 number usually given in the ad and ask for a fact sheet about the product and — if the commercial gives only a post office box as the address — for the company's street address. The operators at the 800 number are probably qualified only as order takers and are not likely to be able to answer your specific questions about the product or the terms of sale. But they can and should pass along your requests to the company.

Sending cash through the mail is a needless risk. You have no proof of payment and face the danger of theft.

If you decide to order, keep a record of the transaction for yourself — including information as to date, time and station; whether you ordered by mail or phone; the guarantee policy and other terms of sale; and how you made payment — whether by check, money order or credit card (again, remember *never* to send cash) and, if by credit card, the specific card you used for the transaction. This is particularly important in the case of a telephone order, since it does not give you the protection of the 30-day Rule.

Once you have ordered, you can sit back and — if all goes well — relax. Your package will arrive in a few weeks — and be satisfactory in every way. But all may not go well. There are a number of legitimate reasons for which there may be a delay in delivery. The company may have been so swamped with orders for a particular item that it ran out of stock — in which case, if the organization sells by mail, it is required by the 30-day Rule to notify you of the delay and give you an opportunity to cancel. Or your shipment may have been sent to the wrong address or lost in transit. In these cases, it is up to you to notify the company that a problem exists.

It is always best to make that notification in writing rather than over the telephone, so that you have a record to which you can, if necessary, refer.

The information you kept about your order when you placed it should form the basis of your letter. State clearly and precisely all the data the merchant will need: what you ordered (the number of items and their description and identification numbers); when you ordered; how much you paid and the method of payment — check, credit card or money order. It is helpful to include backup material that will support your statements: a copy of the ad or order blank; a copy of your canceled check or money order receipt or your credit card bill. Do not send the originals of these documents. And always keep a copy of the letter you send.

Before you mail it, make sure you have included your address as well as your name. A surprising number of people sign their letters but fail to put a return address in the communication. (A sample letter of complaint will be found in Chapter 13.)

A legitimate company will usually respond to your letter within 10 days, telling you what action it has taken to satisfy you, and giving you the option of canceling your order and receiving a full refund. If the company replies by telling you that the merchandise was shipped, remember that the sender is responsible for trying to trace it and, if the package cannot be located, for replacing it or refunding your money. If the company does not reply, follow one of the procedures outlined in "Going Public", below.

CONSUMER ALERT

Sales Tax and Direct Response Purchases

As you have no doubt noticed, there is no set procedure about the payment of state sales taxes on merchandise ordered through direct response. Sometimes you will be asked to make such payment; sometimes you will not. The reason for this apparent inconsistency is simple: the states that have sales taxes have different laws concerning the collection of these taxes from the companies headquartered in them.

The laws will be reflected in statements made on the order forms or in the ads for direct response merchandise. Most direct response companies will be quite explicit. A New Jersey firm, for example, will state "New Jersey residents add 6 percent sales tax." But if neither the ad nor the order form specifically says "Add Sales Tax," you do not have to include it. Moreover, if the statement reads "Add appropriate sales tax" or "Add sales tax where applicable," you have to add it only if you live in the state where the company has its headquarters.

Note that when you do pay sales tax, you pay it only on the cost of the merchandise, and not on the shipping and handling costs.

Cancellations, Returns and Refunds

If merchandise you have ordered through the mail does not arrive within the period prescribed by the 30-day Rule and you decide that you want to cancel, write to the company giving the necessary information about the order and stating that you want to cancel because the merchant has failed to deliver within the time the 30-day Rule allows.

A similar method of action applies if you receive the wrong merchandise or damaged merchandise. Give the same information as in the case of cancellations, and include a paragraph explaining what is wrong with the merchandise and ask for a proper replacement. Under these circumstances, you can ask for a refund only if the merchandise is covered by an across-the-board guarantee that specifically assures you of this right.

Do not do anything more until you hear from the company. It is particularly important not to return or otherwise dispose of damaged merchandise until then. Return policies on damaged goods may vary, and if you are to get an exchange or a refund, you must follow the company's written instructions.

If the company asks you to return the merchandise, be sure to get a receipt from any private delivery service the company chooses to pick it up, or from the post office, if you are asked to send it via mail. If you mail the merchandise, the company should reimburse you for the postage.

You may want to return direct response merchandise for other reasons. Perhaps the product does not live up to its description or the claims that were made for it. A "machine washable" bathrobe that costs $50 and falls apart the third time you wash it has certainly failed to live up to its claims. Here again, send the company a letter of complaint and keep the bathrobe until you receive a response. The firm will doubtless ask you to send back the bathrobe (in this case, you may have to pay the postage) and, once it has confirmed your complaint about the item, will return your money or credit your account.

Or suppose you order a box of assorted cheeses from a mail-order catalog and, when it arrives, find that the products are not of the quality you expect. Whatever the names on the individual packages, all of them seem to you to taste the same. Even though taste is a subjective matter, you should express your dissatisfaction to the company in such a case. Specialty food sales bring in millions of dollars every year to direct response companies, and most are eager to satisfy their customers so that they can look forward to repeat sales. You are, therefore, more than likely to get a refund if you complain. You may not even have to return the uneaten cheeses — which saves you time, effort and postage.

Most reputable direct response firms have liberal return policies, comparable to those found in department stores. You will probably be able to return undamaged merchandise for no other reason than that you have changed your mind — providing, of course, that you do so within the specified time.

Once you have returned mail-order merchandise — making sure always to write the company that the package is on the way, to keep a copy of your letter and to get and hold the receipt for the package if you have accepted it — the ball is in the company's court. It has to send you a refund or — if you have bought through a charge card — credit your account. Except for cancellations under the 30-day Rule, there are no regulations as to the time a company may take to do this. Reputable firms try to act within a week of receiving returned goods, but hitches can occur.

This is one of the reasons it is advantageous to charge mail-order purchases to a credit card, if you have one. The card provides you with an added avenue of recourse and, therefore, additional protection. If the firm to

CONSUMER ALERT

What to Do With Unordered Goods

If you happen to receive something in the mail that you are sure you did not order, the law nevertheless permits you to keep such merchandise without paying for it — unless it is goods associated with your participation in a negative option plan. (See page 156.)

This applies not only to the free samples that manufacturers frequently distribute and to the small articles that charities sometimes include in mailing campaigns to solicit funds, but also to any and every other kind of unordered merchandise you may receive through the mail. You are under no obligation either to pay for or to return such material.

If you are the recipient of unsolicited merchandise about which you are subsequently pressured — whether to return it or to pay for it — report the matter to the Postal Inspection Service.

Such activity is a violation of the law, and action will be taken against the offending company.

which the merchandise was returned has acted promptly, the charge will be removed from your bill in one billing cycle. But if the charge remains, you can — and should — inform the credit card company. Write a letter giving your card number, describing the situation and enclose a copy of the receipt the post office or delivery service gave you when you sent the package back. The credit card company will then get in touch with the mail-order firm to straighten out the situation.

Going Public

If, after a reasonable period — 30 days, for example — you have been unable to resolve a problem with a mail-order company, a number of options are open to you. You can get in touch with your local Office of Consumer Affairs, which may be able to intercede on your behalf (see directory, page 16). The Better Business Bureau may also be able to help (see directory, page 32). If you ordered the merchandise through an advertisement in a newspaper or magazine, or a commercial announcement over a radio or television station, it would be a good idea to get in touch with the advertising acceptance department of the carrier involved. As we have already pointed out, the media cannot be held legally responsible in this area. Nevertheless, a carrier may be willing to put pressure on the advertiser to satisfy your complaint. Moreover, many stations and publications maintain a watch on advertisers, logging the number and type of complaints so that they can keep track of companies that are not living up to their advertising promises.

In addition, there are three agencies particularly interested in mail-order problems.

The Direct Marketing Association (DMA), which was established in 1917 as an advocate for the industry, includes in its membership most of the large mail-order firms in the United States. The DMA is eager to keep the business it represents in the good graces of the public and government regulatory agencies by maintaining and promoting ethical practices and by ridding the industry of unscrupulous operators.

To help consumers, the DMA has established a Mail Order Action Line, which mediates problems between consumers and mail-order companies — not only those that belong to the DMA, but those that do not. (Membership in the DMA does not mean that a company is complaint-proof, any more than nonmembership signifies unreliability. However, according to a DMA spokesman, most complaints are against nonmembers.)

To use the action line, submit your complaint in writing — *not* by telephone — to: DMA Mail Order Action Line, 6 East 43rd Street, New York, New York 10017.

Include in your letter all the details of the transaction and indicate how you would like to have the problem resolved — whether by refund or exchange. Include a copy of your proof of payment — canceled check, money order receipt or credit card statement. Also include any other supporting evidence you may have, such as a copy of the ad from which you made the purchase. If you have already written to the mail-order company, send along a copy of that letter too.

The DMA will contact the company immediately, and then send you a postcard informing you of this fact and asking you to wait four weeks. If your complaint is not satisfied by that time, the action line will take the next step. Although you may have to wait as much as two months for a resolution of your problem, a DMA representative estimates that 85 to 90 percent of companies will solve the problem as soon as it is brought to their attention. "The only time we run into trouble" this representative says, "is when the company has gone out of business."

Just the threat of an investigation will often cause a company to improve its business methods.

Although the Federal Trade Commission (FTC) does not handle individual consumer complaints, you should nevertheless inform the agency about any unresolved problems with direct response merchants. Through the use of a computer system, the FTC regularly tracks the direct response industry to make sure that companies comply with fair-trade regulations and rules. Consumer complaints are fed into its computer, and when any pattern of abuse shows up in connection with a given company, the commission will launch an investigation.

If the company in question is fraudulent or

persists in unacceptable practices, that investigation is likely to lead to prosecution by the U.S. Department of Justice. But often the simple threat of an investigation results in improvement in a company's trade practices. "If they're not keeping good records, if they're not fulfilling their obligations as a seller, they may agree to improve their systems if they hear from us," says a representative of the FTC.

You may file a complaint with the Federal Trade Commission, Office of the Secretary, at headquarters in Washington, D.C. or at the regional office nearest you (see directory, page 199). Your grievance will be entered into the computer system and directed to the appropriate department of the agency.

The U.S. Postal Inspection Service, the government agency most directly involved in mail-order consumer fraud, is prepared to intercede on behalf of individual consumers in cases where they have been unable to resolve mail-order problems on their own. If you have such a complaint against a mail-order company, you can send a letter describing the details of your transaction to the Postal Inspector in your region. (See directory, page 175.) The Postal Inspection Service will then write to the mail-order company and, if the firm is legitimate, you will probably receive a prompt response.

Bear in mind, however, that the Postal Inspection Service can act only on complaints involving the use of the mails. If you placed your order by telephone and received your merchandise through a private delivery service, the postal authorities have no jurisdiction and cannot act in any way.

The Postal Inspection Service does more than merely handle individual consumer problems. It investigates and tracks down all fraudulent use of the mails. The service is a full-fledged law enforcement agency — the oldest in the country — whose origins go back before the American Revolution, when the British colonial authorities named Benjamin Franklin postmaster at Philadelphia. After the Continental Congress in 1775, Franklin named William Goddard as Surveyor of the Post Office; in 1801 Goddard's Surveyors became special agents. As the nation expanded westward, the surveyors moved with the frontier, protecting the fledgling mail service and tilting with mail-train bandits.

Today's postal inspectors are the direct descendants of Goddard's special agents. They have full powers of arrest and, year in and year out, 98 percent of their criminal cases result in convictions. In one recent year alone, the service was responsible for 5,490 convictions and for the collection of $15.8 million in recoveries, restitutions and fines.

The powers of the Postal Inspection Service derive from legislation originally passed by Congress in 1872 in the wake of a rash of mail swindles that erupted after the Civil War. The Mail Fraud Statute — Section 1341 of Title 18 of the U.S. Code — provides for a fine of up to $1,000 and imprisonment of up to five years, or both, for each count of mail fraud. It goes hand in hand with the following section — Section 1342 — which makes it a criminal offense to use false and fictitious names and addresses in operating any business. Together, these sections make it possible for the U.S. Attorney General's office, which prosecutes cases developed by the Postal Inspection Service, to bring very serious charges against defendants in mail fraud cases. Every single piece of mail the Postal Inspection Service collects in any given case can be put in evidence when a case is tried, and each piece qualifies as a separate count of fraud. If the inspectors collect no more than 10 pieces of mail, a defendant could, in theory, be charged with 10 counts of mail fraud and, if convicted, could be fined $10,000 and imprisoned for up to 50 years.

In addition to the Mail Fraud Statute, the Postal Inspection Service makes use of the False Representations Statute — Section 3005, Title 39 of the U.S. Code. This statute authorizes the Postal Service to withhold mail delivery and payment of postal money orders from any firm or individual using false representations to solicit money by mail. It thus enables the service to take effective action against firms it cannot reach through the criminal statutes. By withholding their mail and their money order payments, it can put them out of business.

Mail-order Fraud

However, mail-order fraud is extremely difficult to stamp out. The Postal Inspection Service may not be able to gather enough evidence to make a case that demonstrates a defendant's guilt beyond the reasonable doubt required by criminal law. Regulatory agencies can take civil action against mail-order manipulators, and the Postal Inspection Service can use the False Representations Statute against them. But this may not be sufficient. Mail-order fraud specialists are chronic, repeat offenders. They may consent to stop one promotion only to begin another with a slightly different claim. Or they may close up shop and then resurface later, under a new name and address.

The most effective weapon against such charlatans is our refusal, as consumers, to deal with them. This means that we must be alert and vigilant. For mail-order swindlers sell anything and everything, from the get-rich-quick chain letter, work-at-home and start-your-own-business schemes — which we have discussed in Chapter 3 — to such products as cameras and wigs.

Ads for non-bargains as well as real ones appear in hobby magazines.

Cameras and electronic equipment are often sold at heavily discounted prices through mail-order ads placed by legitimate merchants in the pages of hobby magazines. This very fact acts as a lure to shady merchandisers, who take advantage of readers' expectations that they will find genuine bargains available from reputable merchants.

Some such firms run ads offering a package that, on its face, appears to be a considerable bargain: four related items, for example, one of which is described by a well-known and respected brand name, so that prospective customers are led to believe that the other products are of that brand too. When the packages arrive, buyers discover that they have been deceived *and* cheated. They get the one brand-name item mentioned in the advertisement, but the other three items are of an inferior make. Often the bargain is not a bargain, given the low price at which the unbranded merchandise would ordinarily be retailed.

Sometimes the ads serve as the bait in the illegal marketing practice known as "bait-and-switch": the technique of advertising an apparent bargain and, when customers endeavor to buy it, maneuvering them into purchasing a more expensive version of the same product. A well-known brand of camera, for example, may be advertised for sale by mail at a considerable reduction from the usual retail price. When the consumer sends in money, the company writes to announce it no longer has the advertised model, but *does* have one that sells for a great deal more. You can be sure that customers who do not want the more expensive cameras will have a difficult time getting their money back.

Occasionally, ads for camera sales are nothing more than outright efforts to steal. A few years ago, a mail-order operator offered a very popular family camera for sale in a photography magazine at a price so low that it aroused the suspicions of at least one reader, who notified the Postal Inspection Service. The service caught up with the con artist just in time. He had no cameras in stock, but had already deposited thousands of dollars in his bank account and had additional thousands stashed away in his home. He also had a huge stack of envelopes, which contained nearly $175,000 worth of orders for his nonexistent cameras. But even the quick and efficient work of the Postal Inspectors did not bring restitution to all the victims. Nearly 900 eager camera buffs had been so carried away that they had sent their payments in cash and had failed to enclose their return addresses. As a result, the U.S. Treasury Department was enriched by more than $17,000 — the amount the Postal Service turned over to it.

Women's wigs have also provided swindlers with very tidy incomes. One such cheat relieved nearly 100,000 women of $1.5 million by giving wigs away as "free prizes." Of course, they were not free. To claim them, the women had to buy a plastic head form for $1.50 and two wig stylings for $7.50 each. And when the wigs arrived, the women found that they in no way lived up to the claim that had been made for them: that they were fashioned of 100 percent human hair. They were made of acetate yarn, and fell apart at the touch.

Enraged, thousands of women complained to the authorities, and not too long thereafter the swindler was indicted for and convicted of mail fraud. But while he was still out on bail, he managed to do another $160,000 worth of business — and to generate more thousands of complaints. After he had served a term in prison, he bounced right back into the mail-order business.

Beauty, diet and health "aids" are among the most lucrative of all markets for mail-order swindlers. Useless devices of all sorts are promoted in ads that glitter with a promise all of us would like to believe: that we can have health, beauty, vitality and happiness without expending any effort at all. But there are no magic keys to health and beauty, and no instant ways to achieve them.

Directories and special interest publications are often used as lures in mail-order scams. Con artists send bills to businessmen to pay for listings in some "forthcoming directory," or solicit them for ads in a "forthcoming journal." All too often, the businessmen respond without bothering to investigate, in hopes of generating income for themselves. The publications may never appear, and if they do, they are likely to be poorly printed and have such limited distribution that they bring in no business at all.

One con man made half a million dollars by selling advertisements in a nonexistent magazine that he described as widely read by police officers. He induced businessmen to part with their money by sending them an official looking wallet card that, he said, would save them from getting speeding tickets. The card, of course, did not prevent a single policeman from issuing a single ticket.

Some con men specialize in selling phony insurance through the mail. They are happy to sign up drivers whose poor records make them uninsurable by legitimate companies, and even to give them bargain rates. But the policies offer no coverage whatever, since the insurance companies do not exist, and the premiums go directly into the operators' pockets.

Before buying any kind of insurance by mail, you should always investigate. Ask questions by calling the toll-free number that the ad should list. Or write the company for free brochures and information. The Direct Marketing Insurance Council, a division of the DMA, offers a free booklet, "Ten Do's Before You Buy Insurance by Mail," which you can get by writing the DMA at the address given earlier in this chapter.

Door-to-door Sales

Since the late 18th century, when sturdy Yankee peddlers traveled the countryside from New England through the South and Midwest, door-to-door selling has been a part of American folklore. It has also been the first step in the making of some great American fortunes. Adam Gimbel started out by peddling notions; John Jacob Astor, baked goods; and John D. Rockefeller by selling patent medicine.

Today, shoppers can buy a myriad of products, from small and inexpensive items to high-cost merchandise, through door-to-door salespeople. Cosmetics, encyclopedias, vacuum cleaners, housewares, costume jewelry, home maintenance services, vitamins, food supplements, toys, hobby crafts, photo albums, security systems, cookware and cutlery— all can be purchased right in our own homes. Many of us like shopping in this fashion. We enjoy the convenience of having the merchandise brought straight to the door, the personalized service and attention that we get, the time we save in travel and the fact that we can get a product demonstration in privacy.

If we buy from reputable companies, the products we purchase are of good quality and are supported by the same guarantees and warranties as those offered in retail stores. And the salespeople we deal with — in eight out of 10 cases they are women, usually working as self-employed, independent entrepreneurs who often handle the products of several firms — are eager to see that we are satisfied, since that is the best assurance of repeat business for them.

Buying from Door-to-door Salespeople

Before doing business with any door-to-door salesperson who is a stranger to you, or who represents a firm you do not know, you should make sure that both the product and the person you are buying from are reputable. Check with friends and acquaintances to learn what experiences they have had with that individual or firm. Find out if the company belongs to the Direct Selling Association (DSA), a trade organization of firms that sell their products door-to-door. The DSA has a membership of 200 corporations, all of which subscribe to a code of ethics. A company may, of course, not belong to the DSA and still be entirely legitimate. But DSA membership does offer a measure of consumer protection.

Reputable door-to-door salespersons should immediately identify themselves when they come to your home, tell you what they are selling and give you their name, address and telephone number as well as those of the company they represent. If they do not, you should ask for such identification. But bear in mind that anyone can get a printer to make up a calling card, business letter or brochure. If you have any reason to suspect a salesperson's credentials, do not do any business with that individual until you have personally checked with the company he or she presumably represents.

All salespersons, by definition, are in the business of selling you something, and all will present what they are selling in the best possible light. But reputable salespersons will not force themselves on you and, if they come at an inconvenient time, will ask for a future appointment and leave without making a fuss. If you invite them in, they will leave promptly when their business is finished. They will give you all the information, financial and otherwise, that you need to make a decision. Representatives of Hong Kong tailors, for example, will remind you that their merchandise carries an import duty, which may may add as much as $65 to the price of a $150 suit. And they will answer all your questions courteously and clearly.

Take plenty of time to examine the product and feel free to ask all the questions that occur to you.

Feel free to ask all the questions you think necessary. The beauty of buying products in your own home is that 10 other people aren't standing behind you waiting impatiently to get the same clerk's attention. You are the only customer for the moment.

If you are considering a mechanical product, such as a vacuum cleaner, make sure you ask about the manufacturer's policy on repairs and about the availability of accessories and replacement parts. Check the warranty or guarantee. How long does it last? What parts of the product does it cover? (See Magnuson-Morse Warranty Act, Chapter 7.) Get the company's exchange and refund policy *in writing*.

If you're thinking of buying something that involves a service as well as goods — made-to-order slipcovers, for example, or home repairs — do not sign a contract or in any way agree to have the work done until you have first checked to make sure the firm in question has a store or office with which you can deal. It is also a good idea to ask your local Better Business Bureau if any complaints have been received about the company. Home repair offers, especially, should be investigated carefully: the field generates a large number of consumer complaints.

If you decide to buy a product that will be paid for in installments, make sure that the sales contract is clear and complete. It should specify the terms of the sale, and those terms should match the ones the salesperson described in person. Look for the finance charges, and make sure the annual percentage rate is clearly stated. (Laws regarding credit purchases are discussed in Chapter 9.) Ask about all incidental charges and make sure they are spelled out in the contract.

Do not leave any blank spaces in a signed contract. Draw lines through the blanks, and add your initials. If you make any alterations in the agreement, initial each change, and ask the salesperson to do the same. Most important, *get a copy of the contract, signed by the salesperson, and be sure to keep it.*

One additional safeguard: whether you are paying for your purchase in full or over a period of time, do not pay in cash, and make your check payable to the order of the firm, not the individual salesperson.

If a salesperson uses questionable selling tactics — pressures you, suggests that you cancel a contract you have made with another firm, or disparages the products other firms make — do not do business with that individual. But *do* report the incident to your local Office of Consumer Affairs, Better Business Bureau, and FTC. Since these tactics are violations of the DSA's code of ethics, it is also advisable to inform the Code Administrator at the following address: Direct Selling Association, 1730 M Street, NW, Washington, DC 20036.

The Three-day Cooling-off Rule

It's been a long winter, and you feel sluggish and out of shape. A smooth talking salesman comes to your house by appointment to demonstrate the newest technology in gymnasium-style exercise equipment. He carries with him the machine, which is folded up like an ironing board, flips it open easily and extends it to its full nine feet. Then he lies down on the movable platform that forms part of the machine and pulls himself back and forth along the tension bar, revealing his own superb musculature. His muscles bulge like Tarzan's. His stomach is as flat as a board. He smiles cheerfully as he works out.

A machine that builds your muscles and is fun, also! What could be better? A moment later, he gets you onto the gliding platform to try it out for yourself. Is it possible that your physique has improved in those few minutes that you pushed and pulled?

He has not mentioned the price, and when you bring up the question he says offhandedly, "What would you say if I told you this machine cost $650?"

You are too shocked to say anything. "Well," he continues, "it doesn't. Its total cost is only $325."

You are so relieved that you sign the contract immediately. He eases you through the transaction by suggesting that you pay $100 down and the remaining $225 on delivery.

Even as you affix your signature, you realize that you are responding to his sales pitch, rather than to your need for the machine. But your writing hand seems to have a life of its own. With your name on the dotted line, the salesman flexes his muscles one more time, picks up his sample machine with one hand and departs. Only later do you take a cold, hard look at yourself and realize that you are now the owner of an exercise machine you will probably never use and can't afford.

But what can you do? You asked him to come, and you let yourself be influenced by his well-rehearsed sales skills. You signed a contract, and a contract is a legally binding document.

In fact, you can do a good deal. You can cancel the contract. In recognition of the very human tendency to succumb to skillfully applied sales pressure, the Federal Trade Commission has established the Three-day Cooling-off Rule, one of the most important of all consumer protections.

The Three-day Cooling-off Rule gives you until midnight of the third business day after you have signed a contract to cancel any purchase of $25 or more made in your home or anywhere other than the seller's normal place of business.

It therefore covers many kinds of sales other than those made literally door-to-door: sales at consumer "parties" given in private homes; or in a salesman's rented hotel room; or even in a restaurant or on a street corner. Moreover, it applies whether the salesperson is uninvited or invited, and no matter who issued the invitation. The only circumstances in which the rule does not apply are the following:

- If the sale is made at the seller's permanent place of business or concluded in the home after negotiations were initiated in the business place.
- If it is made entirely by mail or phone.
- If it involves less than $25.
- If the transaction involves insurance, securities or real estate.
- If it involves emergency home repairs for which you have specifically waived your right to the protection.

Nor does it include transactions in which you both initiate the contact and specifically ask a salesperson to repair or perform maintenance tasks on your property. If, for example, you call a firm and ask for someone to come to your house to install aluminum siding and sign a contract for that service, the Three-day Cooling-off Rule does not apply.

On the other hand, depending on where you live, you may have protection in some of these areas. The Three-day Rule is a federal regulation, which is applicable all over the country. But some state and local community laws have been passed that lay down more stringent requirements. Many states, for example, include telephone solicitation under the Three-day Rule. To determine whether your state offers this or any other added protection, check with your local Office of Consumer Affairs or Attorney General's Office. (See directories, pages 16 and 48.)

The Three-day Rule protects more than your right to cancel. It also obligates the salesperson to inform you of that right at the time of sale, requires that he give you a written contract or a fully completed receipt, that your contract include a statement of your right to cancel, and that the company supply you, at the time of signing, with two copies of a cancellation form.

If the salesperson fails to give you a cancellation form, your right to cancel within three business days remains intact. But you will have to write your own letter. And be sure to let the FTC or your local Office of Consumer Affairs know that you were not given the form required by law.

Note that the Three-day Rule also protects your right to return merchandise for which you have paid in full and which the salesperson leaves with you, as long as the sale involves at least $25 and satisfies all the other requirements of the rule. (See additional discussion in Chapter 13.)

Canceling Under the Three-day Rule
To cancel your contract, sign and date one copy of the cancellation form — or, if necessary, write your own letter and sign and date it. You need not give any reason for the cancellation. You have a legal right to change your mind. Then mail or hand deliver your letter to the address given for cancellation any time before midnight of the third business day after the contract date. For your own records, it would be wise to make a copy of the signed and dated letter.

It is important for you to have proof of the date you mailed the cancellation, and proof that the company received it. So unless it is convenient for you to hand deliver the cancellation, send the letter from your local post office by certified mail, with a return receipt requested.

Within 10 days of receipt of your cancellation, the seller must cancel and return any papers you signed, refund any money you paid and return any merchandise you may have given as a trade-in on your purchase. If any merchandise was left with you, the seller must pick it up within 20 days of the date on your cancellation letter, and must inform you when that pickup will be made. If he does not make the pickup, you can dispose of the goods as you will. Or he can pay the expenses for you to ship the merchandise back to him, if that course is agreeable to you. You do not have to assume this responsibility, however, unless you want to.

If, on the other hand, you *do* assume it, you must live up to it. If you do not do so, or if you make it impossible for the seller to pick up the merchandise by failing to be at home at an agreed-on time, you have forfeited your rights under the Three-day Rule and will be bound by the contract. And remember, of course, to keep the merchandise in good condition. If you damage it, you forfeit your rights.

Buying Encyclopedias
Many of the best encyclopedias available are sold only door-to-door. They are expensive items, which often cost $500 or more. So if you are seriously interested in buying an encyclopedia set, it is important for you to do your research carefully, and not make a purchase simply on the basis of a single chance visit from a salesperson who comes to your door as part of a general canvass.

The first step in that research is to decide the kind of encyclopedia your family needs and how much you can afford to pay. Once you have done this, you can consult a volume called *Encyclopedias in Print*, which is available in the reference department of many local public libraries. This publication rates encyclopedias according to reader age, price, readability and subject matter. In addition, talk to your librarian, who will also be able to give you advice, and examine the encyclopedias on the library shelves, looking especially for those whose print size, illustrations and educational level are appropriate for the use you have in mind. If the encyclopedia is primarily for your children, ask one of their teachers to advise you.

Once you have decided which encyclopedia you want — or narrowed your selection to a few possibilities — call or write the publishing company and ask to have a representative visit you.

During the visit, bear in mind that most companies offer, in addition to their encyclopedias, various optional services and merchandise, such as globes or maps. Find out if any additional charges are made for these items. It may seem that you are getting a better deal if you purchase a host of additional material, but remember that your major interest is the encyclopedia — not the extras.

Check the sales contract to be sure it includes all the details of your purchase: a list of each item you ordered, its description and color; a similarly detailed list of all the optional material, whether you are paying for it or getting it as part of your purchase; the date that books and other items will be delivered; the total price, including finance charge, annual percentage rate and charges for shipping and handling; the dates when payments are due; the length of time you have to make payments; and the amount of the monthly payments.

The contract should also spell out how long you have to cancel the purchase. The Three-day Rule gives you three days, but individual companies may give you a longer period.

Read the contract thoroughly before you sign, following all the procedures previously suggested. Many encyclopedia companies will have their representative verify the contract by telephone or letter a few days after it has been signed. The letter or phone call gives you an opportunity to go over the contract once more, making sure that your order is clearly understood. It is also your opportunity to ask any additional questions you may have. But remember that the Three-day Rule begins when you sign the contract.

A reputable encyclopedia salesman will give you all the information you need to make the proper decision. But every business has its scoundrels, and you must always be on the alert for tricks. A manipulative encyclopedia salesperson, for example, may tell you that the encyclopedia is "free" if you subscribe to the company's 10-year updating program, or offer you a "free" set if you write a letter about other books the company publishes that it can use in advertising. Don't believe either the statement or the offer. Encyclopedias are not given away. In both cases, you will be paying for the encyclopedia, although the cost may be hidden in the cost of the updating service or the price of the books to be "endorsed." These unscrupulous sales techniques are used simply to confuse the terms of the sale, so that you are not quite sure what you are buying, or exactly what you are paying for.

Another pressure technique is the offer of a lower price if you agree to buy on the first visit. The offer may be made outright, or by implication only, and it may or may not conform with the facts. Even if it does, don't let a slight discrepancy in price influence your decision. Don't buy until you are ready. If the salesperson tries to pressure you by hinting that you are taking up too much of his time, bid him farewell and ask the company to send another representative to call on you.

Solving Door-to-door Sales Problems

If you have any problems with a product purchased from a door-to-door salesperson, your first step is to check with the company he or she represents. If you cannot get satisfaction, get in touch with your local Office of Consumer Affairs and/or write to the Direct Selling Association. It maintains a service that mediates between consumers and companies belonging to the DSA. Send your letter to the Administrator, DSA Code of Ethics, 1730 M Street NW, Washington, D.C. 20036. Also, inform the FTC. It will not act for you, but *will* add the information to any file it may have on the company or the industry involved, and if there appears to be a consistent pattern of abuse, may undertake legal action.

Charities

Americans are generous. We give to Santa Clauses ringing their bells on street corners at Christmas time and we give through payroll deductions where we work. We give at church and at club meetings, and mail checks to support children in countries we will never visit. Prosperous corporations give, as do families that can barely pay their own bills. Wealthy people set up foundations to support charitable causes they hold dear, and ordinary folk set aside small amounts for organizations whose goals are important to them.

But no matter how much we give, we are always asked for more. The government cutbacks on social programs in recent years have produced an increasing number of appeals to individual donors, and daily our mailboxes are flooded with requests for help — often from organizations whose names and programs sound very much alike. How can we tell which ones to give our dollars to?

Most states and many communities require charities to be registered or licensed. But the fact that a charity is registered does not mean that it has been checked or evaluated, nor does it imply that it has been approved by the authorities. Registration may offer consumers protection against outright fraud — although some particularly brazen charity racketeers have been known to register their crooked operations — but it does not help us to decide which organizations to give to, or indicate either their efficiency or effectiveness.

No one can tell you what kind of charitable program should interest you — one that is devoted to religion, health or education; science, ecology or wildlife preservation; the humanities or the arts. You are the best — and only — judge of your own concerns.

But you should know how much of an organization's income goes to the programs it is designed to support and whether that organization is in the hands of responsible leadership. Registration may not give you that information. You will probably have to get it from other sources.

Judging a Charity

Two organizations are specifically devoted to evaluating charities that appeal to the public for funds. One is the Philanthropic Advisory Service (PAS), a division of the Council of Better Business Bureaus. Its files contain data on more than 7,000 national and international agencies devoted to a wide variety of services, and it will send you free reports on any three of these organizations that you want to know about. The reports describe the background of the agency, its programs and financial structure. PAS publishes a brochure, "Tips on Charitable Giving," which is available free, as well as "Give But Give Wisely," a regularly updated evaluation of the charities most often inquired about, which sells for a dollar.

To receive any of these documents, send a stamped, self-addressed envelope (plus $1, if you want the list) to: Philanthropic Advisory Service, Council of Better Business Bureaus, 1515 Wilson Boulevard, Arlington, Virginia 22209.

The other organization that evaluates charities is the National Information Bureau (NIB), which reports on more than 400 national health, welfare and educational agencies. The Bureau issues a monthly report, "Wise Giving Guide," which is available free of charge and which lists these agencies and indicates whether or not they meet the standards it has established. Individual reports about each listed agency are also available to consumers free of charge from: National Information Bureau, 419 Park Avenue South, New York, New York 10016.

In the event that the information you want is not available from either of these groups, or if for any other reason you want to do your own evaluation, the process is not difficult.

Ask the organization for a list of its Board of Directors. Both NIB and PAS standards require that a reputable charity be governed by an active, responsible board and that its list of board members and their professional affiliations be available to prospective donors.

The NIB and PAS standards further provide that the organization should publish an annual report, including a financial statement audited yearly by an outside public accountant and available to interested members of the public. A newly formed organization may not yet have issued an annual report or a financial statement. But it should have — and be willing to make available — a written budget and an information sheet describing its proposed programs and funding goals.

If you read the financial statement, you can easily determine how efficiently the organization is run. The financial statement will list both the agency's income and its sources (individual donors, government grants, investments and bequests) and its expenses, which fall into three main categories: programs, administration and fund raising.

Guidelines suggest how funds should be employed, but are not the only measure of a charity's efficiency.

The budget will depend on the nature of the organization itself. Research grants to scientists, salaries of doctors and nurses working in hospital missions, food supplies sent to needy families — all these are program expenses. Whatever their specific nature, they show how much of the organization's money is applied directly to the programs for which it is raising funds.

Administrative expenses are those incurred in the day-to-day running of the organization: salaries, office supplies, rent and fees paid to accountants and lawyers, for example. All sizable charities have such expenses, even those that depend heavily on volunteers to help them do their work.

Fund raising expenses include fees paid to professional fund raisers and the costs of mounting fund raising efforts — direct mail campaigns and advertising, for instance.

Look carefully at the program expenses. The PAS guidelines suggest that at least half the money a charity takes in should be spent directly on program services, and the NIB guidelines ask for at least 60 percent. However, there is always some flexibility. For example, very large charities may turn over lower percentages and still contribute significant amounts of money to their programs.

The guidelines limit fund raising and administrative expenses to 40 or 50 percent. But these guidelines should not be taken as the only measure of a charity's efficiency. A newly organized charity, for example, is likely to have to spend a considerable percentage of its income on fund raising — far more than an older, established one.

Note that all these guidelines have been set by private, voluntary organizations and not by the federal government. Some states do limit the fees that professional fund raisers can charge agencies that retain them to conduct campaigns, and the two major voluntary organizations of fund raising professionals — the American Association of Fund Raising Counsel and the National Society of Fund Raising Executives — require members to charge flat fees rather than a percentage of the money they raise. But there is no national standard in this area, and legitimate charities have been known to pay out more to fund raising professionals than would seem proper. Some years ago, one prominent actor publicly announced that he was dropping his support for a well-known charity because its fund raisers received nearly 85 percent of the money the organization collected. Several years before that, a pair of fund raisers bilked another major charity of $13 million by charging the organization more than 50 percent of all funds that were collected through the mails — even though the mailing list used to solicit these contributions consisted at least in part of the names and addresses of individuals already on the organization's own mailing lists.

Credit Card Rip-offs

Now that consumers are increasingly using their credit cards to purchase goods by mail or over the telephone, a new kind of rip-off has emerged: the fraudulent use of credit card numbers by imposters eager to have merchandise but unwilling to pay for it. These thieves manage to get hold of the names, addresses and credit card numbers of unsuspecting consumers and then place mail or telephone orders for the desired items — arranging to have the merchandise delivered as a gift to some name and address that enables the swindlers to receive it and still remain untraceable.

To protect yourself against this scam, make it a point never to discard a credit card statement or purchase receipt without first tearing it up, and never give your credit card number to anyone except when you yourself are ordering merchandise. If you receive a phone call from someone claiming to be the representative of a credit card company and asking for your account number — either directly or in some disguised fashion, as for example, in connection with an inquiry about your card's expiration date — do not reveal this information. No legitimate representative of the company would ask in this fashion.

If, despite all your precautions, you find yourself charged by a credit card company for merchandise you did not buy, call the company immediately.

Responding to Mail Appeals

In an effort to get our attention and encourage us to make contributions, some charitable organizations use gimmicks of various sorts. Some send merchandise to potential contributors — stamps, key rings, pens or other gifts. It is perfectly legitimate for organizations to send such items, but you are under no obligation either to pay for them by contributing or to return anything that may be sent to you. Other groups include "matching checks," which have no value in and of themselves. If you receive such appeals, you need neither return the checks nor make a contribution.

Whatever form a mail appeal takes, it should clearly identify the organization involved and describe its programs in clear and specific language. In addition, it should include an address you can write to for more information, and should state if your contribution is tax deductible.

Responding to Personal Solicitations

Solicitors collecting for a charity door-to-door or by telephone should identify themselves and the organization they represent at once, and should make no attempt either to embarrass or intimidate you. They should answer all your questions about the organization clearly and in full, and should agree to send you an appeal in writing, if you so request.

Unless you are entirely sure of the organization and individual you are dealing with, you should never give on the basis of a telephone appeal alone. Reject the solicitor who offers to send a "runner" to your house to collect your contribution. A legitimate fund raiser can wait for the mail to arrive. And finally, always make your donation by check rather than cash, and payable to the organization, not the solicitor.

Contributions and Federal Taxes

Most of the organizations that solicit contributions from us are themselves tax exempt: they do not have to pay any federal taxes. But this does not necessarily mean that we can deduct from our federal income taxes the contributions we make to them. Contributions are tax deductible only if they are made to organizations approved by the Internal Revenue Service, which include charities; educational, religious, scientific or literary groups; societies for the prevention of cruelty to children or animals; national or international amateur sports competitions; and other groups that meet the established standards. If you have any question about an organization to which you wish to contribute, request a copy of its "Letter of Determination" from the IRS, or ask your local IRS office for a list of those organizations to which contributions are tax deductible.

If you itemize your expenses on your federal income tax return, you are allowed to deduct up to 50 percent of your adjusted gross income for contributions of money or property to organizations the IRS has given tax deductible status. Laws passed as part of the Economic Recovery Tax Act of August, 1981 permit taxpayers who use the 1040 short form to take tax deductions, too, but for different amounts and at different rates in successive years. Check with your local IRS office for specific information about the deductions you can take. Also check with your state's tax department for information about allowable tax deductions for charity on your state income tax.

In figuring your tax deduction for charitable contributions, remember that:

- Only the amount paid *over* the fair-market value for tickets to benefit performances, charity balls, banquets, and so forth, is deductible. If, for example, you pay $50 for a concert ticket that sells for $20 at the box office, the IRS will permit you to deduct $30. Similarly, if you buy food, clothing or other donated merchandise at a charity-sponsored thrift shop or bazaar, you can deduct as a contribution only that portion of what you paid that exceeds the fair-market value of your purchase.
- You can deduct the cost and upkeep of uniforms needed for volunteer duty — a volunteer fireman's uniform, for example, or a hospital aide's — and travel expenses, parking fees, tolls and the cost of meals and overnight lodging while away from home in connection with volunteer service.
- You can deduct the fair-market value of property or merchandise you donate to a charity: if, for example, you give food or clothing to a charity-sponsored thrift shop, you can deduct its fair-market value. But be sure to keep a record of the kind of property you gave, the organization to which you gave it, and the date of your contribution. And when you claim the deduction, you must show how its value was determined. (The IRS defines fair-market value as "what a willing buyer would pay a willing seller when neither has to buy or sell and both are aware of the conditions of the sale.")
- You cannot deduct the value of the time you contribute as a volunteer nor, if you travel for a charitable organization, can you deduct the expenses incurred by an accompanying spouse.
- You cannot deduct expenses incurred while lobbying for any charity group except a church, nor dues paid to any social club, no matter how worthy its purpose. Nor can you deduct direct contributions to needy or worthy individuals, money spent for raffle tickets or bingo, the value of blood you may donate to a blood bank or the appraisal fee you may pay in order to determine the value of property you may donate.

Ways to Contribute

Many charities ask contributors to make pledges — statements that they will contribute specific amounts of money to the agency at a later date. You may make a pledge over the telephone, at a dinner party or meeting, at your office or when a door-to-door solicitor visits you. You may make it in response to a telethon or a drive conducted over the radio.

However you make your pledge, a solicitor will usually follow up by sending you a confirmation that you made it and a mailing envelope in which to send your donation.

Charities use pledges to project their income through the year, and if you make a pledge, you should — if you can — honor it. But pledges generally are not binding. If you find the obligation unduly burdensome or if you change your mind for some other reason, you can cancel your pledge — unless the charity has already undertaken a substantial expense in anticipation of the money you pledged.

Bequests, on the other hand, are binding — at least to the extent that the will containing them is legal. If you are married, most states do not permit you to leave all your money to charity. By law you are required to leave a certain percentage to your spouse. But if in your will you leave a specific, permissible sum of money to a specific charity, that contribution must be made. If, however, your will is not clearly phrased — if, for example, you do not specify the charity you want to give to — the will can be contested and the bequest disallowed. Or if you leave a portion of your estate to a charity that no longer exists when you die, the court may have to decide whether the money should go to another, similar charity or revert back to the estate.

Lotteries and Sweepstakes

Several states use lotteries as a way of raising needed revenues, and in these states such lotteries are entirely legal. But under federal postal laws, it is illegal to mail lottery tickets, and in the eyes of the Postal Inspection Service, lotteries are closely related to chain letters. For this reason, the states that have lotteries cannot sell chances through the mails, and purchasers of lottery tickets would be well advised not to mail them anywhere.

Sweepstakes, on the other hand, do not fall under this federal injunction. Unlike lotteries, which are composed of the three elements of chance, consideration (payment) and prize, sweepstakes do *not* require participants to pay out any money. They are, therefore, legal under the postal laws. On the other hand, many states have laws that govern sweepstakes. In some states, sweepstakes mailings are prohibited; in others, the company sponsoring the sweepstakes is required to post a bond to guarantee the prize; in still others, the winner cannot receive his or her

Regional Offices of the Postal Inspection Service

Central Region — **Illinois, Indiana, Iowa, Kansas, Kentucky, Michigan, Minnesota, Missouri, Nebraska, North Dakota, Ohio, South Dakota, Wisconsin**

Regional Chief Postal Inspector, Main Post Office Building, Room 712
Chicago, IL 60607

Eastern Region — **Delaware, District of Columbia, Maryland, Pennsylvania, Virginia, West Virginia**

Regional Chief Postal Inspector, 1 Bala Cynwyd Plaza, Room E 300
Bala Cynwyd, PA 19004

Northeast Region — **Connecticut, Maine, Massachusetts, New Hampshire, New Jersey, New York, Puerto Rico, Rhode Island, Vermont, Virgin Islands**

Regional Chief Postal Inspector, 633 Broadway, 20th Floor, New York, NY 10097

Southern Region — **Alabama, Arkansas, Florida, Georgia, Louisiana, Mississippi, North Carolina, Oklahoma, South Carolina, Tennessee, Texas**

Regional Chief Postal Inspector, 1407 Union Avenue, 10th Floor
Memphis, TN 38101

Western Region — **Alaska, Arizona, California, Colorado, Hawaii, Idaho, Montana, Nevada, New Mexico, Oregon, Utah, Washington, Wyoming, Pacific Territories**

Regional Chief Postal Inspector, San Bruno, CA 94098

prize through the mail — it must be picked up or delivered personally.

Most sweepstakes are promotional devices to draw consumers' attention to specific products, from magazines to toothpaste — and they are sent out in conjunction with an offer to sell the recipient the product being promoted. But you do *not* have to buy that product in order to be eligible to win. If you were required to make a purchase, you would be dealing with a lottery, not a sweepstakes — and, therefore, with an activity prohibited by the postal laws.

Companies that send sweepstakes mailings use all kinds of means to get recipients' attention. Sometimes the firms send their offers in envelopes decorated in such a way as to make us think we have won a prize even before we have entered the contest.

Such devices — which are perfectly legal — have only one purpose: to get us to read the promotional material in the hope we will find it so persuasive we will buy the product involved. In essence, the advertiser is making a deal with us. In exchange for the chance to win a great deal of money, he is asking us to pay attention to his message.

Another device often used by companies that send sweepstakes mailings is the inclusion of two envelopes — one marked "No" and the other marked "Yes" — and the request that you mail back your entry in the envelope marked to indicate whether you have purchased the product involved. Although most people think that it is a waste of time to send in an entry in a "No" envelope and that only those marked "Yes" stand any chance of winning, this is definitely not the case. In a legitimate sweepstakes, all entries must go into the same hopper and have equal chances to win; the separation into two kinds of envelopes is merely an effort to simplify bookkeeping and process orders quickly.

What to Look for in a Sweepstakes Offer

Although federal regulations cover only certain kinds of sweepstakes, the DMA has laid down standards for its members to observe. In looking over a sweepstakes offer, it would be wise to assure yourself that it adheres to these standards. For example, winners should be selected in a manner that ensures fair application of the laws of chance, according to the published rules and conditions of the particular sweepstakes. All prizes described in the promotional material — or enough money to purchase them — should be set aside by the sweepstakes promoter before the sweepstakes begins, and when the sweepstakes closes, all prizes should be awarded. The sponsoring company should keep all records of the sweepstakes for three years following the termination date. If the sweepstakes offer states that the names of winners will be made public, it should mail to you — at your request, and if you enclose a stamped, self-addressed envelope — the complete list of those who won prizes of more than $25. If the offer does not state this, but the list is nevertheless made public, any winner who so requests can have his or her name removed.

Because sweepstakes are so tempting to consumers, they also have their temptations for unscrupulous operators. Therefore, it is important for you to examine every sweepstakes offer with care.

When any offer comes to you, check to make sure that:

- It does not require you to buy anything in order to be eligible to win.
- It describes every one of the prizes and tells you their actual value and the total number in each category.
- It tells you the geographic area covered by the sweepstakes.
- It specifies the end date for eligibility, where to write for more information and any conditions under which you would not be given a prize.
- If the sweepstakes includes "Yes" and "No" envelopes or boxes, both should be equally conspicuous.
- If the odds can be figured in advance, your approximate chances of winning any of the prizes should be indicated.
- If there are conditions on the sweepstakes — that, for example, the sponsor has the right to verify that winners are eligible to receive awards, or that certain groups are ineligible — they must be clearly stated.

Mail-order and door-to-door merchandising and charitable appeals can be time-saving, convenient and socially useful. But, like every other aspect of our economy in which large sums of money are involved, they attract charlatans. Therefore, the buyer or donor should take the same precautions in this area as in any other monetary transaction.

Chapter 7

Around the Shopping Mall

Every year Americans spend hundreds of billions of dollars in the stores that dot our shopping malls and Main Streets, buying everything from eggs to home computers, clothing to drugs and cosmetics, garden hose to baby cribs. Whether we lay out the money in small sums or in large, whether we pay in cash or buy on credit, the goods we purchase from supermarkets, pharmacies, department stores and other retail outlets take a large bite out of every family's income: groceries alone account for over 15 percent a year.

So it is especially important that we keep our wits about us when we make these purchases. The small sums add up, and although the large ones seem to shrink if we dole them out in monthly installments, they are in fact growing, because of the interest we pay. In this chapter, we turn to problems associated with everyday shopping and to the things we need to know if we are to choose properly from the vast array of merchandise available to us and if we are to get the most from the protections that custom and the law provide. We begin by discussing those protections, as they relate to returning merchandise and to federal legislation covering product warranties. We will talk about the laws and regulations that govern the inspection and labeling of food, drugs and other items of merchandise and about the way to get the maximum of information from labeled products and the maximum benefit from special offers and sales. And we will give particular attention to the things consumers need to know about four specific kinds of products they buy — food, drugs, children's goods and the so-called big ticket items.

Basic Consumer Protections

Of all the protections available to us as consumers, two are the most basic. We ourselves are the first. It is up to us to buy with care, to know what our rights are in the marketplace and to make sure that those rights are respected by the businesses with which we deal. Those businesses are the second. If only because good customer relations and fair dealings with consumers are among the best assurances of business success, it is a matter of enlightened self-interest for manufacturers and retailers to treat buyers honestly.

No retailer, for example, is required by law to take back or exchange merchandise. But because the practice builds goodwill, most stores *do* permit returns, and have clearly stated policies in this area. On the other hand, it is the consumer's job to find out what the policy is in any particular establishment — either by asking or by reading the sign that some states and municipalities require retailers to post — and it is also the consumer's responsibility to take account of differences in policy in deciding where to buy.

For example, most stores that permit returns set a time limit during which the privilege operates. But that time limit can vary. It may be no more than a few days; it may be as much as a month. Similarly, the way returns are handled can differ from store to store. Some places permit exchanges only — the same merchandise in a different color or size. Others offer credit for the amount of the purchase, either in the form of a store credit slip or a credit on the buyer's charge account or credit card. Still others offer a full refund for any purchase made in cash. Clearly, the most advantageous policies for the consumer are those that allow the longest period of time in which to make a return, and those that offer cash refunds or credits on charge accounts or credit cards. But those advantages may have to be balanced against disadvantages. Stores with liberal policies may be more expensive than those whose policies are more stringent. Indeed, stores that do not permit returns at all are often those that regularly sell their goods for considerably less than the prevailing price in other outlets.

Manufacturers' Warranties. The Magnuson-Moss Act. All goods carry a so-called implied warranty: The law requires that any item that is sold be able to perform the function for which it was designed. If you buy a toaster that does not toast or a tennis ball that does not bounce, you have the right to return it and the dealer from whom you bought it has the obligation to make good.

In addition to the implied warranty, however, some carry written warranties. As with a return policy in a store, the practice of offering such warranties is entirely voluntary, and no manufacturer is required to observe it. But it has long been common, especially in connection with products that are complex and relatively expensive — those, in other words, of which consumers have a right to expect durability and which demand special training and knowledge for repair. Such products may carry even further assurances: in an effort to build a competitive advantage, some retailers voluntarily extend the manufacturer's warranty on certain products, or broaden its scope.

In effect, a warranty is a contract between warrantor and buyer, spelling out the rights and obligations of each. In the past, however, that contract sometimes proved to be virtually worthless from the consumer's point of view. Warranties were written in such complex legal jargon that it was often impossible for consumers to know what they meant — for how long they were operative; what parts of the product they covered; precisely what the consumer had to do to ensure that the manufacturer would live up to the warranty terms. Moreover, they sometimes contained loopholes invisible to the untrained eye. Unscrupulous sellers, for example, would simply disclaim the implied warranties that the law automatically grants.

All that changed in 1975, with the passage of the Magnuson-Moss Warranty Act, a landmark piece of consumer protection legislation. Magnuson-Moss does not require manufacturers to offer warranties, but it does ensure that consumers know what they are getting when they buy warrantied goods that cost at least $10 and it does hold manufacturers to the promises they make in their warranties. Its importance to consumers cannot be overstated, and all of us should know its requirements, which follow, so that we can be sure our rights are observed:

- All warranties must be expressed in clear, concise, ordinary language.
- The warranty for any item that costs more than $15 must be included with the product. In addition, a copy must be available at the retail store, for the consumer to read before deciding on a purchase. The retailer must either post the copy on the package containing the product or maintain a file of warranties for inspection by customers.
- The precise terms of the warranty must be spelled out and its nature and duration must be specified at the top of the document.

The warranty itself may be either full or limited, although a single product may contain both types, as long as they are clearly differentiated from one another. A full warranty is the one that gives consumers the

A Year-Round Sales Calendar

According to the National Retail Merchants Association, most retailers follow the same yearly timetable in scheduling sales and promotions, special purchases or combination packages.

These are the sale times to look for:

January: Storewide clearances; resort wear promotions; fur, furniture and white sales.

February: Valentine's Day and Washington's Birthday sales and promotions; furniture, housewares and home furnishing sales.

July: July 4th clearance; sporting goods, sportswear and furniture sales.

August: Furniture and fur sales.

October: Columbus Day sales; women's coats, suits and furs; men's and boys' outerwear and home furnishings sales.

November: Thanksgiving weekend sales; china, glassware, table linen and home furnishings sales.

maximum protection. At the very least, the firm that offers it is obliged to repair without charge an item that proves defective and within a reasonable period of time or, if this is not possible, to give the buyer a choice between a full refund and replacement of the item at no cost. A full warranty can be limited in time, but that limit cannot affect the duration of any implied warranties the item may carry, unless the customer purchases a service contract. Magnuson-Moss requires that the warranty document for an item guaranteed in this fashion for a period of 90 days, for example, carry at its top such a statement as "Full 90-Day Warranty."

A limited warranty provides somewhat less protection. It may, for example, cover only certain parts of the item involved, or it may require consumers to pay certain costs in exercising their rights under it. In addition, the implied warranty on an item carrying a written limited warranty usually need last no longer than the duration of that written warranty. Magnuson-Moss requires that the warranty document for such an item, guaranteed for 90 days, carry at its top such a statement as "Limited 90-Day Warranty," and in addition carry a list of the specific parts of the product it covers and those it does not, and a clear statement of whether or not the warranty covers labor costs, as well.

- Full warranties are transferable during the period of their life. This means that if you buy something that is fully warrantied for a year and after six months give or sell it to someone else, the new owner has the benefit of the warranty for the remaining half year.
- Limited warranties need not be transferable, but if they are not, this fact must be clearly stated in the document. If you give — or sell — an item with a nontransferable warranty to someone during the covered period, that person will not be able to obtain necessary repairs.
- A buyer does not have to send in the warranty card in order to be protected by the warranty. The article is covered even if the purchaser does not register it with the manufacturer. On the other hand, the manufacturer has the right to demand some proof of purchase when such an article is presented for repair. A sales or credit card receipt, or a canceled check with a description of the item, will usually suffice.
- The warranty document must include instructions on how and where the consumer can obtain service on the article. A limited warranty may require the buyer to pay mailing costs if the item has to be shipped back to the manufacturer. In the case of a full warranty, however, the manufacturer or distributor is required to pay any mailing costs necessary for servicing.
- If a buyer complains about a problem during the period of the warranty and the complaint has not been satisfied by the time the warranty expires, the buyer's rights under the warranty remain in force. The company must take care of the problem. If it does not, the buyer has the right to take the matter to court and sue the manufacturer under the terms of the warranty law.

Warranties differ widely in scope and time limit. Read them carefully before purchasing expensive items.

Magnuson-Moss places obligations on the buyer as well as the manufacturer. For example, any warranty is void if the article it covers has obviously been misused. Moreover, the buyer must use only the manufacturer's authorized service centers for any repairs necessary during the warranty period. The use of an unauthorized facility, or a botched repair job performed by the buyer gives the manufacturer the right to refuse to honor the warranty.

By ensuring that written warranties are expressed in language that consumers can understand, that they include all necessary information, that they mean what they say, and that they are enforceable, Magnuson-Moss puts these documents high on the list of factors to be taken into consideration when we make purchases. Often, the most significant differences between products are the variances in their warranty terms. Sometimes these differences are substantial. One brand of a particular item may carry a full 90-day warranty, while another — selling at about the same price — carries only a limited warranty for the same period. The warranty on one make of television set or home computer may offer a temporary replacement if the item has to be sent out for repair during the covered period while another does not. Since repairs on these products can take a considerable amount of time, the warranty that provides a replacement would seem far more desirable.

Even if the differences between warranties are only matters of convenience, they are still worth attention. If the firm that manufactures one brand of electric mixer has an authorized repair service near where you live, and its competitors do not, the first firm's mixer — all other things being equal — is the one for you to buy. In the event that anything goes wrong, you will not have to spend time and energy on packing and mailing.

As all this should make clear, warranty terms deserve your close attention. It is important to read warranties with care; to compare the warranties that different manufacturers offer on similar items and those that accompany different models of the same item. Equally, it is important to find out where in-warranty service is provided, and by whom. The document itself may or may not include the details of this information. If it does not, be sure to ask the retailer before you buy.

Consumer Protection in Credit Transactions

Credit has always played an important role in the American economic system, for consumers as well as businessmen. Since the end of World War II, however, its importance to consumers has skyrocketed. In the past, we borrowed money only for major purchases — our homes and our cars, for example — and bought furniture and household appliances on the installment plan only when we could not afford to pay for them in cash. Moreover, when we *did* borrow or buy on credit, we made use of closed-ended loans: money borrowed in a specific amount and repaid monthly over a specified period of time.

Today, we are urged to buy on credit — and not just our homes, cars, furniture and appliances, but our gas, our restaurant meals, our children's clothes, our vacations, and our records, books, prescriptions and even garden seeds. Open-ended credit — the kind we use when we pay for our purchases with charge accounts or credit cards — has become such a major factor in our lives that some of us could not get through a single week without it, and those of us who are turned down for credit are likely to find our lives very severely affected.

Discounts for Cash

Merchants who accept credit cards pay a fee to the credit card company, and generally raise prices to meet the cost. This means they could offer discounts to customers who pay in cash, lowering prices by the amount saved in credit card fees.

Although this practice is beneficial both to merchants and to consumers, it is not widespread. You can encourage it by expressing interest to the merchants.

The Cash Discount Act, which is administered by the Federal Reserve System, demands that cash discount programs meet the following requirements:

- The merchant must clearly and conspicuously disclose to all customers — generally in the form of a sign at the door or the cash register — that the discount is available.
- The discount must be applicable to *all* customers, not just credit card holders.
- As long as the sign clearly states this fact, the discount can be limited to certain products or certain stores in a chain.

Obtaining Credit. Institutions that lend money or extend credit have several different ways of determining the eligibility of applicants. If you are a steady customer, your local dry cleaner or pharmacy may be happy to open a charge account for you simply on the basis of your request. Banks, department stores and credit card companies, on the other hand, are not likely to be this easygoing. They may — and do — devote large sums of money to promotional campaigns designed to lure us into applying for charge accounts, loans and credit cards. But when the time comes to process those applications, they are both thorough and careful.

They have every reason and right to be so. It is clearly not in their interest to extend loans or credit to people who cannot be counted on to be financially responsible, and clearly in their interest to check applicants carefully to determine their credit-worthiness. There are many different systems through which institutional lenders rate applicants.

One of the most widely used is a credit-scoring system, which assigns a certain point value to each of a series of characteristics that have proved to be reliable indicators of an individual's credit-worthiness. The application forms that these institutions use contain questions whose answers can be rated on this scale. There are, for example, questions about employment: what is your occupation; how much do you earn; how long have you worked on your present job? There are questions about expenses: how many dependents do you have; are you paying alimony or child support? There are questions about assets and additional income: do you have any savings or investments that provide you with income that could be used, if necessary, to pay your debt?

Perhaps most important, potential lenders look at an applicant's credit standing: how much do you owe; how often do you borrow; do you pay your bills on time? If you are applying for a substantial sum — in the form either of a loan or a line of credit — they will probably ask a credit bureau to review your financial history and render a report based on an examination of your bill-paying record over a period of several years.

If your application or the credit bureau search turns up information that indicates to the lender you are not a good risk, that lender has the right to turn you down. The Equal Credit Opportunity Act, which we will discuss in some detail in Chapter 9, prohibits rejection on grounds involving discrimination. But no law exists that establishes specific criteria for credit worthiness or compels any institution to lend money or extend credit to an applicant the institution does not find acceptable. It is up to the institution to make its own decision, based on its own standards. Given the same set of facts about a prospective borrower, two lenders may react entirely differently, one accepting the application, the other turning it down.

Fortunately, the increased use of credit has been accompanied by the passage of a number of laws designed to protect the consumers of this commodity. The Fair Credit Reporting Act provides recourse for consumers who have been denied credit. The Truth in Lending Act requires lenders to give prospective borrowers the information they need in order to make wise choices when they borrow money or apply for credit. The Fair Credit Billing Act establishes procedures through which consumers can dispute any errors they find in credit card or charge account bills. The Fair Debt Collection Practices Act prohibits harassment of creditors by lending institutions or their representatives. And finally, the Equal Credit Opportunity Act ensures that no individual can be denied credit simply on the grounds of sex, marital status, age, race, religion or nationality. Every consumer should be familiar with the terms of these laws, which are discussed in detail in Chapter 9. We are affected by them almost daily, and often need to call on their provisions for our protection.

Buying on Credit. If you are buying with borrowed money — whether through the use of a loan, a charge account or a credit card; or on the installment or layaway plan — be sure to read your contract carefully. It will probably be long and tedious, and you are not likely to find it particularly exciting. But it is important to examine it with care, if only to check the following:

- Do the terms of the contract reflect your understanding of the agreement? For example, if a representative of the lender told you that the interest rate would be 13 percent, the written agreement must specify this same interest rate.
- If you have taken out a loan which requires you to put up collateral as security, is the nature of this collateral clearly stated in the agreement? If, for example, you are putting up your sterling flatware, the precise number of pieces should be specified.
- If you have put up your home as collateral for a loan, does the contract clearly state your right to cancel within three days of signing? Unless the loan involves refinancing, you have this right.
- Have all the blank spaces on the contract been filled in with lines drawn in ink?

Some credit contracts contain terms extremely disadvantageous to borrowers. Try to avoid those that include any of these clauses:

- Waiver of rights: This means that you give up the legal rights that normally protect you against the seizure of certain types of property to satisfy a loan. Once you waive your rights, you have no recourse if the lender seizes that property.

What It Says and What It Means

Although in many states credit contracts must be written in language understandable to the layman, there is considerable dispute about what constitutes clear language. Below are several examples of clauses sometimes found in credit contracts, together with their meanings. If you are presented with a loan agreement that includes any of these clauses, try to negotiate them out of the contract. If you cannot, you would probably do well to find a different source of credit. Not all these clauses are legal in all states, but in some states several of them are.

What It Says — "This note is secured by a security interest in all of the following described personal property and proceeds thereof. If checked at left, Consumer goods consisting of all household goods, furniture, appliances and bric-a-brac, now owned and hereafter acquired, including replacements, and located in or about the premises at the Debtor's residence (unless otherwise stated) or at any other location to which the goods may be moved. In addition, all other goods and chattels of like nature hereinafter acquired by the Debtor and kept or used in or about said premises and substituted for any property mentioned. Proceeds and Products of the collateral are also covered."
What It Means — If you fail to pay the loan on time, the creditor may seize all your household goods.

What It Says — "Each of us hereby both individually and severally waives any or all benefit or relief from homestead exemption and all other exemptions or moratoriums to which the signers or any of them may be entitled under the laws of this or any other State, now in force or hereafter to be passed, as against this debt or any renewal thereof."
What It Means — If you fail to pay on time, the creditor may seize all your possessions, even those ordinarily protected by state law.

What It Says — "To secure payment hereof, the Undersigned jointly and severally irrevocably authorize any attorney of any court of record to appear for any one or more of them in such court in term or on vacation, after default in payment hereof and confess a judgment without process in favor of the Creditor hereof for such amount as may then appear unpaid hereon, to release all errors which may intervene in any such proceedings, and to consent to immediate execution upon such judgment, hereby ratifying every act of such attorney hereunder."
What It Means — You agree in advance that you won't contest a suit brought by the creditor against you. Even if you feel that you are justified in withholding the payments, you have signed away your day in court.

What It Says — "The Creditor may retain the goods as its property or may sell or otherwise dispose of the item pursuant to the (state) Uniform Commercial Code, whereupon the Debtor shall be liable for and shall pay any deficiency on demand."

- Confessions of judgment: This means that if you fail to make a payment on time — for any reason whatever — the creditor can, without informing you or giving you any opportunity to present a defense, go to court, file suit and have a judgment entered against you. Thereafter, the creditor can demand immediate payment of the entire sum or seize any property you may have put up as collateral.
- Assignment of Wages: This permits a creditor to receive a part of your paycheck directly from your employer if you are in default of a debt. In the case of a so-called irrevocable assignment of wages, it is not necessary for a court to authorize the assignment of the sum involved. In the case of a so-called voluntary assignment, you have the right to cancel the arrangement.

Even if you have not agreed to an assignment of wages, a creditor can go to court to "garnish" your wages — to have a portion of your earnings paid directly to the lender — in

What It Means — If you fail to pay on time, the creditor may repossess the item you bought with the loan. If the creditor resells that item and fails to obtain the difference between what you already paid and the amount of the loan, you will owe the difference. If, for example, you bought a stereo on credit for $1,000 and paid off only $300, you would still be liable for $500 if the repossessed stereo was sold for $200.

What It Says — "The undersigned, jointly and severally, waive any right of privacy of any nature in connection with the instrument, regardless of whether or not the debt evidenced hereby may be contested, and agree that the lender may at its option communicate with any persons whatsoever in relation to the obligation involved, or its delinquency, or in an effort to obtain cooperation or help relative to the collection or payment thereof."
What It Means — If you don't make your payment on time, you waive all of your legal rights to your privacy, and that will allow the creditor or his or her representatives to inform your friends, relatives or employer of your negligence.

What It Says — "In addition, if this agreement is referred to any attorney for collection due to any default or breach of any promise or provision hereunder by Debtor, Debtor agrees to pay any attorney's fee of 15 percent of the Total of Payments then due, plus the court costs."
What It Means — You agree to pay the creditor's attorney's fees and all court costs if the lending institution decides to sue you.

What It Says — "If the Debtor(s) fails to pay any installment of any advance secured hereby or part thereof or if there is a breach of any of the covenants, agreements or warranties contained herein or in the Credit Agreement or if the Secured Party shall feel insecure, all sums then owing under said Credit Agreement shall immediately become due and payable without demand or notice."
What It Means — The creditor can call in the loan without notice — demand complete payment of the outstanding balance — for just about any reason at all — even the slightest feeling of nervousness about your ability to satisfy the obligation on time.

What It Says — "Default in the payment of any installment of the principal balance or charges hereof or any part of either shall, at the option of the holder hereof, render the entire unpaid principal balance hereof and accrued charges thereon, at once due and payable."
What It Means — If you miss so much as one payment, the creditor may demand immediate payment of the entire outstanding balance as well as any interest charges then due.

Too many of us are reluctant to admit our lack of true comprehension of legalese. And we are particularly timid about confessing our ignorance when the puzzling phrases are part of what, we are assured, is a standard form contract. Such an attitude can be highly expensive when we are seeking credit. If any part of a contract is not perfectly clear to you, demand that it be translated into understandable layman's English.

the event that you are in default on a debt. In such a situation, however, you have the protection of federal law, which requires that you be given notice of the proceeding and a chance to defend yourself. In addition, state laws have been adopted that provide further protection for the debtor.
• Lawyers' fees: This means that you waive your right to contest any legal fees the lender may charge you for expenses incurred in getting you to pay your loan.
• Balloon payment: Some installment agreements provide for low monthly payments until the very end of the loan period, when a large amount of money is due. In some cases, such arrangements are useful. But they can also produce serious difficulties for a borrower whose financial situation has deteriorated rather than improved.
• Acceleration of payments: This clause gives the lender the right to call in the entire loan if the borrower misses a certain specified num-

ber of payments. Since the number of missed payments can be as low as one installment, the clause can present serious problems.

If You Buy a Defective Product on Credit

Though you may not be aware of it, federal credit regulations offer you a degree of financial immunity if you use borrowed money to buy a product that turns out to be a dud. In any purchase, the seller and the manufacturer are legally required to honor the implied warranty that pertains to all products, as well as any written warranty that may have been included with the purchase. If you use credit, however, additional protections apply.

Let us say, for example, that you buy a new dishwasher from your local appliance dealer. You arrange for an installment loan with the dealer, agreeing to pay off the loan at the rate of $30 per month for 12 months. After the washer is installed it works perfectly for six weeks. Then it suddenly stops washing dishes and begins breaking them instead. You complain to the dealer, who sends a repairman, but after he leaves the machine reverts to its delinquent ways. Nor do things improve after several more visits by the repairman. Indeed, each new repair only seems to make things worse. Exasperated, you inform the dealer you are going to return the dishwasher and discontinue payments. You also ask to be reimbursed for the payments you have already made. The dealer, quite unperturbed, tells you he no longer owns your credit account, but has sold it to a local bank. If you want something done, he says, you'll have to talk to the bank.

A decade or so ago, you would have been out of luck. The bank could have told you it was not responsible. Since it was not the seller but merely the "holder in due course" of the loan agreement, its role was limited to collecting the payments due. This is no longer the case. Since 1976 every installment loan agreement must include the statement: "Any holder of this consumer credit contract is subject to all claims. . . . which the debtor could assert against the seller of the goods or services. . . ." This means that a bank, finance company or any other lending institution that buys a credit contract from a retailer assumes all the obligations the retailer would have had if he had not sold the contract. In this case, it means that the bank must either arrange to have the dishwasher repaired, provide you with a new one, or accept the return of the machine and give you back the money you have already paid.

On the other hand, if you had bought the dishwasher with a loan obtained directly from the bank, the situation would be different. The firm that warrantied the dishwasher — whether manufacturer or retailer — would still be legally bound to fulfill its obligations under the warranty, but the bank would have no obligation unless it had a working arrangement with the dealer under which it automatically handled all credit purchases.

Bank Credit Card Purchases and Defective Products. If you had bought the dishwasher from the same dealer using a credit card, and then found it did not work, under federal regulations you would not have to make monthly payments to the card issuer to satisfy the loan. All you would have to do is call that institution and explain that the dishwasher did not work and that efforts to fix it had failed. The problem would then become a matter for the card issuer and the appliance dealer to work out. There are, however, several restrictions on credit card purchases:

- The item involved must cost at least $50. For purchases of defective products under that amount, the card issuer may demand full payment.
- You must have purchased the item in the state where you live, or within 100 mile of your residence. If you live in Albany, New York, and buy a defective product in Pittsfield, Massachusetts, you cannot be held liable for the credit card purchase, because Albany and Pittsfield are less than 100 miles apart. But if you buy the item in Boston — more than 100 miles from Albany — you are liable for the payments, even if the product proves defective. (See Chapter 5 for a discussion on returning a defective automobile bought on credit.)

The Big Ticket Items

Busy consumers may not find it worth their time and effort to shop around before buying inexpensive items. Such shopping may not even make financial sense. A package of razor blades may cost a few cents more at a store within walking distance of your home or place of business than at one a couple of miles

Buying on the Layaway Plan

Consumers who cannot afford to buy a product outright and do not want to buy on credit can make the purchase on the layaway plan. They make a small deposit to reserve the item and pay the balance in installments at agreed-upon intervals, receiving the merchandise only when it has been paid for in full.

Many consumers find the layaway plan useful, but it can lead to disputes. For example, merchandise may be damaged while it is still in the dealer's possession; unexpected charges may appear on the final bill; customers may lose their money because of misunderstandings about missed payments; the store may go out of business.

No federal laws cover layaway purchases, but some have been enacted in several states. The New York statute, which covers items that cost at least $50 and take at least four installments to pay off, provides a model. Even where the law does not require it, buyers on a layaway plan should ask for the following terms, all part of the New York law:

- Upon completion of payment, the merchant must turn over the product to the customer.
- There must be a written agreement between the customer and the merchant which specifies the total price of the product and the amount and timing of each installment; any extra charges such as installation fees, service fees, freight charges and cancellation fees; gives a complete description of the item, including the name of the manufacturer, brand, color, style, size and model number; the policy of the merchant toward missed payments; and a statement of the merchant's policy about reimbursing the customer for any money already paid if the agreement is cancelled because of missed installments.
- The customer must also be informed of the whereabouts of the goods during the layaway period. If the item is not to be taken out of stock until a specified time — say until after several payments — this information must be disclosed in the agreement.

away. But the cost of using your car will probably wipe out the saving completely.

When you buy expensive items, however, it always pays to shop carefully. Whether you are in the market for a sofa or a refrigerator, you have to make sure you are getting the most appropriate merchandise for your purposes at the best possible price and with the best possible assurance of service, when and if it becomes necessary. This means examining different models, styles and brands of the same item; checking out tests that may have been published in such magazines as *Consumer Reports*; reading warranties carefully and doing comparison shopping for service as well as price.

Appliances. Appliances are available in a wide variety of places — at factory-authorized dealers, appliance stores, discount stores and department stores. Each kind of store may have a different policy with respect to installation and repair services, and these policies are as important for you to take into consideration as price. No matter how attractive a rock-bottom price sounds, it may be worth very little if you have to pay additionally for delivery, installation and service. Nor should you assume that one kind of store always gives you a better price. The refrigerator you want may be on sale at a department store for less than its selling price at a discount outlet.

Appliances come in a wide variety of styles with an equally wide variety of options — each one raising the price by a greater or smaller amount. So it is important for you to decide in advance just how much those options are worth to you — to make a list of the features you actually need and want before you set out to do your shopping.

In addition to the current models of nationally-advertised brands of appliances avail-

Safety Seals for Electric and Gas Appliances

American manufacturers pay private firms (the best known are the Underwriters' Laboratories and the American Gas Association) to make safety tests on thousands of appliances, from electric razors to refrigerators and stoves.

Underwriters' Laboratories may test all — or only some — of the electrical components of a product, checking to see if it is protected against fire, electric shock and related accident hazards. If the motor has been tested, the UL seal may be placed on the housing. The seal may not be visible, so it is wise to inquire when you buy. A tag on the wire means that *it* has been tested and approved; a tag on the plug means that it also meets UL standards. If you are unsure whether the UL seal applies to the entire product or only to some of its parts, ask the sales clerk.

The American Gas Association tests gas appliances for safety; when its seal — The American Gas Association's Laboratories Certificate — is attached to an appliance, it is a guarantee that the product meets national safety standards (both of construction and performance) when used in accordance with directions.

able virtually everywhere, there are some with special characteristics that are often offered for sale, and that are worth examination.

Some stores offer special prices on models that are a year or so out of date. The differences between these older models and the newer ones may be no more than cosmetic; even if they are substantive, the difference in price may make the older model a good buy.

House-brand or store-brand appliances are often good buys. These items are made by the same companies that manufacture nationally-advertised brands and are put together in accordance with specifications supplied by the retailer — who also, in these cases, supplies the warranty.

Reconditioned and rebuilt appliances are also worth examination. Both have been used, but those that are reconditioned have been put through only minor repairs or adjustments while those that have been rebuilt — or reconstructed — have been taken apart and put together again after repair and/or replacement of old, non-working parts. Both reconditioned and rebuilt appliances may carry warranties, but they are generally for a shorter period of time than those that accompany new appliances and the warranties on reconditioned appliances are generally not as good as those on rebuilt ones.

Floor and demonstrator models are somewhat more chancey. A refrigerator marked "as is" may have nothing more wrong with it than a couple of scratches. On the other hand, it may also have serious defects the buyer cannot see. According to the Federal Trade Commission, the phrase "as is" on merchandise releases the retailer from any obligation to repair the item involved after it has been purchased. Unless an "as is" bargain is backed by a written warranty that is still in effect, you will have no recourse if anything goes wrong.

When shopping for major appliances, be sure to check delivery and installation costs. If these are included in the total price, ask the dealer to give you a cost breakdown, so that you can separate the price of the product from the cost of intallation and delivery. Then check to find what those two expenses would cost you if you had to pay for them yourself.

Some installations require the skills of a specialist — a plumber, electrician or carpenter. If the store is going to supply this help for you, the quality of its personnel should be a major factor in your decision. Check with friends and neighbors who have made similar purchases there and with your local Better Business Bureau, if you yourself have had no direct experience with the establishment.

If a problem develops with a major appliance, first try to work it out with your dealer or serviceman, or through your local Better Business Bureau. If you come to an impasse, or have problems concerning your warranty, get in touch with the manufacturer. Many of the major manufacturers have consumer service departments and some have toll-free telephone numbers which can be called for information and action on complaints. If these procedures fail, there are two industry groups you can apply to for help. For problems with major appliances, write to: Major Appliance Consumer Action Panel, Association of Home Appliance Manufacturers, 20 North Wacker Drive Chicago, Illinois 60606.

For problems with electronic devices — television sets, stereos, home computers, etc. — write to: Director of Consumer Affairs, Electronic Industries Association, 2001 Eye Street, NW, Washington, D.C. 20006.

Your letter should include the name and address of the store at which you made your purchase; the model and serial number of the product involved; a description of the problem; a summary of your attempts to solve it and copies of all receipts, including those for service. (See Chapter 13 for additional information about the two organizations mentioned above.)

Furniture. Most furniture costs a good deal of money. Moreover, it is something you have to live with every day. It has to satisfy your needs, your budget and your taste; it has to fit in with your other furniture and into the space available for it; and it has to be durable. So it is a purchase to be made with the greatest care and only after comparison shopping.

Do not buy any major piece of furniture until you have measured it against the dimensions of the room in which you plan to use it. Check upholstery fabrics and colors — not just in the store but in your home. Be sure, also, to measure your doors, hallways and windows — if your purchase must fit through them — to be sure they are large enough to accommodate delivery.

When looking at furniture in the store, it is important to read carefully all the labels it contains. Since 1974, a Federal Trade Commission industry guide has required labeling on all new furniture that describes the materials used in making it. This information is crucial for consumers: few of us can tell one wood from another, or distinguish between natural fabrics and the synthetic counterparts that are often used.

Wood furniture, for example, can only be labeled "all wood" if it contains no metal or any other materials. If it is labeled merely with the name of the wood — "All maple," for example — it is made entirely of solid pieces of maple. If, on the other hand, it is labeled "maple veneer," it is made of several thin layers of wood, of which only the top and bottom need be maple. Because the "ply" construction of veneered furniture increases its strength and its resistance to warping, this process is used in making expensive as well as inexpensive furniture. Some wood furniture is labeled "bonded." This can mean one of several things. Wide boards may have been cut into narrow lengths and bonded back together to make the finished section stronger and less likely to warp. Or each section may be made of blocks of wood glued together and

When buying new furniture, read all labels to learn what materials were used in manufacturing the piece.

then carved or turned to produce the desired shape. Or wood chips or particles may have been bonded together in chipboard, to be used as backing on such articles as dressers and bookcases.

Some woods — oak, walnut, mahogany, maple, birch and teak, for example — are harder and more durable than others; furniture made from them is, therefore, relatively expensive. Soft woods — such as pine, redwood and cedar — can be dented and scratched fairly easily; for this reason, they are likely to be found in relatively inexpensive furniture and in rough, outdoor pieces.

When buying any wood furniture, check to see that the grain of the wood runs parallel to the length of the board, not at right angles to it; that the joints are an integral part of the piece, not screwed on like hardware; that the strongest joints are snugly dovetailed and doweled; and that the finish is consistent in color and has no cracks, streaks or bubbles.

In upholstered furniture, the most important things to check on are the frame, the support for the cushioned seating, the cushioning and the upholstery fabric. Here, too, labeling can be a major help.

Frames may be made of steel; laminated board; strong, rigid plastic or hardwood. You can — and should — find out which by asking the salesperson. Supports for seats can be made of fabric or steel webbing; they may be wooden slats — and they may also be springs. Of these, spring construction obviously supplies the best support, and the best quality of furniture will have oven-japanned, hand-tied coil springs, eight or 12 to a seat: you can find this information on labeling tags. Labels will also tell you the material or materials with which the cushions are stuffed. Down is the most expensive stuffing, but foam — which is far more commonly used — can also be of very high quality, especially if it contains a considerable amount of urethane, which is durable, light in weight and mothproof.

Upholstery fabrics should also be labeled with a grade that indicates how durable they are, how well they respond to cleaning and

If the furniture you buy carries warranties, be certain that they are clearly specified in your contract.

whether or not they have been treated for stain-resistance. But don't rely on the label alone. Before choosing any upholstery fabric, examine a loose swatch. Run your fingernail over it to see if it pills or shreds; pull at it to test its strength; check to see that any printed design goes through to the back: if the design is only surface printed, it will wear away quickly. Since some fabrics fade in sunlight or change color when they are exposed to air pollutants for any long period of time, it is important to read the manufacturer's care instructions thoroughly and to follow them implicitly.

The zippers you may find on the cushion covers of upholstered furniture are not there to enable you to take the stuffing out. They are used to make the cushions themselves easier to put together and to assure that they fit well. Zippered covers are not meant to be removed and should be kept on if the cushions need cleaning. This will prevent shrinkage or damage of any sort.

An extremely important consideration in buying upholstered furniture is its flammability. On the whole, fabrics made of natural fibers — linen and wool, for example — are inherently more flammable than synthetics, although they can be treated with chemicals that make them flame retardant. There are no federal standards governing the flammability of such upholstered furniture as chairs or couches but some manufacturers voluntarily treat the fabrics they use, and will generally indicate this fact on labels. But remember that flammability standards, adopted and enforced by the Consumer Product Safety Commission, *do* apply to all mattresses and mattress pads offered for sale.

When you order furniture, be sure to examine your sales contract carefully. It should contain a detailed description of the merchandise, including the type of materials used, the color and any style or model numbers. Many manufacturers of upholstered furniture offer warranties — one, which generally lasts for five years, covering construction and the second, which generally has a one year term, covering the upholstery fabric. If the articles you buy carry such warranties, they should be specified in the contract.

A chronic complaint among furniture buyers concerns late delivery: the merchandise simply does not arrive on the promised date. To give yourself at least some protection against this, you should ask for a sales contract that contains — in addition to an estimated delivery date — a cancellation clause spelling out the conditions under which you can rescind your order. You may have to pay a fee for cancellation. Find out how much it is and be sure it is written into the contract. And ask, as well, for a statement that you will be notified in writing if the furniture cannot be delivered by the latest estimated date.

Although no federal law or regulation holds the sellers of furniture to any specific responsibility concerning delivery, some states have passed laws in this area, and you should check with your local Office of Consumer Affairs or State Attorney General's office (see directories on pages 16 and 48) to see whether there is any such legislation where you live. One state, for example, gives the seller 30 days beyond the latest estimated date to make delivery. If, by then, the furniture still has not arrived, the buyer has the right to cancel and get a refund.

When your furniture finally arrives, be sure to inspect it carefully. If you have received only a partial delivery, you do not have to accept it if you do not want to. If you are willing to accept it, be sure that the receipt conforms with the actual delivery; if it does not, add a note describing the exact contents, and have the delivery man sign it. If, when you examine the furniture, you find something wrong, ask the delivery man to take it back. If he refuses, do not sign the bill until you have noted the defect on it and the delivery man has signed that notation. If the furniture is sealed in a carton and you cannot adequately inspect it while the delivery man waits, do not sign for it without first writing "approval subject to inspection" on your bill. This will give you protection in the event that you find something wrong with the merchandise when you unpack it.

Complaints about furniture should be taken to the retailer from whom it was purchased; if you cannot get satisfaction there, check with the manufacturer. If the merchandise is warrantied, you should have no trouble. If you do, consult your local Better Business Bureau or Office of Consumer Affairs. (See directory, page 16).

Children's Merchandise. Whether they are expensive or inexpensive, the things we buy for our children should be purchased with particular care. Safety is a vital factor in all of them: if there is trouble to be gotten into, kids can be counted on to get into it.

Fortunately, some safety precautions have been built into the system through federal laws and regulations and through legislation in various states. In most states, for example, the law requires that children below a certain age be strapped in safety seats in automobiles, and the National Highway Traffic Safety Administration has established standards that these safety seats must meet. (See box, page 149.) The Consumer Product Safety Commission (CPSC), which came into being in 1972 under the terms of the Consumer Product Safety Act, has the power not only to set safety standards for a large number of products, including many that are designed for children, but also to compel manufacturers to label packages with consumer warnings, where necessary, and to ban or remove from the market or order the recall of products that do not conform to acceptable levels of safety.

The CPSC is responsible for the ruling that outlawed the use of lead-based paints — which are toxic — both in homes and on children's toys; it administers the Flammable Fabrics Act, which sets safety standards for children's sleepwear (as well as mattresses), and the Federal Hazardous Substances Act, which covers the construction of cribs, bicycles, fireworks, and small parts on toys. In addition, the CPSC has set standards assuring the safety of all electrical toys, whether they are manufactured here or are imported into this country.

Although consumers *can* count on these federal protections in most cases, they must exercise caution when buying for youngsters. Despite every care, some dangerous products *do* slip through. And a product that is safe under one set of circumstances may be harmful in another.

By law, all children's sleepwear must meet tests that assure flame resistance, and labeled with care instructions that indicate how that resistance can be maintained. But no such law applies to other articles of children's clothing and most of the things that kids wear are not treated for flame resistance. So it is important to check carefully before buying, to assure that both fabric and design reduce the danger of fire to the child. Fabrics with loose weaves or high naps are poor choices for children's clothing: they catch fire easily and burn quickly. Fire melts some synthetic fabrics, and thus can cause serious burns. Full and flowing clothing is more likely to catch fire than is clothing that lies close to the body.

Since 1973 the Federal Hazardous Substances Act has required cribs to be made so that mattresses fit properly; slats, sides and ends are properly spaced and side rails latch correctly. But older cribs may not meet these

By federal law, all children's sleepware must be flame resistant.

standards. Moreover, no such protections cover other articles of children's furniture. Here again, it is up to the parents to exercise caution — especially since kids have a genius for getting tangled up in furniture, falling from it and dragging it down on top of themselves. Children's furniture should have a low center of gravity and should stand firmly on the floor without wobbling or tilting. The ladder on a bunk bed should be secure, so that it cannot come away from the rail while the child is in midair, and the entire unit should be firm and secure. Before buying a bunk bed, shake it to make sure it is stable. Even though cribs *are* covered by safety laws, it's a good idea to check them before purchasing, too. Mattresses should fit snugly, so that the baby cannot catch a hand or foot between it and the sides or end of the crib. Safety catches should be secure, and slats should be placed close together, so that there is no chance the baby's head can be caught between them.

Children's toys are a special problem. Be sure to inspect them carefully for construction, finish and durability. If the toy breaks, will it cause an injury? Does it have sharp edges, points that stick up or pieces that can be swallowed? Is there any chance that it might explode? Be wary of dolls' eyes that can come off or out and into a child's mouth; of rough edges that are abrasive; of points that can puncture the skin. All electrical toys should carry the Underwriters Laboratories seal of approval (see box, page 186). Manufacturers are forbidden to use lead based paint on toys, but well-intentioned friends who give your child a toy their child has outgrown, may use such a paint to spruce it up. You should inquire before you let your youngster play with it.

Outdoor playground equipment for children also needs careful inspection. The seats on swings should be made of lightweight material, to prevent them from hurting any child they may accidentally hit. Gym rings should be small enough to keep a child from putting his — or her — head through. Slides should not be too steep, and their ladders should be securely fastened. The ladder treads should be wide and level. The nuts and bolts on all playground equipment should be finished off, to keep the child from being caught on them. And all playground equipment should be anchored firmly.

If you find a safety problem in *any* children's product, be sure to write to the Consumer Product Safety Commission, 1111 18th Street, NW, Washington, D.C. 20207.

As part of its National Advertising Division, the Council of Better Business Bureaus has a Children's Advertising Review unit. If you believe that an advertisement for a children's product is deliberately misleading or downright dishonest, send a letter indicating the brand name of the product; the name of the advertiser; the name of the newspaper, magazine, radio or television station that carried the ad; and the date on which it appeared, to: Children's Advertising Review Unit, Council of Better Business Bureaus, 845 Third Ave., New York, N.Y. 10022.

Food

The foods Americans buy are subject to a number of federal controls before they reach our tables. Federal agencies set standards for grading the quality of raw foods — vegetables, fruits, meats, poultry, milk and eggs. Some types of foods, like meats and poultry, are regularly inspected for safety. Manufacturers of processed foods must adopt inspection procedures and quality controls which conform to federal specifications. Once in a great while, an accident occurs and spoiled food finds its way into the stores, with consequences that can be tragic. But on the whole, we have good reason to be satisfied with the systems and precautions that assure our food is not adulterated, and that it has been produced under sanitary conditions.

Consumers and consumer advocates are, however, somewhat less satisfied with the procedures that govern food labeling and grading. In the first place, they are extremely inconsistent. Labeling is required by law on some food products and not on others; the same grade that signifies the very best chicken signifies only the second best eggs; the date stamped on a package of luncheon meat may have a different meaning from the one stamped on a carton of milk. In addition, the information conveyed on labels is often inadequate and far from clear to the average consumer. Labels may tell us the amounts of certain nutrients in canned, cooked foods, but not of food elements the consumer may wish to avoid. Careful supermarket shoppers have their work cut out for them. It is time consuming — and sometimes confusing — to read and compare the labels on the packaged and processed foods that make up more than half of our national food supply and to compare price and size — or price and grade — to determine which can of stringbeans or carton of eggs is the best buy. But if we are to get the best value and the best nutrition for our food dollars, we must do this work.

Labeling. Certain common food products — among them mayonnaise, canned fruits, milk, cheese, ice cream, macaroni, noodles, bread, margarine and butter — are not required to list the ingredients of which they are made on their packages, although the manufacturer may supply that information voluntarily. The Food and Drug Administration has set so-

What Grading Labels Mean

Not all the foods we buy are graded. Below is a list of those that are and what the grades mean.

Dairy Products

- Butter. All butter, by law, must contain a minimum of 80 percent butter fat. U.S. AA is top quality; A, which usually sells for less, is nearly its equal.
- Milk. Milk and milk products are graded by state officials certified by the Food and Drug Administration. Most of them carry a Grade A label.
- Eggs. There are three grades of eggs — AA, A and B. The first two are virtually equal in quality and the second is the one most commonly sold in retail stores. Grade B eggs are not widely available, but they are entirely acceptable for general cooking and baking. When eggs are graded, they are also checked for size. Extra large, large and medium are most commonly found in stores.

Fruits and Vegetables

- Fresh produce. Although most fresh fruits and vegetables are graded at the wholesale level, consumers seldom see that grading, except on sacks of potatoes. Grades are based on color, shape, maturity and freedom from defects; the typical range is from U.S. Fancy through U.S. No. 1 and U.S. No. 2, although the top grade for potatoes is Extra No. 1. Most fresh fruits and vegetables sold in markets are U.S. No. 1 — the second grade.
- Packaged produce. Most canned, frozen and dried fruits and vegetables are packed according to A, B and C grades, although the grade seldom appears on the label. Grade A products are uniform in size and color; Grade B are not as perfect, nor quite as tender. Grade C are just as wholesome and nutritious as the higher grades, but less esthetically appealing.

Meat, Fish and Poultry

- Meat. Pork is seldom graded, but beef, lamb and veal are. The grades most widely available are U.S. Prime, Choice and Good. There are lower grades available, but they are seldom seen in markets, where the most common grade is Choice.
- Fish. Grading is seldom seen on fresh fish, but is commonly found on packaged frozen fish. The top grade, A, is the one you are most likely to see in your market.
- Poultry. The top grade — U.S. Grade A — is most commonly seen in markets; Grades B and C are reserved for canned soups, luncheon meats and other processed foods.

called standards of identity — specifications of content — for these products, and manufacturers who wish to call their foods by these names must adhere to the FDA specifications. The difference between a product called "mayonnaise," for example, and one called "sandwich spread" is more than a mere matter of words. The two contain different ingredients.

Moreover, the sandwich spread — like all other processed and packaged foods save those named above — must, by law, display a list of its ingredients. Although this list must be arranged in decreasing order of quantity, it does not have to indicate how much of any particular ingredient the product contains. An ordinary can of condensed cream of mushroom soup may have as many as 16 ingredients, starting with water and ending with garlic powder and containing in between some that the ordinary consumer can be expected to know about — corn syrup and tomato paste, for example — and others — dicalcium phosphate, hydrolized vegetable protein — that only a trained nutritionist is likely to understand.

But if the information on ingredient labels is less specific and less comprehensible than consumer advocates would like — people who want to hold down their salt intake, for example, cannot depend on ingredient labels to give them the information they need

CONSUMER ALERT

Breaking the Packagers' Code

A number — but certainly not all — of the packagers of foods, identify some or all of the products they distribute with a clearly understandable statement of the length of time the item can be stored before it will become stale or lose its flavor. This practice is known as open dating.

In addition, practically every can in a supermarket — and many frozen and packaged foods as well — will bear a code symbol that tells the store manager when the item was packed. From this marking — usually a combination of numbers and letters — the manager can determine how long the item, properly stored, will remain fresh and flavorful. If you can decipher the code, you too will be able to know the packing date. (These package dating codes should not be confused with the Universal Product Code — a marking system consisting of lines and numbers, sometimes called the Zebra Code, designed to be read by automatic scanning devices.)

Not surprisingly, each company uses a different dating code. Examples of the codes of several major packagers, and instructions on interpreting them, are given below.

Remember that foodstuffs lose freshness at variable rates according to their type and how they are packaged. Many vacuum packed foods, for example, may last indefinitely, although their flavor may deteriorate after two years or so. Most frozen foods packed with sauce will stay fresh for about a year; frozen foods packed without sauce remain fresh for about eight months.

As a general rule, the more recent the packing date on the product, the greater your assurance that the item has retained maximum flavor and freshness.

Coca-Cola Corporation. The code refers to the date of packaging, and consists of four numbers. The first digit refers to the year the item was packaged, the others to the day of the year. If the code reads, for example, 3072, the food was packaged on March 13, 1983; the 3 refers to 1983, and March 13 is the 72nd day of the year.

General Foods Corporation. Most items are coded with the packaging date: four numerals followed by a letter. The first numeral refers to the year of packaging, the last three to the month and day, the letter refers to the plant where packaging was done. The marking 3 364 B, would mean that the item had been packaged on the 364th day of the year, or December 30, 1983, at plant B.

General Mills. The date of packaging is stamped in a code consisting of a letter followed by three digits. The letter refers to the month the item was packaged, beginning with A for June, B for July, and so forth. The letter I is omitted. Thus, J means February, K stands for March, L is April and M is May. The first digit stands for the year an item was packed and the last two digits for the day of the month. Therefore, a code that reads J422 means that the item was packaged on February 22, 1984.

Kellogg Company. Those products that are not open dated are stamped with the four-digit coded date of packaging. The first digit refers to the year, the last three to the date of packing. A code that reads 3220, would mean the product was packed on the 220th day of 1983, or August 8.

Pillsbury Company. Most items are coded with the packaging date. The marking is in four parts: a letter that refers to the month of packaging, followed by a number referring to the year, then a letter identifying the plant and a number referring to the day of packaging. Months are identified by letters, A (January) through L (December). The code F 3 W 16 would mean that the item was packaged June 16, 1983, at plant W.

Procter and Gamble. Products are marked with a code, only the first four digits of which refer to the packing date. Of these, the first number refers to the year and the next three to the day of the year. Therefore, a product whose first four digits were 4016, would have een packaged on the sixteenth day of 1984, r January 16, 1984.

rogresso Food Corporation. Products are oded with the date they were packaged. The ode consists of three digits, followed by a let- er — signifying the shift during which the em was packaged — and a final digit. The rst three digits stand for the day of the year, ne last digit to the year itself. Thus, an item narked 174G3 was packaged on the 174th day f 1983 (June 23rd), during the G shift.

touffer Corporation. The last two markings n the package identification code are a letter A through L) and a number (0 through 9): nese signify the month and year in which the tem was packed. A code ending in H 3, for example, would indicate that the product was packaged in August of 1983.

Many company codes refer to the day on which an item was packed with a three digit number. The chart indicates how those dates are figured.

Booklets telling how to break the codes of most major food processing companies have been published by the consumer agencies of Connecticut, Maryland and New York. Residents of these states may write for a copy (see directory, pages 16-17).

If you do not live in one of these states but are interested in cracking the code of a processor not listed above, check your food store or supermarket. The manager may interpret the code for you.

ay Of The Year Chart

Day of Month	Jan.	Feb.	Mar.	Apr.	May	June	July	Aug.	Sept.	Oct.	Nov.	Dec.
1	001	032	060	091	121	152	182	213	244	274	305	335
2	002	033	061	092	122	153	183	214	245	275	306	336
3	003	034	062	093	123	154	184	215	246	276	307	337
4	004	035	063	094	124	155	185	216	247	277	308	338
5	005	036	064	095	125	156	186	217	248	278	309	339
6	006	037	065	096	126	157	187	218	249	279	310	340
7	007	038	066	097	127	158	188	219	250	280	311	341
8	008	039	067	098	128	159	189	220	251	281	312	342
9	009	040	068	099	129	160	190	221	252	282	313	343
10	010	041	069	100	130	161	191	222	253	283	314	344
11	011	042	070	101	131	162	192	223	254	284	315	345
12	012	043	071	102	132	163	193	224	255	285	316	346
13	013	044	072	103	133	164	194	225	256	286	317	347
14	014	045	073	104	134	165	195	226	257	287	318	348
15	015	046	074	105	135	166	196	227	258	288	319	349
16	016	047	075	106	136	167	197	228	259	289	320	350
17	017	048	076	107	137	168	198	229	260	290	321	351
18	018	049	077	108	138	169	199	230	261	291	322	352
19	019	050	078	109	139	170	200	231	262	292	323	353
20	020	051	079	110	140	171	201	232	263	293	324	354
21	021	052	080	111	141	172	202	233	264	294	325	355
22	022	053	081	112	142	173	203	234	265	295	326	356
23	023	054	082	113	143	174	204	235	266	296	327	357
24	024	055	083	114	144	175	205	236	267	297	328	358
25	025	056	084	115	145	176	206	237	268	298	329	359
26	026	057	085	116	146	177	207	238	269	299	330	360
27	027	058	086	117	147	178	208	239	270	300	331	361
28	028	059	087	118	148	179	208	240	271	301	332	362
29	029		088	119	149	180	210	241	272	302	333	363
30	030		089	120	150	181	211	242	273	303	334	364
31	031		090		151		212	243		304		365

— some information at least is present on virtually every can, bottle and package of processed food we buy. This is not true of nutritional information. A listing of nutritional elements is required by law only in the case of products that make nutritional claims for themselves — as, for example, fruit drinks that advertise themselves as "high in Vitamin C." As a consequence, consumers who want to know the nutritional value of the packaged foods they buy have to look either for those that carry nutritional claims or those that include this listing voluntarily. Only about 40 percent of the processed foods currently on the market contain this information.

Moreover, consumer groups have argued that the nutritional information required is not adequate. If you examine a nutritional label, you will see that its figures are based on the nutritional content of a single serving — four ounces, or a half cup — of the food concerned, and that it lists the number of servings in each container, the number of calories in each serving, the gram weight per serving of protein, carbohydrate and fat, and the proportion per serving of the U.S. recommended daily allowance (RDA) of protein and seven vitamins and minerals: Vitamins A and C, thiamin, riboflavin, niacin, calcium and iron. But it does not list several elements — cholesterol, fatty acids, sodium and sugar — with which many consumers are concerned. True, sodium and sugar will be listed on the ingredients label, but since that label does not indicate their amounts, consumers who want foods that are low in salt or sugar — and in fatty acids and/or cholesterol — have to look specifically for products that make this claim. And such products are likely to cost more than those that do not.

Labels are also required by federal law to give the weight of the contents of a package or can. But sometimes that weight is deceptive: an item that appears to be a bargain may not be one. Canned fruits and vegetables, for example, contain a considerable amount of liquid, either in the form of syrup or water: to know how much of the fruit or vegetable a given can actually holds, you have to know the drained weight. Some manufacturers give this information voluntarily; others do not. When buying canned fruits and vegetables, a wise consumer compares drained weights, where given, and prices of various brands.

Along with the confusing labels are others — mandated by law — that are quite clear. If you buy a product that claims to have reduced calories, you can be sure that it contains at least one-third fewer calories than the same size of brands of food that do not make this claim; if it claims to be "low calorie" you can be sure it has no more than 40 calories per serving. If you buy something marked "sugar free," you can be sure it contains no table sugar (sucrose). But that does not mean it does not contain sugar in other forms — honey or fructose (fruit sugar) for example. To find this out, you will have to read the ingredients.

Dating. Freshness is another concern of consumers buying food. The huge volume of business in supermarkets and groceries and the desire of food producers and retailers to maintain their reputations offer considerable assurance that the food we buy is fresh. But although there is some state and local legislation on the subject, there is no federal requirement that food packages be labeled as to date. Moreover, even where dating requirements exist, or when producers or sellers supply dates voluntarily, the dates posted on packages do not have a uniform meaning. The products most commonly open-dated — milk, cheese, bread and processed meats, for example — sometimes show the pack date: the day the food was processed or packaged. In other cases, they show the expiration date: the last day the food should be eaten. In still others, they show the pull date — the last day the product should be sold. And in still others, the freshness date: the last day the product can be expected to be fresh. It is still edible for a few days after that — some bakery products, for example, are sold at reduced prices for a short while after the freshness date — but it is no longer at its peak. If you want to know the precise meaning of the date on any open-dated product, you will have to inquire of the store manager.

Although consumers will find open dating on only some products, there is virtually no packaged food sold that does not contain precise information on its pack date. This information, however, is generally in code, and its purpose is to enable the retailer and the manufacturer to identify particular lots of the product in the event of a recall. But code dating is worthless for any consumer who

"Rain Checks"

Supermarkets and other retail stores often offer specials to bring in customers. An FTC rule says that if a grocery store advertises a special, it must have that special available during the sale period, and must clearly identify any branch store that will *not* have the advertised item.

Sometimes a store will misjudge the popularity of an advertised special and sell out right away. Or the delivery truck may be late. If for any reason the advertised special is not available, the store manager, in an effort to comply with the spirit of the FTC rule, may offer you a "rain check," naming the date he expects to have the merchandise at the same sale price. But stores are not required to offer rain checks, nor should they make a habit of falling back on the rain-check system, not only because it is inconvenient for consumers, but because it violates the FTC rule to run out of advertised specials frequently. If your supermarket often does so, write to your local or state consumer protection office, and to the FTC.

does not know how to break the code. Some food companies may be willing to supply this information to consumers who inquire, but this is purely voluntary on their part. The Offices of Consumer Affairs in New York, Connecticut and Maryland have published booklets that explain the codes for some national and local brands of packaged foods, and these booklets are available at no cost to residents of those states (see directory, page 16, for addresses).

Food Grading. Although by federal law raw and processed foods must be inspected several times before they appear on the market, no law requires food to be graded as to quality. This is a purely voluntary procedure, and if done, is paid for by packers and processors and carried out by Department of Agriculture inspectors. As a result, the system is neither standardized nor applied uniformly to all foods. Eggs are graded; bread is not. Top quality chickens are U.S. Grade A, but the best butter and eggs are Grade AA. The best potatoes are called Extra No. 1, while No. 1 apples rank after Extra Fancy and Fancy.

According to a survey conducted by the Department of Agriculture, consumers would prefer a standard grading system to the one that now prevails. But since the grading procedure itself is purely voluntary and packers and processors are reluctant to make any changes, consumers are not likely to get their wish. Those who are concerned with grades of food have to familiarize themselves with the system now in use, which is outlined in the box on page 191.

Fortunately, grading is in reality of only limited value since it does not refer to the nutritional content or the safety of the food in question. Higher grade — and, therefore, more expensive — items may be more attractive to the eye and more pleasing to the palate than those that carry lower grades. Uniform slices of canned peaches look better than broken pieces and slices of uneven size, and a prime steak, with its heavy marbling, is more tender than one graded choice.

Saving Money on Groceries. There are many ways for consumers to save money on food and other groceries. House brands and generic foods are generally less expensive than national brands and are at least roughly the same in nutritional value. Warehouse and limited assortment stores, which offer fewer services and less variety than supermarkets, and which therefore have a lower overhead, can sell goods for lower prices than regular outlets. Cents-off coupons and sales produce bargain prices at supermarkets. But the wise consumer keeps in mind that the stores use these devices as lures. If we do not keep our wits about us, we can easily find ourselves buying products we did not intend to buy and spending more money than we originally planned. According to one survey, coupon users generally run up bigger cash register tapes at the supermarket than do customers who do not use coupons.

Because most packaged goods come in such a wide variety of sizes, probably the most effective way to save money at the supermarket is to make use of the information provided by unit pricing. The unit price, generally posted on a shelf card under the product in

Safety Precautions in Using Prescription Drugs

Although all drugs — prescription and nonprescription — are tested for safety before they are put on the market, many have side-effects. Some are unpleasant but essentially harmless: the benefits the drugs produce far outweigh the difficulties they cause. On the other hand, some drugs can have still untoward — and sometimes dangerous — effects on patients. Some drugs interact badly with one another. Taken alone, each may be entirely safe. Taken together, they may produce difficulties for the patient.

According to a national survey conducted by the FDA, nearly 80 percent of patients are not adequately advised, either by pharmacists or physicians, of the proper precautions to use in taking prescription drugs. But the problem does not seem to be entirely the professionals' fault: the same survey indicates that patients tend to be embarrassed about "wasting" their doctor's or druggist's time by asking questions. Such reluctance is foolish. It is important to ask questions and to get adequate information about any drug.

Printed information on prescription drugs is also available to patients. Manufacturers supply an information leaflet that describes the drug's properties and possible side effects. In addition, a more detailed and technical leaflet is available — the professional "package insert," which is directed toward physicians and pharmacists. Every drug carries such an insert, but it is not usually passed along to consumers. You have, however, every right to ask your pharmacist for it if you think it will be helpful. The most important paragraphs to read are those headed "Indications," "Contraindications," "Side Effects" and "Precautions." If you cannot obtain the package insert, you can find the same information in the reference department of your public library, in a volume entitled *The Physicians' Desk Reference*.

question, indicates how much a given unit — whether an ounce, a pound or some other standard — of the item costs. It may take some calculating to determine whether one size of a given product is a better buy than another, but the effort is worth while. Even though larger sizes are generally more economical than smaller ones, this is not always the case. Moreover, sizes sometimes vary from one brand to another. Tinned fish and meat, for example, come in both six-and-a-half and seven-ounce cans. Although unit pricing is mandatory only in some states and even in those may apply only to stores that do a certain minimum volume of business, large supermarkets throughout the country voluntarily offer this service as an aid to their customers.

Drugs and Cosmetics.
Every medicinal drug sold in this country — whether by prescription or over the counter — falls under the control of the Food and Drug Administration (FDA), and none can be sold until it has been demonstrated, by test, to be both safe and effective. The FDA also has jurisdiction over the $10-billion-a-year cosmetics business. But its control over cosmetic products is less stringent than its control over drugs: the law does not require that cosmetics be tested for safety before they are marketed. With the exception of color additives, ingredients used in cosmetics need not be cleared in advance with the FDA. On the other hand, the FDA requires manufacturers to provide a warning label on cosmetics containing ingredients that have not been adequately substantiated for safety.

Prescription Drugs. Prescription drugs can represent a significant expense for many consumers, especially older people with chronic diseases that require daily medication. Moreover, the cost of prescription drugs has always been notoriously high. Part of the reason is that it costs drug manufacturers a great deal, both in time and money, to bring a new drug to the market: according to one reliable estimate, 10 years and $50 to $70 million. Because the FDA requires that all drugs be both safe and effective, every new drug must be extensively tested after it has been developed. The tests themselves are strict and conducted according to rigid standards. Some are so-called single blind tests: ones in which some patients are given the drug while others are given a placebo — a harmless, ineffective substance, such as a sugar pill — and in which, although the doctor knows what the patient is getting, the patient does not. Others are double blind tests: neither doctor nor patient knows who is getting what. When all the results of this testing are in, the drug company submits its evidence to the FDA in the form of a New Drug Application — a long and detailed document — and the agency then reviews it carefully, a process that itself takes two to three years.

Once a drug has been approved, it must thereafter be manufactured in strict accordance with the specifications and standards laid down in the application, and the FDA regularly and periodically collects samples of all drugs on the market and tests them for purity and strength. If a drug is discovered to be adulterated or misbranded, the manufacturer will be asked to recall it voluntarily; if the drug is not withdrawn, the FDA has the authority to seize it and remove it from the market.

Generic Drugs. For the first 17 years after a new drug is patented, it receives special protection. The company that developed and manufactured it has a monopoly, and can set the wholesale price at whatever level it chooses. A patient for whom this drug has been prescribed may be able to save a little money by comparison shopping among pharmacies. But for the term of the patent, the medication itself has no competition in the marketplace.

On the other hand, once the patent runs out, *any* pharmaceutical company can manufacture and sell the drug — provided it goes through the same process as the original developer, conducting the necessary tests and making the necessary application to the FDA. These drugs, whether sold under different brand names from the original or under the general — or generic — name that describes their chemical composition or class, usually sell for about one-third less than the medications they duplicate and are identical to the originals in every way save name and sometimes appearance. The original tablet may be round, for example, while some of the new drug tablets are oval. Achromycin, for example, is the brand name for the first of one specific class of antibiotics to be developed. Now, that same drug is marketed by a number of different companies, some of which sell it under brand names of their own, such as Sumycin and Tetracyn, and others of which sell it under its generic name: tetracycline.

In the view of the FDA, there is no consistent difference in quality between prescription drugs sold by brand name and those sold by generic name, or between prescription drugs made by large and widely known pharmaceutical houses and those made by smaller firms. So, for the economy-minded consumer, the generics are likely to be the better buy. On the other hand, doctors tend to prescribe a drug by the brand name used by the original manufacturers, since that is the name with which they became familiar during the life of the patent. In all states save Indiana, doctors and, in some states, pharmacists can substitute a generic for a brand-name prescription drug. But consumers who want generics should not rely on their pharmacists to make the suggestion. If a drug that has been prescribed for you is no longer covered by a patent and you want to save money by buying a generic, be sure to tell this to your doctor and pharmacist. And, of course, remember that prices among generics can vary also, as can prices for the same drug in different pharmacies. In buying prescription drugs, it is important to comparison shop not only among the various brands and generics available, but also among stores.

Over-the-Counter Drugs. More than 250,000 different drugs — pain killers and cough syrups; antacids and antihistamines — are offered for sale over the counter in the United States. None is designed to cure illness, and none is a substitute for professional medical treatment. Over-the-counter medications are designed only to relieve the symptoms of minor illnesses — coughs, colds and indigestion, for example.

Safety Packaging of Over-the-Counter Drugs

Two of the most important safety requirements the government imposes on the manufacturers of over-the-counter drugs had their origins in tragedies. The Poison Prevention Packaging Act requires many prescription and over-the-counter drugs be placed in containers with caps that children cannot remove. It was passed only after a number of youngsters died as a result of swallowing aspirin tablets they found in bottles around their homes. Because these child-proof caps can be a problem for adults too, the law permits manufacturers to market some containers with easy-to-open tops. If you want such a container but do not find it, ask the pharmacist to transfer the medication to a conventional container. This is entirely within the law.

An FDA regulation which became effective in 1983 requires that most over-the-counter drugs be sealed in tamper-resistant packages before they leave the factory. This regulation, too, was prompted by tragedy: the deaths of several persons after they had taken capsules of an over-the-counter pain killer that was laced with strychnine after it left the factory.

Before 1962, the law required the manufacturers of over-the-counter drugs to demonstrate only that their products would produce no adverse side effects. Since then, a stronger requirement has been imposed — not only on medications created since that date, but on those that were already on the market. All over-the-counter drugs must now be tested for safety, effectiveness and labeling by the FDA. As a consequence, changes have been made in the ingredients and claims of some nonprescription remedies, and as the review process continues, additional changes may be made as well.

On the other hand, because these medications are freely available to anyone and because the improper use of any drug can have harmful consequences, strict federal regulations have been enacted that require clear and careful labeling of all over-the-counter drugs. The information on the label is important, and every consumer should read it with care. It includes:

- A list of the active ingredients and their quantities.
- Complete directions for use.
- The purpose (or purposes) for which the medication is intended.
- How much to take for each purpose.
- How often to take it.
- When not to take it.
- Any cautions or warnings.
- The names and quantity of any habit-forming drug contained in the product and the properties of that drug.
- Storage instructions, when necessary.
- An expiration date after which the drug should no longer be used.

Economy-minded consumers would do well to compare the ingredients list of different brands of over-the-counter medications designed for the same purpose. Aspirin, for example, is aspirin, no matter what the brand name. And this is true of many other nonprescription medications, which differ in name but contain the identical ingredients. Prices among brands may, however, differ substantially and some products may contain ingredients their names would not necessarily lead you to suspect . . . "Buffered aspirin," for example, is aspirin plus a buffering agent — a fact the ingredients label is required to disclose.

Cosmetics. As mentioned earlier, the law does not impose the same rigorous safety standards on cosmetics manufacturers as it does on the manufacturers of medicinal drugs, although the FDA has prohibited the use of certain specific ingredients in some cosmetics products. The only cosmetics ingredients that require prior approval by the FDA are colors. The agency has a list of approved coloring substances from which manufacturers must choose, and no manufacturer can receive a shipment of any of these materials until the FDA has tested and certified sample batches.

The reason the FDA makes relatively few testing demands on the cosmetics industry is simple: except for coloring materials, the ingredients used in cosmetics are generally considered safe. Most manufacturers of na-

(continued on page 202)

Regional Offices of the Federal Trade Commission

Main Office	**Federal Trade Commission, Washington, DC 20580**
Atlanta Regional Office	**Alabama, Florida, Georgia, Mississippi, North Carolina, South Carolina, Tennessee, Virginia** 1718 Peachtree Street, NW, Suite 1000, Atlanta, GA 30367
Boston Regional Office	**Connecticut, Maine, Massachusetts, New Hampshire, Rhode Island, Vermont** 150 Causeway Street, Room 1301, Boston, MA 02114tl
Chicago Regional Office	**Illinois, Indiana, Iowa, Kentucky, Minnesota, Missouri, Wisconsin** 55 East Monroe Street, Suite 1437, Chicago, IL 60603
Cleveland Regional Office	**Delaware, Maryland, Michigan, New York (West Of Rochester), Ohio, Pennsylvania, West Virginia** 118 St. Clair Avenue, Suite 500, Cleveland, OH 44114
Dallas Regional Office	**Arizona, Louisiana, New Mexico, Oklahoma, Texas** 2001 Bryan Street, Suite 2665, Dallas, TX 75201
Denver Regional Office	**Colorado, Kansas, Montana, Nebraska, North Dakota, South Dakota, Utah, Wyoming** 1405 Curtis Street, Suite 2900, Denver, Co 80202
Los Angeles Regional Office	**Arizona, Southern California** 11000 Wilshire Boulevard, Los Angeles, CA 90024
New York Regional Office	**New Jersey, New York (East of Rochester)** 26 Federal Plaza, Room 2243-EB, New York, NY 10278
San Francisco Regional Office	**Hawaii, Nevada, Northern California** 450 Golden Gate Avenue, San Francisco, CA 94102
Seattle Regional Office	**Alaska, Idaho, Oregon, Washington** 915 Second Avenue, 28th Floor, Seattle, WA 98174
FTC Field Station	P.O. Box 50169, Honolulu, HI 96850

Regional Offices of the Food and Drug Administration

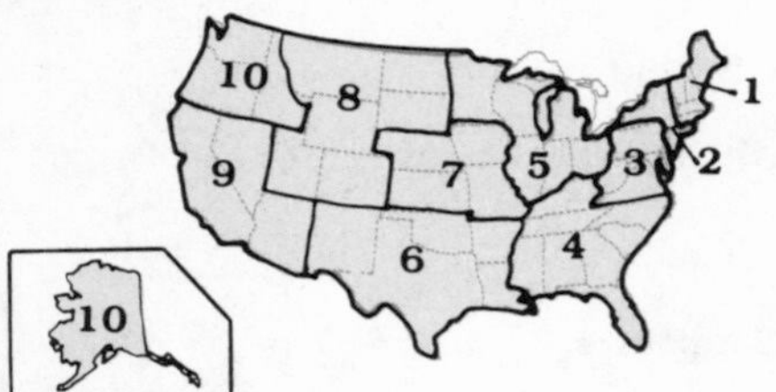

Main Office **Consumer Affairs and Small Business Staff (HFO-22), Food and Drug Administration Department of Health and Human Services**
5600 Fishers Lane, Rockville, MD 20857

Region 1 **Connecticut, Maine, Massachusetts, New Hampshire, Rhode Island, Vermont**
585 Commercial Street, Boston, MA 02109

Region 2 **New Jersey, New York, Puerto Rico**
850 Third Avenue, Brooklyn, NY 11232
599 Delaware Avenue, Buffalo, NY 14202
20 Evergreen Place, East Orange, NJ 07018
P.O. Box 54427, Old San Juan Station, San Juan, PR 00905

Region 3 **Delaware, Maryland, Pennsylvania, Virginia, West Virginia**
Room 900 U.S. Customhouse, 2nd and Chestnut Streets, Philadelphia, PA 19106
Pittsburgh Resident Inspection Post, 7 Parkway Center, Suite 645, Pittsburgh, PA 15220
900 Madison Avenue, Baltimore, MD 21201
Falls Church Resident Inspection Post, 701 West Broad Street, Room 309, Falls Church, VA 22046

Region 4 **Alabama, Florida, Georgia, Kentucky, Mississippi, North Carolina, South Carolina, Tennessee**
1182 West Peachtree Street, NW, Atlanta, GA 30309
P.O. Box 118 Orlando, FL 32802
297 Plus Park Boulevard, Nashville, TN 37217

Region 5 **Illinois, Indiana, Michigan, Minnesota, Ohio, Wisconsin**
433 West Van Buren Street, 1222 Main Post Office Building, Chicago, IL 60607
1141 Central Parkway, Cincinnati, OH 45202
U.S. Courthouse Building, 85 Marconi Boulevard, Room 231, Columbus, OH 43215
Cleveland Resident Inspection Post, 601 Rockwell Avenue, Room 453, Cleveland, OH 44114
1560 East Jefferson Avenue, Detroit, MI 48207
Indianapolis Resident Inspection Post, 575 North Pennsylvania, Room 693, Indianapolis, IN 46204
240 Hennepin Avenue, Minneapolis, MN 55401
Milwaukee Resident Inspection Post, 615 East Michigan Street, Milwaukee, WI 53202

Region 6	**Arkansas, Louisiana, New Mexico, Oklahoma, Texas** 500 South Ervay, Suite 470-B, Dallas, TX 75201 4298 Elysian Fields Avenue, New Orleans, LA 70122 Houston Station, 1440 North Loop Suite 250, Houston, TX 77009 San Antonio Resident Inspection Post, 419 South Main, Room 301, San Antonio, TX 78204
Region 7	**Iowa, Kansas, Missouri, Nebraska** 1009 Cherry Street, Kansas City, MO 64106 St. Louis Station, Laclete's Landing, 80B North Collins Street, St. Louis, MO 63102 Omaha Resident Inspection Post, 1619 Howard Street, Omaha, NE 68102
Region 8	**Colorado, Montana, North Dakota, South Dakota, Utah, Wyoming** 500 U.S. Customhouse, 19th and California Streets, Denver, CO 80202
Region 9	**Arizona, California, Hawaii, Nevada** 50 United Nations Plaza, Room 518, San Francisco, CA 94102 1521 West Pico Boulevard, Los Angeles, CA 90015
Region 10	**Alaska, Idaho, Oregon, Washington** 909 First Avenue, Federal Office Building, Room 5003, Seattle, WA 98174

Regional Offices of the U.S. Consumer Product Safety Commission

Main Office	**Washington, DC 20207**
Midwestern Regional Office	230 South Dearborn Street, Room 2945, Chicago, IL 60604
Southwestern Regional Office	1100 Commerce Street, Room 1C10, Dallas, TX 75242
Southeastern Regional Office	800 Peachtree Street, NE, Suite 210, Atlanta, GA 30308
Western Regional Office	555 Battery Street, Room 416, San Francisco, CA 94111
Northeastern Regional Office	6 World Trade Center, Vesey Street, 6th Floor, New York, NY 10048

The Commission also maintains Resident Posts in the following cities:

Boston, Massachusetts • Bridgeport, Connecticut • Buffalo, New York • Charlotte, North Carolina • Cincinnati, Ohio • Cleveland, Ohio • Denver, Colorado • Detroit, Michigan • Honolulu, Hawaii • Houston, Texas • Indianapolis, Indiana • Kansas City, Missouri • Los Angeles, California • Miami, Florida • Philadelphia, Pennsylvania • Phoenix, Arizona • Pittsburgh, Pennsylvania • Portland, Oregon • Rockville, Maryland • San Juan, Puerto Rico • Seattle, Washington • St. Louis, Missouri • St. Paul, Minnesota • Tulsa, Oklahoma

Precautions in Using Over-the-Counter Drugs

- Only use over-the-counter (OTC) drugs when you need them. Make sure you know what you are taking.
- Follow the directions on the label to the letter, pay particular attention to the WARNING section and read carefully any circular that comes with the product.
- Do not take any OTC drug over an extended period of time without medical supervision.
- If you are receiving treatment for any chronic illness, consult your doctor before taking OTC drugs.
- If you experience a side effect from any drug, stop using it and call your doctor.
- Some drugs deteriorate quickly. Check the expiration date on medications and discard them when that date arrives. Flush old drugs down the toilet, and throw away the containers.
- Alcohol and certain pills don't mix. Combined with sleeping pills, tranquilizers and some antihistamines, it can produce dangerous effects. Alcohol can also reduce the effectiveness of antibiotics.
- Never combine several drugs, whether they are OTC or prescription, without consulting your doctor.

tionally advertised brands test products carefully before marketing them — either in their own laboratories or at consulting laboratories.

Despite these precautions, some consumers *do* have cause for concern. The government estimates that 60,000 people a year are injured by cosmetics, through irritations or allergic reactions. Indeed, allergic reactions are so widespread that many manufacturers make a special effort to remove all common allergy-causing substances from their products. In addition, the FDA has mandated a series of regulations that must be observed, designed to provide consumers with the information needed to protect themselves from being harmed by their cosmetics. All cosmetics must carry a list of all their ingredients, save those that make up its flavor or fragrance, in descending order of weight: the list may be on the label or in an accompanying brochure – and can be studied to see if the product contains any substance to which the user may be allergic. All products in aerosol cans must carry warnings that aerosol sprays held too close to the body can produce itching, blistering and burning. Certain coal tar hair dyes must carry a conspicuous warning that they may be irritating to the skin and that they have been determined to cause cancer in laboratory animals. Also, the label on these dyes must give the consumer directions for doing a preliminary sensitivity test, called a patch test, to determine whether irritation is likely to develop. Finally, cosmetics described by their manufacturers as hypoallergenic — unlikely to cause allergic reactions — must be submitted to a series of stringent tests in order to demonstrate to the FDA that they produce significantly fewer adverse reactions in users than do other comparable products.

The kinds of purchases discussed in this chapter — big ticket items; children's goods; foods and drugs — are so much a part of our lives that we seldom stop to consider the number of consumer-related issues they involve. Certainly we are aware of their cost, and of the use we make of them; we are aware of their quality and of the service we expect from the merchant if we are dissatisfied. But virtually all of them also involve important matters of safety and health. Manufacturers and retailers have a major responsibility to ensure that the goods they sell are made according to acceptable standards, and the federal government has enacted laws and regulations designed to hold business to those standards and to protect consumers. But that does not mean that we, as consumers, have no responsibility. Precisely because we do not have the technical knowledge that may be necessary to make informed decisions on questions of health and safety, it is up to us to see to it that business and government carry out their obligations in this area. Also, it is up to us to exercise intelligence and caution when we buy: to ask questions; to pay attention to — and use — the information the government requires manufacturers and dealers to give us; to comparison shop and — if anything happens to go wrong with a purchase we make — to know our consumer rights and exercise them.

Chapter 8

Business Services

This chapter concerns such service businesses as dry cleaning, plumbing, gardening, pest control, employment counseling and a host of others we so frequently need and use. (Professional services — legal, medical, dental and others — are the subjects covered in Chapter 12.)

All of them can present difficult problems for consumers. When you buy merchandise of any kind, from a pair of shoes to an automobile, you have something tangible to look at and examine — to try on or even try out. On the other hand, when you buy services, you are dealing primarily with people — whose skill, honesty and responsibility are not always easy to evaluate. It is, therefore, particularly important to shop around carefully before committing yourself to a service transaction — to get recommendations from friends and neighbors; to check into the reputations and credentials of the individuals or firms you are considering; to compare the terms and offers of various suppliers and to steel yourself against the lure of high-pressure methods and apparent bargains.

In addition, it is a good idea to check with your local Better Business Bureau about any firm you are considering — even one that has been recommended to you. The BBB will not evaluate a company for you, but it *will* tell you if it has received any complaints about it. If the consumer affairs agency in your area is active and effective, it, too, will have files on firms about which there have been complaints. If your consumer affairs agency is not active, try the nearest office of your state's attorney general, which will certainly know if complaints have been received and can describe any action it may have taken. You should also check to see whether the firm belongs to its industry's trade association. Membership in such a group is not an automatic assurance either of competence or honesty but, taken together with other recommendations, it should have some weight.

Contracts

In dealing with a company supplying services that are relatively complicated and expensive and take a fair amount of time to carry out — home repairs, for example — you should always insist on having a written contract. Suppliers often have standard forms that they ask their clients to sign. But even if the supplier with whom you are dealing does not have such a document, you should demand that one be drawn up. A written agreement, properly detailed, goes a long way toward forestalling arguments.

A contract does not need to be complicated. At a minimum it should describe the work to be done and the payments you are to make. But in order best to protect yourself, other information should also be included. Following is a suggested check list. Some items may not apply to the job you want done. You may have to negotiate for some of the things you want, and you may not get all of them. You may be willing to give up one demand or another in order to obtain the services of a particularly well-qualified or responsible individual or firm. But even if you cannot get everything you want, you should always try.

- The names and addresses of the parties to the agreement.
- A precise and detailed description of the work that is to be done.
- The date on which the work will begin and the date on which it will be finished.
- The total amount to be paid.
- The form in which payment is to be made (check, cash, credit card, for example).
- A payment schedule. Contract work should never be paid fully in advance, and you should strive for a payment schedule in which each installment is paid on *satisfactory* completion of a specifically spelled-out portion of the work. The largest installment should, if possible, be reserved for the last. You might, for example, suggest paying one-quarter on signing; another quarter when half the work

has been satisfactorily done and the balance when the job has been satisfactorily completed, provided that completion occurs no later than the agreed-on final date. Suppliers may not like such an arrangement. For one thing, many want to be paid for materials as they are purchased or needed. They also prefer schedules that bring them as much money as possible early in the game and that link payment to time, rather than work — as, for example, one-half on signing the contract; one-quarter half-way through the agreed-on period; and the final quarter on the completion date mentioned in the contract, even if the work has not been completed by then. Given this disparity of interest between consumers and suppliers, payment schedules are likely to become matters requiring considerable negotiation and compromise.

- A penalty clause. Under the terms of such a clause, the price of the job is lowered by a specific percentage or amount if the agreed-on time schedule is not met. Some suppliers do not like penalty clauses, and you may have to negotiate for one.
- A statement of who is to pay for any materials that may be necessary to the job. If you have to bear the cost, the contract should spell out whether you will be required to pay the retail or wholesale price or whether you can buy the materials yourself.
- A statement that the supplier will obtain any permits that may be required.
- Proof that the supplier is bonded and insured. This is especially important in the case of any work done in or around the house.
- A warranty: a statement of the specific aspects of the work the supplier guarantees — parts, labor, the job as a whole — the length of time the warranty holds and the nature of the redress to the consumer for any defects. This last provision can be especially important. If, for example, paneling falls off a wall because the adhesive used on it was faulty, the cost of new adhesive would hardly be adequate redress. All the paneling would have to be removed; the old adhesive would have to be stripped from the wall; new adhesive would have to be applied and then the paneling would have to be put in place again.

Under certain circumstances, the agreement may be based on a written offer — the supplier's estimate or appraisal of the job while it is still in the discussion stage. In this case, the offer should include a clear statement of the length of time for which it holds. Otherwise, when you agree to go ahead, you may discover that the price has increased by a considerable amount.

Appliance Repair

Nothing lasts forever, and you can be sure that even the best and most durable appliance in your household will break down at some point. The average life span of a dishwasher is 9 years; a refrigerator, 15; a washing machine, 11; and a dryer 14 years. A good sewing machine should keep on working up to 24 years, and sometimes longer. Of course, few appliances keep neatly to this schedule, and you can never tell when one will need minor — or major — repairs.

If an appliance breaks down while it is still protected by the warranty, the terms describe what you must do in order to have it repaired. (Chapter 7 contains a full discussion of this matter.) But if the problem develops after the warranty has expired, the responsibility for repair is yours.

The most reliable repair shops are usually those that offer factory-authorized service. Manufacturers are selective about the people they permit to service their products, and factory-authorized dealers usually receive special training, which is updated periodically. But check carefully. Firms that offer factory-authorized *parts* do not necessarily offer factory-authorized service. If you do not find the names of factory-authorized dealers in the phone book, write to the manufacturer.

Be sure to get a detailed estimate before having any appliance repaired. Repairs can be expensive, and if the appliance is old, it may not be worth the investment. If you do not have the work done, you will probably have to pay for the estimate, but if you *do* have the repairs made, the estimate should cost you nothing. Be sure to find out whether the estimate is binding; if it is not, ask the repair shop to telephone you about any additional work that may be necessary before undertaking it.

Appliance repairs seldom require a detailed contract, but be sure to get a written statement of the delivery date. And when the work is finished, check over the bill to make certain the charges have been itemized. Do not forget to get a written guarantee, both for parts and labor, if possible. You are also entitled to the return of any parts that have been replaced.

Service contracts are available for some appliances, and many stores offer them at the time of sale, calling them extended warranties or additional warranty coverage. Even if you want such a contract, immediate action is not necessary. Most dealers will make the service contract available up to the time the warranty expires.

Beauty Services

Some skill is required in the performance of all beauty services. But there are three specific aspects of the field that require particular expertise: permanent waving, hair coloring and electrolysis. The first two involve the use of strong chemicals, and if either is done improperly, the hair can be seriously damaged. Similarly, electrolysis can damage the skin if it is performed on certain people under certain circumstances. Hairdressers must be licensed in all states. But in some, there are no requirements at all for electrolysists, while others permit only medical specialists in dermatology to perform this service. Whatever the requirement may be in your state, it is particularly important to check the qualifications of anyone who is going to give you a permanent wave, color your hair or perform electrolysis on you.

A good way to judge competence and professionalism is to see how careful a hairdresser or electrolysist is before beginning a job. A good hairdresser will examine a client's hair carefully before coloring it or giving a permanent wave.

If the hair is to be colored, the hairdresser will first perform a patch test to see whether the dye will prove irritating. If the hair is to be waved, a series of questions is in order, to determine whether the permanent will take. Is the hair dyed? Is the client pregnant or taking medication of any kind? Is the client due for surgery that requires an anesthetic? A client who insists on having a permanent despite the hairdresser's warning that it may fail may legitimately be asked to sign a release exonerating the hairdresser in the event the wave does not take.

Electrolysis — the application of heat to the hair root by means of a tiny wire — is the only known method of permanently removing excess body or facial hair. The process should be safe and painless, but it must be repeated several times; in particularly stubborn cases, treatment may be necessary for as long as two years. Moreover, there are some circumstances under which electrolysis may not be advisable, and a good electrolysist will check to discover such conditions in advance. Pregnancy and childbirth temporarily increase hair growth in some women, as does regular use of a contraceptive pill. People who take aspirin regularly are more likely to bleed than those who do not. Certain illnesses — diabetes, for example — carry with them a tendency to develop minor or serious infections. Some individuals — especially black people — tend to develop raised and visible scar tissue.

Carpet Cleaning

Today, 80 percent of carpets can be cleaned just as well in the home as at a carpet-cleaning plant. If you are moving, or want to have your floors waxed or refinished, it may be to your advantage to send your carpets out to be cleaned. Otherwise, all but the most fragile carpets, or those that are light and move easily on the floor, can be cleaned in the house.

A good carpet cleaning, whether done by steam, shampooing or the use of foam, should get out all the dirt — even soot from the fireplace. But some stains may not be completely removable. The carpet cleaner should examine for such stains beforehand, and warn you.

Carpet seams sometimes split under the force of a cleaning machine, and occasionally the machine can produce a tear. The cleaning company should repair those damages at no cost. Sometimes, wall-to-wall carpeting shrinks when it is cleaned, either because it was improperly installed or because too much shampoo has been used. The first is not the cleaner's responsibility. The second is. Once in a great while the cleansing agent combines with the carpet dye in such a way as to produce a stain. The cleaner's responsibility for this depends on whether or not the difficulty could have been anticipated.

Most carpet cleaners give estimates over the telephone at no cost. But remember that the accuracy of the estimate depends on the the information you supply — the size of the carpet, its condition and any special stain problems.

Dry Cleaning

Of all the services consumers use, dry cleaning is the one with which they seem most dissatisfied. Most complaints concern shrinkage, pilling of woolen goods, the spreading of stains, fading, disintegration of fabrics and clothes that are lost and never found.

An FTC regulation requires most items of clothing, except such things as shoes and gloves, to carry a permanent label describing the appropriate way to clean them and any special care that may be necessary.

But even when instructions are followed to the letter, problems can arise. Luxury fabrics, such as cashmere and mohair, are fragile and have a naturally short life span. Fusible interfacings in suit and jacket lapels can pucker when they are cleaned. Bonded linings tend to separate from the fabric. Polyester knits may shrink or sag; some knit fabrics tend to stretch when they are steamed. And there are a host of other possible difficulties. So it is important for the cleaner to examine any garment thoroughly when it is brought in and point out any problems that may arise. Similarly, it is your responsibility to tell the cleaner about any special conditions of which you may be aware. Point out any spots that may require special attention. Check to be sure that buttons and decorations can be safely cleaned; if not, it may be worthwhile to remove them. Ask the cleaner's advice if you have any question about the advisability of having a garment cleaned; if the cleaner assures you that there will be no problem, ask for a guarantee in writing.

When you pick up clothing from a dry cleaner, examine it carefully the moment you get it home. If you have a complaint, it is wise to register it as soon as possible.

If clothes are lost or damaged through the cleaner's negligence, you are entitled to reimbursement. It is in figuring this amount that consumers and dry cleaners are most likely to disagree. Reimbursement is not calculated on the basis of the original cost of the garment, but on the amount of future wear you can be expected to get from it.

Every state and many cities have their own local dry cleaning trade associations, which function under a variety of names. All these groups work actively to try to resolve consumer complaints. You can get the name and address of your local dry cleaners' association from the Better Business Bureau in your community. If the association is unable to solve a problem to your satisfaction, you may get help from the grievance committee that has been established by the Better Business Bureau. However, both the trade associations and the BBB have better records in dealing with cleaners affiliated with them than they have in other cases. And unfortunately, most complaints are brought against cleaners who do not have these affiliations.

Employment Agencies and Career Counseling Firms

A great many organizations offer individuals help in planning careers and getting jobs. Their services and fees, however, vary widely — as, unfortunately in some cases, do their ethics — so it is wise to investigate before taking action.

To get a job, of course, you can always apply directly to the employer you want to work for or consult the help-wanted ads in the classified sections of newspapers and business and professional journals. Other sources of free information and assistance include local human resources agencies and referral services, which may help with placement or, if they do not, can give you the names of groups that do. The career-service offices of colleges and universities usually limit their assistance to students and alumni, but some give outsiders access to job listings or give general advice.

A major source of job opportunities is the nationwide network of 1,800 employment offices maintained by state governments with partial funding from the federal government. These offices operate at no charge to job seekers or employers looking for workers. You will find your local office listed in the telephone book under state government — in some cases as Job Service Offices, or as State Employment Services or as Employment Security Commissions. Applicants are interviewed, classified according to training and experience and shown a list of appropriate openings in their region. If one seems like a good match, the interviewer may arrange an appointment with the prospective employer. For those unsure of the work they are suited for, counselors can test aptitudes and skills and recommend a course of action, including added training if necessary. Particular attention is given to job seekers with special problems, including school dropouts, women returning to the job market, veterans, older workers and the handicapped.

Private Employment Agencies. Millions of Americans each year seek jobs through private employment agencies, which charge fees for the services they perform. In almost all states such agencies must be licensed and in many they are regulated as to the maximum fees they can charge, generally a specified fraction of the first month's salary or a percentage of annual salary, spread over a period of months. Under the laws of most states, an agency cannot demand a fee until the client actually accepts a job.

Some jobs are advertised by agencies as "fee paid," meaning that the employer will pick up the agency's tab at no cost to you. No matter who is supposed to pay the fee, however, if you accept a job and do not report for work, or if you leave or are fired within a specified period, you may be required to pay. It would be wise, therefore, to check the agency's policy in this regard before signing on with it.

You should accept any job that comes through an employment agency only after careful consideration. It is your obligation to pay the fee upon acceptance, not when and if you actually start the job.

Most complaints about employment agencies arise from the applicant's failure to read and understand the terms of the agreement. Never sign a contract you do not completely understand; make certain you receive a copy of anything you sign and, of course, keep it in a safe place.

A good employment agency should not only provide details of specific job openings listed with it, and information about the employing companies, but should counsel you on writing your résumé and preparing for an interview. If indicated, the agency should also submit your résumé, arrange interviews and keep your résumé on file so that it can search for other jobs on your behalf. Some agencies specialize in particular fields, such as publishing, engineering or general business. If you build a good working relationship with an agency in your field, you will be more likely to have access to better job openings as they appear.

If you have any doubts about the competence or reputation of an employment agency, check with your local Better Business Bureau to see if it has received complaints.

Jobs for Executives. In the last decade or so a multitude of firms have sprung up to cater to the lucrative executive market. Although many of them render useful services, others engage in deceptive practices or outright fraud. Some call themselves "executive counselors" or "career counselors," others, "executive search," "executive marketing" or "outplacement" firms. No matter how high-sounding their labels or their advertising, however, it is what they do, and cannot do, that matters.

Executive search experts — also known as executive recruiters or headhunters — are essentially management consultants or agents who specialize in finding qualified individuals to fill job openings in their clients' companies and whose fees are paid by the companies. While some search firms are willing to talk to executives looking for new jobs in their fields, and will keep résumés on file against the possibility of a future "match," many are too busy filling specific current assignments for their clients to be of much help to executives who are looking for jobs. A better bet may be an employment agency that specializes in placing executives in a particular field — or has direct contacts with the companies themselves.

Quite different are the firms that style themselves as "career counselors," "job search specialists" or "executive marketing" experts — and who may offer to show you the way to the "hidden job market," a fabled utopia filled with high-paying, fascinating positions that no one else knows about. Experienced bona fide career counselors can provide a good deal of help to people who need to develop a better sense of what they really like to do and what they are good at, and can show them how to reach their objectives through specific job-hunting skills and techniques. But others can — and do — take their clients' money and do little else.

Responding to a growing number of complaints in recent years, consumer protection agencies have been cracking down on some of the worst offenders. In New York, for example, the state attorney general enjoined several firms from engaging in deceptive and fraudulent practices, and the court ordered offending firms to give back the money victimized clients had paid.

Undercover investigations revealed that these firms charged their clients advance, non-returnable fees, which ranged from $1,500 to $8,000, by assuring them of interviews and contacts otherwise unavailable, and offering them psychological testing, counseling, résumé and letter preparation and extensive job market research. In reality, the investigators found, individual job "campaigns" were slow to get off the ground, and the services often consisted of little more than preparing a standard résumé and cover letter for the client to distribute, at his or her own expense, to a list of employers culled from standard business directories that frequently included the names of companies no longer in business and executives who had left their firms or died.

Worse still, as the attorney general's office pointed out, the firms were preying on people at highly vulnerable periods in their lives — often when they were unemployed and had to scrape the bottom of the barrel to pay the substantial fees. Said a victim of one of the firms in his letter to the attorney general's office: "I feel used. I would feel better had someone robbed me at gunpoint. At least that doesn't involve fakery and hypocrisy." Said another: "Frankly, trying to find gainful employment in this society is becoming a heartache enough without having to be lured, lied to and entrapped by unscrupulous firms."

State officials, Better Business Bureaus and the Federal Trade Commission have sound advice for people considering a career counseling firm — or any other agency promising to provide better jobs:

- Check the firm's reputation, the qualifications of its staff in career guidance, the length of time it has been in business and whether the local Better Business Bureau or consumer agency has any complaints on file against it.
- Ask for the names of satisfied clients and for examples of materials prepared for other clients with backgrounds similar to yours.
- Get a clear explanation of what the firm will and will not do, what the costs are going to be, the time periods in which each of the services are to be delivered and the provisions for refunds.
- Insist that all these details be spelled out in a contract and, if you have any doubts at all, have the contract checked by a lawyer before signing it.
- Watch out for clauses requiring you to sign periodic statements that you are satisfied with the firm's services or demanding that you send it a certified letter each month reporting on your job interviews. Such clauses could jeopardize your chance of ever getting your money back in the event that you are dissatisfied, since your failure to live up to their provisions in even one instance could invalidate the contract. Don't listen to a salesman's claims that such provisions or any others are "unimportant" or "just routine." They *could* land you in trouble.

Home Improvements, Repairs and Maintenance

In Chapter 4, we discussed the problems and procedures associated with the *major* job of home remodeling. Here, we want to discuss more repair and maintenance services, from basement waterproofing to painting, and specific home improvements, from security systems to swimming pools. All these fields get more than their quota of consumer complaints. The box on page 82 describes the techniques most commonly used by unscrupulous operators to manipulate consumers into deals that are bound to prove, at best, unsatisfactory and, at worst, an outright fraud. The first and most important rule to follow when making arrangements for any kind of work to be done on your house is to shop around and to check carefully the credentials of any company you plan to employ.

Alarm Systems. Both the increasing number of burglaries and the frightening statistics on residential fires — they occur in more than 13 million American homes each year — have brought consumers to a sharp awareness of the importance of taking protective measures. Sales of smoke and burglar alarms have been steadily increasing. A number of different types of systems are available, and their costs vary widely, depending on the type of equipment used, the amount of wiring needed, the size of the house or apartment, the structure of the building and whether the consumer buys or leases the system.

All these questions need investigation before you make a decision. You can get valu-

CONSUMER ALERT

Home-Improvement Loans

Home repairs and improvements — even simple ones — can prove to be very costly. If you need to borrow money to pay for the work, you will have to shop for the cost of credit as carefully as for the home improvement service itself.

There are several sources for home-improvement loans: banks, credit unions, the contractor and — generally most expensive — loan companies. The contractor often sells the finance contract to a bank after the job is done, and can also negotiate interest rates.

There is a variety of financing plans available to property owners, and rates will vary among lenders. A homeowner may seek a personal loan, may use the home as collateral for a second mortgage, or, in some instances, may refinance the first mortgage.

The first step in getting a home-improvement loan is to obtain cost estimates of the job to be done. This is important for you, not only because it enables you to compare prices, but because some lenders will require two or more written estimates before considering loan applications. At the time you interview contractors, ask for estimates and find out if the contractor can get you financing, and at what rate.

Nowadays, homeowners with good credit histories and enough equity in their homes can bargain for lower rates, longer terms and larger amounts. The blanket term "home-improvement loan" covers all types of borrowing for the purpose of fixing up, remodeling or adding on to a house, and applies to both secured and unsecured loans.

Unsecured loans are usually limited to $20,000 and the lender generally stipulates that repayment must be made within five years. The banks rely solely upon the borrowers' income and willingness to repay, as shown by their credit histories. Since you do not pledge any assets, a lien cannot be placed on your house that might prevent you from selling it.

For a secured home improvement loan, sometimes called a "home-equity loan," a lien is placed against the house until the loan is repaid. Such a loan is similar to a second mortgage, but usually has a shorter term.

Loans insured by the Federal Housing Administration (FHA) are based primarily on the borrower's credit-worthiness; the amount of equity in the house is of lesser importance. This is an advantage for new homeowners who may have only a small amount invested in their houses or who, for some other reason, have little equity.

Carefully examine all the conditions of any loan agreement. The federal Truth in Lending Law, which is discussed in detail in Chapter 9, requires that the borrower be informed about a number of items, including the annual rate of interest in percentages (APR), the finance charge in actual dollars, the amount of each installment, the number of payments and the penalties for pre-payment, late payment or default.

If a contractor finances your loan and later sells it to a finance company, or if the contractor regularly arranges loans with a particular company (called a "holder in due course"), federal law makes both the contractor and the lending institution responsible to you. If there should be problems with the job — defective materials, workmanship or abandonment, for example — and, despite your best efforts, you cannot work them out either with the contractor or the financing company, you may withhold installment payments. If you are taken to court for nonpayment, you may plead as your defense your dissatisfaction with the contracting job.

Clearly, it would be preferable to avoid court proceedings, if at all possible. Before matters reach the point where you are prepared to withhold payment, get in touch with your local or state consumer protection agency and describe the problem to a staff member.

able information from your local police and fire departments, your local Better Business Bureau and the National Burglar and Fire Alarm Association, 1133 15th Street, NW, Washington, D.C. 20005. All of them will provide you with literature and will help you locate reputable alarm firms in your area.

If you want only a simple protection system, you should be able to install it yourself. But if the job is more complex, you would be well advised to have it done by an expert.

To protect against fire, an expert will probably advise the installation both of heat detectors, which respond to an abnormally high temperature in the immediate area around them, and smoke detectors, which respond to the presence of smoke. If you want only one kind, the expert will undoubtedly recommend that you get smoke detectors. Whatever kind — or brand — you buy, make sure it bears the UL seal: the guarantee that it conforms to standards set by the independent testing group, Underwriters Laboratories. And when the equipment is installed, make certain that the individual detectors are placed properly: outside all bedrooms (and inside the bedroom of any family member who smokes) and at the base of each stairway, and that none are installed within three feet of a heating register, or in the kitchen, where cooking can cause false alarms.

Protection against burglary is a more complex — and more expensive — problem. The most effective system will fail if the householder neglects to lock windows and doors, or if the system has not been properly installed. For this reason, it is urgent that you investigate thoroughly before you buy, and that you purchase the kind of system that is most appropriate for your family's needs and situation. Do you, for example, want an alarm that issues its warning at your residence, or somewhere else? If you live in a well-settled area, a noisy alarm in your own home may be enough to frighten a burglar off or bring timely help. If, on the other hand, your house is in an isolated spot, such an alarm is not likely to do much good. If the alarm is to be registered somewhere else, where should it be — the police station or a security company? You may not be able to make the former arrangement. Some communities do not permit alarms to be hooked into police stations. Check with your local police or sheriff's office.

Do you want a system that works *before* the burglar has entered your home, or one that goes into action only after entry has been achieved? If you have pets or children, inside alarms can create a problem. Youngsters, dogs and cats can inadvertently trigger the sensors that set the alarm in operation. Ultrasonic sensors, which emit sound waves beyond the range of human hearing, can be extremely distressing to animals — and to some people with unusually sensitive hearing, as well.

All these questions should be subjects of discussion with the security company from which you plan to buy. A reliable firm will help you decide which kind of system is most sensible for your particular situation and will itemize costs, breaking them down into two divisions — installation and customizing charges and the monthly service charge. The contract it offers should indicate precisely where protective devices will be placed and should itemize all the equipment to be installed. In addition, the contract should give the details of labor costs and maintenance and service commitments, and should include a description of the warranty terms. If the system you are getting involves a remote alarm answering service, you will probably be required to sign up with the company — and pay service charges — for a period of two to five years.

Before buying any burglar alarm system, get the advice of an expert who can analyze your family's needs.

Locks are a major component in any plan for home security, and they are especially important for consumers who do not want to go to the expense and trouble of installing complex burglar alarm systems. A good locksmith is well qualified to evaluate the security problems your home presents, and to propose methods of dealing with them. But speak to several candidates; both prices and opinions of what needs to be done can vary widely in this competitive field.

Because all locksmiths are expert at opening locks without damaging them, most cities require these craftsmen to be fingerprinted and to supply character references to the police department before they can go into business. If they are found to have no criminal record, and their references are satisfactory, they are issued registered, specially numbered permits, which must be prominently displayed in their shops. If you have any doubts about a locksmith's honesty, you can cross-check the permit number at your police department. Another indication of a locksmith's honesty — and skill — is membership in Associated Locksmiths of America (ALOA), a trade association which requires its members to have supplied, serviced or installed locks for at least two years, and to provide both reliable character and business references.

Basement Waterproofing. If your house was improperly waterproofed at the time it was built, or if the site on which it stands has poor drainage, you are more than likely to find yourself with a damp — or even wet — basement at some time. If the problem is serious, it will require diagnosis and repair by an expert.

Because any number of conditions can create a wet basement, and different causes require different kinds of treatment, the job is likely to be complicated and expensive. To make things more difficult for the householder, the waterproofing business is entirely unregulated, and if you find yourself in the hands of the wrong person, you can wind up in serious trouble. It is therefore imperative to shop around with great care before making any commitment.

Look for someone who is familiar with a number of different methods of waterproofing and knows which one is appropriate in a given situation. A slow, small leak from the outside can sometimes be remedied by sealing cracks with a watertight hydraulic cement; slow seepage over a large area can sometimes be stopped by the use of water-resistant paint on the affected area. Poor drainage from the roof may require plastic piping to carry off the water and a slight regrading of the land around the house, so that it slopes away from the foundation. Leakage due to groundwater may require a major excavation to expose the foundation and cover its walls with a membrane coating or a plastic film. Leakage through the basement floor may call for a sump tank, a drain system and an electric pump.

As the above list indicates, it is a poor idea to deal with a firm that offers only one solution to all waterproofing problems, or one that proposes methods — clay injection and pressure pumping, for example — that have not been demonstrated to have value. You want an individual or firm with broad experience and sufficient familiarity with the topography of the area and the immediate terrain to be aware of the problems that can be caused by a poor choice of site.

Carpentering. The best recommendation for a carpenter is the work he or she has done. Before hiring anyone — whether a professional with long years of experience or a college student looking for summer work — make arrangements to inspect a few previous jobs. A good carpenter will leave edges rounded and sanded, and surfaces finished. The saw marks will be clean, and there will be no hammer marks on the wood where nails have been driven in. Joints will be tight and neatly made, and patches will be spliced in, sanded and finished so that they do not stand out from the surrounding wood.

You have a right to demand this kind of competence from any carpenter you hire. But to build a couple of bookcases you hardly need a journeyman, who is experienced in everything from restoring antiques to putting up house frames. For simple jobs, you will probably be able to find an adequately trained carpenter by applying to a small general-contracting firm.

A responsible carpenter should be prepared to give you a free, detailed estimate for any custom job. If the carpenter is well-established, you may not be required to pay for materials up front; any carpenter who has been in business for an appreciable length of time should have an established line of credit with local suppliers.

The most common consumer complaints about carpenters concern the quality of their work and their inability to keep to a schedule. This means that you have to monitor the job carefully as it goes along, and that you should press for the inclusion of a penalty clause in your contract — if only to give the carpenter an incentive to get the job done on time.

Driveway Installation and Repair. Residential driveways are usually made of concrete or asphalt, and occasionally of crushed stone.

Each type requires a different kind of specialist to install or repair it — a mason, if the driveway is concrete; an asphalt-paving contractor, if it is made of asphalt; a general landscaper, if it is made of crushed stone. In some municipalities, local licensing boards require driveway contractors to register. Be sure to check the requirements where you live. If there are no registration requirements, you will have to be especially careful in choosing someone to do driveway repairs. This is a favorite business for unscrupulous, fly-by-night operators.

No driveway work should ever be done in the rain or snow, or in freezing temperatures. Driveway work of any kind should always be done in fair weather. Moreover, if you live in an area of hot summers and cold winters, special care will have to be taken both in building and repairing a concrete driveway, since the material tends to expand and contract with sharp changes in the temperature. If you plan to use salt or a de-icing compound to melt snow on a concrete driveway, the contractor may refuse to warranty the work; salt and de-icing compounds make concrete crumble.

The major consumer complaint about driveway installations and repairs has to do with thickness; in the case of asphalt driveways, especially, there may be an insufficient number of layers. Be sure, therefore, that your contract specifies the thickness of the surface and the foundation material to be used, and observe the progress of the job daily, to make sure that the contractor actually lays down the amount of sub-base and paving material that has been specified.

Electrical Work. All qualified electricians, whether they are union members or not, have trained as apprentices for four or five years. To be licensed, they must have a certain number of years of additional experience (the number required varies from place to place) and must pass an examination. Licensed electrical contractors who are affiliated with the National Electrical Contractors Association (NECA) are required to subscribe to the detailed NECA Standards of Installation. You can get the names of licensed NECA members in your area by writing to the organization at 7315 Wisconsin Avenue, Washington, D.C. 20014.

CONSUMER ALERT

Aluminum Wiring

Of the homes and apartments that were built between 1965 and 1973, some two million were wired with 15 and 20 amperes aluminum wiring systems. All of these carry the possibility of serious danger.

Aluminum wiring has proved a fire hazard: within a 10-year period, it has been the cause of over 500 home fires, many resulting in death.

If you suspect that your home or apartment may have aluminum wiring, do not attempt to check the switchboxes or wiring in your living area. Instead, look in the basement for exposed wires to see if "AL" is stamped on them; ask the resident manager or superintendent of your building about it; or check with the electrical contractor who did the original installation in the building.

There are other signs of possible trouble: switches or outlets that are warm or hot to the touch; outlets that glow, smoke or shower sparks; strange odors, such as the smell of burning plastic around outlets or switches; outlets, lights or entire circuits that fail to operate; or lights that flicker periodically.

The trouble may be hidden in an inconspicuous outlet that has nothing plugged into it, because the current passes through it on the way to other outlets and overheating can occur at many places along the line.

If your residence *does* have aluminum wiring and you notice any of the trouble signs mentioned above, call a qualified electrician; *do not* under any circumstances try to make any repairs, even simple ones, by yourself. There are a number of things an electrician can do to ensure the safety of an aluminum-wired house without having to rewire it entirely, and the cost of this protection may not be very high. If you would like more detailed information, write: AMP Special Industries, Valley Forge, Pennsylvania 19482, or U.S. Consumer Product Safety Commission, Washington, D.C. 20207.

Safety, of course, is the single most important consideration in any electrical work. Less current than that used by a 10-watt bulb can kill. All electrical installations must conform with local safety codes, which you can check with the building department in your municipality. And remember not to sign any contract with an electrician — or accept any estimate for electrical work — unless it includes a provision that all materials will be UL listed (approved, in other words, by the independent Underwriters Laboratories) and all work and materials will conform strictly to the National Electrical Code and to all local codes.

Extermination (Pest Control). For homeowners, termites are the most worrisome and dangerous pests; for apartment dwellers, cockroaches are the major concern. It is sometimes — although not always — possible to deal with cockroaches yourself, but termites always require professional treatment.

An annual termite inspection is a good investment for any homeowner, and an immediate inspection is a necessity if you have any reason to suspect an infestation. A good exterminator should be able to identify any pests that may be present, determine the degree of infestation, locate entry points and nesting areas and recommend safe, effective treatments. A careful inspection should cover not only the kitchen, bathroom and other areas inside the house, but also the foundation and all damp or dark places.

If no infestation is found, the exterminator should give you a certificate of inspection, with a guarantee promising a free job of extermination if pests show up within a specific time, usually three months. If inspection uncovers an infestation, make sure you fully understand the nature and extent of the problem and the work necessary to solve it before you sign an agreement. A serious termite problem, for example, requires that the ground around the house be treated chemically. In addition, it may be necessary to remove all wood from underneath the building; chemically impregnate any wood that enters the soil line; cut away and replace heavily damaged wood, such as sills, joints and flooring; improve drainage and ventilation; and seal cracks in concrete masonry.

A reputable exterminator should be willing to give you a warranty for any work done. There are no standards for such warranties: they vary widely according to the species of pest, conditions of construction and pesticides used. But you should ask for a six-month warranty on treatment for cockroaches and a one-year warranty for termite treatment.

Federal regulations permit exterminators to use certain chemicals in their work that are not available to ordinary consumers. To use these restricted chemicals, however, the exterminator must, by federal law, be certified according to the standards established by the state in which he or she works. The individual states also establish their own rules in regard to the use of these restricted chemicals, and in some states, certain pesticides cannot be used even though they have been approved by the federal Environmental Protection Agency (EPA). You can get a list of the federally restricted chemicals by writing to the Office of Pesticide Programs of the EPA, Washington, D.C. 20460, and can find which are approved for use in your state by contacting your state or local health department or your county office of the U.S. Department of Agriculture, which you will find listed in the telephone book. In addition, you can write to the National Pest Control Association, 8150 Leesburg Pike, Vienna, Virginia 22180, to check the effectiveness of both the methods and the chemicals an exterminator plans to use.

Floors and Floor Covering. Floors can be covered with wall-to-wall carpeting or with vinyl or ceramic tile; wood floors can be left bare and kept in shape by sanding and finishing.

If you rent your housing, wall-to-wall carpeting may be impractical. You may not be able to sell it to the new tenant when you move; if you cannot, you will have to have it removed and then recut, and either fitted into your new residence or turned into room-size rugs. But if you own the place you live in, wall-to-wall carpeting can be a good investment, provided you choose the right kind of carpeting for each room and have the right person lay it for you. That person can be an independent installer, but most carpet dealers have their own installation services. For this reason, it is particularly important to make a careful check of the credentials of the retailer.

When you shop for carpeting, remember that the kind you buy should be appropriate to the area in which you plan to use it. High traffic areas — the kitchen, family room and bathroom, for example — require carpeting that is durable and easy to clean, while the floors of adults' bedrooms, which get less traffic — and fewer spills — can be covered with more delicate carpeting.

Carpeting comes in all grades and all prices and may be made of different fabrics. Wool, the most expensive, is resilient, durable, easy to clean and fire resistant. Nylon is less resilient, but very durable and can be easily cleaned of water-soluble stains. On the other hand, unless it contains a metal fiber, it tends to generate static electricity. Acrylics look like wool and wear like nylon, resist soil and fading and clean easily. Rayon is the least expensive of carpet fabrics, but it does not stand up under the wear and tear of high-traffic areas. All carpeting and rugs — except such one-of-a-kind pieces as antiques — must live up to the standards set by the Consumer Product Safety Commission in accordance with the federal Flammable Fabrics Act. In deciding on a fabric, therefore, you can feel equally safe with any one you choose.

When buying carpet, examine the sturdiness of the construction and backing. Bend back a corner to check the length and density of the pile and the number of strands of fiber twisted into one strand of yarn. In a good carpeting, the pile is closely packed and tightly secured to the backing.

The density of the surface yarn is more important than its height. A thin pile may feel soft, but crushes easily and will not hold up in a high-traffic area. A medium-height dense pile is a good choice for living rooms, hallways and stairways. A short, dense pile will not show crush marks. Further information on the proper way to buy carpeting and what to look for when you buy it is available from the Carpet and Rug Institute (CRI). Write to: Carpet and Rug Institute, Director of Consumer Affairs, 1629 K Street, NW, Suite 700, Washington, D.C. 20006.

Padding is installed underneath wall-to-wall carpeting to absorb wear and tear and help prolong the life of the carpet. Padding is frequently offered free when you buy carpeting, but you are not likely to be offered any selection and if you want a better quality, more expensive padding, you will probably have to pay extra for it. The most commonly used paddings today are sponge rubber, foam rubber and urethane foam, all of which give good resilience and soft but uniform support underfoot.

Before committing yourself to the purchase of any wall-to-wall carpet, read the contract carefully, paying particular attention to the terms of the guarantee. Precisely what does it cover? Does it include installation as well as materials? And do not buy any wall-to-wall carpeting until you are absolutely sure of how much you will need.

When the carpet is installed, be sure that someone is at home who can inspect the work before the installers leave. Look particularly for any buckles in the carpet surface: they indicate it has not been evenly or tightly stretched.

Check wall-to-wall carpeting carefully after installation. Make certain there is no surface buckling.

If you plan to have your floors covered with roll vinyl or tiles, bear in mind that the installation is likely to be expensive; the work is both exacting and time-consuming. Before you make any purchase, you should have the installer come to your home to inspect the underflooring and its covering, as well as to estimate the amount of material you will need. Unless you have already decided on the specific covering you plan to use, you may not be able to get a cost estimate then and there; the installer will have to work out costs after you have decided on the material to be used. Although you will have to pay for the vinyl — or tile — before the installer starts work, you should not pay for the actual installation until it has been completed to your satisfaction. This arrangement gives you some leverage with the installer if any problems should develop. Reputable flooring installers will give you a guarantee, both for materials and for labor.

The flooring work most difficult for consumers to assess is refinishing. It is easy to make floors look good — at least for a short while — even when the job is not done properly, if only because refinishing puts a shine on the floor.

Refinishing a floor involves three steps

— sanding (or scraping), coloring and finishing. The number of sandings a floor requires depends entirely on its condition. It may need only one; it may need as many as three. Once it is sanded, you may want to have the floor stained or bleached — unless it is oak, in which case it can be left its natural honey color. Since staining shows up any scars left from sloppy sanding, floor refinishers who have little confidence in their own work shy away from doing the job. This means that it is always a good idea to get an estimate on staining, whether or not you plan to have the job done. The workman's willingness — or unwillingness — to quote a price provides a clue to his competence. Today, most floors are finished with polyurethane, which should be applied in two coats, at least six hours apart. Almost all refinishers promise to apply two coats of finish, but in fact many apply one coat of sealer and one of polyurethane. You should insist on two coats of the latter, even if you have to pay extra for it.

Floor refinishers sometimes offer to make estimates on the telephone. Such estimates are almost always inaccurate and unsatisfactory. If it is at all possible, you should insist that the workman come to your home.

Gardening and Landscaping Rip-Offs

The landscaping business has its own particular group of unscrupulous operators, who wander from house to house offering their wares. They may introduce themselves by saying that they "just happened to be in the neighborhood," and by the greatest of good fortune "just happen to have" quantities of sod or topsoil for you to buy. Before you deal with such individuals, you would be wise to check on their credentials and references. If you do not, you may find that the sod is of an inferior quality and the top-soil overpriced.

Similarly, check on so-called arborists, who "just happen" to be pruning trees in your neighborhood, and on lawn-maintenance people who offer their services door-to-door, proposing to spray for insects or apply feeding treatment on a per-application basis. Their services seldom offer written contracts. But they often do offer the possibility that your bushes and shrubs will be killed as a result of improper feeding or over-spraying.

Landscaping and Lawn Maintenance. You may arrange with any number of different kinds of people to work in your yard — from landscape contractors, contract nurserymen, sprinkler specialists and lawn maintenance specialists, to the teenager who lives in the house next door.

Some nurserymen and landscape contractors do everything, from analyzing your property and installing an underground sprinkler system to actually growing the plants and setting them in place. Others rely on specialists to perform particular aspects of the job: a landscape contractor may buy plants from many different sources and put them in the ground according to your specifications.

Both landscape contractors and contract nurserymen should be able to give you a full evaluation of your property and propose a design plan for it that covers 12 months of the year. Once the design has been determined, the landscaper may carry out the entire plan or only some part of it. Landscaping does not have to be done all at once. It can be a gradual process, taking several years to complete.

If you are having an underground sprinkler installed, the contractor should submit a plan showing where the pipes will be laid, and what coverage the system will provide. In order to lay the pipes for the system, workmen will have to trench your lawn. Your contract should specify that the installer will clean up and replace the sod after the trenches are dug. The contract should also specify that the pipes will be laid in conformity with all local building and plumbing codes.

A number of different kinds of lawn maintenance services are available which are sold on the basis of yearly contracts, and provide patented lawn services that include everything except cutting and watering. Before you sign such a contract, compare its cost with the cost of a pay-as-you-go service provided by a local gardener and check with your county or state agriculture office.

Painting and Paperhanging. Except by observation, it is difficult to judge the professionalism of painters and paperhangers. Union members have been trained for up to three years, but since they spend much of this time fetching and carrying for the more experienced men on the job, they themselves usually do not become expert until several years after they have completed their apprenticeships. So, aside from recommendations, the only way to judge painters' and paperhangers' competence is to watch them at work.

Professional painters use heavy canvas drop-cloths, long-handled brushes and rollers and work from big two-gallon buckets. Competent paperhangers bring portable pasteup tables and may use strap-on stilts or scaffolds for work in high-ceilinged rooms.

Virtually all painters and paperhangers give free estimates and product samples and, of course, work on a contract basis. A well-drawn contract will specify the area to be worked on; the way the walls will be prepared; materials — listed by manufacturer, type, color and, if possible, product number. The contract should estimate the amount of material needed to do the job, and before you sign it, you should check that estimate against the measurements of the area to be painted or papered. One gallon of paint covers approximately 200 square feet; a 36-inch-wide roll of wallpaper will cover about 30 square feet. In addition, the contract should include statements of the completion date and of the contractor's insurance coverage. Do not sign a contract that asks for payment in full before the completion date. A final payment arrangement is your ace in the hole to ensure that the work is done properly.

Plumbing. Not all plumbers are licensed. But all states — and some municipalities — *do* issue licenses to plumbers who meet the specific requirements the state or municipality has established. Always deal with a licensed plumber if possible. Licensed plumbers are familiar with the local building codes and inspection requirements; they know what permits are necessary for a given job and how to obtain them. Most important of all, they are responsible to the board through which they have obtained their licenses. Since these boards have the power to revoke licenses, as well as issue them, they provide consumers with a valuable bargaining tool in the event of a dispute about the quality of plumbing work.

Many plumbers are union members and belong to the United Association of Plumbers and Pipe Fitters (UAPPF). All union members serve as apprentices for four years. Then, after passing an examination, they can be promoted to the grade of journeyman. Five years' service as a journeyman entitles a candidate to take the examination for master plumber. Those who have passed this test are eligible for membership in the National Association of Plumbing-Heating-Cooling Contractors (NAPHCC), a trade association which also offers training programs.

The office of the union is at 901 Massachusetts Avenue, NW, Washington, D.C. 20001, and NAPHCC is headquartered at 1016 20th Street, NW, Washington, D.C. 20036. Both of these organizations can supply you with the names and addresses of members who work in your area. The union local will also help settle disputes over workmanship with any of its members.

If you wish to find out if the plumbing contractor you may be doing business with has participated in a registered training program, you can write to the Department of Labor, Bureau of Apprenticeships and Training, 601 D Street, NW, Room 5000, Washington, D.C. 20213.

Any contract you make with a plumber should include his license number, assurances that he will assume responsibility for property damage and a statement that he is covered by personal liability insurance, a detailed description of the work to be done, assurances that the work will be performed in accordance with local codes, and a guarantee that should run for at least a year.

Roofing. Any roof that is leaking demands careful inspection by an expert. A single glance will give no clue either to the cause or the cure. The problem may be relatively simple, with a relatively simple solution: loose flashing around the chimney, for example, or a puncture somewhere. On the other hand, it may be more complex — a condition connected with widespread deterioration of some sort. In this case, you may need more than a simple repair. You may need a new roof.

If your roof is flat or has a slope of less than three inches per foot, and if deterioriation is not severe, it may be possible to use a coating or roof cement to cover the seams that permitted the leak. But the distressed areas must first be repaired, and the coating must first be tested, to be sure it is chemically compatible with what is already on the roof. If your roof is high-sloped, it is unlikely that any kind of waterproof coating will be effective, unless you live in an area with a relatively constant climate. In any place where temperatures vary widely, the roofing material will expand and contract in response to changes in the weather, and the coating will crack.

A good roofer works with many different methods of installation and has the special skills to handle a variety of roofing materials — not only shingle, but rounded terra-cotta barrel tile, copper sheeting and slate.

When you sign a contract with a roofer, be sure it includes the dimensions of the areas to be covered, and describes everything that is to be done, including necessary preliminary steps and the installation of flashings and edgings. All materials should also be described and specified. If the roof is to be shingled, the contract should name the type, color, weight, fire rating and brand of shingles to be used, the number of squares that will be required and the price per square installed. And, of course, the contract should spell out the total cost and a completion date. Since most roofing jobs do not take very long — a competent crew can frequently do the work in only one day — that date should be relatively firm. Still, it is a good idea to keep the deposit small and reserve the largest payment until the job is done.

The roofer should give you the manufacturer's warranty on the materials, and should provide his own guarantee of the workmanship, which should have a term of at least five years. Any leakage that occurs before then should be repaired at no cost.

Siding. New siding can cover flaws, increase durability and decrease maintenance costs on your house. But it cannot conserve energy or provide insulation, thereby lowering your fuel bills. Siding salesmen sometimes make such claims but they have little value. The thin panels — so-called backerboard and drop-in panels — that they offer as part of their packages provide only a very small energy-saving benefit. Real insulation benefit can only be achieved by the installation of large sheets of foamed plastic — polystyrene, polyurethane or polyisocyanurate.

The cost of siding for a house is quoted in terms of the "square" — 100 square feet of siding. When you get an estimate, make sure it covers all the squares necessary to side your entire house. The house dimensions should be stated clearly, so that you can check the total cost of materials. And be sure the estimate includes installation costs, as well as material.

The contract should specify the type of siding — wood, asphalt, steel, vinyl, aluminum — its composition and thickness, the name of the manufacturer and all warranties that apply to the materials. Other relevant details — door and window facings, backerboard or aluminum breatherfoil, if required — should also be detailed and their prices spelled out. Once your contract has been signed, there should be no surprises when the time comes to make the final payment on the bill: the cost of siding and its installation can be figured precisely in advance.

Swimming Pools. In addition to the hours of enjoyment a swimming pool brings, it is one improvement that usually earns back its cost when the time comes to sell your house. But a pool — whether large or small, above-ground or in-ground — is an expensive proposition, which goes on costing money long after it has been installed. An in-ground pool, which may be more attractive than its above-ground cousin, is, of course, a permanent installation. But such an improvement may increase your property taxes as well as the value of your property.

A young family with small children may want to purchase an above-ground pool, which can be taken down and stored, or moved to a new location, and which is not likely to be taxed as a property improvement.

Local ordinances often require security fences to be installed around a yard that contains a swimming pool, and your local health department may have established restrictions on piping, water supply and drainage. Before considering the purchase of any swimming pool, be sure you look carefully into these areas. Even if the law does not require a security fence, it is wise to put one up — or, at the very least, to get a cover for the pool. If anyone — even a trespasser — drowns in a pool which does not have some kind of protective device, the owner of that pool may be held liable under the legal doctrine of "attractive nuisance."

The installation of an in-ground pool is a major construction project, and although you may initially deal with a salesman, once you have made the decision to go ahead, you should talk with the pool builder and go over every clause of the contract before signing it.

The builder should help you select the proper site for the pool, choosing a spot where the composition of the soil will permit the pool to settle without cracking or leaking, and should describe the various materials available to line the pool, their advantages and disadvantages and their respective costs. All materials and labor costs, including optional equipment, should be itemized on the contract, along with the starting and finishing dates, the total cost and the financing arrangements. You probably cannot take the completion date literally: pool construction is so complicated, and involves so many plans, permits and special finishing techniques — not to mention cooperative weather — that the job is seldom completed on time.

The contract should hold the builder responsible for any damage that may occur to your property or your neighbors' in the process of constructing the pool. In addition, it should provide evidence that the contractor is insured against accidental damage.

When the job is finished, the contractor should supply you with all manufacturer's warranties, along with instructions on how to obtain service or repairs, and literature from the manufacturer describing care and maintenance — how to use the cleaning equipment, maintain the filter and heating systems, etc. Some pool companies offer maintenance services as well as construction, but you are under no obligation to sign up with the company that built your pool if you do not want to.

It is important never to pay a deposit to a salesperson for a pool company. You should not pay anything until you have a signed contract and, since pools have to be built — or installed — according to individual specifications, a proper contract cannot be drawn until you have consulted with the builder. If by any chance you make the mistake of signing a contract for a pool with a door-to-door salesman, you can withdraw from the deal if you act on time, by making use of the Federal Trade Commission's Three-Day Rule, which is described in detail in Chapter 6. Likewise, you can withdraw within three days if you buy on credit and agree to use your residence as security.

The trade association of the pool-building industry will help in the resolution of disagreements that pool companies and consumers cannot work out for themselves. Write to the National Spa and Pool Institute (NSPI), 2000 K Street, NW, Washington, D.C. 20006.

Buying Skills

If you are in the market for the kinds of services discussed in this chapter, take all possible precautions.

- Be a thorough comparison shopper to be sure you are getting the best buy available.
- Get as much information as you can about the competence, honesty and reliability of the individual or company you plan to employ.
- Make certain your interests are protected before signing any contract. If you are uncertain, consult your lawyer.
- Be a firm but reasonable negotiator if problems arise due to misunderstandings, failures of communication or other honest mistakes.

Chapter 9

Banks, Credit and Credit Cards

Scarcely a decade ago, banking was still a relatively cut-and-dried business. Except for your convenience, it didn't make much difference which bank you dealt with: interest rates, loans and other services were pretty much the same.

All that has changed. Today, thanks to continuing government deregulation and superheated competition among all sorts of financial institutions, banking is in the throes of a revolution and important changes are taking place constantly. "What you have now is a free-for-all," says one industry analyst. "Virtually any kind of business can go into banking, while banking is making important inroads where it has been forbidden before."

The battle to woo customers, especially those with good incomes and/or substantial amounts of money to invest, can be followed in newspaper advertisements and broadcast commercials every day. One institution upstages another with higher interest rates, more lavish "free gifts" or more tempting promises of attention from your "personal banker."

Many institutions offer their clients "instant access" to their money through conveniently located, 24-hour machines. These electronic marvels provide cash on command, even on a deserted street at 2 A.M. when you're broke and need money for a taxicab to get home. Some banks, indeed, make it clear that they prefer their less affluent depositors to use the machines regularly, even during banking hours — so that the banks can reserve the costlier services of human tellers for those with enough money on deposit to maintain "express" or "priority service" accounts.

Increasingly, banks and other financial service companies are merging and maneuvering toward regional networks and "one-stop-shopping" for all a consumer's financial needs, with the result that old distinctions among financial institutions are becoming blurred. In addition to different kinds of checking and savings accounts, money market accounts, certificates of deposit, loans, credit cards and 24-hour cash machines, more and more financial institutions are offering such services as automatic check depositing and bill paying. A few are even offering discount stock brokerage services, some types of insurance and a host of other enticements.

Both banks and brokerage firms, trying to intrude on each other's traditional territories, have been pushing comprehensive accounts that combine banking and brokerage services. In return for depositing some specified minimum in cash, or a combination of cash and securities, and for the payment of an annual service fee, a customer gets the following: a high-yielding money market fund (into which all idle cash in the account is periodically swept); check-writing privileges; the buying and selling of stocks and bonds; a credit or debit card for cash withdrawals or purchases and a line of credit against which to draw. If present trends continue, some industry observers see the day when banks will be able to offer an even wider range of services, including data processing, all kinds of insurance and the buying and selling, as well as financing, of real estate.

In all, banking has become a decidedly lively, if sometimes bewildering, affair. In today's financial landscape, the choices are not only broader and potentially more rewarding, but often far more complex than in the past. It pays not only to shop around, but to look carefully at the fine print behind the glowing offers and to ask questions if you don't understand. What services are actually rendered, and at what actual total cost? How much do any hidden fees and charges add?

The Case of the Stolen EFT Card

A bank customer standing in line one evening to buy some theater tickets, discovered, when he got to the window, that his wallet was missing. In the jostling crowd, a professional pickpocket, Jimmy the Lift, had deftly removed the wallet, which contained several credit cards and a bank electronic fund transfer (EFT) card and personal identification number (PIN). The victim immediately called the credit card companies to notify them of the loss, but did not call the bank, on the assumption that it was closed.

Jimmy the Lift, being conversant with electronic banking, made his first stop at a nearby branch of his victim's bank. He let himself into the bank's 24-hour vestibule with the card, then withdrew $300, the maximum permitted in cash withdrawals at one time.

The next morning the victim called the bank as soon as it opened for business. Because he notified the bank within 48 hours of his loss, his personal liability was limited to $50 and the bank restored the remainder of $250 to his account.

Not so alert, or fortunate, was another of Jimmy's targets, who also lost his EFT card and PIN to Jimmy's educated hands. Unlike the first victim, this man neglected to notify his bank, and Jimmy made off with his savings as well as $1,000 from his automatic line of credit. Moreover, because the victim did not look at the bank statement on which these withdrawals appeared, but simply filed it away for examination several months later, he could not recover any of the stolen money. Since more than 60 days had by then elapsed between the time the bank sent him the statement and he reported the error, his liability was unlimited. (See discussion of Electronic Funds Transfer Act on page 230.)

Moral: Never carry both your EFT card and your PIN together in your wallet or purse, and notify your bank immediately if your card has been stolen or misplaced.

How long do advertised interest rates apply, how often can they change and to what index, if any, are they tied? Perhaps most important, which basic services and which extras do you really need, and which can you easily do without — or get elsewhere at a reasonable price if the need arises?

Financial institutions are not charitable organizations, and what they lose in one area they have to make up for somewhere else. Higher rates offered for savings may be reflected, eventually if not immediately, in higher rates demanded for loans. Some bank services that were provided free in the past are already carrying new charges in order to pay their way. Fixed rates may have to yield to more realistic, variable rates on loans and credit cards — indeed, they are already doing so, particularly in the area of real estate loans.

Shopping for a Bank

In looking around for the financial institution that best serves your purposes — assuming there is more than one commercial bank, savings institution or credit union to choose from where you live — first determine what you really want to use it for: savings, checking, a credit card, 24-hour cash, a personal loan or home mortgage, stock purchases or a combination of several or all of these. Compare each bank's offerings and policies on minimum balances and fees.

Some people search out a bank about as seriously as they look around for a mailbox or trash can: the nearest one is fine. But it really is not wise to be overly swayed by convenience. It's always helpful to have a bank branch reasonably handy to your home or place of business, but what you should look for is a bank whose staff is the most knowledgeable and responsive to your needs.

On the other hand, if you like the idea of being able to get cash or conduct other financial business at odd hours, or wherever you happen to be, you may want to consider a network: either one owned by a large institution or one shared by a number of smaller banks. In New York City, for example, depositors at any one of more than 20 local savings banks can use a special card to draw cash from "Express Banker" automatic tellers scattered around town. In Connecticut, a number of major state banks have interconnected their ATM's, numbering more than 250, and have

Credit Unions: A Good Banking Buy

If you are looking for higher interest rates on your money, along with lower minimum deposits, fewer service charges and reasonably priced loans, you may be able to get them by joining a credit union through your place of employment or a group to which you belong.

Credit unions — there were some 22,000 of them around the country in 1983 serving more than 48 million people — are nonprofit cooperatives made up of individuals who have some kind of common bond, whether because they hold jobs in the same company, are members of the same labor union, professional or religious organization, or simply live in the same geographical area.

Originally conceived as a means of providing low-cost consumer loans and financial advice to workers, more and more credit unions are expanding into other financial services: a variety of savings and checking accounts, money market accounts, certificates of deposit, credit cards, point-of-sale terminals, automatic teller machines and long-term mortgage loans. Federal credit union accounts are insured by a fund administered by the National Credit Union Administration. State chartered credit union accounts are also insured, either by this agency or a state mechanism.

Because they are nonprofit and thus, so far at least, exempt from federal taxation, and because they are not subject to the same restrictions as other banking institutions, credit unions are often a step ahead of the competition in offering their members attractive financial deals. Moreover, since members are considered shareholders rather than simply depositors, they are part owners of the credit union and have something to say about how the organization is run.

Some typical advantages of this arrangement are illustrated by a 1983 survey of one credit union and its competing institutions in the Poughkeepsie, New York, area. While holders of conventional passbook savings accounts were receiving 5 to 5¼ percent interest and were required to maintain minimum balances of $10 to $100, local employees of International Business Machines who belonged to the IBM Poughkeepsie Federal Credit Union were getting 7¼ percent in dividends and had to keep only $5 in their "share" accounts. Other banks were paying 5¼ percent on NOW accounts with minimums ranging from $150 to $3,000, and often imposed maintenance fees; the credit union paid its members 6¼ percent on comparable "share draft" accounts and had no minimum requirements or service fees.

Standard rates in banks and savings banks for money-market accounts ranged from 7.6 to 9 percent, with lesser interest and penalty charges if a balance dipped below $2,500; the credit union's money market account paid a full 9 percent on the same minimum and imposed no fees. The IBM organization also offered a variety of loans at both fixed and variable rates of interest, in many cases beating the price of money at local banks.

Thanks to recent liberalization of membership requirements by the federal government, credit unions are now permitted to take in both individuals who were formerly ineligible, and groups with too few people to form CU's of their own.

Some credit unions originally chartered to serve teachers, for example, have been allowed to expand their base to include students and their parents as well. In the past, relatives of credit union members could join only if they lived in the same household, but now any relative of a member is eligible no matter where he or she lives. If you wish to find out if there is a credit union in your area that you might be able to join, check your employer, any associations, clubs or church groups you belong to (or could join) and make inquiries among relatives and friends.

been installing additional units in shopping centers and supermarkets to make the system even more accessible. An interstate network enables a customer of any of the member banks to use other members' machines for any routine banking transaction, including depositing or withdrawing money. The holders of one main credit card have their own growing system: they can draw cash or travelers checks from 24-hour machines at more than a thousand locations around the country at airports, supermarkets and banks. An increasing number of savings and loan companies and credit unions are also making use of electronic tie-ins.

If you expect to be depositing your paychecks, pension or dividend checks, or conducting other business regularly in person, observe the lines at the counters during peak hours when everyone else is apt to be doing the same thing — from noon to 3 P.M. on Fridays, for example, particularly those falling on major paydays around the 15th and 30th of the month. If the lines look intolerably long — there can be more than a half-hour wait at some big-city banks — you might find faster, less harried service on Tuesdays or Wednesdays, generally the quietest days of the week. Or you can inquire if the bank will arrange for automatic deposit of your checks so that you do not have to go there at all.

In comparing banks, don't overlook the length of time each holds different kinds of checks deposited in your account before permitting you to draw on the funds they represent. Most banks clear a local check immediately or in a day or two, but others can take as long as 10 days; in a few instances out-of-town checks have taken as long as three weeks to clear.

Banks have claimed that they maintain waiting periods in order to prevent losses on bad checks, but critics have pointed out that only about 1 percent of all checks passed turn out to be no good. Moreover, banks can get credit for checks from the Federal Reserve usually within 24 to 48 hours, then invest the money to make more money for themselves, a strategy known as "playing the float." In effect, depositors are giving the bank free loans of their money for days or even weeks. Public and legislative pressure has already forced banks to cut down on their holding time, but it still pays to compare. Ask also if a bank officer

An Automatic Teller Scam

The proliferation of automatic teller machines (ATM's) prompted criminals to find ways to put them to their own use. One New York City bank, for example, placed pairs of ATM's in the lobbies of its branches, along with a telephone linked to a clerk who answered questions about the new machines. A depositor wanting to use an ATM would often find another "customer" already present, talking on the phone. Before the depositor finished his transaction, the other person would say that the clerk had just told him the depositor's ATM was malfunctioning, but the other was working. Unsuspecting, the customer would take his card from the first ATM and move over to the other.

The phone user would then surreptitiously watch the customer punch his personal identification number into the second machine and make a note of it. When the depositor had completed his transaction, the thief would say that the clerk wanted the depositor to insert his card in the supposedly malfunctioning ATM so that bank officials could figure out what was wrong. In complying, the depositor would activate the ATM — enabling the thief, once the depositor left, to use the victim's identification number to withdraw money from his account.

This scam cost New York bank patrons many thousands of dollars before it was discovered. At first the bank refused to take responsibility, contending that it was up to its customers to exercise due caution in the use of the automatic tellers. New York State's Attorney General disagreed and threatened suit against the bank under the Electronic Funds Transfer Act. The bank finally agreed to make restitution to the victims, and to pay interest on the funds fraudulently withdrawn. The bank hastened to adjust the machines so that it was no longer possible to work the scam. But all banks in the United States may not have taken this precaution, so beware.

can give clearance to make needed funds immediately available in emergencies, or to cover checks written against deposits you were given to believe had already been credited to your account.

If there is a chance that you will need a personal loan or a new mortgage within the next year or two, by all means inquire now about a bank's rates and policies. Many banks will give their depositors preference over others, particularly when loan money is tight. If you are a good customer — and if you ask — you may even be able to get a preferential rate as much as 1 or 2 percent lower than that offered outside applicants.

In picking a bank, it is well to bear in mind two facts of financial life. One is that bankers, especially when they are parting with depositors' money, like to deal with someone they know. The second is the Golden Rule of 80-20: some 80 percent of a bank's income, on average, derives from 20 percent of its clients — so it pays the bank to be particularly cooperative with that top one-fifth. Putting those facts together before starting to deal with a bank at least starts a customer on the right track. To the two banker's canons you might add one of your own: banks need you at least as much as you need them.

The Valued-Customer Approach

In doing business with a bank, the first step is to try to establish yourself in its mind as a valued, or at least potentially valuable, customer, and to do it on a businesslike basis. It is important to get this impression across at the start. "Never, never start a relationship with a bank by 'walking in' and going to the nearest bank officer and announcing 'I want to open an account,' " says John A. Cook, an experienced New York bank officer and coauthor with Robert Wool of *All You Need to Know About Banks*. "Do that, and you are, in his mind, a 'walk-in,' and you lose. You are interrupting his work, and worse, coming at him unexpectedly. Beyond that, you are not being what he considers 'businesslike.' If he can spin you off down into the vulgar pits of the Special Checking Accounts, he will."

Instead, Cook and Wool advise, first learn as much about the bank and its services as you possibly can. Talk to friends, relatives, business associates, your lawyer, your accountant. Above all, ask someone in your company's treasurer's office, particularly if the company does business with the bank. If any of these people seems a particularly good reference, and is satisfied with the bank, ask for the name of a specific officer to whom you can speak, using your reference's name — and, thus, his or her clout.

Don't pop in to see the officer unannounced. Call and make an appointment, preferably at the officer's convenience. If you are capable of doing significant business with the bank — one or more family accounts, a separate business account, possibly trust or investment services — convey these facts immediately. The officer who sees you as someone with "potential," is apt to give you full attention. Don't try to impress the banker by spouting off numbers, and don't launch into an angry attack on your present bank. If you do, you may be instantly labeled as a "bouncer," one who unhappily goes from one bank to the next and might well choose another again in a month or two.

If you like the bank and are able to work out the details to your satisfaction, open a checking account, and a savings account too, if

Privacy in Banking

Although information about your bank accounts and transactions is usually a matter between your banker and yourself, there can be exceptions. State laws vary on bank-account privacy. In some states banks are allowed to reveal to merchants whether a customer has sufficient funds to cover a large check a retailer has just been given for a purchase. Some banks will even reveal the exact balance in an account over the telephone. Check with your own bank as to its policy in this area.

On the other hand, the 1978 Right to Financial Privacy Act places limitations, in certain circumstances, on disclosure of your private bank records to federal officials. Not all requests by the government need be honored. Moreover, if a bank is asked or required to turn over your records to a federal agency, you will usually be notified of that fact.

necessary, with as large a balance as you can reasonably afford. You are probably much better off putting all your accounts in one bank and doing business with it as a regular customer than spreading yourself thin over two or three banks, where you won't mean much to anyone. Money talks. Even if you have only $1,000 in savings, deposit it all in one bank and let it talk for you there. If you have approached the bank correctly to begin with, you will indeed have a "personal banker" in the officer who signed you up. He or she may turn out to be the financial friend you need, bending the bank's rules in your favor, if necessary, to get you a loan or offering sound financial advice.

Comparing Bank Services

Among the most familiar bank services to a majority of Americans are ordinary savings accounts, in which they can place their hard-earned money and know that it will be both safe and available on request. Savings accounts, like most other accounts, are insured by federal agencies — the Federal Deposit Insurance Corporation (FDIC) or the Federal Savings and Loan Insurance Corporation (FSLIC) — for up to $100,000 or by state insurance agencies for amounts set by state law. Traditionally, savings accounts have paid minimal interest, but this is changing, too. Savings accounts come in several forms.

Passbook Accounts. In this time-honored arrangement, you deposit and withdraw money in any amount and as many times as you wish, with a bank teller recording the transactions, as well as accumulated interest, in a passbook provided to you by the bank. Though the rates have been fairly standard, actual yields can vary depending on the way the interest is compounded — yearly, quarterly, monthly, daily or from day of deposit to day of withdrawal. There may, however, be a small loss of interest if funds are withdrawn before a certain time has elapsed.

Be careful to read the terms of the passbook contract and ask questions if you are uncertain about any detail. If one bank offers a quarter percent lower interest rate on passbook accounts than a competitor, but compounds interest daily, it may actually provide a higher yield than the competitor's if the money is left on deposit for a full year.

On passbook savings accounts, as well as statement and club accounts (see below), a bank may require as much as 30-days notice before a withdrawal is made. If this is the case, a statement to that effect is included in the contract that sets up the account. As a practical matter, however, banks rarely enforce this injunction and depositors usually have total access to their cash.

Banks do, however, look askance at people who use savings accounts as if they were checking accounts; some institutions limit the number of withdrawals that can be made in a week or month. A bank may even insist that an account be closed if the depositor makes too many withdrawals within a specified period. Another method banks use to limit withdrawals is to charge a service fee for each such transaction in excess of an agreed-upon number per month. In a typical situation, a bank might charge a $1 service fee per withdrawal after the customer has made five withdrawals in a two-month period. A bank may also charge a similar fee if the customer closes out the account within three months of the opening date.

Statement Savings Accounts. These are much like passbook accounts, the difference being that customers keep track of their own deposits and withdrawals on a form provided by the bank. The customer, however, receives a periodic statement from the bank, which includes accrued interest as well as the bank's own records of deposits and withdrawals. Because they involve slightly less work for a bank, a few pay a slightly higher rate of interest for statement savings than for passbook accounts.

Specific-Purpose Savings Accounts. The prime examples are the familiar "Christmas Clubs" or "Vacation Clubs." A person joining a Christmas Club, for example, might agree to deposit $10 per week over a 40-week period; at the end of that time, he or she would have $400 plus interest to use for Christmas spending. In the meantime the bank has the use of each deposit to invest or lend as it pleases.

Originally, club accounts paid no interest. They were simply regarded as a convenient way of encouraging thrift. In recent years, however, some states have adopted regulations that force banks to pay interest on club accounts, at a rate usually one-quarter percent lower than the interest paid on passbook savings accounts. A depositor who fails to maintain the account with regular payments as agreed may forfeit the accumulated interest.

Checking Accounts

In the not so distant past, checking accounts were also thought of as a convenience to the customer and paid no interest. In return for the privilege of writing checks, a so-called "regular" checking account required a customer to maintain a minimum monthly balance in order to avoid a service charge or per-check fee. A "special" checking account did not require a minimum balance, but the bank levied both a monthly service charge and a per check fee.

Today, however, competition among banks has resulted in a variety of checking accounts, among them NOW accounts (Negotiated Orders of Withdrawal), which offer the customer an opportunity to combine the thrift advantages of a savings account with the convenience of checking.

Regular Checking Accounts. Such accounts require you to maintain a minimum balance at all times. The amount of the balance varies, depending on the bank, but typically it ranges from $300 to $1,000. In exchange, the bank offers "free" checking: you can write as many checks as you like each month and will not be charged a per-check or a monthly service fee. When you open a regular checking account, you place at the bank's disposal a certain amount of money it can lend or invest to offset the cost of its services to you. A minimum balance account may be a good arrangement for you if you can afford to maintain the amount, and if you write a fairly large number of checks each month. It may not be a good arrangement if you cannot easily maintain the balance or if you write few checks.

Even if you write a great many checks, it pays to shop around among the banks in your community for the best possible deal, not only in terms of the required minimum balance but also of the way the balance is figured. For example, Bank A may require an *average* balance of $500 each month: this permits you to have less than the minimum on deposit at various times as long as your average daily balance for the whole month is $500 or more. Bank B, on the other hand, may require a minimum balance of $500 at all times. All other factors being equal, Bank A offers a better arrangement for the consumer.

Another factor to think about is whether the bank you are considering offers automatic transfer privileges for regular checking customers who also maintain passbook or statement savings accounts with the institution. Banks offering this privilege will transfer funds from your savings to your regular checking account whenever the checking balance falls below the minimum, thus maintaining your balance so that you will not have to pay service or per-check charges.

Finally, and most important, you should consider whether a regular checking account makes sense for you at all. If the account requires you to maintain a $500 minimum balance and you write an average of only four checks a month, you are losing the $27.50 in interest per year the money would earn at 5½ percent in a passbook savings account. However, if you open a special checking account at the same bank, which demands no minimum balance but charges 15 cents a check, you would spend $7.20 for your 48 checks annually, and you would earn the $27.50 in annual interest on the $500 in the savings account.

If, on the other hand, you write an average of 25 checks per month, a regular checking account makes a great deal of sense, because a per check charge of 15 cents would bring your total yearly outlay to $45, considerably more than the $27.50 you would earn in yearly interest on a $500 savings account.

Special Checking Accounts. These are sometimes called "economy" or "budget" accounts. They require no minimum balance, but the depositor is charged either a fee for each check issued or a monthly maintenance fee, or, in some cases, both. This kind of account makes sense for someone who writes few checks or cannot conveniently maintain a minimum balance. Again, shopping around, reading contracts and asking questions can save you money. One bank may charge 20 cents per check and another only 10. But the bank that charges 10 cents may also impose a $1.50 service fee per month, while the bank that charges 20 cents per check may charge no service fee at all. And some banks levy a service fee but make no charge per check.

NOW Accounts. Some years ago, federal regulations were significantly eased to permit banks to pay interest on checking accounts. Both savings and commercial banks offer a variety of NOW (Negotiable Order of Withdrawal) checking accounts, all of which have two things in common. Each pays interest on the funds that are in the account, and each requires a depositor to maintain a minimum balance that is usually greater than the balance needed for maintaining a regular checking account.

As with other types of accounts, the customer should shop around to determine which institution provides the most benefits. Among the several factors to be considered are the following:

- **Free checking.** Some NOW accounts involve no monthly or per check fees as long as the minimum balance is maintained.
- **Minimum balances.** These vary from bank to bank. As with a regular checking account, a NOW account from Bank A may require that you maintain $300 in your account while Bank B may require $1,000. However, Bank A may demand that the balance never fall below the $300 mark during the calendar month, while Bank B may average the balance for the month and allow full privileges if the average does not drop below $1,000.
- **Penalties.** If you fail to maintain the required minimum balance, some banks will levy a per check charge, others a service fee; some will levy both. These fees will usually match those the bank charges its special checking account customers, for example, 20 cents per check. In addition, some banks will charge a service fee linked to the amount on deposit, such as $4 per month when the average monthly balance falls to between $1,000 and $2,000, and $8 per month when the balance falls below $1,000.
- **Interest payments.** Most banks will continue to pay interest on the balances in NOW accounts even when those balances have fallen below the level required for free checking. Some banks, however, require that a smaller balance — $100 or $200, for example — be maintained if interest is to be paid.
- **Transfers of funds.** Some banks offer automatic transfer of funds from savings to NOW accounts in order to ensure a minimum balance in the latter. This offer may apply only to statement savings accounts.

Special Charges

All banks charge extra fees for stop payment orders on checks, as well as for processing checks that have been returned because of insufficient funds. Since the fees vary widely from bank to bank, inquire about them before opening an account. Some banks charge $5, others $10, others as much as $30 when they must return a check to a depositor because of insufficient funds. Stop payment orders similarly vary in cost — from as little as $4 to as much as $15, depending on the bank.

Other Bank Services

Most banks offer depositors, and in some cases non-depositors as well, a variety of convenience services. Here are some typical examples and their relative costs.

- **Safe-deposit boxes.** Millions of consumers find these boxes, which are locked and kept in bank vaults, useful for the safekeeping of stock and bond certificates, valuable personal papers, jewelry, sterling silver and other precious objects. Only those whom the renter of the box has designated are allowed entry. (An exception to this rule: law-enforcement officials who have obtained a court order.) The boxes come in a variety of sizes; yearly rentals vary according to size from as little as $10 to as much as $200 or more.
- **Money orders.** People who do not have checking accounts but wish to pay their bills with a check-like device have the option of purchasing money orders at most banks. The cost — usually $1 or more — is greater than the normal charge for handling a depositor's personal check.
- **Certified checks.** Often used in business transactions, a certified check is drawn against the depositor's personal account and then taken to the bank for certification — a guarantee by the bank to the payee that the check will be honored. The bank does this by freezing the amount of the check in the depositor's account until the certified check has cleared. The bank often charges a small fee for this service.
- **Cashier's Checks.** Perhaps the most common financial instrument issued by banks, a cashier's check is one that is drawn on the bank's own account. Since it is the bank that is liable for payment, a cashier's check assures the payee that it will be honored.
- **Automatic account transfers.** As a service to

customers who have both savings and checking accounts, many banks will automatically transfer money from the former to the latter to cover an overdraft. The fee for each transfer is usually about $1. Some banks will also make such a transfer on a depositor's telephoned request.

• **Copies of documents.** If you lose your copy of a bank account statement or other document, your bank will supply you with a duplicate copy — generally at a cost of $1 to $7.

• **Travelers' checks.** Some banks issue travelers' checks without charge to their customers. Other banks charge a fee, for example, either 1 percent of the face value of the travelers' checks or a flat fee such as $2.50, whichever is greater.

Investment Accounts

While safety of deposits remains a key element in all types of bank accounts, more and more banks are offering interest rates that match and even exceed those of money market funds promoted by brokerage houses. These high-yield, investment-type accounts have become increasingly available to the average person as the deposit requirements have been lowered during recent years. The primary types are Certificates of Deposit (also called time deposits), Money Market Savings Accounts and Money Market Checking Accounts, sometimes referred to as "Super-NOW" accounts.

Certificates of Deposit. There are many types of certificates of deposit, but all share a common characteristic: the money deposited must remain in the account for a specified time, with severe penalties for early withdrawal (see below). On most CD's the interest remains the same throughout the life of the certificate. By and large, the longer the life of the certificate the higher the interest rate, except, in some cases, very long term certificates. At one time, stringent regulations governed CD's in denominations less than $100,000, making them somewhat unattractive investments. In recent years, these regulations have been eased, and the purchase of lower priced CD's has become a desirable investment for many people.

The main advantage of fixed-interest CD's is that the interest rate is guaranteed for the life of the certificate, whether or not prevailing rates of interest fall. This, of course, can become a disadvantage if general interest rates rise.

The primary drawback of a CD is that your money is tied up for a specified period. If you decide to withdraw your funds from a CD before its maturity, you must first get the bank's approval and then be prepared to pay a significant penalty. Under current federal rules, early withdrawal penalties for CD's issued after October 1, 1983 amount to three months' loss of interest for certificates maturing in more than a year, and 31 days loss of interest for certificates that mature in less than a year. (Penalties are not exacted if a CD is redeemed early because the owner has died or has been declared legally incompetent.) A CD owner who is pressed for cash may have an alternative to early redemption. Many banks will accept CD's as collateral for a loan. The rate charged on such a loan, however, may be so high that it is more economical to cash in the CD and accept the penalty. In other instances, it may be worthwhile to take out a loan to avoid the penalty. The determining factor is the length of time for which the loan is needed.

Fluctuating-Rate CD's. Many banks offer special certificates of deposit that pay variable rates of interest. Depending on the bank, they may be called "Premium Rate Certificates" or "Investment Accounts," or some similar name. Like ordinary CD's, they are sold for specific lengths of time and interest penalties are exacted for early redemption. However, the interest rates are not fixed but are linked throughout the life of the certificate to some other indicator of the bank's choosing — the average yield on U.S. Treasury securities, for instance. If that yield rises, so does the interest rate on the certificate; if it falls, the rate of the CD declines as well.

A variable-rate CD is a bit riskier than an ordinary certificate in terms of interest payments, but it does offer the possibility of higher profits if interest rates rise. Like a fixed-rate CD, principal and accumulated interest are guaranteed by the FDIC or FSLIC up to $100,000, or in some states, by a state agency up to an amount determined by state law. Now that banks are permitted to offer money market savings accounts (see below), it is likely that investor interest in fluctuating-rate CD's will decline. For small investors, however, they offer one major advantage over money market accounts: they usually require a much smaller deposit.

Reinvesting a Certificate of Deposit. During the life of a certificate of deposit you should discuss with an officer of your bank what you want done with the funds in the account at maturity. If you fail to make provision for taking the cash or reinvesting it, depending on bank policy and the law in your state, one of several things may happen: the cash could be transferred to a passbook account paying lower interest; it could be held by the bank at no interest; it could be reinvested in a new CD for the same time period. Check over your certificates of deposit at regular intervals to remind yourself of their dates of maturity. It is a wise idea to keep a calendar noting their maturity dates a week in advance.

Bank Money Market Accounts. As part of the continuing deregulation of banks to allow them to compete more successfully with other financial institutions, federal authorities in late 1982 authorized them to offer money market rates to their customers. This has brought banks into direct competition with private brokerage houses, for whom these funds have been a primary source of income in a period of high inflation and high interest rates. For consumers, the benefit of such funds in recent years has been the high interest rates they have paid. Although these rates are not guaranteed — they traditionally vary with the rates being paid on such federal securities as Treasury bills — in the early 1980's their yields were, on the average, significantly higher than yields offered by most other forms of investment.

In the competitive atmosphere of late 1982, when bank money market accounts first became available, both commercial and thrift institutions were offering initial interest rates in excess of the rates offered by brokerage houses — inducements to tempt investors to transfer their funds from the brokerage houses to the banks. The high rates were guaranteed for only a short period, often no more than a week, after which they often dropped into line with the rates offered by the investment concerns.

In one respect, at least, banks have a significant advantage over investment houses in attracting investors to their money market accounts: bank deposits are insured by the federal or state agencies while the investment houses can offer no such guarantee of safety. However, it should be noted that as of mid-1983, no investor had lost a penny through money market funds operated by brokerages.

Features of Money Market Accounts. Like other bank services, money market savings accounts are subject to government regulations. Individual banks, however, may offer special inducements within prescribed limits. Here is a summary of the main features offered by a typical money market account:

- **Minimum investment.** To open and maintain a money market savings account, a minimum of $2,500 is legally required, although some banks require a higher initial investment but thereafter sometimes permit the depositor to reduce the account to $2,500. So long as this minimum remains in the account, money market interest rates will be paid. There is usually no charge for servicing the account.
- **Interest rates.** There is no maximum interest limit and rates can either be linked to some other marketplace factor such as the rates being paid by the federal government on its Treasury bills, or can be set at any other level the institution may choose. New interest rates are generally posted every seven days. Some banks pay investors a bonus for maintaining large deposits, for example, an additional 1 percent interest on accounts of $25,000 or more. However, if the average deposit in any month falls below $2,500, interest rates for that period drop to the rate the bank pays on passbook savings — usually 5¼ percent. Interest on money market savings accounts is generally compounded daily and paid monthly, and an investor who closes an account before the end of the monthly statement cycle generally loses all interest for that month.

Super-NOW Accounts. Scarcely had the federal government authorized banks to offer money market savings accounts than it also granted them permission to introduce checking accounts that pay money market interest rates — accounts known as "Super-NOW's." Depending on the policy of the individual bank, Super-NOW accounts may offer all of the features of regular NOW accounts, including free check-writing privileges and no service fees as long as a minimum balance is maintained. If you are to earn money market rates, you must maintain the legal minimum of $2,500 in your Super-NOW account. If you are to benefit from free check-writing privileges, the bank will generally require you to maintain the same balance as is required for a regular NOW account. The interest paid on Super-NOW accounts usually varies from day to day, but in general is a point or so below that paid on money market savings accounts. Should a Super-NOW account fall below the $2,500 minimum, most banks will continue to pay interest, though it will be reduced to the rate paid on regular NOW accounts.

While a Super-NOW pays slightly lower interest, its major advantage over a money market savings account is that it offers unlimited checking privileges. One banker has gone so far as to say that with these new high-yield accounts there is no reason for anyone with $2,500 ever to maintain a passbook or an ordinary checking account. Indeed, it is quite possible that the minimum deposit for Super-NOW's, as well as money market savings accounts, will be reduced in the near future.

Brokerage Services

Just as large brokerage chains have been moving in on the banking and credit area, banks are now invading territory once reserved exclusively for brokers.

At an increasing number of banks you can invest not only in certificates of deposit and money market accounts, you can also buy or sell corporate stocks and bonds, generally paying less in commissions than you would at a full-service brokerage house.

This latest addition to bank services began when some of the giant banking institutions made arrangements with, or acquired, discount brokerage firms to serve their depositors, and other banks thereafter followed suit.

To buy shares of a given stock, the depositor simply calls his or her bank, and it takes the necessary money from the depositor's accounts. Although the customer will not get the investment advice provided by a full-service broker, the fee can be much lower than that charged by a brokerage house.

Commercial banks are entering the discount securities business so enthusiastically and with such success that some industry analysts believe banks will account for a quarter of such trades in 1984 and half in 1985.

Electronic Fund Transfers (EFT)

By now, most depositors have some familiarity with the machines in bank lobbies that enable customers to make withdrawals from, or deposits to, savings and checking accounts without the aid of a human teller.

But such machines are only one aspect of electronic fund transfers. An increasing number of other transactions are also being handled by computers. Here are descriptions of a few of the electronic services available in a number of banks.

Preauthorized Payments. One of the relatively new forms of electronic banking is the preauthorized payment, in which money is *automatically* deposited or withdrawn from an individual's savings or checking account. For example, an employer who is authorized by an employee to do so, may place the employee's paycheck in his or her account through an electronic fund transfer. Some major companies deposit a single payroll check (actually a computer tape authorizing payment) for all their employees who are patrons of a particular bank. The bank's computer has already been programmed to divide the payment according to each employee's salary. A more sophisticated method now coming into use is for the employer to route the total payroll tape to a regional automated clearinghouse, where a computer not only divides the tape into individual payment orders but dispatches these orders — again via computer — to all of the participating banks in the area in which the employees have accounts. Other regular payments, such as Social Security checks or dividend checks, can be, and often are, deposited electronically via automated clearinghouses.

Similarly, an account holder may authorize the bank to transfer money electronically from his or her checking account on a certain day each month to pay the mortgage, the telephone bill and other regular expenses.

Point of Sale Terminals (POS). These are electronic fund transfer machines located in shopping centers and department stores. Instead of paying for a purchase with a check or cash, or charging it to a credit card, a bank depositor can activate the POS terminal and transfer funds electronically from his or her account to that of the merchant. This is one of the newest forms of electronic fund transfers, but it will probably be some years before the service is available on a nationwide basis.

Your Rights as an EFT Customer

Like anything else, electronic fund transfers are subject to error. A malfunction in a computer or a mistake by a programmer could, for example, transfer $1,000 from your account to the account of your utility company when in fact your bill was $100. If you lose your automatic teller card and it is found by someone who discovers your personal identification number, that person is in a position to empty your account. To protect bank customers and banks alike, Congress passed the Electronic Fund Transfer Act, which is implemented through Regulation E of the Federal Reserve Board. Following are your rights as an EFT customer.

Statement of Terms. When you open an account with an EFT feature, you are entitled to receive a statement listing all of the terms and liabilities associated with the account.

Receipt. Both automatic teller machines and point of sale terminals must provide you with receipts of all transactions. A receipt includes information on the amount of money transferred, the date of the transfer, the type of account from which the money was withdrawn or in which it was deposited, the name of any financial institution or other party to which funds were transferred and the number of the encoded card that was used to make the transfer.

The monthly statement you receive from the bank must also list all transfers, giving their amounts and dates, including information on preauthorized transfers and those made via telephone. The statement must include the names of the holders of accounts to which you made EFT payments and show all bank fees involved, as well as your balances during the period covered. In addition, it must specify the name and address of the person to whom inquiries are to be directed.

Remember that electronic fund transfers, unlike checks, are recorded immediately and thus should be noted immediately in your deposit and withdrawal records. For example, if you make a POS payment from your checking account directly to a merchant's, you must have the money available in your account if you are not to be charged for an overdraft.

On the other hand, if you have authorized an EFT transaction in advance, you can stop it, either by oral or written notice, provided you act at least three days before the transfer is scheduled to take place.

If a bank fails to make an EFT transfer when it has been authorized to do so and when the depositor has sufficient funds to cover the transfer; or if it fails to stop payment when it has been properly instructed to do so, it may be held liable for any damages caused to the depositor.

Errors. If you suspect that an error has been made in an electronic transfer of funds, call your bank immediately. The law requires that you make the call within 60 days, but the sooner you give notice the easier it will be to correct any error. Unless the bank asks you to, you need not follow your call with a written description of the error, although it is good practice to do so, since it will provide you with evidence that you notifed the bank. Include your name and account number, the date of the error and a description of the discrepancy. The bank is required to investigate and resolve the problem within 45 days of receipt of your notification. If, however, the bank has not completed its investigation within 10 days, it must provisionally credit your account for the amount you claimed you lost through the error, plus the interest on that amount.

If the bank discovers that your claim is correct, the credit must be made permanent. If the bank disputes your charges, it must inform you of this fact and, at your request, provide you with the documents it used to reach this conclusion.

If you are unable to reach an agreement with the bank, you may take your case to: Division of Consumer and Community Affairs, Board of Governors of the Federal Reserve System, Washington, D.C. 20551.

If your specific complaint falls outside the jurisdiction of the Federal Reserve, it will direct you to a state body that can help.

Your state banking commission is another

source of assistance (see directory, page 246), as is your state attorney general's office (see directory, page 48). Should all else fail, you have the right to go to court and sue the bank for relief.

If your EFT card is lost or stolen and someone else uses it, your liability is limited to $50. But this limitation applies *only* if you notify the bank within two business days after discovering the loss. If you wait more than two days, your liability may be as much as $500, and if you fail to notify the bank of any unauthorized transfers that appear on your statement within 60 days of the date the statement was sent to you, you could lose everything that was taken.

Since your EFT card can be used by an unauthorized person only if he or she also knows your personal identification number, do not carry a notation of your number in your wallet or handbag, but memorize it instead.

Types of Bank Loans

Bank credit for consumers falls into two general categories, closed-ended and open-ended. A mortgage, for example, is considered a closed-ended loan because it is for a specific amount and must be paid off over a specified period. (Mortgages are discussed in Chapter 4.) A bank credit card provides an open-ended loan: it gives the cardholder a specific amount of credit against which he or she may draw in making purchases.

Installment Loans. These are closed-ended credit agreements. The borrower receives a certain amount of money and agrees to repay it over a stated period, usually month by month, at a predetermined rate of interest that will neither rise nor fall during the period of the loan. Because the loan is amortized, the borrower has the full use of the funds only for the first month.

The interest charged on installment loans varies from bank to bank and with the purpose for which the loan is to be used, so consumers should shop around for the lowest rate.

Higher rates are usually charged for personal loans that have no particular purpose specified and that are "unsecured" — i.e. have no collateral in the form of property, such as an automobile or a boat, that the bank can take over in case of default. In contrast, a loan that is specifically written for the purchase of an automobile, in which the car itself serves as the security or collateral, can usually be obtained at a point or two lower interest. The lowest rates of all are generally offered on government-subsidized loans, such as those taken out by students for their college or postgraduate education.

Lines of Credit. These are open-ended loans, often given names like "Credit-Line Checking." Whatever they are called, the bank provides the customer with a stated amount of credit that may be called upon, in whole or in part, at any time. Most loans of this type are linked to the customer's checking account. To use the credit the customer writes a check. If there are insufficient funds to cover the withdrawal, funds from the credit line are automatically transferred to the checking account.

If you use a line of credit, you are billed each month for the credit you have used and are required to make payments monthly against the principal and accrued interest charges. As the principal is reduced by a given amount, that amount is restored to your credit line. The interest on this "revolving credit" is usually higher than the interest on installment loans, but you can often arrange with the bank to have a specific sum taken from your checking or savings account each month to pay off the obligation.

Bank Credit Cards. Credit cards, whether issued by banks or other institutions, are another form of revolving credit. These cards entitle their holders to a predetermined maximum against which they may borrow, and the principal repaid is automatically restored to the credit line.

You can use a credit card to pay for goods and services from participating stores, restaurants, airlines and the like and can also borrow cash against it. Interest rates on bank-card purchases tend to be high, and the rates for cash advances even higher. Business institutions that accept credit cards pay a fee to the issuer — the bank, for example — to help defray the cost of credit card transactions, while on a cash advance the customer must bear the entire cost.

Thousands of banks around the country offer major credit cards and until recently, most of them were issued without charge. Many customers made use of their cards to

(continued on page 234)

How Good Is Your Credit Rating?

In the days before computers and credit cards, loan officers usually sized up applicants on the Three C's of Credit: Character (a moral commitment to pay the money back), Capacity (the means to do so) and Collateral (property that could be seized and resold in the event repayment was not made). The Three C's are still important in securing loans, but creditors today are more apt to rely primarily on computer models and statistical graphs that rate by points the typical characteristics of people who do, and don't, repay their debts.

According to a California firm that develops such systems for banks and other creditors, only about 20 to 30 percent of all credit applicants get enough points to be approved. While each institution has its own system, Consumers Union, publisher of the magazine *Consumer Reports*, analyzed some common denominators and came up with the hypothetical scoring test shown below.

Generally, the older you are the better credit risk you are in a lender's eyes. The points, however, drop noticeably for people in their mid-30's, a group that often faces the unforeseen expenses of young children, divorce or other causes of financial stress.

The longer you have lived in one place the more lenders see you as a "stable" person, and if you own rather than rent your home, you score extra points. People with cars rate higher than those without, and the newer the car the more points you are apt to get.

Another consideration is how long you have held the same job. What kind of job you have — an executive rates higher than a cab driver — and your income, of course, make a difference.

Having a savings account is better than having a checking account, and you are considerably more desirable if you have both. If you have taken out an installment loan from your bank, and are repaying promptly, you will get a few more points.

People who already have one or more credit cards in good standing are considered better risks than those with none. Department store charge cards, travel and entertainment cards and oil company cards rate somewhat lower, and off-the-cuff credit with, for instance, the local drug store, which is not punched into a national credit-reporting system, ranks even lower than that.

If you have been desperate enough to have borrowed recently at high interest from a small-loan or finance company, you will probably be docked a number of points. If you have applied and been turned down for credit more than once in the last six months, and that fact appears on your computerized record with a credit-reporting agency, you may have difficulty getting new credit, as you may if your record indicates that you have not been prompt in paying your bills.

If you have gone through bankruptcy in the last few years, you may have to forget credit completely, unless you have solid evidence that you are back on your financial feet.

The "test" given here can indicate only your relative credit-worthiness. It cannot tell you whether you will actually get credit from particular lenders, whose policies may vary widely according to their experiences, profit targets and tolerance of risk under different economic conditions at different times. One lender, for example, might sign you up if you scored a total of 75 or more points, while another might approve you only if you exceeded 125 points.

Before applying for credit, especially a major loan, it is a good idea to see for yourself just what your credit history is. You have the right under law to ask the lender for the name of the credit reporting agency the institution uses, and to obtain a copy of your record from that agency so you can weigh your chances, correct any errors or append your side of the story. Then discuss your prospects with an officer of the institution where you hope to get a loan. Be leery of outside organizations that claim they can help you get credit or "fix" your credit report. For a fee, often a substantial one, such operators usually just tell you what your rights are in investigating and amending your report — something you can do yourself at little cost.

A Hypothetical Credit-Scoring Scheme

1. *What is your age?*
   Under 25 **(8)** 25-29 **(12)** 30-34 **(10)** 35-39 **(6)** 40-44 **(14)** 45-49 **(18)**
   50 or more **(25)** ______
2. *How many years have you lived at your current address?*
   Less than 1 **(-10)** 1-2 **(-3)** 2-3 **(0)** 3-5 **(4)** 5-9 **(14)** 10 or more **(26)** ______
3. *Do you own your home or do you rent?*
   Own **(30)** Rent **(-32)** Other **(0)** ______
4. *How many years have you held your current job?*
   Less than 1 1/2 **(-14)** 1 1/2-3 **(0)** 3-6 **(5)** 6-8 **(9)** 9 or more **(16)** ______
5. *What bank accounts do you have?*
   Checking & Savings **(24)** Savings only **(11)** Checking only **(6)** Neither **(0)** ______
6. *Do you have a current bank loan?*
   Yes **(3)** No **(0)** ______
7. *Do you have a phone?*
   Yes **(9)** No **(0)** ______
8. *How many bank and travel-entertainment cards do you have?*
   0 **(0)** 1 **(12)** 2 or more **(21)** ______
9. *How many major department-store credit cards do you have?*
   0 **(0)** 1-2 **(5)** 3 or more **(8)** ______
10. *How many loans from a small-loan company do you have?* [1]
    0 **(0)** 1 **(-4)** 2 or more **(-12)** ______
11. *How many marginal credit references would you have to use?* [2]
    0 **(0)** 1 or more **(-6)** ______
12. *What is your family income?*
    0-$10,000 **(-7)** $10,000-15,000 **(0)** $15,000-19,000 **(5)** $19,000-25,000 **(8)**
    $25,000 or more **(13)** ______

Total ______

Do not include loans from automobile-finance companies such as GMAC.
In filling out an application form, a certain number of credit references are required. If you have to use small stores without an organized credit-reporting system, you'll lose points.

Scorecard

If you scored	You'd be in the top	Your bad-debt ratio	If you scored	You'd be in the top	Your bad-debt ratio
51 to 175	3%	0.4%	26 to 50	67%	11.0%
26 to 150	8%	1.0%	to 25	84%	14.7%
01 to 125	16%	2.5%	-24 to 0	93%	19.2%
76 to 100	28%	5.1%	-49 to -25	98%	22.7%
51 to 75	46%	8.0%	-75 to -50	100%	29.1%

purchase goods and services and then, by paying in full during the first billing period, avoided all interest charges. In effect, these people were taking out short-term, interest-free loans. As this practice defeated the banks' purpose in issuing credit cards — to encourage purchases on credit so that the bank could earn interest — many institutions began charging membership fees of $15, $20 or more a year for the use of their cards. Some banks have waived fees in order to attract new customers, and others offer cards free of charge to those who maintain accounts with the bank. Because the interest rates on credit card purchases may vary from one institution to another, it is a good idea to check with a number of banks before deciding to sign up for a credit card.

Debit Cards. Less common than credit cards are debit cards, now offered by an increasing number of banks and savings institutions. You can use them like credit cards in making purchases but, unlike credit cards, which bill you later for the amount you have been charged, debit cards transfer your money immediately and directly out of your account with the bank. With a debit card you can draw on a checking account, a savings account, and, with some, a personal line of credit extended by the bank as an overdraft privilege — you can even draw from a predetermined loan that is secured by your home or other property as collateral.

Debit cards are being used more and more in such places as department stores and supermarkets. Instead of having to cash a check with the manager's approval, or using the store's own charge card, a clerk inserts your debit card in a point-of-sale terminal and types in the information, and the amount is immediately deducted from your account at the bank.

Passbook Loans. The least expensive form of credit available at banks is usually a passbook loan which uses the borrower's savings at a bank as collateral. Most passbook loans are written as installment loans and specify a repayment schedule.

Getting a Loan

Before applying for any kind of loan, it is prudent to analyze just how much money you need and precisely how long you need it for. Then compare the rates and conditions you will have to abide by for the use of someone else's cash.

Financial institutions offer many types of loans under many different names. In addition to auto loans and home mortgages, there are, for example, home improvement loans, used for financing repairs, remodeling, additions or other improvements to a house; small business loans, made to individuals who own their own companies to finance operations or buy new equipment; special short-term loans for a variety of purposes; "demand loans" or "time notes" that can be used to tide a person over a number of months or until a specified date when expected funds will have come in and the loan can be paid in full; "swing" or "bridge" loans to enable a house buyer to close on the contract for a new home while waiting for the money due on the purchase of his or her old one.

In all loans — particularly the most common ones, "consumer" or "personal" loans that are ordinarily paid back in monthly installments — bankers are mainly interested in two things: the purpose of the loan and the borrower's ability to repay it. They are usually less willing to lend $5,000 for an extended vacation in Europe than to lend the same amount for the payment of medical bills or the installation of a brand new heating system for the home.

As a practical matter, a loan officer may have a hard time knowing what the money actually went for; your ability to repay is the primary concern. Though the figures vary, most banks do not like to lend you a sum that exceeds 20 or 25 percent of your gross income — $6,000 to $7,500 on a salary of $30,000, for example — or an amount that would make your total monthly payments larger than a week's salary, including your debts (and in the case of mortgages, including payments towards taxes and insurance on your home). But, again, banks don't make a fetish of verifying people's stated incomes. They are likely to pursue the matter in detail only if the loan is for a large amount and the collateral or security interest is inadequate or shaky. Moreover, if they have any misgivings about you, they can scrutinize your credit history to see how well you have handled credit in the past.

The Perils of Cosigning

There may come a time when a friend or relative applies for a loan and the lending institution refuses unless the applicant can find a cosigner. If someone you know asks you to cosign a loan, consider the request very carefully before you agree. Chances are that the lender would not have required a cosigner if the applicant's credit rating was good. If you do cosign, you are not simply doing your friend a favor; you are agreeing to pay off the loan in full in the event that your friend cannot. In fact, if you are accepted as a cosigner, the lender may be more persistent in dunning you for repayment than in pursuing the borrower, on the assumption that your financial resources are greater. As a cosigner, you have few rights but possibly crushing obligations — and all this without having received a penny from anyone.

Protections For Users of Credit

Like millions of Americans, you probably make at least some of your purchases on credit. The practice of buying now and paying later, though vital to both individual and national economies, can be dangerous if abused. Each year hundreds of thousands of people find themselves over their heads in debt and unable to meet all their monthly payments. Often they resort to desperate means — trying, for example, to consolidate their debts by incurring a single new one, a tactic that sometimes makes matters worse. In some cases they wind up in bankruptcy court, their credit ratings shattered and their property forfeit (see Chapter 15).

Neither federal nor state governments can prevent people from overextending themselves financially, but the governments can, and do, provide consumers with some protection in the credit marketplace. Because banks are the primary source of credit, they come under particularly close scrutiny.

There was a time, not too long ago, when a bank could turn down a credit applicant for any reason, or for no reason at all. A person might be denied a loan on the basis of sex, race, marital status or just because the loan officer took a dislike to the applicant. Similarly, banks and other lending institutions could conceal the true interest they were charging for loans by stressing the monthly rate and obscuring the total yearly cost. Credit reporting agencies, upon which lenders depend for determining the credit-worthiness of an applicant, were so loosely governed that they could report mere rumors as evidence of a person's lack of financial responsibility. All such practices, and a host of other dubious credit procedures, have been outlawed.

The Truth in Lending Act. The primary purpose of this federal legislation, enacted in 1968, is to make the borrower aware of exactly how much a loan will cost. There was a time when lenders could simply advertise "8 percent interest." Unless the borrower carefully examined the exact terms of the loan — often written in difficult-to-understand legal terminology — he or she was unlikely to realize that "add-ons" might effectively double the interest being charged. Such tactics are now illegal. Today a borrower must be provided with information, written in terms that a layman can understand, which includes the following facts:

- The finance charge: All lenders — except those lending mortgage money — must state clearly in their contracts the total amount the loan (or line of credit) is going to cost the borrower. This amount may include sums other than interest: there may also be points, handling, appraisal, loan and/or insurance fees and similar expenses.
- The annual percentage rate (APR): All lenders must disclose their cost of credit as a yearly rate. Unless the information is given in these terms, consumers can end up paying considerably more for either closed or open-ended loans than they expected. If, for example, you borrow $1,200 for a year at 10 percent interest with the understanding that you will repay the total sum plus interest at the end of the year, you will have had the use of the full $1200 at a cost of $120. But most consumer loans are repaid in monthly installments. You therefore do not have the use of the money in full, and the interest rate is thus increased. For instance, $1320 paid back in 12 equal installments of $110 a month represents an 18 percent annual rate of interest.
- Late payment penalties: In order to assure themselves of an adequate profit, most lenders levy penalties on borrowers who are tardy in making scheduled payments. This practice is entirely legal, but under Truth in Lending, institutions that engage in it must disclose

that fact, and must also disclose the terms of the penalties.

In addition to the general disclosure requirements of the Truth in Lending law, there are others that relate specifically to closed and open-ended loans. Closed-end loan agreements, for example, must include the following information:

- The date on which each payment for the loan is due.
- The total amount the borrower will have paid out once his or her obligation has been fulfilled.
- Whether or not a prepayment penalty — a percentage of the money still outstanding — will be levied against borrowers who pay their loans in full before the due date; and if it is levied, the amount.
- If the interest rate is variable, the circumstances under which it changes and on what basis the rate is determined.
- The total number of payments to be made.
- Whether or not the loan contains a demand feature and, if it does, the terms.
- An accurate description of any property that may have been used to secure the loan and the terms under which that property may be forfeited.

Open-ended loan agreements must include the following information:

- Whether or not borrowers can avoid interest charges, and if so, how. Most credit card companies do not charge interest on bills that are paid in full, and under Truth in Lending, the holders of such cards must be given at least two weeks from the opening of the billing period to make their payments.
- The differences — if any — in interest rates for different kinds of loans. Credit card companies often charge a higher rate of interest for cash advances than for purchases; if they do, this information must be given in the credit agreement. Similarly, if there is a variable rate of interest, the circumstances under which the rate may vary and the limits on the amount by which it can vary must be disclosed. Finally, any changes in interest rates must be reported to card holders, and transactions completed before the rate change is in effect must be billed at the earlier rate.
- The lender must send the borrower a monthly statement detailing the following: previous balance; payment received; amount owed; interest; principal and date or time by which the new balance or a portion of it must be paid to avoid additional charges. The statement must also itemize all purchases made during the billing period.

Failure on the part of a lender to make the disclosures required by the Truth in Lending law gives a borrower grounds for legal action — a suit for damages, plus double the finance charges up to a maximum of $1,000. If the suit is successful, the defendant will be required to pay court costs and the plaintiff's legal fees.

If you think any bank has violated the terms of the Truth in Lending Act, get in touch with your state banking commission (see directory, page 246); if your complaint concerns a credit card company or some other lender, report it to your state attorney general's office (see directory, page 48).

Advertising Restrictions. The Truth in Lending Act also imposes restrictions on those who advertise credit. A bank, for example, may advertise that credit is available to "qualified customers," but if it goes beyond that to mention specific credit terms, it must describe other basic requirements. An ad for a new home, for example, cannot merely advertise "12 percent credit" unless it also mentions the annual percentage rate. Nor can the ad state the amount of finance charge without also stating the amount of the down payment, if any, the terms of repayment and the APR.

The Equal Credit Opportunity Act: Before 1975, when the Equal Credit Opportunity Act became effective, a considerable number of Americans — women, older people and minority group members — often had difficulty in obtaining loans and credit. Since then, discrimination on these bases has been forbidden by law. Prospective lenders no longer have the right even to ask borrowers about their race, religion or nationality — except, for monitoring purposes, in the case of real estate loans, and even in this case, the borrower is under no obligation to respond. Older people cannot be rejected on the grounds that their age prevents them from obtaining credit insurance and in determining their financial status, prospective lenders must take into account such various sources of income as Social Security, annuities and pension payments.

CONSUMER ALERT

Lost Checks or Credit Cards

If you lose your checkbook and a check is forged in your name, you are generally not liable; it is the responsibility of the bank to know the depositor.

Of course, it is in your own best interest to report the loss immediately to your bank. There are some special circumstances under which you might have trouble. For example, a skilled forger who has a sample of your signature may conceivably withdraw your entire balance. Informing the bank promptly will save you problems and, possibly in some limited circumstances, loss of funds.

Make certain to check the next monthly statement that you receive to discover whether you have been charged for a forged check.

Lost or misplaced bank credit cards or department store charge cards should be reported as soon as the loss is discovered. While the original card holder may be liable for a maximum of $50 (per card) — card issuers buy insurance against a thief's shopping sprees or purchase of a first class flight to some distant pleasure island — it is nevertheless to your benefit to have those accounts closed and new registration numbers issued to you (and anyone else authorized to charge purchases on those accounts). If there have been charges which you did not make, you will have to go through the burden of having the billing corrected, including having to demonstrate that the purchases were not in fact made by you. To the extent that credit card issuers bear losses due to forged credit card purchases, there may be increased fees associated with procuring credit cards for all customers. And finally, there is a civic responsibility to report crime to appropriate officials.

It is important, therefore, to have an up-to-date list of your credit card numbers in a safe place other than the wallet or purse in which you carry your credit cards.

Holders of several cards may wish to purchase credit card insurance. For a modest fee, the insuring company retains the list of all of your account numbers and immediately notifies all of the issuers once you call to report a loss or theft. These companies also supply warning labels to paste on your credit cards, which, it is hoped, will deter a thief from making criminal use of the accounts.

Perhaps most dramatic are the changes the law has brought about in the treatment of women. In the past, married women often could not get credit unless their husbands acted as co-signers; unmarried women were often held to much more rigid credit tests than men; young married women without children were often turned down on the grounds that when — and if — they became mothers, they would no longer be acceptable credit risks. Under the provisions of the Equal Credit Opportunity Act, all these forms of discrimination are outlawed. Specifically, the law provides that:

- A lender may not reject a female applicant for credit because of her sex or marital status, and any woman whose application is denied has the right, within 60 days, to ask for the reasons in writing. A lender who refuses to supply this information is subject to court suit and could be forced to pay the plaintiff's actual charges plus punitive damages, attorney fees and court costs.
- In applying for credit, married women may use their maiden names, if they choose.
- Divorced or legally separated women are not obliged to list such sources of income as child support and alimony when applying for credit. But those who believe that mention of these resources will improve their chances of getting the money can do so, and although prospective lenders are entitled to determine if these sources of income are reliable, they must be taken into consideration when making a decision.
- A lender may not ask a woman whether she intends to have children.
- A lender can ask a woman's husband to co-sign a loan only when it is clear that her income alone is insufficient or when property

jointly held is to be used as collateral.
• Lenders may not ask women about their marital status except in states with community property laws — specifically, Arizona, California, Idaho, Louisiana, Nevada, New Mexico, Texas and Washington — where the spouse can use the account or will be contractually liable for it, or where the spouse's income is used to help qualify for the loan.

Lenders who violate the Equal Credit Opportunity Act are subject to severe penalties, including actual damage, up to $10,000 in punitive damages along with attorney fees and court costs.

Violation of the law can be difficult to prove, especially in cases where the applicant's credit-worthiness can be considered marginal, whether because of a relatively low income or a short period of employment or residence in the community. Under the terms of the law, applicants who are rejected for credit must be given the reasons for this action in writing. If, after you have examined the lender's statement, you remain convinced that you are the victim of discrimination, the next step is to write a letter describing the situation in full. Your complaints about commercial banks should go to the nearest regional office of the Federal Reserve System.
• Complaints about federally insured savings and loan associations should go to: General Counsel, Federal Home Loan Bank Board, 1700 G Street, NW, Washington, D.C. 20552.
• Complaints about credit unions should go to: National Credit Union Administration, 1776 G Street, NW, Washington, D.C. 20456.
• Complaints about credit card companies, finance companies and retail stores should go to: Federal Trade Commission, Equal Opportunity Division, Washington, D.C. 20580.

Or, if you prefer, you can send your complaints — no matter what kind of lending agency is involved — to your state's consumer protection office or attorney general's office. (See directories, pages 16 and 48.)

The Fair Credit Reporting Act. When you apply for credit, the lender may ask a credit reporting agency for a summary of your financial history before deciding whether to grant the loan. This is standard procedure, particularly when substantial sums are involved, and every day, thousands of such credit reports are issued to lenders throughout the country. The majority of them deal solely with your bill-paying record in connection with the credit transactions in which you have been involved over the last several years.

On the other hand, if you apply for a job that carries considerable financial responsibility or a large amount of life insurance, you may be examined much more thoroughly. In a so-called investigative credit report, the agency may also get in touch with your friends, neighbors and business associates to discover as much as possible about the way you live. But if such a report about you is contemplated, you are entitled to be notified of this fact within three days of the time the request for the report is made — unless the investigation is in connection with a job for which you have not specifically applied. And you are also entitled to obtain a complete and accurate description of the nature and scope of the investigation request.

If you are rejected for a loan or credit, you have the right to invoke the protections offered by the Fair Credit Reporting Act. This law requires lenders to inform rejected applicants of the reason for the rejection, and if that reason is a negative credit bureau report, the law gives those applicants a number of important rights.

First, they have the right to know the name and address of the credit bureau that issued the report and to know precisely what information about them the credit bureau has in its files. Applicants who request this information, either by mail or phone, within 30 days of the time that credit was denied them must be given it free of charge; thereafter, the credit bureau may demand a small payment.

It is up to the credit bureau to decide how to make that material available. Most permit applicants to examine the file itself, by coming to the bureau office — and the law permits them to bring their lawyers or other persons with them, if they choose. If that is not convenient, the bureau will supply either a copy of the material in the file or a written description of it. If the applicant has any difficulty understanding this material, the bureau is obliged to explain and interpret it.

In addition, the Fair Credit Reporting Act gives credit applicants these important rights:
• The right to know the names and addresses of all companies to which the report was sent during the preceding six months.

• The right to challenge any information in the credit report on the grounds either of its accuracy or its date, and to compel the credit bureau to reexamine such information, by consulting with the creditor in question, if necessary. Generally, any negative information — arrest records, paid tax liens, adverse lawsuits or judgments, for example — that is more than seven years old must be removed. One exception is a previous declaration of bankruptcy, which may stay in the files for 10 years. Another is the case of an individual applying for credit on life insurance worth more than $50,000 or a job paying more than $22,000 a year. Any information that proves to be incorrect must be stricken from the record.
• The right to have all changes made as the result of investigation sent to any companies that received the inaccurate report.
• The right to enter into the file, in the event that investigation does not alter it, a short statement giving the applicant's side of the story. This statement — or a summary of it — must be included in all future reports the agency sends about the applicant.

These protections are extremely valuable. Applicants who discover errors in the report are in a good position to reopen their previously failed negotiations, and this time they may be successful. Even if there is no error, it is often helpful for applicants to enter their own statements with the report. There may be extenuating circumstances — a temporary loss of employment; a one-time major and unexpected expense — that will make them more attractive prospects to lenders who might otherwise reject them.

Most credit bureaus adhere strictly to the requirements of the Fair Credit Reporting Act and cooperate willingly with consumers. But if you have any difficulty with an agency, you should report it in writing to: Bureau of Consumer Protection, Federal Trade Commission, Pennsylvania Avenue and Sixth Street, NW, Washington, D.C. 20580.

The Commission will not intercede for you, but a number of complaints may trigger an investigation and, possibly, legal action that halts the company's offensive practices.

You should also report any problems to the credit bureau trade organization, which will attempt to settle the dispute. Write to: Associated Credit Bureaus, Park Ten Place, Houston, Texas 77036.

If this intercession fails, and you believe that a credit agency has violated your rights under the law, consult an attorney. You may have grounds for legal action under the law and your suit, if successful, will bring you damages as well as court and attorney's fees.

Another source of help in disputes with credit agencies is your state attorney general's office (see directory, page 48). In situations where you are unable to reach an agreement, you may bring suit. If you are successful, you may collect damages as well as court and attorney's fees.

The Fair Credit Billing Act

This important piece of legislation is designed to give consumers a method of dealing with the errors in — or disputes about — billing that are almost certain to occur from time to time in credit card accounts. The difficulties can arise for any number of reasons. The company may fail to credit you for a payment you have made. It may charge you for an item bought on someone else's card. It may fail to credit you for an item you returned. Sometimes, such errors can be corrected informally, through a phone call to the credit card company. But a phone call will not trigger the safeguards that the law provides, and for this reason wise consumers stick scrupulously to the procedures the legislation outlines.

First, the law permits you to withhold payment for any item while it is the subject of a dispute, and also to withhold payment of any minimum fees or finance charge that may be associated with it. But you are required to pay all other charges, and should. Then, the law requires you to write a letter to the company that issued the card, directing it to the office listed on your bill as the one authorized to deal with inquiries and complaints. The letter — which should be sent separately from your payment — should include your name, account number and date and should clearly and specifically describe the problem about which you are complaining, indicating the item you question, the amount of money involved and why you believe the company is in error in making the charge.

The law requires that the company receive this letter no later than 60 days after your bill was mailed to you; if you delay sending the message until nearly the end of that 60-day period, it might be advisable to send it by

CONSUMER ALERT

When to Pay Credit Card Bills

Although most credit card accounts carry the same annual interest rates, they do not all calculate monthly interest charges the same way. Consequently, consumers may find themselves paying differing amounts in interest on the same purchases.

For example, if the interest is calculated on the basis of the consumer's *average daily balance*, a cardholder who owes $200 at the beginning of the 30-day billing cycle and pays $100 on the 15th day will be charged interest on $150 (15 days at $200 plus 15 days at $100, divided by 30). This means that average daily balance accounts should be paid as early in the month as possible, since this reduces the amount on which interest is owed.

On the other hand, if it is calculated on the basis of the *adjusted (or unpaid) balance*, that same cardholder will pay interest only on the $100 owed at the end of the cycle. In this case, therefore, cardholders can safely wait to the end of the cycle to pay their bills — provided, of course, that they are careful not to make purchases at that time.

The third method of calculation, based on the *previous balance*, is illegal in some states and, in any event, undesirable for consumers, since it charges consumers the amount owed when the cycle opens — in this case, $200.

certified mail, requesting a return receipt.

The company cannot threaten your credit rating or dispute your account because you question a bill, and it must acknowledge your letter in writing within 30 days and inform you of its decision no later than 60 days thereafter. If the decision is in your favor, your account must be corrected to reflect this fact. The charge — and any fees you may have paid in connection with it — must be removed or the credit entered. If the decision is not in your favor, the company must send you a letter providing you with proof — a copy of the sales receipt, for example — that the company is correct, together with a statement of what you owe, which may include any finance charges that have accumulated and any minimum payments you did not make during the period of the dispute.

If you find the company's decision unacceptable, the law gives you at least 10 days to write again. But it also gives the company the right to report you as a delinquent and to take action to collect. Even then, however, you have the right to disagree in writing, to obtain from the company the name and address of every firm to which your delinquent status has been reported and to enter your side of the story in your credit record. When the matter is finally settled, the company must report the outcome to every organization that has received information about it.

If the error concerns a charge for goods not yet delivered, the credit card company cannot conclude that there is no mistake in the billing until the goods have actually arrived. If you fail to reach a satisfactory solution, contact your state banking commission (see directory, page 246) if the card was issued by a bank in your state. Otherwise, write to your state attorney general's office (see directory, page 48). For more information on the Fair Credit Billing Act, write to: Fair Credit Billing, Room 720, Federal Trade Commission, Washington, D.C. 20580.

The Fair Debt Collection Practices Act. If you find yourself in financial difficulties, there are several specific steps you can take to protect your credit standing. Although creditors can always turn over your account to a collection agency, some prefer not to do so and would rather make an arrangement for repayment with you. They may be willing to accept reduced payments, extended over a longer period of time; they may be willing to accept a delay or postponement in your payment schedule. Such arrangements will, in the long run, cost you money, since the interest on your debt will continue to accumulate. But they are worth it, since they maintain your credit standing.

The particular arrangement you make with any given creditor can only be determined in conversation between you. It is important to visit your creditors personally, if you can, and to explain your financial situation with complete honesty. (This subject is discussed in more detail in Chapter 15.)

(continued on page 248)

General Banking Inquiries

American Bankers Association
1120 Connecticut Avenue, NW
Washington, DC 20036

Credit Union National Association
1730 Rhode Island Avenue, NW
Washington, DC 20036

National Association of Mutual Savings Banks
200 Park Avenue
New York, NY 10166

Offices of the National Credit Union Administration

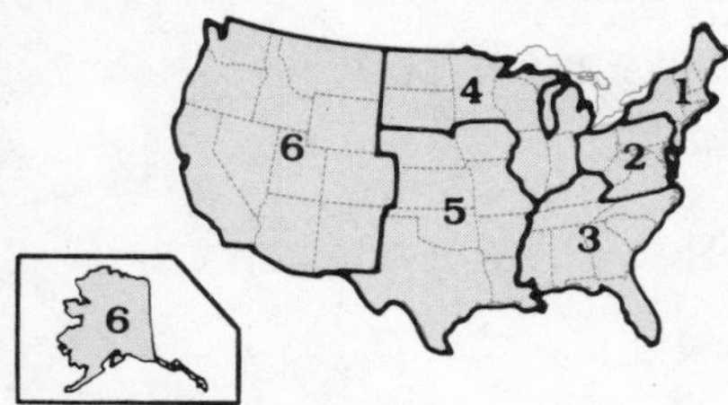

Main Office **Office of Consumer Affairs, National Credit Union Administration, 1776 G Street, NW, Washington, DC 20456**

Region 1 **Connecticut, Maine, Massachusetts, New Hampshire, New Jersey, New York, Puerto Rico, Rhode Island, Vermont, Virgin Islands**
National Credit Union Association, 441 Stuart Street, Boston, MA 02116

Region 2 **Delaware, District of Columbia, Maryland, Pennsylvania, Virginia, West Virginia**
National Credit Union Association, 310 North Second Street, Harrisburg, PA 17101

Region 3 **Alabama, Arkansas, Florida, Georgia, Kentucky, Louisiana, Mississippi, North Carolina, South Carolina, Tennessee**
National Credit Union Association, 1365 Peachtree Street, Atlanta, GA 30367

Region 4 **Illinois, Indiana, Iowa, Michigan, Minnesota, Missouri, North Dakota, Ohio, South Dakota, Wisconsin**
National Credit Union Association, New Federal Building, 234 North Summit Street, Toledo, OH 43604

Region 5 **Arizona, Colorado, Idaho, Kansas, Montana, Nebraska, Nevada, New Mexico, Oklahoma, Texas, Utah, Wyoming**
National Credit Union Association, 611 East Sixth Street, Austin, TX 78701

Region 6 **Alaska, American Samoa, California, Guam, Hawaii, Oregon, Washington**
National Credit Union Association, 77 Geary Street, San Francisco, CA 94108

Offices of the Federal Deposit Insurance Corporation

Main Office	**Federal Deposit Insurance Corporation, Office of Consumer Compliance Programs, 550 17th Street, NW, Washington, DC 20429**
Atlanta Regional Office	**Alabama, Florida, Georgia, North Carolina, South Carolina,** Federal Deposit Insurance Corporation, 233 Peachtree Street, NE, Atlanta, GA 30043
Boston Regional Office	**Connecticut, Maine, Massachusetts, New Hampshire, Rhode Island, Vermont** Federal Deposit Insurance Corporation, 60 State Street, Boston, MA 02109
Chicago Regional Office	**Illinois, Indiana** Federal Deposit Insurance Corporation, 233 South Wacker Drive, Chicago, IL 60606
Columbus Regional Office	**Kentucky, Ohio, West Virginia** Federal Deposit Insurance Corporation, 1 Nationwide Plaza, Columbus, OH 43215
Dallas Regional Office	**Colorado, New Mexico, Oklahoma, Texas** Federal Deposit Insurance Corporation, 350 North St. Paul Street, Dallas, TX 75201
Kansas City Regional Office	**Kansas, Missouri** Federal Deposit Insurance Corporation, 2345 Grand Avenue, Kansas City, MO 64108
Madison Regional Office	**Michigan, Wisconsin** Federal Deposit Insurance Corporation, 1 South Pinckney Street, Madison, WI 53703
Memphis Regional Office	**Arkansas, Louisiana, Mississippi, Tennessee** Federal Deposit Insurance Corporation, 1 Commerce Square, Memphis, TN 38103
Minneapolis Regional Office	**Minnesota, Montana, North Dakota, South Dakota, Wyoming** Federal Deposit Insurance Corporation, 730 Second Avenue, S, Minneapolis, MN 55402
New York Regional Office	**New Jersey, New York, Puerto Rico, Virgin Islands** Federal Deposit Insurance Corporation, 345 Park Avenue, New York, NY 10154
Omaha Regional Office	**Iowa, Nebraska** Federal Deposit Insurance Corporation, 1700 Farnam Street, Omaha, NE 68102

Philadelphia Regional Office

Delaware, District of Columbia, Maryland, Pennsylvania, Virginia

Federal Deposit Insurance Corporation, 1900 Market Street, Philadelphia, PA 19103

San Francisco Regional Office

Alaska, Arizona, California, Guam, Hawaii, Idaho, Nevada, Oregon, Utah, Washington

Federal Deposit Insurance Corporation, 25 Ecker Street, San Francisco, CA 94105

Offices of the Federal Home Loan Bank Board

Main Office

Department of Consumer and Civil Rights, Office of Examination and Supervision, Federal Home Loan Bank Board, 1700 G Street, NW, Washington, DC 20552

Atlanta Regional Office

Alabama, District of Columbia, Florida, Georgia, Maryland, North Carolina, South Carolina, Virginia

Federal Home Loan Bank Board, P.O. Box 56527, Peachtree Center Station Atlanta, GA 30343

Boston Regional Office

Connecticut, Maine, Massachusetts, New Hampshire, Rhode Island, Vermont

Federal Home Loan Bank Board, P.O. Box 2196, Boston, MA 02106

Chicago Regional Office

Illinois, Wisconsin

Federal Home Loan Bank Board, 111 East Wacker Drive, Suite 800 Chicago, IL 60601

Cincinnati Regional Office

Kentucky, Ohio, Tennessee

Federal Home Loan Bank Board, 2500 DuBois Tower, Cincinnati, OH 45202

Des Moines Regional Office

Iowa, Minnesota, Missouri, North Dakota, South Dakota

Federal Home Loan Bank Board, 907 Walnut Street, Des Moines, IA 50309

Indianapolis Regional Office

Indiana, Michigan

Federal Home Loan Bank Board, P.O. Box 60, Indianapolis, IN 46202

Arkansas Regional Office

Arkansas, Louisiana, Mississippi, New Mexico, Texas

Federal Home Loan Bank Board, 1400 Tower Building, Little Rock, AR 72201

New York Regional Office

New Jersey, New York, Puerto Rico, Virgin Islands

Federal Home Loan Bank Board, One World Trade Center, New York, NY 10048

Pittsburgh Regional Office

Delaware, Pennsylvania, West Virginia

Federal Home Loan Bank Board, 11 Stanwix Street, Gateway Center, Pittsburgh, PA 15222

San Francisco Regional Office **Arizona, California, Nevada**

Federal Home Loan Bank Board, P.O. Box 7948, San Francisco, CA 94120

Seattle Regional Office **Alaska, Guam, Hawaii, Idaho, Montana, Oregon, Utah, Wyoming, Washington**

Federal Home Loan Bank Board, 600 Stewart Street, Seattle, WA 98101

Topeka Regional Office **Colorado, Kansas, Nebraska, Oklahoma**

Federal Home Loan Bank Board, P.O. Box 176, Topeka, KS 66601

Board of Governors of the Federal Reserve System

Main Office **Division of Consumer and Community Affairs, Board of Governors of the Federal Reserve System, 20th and C Streets, NW, Washington, DC 20551**

District 1 **Connecticut, Maine, Massachusetts, New Hampshire, Rhode Island, Vermont**

600 Atlantic Avenue, Boston, MA 02106

District 2 **Central and Northern New Jersey, New York**

33 Liberty Street, New York, NY 10045

District 3 **Delaware, Southern New Jersey, Central and Eastern Pennsylvania**

10 Independence Mall, Philadelphia, PA 19106

District 4 **Eastern Kentucky, Ohio, Western Pennsylvania, Northern Tip of West Virginia**

P.O. Box 6387, 1455 East 6th Street, Cleveland, OH 44101

District 5 **Maryland, North Carolina, South Carolina, Virginia, West Virginia except Northern Tip**

701 East Byrd Street, Richmond, VA 23261

District 6 **Alabama, Florida, Georgia, Southern Louisiana, Southern Mississippi, Central and Eastern Tennessee**

P.O. Box 1731, 104 Marietta Street, NW, Atlanta, GA 30303

District 7 **Northern Illinois, Central and Northern Indiana, Iowa, Michigan (except Upper Peninsula), Wisconsin (except Northwestern portion)**

230 South LaSalle Street, Chicago, IL 60690

District 8 **Arkansas, Southern Illinois, Southern Indiana, Western Kentucky, Northern Mississippi, Central and Eastern Missouri, Western Tennessee**

411 Locust Street, St. Louis, MO 63102

District 9 **Upper Peninsula of Michigan, Minnesota, Montana, North Dakota, South Dakota, Northwestern Wisconsin**

250 Marquette Avenue, Minneapolis, MN 55480

District 10 **Colorado, Kansas, Western Missouri, Nebraska, Northern New Mexico, Oklahoma (except Southeastern portion), Wyoming**

925 Grand Avenue, Kansas City, MO 64198

District 11 **Northern Louisiana, Southern New Mexico, Southeastern Oklahoma, Texas**
400 South Akard Street, Dallas TX 75222

District 12 **Alaska, Arizona, California, Hawaii, Idaho, Nevada, Oregon, Utah, Washington**
101 Market Street, San Francisco, CA 941051

Offices of the Comptroller of the Currency

Main Office **Deputy Comptroller for Customer and Community Programs, Comptroller of the Currency, Department of the Treasury, 490 L'Enfant Plaza, Washington, DC 20219**

Region 1 **Connecticut, Maine, Massachusetts, New Hampshire, Rhode Island, Vermont**
Harbor Plaza, 470 Atlantic Avenue, Boston, MA 02110

Region 2 **Delaware, New Jersey, New York, Pennsylvania, Puerto Rico, Virgin Islands**
1211 Avenue of the Americas, New York, NY 10036

Region 3 **Indiana, Kentucky, Ohio**
1 Erieview Plaza, Cleveland, OH 44114

Region 4 **District of Columbia, Maryland, North Carolina, Virginia, West Virginia**
F & M Center, Richmond, VA 23277

Region 5 **Florida, Georgia, South Carolina**
Peachtree Cain Tower, 229 Peachtree Street, NE, Atlanta, GA 30303

Region 6 **Illinois, Michigan**
Sears Tower, Chicago, IL 60606

Region 7 **Alabama, Arkansas, Louisiana, Mississippi, Tennessee**
165 Madison Avenue, Memphis, TN 38103

Region 8 **Minnesota, North Dakota, South Dakota, Wisconsin**
800 Marquette Avenue, Minneapolis, MN 55402

Region 9 **Iowa, Kansas, Missouri, Nebraska**
911 Main Street, Kansas City, MO 64105

Region 10 **Oklahoma, Texas**
1201 Elm Street, Dallas, TX 75270

Region 11 **Arizona, Colorado, New Mexico, Utah, Wyoming**
1405 Curtis Street, Denver, CO 80202

Region 12 **California, Guam, Hawaii, Idaho, Montana, Nevada, Oregon, Washington**
1 Market Plaza, Stuart Street Tower, San Francisco, CA 94105

State Banking Authorities

The following authorities have the responsibility for the supervision and regulation of state chartered banks. You may also find them very helpful for answering any questions or for referring problems that may pertain to other types of banks.

Alabama
Superintendent of Banks
64 North Union Street
Montgomery, AL 36130

Alaska
Director of Banking
and Securities
Pouch D
Juneau, AK 99801

Arizona
Superintendent of Banks
Commerce Building
1601 West Jefferson Street
Phoenix, AZ 85007

Arkansas
State Bank Commissioner
1 Capitol Mall
Little Rock, AR 72201

California
Superintendent of Banks
235 Montgomery Street
San Francisco, CA 94104

Colorado
State Bank Commissioner
State Office Building
Denver, CO 80203

Connecticut
Bank Commissioner
State Office Building
Hartford, CT 06115

Delaware
State Bank Commissioner
Kirk Building
15 the Green
Dover, DE 19901

Florida
Comptroller of Florida
State Capitol Building
Tallahassee, FL 32304

Georgia
Commissioner of Banking
and Finance
2990 Brandywine Road
Atlanta, GA 30341

Guam
Director of Revenue
and Taxation
Government of Guam
P.O. Box 2700
Agana, GU 96910

Hawaii
Director of Regulatory Agencies
P.O. Box 541
Honolulu, HI 96809

Idaho
Director of Finance
Statehouse Mall
Boise, ID 83720

Illinois
Commissioner of Banks and
Trust Companies
310 South Michigan Avenue
Chicago, IL 60604

Indiana
Department of Financial
Institutions
Indiana State Office Building
Indianapolis, IN 46204

Iowa
Superintendent of Banking
418 Sixth Avenue
Des Moines, IA 50309

Kansas
State Bank Commissioner
818 Kansas Avenue
Topeka, KS 66612

Kentucky
Commissioner of Banking
and Securities
911 Leawood Drive
Frankfort, KY 40601

Louisiana
Commissioner of Financial
Institutions
P.O. Box 44095, Capitol Station
Baton Rouge, LA 70804

Maine
Bank Superintendent
State House Station No. 36
Augusta, ME 04333

Maryland
Bank Commissioner
1 North Charles Street
Baltimore, MD 21201

Massachusetts
Commissioner of Banks
100 Cambridge Street
Boston, MA 02202

Michigan
Commissioner
Financial Institutions Bureau
P.O. Box 30224
Lansing, MI 48909

Minnesota
Commissioner of Banks
Metro Square Building
Seventh and Roberts Streets
St. Paul, MN 55101

Mississippi
Commissioner
Department of Banking and
Consumer Finance
P.O. Box 731
Jackson, MS 39205

Missouri
Commissioner of Finance
P.O. Box 716
Jefferson City, MO 65101

Montana
Department of Business Regulation
805 North Main Street
Helena, MT 59601

Nebraska
Director of Banking and Finance
301 Centennial Mall, South
Lincoln, NE 68509

Nevada
Superintendent of Banks
406 East Second Street
Carson City, NE 89710

New Hampshire
Bank Commissioner
97 North Main Street
Concord, NH 03301

New Jersey
Commissioner of Banking
36 West State Street
Trenton, NJ 08625

New Mexico
Financial Institutions Division
Commerce and Industry Department
Lew Wallace Building
Santa Fe, NM 87503

New York
Superintendent of Banks
2 World Trade Center
New York, NY 10047

North Carolina
Commissioner of Banks
P.O. Box 951
Raleigh, NC 27602

North Dakota
Commissioner of Banking and Financial Institutions
State Capitol
Bismarck, ND 58505

Ohio
Superintendent of Banks
Borden Building
180 East Broad Street
Columbus, OH 43215

Oklahoma
Bank Commissioner
Malco Building
4100 North Lincoln Boulevard
Oklahoma City, OK 73105

Oregon
Superintendent of Banks
Department of Commerce
Busick Building
Salem, OR 97310

Pennsylvania
Secretary of Banking
P.O. Box 2155
Harrisburg, PA 17120

Puerto Rico
Secretary of the Treasury
Commonwealth of Puerto Rico
P.O. Box 4515
San Juan, PR 00905

Rhode Island
Bank Commissioner
100 North Main Street
Providence, RI 02903

South Carolina
Commissioner of Banking
1026 Sumter Street
Columbia, SC 29201

South Dakota
Director of Banking and Finance
State Capitol Building
Pierre, SD 57501

Tennessee
Commissioner of Banking
James K. Polk State Office Building
505 Deaderick Street
Nashville, TN 37219

Texas
Banking Commissioner
2601 North Lamar
Austin, TX 78705

U.S. Virgin Islands
Chairman of the Banking Board
Government House, Charlotte Amalie
P.O. Box 450
St. Thomas, VI 00801

Utah
Commissioner of Financial Institutions
10 West Broadway
Salt Lake City, UT 84101

Vermont
Commissioner of Banking and Insurance
State Office Building
Montpelier, VT 05602

Virginia
Commissioner of Financial Institutions
701 East Byrd Street
Richmond, VA 23219

Washington
Supervisor of Banking
General Administration Building
Olympia, WA 98504

West Virginia
Commissioner of Banking
State Office Building 6
1900 Washington Street, East
Charleston, WV 25305

Wisconsin
Commissioner of Banking
30 West Mifflin Street
Madison, WI 53703

Wyoming
State Examiner
819 West Pershing Boulevard
Cheyenne, WY 82002

If a bank or finance company is among your creditors, one of its officers may try to talk you into taking out a consolidation loan, which will enable you to pay off your outstanding debts immediately and will give you a long period in which to make repayment. The proposition may sound tempting, but you should think very carefully before agreeing to it, since it merely postpones your problems and charges a high interest rate for the privilege. On the whole it is wiser to reschedule payments of existing debts than to borrow new money to pay them off.

If, despite your best efforts to come to a satisfactory arrangement with a creditor, your account is turned over to a collection agency, you are protected by the provisions of the Fair Debt Collection Practices Act. This law prohibits a number of practices that were previously standard in the debt collection business. Among other things, it prohibits bill collectors from:

- Placing telephone calls to debtors at unusual places or times, generally before 8 A.M. or after 9 P.M.
- Harassing debtors and their families by telephoning frequently.
- Being personally abusive towards debtors or members of a debtor's family.
- Threatening to expose debtors to their friends, neighbors or employers. A collector may get in touch with other people, but only to find out where the debtor lives or works and may not tell anyone other than the debtor and the debtor's legal counsel that any money is owed.
- Pretending — whether in writing, in person or on the telephone — to represent any agency of local, state or federal government.
- Engaging in any other misrepresentations — as, for example, pretending to take a survey in order to obtain personal financial information about the debtor.
- Making any attempt to humiliate the debtor in some manner — as, for example, by stationing in front of the debtor's house a car with the words "debt collector" on it.
- Demanding payment in excess of the amount actually owed.
- Instituting legal proceedings against the debtor except in the debtor's home town, where the contract was signed, or in an action involving real estate, in an area where that real estate is located.

You may legally break off all contact with a debt collector by informing the agency — or individual — in writing that you have turned the matter over to an attorney, or that you simply will not deal with the collector or the agency. In that case, the collector has the right to notify you that he or she will go to court to force collection. But having told you this once, the collector cannot continue to make any contact with you, either personally or in writing.

These requirements apply only to collection agencies. They do not apply to creditor companies or institutions, to their lawyers, federal or state officials or legal process servers — except in the case of those localities that have imposed their own specific legal restrictions.

In the event you are bothered by a collection agency that acts in violation of the Fair Debt Collecting Act, make sure you notify your local Better Business Bureau (see your telephone directory). In addition, it is a good idea to write to the Bureau of Consumer Protection of the Federal Trade Commission (see directory, page 199). If the FTC commission receives several complaints against a particular agency, it may bring suit against it. You, too, have the right to bring suit, and if you are successful, you can collect actual damages, additional damages up to $1,000, court costs and attorney fees.

Chapter 10

Insurance and Investments

Insurance and investments — the two topics discussed in this chapter — play equally important but very different roles in our lives. Virtually everyone needs insurance of some sort. Few of us have the financial resources necessary to pay the costs of all the calamities that can overtake us. Insurance gives those resources to us. By setting their premium rates on the basis of carefully analyzed statistics and by pooling and investing their policyholders' premiums, insurance companies can offer us the protection against life's hazards we could otherwise not afford.

Investments, on the other hand, are a somewhat different matter. In the first place, they are not necessities. Moreover, until fairly recently consumers with only modest amounts of cash to spare had a very limited number of investment options open to them. But in the 1970's, as inflation began to erode the value of people's savings, investment became part of the consumer market and a wide variety of financial services became available, for the first time, to ordinary consumers.

In this chapter we will talk about the choices now open, both in insurance and investments, and about the things you need to know in order to make selections wisely. We will begin with a discussion of life insurance and the various benefits it can offer you above and beyond payments to your survivors when you die. Next, we will tell you about your choices in shopping for protection against the hazards of life — health, homeowners' and automobile insurance policies.

Then we will turn to the many ways of making your nest egg grow by becoming an investor. The possibilities are rich. There is the stock market, with its shares in high-tech industries and blue chip corporations. There are bonds issued by corporations and by governments and government agencies. There are short-term and long-term notes of indebtedness and other so-called "money-market instruments;" mutual funds (great pools of money in which you buy a share) and special accounts and packages that banks and brokerage houses can establish to manage your money in accordance with your particular needs.

We will also briefly discuss pensions and other retirement plans as well as cautions to be observed in drawing up a will.

Throughout, we will discuss safeguards against fraud — the federal laws and agencies designed to protect us from the sharks that are attracted to the financial waters — and tell you how to make use of these safeguards.

Insurance

Because it is so intimately concerned with the public interest, insurance is a regulated business — not on the federal level, but on a state-by-state basis. Each state has an Insurance Commission or Department of Insurance, whose head — variously called commissioner, director or superintendent — oversees a staff of technicians and experts responsible for protecting the interests of both the insurance companies and those they insure.

The specific functions of insurance departments vary from one state to another, but all have the following basic responsibilities:

- Licensing insurance companies and their agents.
- Examining companies for their financial condition.
- Responding to consumer complaints.
- Enforcing laws against false and misleading advertising and representations.
- Ensuring that insurance rates are not excessive, inadequate or discriminatory.
- Approving the form of insurance policies to assure that they comply with state statutory requirements before being sold to the public.

By their nature, state Insurance Departments — like state Public Utility Commissions — are engaged in a balancing act, weighing the needs and interests of both business and consumers. Although they do not, as a general matter, pass on the merit of particular policies, they *do* regulate rates for some lines of insurance and they *are* responsible for dealing with consumer complaints. Any problems you have not been able to resolve satisfactorily with an insurance company should be taken to your state insurance department. You will find a directory of these agencies on page 272.

Choosing an Insurance Agent

A reliable insurance agent may work for a particular insurance company or may handle policies for a number of different companies. In either case, he or she will be licensed by the state. Some agents have special qualifications, earned after completing a course of study and passing examinations which permit them to designate themselves as Chartered Property/Casualty Underwriters (CPCU) and/or Chartered Life Underwriters (CLU).

Before deciding on an agent, ask for recommendations from trusted friends and from business and professional people of your acquaintance who have significant insurance needs and in whose practical judgment you have confidence. And pay close attention to the way the agent deals with you. A competent agent will see to it that your insurance purchases mesh with your needs and your financial situation, and will offer you options among various available policies.

It is also a good idea to check into the companies the agent represents. Your library should have a copy of *Best's Insurance Management Reports*, a publication that lists insurance companies, describes their financial record and rates them according to a letter scale. The best — and the ones you should deal with — are those rated A or A plus.

Life insurance. The first questions about life insurance to which you need answers are: how much and what kind? The answers depend on your circumstances and situation, which will change over time.

If you have no dependents, for example, you may need little if any life insurance. On the other hand, if you are young and have a small bank balance and a large family, you need a generous amount — enough to assure that in the event of your death, your family has income to replace yours, and that your children will be properly reared and educated.

But as you get older, your responsibilities decrease. Your children grow up and your family's savings and assets — pension and profit-sharing plans, the equity in your home, and Social Security benefits — increase, with the result that you need less insurance to cover the gap.

Because your insurance requirements change with your responsibilities and income, you should review your insurance program every year if possible, and certainly every two or three years.

Once you have an idea of the amount of protection you need, the time has come to consider the kind. Some newer forms of life insurance are now available, but traditionally two kinds have been most popular: term insurance and whole — or straight — life.

Term insurance. A term insurance policy is a contract between you and an insurance company in which you pay for protection for a specific number of years — 1, 5, 10, or 20. In return for your premium — paid quarterly, semi-annually or annually — the company guarantees that if you die during the period the policy is in force, it will pay your beneficiary the amount stated on the face of the policy. If, on the other hand, you survive the term of the policy, you get nothing back. Term insurance has no savings feature. It brings in no income nor can you borrow against it. There is only a death benefit. For this reason, it generally carries lower premiums than any other kind of insurance. Premium rates on term insurance vary widely from one company to another and the least expensive is not necessarily the best buy.

The company may ask you to take a medical examination before selling you a term policy. Thereafter, however, your policy should be renewable without examination. Any policy that does not offer this feature should be rejected. When you renew your policy, the premiums will be higher: the older you get the more statistically likely it is that you will die during the term of the contract. Many policies are not renewable after age 65, and those that are carry very high premiums.

Term insurance is considerably cheaper as part of a group policy than as an individual purchase, and when it is bought through a group, usually no medical examination is required. Group term insurance is often available through unions, professional associations, fraternal lodges and other organizations. It may also be available through the company you work for and may even be a fringe benefit of the job, with the employer paying part or all of the premium.

In addition to the standard term insurance, two other types deserve mention. *Decreasing* term insurance, often used to protect a long term decreasing debt, such as a home mortgage, pays less and less to the beneficiary as time passes although the premium remains level. *Increasing* term insurance, on the other hand, may offer an "inflation guard" option, which increases the basic insurance benefit by 10 percent of the initial amount at the end of each of the first 10 years so that an original benefit of $50,000 will increase to $100,000. Or increasing term insurance policies may offer "cost of living" options tied to the consumer price index. In all such policies, of course, the premiums increase along with the benefits.

Still another form of term insurance is credit insurance: on payment of a premium tied to the balance on the account, this policy pays off the amount due a creditor if the debtor dies before the term has expired.

Almost all life insurance companies sell term policies, and they are also for sale in some states by savings banks and by savings and loan associations.

Whole life insurance. Whole life insurance, like term insurance, pays a specific amount to the beneficiary on the policyholder's death. But it has a savings feature, as well. Part of the policyholder's premium pays death benefits, while another part builds up a cash value.

For this reason the premiums for whole life insurance are higher than those for term insurance. On the other hand, they usually remain constant, and do not increase as you age. If you buy whole life insurance while you are still young, you are at first paying more than is actually required for the amount of protection you have bought — and it is that extra sum that builds the cash value of your policy. But once you have passed your mid-50's, you pay a lower premium than you would for the same amount of term insurance.

What, then, are the advantages of a whole life policy? For one thing, it makes life insurance more easily affordable as you age. In addition, it is a form of compulsory savings, and therefore useful to people who have difficulty setting surplus money aside.

Moreover, you can always take advantage of the fact that the policy has a cash value by cancelling it and taking the money when you no longer need the insurance protection.

In addition, if you are in need of money, you can borrow up to the full amount of the cash value of a whole-life insurance policy in the form of a policy loan, which you pay back to the company — with interest — at a rate fixed in the policy. If you die before your loan is completely repaid, the amount outstanding — plus any unpaid interest — is deducted from the payment to the beneficiaries.

Whole life insurance has two other advantages. If you miss a premium, the company can, if you authorize it, draw from the cash value of your policy to keep the insurance in force. If you wish to stop paying premiums, the accrued cash value of your policy can be used to continue your insurance, probably in a reduced amount.

Limited payment life policies. Some life insurance policies permit you to set a limit to the length of time during which you will pay premiums — your working years, for example. Among these are paid-up policies which require no premium payments beyond a certain age, usually 65; 20-pay or 30-pay policies, which require payment of 20 or 30 annual premiums (or some other number) and remain in force thereafter; endowment policies, which return their face value to you at the end of a fixed period — or to your beneficiary if you die before then. Endowment policies are ways to guarantee that you will receive a fixed sum at a specified future date, and can be useful in planning payment for such major expenses as a child's education.

The premiums for these limited-payment policies are higher than for those forms of life insurance that require you to pay throughout your lifetime, and their cash value therefore increases more quickly. In other words, they involve a trade off: more cash value per premium dollar for less protection.

Universal life insurance. In 1978, insurance companies devised a policy, still controversial in the industry, called universal life.

Universal life differs from other whole life policies in that it separates the insurance cost of a policy from its cash value and thus transforms it into something of an insurance-plus-savings arrangement. The part of the premium that goes into building its cash value is typically invested in securities earning interest at higher rates than those paid by most whole-life insurance investments. Moreover, holders of universal life policies can increase or decrease the amounts they invest by raising or lowering their premium payments within limits stated in the policy, and when the money invested — the accumulation fund — is large enough, it can be used to pay premiums. When the policyholder dies, the beneficiary usually gets both the death benefit and the interest earned on the policy's cash value. The interest rate, which was about 10 percent in 1983, is disclosed in an annual statement sent to all policyholders. The statement also includes a list of the amounts used for insurance, investment and fees.

In 1982, as a result of legislation that granted the death proceeds of qualifying universal life the same tax-free status enjoyed by other whole life policies and safeguarded their value as insurance by limiting their cash value, sales of this form of insurance accounted for some 10 to 12 percent of new policy premiums and, by the end of the year, it was being sold by approximately 100 companies.

Variable life insurance. Another version of insurance-plus-investment is called variable life insurance. Unlike universal life, whose policyholders are not consulted about the investments their premiums buy, variable life offers policyholders a choice among investments. For this reason, the sale of variable life insurance policies is regulated by the Securities and Exchange Commission (SEC), the federal agency that oversees the securities market to protect investors. Variable life policies can be offered for sale only by a prospectus, just as are new issues on the stock market, and salesmen must be registered with the National Association of Securities Dealers.

Variable life policies offer a broad range of investments — stock funds, corporate bond funds, government bond funds and shares in money market funds — and policyholders have to decide how to split the cash value of their policies among these different securities. It is a major responsibility, since the markets are volatile and a wrong choice can do considerable damage to the cash value of a policy. However, policyholders have the right to change their choices (within certain limits) at fixed periods, usually twice a year.

Still, variable life remains a form of insurance, with fixed premiums and a guaranteed minimum death benefit, which can increase, depending on the policyholder's earnings and surrender rights. On the average, variable life premiums are higher than those charged for whole life and term insurance.

Shopping for life insurance: term or whole? In deciding whether to buy term or whole life insurance you must consider both the amount of money available to you for the payment of your premiums and the amount of insurance money it will take to meet your family's minimum needs — keeping up the mortgage, paying medical and school bills, and so on — if you die prematurely.

A family's insurance needs are usually highest when all its members — parents and children — are young. During this early period, term insurance provides five to eight times more protection for every premium dollar than does whole life. So the money savings can be considerable.

But, as we pointed out earlier, although our insurance needs usually decrease as we approach retirement, the premiums on term policies increase with each renewal and a company may even refuse to sell a term policy if the buyer is beyond a certain age. The premiums on whole life policies, in contrast, remain the same. But it should be remembered that the increase is slow. If you buy a term policy at age 35, it will, on the average, be about 20 years before the amount you have to pay in premiums is greater than it would be for a whole life policy. Moreover, you might then reduce your insurance cost by reducing the amount of your term insurance coverage.

Combining term and whole life policies. An experienced and knowledgeable insurance agent may suggest to you some ways to combine high protection when you're young with guaranteed insurance when you're old, and at a price within your budget. For example, you might buy a renewable term policy that is also convertible — one that permits you to trade it for a whole life policy of the same or lower face value up to a certain age without taking a medical examination which, as you get older, you are less likely to pass. The premiums for this policy will be higher than those for simple term insurance, but it may well be worth the expense. Or you might consider adjustable life, a new type of policy that permits its holders to move freely between term and whole life insurance as their needs change, without having to cancel old policies or take out new ones.

You can also buy a combination policy — a whole life policy with a term rider attached that provides for additional death benefits if you die before a certain age. Or you can buy term and whole life policies separately and reduce or drop the term policy at renewal time. These procedures, too, will cost more than term insurance alone, but they provide the benefits of a whole life policy with its enforced savings.

The importance of the savings component of a whole life policy varies from individual to individual. Many experts consider it insignificant because insurance companies have, in the past, paid low interest rates. J. Robert Hunter, president of the National Insurance Consumer Organization says: "Our fundamental advice is to buy term and invest the difference." But a savings program is a matter of personal style as well as profitability and for those who do not wish to undertake the responsibility of choosing among investments, or who find it difficult to put money away without the incentive of a premium notice, whole life may be a good option.

Bringing down the costs. In calculating the actual price of a whole life insurance policy it is important to remember that its cash value does not build appreciably for several years. In the first year, the bulk of every premium dollar goes to pay administrative costs and the agent's commission, which itself is often more than half the premium. This means that if you drop the policy within two years, your money will have bought you nothing more than extremely expensive term insurance. And yet some 20 percent of all new whole life policies bought in the United States are allowed to lapse during this period, and by the 10th year, about 45 percent have either been cancelled or allowed to lapse, despite the fact that until that time, the cash value of most whole life policies does not even equal the total of premiums paid in. The obvious moral is that you should never buy a whole life policy unless you know with certainty that you will be able to afford the premiums.

Still, no matter how careful you are, emergencies can arise that make payment virtually impossible. Some policies — term as well as whole life — contain a waiver-of-premium provision which costs relatively little and assures that your premiums will be paid if you become totally disabled. If you do not choose to take advantage of that provision, or if the emergency is of a different nature — if, for example, you lose your job — there still are ways of keeping your policy in force, provided you have asked the proper questions before buying and have chosen the right company with which to deal. If you have, your policy may contain a provision that permits you to pay your premiums out of the accumulated cash value or one that makes it possible to alter the premium schedule to conform better with your budget.

You should also check into the possible advantages of buying a participating (par) policy, which entitles you to receive a dividend, in an amount determined by the company's Board of Directors, if the company shows a surplus at the end of the year. You can take your dividend in cash; use it to reduce your premium, or to increase the face value of your policy; or let it sit and accumulate interest. The dividend is not taxed because it is a form of premium refund to you.

The premiums on a participating policy may be higher than those on a non-participating (non-par) policy, but if the dividends are regular, it may cost less in the long run. If you are considering such a policy, you will be shown the so-called illustrated dividends — the expected dividends per year. Although in recent years the dividends paid on most par policies have actually been higher than those illustrated at the time the policies were sold, the illustrated figures cannot be guaranteed, because no company can predict its costs and income with absolute accuracy. So before you buy any par policy, you should know something of the company's past record.

Lifestyle discounts. Under certain circumstances, your occupation can be a significant factor in the cost of your insurance. If you are a test pilot or a wire walker or in some other profession that insurance companies consider to carry extra risks, you will doubtless pay a higher premium than your neighbor who has a desk job. On the other hand, if you subsequently change to a less dangerous occupation, you will be eligible for a reduction in premiums.

Some insurance companies are now offering inducements to their policy holders to stay healthy by lowering premium rates for non-smokers and for policy holders who engage in physical fitness programs and have regular medical examinations. If you meet these qualifications, such policies will obviously be of advantage to you.

Medical and Health Insurance

Health insurance is a necessity for everyone, if only because of the constant — and enormous — rise in health care costs. Fortunately, millions of Americans are covered by group health insurance plans through their jobs. But other millions are not. And even those who *are* insured may need additional coverage if they and their families are to be saved from the frightening financial consequences of serious and long term illness. Additional insurance is equally a necessity for the millions of Americans over 65 who are covered by Medicare, not only because the program provides only partial coverage, but because older people usually have more medical expenses than younger ones.

Group and Individual Contracts

Even if they provide precisely the same kind and amount of coverage, there is one major difference between group and individual health insurance policies: the group policies are generally less expensive. If you are interested in buying medical insurance on your own — whether as your primary source of coverage or as a supplement to the protection your employer's policy offers — check with your state insurance office (see directory, page 272). It may have available names and addresses of organizations — clubs, professional groups, unions, fraternal orders, etc. — with group plans that you may be eligible to join.

Husband and wife coverage. Most group policies provided through a job cover husband, wife and all children up to age 19 — or 23 if they are college students. Divorce terminates the ex-spouse's coverage, but some policies pay benefits to him or her for a fixed period and some offer a conversion policy — generally at a fairly high rate — that continues the protection.

If both husband and wife are covered by policies through their employers, they cannot collect double benefits. Each must inform the insurance company concerned that he or she is carried on the other's plan so that their benefits can be coordinated. But this coordination can still produce a benefit. If each spouse is covered for 80 percent of a given medical expense, and both file claims when that expense is incurred, the primary claimant will be reimbursed 80 percent and the spouse 20 percent, so that the expense will be 100 percent covered.

The basics of health insurance policies. The material below describes the coverage provided by most health insurance policies. This is, at a minimum, the coverage you should look for if you do not already have medical insurance. And if you *do* have it — whether at work or through some other group or individual plan — it would be a good idea to check the provisions of your policy against this information so that you can, if necessary, buy additional coverage.

Deductibles. The greatest number of plans have a deductible — an amount you must pay before your coverage comes into effect. The deductible may be as small as $100 or as large as $1,000, and it refers to yearly medical expenses involved in each individual claim. In group policies, the amount of the deductible is fixed by the terms of the arrangement, but if you buy an individual policy, you may have a choice in this area. A higher premium will buy you a lower deductible. If you want to pay a lower premium, you will have to absorb a higher deductible.

Some individual policies contain a stop-loss protection clause. This provides a very important benefit by limiting out-of-pocket expenses for the deductible part of medical bills. After the policy holder has paid a specific amount — $1,500 for one person, or $3,000 for a family, for example — the policy pays 100 percent of medical bills. People who have to use their medical insurance with some frequency — whether because their families are large or because there is some serious medical problem — can find themselves paying a considerable amount in deductibles. This cap on such expenses may therefore be well worth the additional cost in premiums, which runs from about $60 a year for individuals to $180 a year for a family of four. Stop-loss protection is often a part of on-the-job health protection. Where it is not, employers should be urged to add it to their policies.

Outpatient benefits. After the deductible is paid, most health policies — except major medical — cover 80 percent of bills for doctor's appointments, prescription drugs, laboratory tests, and other out-of-hospital care.

Hospital care. Some policies cover only part of the hospital bill, but others pay 100 percent of the cost of a stay in a semi-private room — for a period that varies from 21 to 120 days. Thereafter, some — but not all — policies pick up 50 or 80 percent of the charges.

Surgical benefits. Most policies pay 80 percent of a doctor's "reasonable and customary charges," based on the going rate in the particular area. Others set a fixed amount for various surgical services. These latter plans are less likely to provide adequate coverage. They may give you only $529 for an appendectomy even though it costs $1,000.

Maximum benefits. Most policies have limits on the total benefits you can receive in your lifetime — some as low as $25,000, others as high as $1 million. The Health Insurance Association of America recommends that every person covered by a policy be entitled to at least $250,000 in benefits. If the policy you have pays a lower maximum benefit than you would like, you can increase the benefit at fairly low cost through the purchase of additional coverage with the issuing company.

Additional benefits. Some health insurance policies offer coverage for treatment by a psychiatrist, although such coverage is usually limited by the amount of the reimbursement paid per visit and/or by the number of visits that are reimbursed. Few plans, whether individual or group, pay more than 50 percent of the cost of mental illness, and some also limit their payments to $1,000 a year, which will not go very far.

Increasingly, group plans now include dental care. Such coverage is also available to those who buy individual policies, but it is expensive and often covers no more than 25 to 50 percent of the actual cost of treatment. Before buying dental coverage you should therefore make a careful estimate of your family's future dental costs, based on your experience and your dentist's analysis.

Major medical. A major medical plan is a provision for the extra costs, often catastrophic, of the serious, long-term illnesses or injuries that require extensive treatment and many months in the hospital. Some company health insurance plans include major medical coverage; if yours does not have it, you should, if at all possible, buy major medical coverage for yourself and your family on your own.

Additional information on health insurance benefits and needs is available in "What You Should Know About Health Insurance," a free booklet published by the Health Insurance Association of America, 1850 K Street, NW, Washington, D.C. 20006.

Supplementing Medicare

Age 65 is a major landmark in health insurance protection. It marks the date of eligibility for Medicare, a major benefit without which many older people would literally be unable to get along. But it has its limitations. There are very definite limits to the amounts by which Medicare reimburses recipients for their outlays to doctors, laboratories, hospitals and pharmacists. And, of course, these outlays increase as health problems multiply with age. Nor is additional insurance always an adequate solution, since most policies pay only supplementary benefits which do not cover all the gaps. So it is especially important for older people to hold on to any major medical policies they may have purchased, even if they have to transfer from the group policy that covered them at work to an individual policy. Few new major medical policies are available to people over 65.

If you are planning to buy additional health insurance to supplement Medicare:

• Be certain you know exactly what your Medicare coverage provides.
• Check out carefully the extent of your existing coverage.
• Determine how much you can afford to pay for medical care out-of-pocket and the amount you can afford to pay in premiums, and weigh the two against one another to decide whether it is to your advantage to pay a lower premium in return for a higher deductible, or whether you are better off paying a higher premium and a lower deductible.
• Bear in mind those aspects of your situation that will influence the benefits you need to have. For example, if you live in a rural area, you may need transportation in case of illness. If you live alone, you may need a housekeeper or nurse.

Remember that you do not have to purchase supplementary insurance on an individual basis. Group plans are available through membership in such organizations as the American Association of Retired Persons (AARP), 1909 K Street, NW, Washington, D.C. 20049 or The National Council of Senior Citizens (NCSC), 925 15th Street, NW, Washington, D.C. 20005, and membership in these organizations is not difficult to obtain.

Whatever policy you plan to buy, be careful. Some group plans are not less expensive than individual coverage and some policies do *not* fill the gaps in Medicare. For this reason, in some states such policies must by law be labeled "Limited Benefits Health Insurance," Moreover, there are also fraudulent schemes that cruelly play on the fears of the elderly. Although the policies sold through these schemes may be legitimate, they are limited in scope, and these limitations may not be made clear either by the advertisements or by the agents. To make things worse, unscrupulous agents have no qualms about using scare tactics to persuade elderly people to drop perfectly good supplementary policies to take on new ones that may not be as comprehensive. If you believe you need additional health insurance and have responded to an ad for such a policy, be very cautious in dealing with agents who:
• Don't live in your area;
• Push a sale by saying that the "enrollment period" is closing;
• Suggest that you buy a number of different policies;
• Tell you to drop a comprehensive policy in favor of an indemnity policy.

It is not a good idea to try to extend your coverage by purchasing several small insurance policies, such as hospital income policies or policies that cover only one kind of illness. The cumulative premium payments are a costly way to pay your bills. You are better off using the money for more comprehensive coverage.

So-called "catastrophic" coverage, on the other hand, is worth looking into. It starts paying after $12,000 or $25,000 of expenses and may be unlimited in what it will pay for the rest of your life.

Finally, your local Social Security office can be of help. If you do not already have it, ask for the free pamphlet "Guide to Health Insurance for People with Medicare."

Homeowners Insurance

Homeowners insurance is another necessity for virtually all of us. It provides protection against the calamities that can befall our homes and possessions, helps pay for the living expenses we may incur if those calamities are severe enough to drive us temporarily from our homes, and offers liability and medical coverage for injuries or damages that others may suffer while in our homes or on our property.

If you are a tenant — or the owner of a condominium or cooperative — the policy you buy is not, in the strictest sense, a homeowners policy. It will cover only the contents of your dwelling; the dwelling itself is insured by your landlord — or by the condominium or cooperative association. But if you own your own house, your policy covers it as well as its contents.

Types of homeowners insurance. All homeowners policies make their reimbursements on the basis of schedules: the amounts they pay for specific losses are tied both to the amount of the policy and its type. The box on page 257 indicates the amount of protection for specific items that a typical homeowners policy provides. The amount of insurance you will need depends on several things. After you have owned a home for several years, for example, it is likely to be worth more than it was when you bought it, both because of increases that may have occurred in real es-

Coverage in a Standard Homeowner's Insurance Policy

1. Except for tenants and the owners of cooperatives and condominiums, your house and the structures attached to it are covered up to the limit of your policy.
2. Personal Property — coverage for complete destruction or loss of furniture, clothing, etc., is usually 50 percent of the amount of the policy, but in newer policies can be as much as 70 percent.

The most common upper limits for the loss or destruction of valuables likely to be in and around your home are:

- $100 for money, coins, gold, silver and medals;
- $500 for securities, stamps, deeds, etc.;
- $500 for trailers, jewelry and furs;
- $1,000 for silverware, pewter-ware, goldware, guns and firearms.

3. Loss of Use. Expenses of living away from home during a period of repair are covered up to 20 percent of the coverage in your contract.
4. Personal Liabilty. Generally, the minimum liability in a homeowners policy is $25,000. Some companies have raised the minimum to $100,000 and consider a more reasonable limit to be $300,000. Typical deductible base is $250.
5. Medical Payments. Basic amount per person injured is usually $1,000, and you can buy larger amounts of coverage. Because this is part of your liability coverage, it will not pay for injuries to you or members of your family.
6. Damage to others' property. Usually $500 for any one accident.

tate values and because of improvements you yourself have made. So you may want additional insurance to reflect your increased stake. Some companies offer special modifications of the basic policy — endorsements — that automatically increase its amount at regular intervals. But these are primarily inflation guards, and do not take account of other factors. You can, however, figure them in yourself by reviewing your policy periodically to see if it provides the amount of insurance you need.

The type of policy you will want depends not only on the number of perils against which you need protection, but also on the extent of the damage you believe these perils can do. The maximum protection against damage is offered by so-called Replacement Cost Insurance — first introduced in the 1970's and now carried by nearly one third of all policyholders — even though it is the most expensive to buy.

Replacement cost insurance is available in two forms. A full replacement cost policy gives the homeowner the full amount — less deductible — it costs to replace his or her dwelling if it is totally destroyed by any one of the perils covered in the policy — provided, of course, that the cost of replacement does not exceed the amount of the policy. But this does not mean you must purchase insurance for the market value of your home, since that value includes the land the house sits on as well as the building itself. You need only the amount of insurance that will cover the cost of rebuilding your home. Most insurance companies publish guides that will help you estimate that cost. Or you can have the estimate made by a professional appraiser.

At a somewhat lower cost in premiums, you can also purchase 80 percent replacement cost insurance, which guarantees the full replacement cost — again, less deductible — of any *part* of your house that is destroyed. Such a policy has several advantages over one that provides full replacement cost. It is less expensive and it does not require as much coverage. Moreover, it is far more probable that part of your house will be destroyed than that all of it will be.

If you want to pay less in premiums and are willing to settle for less protection, you can buy a policy that takes depreciation into account and reimburses losses not on the basis of the cost of replacing them, but on the basis of the actual cash value (ACV) of the item involved, as determined by tables kept by the insurance company. Some policies of this type pay only a percentage of the ACV; others include a co-insurance provision, which guarantees that if you insure your property for at least 80 percent of its actual cash value, you will collect the full ACV payment for any given loss, up to the amount of the policy.

To see what co-insurance actually means, let's take the example of two houses, each with an actual cash value of $40,000. If one is insured for $32,000 (80 percent) and the other for $16,000 and both suffer a $2,000 loss, the first policyholder will be reimbursed for the full amount — less, of course, the deductible — while the second, who is insured for only half the co-insurance requirement, will get considerably less — $1,000, minus both the deductible and depreciation. Clearly, it is advisable to carry at least enough insurance to meet the co-insurance threshold.

Although Replacement Cost Insurance offers significantly more in reimbursements for property damage than does ACV insurance, neither offers total reimbursement for loss of personal possessions. The most you can expect a replacement cost policy to return to you for the loss of *all* your household goods is 50 to 70 percent of the amount of the insurance. Moreover — and this is true for tenants and the owners of condominiums and cooperatives, as well — coverage for expensive property that is especially susceptible to theft — cash, securities, jewelry, furs, and silverware, for example — is even further limited. You can, however, increase that coverage by purchasing an additional endorsement known as a floater, the yearly cost of which varies depending on where you live and the company from which you buy. To set an appropriate value on the items you want to have insured, it is wise to have them appraised. But be sure the appraiser charges by the hour — hourly rates generally run from $50 to $100 — rather than by relating the fee to the value of the items being appraised. A percentage fee encourages the appraiser to inflate the worth of your possessions, and insurance companies are extremely careful in checking claims on items covered by a floater. You can locate an appraiser in your area by writing to the American Society of Appraisers, P.O. Box 17265, Washington, D.C. 20041, a trade association that publishes a free directory of its members.

Homeowners policies normally include what is known as liability coverage, which provides payment, up to some stated limit, in the event that a visitor to your home is injured and files a claim against you. You may want to purchase additional coverage in this area, especially if there are small children in your family who leave toys around on which people may trip; if you own a pet given to biting or scratching; or if you are in a business or profession that makes you a likely target for a damage suit.

Saving on homeowners insurance. There are several ways to bring down the cost of your homeowners policy. One is to set the deductible at a fairly substantial amount — one week's worth of the total family take-home pay, for example. If you are prepared to do this, you may be able to make a substantial saving on the cost of your policy. But bear in mind that the higher the deductible, the greater the loss you will have to absorb if you become the victim of any covered peril. Nor can you deduct that loss from your federal taxes unless it exceeds 10 percent of your adjusted gross income.

In addition, check with your insurance agent about a policy that will give you a discount if you are 55 years old or older; if your house is brand new; if you etch your property with your personal identification number (your local police department may have such an identification program); or if your house is equipped with:

- Burglar alarms
- Deadbolt locks
- Solid doors
- Window locks
- A sprinkler system
- Smoke detectors

Filing a claim. The fire has blazed and been put out. The burglar has gone and you've called the police. What do you do now?

First, notify your agent or insurance company by telephone, and follow up with a letter describing what happened and what losses you suffered. If the problem is damage, an adjuster will be sent to look over the situation, make an estimate of the repair or replacement costs, help you fill out the claim form and gather the materials necessary for formal proof of the loss.

Unless you are prepared simply to accept

the insurance company's offer, you would be wise to get your own estimate of the repair costs from a contractor, to compare with the company's estimate. You may be charged a fee for this service, but if the contractor who makes the estimate does the repair work, that fee will usually be deducted from your bill.

If the damage is extensive and the insurance company's offer appears to you to be inadequate, it may be worth your while to consult a public adjuster, a licensed professional who will act as your agent in negotiating a settlement with the insurance company. Public adjusters, who are listed in the yellow pages of the telephone directory, charge fees based on a specified percentage of the insurance settlement, and generally ask for partial payment in advance as a retainer.

Whether your home has been burglarized or damaged, one of the first things you must do is protect it against further damage by boarding up any broken windows, replacing any broken locks and otherwise assuring that it will be safe from further harm. If you do not do this and you suffer additional damage, the insurance company may have the legal right to refuse to pay for it. Be sure to keep receipts for the money you spend on these temporary repairs, so that you can get reimbursement from the insurance company. But do not make any *permanent* repairs until the company has looked at the damage and you have reached an agreement on cost. The insurer can refuse to pay you for any work done before it has exercised its legal right of inspection.

If the damage is so extensive that you cannot live at home, notify your agent of this fact and keep a record of all the expenses you incur during this period. The insurance company will reimburse them up to the amount listed in your policy.

You should already have a list of your insured possessions and their cost — with at least one copy kept outside your home, in a safe place such as a safety deposit box. Use it to make out the inventory of damaged or lost possessions for which the insurance company will ask you. If you have bills or other documents that substantiate your claim as to the value of the items involved, submit them along with the inventory.

If you and the insurance company cannot agree on the amount of a settlement, the next step is to take your case to your state insurance department (see directory, page 272). Many policies provide for the resolution of disputes through binding arbitration by a three-person board, one of whose members is selected by the consumer, another by the insurance company and the third by the first two. Other policies provide other arrangements; still others provide none at all — in which case the consumer can propose arbitration, or take the company to court.

Recovery of stolen property. There are several things you can do to increase the chance that you will get your property back if it has been stolen. We have already mentioned one: engraving your valuables with an identifying mark of some kind. The second — most useful in the case of jewelry and other possessions you do not want to mark up in any way — is to photograph the items so that they can be recognized if they are recovered.

If stolen property is recovered after you have received a settlement from the insurance company, talk to your agent. The property is no longer yours if the insurance company reimbursed you for it in full; you have only a part interest in it if the reimbursement was only partial. But the insurance company will doubtless agree to let you buy it back for the amount of the settlement.

Responding to a claim against you. If someone is injured on your property or by a member of your household, or if you damage the property of others, a claim may be filed against you. You will receive papers in the mail notifying you of this fact. As soon as you receive them, make copies for yourself and forward the originals to your insurance company.

If the claim involves an injury to someone, your insurance company will demand proof that medical payments were made. It is up to you to get the necessary documents and send them to the insurance company. The company will also want to obtain copies of relevant medical reports from physicians and hospitals and may require that the claimant be examined by its physician.

Different insurance companies follow different procedures in connection with claims filed against their policyholders for damaging the property of others. Often the company asks the policyholder for a sworn statement about the incident, which must be provided

Federal Insurance Programs

Private insurance companies do not issue homeowners policies against earthquakes, power outages, war, nuclear accidents or floods. These calamities affect hundreds, even thousands, of homes at a time and protection against them would therefore be prohibitively expensive. Similarly, as the crime rate has steadily risen over the past decades, insurance companies have become increasingly reluctant to issue homeowners policies to residents and businesses in particularly high-crime areas.

Fortunately, the federal government has stepped in with subsidized programs designed to help consumers who need — but cannot obtain — private insurance protection against two of these hazards: crime and floods.

The Federal Crime Insurance program, part of the Department of Housing and Urban Development, offers residential crime insurance to homeowners and tenants in amounts from $1,000 to $10,000, with a deductible of $100 or five percent of the amount of the loss, whichever is greater. The full $10,000 coverage costs between $60 and $120 a year.

The policy has several limitations. Loss of cash is covered only up to $100 and no item is covered unless the policyholder can show evidence that the premises were entered forcibly. Moreover, policyholders must meet minimum protection requirements by installing locks on windows and half-inch deadbolt locks on doors. If you cannot obtain crime insurance from a private company, ask your insurance agent about federal crime insurance or write to the Federal Crime Insurance Program, P.O. Box 41033, Bethesda, Maryland 20814.

The National Flood Insurance program enables the residents of endangered communities that meet certain federal land-use and flood-plain management standards to obtain homeowners insurance against flood damage. The policies are issued for one or three years and can be purchased on either an emergency or permanent basis. The first insures a single family residence up to a value of $35,000 and its contents up to $10,000; the second insures the house up to a value of $185,000 and its contents up to $60,000. The National Flood Insurance program is presently available in 17,000 communities and, as of mid-1983, almost two million policies were in force. To purchase flood insurance, speak to an insurance agent. For further information, write the National Flood Insurance Program, Federal Insurance Administration, Washington, D.C. 20472.

within 60 days. The company may also ask to examine the property involved.

Automobile Insurance

Automobile insurance is not only a desirable purchase; in many states, it is mandatory. Different states have different laws in this respect, and there are also variations among the states in the laws governing the way liability claims in automobile accidents are handled. In the jurisdictions with no-fault insurance laws, policyholders who are involved in accidents and whose claims are for sums under a specific level set by the law, file these claims with their own insurance companies, which pay them. In states that do not have no-fault, the victims file their claims against the other driver, whether or not that driver is insured, and are paid only if it can be proved that the other driver was responsible for the accident. There are many other differences among the states in their requirements concerning automobile insurance. You can find the specifics in your state by checking with the Department of Insurance (see directory, page 272).

Types of automobile insurance. Liability coverage is the heart of every automobile insurance policy. It covers the following:

• Bodily injury liability: In those states which do not have no-fault insurance and in no-fault states when the claim is above the maximum covered by the law, this part of the policy covers death, injury and sometimes pain, suffering and mental anguish accidentally inflicted on someone by your car.
• Property damage liability: Covers virtually any property your car accidentally harms, from other automobiles to fences and cargo on a truck.

In addition to liability coverage, automobile insurance also offers medical payments coverage — for you and your passengers, not only for car accidents but for such mishaps as slamming a door on a finger and for injury that may be inflicted by a car on you as a pedestrian. (In this case, the company will, of course, try to collect from the driver's insurance company if the accident is not your fault.)

You can also purchase uninsured motorist's coverage, which pays your medical bills if you are a victim of an uninsured motorist or a hit-and-run driver. In some, but not in all states, this insurance also covers injuries caused by under-insured motorists. This kind of coverage is most valuable for those who do not have adequate medical or disability insurance in other policies.

Collision insurance is also available. It pays for damage to your car, and will pay the cost of repair or its cash value, whichever is less. If your car is four or five years old, for example, your insurance will pay only its "book value" or the repair cost, minus depreciation, if that is lower. A small number of companies sell replacement cost collision insurance, which offers higher benefits, but it is considerably more expensive.

You can also purchase comprehensive coverage, which encompasses fire, theft, glass breakage, flood and a host of other things. But although this insurance will pay your car's book value if it is stolen, or may pay for car rental for a specified amount of time, it will not pay for damage incurred in a collision with another car, for wear-and-tear, engine failure or other mechanical difficulties.

Both collision insurance and comprehensive insurance will considerably increase your premium costs. A lender may require you to carry them if you are still paying off the cost of your car. But if this is not the case, and your car is five or more years old, one or both of these options may cost more than they are worth, given the rapidity with which automobiles depreciate in value.

How much automobile insurance do you need? Given the sky-high costs of medical care and the generosity of juries in those automobile accident cases that go to court, you will want to purchase as much liability insurance for your car as you can possibly afford. Even if you are insured, you can lose many of your personal holdings and possessions if a judgment against you exceeds the amount of your insurance. You can increase your liability coverage by purchasing a so-called "umbrella policy" which provides protection for one million dollars or more over and above the basic limits of your policy. It costs less than you might think — about $100 a year.

You may not need collision insurance or comprehensive insurance at all, for the reasons discussed above. But you should give serious consideration to purchasing at least some uninsured — or under-insured — motorists coverage, if only as a protection against injury to yourself. In some states, such insurance will bring the other party's coverage up to the bodily-injury liability limits of your policy, provided they are no higher than $100,000/$300,000.

As with other forms of insurance, you can trade off high deductibles on your automobile insurance for lower premiums, absorbing modest bills and insuring yourself only for those losses you cannot afford to pay.

Saving money on auto insurance. The insurance companies themselves can help you save money if you fit into a low-risk category or otherwise help them financially. For example, if you own more than one car, you can often get a discount by insuring all your cars with the same company. Similarly, discounts are available from some companies to owners of small cars, which are cheaper to repair and replace than standard size models; drivers who participate in carpools or who make only limited use of their cars.

Certain groups have statistically better accident records than others, and therefore qualify for special discounts. Age, for example, is a significant factor in all automobile premiums. The younger the driver, the higher the risk for the insurance company and therefore the higher the rate. Unmarried men under 25 have a poor safety record as a group, and therefore premiums are much higher for them. But beyond that age, and if they are married, the premiums drop. Such changes should therefore be immediately reported to the insurance company.

Some companies reduce premium rates for drivers who take driver-education courses — especially for young drivers — or whose records are free of violations or accidents for three years, for example. If you install certain anti-theft devices, or garage your car in a low-crime area, the rate for your comprehensive coverage may be cut. If you move from a large city to a less congested suburban town, your premiums will go down. (Of course, they will go up if you move back to the city.)

But the best way to save money on automobile insurance is to shop around. There is a wide variation in premium costs from company to company.

But price, of course, is not the only consideration. You will also want to know the company's claim practices, its record with respect to prompt service, its convenience, the discounts it offers and the length of time — six months or one year — its policies run. You also want to find out if it has been the subject of many complaints. You can do so by writing to your state insurance department (see directory, page 272); it may publish figures on this subject.

The insurance company may cancel your policy if you are found guilty of drunken driving, speeding or recklessness that results in injury or death, or for other specified serious violations of the law. If you are refused renewal and no other company will give you insurance or if, as a new driver, you are unable to find a company willing to provide insurance, you will probably have to go into the "shared" market, also known as "assigned risk plans." Your insurance will probably cost you more, but even here, prices vary. And remember, if you then maintain a spotless record, you should be able to get regular insurance after a period of time.

What to do if you are in an automobile accident. To file — or respond to — a claim in the event of an automobile accident, you will need the following information:

- The other driver's name, address and phone number and the name of the owner of the car, if it is not the same as the driver's.
- Driver's date of birth.
- Driver's license number.
- Driver's license plate number.
- Make of car, color, model and year.
- Insurance company and policy number.
- Scene, date and time of the accident.
- Weather and road conditions.
- Damage to the other car.

If there are passengers in any of the cars involved in the accident, or if there are eyewitnesses, get their names and addresses, if possible, and make a diagram of the accident, showing where the cars were when the accident occurred and the directions in which they were moving.

If any passengers in your car or the other cars in the accident are injured, make a note of the nature of their injuries as far as you can tell — and of any statements they may make about them.

If a police officer arrives, get his name and precinct number and give him a report on any damage there may be to your car. Ask if any citations were issued and if so, to whom and for what. Also ask how to obtain a copy of the official accident report.

Filing a claim. Your insurance agent or your state insurance department can tell you what specific requirements, if any, there are in your state regarding the length of time an automobile insurance company has to respond to a claim when you file it — something that you should do immediately when a problem arises.

If your claim is for damage to your car, the company may ask you to get an estimate from a body shop or may send its own representative to inspect the vehicle and give you a detailed estimate of the cost of repairs and the amount the company is willing to pay you under the policy. The representative may even give you the name and address of a convenient repair shop that will provide a written guarantee of its work. You do not have to use this facility; you can take the car to a repair shop of your choice. But if your shop charges more than the insurance estimate, you will have to pay the difference.

On the other hand, you are entitled to have your financial losses covered — indeed, the purpose of your policy is to restore you to the same financial condition you were in the second before the accident. So if no shop is willing to do the work in a satisfactory manner for the insurance company's estimate, you should advise the company of that fact and ask for a higher amount. And until you have found a shop that will satisfactorily repair your car at a price the insurance company is willing to meet, you should neither accept payment nor sign away your rights to an additional claim. Moreover, you may accept the payment and not have the work done on the car.

If your claim is for a car that is stolen or "totalled," the company must either replace it with a substantially similar car or pay its retail value as determined by standard dealer tables — plus whatever sales tax is applicable where you live. If your stolen car is subsequently found by the police, the company must pay the cost of towing it to a place of safe-keeping until you claim it. If you have already settled with the company by the time the car is found, you may be able to work out a repurchase arrangement, if that is what you would like.

Some insurance companies deduct the salvage value of a car that has been totalled from the settlement offer they make. If they do, they must provide you with the name and address of a salvage dealer who will buy the wreck from you at that price.

In any of these cases, and if your policy contains such a clause, the insurance company should pay you for the rental of a car for a stated period, while you are waiting for your new car or the repair of your old one.

If you live in a no-fault state and have an injury claim to file, give prompt written notice to the insurer of your car if you were riding in it at the time of the accident, or of the car that hit you, if you were a pedestrian. The company will then explain your rights and obligations and advise you of the procedure to follow in applying for benefits.

Appeals and protections. If you feel you have been unfairly denied renewal of your automobile insurance, or that you have been offered an inadequate settlement — or if you have any other complaint about the company you have been dealing with, the first place to turn is your state Department of Insurance (see directory, page 272).

In addition, you can get general information on homeowners or automobile insurance from the The Insurance Information Institute 1025 Vermont Avenue, NW, Washington, D.C. 20005. For information on life insurance, write the American Council of Life Insurance, 1850 K Street, NW, Washington, D.C. 20006. You may also wish to contact The National Association of Insurance Commissioners (NAIC), an organization of the chief state insurance regulatory officials, at 1125 Grand Avenue, Kansas City, MO 64106.

Investments

Before the 1970's, people with relatively small amounts of money who could not afford to gamble with their nest eggs had only one choice of where to put it — a savings account. But the same galloping inflation that wiped out the earning aspect of savings accounts changed the shape of the banking and securities businesses, encouraging them to find ways of making their enterprises more attractive to those small investors. Today's investor has many choices — not only among investment instruments offered by banks (see Chapter 9) and other private firms, but among the various securities offered by our national, state and local governments.

U.S. government securities. The U.S. government and its agencies offer investors a number of opportunities to earn money at virtually no risk through the purchase of bonds — loans that investors make to the government at a fixed rate of interest and that the government guarantees to repay at a specified time.

Probably the best known are U.S. Savings Bonds, which can be purchased only through employers — usually as part of a payroll savings plan — through banks, or through other sources authorized by the U.S. Treasury. Unlike other bonds, which can be traded back and forth many times before they reach maturity, U.S. Savings Bonds are not negotiable — although, of course, they can be redeemed, at a loss in interest, before they reach maturity.

Series EE Savings Bonds, which come in various denominations from $50 to $10,000, pay interest through a process called discounting. Each bond is purchased for half its face value — a $50 bond costs $25 — and at the end of its full ten year term pays at least $50 — which represents 7.5 percent interest compounded twice a year. It may even pay more. Since November, 1982, Series EE bonds, if held five years or longer, pay interest at the rate of 85 percent of the average interest rate of five-year marketable Treasury securities.

Series HH Savings Bonds, which are issued in face amounts from $500 to $10,000, are not discounted, but are bought at their face value and pay interest at the rate of 7.5 percent a year through a check mailed to the owner semi-annually. Like EE bonds, series HH bonds mature in 10 years.

Series EE and HH Bonds have four important advantages:

- Safety. They are guaranteed by the U.S. Government, and if they are lost or stolen, can be replaced without charge.
- Affordability. The least expensive EE bond costs only $25. Moreover, through your company's payroll savings plans, they can be purchased in installments.
- Liquidity. Both EE and HH bonds can be cashed in any time after they have been held for six months.
- Partially tax-free interest. The interest on these bonds is tax free until they are redeemed; thereafter, although the interest is subject to federal taxes, it is exempt from state and local income tax.

The federal government also issues Treasury Bonds and Treasury Notes. The difference between the two is the length of time it takes them to mature. The notes mature in two to 10 years, the bonds in 10 years or more, and both are issued in denominations that run from $1,000, to $1,000,000.

Unlike savings bonds, U.S notes and bonds are traded and can be bought and sold, usually for a fee of $25-$40, through banks and brokers. Their yields vary, depending on other interest rates. When money is tight, interest rates in general rise, and the yields on Treasury notes and bonds tend to go up.

The United States also borrows money for immediate cash needs through short-term securities called Treasury Bills, which mature in three, six or 12 months. Every week a number of them are sold at a discount by competitive bid, and each week the interest rate depends on the price, which is set by the high bid. If, for example, the top bidder offers 90 cents for every dollar of face value, the discount is 10 percent, and an investor who can put up $18,000 for three to six months will get back $20,000 at the end of that time. For small investors, that's the rub: the smallest denomination in which a Treasury Bill can be purchased is $10,000.

In addition to the securities issued by the Treasury Department are those issued by quasi-governmental or government-sponsored agencies. Unlike Treasury securities, which have the full faith and credit of the U.S. government behind them, most of these are secured only by the government's moral obligation. But in return for taking this very slight risk, an investor can earn a higher interest rate than is paid on any Treasury issues.

For example, the Federal National Mortgage Association, or FNMA, whose purpose is to stimulate homebuilding, buys mortgages from banks, thus providing these institutions with cash they can use for other investments whose profits enable them to grant additional mortgages.

The FNMA gets the money to buy these mortgages by selling securities known as Fannie Maes whose minimum denomination is $10,000. The agency pays the holders of these securities through the mortgage payments it collects and since it can, if necessary, borrow up to $2.25 billion dollars from the Treasury, its securities are extremely safe.

The Federal Home Loan Mortgage Corporation and the Government National Mortgage Association also sell mortgage-backed obligations — Freddie Macs and Ginnie Maes. Freddie Macs are truly costly — the cheapest is $25,000; the most expensive $5 million. Ginnie Maes have a minimum denomination of $25,000, but a partially paid-off Ginnie Mae can be had for less, and recently the establishment of Ginnie Mae investment trusts has made units available to the public for as little as $1,000 each.

Many other Federal agencies are authorized to issue marketable securities as a way of achieving some goal that Congress thinks desirable. Among them are the Tennessee Valley Authority (TVA) and the Federal Land Banks.

State and municipal securities. States and municipalities also borrow money through bond issues. There are several different kinds of such bonds. General obligation bonds are used, as their name indicates, to pay general obligations, and are backed by the credit and taxing power of the government that issues

Rating Municipal Bonds

Investment Grades

Moody's	S. & P.	Description
Aaa	**AAA**	Highest quality bonds with the least amount of risk and a strong ability to pay interest and principal.
Aa	**AA**	High quality bonds, but with slightly less financial strength than triple-A issues.
A	**A**	Strong capacity to pay interest and principal, but more vulnerable to changes in economic conditions.
Baa	**BBB**	Adequate current ability to pay interest and principal, but may be threatened by changes in the economy.

Speculative Grades

Moody's	S. & P.	Description
Ba	**BB**	Currently paying interest but with an uncertain future. Not well guarded during good and bad economic times.
B	**B**	Little assurance that interest and principal will continue to be paid.
Caa to C	**CCC to C**	Highly speculative issues that may be in or near default. Caa/CCC rated issues are the most speculative. Very few municipal bonds receive these ratings.
D		Used only by S. & P. for issues in default.

them. Revenue bonds are issued for specific projects — a subway or bridges, for example — and are paid off from tolls, fares or user's fees. Special revenue bonds finance other civic undertakings: attracting industry, building hospitals, fighting pollution or similar projects.

All municipal bonds share one important advantage. The interest they earn is exempt from Federal income tax. In addition, some states and cities that have income taxes also exempt the interest on municipal bonds from taxation for their residents and the bonds are, therefore, triple tax exempt.

This can be a significant advantage for the taxpayer. Someone in the 40 percent bracket who buys a non-tax-exempt $1,000 bond at 10 percent, will have only $60 in interest left at year's end, while a tax-exempt bond at eight percent will have earned $80 free and clear.

Like other government bonds, municipal bonds come in many denominations — $5,000 is the most common — and yields. In addition, they carry different degrees of risk, depending on the fiscal health of the issuing municipality. Several rating services grade bonds on their relative safety. You can discover their findings by consulting such publications as *Bond Buyer*, *Credit Week*, and *Moody's Bond Survey*, which can usually be found at your library.

Corporate bonds. Like the various levels of government, private corporations also issue bonds, using them as a way to raise very large sums of money for needed expansion or other capital costs and to spread their debt among hundreds of thousands of buyers. Corporate bonds, which usually have a face value of $1,000, are unlike municipal bonds in that they are not tax exempt. But like municipal bonds, they are a somewhat more chancey investment than federal government bonds. Corporations, like municipalities, can get into financial difficulties, and before buying any corporate bond, you should investigate the issuing company carefully in such a publication as *Moody's* or *Standard & Poors*.

The primary advantages in buying a bond are that almost all guarantee regular interest income twice a year and the knowledge that at the end of a set term, when the bond matures, it can be redeemed for its full face value. If you buy a 20-year, six percent, $1,000 bond in 1985, you will get $30 twice a year until 2005, when you will get your $1,000 back. The interest rate cannot change during the life of the bond. Be sure to check, however, whether the issuer reserves the right to call in the bond. If so, and the right is exercised, your interest payments will stop — although you will be paid the full face value of the bond.

Because bonds are negotiable instruments and can be bought and sold many times before maturity — usually through brokers, who charge a commission, generally $10 per $1,000 — and because their sale price fluctuates with supply and demand, their actual rate of interest can be higher — or lower — than the one at which they are issued. If you buy a bond when it is selling for less than its face, or par value, the rate of return will be higher, while if you buy it when it is selling for more than its par value, the return will be lower. Therefore, under some circumstances, bonds can turn out to be a poor investment. If, for example, a financial emergency compels you to sell a bond before it has matured and its price is low at the time, you will not get back the full sum you paid.

Unit trusts and money market funds. As we have seen, most bonds are available only in fairly large denominations and, except for savings bonds, their rates of return vary. They therefore demand special knowledge and expertise if they are to be bought wisely.

Fortunately, however, two kinds of institutions exist that enable small investors to buy such securities — and others — without having any special financial knowledge in the field. One is the so-called unit investment trust — a pool of a particular kind of bond established by a bank or a brokerage firm. You can purchase a share in such a trust for as little as $1,000; in return, you will earn a fixed rate of interest — paid monthly, quarterly or semiannually — until the maturity date, when your initial investment is returned to you.

A more common way for the small investor to cash in on the advantages of the market rate of interest is through participation in a money market fund, a special variety of mutual fund that invests in short-term, low-risk securities. Since these securities mature quickly, they are highly sensitive to interest rates and thus give their investors an opportunity to earn the highest rates the market pays. Money market funds invest in such short-term securities as Treasury bills, short-term corporate debt, commercial bank certificates of deposit and repurchase agreements. Some money market funds hold general portfolios, others restrict themselves to particular types of securities — those of the U.S. Government, for example.

Money market funds achieved their tremendous popularity — there were 15 in 1974; by mid-1983, there were over 300 — by introducing new ideas. They lowered the minimum amount for participation to $500 or less. They permitted members to write checks against their holdings and continued paying interest on that money until the checks actually cleared. Moreover, most money market funds are no-load: they levy no charge on their participants, either for entrance or withdrawal.

The advantages of a money market fund are obvious. It is easy to get in and out of. Although its yield goes up and down with the daily interest rate, it is generally relatively high. If the fund invests broadly, the interest rate is likely to fluctuate quite widely. If it invests only in government securities, interest will tend to be one or two percentage points lower. But in both cases, interest is usually compounded daily so your money grows until the day it is withdrawn. Some money market funds offer tax advantages, as well, by investing only in tax exempt bonds.

You can buy into a money market fund either through a broker, or directly. To choose among them, write for copies of their literature. Every fund publishes a prospectus — a document setting forth the nature and object of the shares the company has created and inviting the public to purchase them, and the prospectus will indicate the way the fund has performed. A list of all money market funds is available at no cost from The Investment Company Institute, 1775 K Street, NW, Washington, D.C. 20006.

CONSUMER ALERT

Investing in a Business of Your Own

Every night, thousands of Americans go to sleep dreaming of the day when they can start a business of their own. And when they wake up, some actually *do* go into business for themselves. Far too many are doomed to failure. According to the Small Business Administration, about 65 percent of business start-ups collapse within five years.

The record is considerably better for franchised businesses. A 1982 Congressional committee report found an average failure rate among franchises of only two to six percent.

If you are thinking of buying a franchise, or dealing with any company that offers assistance in starting a business, you *must* investigate that company thoroughly. You need the following information — in writing, if possible:

- Business background of the principals.
- An audited financial statement.
- A complete list and description of all charges and obligations you will incur.
- Conditions of any contracts you may have to sign.
- Any buy-out options held by the issuer of the franchise.
- Any terms relating to supplies, management, advertising, construction, etc.
- Names and addresses of others who have franchises with the company.
- Any restrictions on sales.
- A list and description of any help you might get from the company.

A great deal of information is available on various businesses that can be started with a small capital investment.

Two booklets — "Franchise Opportunity Handbook" and "Franchising in the Economy" are available from Bureau of Industrial Economics, Service Industries Division, Department of Commerce, Washington, D.C. 20230. The U.S. Small Business Administration, 1441 L Street, NW, Washington, D.C. 20416, issues a publication "Franchised Businesses," for which you can also write.

The International Franchise Association (IFA), 1025 Connecticut Avenue, NW, Suite 1005, Washington, D.C. 20036, publishes a booklet *IFA Directory of Membership*, which includes a valuable section called "Investigate Before Investing," and is available for $1.95 to cover postage and handling.

But remember that money market funds carry no federal insurance and, therefore, no guarantee. On the other hand, many are insured by the Securities Investor Protection Corporation up to $100,000 per investor, and most put their money in very safe investments and carry only a minimal risk. They are likely to pay a slightly higher rate of interest than their insured competitors — the bank money market accounts discussed in Chapter 9.

Cash management accounts. Cash management — or financial management, or resource management — accounts are convenience accounts that give consumers with $10,000 or more the opportunity to purchase stocks, bonds and other securities, all of which are kept in one umbrella account. The income from those securities is transferred into a special fund on which money market interest rates are paid. The investor can write checks against that fund and is also issued a credit or debit card (see Chapter 9), backed by the account. In addition, these accounts permit investors to borrow up to 50 percent of the market value of their common stocks and 70 percent of the value of their bonds. These accounts, now offered by many major brokerage houses, have their own specific features, charges and investment minimums.

Stock Market Basics

Investing in stocks is a more risky business than investing in bonds or money market funds. When you buy stocks, you are taking a chance on the ability of the company involved to make money — to manage its affairs well, and to grow in prosperity — and on the way investors value the company's future prospects. But you are not taking the chances investors took in the 1920's, before the stock market crash. That calamity led, in 1934, to the establishment by Congress of the U.S. Securities and Exchange Commission (SEC) as a watchdog over the securities markets. Today, every company involved in interstate commerce that offers shares for sale to the public must register with this agency, and must make available to any potential investor complete and accurate information about the business it conducts or proposes to conduct. A company involved in making an offering in only one state generally has to register with that state's securities agency.

In general, SEC regulations are designed to guarantee that full disclosure is made to all investors, and that no entrepreneur be able to take unfair advantage of others. For example, SEC rules prohibit the directors, officers and employees — and often such outside personnel as legal counsel, accountants, etc. — from trading in stock on the basis of information about the company's financial situation obtained before that information is made public. Moreover, the agency has the legal power to sue companies that violate securities regulations, either in the civil or criminal courts, depending on the violation involved. But although the SEC has the authority to require fair and full disclosure and to punish those who do not meet its standards, it has no authority to evaluate the quality of any potential investment or to give advice on the merits of any offering.

In addition to the protections provided by the SEC, the Securities Investor Protection Corporation (SIPC) was established in 1970. SIPC is a federally chartered membership organization that insures the brokerage accounts of individual investors by providing $500,000 protection for securities and $100,000 for cash in each account. The SIPC, whose offices are at 900 Seventeenth Street, NW, Washington, D.C. 20006, has a $1 billion line of credit with the U.S. Treasury. Large brokerage firms also provide substantial insurance for their customers' accounts.

Stocks. When you buy a corporate bond, you are a lender, giving the use of your money to a company in return for the payment of interest. When you buy a company's stock, you are buying part ownership of that company. For the ordinary investor, that ownership is only a microscopic share. Still, it confers the right to vote — the weight of which is proportionate to the number of shares held — for members of the Board of Directors, and the right to a proportionate share of any yearly dividends the company may pay. Even if a company has earned a profit during the course of a business year, it is not legally required to pay dividends. The directors may choose to put that profit back into expanding the company. On the other hand, the company may choose to pay dividends, even if it makes no profit in a given year, taking the money out of cash reserves.

In general, however, when a company prospers it pays dividends. And some secure, established companies have paid dividends without a break for several decades. The dividends must first be paid to the owners of preferred stock, if the company has issued it. This stock, like bonds, carries an interest rate that has been fixed in advance. Preferred stocks are, therefore, a relatively safe investment. But they do not hold as high a promise of profit as do common stocks — the kind that most of us buy. The dividends paid on common stocks are not fixed in advance and may be raised or reduced in accordance with management decisions.

Buying and selling. Although every share of stock is issued at a particular face value, its actual price depends on the daily trading that takes place at a stock exchange or over the counter between brokers. A share you bought last week at $100 may be selling at $85 or $125 today. These changes in the trading price of stocks can be tracked on a minute-by-minute basis by a broker or on a daily basis in the newspapers. In addition, there are special indices, of which the Dow-Jones is the best known, which provide a daily report on the overall price movement of a selected group of stocks, and thus a regular reflection of investor confidence in the economic health of a particular industry or the economy as a whole, or reactions to world events.

If you buy stocks not only to collect dividends, but to do some trading as well, you too, will have to make certain kinds of economic judgments. What stocks are likely to go up and are, therefore, worth buying? What stocks are ready to drop and should be sold? How much should you rely on the experts' forecasts, how much on tips, how much on your own evaluation? These questions and others like them make the stock market fascinating for some people — and frightening to others.

Income and growth, long run and short. Before buying any stock, you should always have a clear idea of your investment goal. In large measure, that goal will determine the stocks you choose to buy.

If, for example, your primary interest is to add to your current income, you will want a good blue chip stock — stock in a company that has been around for years, dealing in something that people are always going to need and paying dividends regularly, except, perhaps, during periods of general economic decline. If, on the other hand, your purpose in buying stock is to increase the value of your investment in a short period of time, you will want stock in a so-called growth industry — a field whose importance appears to be increasing. In recent years, the computer business, cable televison and new prescription drugs have been among the best-known growth industries. But new developments in technology keep tumbling on one another, and tomorrow some other area may be the one to watch. Bear in mind that these stocks are often expensive. The larger the number of people who share your optimism about a given company, the higher the price of its stock is likely to go.

You can also pick stocks on the basis of their long-term growth prospects, as evidenced by some continuing economic or social trend. For example, older people already constitute a significant element of our population, and their proportion among us will increase well into the 21st century, when the children who were born during the baby boom of the 1950's reach their sixties. A company that builds retirement communities, for example, might therefore be a steady and gradual gainer.

You may even decide to take a gamble on a stock that will either pay off handsomely and quickly or not pay off at all. In that case you will look for a high-risk stock — as, for example, stock in a company set up to explore for new sources of oil. If the company hits a gusher, your stock will skyrocket, but it will be worthless if the drilling site turns out to be a dry hole, although you may get a tax break on your losses.

When you buy stock, you are investing in an industry and a company. You will, therefore, want to know as much as you can about trends in the industry and about the company. Has it a track record? What can you learn about its management? Its assets? Its credit rating? These are all on record and you should look them up before you invest.

Whether your goal is to add to your income or increase the value of your investment, you should be aware that dividends from stock investments and gains from stocks held for less than a year are taxed as ordinary income, while gains made from holding stocks for more than a year are taxed at the lower, long-term capital gains rate. You have an additional option. You can divide your investment among several kinds of stocks, each of which serves a different investment purpose. And you can build such a diversified portfolio either on your own, working with a broker or through participation in a mutual fund.

Mutual funds and brokers. One way to avoid some of the anxiety of stock investment is to buy shares in a mutual fund, an organization whose portfolio includes a number of different stocks and thus offers the investor a measure of protection in the event that one particular stock fares poorly. Some mutual funds specialize in a specific area — stocks of high tech industries, for example, or multi-national corporations, while others hold more varied portfolios.

Most mutual funds are no-load: they do not charge participants any per-transaction fee. Some are low-load: they charge a two or three percent fee for the first investment and a one percent fee for any shares redeemed. Many newly established funds use a small percentage of their assets to cover marketing costs. This fact must be noted in their prospectuses, since it is comparable to a load charge. The majority of mutual funds are, in the jargon of the financial market, open-end: they will sell new shares or redeem existing shares at all times. A few, however, are closed-end: they are corporations which issue only a limited number of shares, which can be bought and sold only through a broker, who will charge a commission. Moreover, the value of the shares in such a fund fluctuates over time.

You can get help in choosing a mutual fund by consulting the issue of *Forbes Magazine* published yearly at the end of August. This issue contains the publication's annual survey of the best-performing mutual funds.

Whatever mutual fund you buy into, you have purchased something more than participation in a stock portfolio. You have purchased the services of the fund management, which will do some of your worrying and choosing for you.

Another way to purchase such management is to work through a stockbroker — someone associated with a brokerage house which has purchased a seat on one or more of the various stock exchanges and who therefore has the ability and right to trade stocks on the exchange floor. A good broker not only buys and sells securities for you, but also has up-to-date information on investment problems and opportunities and will act as an adviser, as well. In addition, he or she will do the bookkeeping and reporting connected with your securities transactions, and will — if you desire — set up a cash management account for you and render other bank-like services. The broker will even lend you — at interest, of course — part of the money to buy your stocks, which will then become the security for the loan. This process, which is called buying on margin, is strictly controlled: the legal minimum, or margin requirement, is that the investor put up at least 50 percent of the initial investment. But buying on margin can be risky. If your investments do not pan out as expected, you will be responsible for any losses that are incurred.

As a matter of convenience for you, the broker will send you your stock certificates, if you want them in your name, or hold them for you in the "street" name — the name of the brokerage firm — thus providing both safe storage and speed: you cannot sell stock unless the broker has possession of the stock certificate, and it could take time for you to deliver it or — if it is lost, replace it. In addition, large brokerage firms maintain research staffs that compile information to guide their clients' purchases, and publications staffs that make this information available through newsletters and pamphlets of various sorts.

For all these services, brokers charge a commission, the amount of which varies with the firm, on each transaction a client makes. If you find that the fees of a full-service broker are more than you are willing to pay, you may want to work through a discount broker. Like other brokers, discount brokers are licensed to trade on the stock exchanges. But they offer fewer extras than full-service brokers.

You should choose a stockbroker as you choose any other professional — on the basis of his or her public reputation and standing in the field and on the basis of advice from friends whose judgment in these matters you trust. Financial publications — *The Wall Street Journal* and *Barron's*, for example — which carry articles that will help you sharpen your own expertise in stock selection, also carry advertisements for brokers and investment advisory services. The New York Stock Exchange offers a free booklet listing firms handling small investor accounts. Write for: Individual Investor's Directory, Department F, New York Stock Exchange, 11 Wall Street, New York, New York 10005.

If your expectations are reasonable and you yourself are cautious, stocks can be a very good investment. Although their prices rise and fall with general economic conditions, you do not have to hold onto them a day longer than you wish and, if you have chosen wisely and spread your risk, you need not lose large sums, even in a bad market or if something goes wrong with one particular company whose stock you own. Stocks always involve risk, but they can outperform any other kind of investment you make.

Pensions and Other Retirement Funds

About half of all American workers are covered by some kind of pension plan where they work. If pension benefits are part of your job, you should find out as much as you can about the specifics of your plan.

How long do you have to stay on the job before you are vested — guaranteed that you will take some pension money with you when you leave? At what age will you begin to collect your pension? How large will it be? What benefits does it carry for your spouse in the event of your death?

The company you work for doubtless has published a booklet describing your pension plan in some detail. If you read it with care, you should be able to determine how much money, beyond your pension and Social Security benefits, you will need for a reasonably comfortable retirement.

In addition to pensions, there are three tax-sheltered sources of retirement income available: annuities, Individual Retirement Accounts (IRAs) and Keogh Plans. The first two are available to everyone; the third only to the self-employed.

Annuities. An annuity is a contract with an insurance company under the terms of which the purchaser pays a specific sum of money, either in installments or in a lump sum, and the insurance company guarantees, in return, to pay a fixed, regular income to the purchaser from a specific date to the end of his or her life. Some of those who hold annuities will die before they have collected all they paid in while others will collect much more than they paid. Statistics tell the insurance company how these numbers balance out, and, therefore, how to set annuity rates.

Annuities are available in several forms. Some are payable to beneficiaries if the annuity holder dies before completing his or her payments or, thereafter, before the total invested has been paid back.

Although most annuities pay a fixed monthly sum, so-called variable annuities are also available. The premium payments for these annuities may be put in a portfolio of stocks, or moved among a stock fund, a bond fund, and a money market fund, according to a program the policyholder chooses. The return to the policyholder will thus vary with the fortunes of the markets chosen.

Individual Retirement Accounts (IRAs). More than 100 million wage and salary earners, including the self-employed, are eligible for Individual Retirement Accounts (IRAs), which permit them to invest up to $2,000 annually and pay no taxes either on that sum or on its earnings until the money is withdrawn. Withdrawals can be made in a lump sum or gradually, beginning at age 59½, and must be made by age 70½, at a rate that guarantees the entire account is closed within a fixed number of years.

Both spouses can open their own IRAs if both are working; if one is not, the working spouse may invest an additional $250 in his or her IRA.

Because Congress' purpose in permitting wage earners to establish IRAs was to encourage private investment, and thus stimulate the economy, IRA money cannot be used to buy life insurance, precious metals, or collectibles or any other vehicle that plays no role in the investment business. But within these restrictions, there are many choices.

For the most worry-free use of your IRA, you can open one with a bank. You will probably have some choice of how your money will be handled — through the purchase of certificates of deposit, for example, or a money market account. But you will be restricted to the kind of conservative investments the banks themselves are held to, in order to qualify for the deposit insurance — up to $100,000 per account — that guarantees the safety of your money.

You can also use your IRA to purchase an annuity, which typically will cease when you die — unless that event occurs within 10 years of your first payment, in which case, your spouse will continue to receive benefits. You may purchase either fixed-rate or a variable annuity. Such an IRA has one drawback: some of your money will go into agents' commissions and other forms of sales charges.

Mutual funds also accept IRAs and the returns they pay can be quite good. If you choose a fund that consists of families of investments, you will be able to switch from one investment to another, within specific limits, in order to earn the highest return. But unless the brokerage has SIPC insurance, you do not get the safety of a bank IRA.

Finally, you may open an IRA with a stockbroker, thus providing yourself with a whole range of brokerage services. If you enjoy managing money, this kind of IRA will be most attractive to you. But remember that you will be paying fees and commissions, and that you will not be covered by insurance.

If you choose, you can spread your IRA money among these different vehicles or switch it from one kind of investment to another without penalty, as long as you do not actually withdraw any of it. You can open a different IRA each year or keep adding to the same one until it reaches some predetermined sum with which you can buy a relatively expensive security — a $10,000 Treasury Bill, for example.

Be aware, however, of some problems about IRAs. If you withdraw all or part of your money before you are 59½, you will have to pay a penalty of 10 percent of the amount you withdraw, as well as the tax on your with-

(Continued on page 274)

State Insurance Offices

Alabama
Commissioner of Insurance
64 North Union Street
Montgomery, AL 36130

Alaska
Director of Insurance
Pouch D
Juneau, AK 99811

Arizona
Director of Insurance
1601 West Jefferson
Phoenix, AZ 85007

Arkansas
Insurance Commissioner
400-18 University Tower Building
Little Rock, AR 72204

California
Insurance Commissioner
600 South Commonwealth
14th Floor
Los Angeles, CA 90005

Colorado
Commissioner of Insurance
106 State Office Building
Denver, CO 80203

Connecticut
Insurance Commissioner
State Office Building
165 Capitol Avenue
Hartford, CT 06106

Delaware
Insurance Commissioner
21 The Green
Dover, DE 19901

District of Columbia
Acting Superintendent of Insurance
614 H Street, NW
Washington, DC 20001

Florida
Insurance Commissioner
State Capitol, Plaza Level Eleven
Tallahassee, FL 32301

Georgia
Insurance Commissioner
200 Piedmont Avenue, SE
Floyd Memorial Building
West Tower—7th Floor
Atlanta, GA 30334

Hawaii
Insurance Commissioner
P.O. Box 3614
Honolulu, HI 96811

Idaho
Director of Insurance
700 West State Street
Boise, ID 83720

Illinois
Acting Director of Insurance
320 West Washington Street
Springfield, IL 62767

Indiana
Commissioner of Insurance
509 State Office Building
Indianapolis, IN 46204

Iowa
Commissioner of Insurance
State Office Building, G23
Ground Floor
Des Moines, IA 50319

Kansas
Commissioner of Insurance
420 SW 9th Street
Topeka, KS 66612

Kentucky
Insurance Commissioner
151 Elkhorn Court
Frankfort, KY 40601

Louisiana
Commissioner of Insurance
P.O. Box 44214
Baton Rouge, LA 70804

Maine
Superintendent of Insurance
State Office Building
State House, Station No. 34
Augusta, ME 04333

Maryland
Insurance Commissioner, Acting
501 St. Paul Place
7th Floor South
Baltimore, MD 21202

Massachusetts
Commissioner of Insurance
100 Cambridge Street
Boston, MA 02202

Michigan
Commissioner of Insurance
1048 Pierpont Street
P.O. Box 30220
Lansing, MI 48909

Minnesota
Commissioner of Insurance
500 Metro Square Building
Fifth Floor
St. Paul, MN 55101

Mississippi
Commissioner of Insurance
1804 Walter Sillers Building
P.O. Box 79
Jackson, MS 39205

Missouri
Director of Insurance
515 East High Street
P.O. Box 690
Jefferson City, MO 65102

Montana
Commissioner of Insurance
Mitchell Building
P.O. Box 4009
Helena, MT 59601

Nebraska
Director of Insurance
301 Centennial Mall South
State Capitol Building
P.O. Box 94699
Lincoln, NE 68509

Nevada
Insurance Commissioner
Nye Building
201 South Fall Street
Carson City, NV 89710

New Hampshire
Insurance Commissioner
169 Manchester Street
P.O. Box 2005
Concord, NH 03301

New Jersey
Commissioner of Insurance
210 East State Street
Trenton, NJ 08625

New Mexico
Superintendent of Insurance
PERA Building
P.O. Drawer 1269
Santa Fe, NM 87501

New York
Superintendent of Insurance
Two World Trade Center
New York, NY 10047

North Carolina
Commissioner of Insurance
Dobbs Building
P.O. Box 26387
Raleigh, NC 27611

North Dakota
Commissioner of Insurance
Capitol Building, Fifth Floor
Bismarck, ND 58505

Ohio
Director of Insurance
2100 Stella Court
Columbus, OH 43215

Oklahoma
Insurance Commissioner
408 Will Rogers Memorial Building
Oklahoma City, OK 73105

Oregon
Insurance Commissioner
158 12th Street, NE
Salem, OR 97310

Pennsylvania
Commissioner of Insurance
Strawberry Square, 13th Floor
Harrisburg, PA 17120

Rhode Island
Insurance Commissioner
100 North Main Street
Providence, RI 02903

South Carolina
Chief Insurance Commissioner
2711 Middleburg Drive
P.O. Box 4067
Columbia, SC 29204

South Dakota
Acting Director of Insurance
Insurance Building
Pierre, SD 57501

Tennessee
Commissioner of Insurance
114 State Office Building
Nashville, TN 37219

Texas
State Board of Insurance
1110 San Jacinto Boulevard
Austin, TX 78786

Utah
Commissioner of Insurance
160 East 300 South
P.O. Box 5803
Salt Lake City, UT 84110

Vermont
Commissioner of Insurance
State Office Building
Montpelier, VT 05602

Virginia
Commissioner of Insurance
700 Jefferson Building
P.O. Box 1157
Richmond, VA 23209

Washington
Insurance Commissioner
Insurance Building AQ21
Olympia, WA 98504

West Virginia
Insurance Commissioner
2100 Washington Street, East
Charleston, WV 25305

Wisconsin
Commissioner of Insurance
123 West Washington Avenue
Madison, WI 53702

Wyoming
Commissioner of Insurance
2424 Pioneer Avenue
Cheyenne, WY 82002

drawal. If you are in the 40 percent tax bracket, you would normally pay $400 on $1,000 withdrawn. But the penalty adds another 10 percent, or $100, for a total of $500.

For this reason, young people should do some careful figuring before opening IRAs. The tax saving is less for those with low to moderate incomes than those who earn more and are in higher brackets — and few of us reach the peak of our earning power when we are still young. In addition, young people often have major expenses still ahead of them — the down payment on a first home, for example, and may not have the necessary cash if they put $2,000 into an IRA every year. For these reasons, they may find it advisable not to make the maximum IRA contribution but to invest only part of that sum.

Keogh accounts. Both employees and the self-employed can open IRA accounts. But only those who are self-employed can open Keogh Accounts, as well. In most respects, Keoghs and IRAs are similar. The money involved can be invested in the same ways; the interest the money earns is tax-free until it is withdrawn; early withdrawals are penalized 10 percent; the money can be withdrawn wihout penalty starting at age 59½; and withdrawals must commence by age 70½. But Keoghs permit a much higher annual maximum deposit than do IRAs — 25 percent of net income, up to a maximum of $30,000 for 1984 and 1985, and thereafter, an amount tied to cost-of-living increases. In addition, holders of Keogh accounts who are themselves employers — doctors and dentists, for example, who have receptionists and nurses working for them — must open such accounts for those employees, as well.

Estate Planning

No matter how small your estate, it is generally a good idea to have an up-to-date will. A will permits you — within certain limits of the law — to distribute your estate as you want and may be helpful in limiting the amount of taxes that must be paid. If you die without a will, state law will determine what happens to your estate. Your will does not have to be complex or written in legal language. You can make it out yourself, in your own words, or preferably, buy a blank will form and fill it in. As long as a will is drawn up according to state law and witnessed by two or three people, none of whom is among your beneficiaries, it is perfectly acceptable.

You can, of course, also have your will drawn up by a lawyer, and if your estate is large or your bequests complicated in any way, such a procedure would be advisable. A lawyer can help you write provisions that will reduce or avoid the sizeable bite that state and federal taxes can take out of your estate.

One way of reducing estate taxes is through the creation of a trust, which appoints someone to invest and manage all or part of your property for a certain period of time, and to distribute the income from that property and eventually its principal to the beneficiaries named in the will. Many banks and savings institutions have excellent trust departments.

All property passing to beneficiaries by means of a will must go through probate — the legal procedure for validating a will. Depending on the law in your state, probate can be costly and time consuming, sometimes tying up an estate for a year or more. It is therefore important to find some way of bypassing probate for at least part of your estate, so that your family will have some income to tide it over and pay the immediate expenses of a funeral, legal fees, etc. Among the most effective ways of bypassing probate are by title, by contract and by trust. For instance, if a husband and wife have joint ownership or tenancy of a home or savings account, that property would pass to the survivor by title; life insurance proceeds are paid to the beneficiary by contract; and death benefits from an employee's pension plan are passed to the family by trust.

All of us are well aware of our responsibilities as consumers when we are in the market for milk or home appliances or automobiles. But when it comes to buying insurance and investing our money, too many of us are far less careful than we should be.

In this chapter, we have tried to set some realistic guidelines in these areas, describing the pros and cons of the various kinds of insurance and investment options that are available. It is up to you to analyze these options in terms of your family's needs and situation, and to keep a continuing watch as those needs and that situation change, so that you can make the necessary adjustments in both your insurance and investments.

Chapter 11

Leisure-Time Activities

With shorter working days, longer vacations, frequent three-day weekends and early retirement options, we Americans now have more leisure time than ever before in history. Providing activities for the use of that time has become big business — an estimated $200 billion per year spent for everything from travel to cooking classes. We join health spas and country clubs, buy boats and snowmobiles, seek out ski slopes and semitropical islands, patronize luxurious resort hotels and go backpacking into the wilds, roll a few games at the neighborhood bowling alley and brave the white waters of the Colorado River, enjoy the relaxed atmosphere of a cruise ship and board a jet airliner that can whisk us to any part of the globe within hours. The variety of ways in which we use our leisure time is almost unlimited.

Because a substantial part of our disposable income is spent for recreation, we should be as knowledgeable about getting our money's worth in this field as in any other. As sophisticated consumers, we should clearly define what we want and be realistic about what we are willing — and able — to spend for it. We need to develop the ability to distinguish between true bargains and bright but empty promises. We should also be aware that any big enterprise attracts a certain number of shady characters out to fleece the gullible and that the lucrative recreation and leisure business is no exception.

Because a vacation is likely to take the largest bite from an individual's or a family's annual recreation budget, let's begin there.

Planning a Vacation

Start making plans as far ahead as possible. You will not only reduce the chances of disappointment but quite possibly save money. Obviously, the first question is what kind of a vacation you want this year. If you have only yourself to consider, the decision can be relatively simple. If a family or friends will be involved, conferences will help decide such key questions as:

- Where to go; a rough itinerary.
- Whether you want to be on your own or part of a group.
- What kind of lodging to expect — visiting friends, staying at hotels or motels, camping out, etc.
- What kind of activities to indulge in.
- How much money you should allocate.

With such basic matters agreed on, the next step is to learn as much as possible about where you will be going.

Obtaining Information

Free information is readily available from foreign tourist bureaus, federal and state agencies and private facilities. Write to them for maps, directions and details of the attractions that might be of interest to you. Be sure to specify what you particularly want to find out, for example, rates, family plans or group programs, activities for children, transportation, facilities for the handicapped, special diets. A postcard, rather than a letter, with the sender's name, address and questions clearly written will usually bring forth an abundance of descriptive material which, in its turn, may bear names of additional sources to call upon. You may also find valuable information at your local library. Your travel agent can also be of enormous assistance in this area.

Narrowing the Choices

Examination of your growing wealth of travel literature will help you to define your vacation in practical terms of time, place and money. For example:

- A family of four hoping to spend the first two weeks in August on an inexpensive camping trip in a popular scenic wonderland, say Yellowstone National Park, learns that these are the most crowded weeks of the year there, but the same activities can be enjoyed in comparative comfort at lesser-used parks.

• A couple planning a tour of Spain and Portugal discovers that if they delay their trip one week — which they can easily do — they will be traveling off season and, therefore, at substantial savings.
• If one member of a family needs rest while the others crave excitement, they may find that a cruise which stops at several ports will allow the adventurers to sightsee, explore and shop while the other remains on deck to bask in the sun.

Money-Saving Travel Tips

• Rural areas of the United States and Canada are usually the least costly to visit all year round, as are southern European countries and the underdeveloped nations.
• The more sophisticated the metropolis, the higher the cost of visiting.
• By traveling off-season — at times other than the most popular weeks or months — you can enjoy the same countryside, landmarks, cultural attractions and shops, *minus* the crowds and inflated prices.
• Air fares during the week (Monday through Thursday) may be cheaper than on weekends; air fares and train fares may be lower during nonpeak hours. Inquire.
• Traveling at night — when you can sleep on the plane, train or bus — eliminates the cost of that night's hotel and gives you more useful time at your destination.
• Since most airlines serve complimentary food, flights scheduled at mealtimes save the cost of eating at a restaurant.
• Purchase of a vacation package which offers transportation, accommodations and some sightseeing and meals at an all-inclusive special price, may be less expensive than buying the elements separately.
• Buses and trains generally sell special-price tickets to be used within a stated time period; ask about 60-day passes, two-week rates and the like.
• Bed-and-breakfast establishments are usually less costly than hotels and offer the opportunity to meet people who live in the community rather than the formal hotel staff.
• Hostels offer unusually low-cost accommodations both in the United States and abroad.

Professional Help

The services of a travel agent cost you nothing and can save hours of time and trouble.

The ideal travel agent is knowledgeable, enthusiastic, accessible and, above all, helpful. Constant contact with carriers and hotels gives him or her firsthand knowledge of prices and places, schedules and special events. An agent can make almost any kind of reservation for you and, with direct lines to reservations personnel worldwide, can accomplish within minutes many bookings that could involve hours of a novice's time. A good travel agent:

• can recommend substitute hotels if the one you've requested is unavailable or too costly for your budget;
• knows which places have changed hands and whether service has improved or seriously deteriorated;
• should know which tours and resorts have satisfied customers and which to avoid because they fail to live up to the promises set forth in a glossy brochure;
• knows about the availability of travel bargains and the suppliers' financial stability;
• can tell you which times are on and off season, worldwide;
• can advise what to wear, what to pack, what to tip;
• can custom-create a trip exactly to your needs.

If you are planning to go abroad, the travel agent can advise on getting passports, knows whether visas and/or immunizations are required and can aid in the process.

You may be asked to pay for special long distance telephone calls or telegrams, or for reticketing if you change your plans repeatedly, but except under these circumstances you are not charged for the services that travel agents provide. They earn their money through the commissions paid by carriers, hotels and tour operators. But bear in mind that the amount of the agent's commission is related to the amount of money you spend.

Finding a Travel Agent

Travel agents are listed in the classified section of the telephone book, but you may be well advised to ask for recommendations from friends and business associates. If the agent you are considering is a stranger, check with your local Better Business Bureau to learn whether any complaints have been filed against the agency.

You may also want to inquire if the agency

is a member of ASTA (the American Society of Travel Agents). Membership signifies that the agent or agency has been in business for more than three years, has had billings of at least $500,000 the year before certification, and conforms to the organization's standards of practices and ethics.

Doing It Yourself

It is possible — although time consuming — to handle the details by yourself. If you call the major airlines during nonrush hours, you will reach reservations clerks more readily. They can tell you the schedules and rates offered by all the airlines, but generally will be able to take reservations only for their own flights. Major hotel and motel chains around the world have toll-free telephone numbers through which you can book space — using a credit card, if you desire. You will then receive a confirmation by phone or through the mail. Amtrak will take train reservations over the phone if they can be charged to a major credit card.

If you want to stay at a country inn or a bed-and-breakfast establishment, or at a national or state park, or if you need special equipment, a phone call may not be enough. You may need to write a personal letter as well.

To be on the safe side, be sure to keep records of your correspondence, your reservations, prices, deposits paid and amounts remaining to be paid. Above all, keep copies of the confirmations of all arrangements.

Payment in Advance

Hotels and motels in this country generally demand the cost of one night's lodging as an advance deposit; foreign establishments sometimes request payment for your entire stay. Tours, charters and cruises must be paid for in full at the time the ticket is written. If you are booking your trip many months in advance, it may be possible to pay a portion of the fare as a deposit, with the remainder paid 30 to 45 days before departure. Airline tickets, which may be purchased at flight time, are charged at the time they are issued. Bus fares, which are usually purchased by the traveler, are paid for at the time of the trip.

The Need for Awareness

It can be comforting to enjoy a trip with no fear of returning to face a slew of bills. Similarly, prepayment ensures that suppliers will not have to chase clients for money due. However, before paying the often substantial amounts of money involved in a trip, make certain that you will get what you are paying for. Your travel tickets are like contracts — binding agreements between you and the organizations or individuals supplying the services you want.

Take the time to read the fine print on everything — your brochures, your tickets, your confirmations. Understand the cancellation/refund stipulations: If you must cancel your trip at the last minute, will you be able to ask for and receive a refund? (Ordinarily, no.) Does the supplier have the right to make substitutions in accommodations or destinations, or to change the departure date? (The traveler is supposed to be notified of changes by the tour operator and is supposed to have seven days to cancel the reservation.) But what if "conditions beyond our control," such as weather or mechanical difficulties, cause delays that result in missed connections or the loss of other reservations? (You may receive restitution, but some authorities say it is the traveler's responsibility to allow enough leeway if arrival time is of such importance.)

Because of the nature of the travel industry — the airlines' complicated fare structures, the widespread use of computers into which reservations can sometimes seem to disappear, the unprecedented volume of transactions and the lack of consistent overall regulation — any one of a score of details can go awry.

Perhaps it is amazing that so much does go exactly according to plan. Only a very small percentage of travelers miss connections, or arrive at a brand new hotel that has not been completed in time to receive them. However, to the man whose luggage went to Reno while he and his bride took the plane to Niagara Falls, the highest traveler-satisfaction statistics are immaterial, and legal action, while it offers the hope of restitution in a possibly distant future, does not solve the immediate problem — your ruined vacation.

Travel Precautions

It is to ensure against such mishaps that you should deal with recognized, reputable professionals whenever possible. You can also buy travel insurance. For a small price, you

Consumer Victory Over Fraudulent Tour Operators

For many years the travel industry was a fertile field for unscrupulous entrepreneurs. Distraught travelers returning from what had been billed as "dream" vacations told nightmare tales of planes that never took off, hotel rooms that did not exist, Super Bowl tickets that were never delivered, unsanitary cruise ships and, worst of all, vanishing tour operators who took all of the travelers' prepayment money with them. Worse yet, there seemed to be nothing to do but say "Never again." The amount of money involved for an individual was rarely large enough to justify legal expense: the cost of the action would be many times greater than the amount at stake.

That such things are much less likely to happen today is due largely to protective measures enacted by the now defunct Civil Aeronautics Board (CAB). Tour operators are now required to establish escrow accounts for consumer deposits. Tour operators must also obtain surety bonds, guaranteeing the performance and delivery of those services promised and paid for.

In addition, travel law has become a recognized area for group legal action, in part because of the successful prosecution of travel liability cases by New York attorney Thomas A. Dickerson, who was himself the victim of a fraudulent tour operator. Along with about 250 other vacationers who had paid $300 to $480 each for a week's vacation, Dickerson was flown to a "resort" in Jamaica during the Christmas holidays of 1975. He and his companions found no "resort" but a collection of unfinished villas with nonworking toilets, inadequate hot water, inedible food and a huge colony of rodents that enjoyed leaping from the adjacent banana trees through the thatched roofs to scamper across the floors of the huts. A five-mile trek along a narrow jungle path led to a tar-stained strip of sand — the "nearby beach." Nor was there any telephone service.

Mr. Dickerson represented the vacationers in court. After three years of litigation he succeeded in getting most of their money back. Persuading the New York state courts to accept his suit as a class action — one person suing for a "class" of 219 — was in itself a precedent-setting achievement in the travel field and paved the way for his eventual victory.

Now that airlines, bus companies and railroads have been deregulated, the rights of passengers are governed by common law, so that the liability of the carriers is no longer limited. Dickerson is certain that travel litigation will increase as consumers realize they are not powerless in the face of delays, discomfort, the loss of baggage, misrepresentation and/or misinformation.

Travelers wishing to lodge a complaint may get help from local Better Business Bureaus, municipal consumer affairs departments or the U.S. Tour Brokers Association, 211 East 51st Street, New York, New York 10022.

can now purchase a policy that covers trip cancellation, baggage loss and/or misdirection, even weather conditions. Insurance is available that protects against employees' strikes that force you to change your plans, against hijacking and even against the loss of your prepayment should the tour operator or carrier go out of business. Your travel agent knows about such coverage and is often authorized to sell the policies.

The airlines' traditional limitation of two pieces plus a carry-on bag is a good guideline for travel on any vehicle. If you are flying outside the United States, ask your travel agent if there is a weight limit; overweight charges can be significant.

Attach an identification tag to each piece of luggage whether or not it is checked. The tags should bear your name, and your *office address* and *telephone number.* Use of your home address is unwise; it may alert a professional burglar to your departure. Place a second identification tag inside each piece and include the travel agent's or tour operator's name and number so that one of you can be reached if your bag is found.

Always remove old travel destination tags from your valises before each trip. Otherwise, a busy baggage handler may become confused and route your suitcase to the wrong destination.

Because much luggage looks alike, identify your cases with a brightly colored tape or tie — a loop of yarn around the handle will suffice — to prevent an accidental switch.

Remember how many pieces of luggage you have checked, so that you do not leave a piece behind in the baggage claim area.

If your luggage is lost, misrouted or damaged, put in a claim immediately. Take any damaged suitcase to the baggage service area, fill out a Property Irregularity Report, describe the damage and ask to have arrangements made for the necessary repair. If your luggage is missing, report the loss, and put in a claim for the suitcase and its contents. While carriers have historically attempted to limit their liability to $750 per passenger on domestic flights and $9.04 per pound of baggage on international flights, this limitation has been challenged successfully. And luggage insurance allows you to purchase excess value insurance before departure.

If your luggage has been sent to the wrong destination, find out when it will be flown to you. You can ask to have it delivered directly to where you are staying.

Security Measures for Travelers

No city has a monopoly on hotel theft, nor is any locality free from it. Burglaries occur in exclusive, luxurious establishments as well as in inexpensive lodgings. Take precautions:

- Traveling with a lot of cash or jewelry or a glut of credit cards is always dangerous.
- If you must take some valuables with you, keep them in the hotel's safe-deposit box except when needed. Never leave them on your dresser or night table.
- Watch your luggage while you are waiting to check in, or as it sits on the curbside before departure.
- Always lock your hotel room door, especially when you are sleeping.
- Don't turn in your hotel room key when you go out for the day; keep it with you at all times.

If you are driving:

- Keep luggage out of sight — locked in the trunk.
- Lock all car doors at all times.
- Keep your car key on a separate chain, and hand only that to the parking attendant.
- Park in well-lit areas.

Traveling with Children

When making reservations, indicate that you will be traveling with children and ask about discount or family plans. Airlines usually permit children under two to travel free and charge half-fare for youngsters up to age 11. On trains and buses children under five traveling with an adult usually ride free; children aged five to 12 are charged half-fare. Deregulation and the resulting price competition may alter these policies; check to find out what the lowest prices are.

Your travel agent will know about hotel policies regarding additional charges for children. Some chains permit children to share their parents' room at no extra charge; others add a modest fee for the use of a rollaway cot or other sleeping equipment.

Senior Citizens

Hotels and carriers are offering an increasing number of bargains to older Americans — in some cases, starting at age 55. These senior citizen rates are not always publicized, however, so anyone desiring to benefit from them should inquire about them at the time the reservation is made.

In many cities an identification card proving the traveler is over 55 will entitle that person to discounts on local transportation and at participating restaurants, theaters, shops or special attractions. Lists of participating facilities are usually available from the local chamber of commerce, convention and visitors bureau or related municipal office.

Discount fares are offered by Amtrak, by Trailways and Greyhound (and possibly some of the short line bus companies); some domestic airlines also offer discounts to passengers over 65, but they may not take reservations for those seats more than a day in advance.

Organizations offering travel advice to senior citizens include:

• American Association of Retired Persons, 1909 K Street, NW, Washington, D.C. 20049.
• National Council of Senior Citizens, 925 15th Street, NW, Washington, D.C. 20005.

A Vacation Abroad

For travel outside the United States a certain extra amount of preparation is necessary, and sufficient time should be allotted for it.

You will probably need one or more of the following documents: passport, visa, tourist card. Some countries will also want proof that you have enough money for your visit as well as an indication — in the form of ongoing travel tickets — that you are not planning to stay on.

Passport. To depart from or enter the United States and to enter most foreign countries, U.S. citizens need a passport. (Passports are not generally required for travel between the United States and Canada, Mexico or Bermuda; your travel agent will know of other exceptions.) You should apply for this document well in advance of your departure date.

Application for your first passport must be made in person at a passport agency or at one of the thousands of U.S. Post Offices or federal or state courts that accept passport applications. Be aware that some passport offices in major cities become badly crowded in late spring and early summer, so allow enough time. You will need:

• The completed passport application form.
• Proof of U.S. citizenship, such as a birth certificate, hospital birth record or baptismal certificate. Persons born abroad should have a Certificate of Naturalization, Certificate of Citizenship or a Report of Birth Abroad of a Citizen of the United States (Form FS-240).
• Two identical photographs of yourself, taken within the last six months. The photos should be two inches square, front view, against a light background. They may be in color or black and white. The blank area to the left of the image must bear your signature. There is usually a photography shop specializing in passport photos near the passport office; your pictures — which will cost between $5 and $10 — can be taken and developed within a short time on the day you apply for the passport. Vending machine photos or newspaper or magazine reproductions are *not* acceptable.

The passport fee is $35 for persons 18 or over, $20 for children up to age 17. There is a first-time execution fee of $7.

When you apply for your passport you will also have to establish your own identity to the satisfaction of the passport official. A driver's license or identifying card with your signature and photograph or description is acceptable identification.

Applicants 13 years of age or older must apply for the passport in person. However, a parent or guardian may apply for children under age 13.

Allow at least four weeks for processing of your application. Even more time is usually required in spring and early summer.

When you receive your passport, be sure to sign it and fill in the personal data.

Passports by Mail. You may apply by mail to renew a passport, or reinstate an expired passport that was issued within the previous eight years but not before your 18th birthday. The Application for Passport by Mail Form (DSP-82) may be obtained from any passport office. Complete the application, sign and date it, attach your previous passport; two recent, signed photos (as above); and the $35 passport renewal fee, and mail the materials to a passport office for processing. Your renewed passport will be mailed to you. Allow at least four weeks for processing.

Length of Use. As of January 1983, an adult passport is valid for 10 years from the date of issue; passports issued to minors are valid for five years, or until the child reaches age 17.

Alterations of a Passport. The only permissible alteration on a passport is a change of such personal data as your address. Any other changes may be considered mutilation and render the passport invalid. If your passport is damaged — by water or fire, for instance — turn it in to your passport office (or the nearest consular office if you are abroad) so that a replacement can be issued to you as soon as possible.

Loss or Theft. U.S. passports, which guarantee that the bearer is an American citizen, are valuable documents and should be treated as such. Keep your passport in a safe place and keep a separate record of its number. The loss of a passport in the United States should be reported immediately to the nearest passport agency or the Passport Service, Department of State, Washington, D.C. 20520. Theft of a passport should also be reported to local police authorities.

Loss or theft of a passport while you are overseas should be reported immediately to the local police authorities and to the U.S. embassy or consulate.

Visas. A visa is an endorsement, or stamp, placed by officials of a foreign government on a U. S. passport, permitting the bearer of the passport to visit that country.

Many governments, such as France, Great Britain, Italy and Uruguay, require no visa for visits as long as three months, and will simply stamp the tourist's passport upon arrival. Other nations, such as South Africa and Brazil, require travelers to secure the visa in advance, sometimes charging a fee of several dollars for it.

The visa may be valid for days, months, years or just the length of the visit.

It is the traveler's responsibility to find out whether a visa will be needed, and to obtain it in advance of his or her trip from the particular embassy or consulate.

If you are traveling in a tour group you can usually rely on the tour operator or travel agent to look after such details, but you should always make sure. A booklet entitled "Visa Requirements of Foreign Governments," is available from the Department of State, Bureau of Consular Affairs, Washington, D.C. 20524. It lists the entry requirements of those countries that require visas, and tells how to apply for them. Because requirements may change, direct inquiry at the particular consulate is recommended.

The visa request must always be accompanied by the passport (and, if requested, by additional passport photos). As it is sometimes necessary to send the application overseas, it is important to allow yourself sufficient lead time for all this paper work if your trip requires several visas.

Most foreign consulates are located in the major cities — Washington, New York, Los Angeles, San Francisco, Chicago and New Orleans. Elsewhere, information on foreign consulates can be found in most city telephone directories.

Innoculations and Immunization. No vaccinations are required to return to the United States from any country. However, depending upon health conditions at the time, other countries may require immunizations before they will admit you. Specific information can be obtained from your doctor, your local health department or from the Public Health Service.

International Driving Permits. Any licensed driver at least 18 years of age who holds a valid U. S. passport is eligible for the International Driving Permit and, for driving in Latin American countries, the Inter-American Driving Permit. Your local AAA club will be able to tell you whether such a license is required in the country you are planning to visit and, if it is, will be able to supply you with an application form. Because it is necessary to submit your driver's license and two passport-size photos along with the completed application form and the $5 fee, the matter is more easily handled in person than through the mail. Once you get to the appropriate office the entire procedure normally takes only minutes.

The Matter of Money

All travelers are cautioned *not* to carry large amounts of cash. Traveler's checks are preferable by far.

Traveler's checks, which may be purchased at banks, savings and loan associations, AAA clubs and from such large travel agencies as Thomas Cook and American Express, are virtually tantamount to money. When you purchase them, you write your signature at the top of each check; later, when a check is to be spent or redeemed, you sign it again. The double signature acts as a safeguard against redemption by anyone except the owner. Traveler's checks are numbered; the traveler is advised to keep the receipt and the list of numbers in a secure, separate place and, in the event of loss or theft, to report the numbers immediately to the local office of the issuing company. Replacement of the checks can then be made with little inconvenience to the traveler.

Traveler's checks never lose their value, so even if they are not spent on the trip, they may be used at home or, possibly, saved until the next vacation. (If the amount is large, however, remember you're not receiving any interest on your money.)

There is generally a charge of $1 per $100 for traveler's checks. However, no-charge traveler's checks can be obtained from some sources. Call your local banks or ask your travel agent.

Cashing Traveler's Checks Abroad. The best exchange rate is usually offered at banks in the country you are visiting or at the local American Express office. If you are in a hurry or need only a small amount of cash, your hotel will usually oblige, but often at a less favorable rate. Restaurants and shops, for which the exchange represents a labor cost, usually give still less favorable rates. (Traveler's checks can be obtained in foreign currencies. If they are purchased in the United States, a less favorable exchange rate is applied. Unused checks will have to be converted back to U.S. dollars at the conclusion of the trip — again at a less favorable exchange rate. Therefore, consumers should be alerted not to buy more than they will need.) Under no circumstances should you be lured into any private or blackmarket transaction. You risk being swindled, arrested, stuck with counterfeit bills, even personally endangered. Obey local currency laws.

Foreign Currencies. Travelers who are not on an all-inclusive package tour will need local currency for ground transportation and tips upon arrival. Small amounts of foreign currency can usually be purchased at your local bank, although an advance request may be necessary.

Credit Cards

Credit cards, which can now be used for almost any kind of purchase almost anywhere, are a great convenience. Credit card companies will be glad to furnish travelers with lists of establishments around the world that accept their cards. But when you use a credit card outside the United States, you must be aware that the rate of exchange fluctuates daily and that your account is not charged for a purchase on the day you make it. If, for example, you buy a pair of rain boots in London for £10, charging the purchase to your credit card, and the pound is worth $2 on that day, your boots would seem to have cost $20. But if the pound is worth $2.10 on the day the purchase is actually entered on your credit card account, you will be billed at $21 — a dollar more than you thought you were paying. Of course, if the pound is worth $1.90 on that day, your boots will have cost $19.

European Railroads and Buses

European trains go just about everywhere, and beyond a routine customs check there are no problems about leaving one country and entering the next. Two classes of train travel are available: first class — for which reservations are necessary — is more costly, and is advisable for longer trips when sleeping accommodations are needed. Second class (the equivalent of our coach) is fine for short rides. Travelers intending to visit several cities may save money by buying the Eurailpass, a ticket that permits around-the-clock first-class train travel throughout Europe. The Eurailpass is issued for a set period of time (1983 prices are quoted): 15 days ($260), 21 days ($330), 30 days ($410), 60 days ($560) or 90 days ($680). The pass may be obtained as much as six months in advance and is sold only in the United States; it cannot be purchased in Europe. The travel-time period is computed from the date of the first train trip.

Travelers under 26 years of age are eligible to buy the economical Youthpass, good for second-class train travel for periods of 30 days ($290) or 60 days ($370). It, too, must be purchased in the United States.

Information about both Eurailpass and Youthpass is available from French National Railroads, 610 Fifth Avenue, New York, New York 10020.

BritRail and the BritRail Youth Pass, for those aged 14 through 26, are the equivalent bargains offered in the British Isles. Both must be purchased before leaving the United States, either from your travel agent or from BritRail, 630 Third Avenue, New York, New York 10017.

The Europabus network offers economical travel throughout all of western Europe except Spain. Excursion passes are not available; tickets are purchased at the time of the trip. Travel information is available from Europabus, 747 Third Avenue, New York, New York 10017.

Food is not included in the price of train or bus travel. Not all of the first-class, long distance trains carry dining cars; inquire at the train stations. Vendors hawking local products generally rush onto the platforms as the trains pull into a station. If you expect to be enroute at mealtimes and do not want to trust to chance, you can ask your hotel to provide you with a box meal.

Buses usually stop for meals and/or snacks along the road. Passengers may bring their own food if they wish.

Driving

An automobile offers independence and flexibility — the freedom to linger at the places that appeal to you. If your accommodations are on the outskirts of a city, a car may be a necessity. Four or more people traveling together may also find that driving is the most economical way to go.

Members of AAA can request country-by-country information about car rental overseas, as well as detailed road maps. Most countries have some sort of automobile club affiliated with AAA; carry the names and numbers for your protection.

Buying a Car Overseas. In the past, Americans have found it both convenient and financially advantageous to purchase a car overseas, drive it on the Continent and ship it back to the United States. Anyone considering this procedure today must add to the cost of the car and shipping the amount of duty that will have to be paid on the purchase and the cost of cleaning the vehicle once it arrives here (a Department of Agriculture requirement). As the car will also have to conform to U. S. safety and emissions standards — which differ from those of Europe — and it is expensive to have a car retrofitted to achieve this conformity, it is important to check that the car you are purchasing is in compliance with U.S. standards, and to get a certificate to that effect from the dealer. An alternative is to purchase the car overseas and resell it to the dealer at the end of the trip for a prearranged amount, minus the depreciation.

Car Rental. The major car-rental companies maintain offices around the world. In most countries there are also local car-rental agencies which will probably be less expensive than the international firms. Rental cars overseas do not always have an automatic shift, air conditioning, or power brakes or steering. Additional fees may be charged for the convenience of renting the car in one city and dropping it off in another.

Hiring a Car. Travelers who want the convenience of a private car, with none of the responsibility or strain of driving, may find it worthwhile to hire a local car and driver. It will probably cost less to pay the driver a daily rate than to take a series of taxis. In addition, you will have a knowledgeable guide. Inquire at your hotel or local tourist office.

Biking. The least expensive means of travel is the bicycle. Touring bikes are easy to buy or rent overseas. This form of travel is obviously not for everyone — biking on a busy highway can be perilous — but an experienced biker who travels light can enjoy a vacation almost anywhere. Members of AYH (American Youth Hostels) have access to one of the least costly of all ways to "see the world."

Accommodations

Many hotels, motels, inns and resorts abroad are regularly inspected by representatives of tourist boards and such travel services as Michelin, AAA and Frommer. Establishments are evaluated for cleanliness, comfort, atmosphere, service, food and security; they are also classified according to cost. The reports are then published in travel guides which the traveler is advised to examine before embarking on the trip.

Even though the guides may say that certain hotels require no reservations, it is a safer course to assume that reservations *are* necessary. The wonderful little out-of-the-way place that your closest friend happened on last year will, nine times out of 10, have been discovered by Baedecker and be fully booked by the time you arrive.

Understand, too, that the term *first class*, while it means *the best* in terms of transportation, does not have the same connotation where hotels are concerned. The truly *best* hotel in most cities is labeled deluxe or superior; the rare ranking of world class connotes the ultimate in service and luxury. Someone who requires the convenience of 24-hour room service, wants to step from the hotel lobby out onto the city's main thoroughfare or dreams of gazing out the window at the city's

Bumping and What You Can Do About It

Each year some 100,000 ticket-holding airline passengers in the United States appear at the airport in plenty of time to make their scheduled flight but are required to take a later plane to their destination. There is nothing the matter with their scheduled plane; there are just more passengers than seats. Some people have been bumped. Passengers complain bitterly that bumping is a direct result of over-booking. Airlines claim that bumping results from problems with no-shows. Both are correct.

Because a great number of people who reserve seats on airplanes do not use them and do not take the trouble to cancel their reservations, the airlines, loath to find themselves with empty seats at flight time, accept more flight reservations than they have seats. In the majority of cases the airlines estimate correctly and there are enough seats to accommodate all ticketed passengers.

Sometimes, however, more passengers than anticipated check in at the flight desk so some ticket holders must be bumped. In that event, flight personnel usually ask for volunteers — passengers who are willing to take a later flight. A sum of money is customarily offered as an inducement.

If there are not enough volunteers, the airlines must bump passengers arbitrarily. In that case the carrier is obliged to book every bumped passenger on another flight and also pay him or her the face value of the one-way trip (up to $200). If the substitute flight arrives more than two hours later than the original flight, the penalty is doubled (up to $400). Substitute international flights must arrive within four hours of the original time.

Bumping is a frustrating, maddening experience, but certain amenities — plus the money you get — will or should be provided. You will be able to telephone, cable or ask the carrier to send a telex informing your family or friends of your late arrival. If the delay continues for many hours you may request a meal and, in cases of especially long detainment, overnight accommodations.

Remember, of course, that your checked luggage, already stowed in the baggage compartment of your original flight, will be waiting for you when you finally reach your destination.

Bumping *up* (upgrading), an occasional and pleasant experience, can occur when a tourist cabin has been overbooked and a tourist passenger is provided a vacant first-class seat at no added cost.

most famous landmarks, should know that those are the hallmarks of luxury and be prepared to pay a premium for them. However, a traveler who doesn't mind walking a couple of blocks to the main attractions, enjoys the quiet of a side-street location and has no need for a cheese sandwich and chocolate at 3 A.M. will be content in what the Europeans and guidebooks term a *first-class* hotel.

Hotels in lower categories may be less conveniently situated, have washbasins in the room, baths down the hall, and lack restaurant facilities.

Overbooking or Other Errors. Hotel owners, like airline operators, claim that overbooking — taking reservations for more people than they can accommodate — is their protection against last-minute cancellations and no-shows (the inconsiderate people who reserve space but fail to arrive). If you arrive at your hotel with your confirmation voucher in hand and find that no room is available at the confirmed rate, you have every right to expect that you will be upgraded to the next higher price available, at no added cost to you. And if the management appears unwilling to do this, you have every right to raise a fuss.

If, as sometimes can happen, there is no room at all — expected departures have not taken place, for example — the management is obliged to find you equivalent accommodations nearby and take you and your luggage to them. Major hotel chains sometimes even pay for your first night at the substitute lodgings.

If the establishment at which you have booked does not live up to this obligation, report the incident to your travel agent or the tour operator immediately upon your return home. In addition, if the establishment is part of a hotel/motel chain, write a letter of complaint to the president of the chain; be specific as to name, dates and times.

Tipping. Most hotels and restaurants abroad will add to your bill a service charge that substitutes for a tip. If service has been satisfactory, however, you may want to add an extra tip for the people who have done especially well for you. About 10 percent is considered sufficient; those who have impressed you with their extra care and vigilance may deserve more. It is best to tip in cash, in the currency of the country, not by writing an additional amount on the bill or check. Give the gratuity directly to the person who has earned it. Bear in mind that in some establishments tips are the only income that the help receives.

Vacationing in the United States

A vacation in the United States offers the advantages of convenience and, usually, lower initial cost than a trip abroad. And for budget-conscious Americans, federal and state public lands offer some great bargains.

The scope of America's network of public lands is unique. Hundreds of millions of acres have been set aside for the benefit and enjoyment of the public. Within them are opportunities for swimming, camping, fishing, hunting, boating, skiing and other activities.

Like recreational facilities throughout the world, our public lands are experiencing record numbers of visitors. Park personnel advise would-be vacationers to avoid the peak attendance months of July and August. If travel at those times is unavoidable, try to visit the lesser-used parks. Although they may lack the spectacular aspects of Yellowstone or Yosemite, they can provide an exhilarating vacation experience.

Travel Information. Planning a vacation on the public lands is essentially a do-it-yourself job. Travel agents do not ordinarily involve themselves in requesting campsites or directions to nature trails. The process of planning and arranging for such a vacation is the same as that outlined at the start of this chapter. Instead of international organizations, you will be dealing with parks personnel or private concessionaires, whose job it is to assist you whether you are at home or stopping at the park visitors center.

The Need for Reservations. Reservations will be necessary in most areas, and it is sensible to make them well in advance. A year ahead is not too soon — particularly in the case of such group activities as ski outings or white water trips, or when special equipment is needed or overnight accommodations are required. Such services are generally supplied by private companies or individuals under an arrangement with the administrators of the site. Concessionaires doing business in the National Park System are listed in the booklet "Visitor Accommodations, Facilities and Services," which is available from the Superintendent of Documents, Government Printing Office, Washington, D.C. 20402. Information on accommodations and services at other public lands may be obtained from the facilities. Remember that prices, hours and holidays are subject to change; always verify the figures when you make your reservation. And keep the confirmation slips together, in an easy-to-reach place.

Entrance Fees. Many parks now charge entrance fees, ranging from $1 to $3 per passenger vehicle. The charge usually covers the length of the visitors' continuing stay in the park. Persons who leave the park and then reenter on another day may be charged an additional entry fee. Visitors under age 16 are admitted free.

Recreation Use Fees. These are charges for special sites, special equipment or special services such as parking places, campsites, boat-launching areas or special guides. Rates vary at each park; fees are usually posted.

Special Permit Fees. Extra charges are often made for use of group campsites, back-country camping trips or other special activities. Information about costs is available from the superintendent of the park you intend to visit.

Golden Eagle and Golden Age Passports. Congress has authorized two kinds of entrance passes for use at federally operated recreation sites. The Golden Eagle Passport, issued to anyone under age 62, costs $10 and is good for one calendar year. It admits the holder and all his or her companions traveling in the same vehicle to any federal recreation area.

The passport may be obtained by mail or in person at offices of the National Forest Service. It may also be purchased upon arrival at any park where an entrance fee is charged.

The Golden Age Passport is issued free of charge to citizens or permanent residents of the United States who are 62 years of age or older. It is a lifetime pass to areas where federal entrance fees are charged. The passport admits the holder and everyone accompanying him or her in a private vehicle; or holder, spouse and children if they are all traveling together.

In addition, holders of the Golden Age Passport are entitled to a 50 percent discount on federal recreation use fees, parking, campsites and the like. Fees charged by private concessionaires are not covered, however.

Application for Golden Age Passports must be made in person. They are available at most recreation sites where federal entrance fees are charged, at the headquarters and regional offices of the National Park Service and the National Forest Service, and at most offices of the Bureau of Land Management and the Fish and Wildlife Service.

Applicants are required to show proof of age — a driver's license or passport will do. Persons without proof of age may be asked to sign an affidavit attesting to their age.

State Recreation Lands

Supplementing the wealth of federally administered recreation sites are the public lands maintained by the states. They include parks, forests, monuments, wildlife reserves, wilderness areas and historic sites. Activities range from picnicking or camping to organized gatherings of hobbyists.

Vacations on state facilities are comparatively inexpensive. Accommodations go from spartan to surprisingly luxurious; some states are able to maintain resort inns with elaborate cocktail lounges, air-conditioned suites, 18-hole golf courses, marinas and private airstrips. As with the federally administered areas, plan your vacation ahead and, if possible, select non-peak seasons.

Reservation procedures vary from state to state; some places set minimum and maximum lengths of stay. At some locations lower rates may be available for state residents.

Brochures, maps and any other information you might find necessary will be available from the individual state park commissions. A postcard will usually bring a flood of material.

Seeing America

Each year millions of Americans, eager to see more of their own country, crisscross the continent in cars, recreational vehicles, planes, trains, buses and even on bicycles. Obviously, time, convenience, personal preference and cost are among the factors that determine the choice of transportation. Before you make your selection, you would be well advised to do some comparison shopping — especially if the financial outlay is important to you.

Once you have an approximate estimate of the distance you plan to go, figuring the cost of **driving your own car** should be relatively simple (see Chapter 5). But before you make up your mind, consider alternatives and compare prices.

If you will be covering a lot of territory, a **fly-drive vacation** — taking a plane to each city and renting a car there for side trips — may be a better bet. Airlines, in conjunction with major car-rental companies, frequently offer such combinations at attractive prices, and your travel agent may be able to help you spot a bargain.

On relatively long trips, **buses** are usually the least expensive form of public transportation. If your journey is extensive, you can usually break up the trip, stopping at various cities en route and renting a car for sightseeing, a variation of the fly-drive vacation.

In an attempt to restore **trains** as a popular form of travel, Amtrak is modernizing its long-neglected equipment, stations and roadbeds. Thanks to the track improvements, travel time is being cut. The management is beginning to offer tours in conjunction with hotels, national parks and other attractions adjacent to some stations.

The success of the Eurailpass and the BritRail pass has prompted Amtrak to experiment with a similar program in the United States. For further information, consult your travel

Time Shares

During the severe real estate slump of the mid-1970's, builders of luxury resort condominiums found few purchasers for the expensive accommodations. To save themselves from ruin, the developers came up with an ingenious, multi-owner plan. Instead of selling an apartment, suite or cabana to one person, they offered it to several, each purchasing a specific portion of time when he or she could occupy the premises. The cost per buyer was, of course, far lower than full ownership. The idea made sense to a lot of people: why invest a large sum of money in quarters one occupied only a few weeks of the year?

Time sharing became a boom industry when Resort Condominiums International and Interval International introduced a variation of the original concept: exchange of accommodations. The buyer would not necessarily have to occupy the quarters of which he or she was part owner. Space and time purchased at one resort could be swapped for equivalent accommodations at a member facility in another location. For example, one woman who bought two weeks in a condominium in New Jersey has never occupied those premises. She has traded that time and space for vacations in Aruba, Florida and Cape Cod. The company handles all arrangements. Membership and maintenance fees are charged each year.

Inevitably, a certain number of high-pressure hucksters and fraudulent operators moved into this lucrative field. Horror stories of shares sold in condominiums that never got beyond the planning stage, and of buildings so poorly constructed that they were uninhabitable forced a number of states, including Florida, New York and Ohio, to pass laws regulating time share sales and development. The Federal Trade Commission has also taken action against some promoters. A helpful booklet, *Timeshare Tips,* is available free from the FTC (see directory, page 199).

Although consumers now have some protection against time-sharing scams, caution is still advisable. If you are considering time-share ownership, check with your local Better Business Bureau and with the state attorney general's office. Make certain you have ample information about the promoter's track record and financial stability and know exactly what you are buying. Consult your lawyer if you have unanswered questions.

agent or the Amtrak office nearest you.

Any complaints about accommodations or other aspects of a specific Amtrak trip should be accompanied by as much documentation as possible: the ticket, the conductor's name, his version of the problem, your recounting of the facts and a refund request form if any facility has proven unusable. Complaints should go to: Amtrak Customer Relations, P.O. Box 2709, Washington, D.C., 20013.

Bicycling is the least expensive way to see the United States and foreign countries. Hosteling makes it possible for bikers to be sheltered in plain accommodations — usually group dormitories — with some kind of kitchen privileges and access to bathing facilities. Membership in American Youth Hostels is open to families, senior citizens and juniors (travelers under 18). At a nominal cost it provides a passport to a network of hostels across the country and throughout the world. For details write: American Youth Hostels, National Office, 1332 "I" Street, NW, Washington, DC 20005.

There are 32 councils around the country. The national office will direct you to the one nearest you.

For millions of Americans the best way to travel is to take your house with you by using a **Recreational Vehicle** (RV). "Home is where you park it," say the owners and users of such RV's as campers, trailers, motor homes, motor coaches, vans and minihomes. Sometimes RV drivers will simply pull off the highway into a rest area to spend the night, free of charge. For the most part, however, they reserve space at private and public campgrounds where they can be certain to find such amenities as electrical hook-ups and disposal facilities. To attract vacationers, some of the newer trailer parks offer swimming pools, tennis courts, playgrounds, golf courses and elaborate recreation programs.

If you wish to enjoy an RV open-road vacation, first experiment with a rented vehicle on a relatively short trip. If the experience is appealing, leasing an RV may still be preferable to a long-term financial commitment.

For further information, write to one or more of the following:

- Family Motor Coach Association, 8291 Clough Pike, Cincinnati, Ohio 45244.
- Loners on Wheels, 2940 Lane Drive, Concord, California 94518.
- Motorhome Travelers Association, P.O. Box 6279, Pensacola, Florida 32503.
- National Association of Trailer Owners, Box 1418, 2015 Tuttle Avenue, Sarasota, Florida 33578.

Vacations at Sea

Each year more than a million Americans board **cruise ships** for vacations that range from three- or four-day "trips to nowhere' to months-long voyages around the world. As an escape from routine activities and responsibilities, almost nothing can compete with these floating cities. Your fare, though hardly inexpensive, takes care of just about everything: travel, accommodations, meals, recreation, entertainment. The numerous, diversified activities aboard can fill your every waking moment, or you can choose the passive life and scarcely move from your deck chair.

A reliable travel agent is an invaluable ally in booking your cruise. He or she is likely to know, often from firsthand experience, almost everything you will want to learn about the various ships: the comfort of the cabins, the quality of the food, the efficiency of service, the recreational facilities and entertainment offered.

If you prefer to make your own plans, here are a few tips to keep in mind:

- Remember that ads usually quote minimum prices. The spacious, comfortable cabin you may prefer probably costs more.
- Note the ratio of ship's personnel to passengers. The higher that ratio, the better the service is likely to be.
- If you are traveling alone, find out if there is a single traveler surcharge. This can be quite a significant item. Usually, it is possible to be booked "Guaranteed Share" — in which case the company either finds you a cabin mate or charges you the lower shared-cabin rate for one you occupy alone.
- Make certain that your ship has been inspected for cleanliness and safety. If you have any doubts, request a Vessel Sanitation Report from: Chief Sanitation Officer, U.S. Public Health Service, 1015 North American Way, Miami, Florida 33132.
- To experience the least amount of motion, select a cabin close to the center of the ship, on a lower deck.

If your time is ample, your schedule flexible, and if you are adventurous and self-sufficient, you may be interested in booking passage on a **freighter.** Little provision is made for the entertainment of passengers — the cargo is what's important — but there is rarely a crowd. Meals are taken with the crew, and they can be both hearty and tasty. But when the vessel is in port you're on your own. Casual is one operative word; another is economy. Freighter travel costs much less than a conventional cruise. For this reason — and the fact that the ships visit some exotic places — space on freighters is usually booked far in advance.

For further information write:

- TravLtips Freighter Travel Association, 40-21 Bell Boulevard, Bayside, New York 11361.
- Ford's Freighter Travel Guide, P.O. Box 505, Woodland Hills, California 91365.
- Pearl's Freighter Tips (Pearl Hoffman), 175 Great Neck Road, Suite #306-A, Great Neck, New York 11021.

Vacation Plus Education

The realization that learning is a lifelong process has generated an increasing number of vacation-study opportunities that are offered by colleges, universities and private and non-profit organizations. Those people who might never have dreamed of matriculating for a degree can now look forward to spending the summer on a college campus, enrolled in a program that will permit them to combine their vacation with some type of self-improvement.

CONSUMER ALERT

Safety at the Stadium

Suppose you and your family decide to spend a summer Saturday at a baseball game. The man at bat hits a foul ball into the stands and it strikes your daughter's arm. She is painfully bruised.

Is the management of the stadium legally liable?

Courts have ruled that it depends on the circumstances.

If your seats were in the sections behind the catcher and under the protective wire netting behind home plate, and if the ball passed through an unpatched hole in the netting or screen, then the park management would be at fault and could legitimately be accused of negligence.

However, let's assume that your seats were not in the area protected by the screen but were in an open area, say, behind third base. In that case the spectator is assumed to know and accept the risk and to be responsible for his or her own welfare.

Many of these seminars require no previous academic work; others are designed for university-level participants. Many involve living and studying in a particular location, while others consist of tours to foreign countries. The range is wide — from courses in language, arts and literature to archeology, photography and international business.

Information about continuing education programs is available from the college or university nearest you and in Barron's *Compact Guide to Colleges*, available at your local library.

For information on study programs overseas, write to: Council on International Educational Exchange, 205 East 42nd Street, New York, New York 10017.

Refer also to the travel, education or school sections of newspapers and magazines. Your travel agent may be an additional source of information.

Year-Round Leisure Activities

Running, jogging, swimming, aerobics, calisthenics — staying young by keeping fit has always been a sound practice. Suddenly it has become almost a national obsession. **Health clubs** are springing up throughout the nation and their advertising budgets are often large.

What they offer is the availability of a well-equipped facility for as long a period as you like — enabling you to swim, loll in a steam bath, bake in a sauna and enjoy various forms of exercise. Many establishments are handsomely decorated, with Olympic-size pools, tennis and squash courts, jacuzzis and day and night classes in the many modern dance and exercise techniques. There are frequently impressive banks of stationary cycles and collections of muscle-firming, weight-reducing machines. It is easy to envision yourself becoming lithe and trim soon after you become a member. But take time to investigate before joining such an organization.

Frauds at Health Clubs

The majority of health club proprietors are honest businessmen looking to make a decent profit on their investment. There have, however, been some blatant deceptions in the industry. Most obvious is the establishment of a gorgeous, lavishly-equipped spa whose entrepreneur embarks on a heavy advertising campaign and succeeds in signing up scores of members — whereupon he promptly disappears with their membership fees. The club is still there but no one is running it, and within a very short time the brand-new equipment is carted away by suppliers who were never paid.

A variation of this scheme is the offer of a reduced price membership to people who join *before* the club is ready for use. Actually, the health club exists only in the drawings in the ads and in the salesman's prospectus. Once enough money has been collected, the salesman disappears, along with all the dues.

To guard against the possibility of this kind of swindle, it is essential to:

- Know exactly with whom you are dealing and the company's track record;
- Make inquiries at your local Better Business Bureau;
- Check with your local attorney general's office and/or consumer agency (in many areas they operate from the same desk);
- Find out if the club has branches in the area and if you may use those facilities until your club opens.

Before joining an existing club:

- Make a trial visit at the hour you expect to use the club. Is it badly overcrowded?
- Find out whether you can buy a short-term trial membership whose cost may be applied to a long-term membership. The long-term commitments are usually more economical, but many people fail to keep up with exercise programs once the original burst of enthusiasm subsides. This may prove to be your experience, too.
- Talk to the other members using the club when you visit; ask them about service, cleanliness, upkeep, courtesy.
- Check out the quality and sturdiness of the equipment.
- Ask if there is a place to secure valuables while you are working out.
- Find out whether you will be able to sell your membership or return any unused portion for a refund.
- Inquire whether you can put a "hold" or "freeze" on your membership in case you have to be away on a long business trip or vacation.
- Ask if there is a family plan.
- Ask if there is a group rate if your friends join with you.

Short Educational Courses

On a less serious and intense level than the learning vacations mentioned above are the special-interest seminars currently offered by private and professional organizations, by community colleges and by the continuing education departments of some universities. Movie buffs, for example, gather for marathon cinema weekends, where they view the works of a particular director, writer or star, often with the celebrity joining in the ensuing discussions. The current interest in the cuisines of the world has led to a spate of gourmet cooking and wine tasting seminars offered in kitchens, restaurants and resorts in this country, in Europe and even aboard some cruise ships. You can improve your needlework or your knowledge of opera; learn hypnosis, belly dancing, how to handle a hot air balloon. The courses offer an inexpensive mix of diversion and education in proportions that vary according to the seriousness of the subject and the zeal of the participants.

Such courses generally involve a small group with an instructor who knows the subject well. One need not feel foolish about being a novice. The classes serve as good places to meet people who share similar interests as well as to test one's own enthusiasm for a hobby. The brief taste may tell whether additional time and money would be wisely invested in futher pursuit.

Information on such informal learning programs is usually available in special interest magazines, in newspapers and through related clubs and professional organizations which are listed in the telephone directory. Community colleges and neighborhood YM/YWCA and YM/YWHA branches offer many such courses at modest cost.

Investigate Before You Invest

That is obviously sound advice for anyone entering the financial field. It is equally valid counsel for the individual who is prepared to spend money for vacations and other leisure-time activities. Many consumers waste large sums of hard-earned cash each year because of failure to plan adequately, make price comparisons, read advertisements and contracts carefully, consult reliable travel agents when they could be useful, and seek guidance from Better Business Bureaus and similar organizations when dealing with unfamiliar agencies and promoters.

Vast quantities of information are readily available from public and private sources about travel and other subjects that are discussed in this chapter. You have effective allies to assist you with various kinds of problems. The only thing you need is the determination to be a knowledgeable and careful consumer.

Chapter 12

Selecting Professionals

Americans spend billions of dollars each year for professional services — for help from doctors, dentists, attorneys, accountants and other dispensers of necessary aid, up to and including funeral directors.

While much of this money is well spent, much is not. Far too many of us choose and use professional services with less care than we put into buying a new car or a color television set. Perhaps one reason is that we usually do not call on professionals unless we are in some kind of trouble, and we are rarely careful and cautious judges at such times. Or perhaps it is because the professionals often envelop themselves and their work in a cloak of mystery, jargon and authoritarianism, and we, whether awed, desperate or simply confused, feel incapable of setting standards.

True, there are certain basic protections built into our dealings with most professionals. Virtually all of them come under specific licensing laws and regulations established by the states in which they practice, and all are required to meet certain standards of training and conduct on pain of losing their licenses. But a license to practice a profession is not an automatic guarantee of high competence and ethics. Nor is the penalty of losing it invoked very often. It is up to us, as clients, to protect our own interests by taking an active and constructive part in our dealings with the professionals we hire to work on our behalf.

In this chapter, we will discuss the most important professional services we purchase. We will talk about how to choose a practitioner; how to work effectively with him or her; the rights we have in these dealings, and what to do if things go wrong. We will also examine the institutions with which professionals are affiliated, from hospitals and nursing homes to legal clinics, and will discuss specific ways of dealing with them.

Health Services

The professionals with whom Americans come into most frequent contact are those involved in medical care — a total of more than 5 million people, of whom nearly 2 million deal directly with patients. By this measure, health care is the third largest industry in the United States — and one of the costliest to consumers. In a little over three decades, total annual expenditures for health have risen from $12.7 billion, or $81.86 per capita, in 1950 to $286.6 billion, or $1,225 per capita, in the early 1980's, a figure equal to almost 10 percent of the gross national product, and about 10 percent of the total spent by Americans on all personal needs.

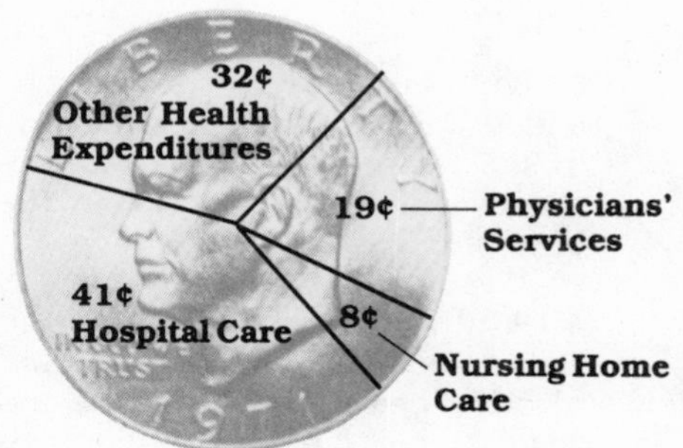

Of each dollar spent on health, 41 cents goes toward hospital care, about 19 cents for physicians' services, 8 cents for nursing home care and 32 cents for all other health expenditures. About 68 percent of the health-care bill is paid by private health insurance and government programs, leaving the average consumer to pick up the remaining 32 percent.

Moreover, the cost of health care is constantly rising, at a rate far outstripping inflation in general. In one recent year the cost of health insurance premiums rose nearly 16 percent — more than any other medical item,

The Physician's Code

Because of the very nature of their profession, physicians have always been expected to live up to the highest principles. Since the time the Oath of Hippocrates was formulated to protect patients and provide a guide for physicians' conduct — around the 5th century B.C. — the Code of Medical Ethics has been steadily evolving.

In its current form, it is stated in the seven Principles of Medical Ethics laid down by the American Medical Association in 1980:

1. A physician shall be dedicated to providing competent medical service with compassion and respect for human dignity.

2. A physician shall deal honestly with patients and colleagues, and strive to expose those physicians deficient in character or competence, or who engage in fraud or deception.

3. A physician shall respect the law and also recognize a responsibility to seek changes in those requirements which are contrary to the best interests of the patient.

4. A physician shall respect the rights of patients, of colleagues and of other health professionals, and shall safeguard patient confidences within the constraints of the law.

5. A physician shall continue to study, apply and advance scientific knowledge, make relevant information available to patients, colleagues and the public, obtain consultation, and use the talents of other health professionals when indicated.

6. A physician shall, in the provision of appropriate patient care, except in emergencies, be free to choose whom to serve, with whom to associate, and the environment in which to provide . . . services.

7. A physician shall recognize a responsibility to participate in activities contributing to an improved community.

These principles are not the only ones that guide physicians. The Judicial Council of the American Medical Association periodically issues formal opinions on a wide range of issues, including records, fees, matters of practice, professional rights and responsibilities, hospital and interprofessional relations, confidentiality of information, physician advertising and on social policy issues such as organ transplants, genetic engineering and terminal illness.

Specifically, the American Medical Association considers it to be unethical for a physician:

- To provide or prescribe unneccessary services.
- To split fees with another physician, clinic or laboratory to which he or she refers a patient.
- To accept any kind of payment from a pharmaceutical company, pharmacist or other medical supplier for referring a patient for goods or services.
- To send a patient to any clinic, nursing home or other health facility in which he or she holds a financial interest without disclosing that fact first.

In connection with financial matters, the AMA is quite clear: "Under no circumstances may the physician place his own financial interest above the welfare of his patients. The prime objective of the medical profession is to render service to humanity; reward or financial gain is a subordinate consideration."

including a 13.3 percent rise in rates for hospital rooms. In such a situation it is urgent for consumers to make their health dollars go as far as possible.

The Physician — Training and Credentials. There are more than half a million physicians in the United States. Of these about 485,000 are the familiar doctors of medicine, or M.D.'s; the remaining 19,000-plus are doctors of osteopathy, or D.O.'s. To obtain either an M.D. or a D.O. degree, a candidate must complete college-level premedical courses, graduate from a four-year course at an accredited medical or osteopathic school and then pass a state or national board examination to become licensed to practice. In addition, most states require physicians to complete at least one year of graduate on-the-job training as hospital interns or residents.

Both M.D.'s and D.O.'s utilize all scientifically accepted methods of diagnosis and treatment, including drugs and surgery, and in most states both are examined by the same licensing board. In addition to practicing the orthodox medicine of M.D.'s, D.O.'s are also trained in methods of relieving pain and correcting disorders by manipulating the musculoskeletal system — the bones, joints, muscles, ligaments and tendons that make up most of the body's mass. According to the osteopathic view, these parts not only reflect signs of illness but, if malfunctioning, may aggravate the problem. All 50 states and the District of Columbia permit osteopaths an unlimited practice of medicine and surgery.

Once a physician has received a degree and a license, he or she is legally entitled to practice in any field of medicine. If, for example, he wants to practice surgery, nothing prevents him from calling himself a surgeon. But the vast majority of physicians do not claim their titles so offhandedly. They voluntarily complete anywhere from two to seven or more years of postgraduate on-the-job training in their chosen field, after which they take certifying examinations administered by such national specialty boards as the American Board of Internal Medicine, the American Board of Family Practice or the American Board of Surgery. There are now 22 such specialty boards in the United States (see box, Medical Specialists, page 294). A physician who passes the board examination in his or her specialty becomes "board certified" and is known as a "diplomate" of that board. One who has completed the requisite training but who has not yet passed the examination is referred to as "board eligible."

Most physicians also belong to one or more professional societies — the American Academy of Family Physicians (AAFP), for example, or the American College of Surgeons (ACS). The criteria for membership in these groups vary and membership is not a guarantee of a physician's skill. But initials such as AAFP or ACS after a physician's name are some assurance he or she is trained in the field. If the doctor has met additional criteria, he or she may be elected a "fellow" of the society and permitted to use that designation — for example, FACS (Fellow of the American College of Surgeons). Some societies require their members to complete a minimum number of hours of ongoing training annually to keep up with new medical developments, and nearly half the states also have continuing-education requirements for license renewal.

Choosing a Primary-care Physician. The first step in looking out for your health and that of other family members is choosing the right primary-care physician. He or she is the one that you and your family will depend on for your routine medical treatment, and also the one who will refer you to a specialist or admit you to a hospital, should that ever become necessary.

Given the central role the doctor plays, it is particularly important that you look for and find one *before* you or other members of your family get sick. The physician who has a chance to examine you, explore your medical history and get to know you while you are healthy is the one who will be best able to treat you when something goes wrong.

According to Lewis Miller, a long-time observer of medicine and author of *The Life You Save*, one of the biggest mistakes a person can make in selecting a doctor is to go directly to a specialist to fit the ailment the patient *thinks* he or she has, rather than to pick a primary-care physician to handle most medical problems and refer the patient to a specialist when necessary.

Attempting to diagnose your own ailments and selecting a different doctor for each one is a dangerous business. Specialists tend to see

Medical Specialists: Who Does What

There are now some 57 specialties and subspecialties of medical practice, grouped into 23 major areas of certification for doctors of medicine and 18 for doctors of osteopathy. Specialists a patient is most likely to encounter are:

Internist. A practitioner of internal medicine, who may diagnose and treat a broad range of adult diseases, or specialize in a particular aspect of the field. The cardiologist, for example, treats the cardiovascular system, including the heart and blood vessels. The gastroenterologist focuses on the stomach, intestines, pancreas and other parts of the digestive system. The endocrinologist deals with the hormone-producing organs and treats metabolic disorders. The rheumatologist is concerned with diseases of the joints, muscles and ligaments. The nephrologist treats problems of the kidneys and the urinary system; the hematologist handles blood disorders. Other internists treat infectious or respiratory diseases.

Family practitioner. Like the old general practitioner, but with more training, the F.P. treats all members of a family.

Pediatrician. A specialist in child development from birth through adolescence and in the treatment of childhood diseases. The subspecialties of pediatrics include neonatal-perinatal medicine, the care of newborn and premature babies and their mothers; pediatric cardiology, the treatment of children with cardiovascular problems; pediatric nephrology, the care of children with kidney disorders; and pediatric hematology and oncology, the treatment of children with blood diseases or tumors.

Obstetrician. The physician who cares for mothers and their infants during pregnancy and delivery, as well as immediately after. Obstetricians are often gynecologists also, and treat disorders of the female genital and reproductive system.

Allergist. A specialist who deals with persons suffering from allergies — negative bodily reactions to such otherwise harmless agents as pollen, fur or foods. Some are also immunologists, whose concern is the ability of the body's immune system to deal with truly threatening agents — viruses and bacteria, for example.

Dermatologist. A specialist in the diagnosis and treatment of disorders of the skin.

General surgeon. The surgeon performs operations designed to treat a variety of diseases and injuries. Subspecialties include colon and rectal surgery; neurosurgery; plastic surgery; thoracic surgery. The otolaryngologist performs diagnostic and surgical procedures on the ears, nose and throat. The urologist treats disorders of the female urinary tract and the male urinary and genital tract.

Ophthalmologist. The specialist who deals with the medical and surgical treatment of eye and vision disorders.

Orthopedist. A specialist in disorders of the skeletal system, which includes the bones, joints, muscles and tendons, who uses medical, physical and surgical treatment methods. The physiatrist practices a related skill. This specialist in physical medicine and rehabilitation uses various forms of therapy, which includes exercise, to help restore function to disabled patients.

Other specialists may confine their work to adolescent medicine, which deals with patients too old for pediatric care and too young for adult medicine; geriatrics, which focuses on problems of the elderly; oncology, which involves the diagnosis and treatment of malignant tumors (cancers); and radiology and nuclear medicine, which use X rays and radioactive substances for both the diagnosis and treatment of disease.

In addition, there are the neurologist, who deals with disorders of the nervous system; and the psychiatrist, who treats patients with mental, emotional and behavioral problems.

problems in terms of their own specialties and, lacking any information from a primary-care physician, may misdiagnose ailments. Moreover, a specialist acting independently may prescribe a therapy or drug that conflicts with the treatment another doctor has prescribed for a different ailment. The two medications may either cancel one another out or create even more serious difficulties than those they were designed to solve.

Until about half a century ago, some two-thirds of all doctors in the United States were G.P.'s, or general practitioners, and it was they who acted as primary-care physicians. Today, only about 15 percent bear this title. Certain specialists, however, now serve their patients in much the same way as G.P.'s. The family practitioner, or F.P., for example, is a relatively new specialist whose training goes well beyond that of the G.P. A general practitioner usually has only a relatively brief period of formal training beyond medical school. A family practitioner, on the other hand, must have three years of residency training after receiving an M.D. and then pass qualifying examinations. The F.P. is familiar with a broad range of fields, with emphasis on internal medicine, pediatrics, obstetrics and gynecology, surgery and psychiatry, and is thus equipped to deal with most problems of diagnosis and treatment for all members of a family, young or old, or to refer them to other specialists, if needed. An F.P. is a particularly useful primary-care physician for families with small children who want one doctor to treat most problems.

Other specialists may play the role of primary-care physicians during particular periods in an individual's life. A pediatrician cares for children from infancy until they are well into their teens. An obstetrician-gynecologist is frequently the major medical adviser for a woman during her child-bearing years. The specialist in internal medicine, or internist, is concerned with a broad range of diseases affecting adults' internal organ systems — the cardiovascular system, the digestive system, the lungs, kidneys and endocrine glands — and is therefore particularly well suited to serve as primary-care physician for patients who are middle-aged or older and who may suffer from such chronic illnesses as arthritis, ulcers, diabetes, hypertension and heart disease.

But not all internists perform this function. Some further specialize, limiting their practices to such specific areas of internal medicine as cardiology or gastroenterology.

Looking Over Candidates. Many people depend too heavily on the advice of friends or neighbors when picking a primary-care physician. While this method may provide some good tips, it should not be your only criterion: you may simply wind up with nothing more than highly personal opinions, pro or con. Nor is it advisable to choose a physician on the basis of personality alone. As Lewis Miller points out, no matter how pleasant it is to have a doctor with an engaging manner, professional competence is far more important for the patient.

A better approach is to use a combination of several informed professional sources. If you are about to move to a new community, ask your present doctor for the names of candidates; he or she may know some personally or by reputation. If not, the physician can look up likely ones in a medical directory. If you are already living in an area and are looking for a new doctor, check with people in the health-care field or ask your company's medical department, if it has one. Ask a dentist, pharmacist or nurse. If you are already dealing with a specialist — a dermatologist or an ophthalmologist, for example — ask him or her for recommendations. Or call the local county medical society for the names of two or three primary-care physicians. Many medical societies simply give out names on a rotating basis from a list of available members in good standing, but some publish physician directories and a few, like the Montgomery County Medical Society in Maryland, have organized helpful patient referral services that actually try to match physicians to the patients' individual needs.

Also call the administrator's office of your local hospital (or the most prestigious hospital in your area, if there are several) and ask for the names of physicians who have staff privileges there. Affiliation with a good hospital, especially one connected with a medical school, indicates that a doctor has high standards of practice, acceptable to the institution's credentials committee, and that he or she is working in the mainstream of contemporary medicine and keeping up with the latest developments. In addition, you will be able to go to that hospital for treatment, if necessary. Except in an emergency, you cannot enter a hospital unless your doctor has privileges there.

You can also check a doctor's standing and credentials by looking in such sources as the *American Medical Directory* or the *Directory of Medical Specialties*, which should be available in the reference section of your local library. The latter book is especially useful. Organized by state and town as well as alphabetically, it includes brief medical biographies of a quarter-million physicians — roughly half of all those in the United States — who have met the certification requirements of their respective specialty boards. Finally, in some areas consumer groups have published their own directories of local physicians. Not all of them contain the name of every available physician, however, since some doctors may not have agreed to be listed.

In using any directory, be sure to check its date of publication; the information may be outdated if the directory has not recently been revised.

When checking credentials, find out if the doctor maintains a private practice or belongs to a group.

At the same time you are investigating a physician's credentials, check to see whether he or she is in individual practice or is a member of a medical group. If you choose one who practices alone, you should be able to build up a long-term, personal relationship with him or her. On the other hand, you may want to choose one who is a member of a group practice — an association of several doctors who usually practice in a variety of fields. Some group practices offer a patient the same opportunity to establish a personal relationship with one physician as do individual practices, but this is not always the case. Still, the group practice guarantees that you will always be able to see a doctor when necessary and also enables the physicians who belong to it to consult with one another on difficult medical problems, thus giving the patient the benefit of several independent opinions rather than only one.

Large group practices often include a number of different kinds of specialists — internists, gynecologists, pediatricians — who can take care of a broad range of family needs. Since the group may have its own clinics, laboratories, X ray and other diagnostic services, you can also be saved trips to outside specialists or to a hospital for tests. But you may not be able to see the same doctor on every visit and may find yourself being shunted from one physician in the group to another for consultations (see box, Health Maintenance Organizations, page 300).

The First Office Visit. Once you have zeroed in on a primary-care physician who seems to meet your needs, make an appointment. You may want no more than a preliminary get-acquainted visit, and the doctor may be willing to see you on this basis — with the understanding that you will pay the regular office fee. On the other hand, you may be required to undergo a physical examination and give a detailed medical history — for which you will obviously have to pay. Before you go, and whichever arrangement you have made, draw up a list of the questions you want answered, including any that your previous research has not revealed.

When you arrive, look around the waiting room: adequate space, comfortable chairs, current magazines and polite office personnel may not equate with medical skills, but they suggest that the doctor is at least thoughtful enough to care about his patients' feelings while they wait. Also check whether the doctor has supplied a printed information sheet for patients, giving the answers to some of the most common questions about fees, billing procedures and payments, policies on Medicare and Medicaid, and preparation of insurance and legal forms.

When you meet the doctor face to face (note the time you had to wait), size him or her up as a person as well as a technician. Would you feel comfortable bringing your problems to this physician over a long period of time? Are you given full attention or does the doctor seem rushed or preoccupied? Does he or she seem interested in you as a person — or are you just another problem to process for a fee? Is he or she open in answering questions about his or her approach to medicine, hospi-

CONSUMER ALERT

How Often Should You Have a Medical Checkup?

For many years, it was the policy of the American Medical Association to recommend that all adults — no matter how fit and healthy they felt — have a complete physical examination every year. Recently, however, as a result of long and extensive study — and in line with recommendations previously put forward by many other medical organizations and authorities — the AMA has changed its view. According to an article in the March 25, 1983 issue of "The Journal of the American Medical Association," "Healthy young adults, for whom morbidity and mortality rates are generally low, except for traumatic injuries, should have medical evaluations at intervals of five years until they are 40 years old." Thereafter, the article recommends "periodic evaluation at intervals of one to three years, depending on the individual's occupation, present health status, medical history and other personal characteristics."

In the case of children and young people from two to 20 years old, the recommendations call for a regular examination every one or two years. And infants up to a year old should be examined two to four weeks after birth and then every two months or so.

Obviously, these recommendations do not apply to people with recognized health problems or those known to be predisposed — through family history, for example, or the kind of work they do — to the development of particular kinds of serious illnesses.

tal affiliations, ability to treat you and other family members for a range of needs? Is the doctor frank in discussing the details of fees — for office visits, physical examinations, routine tests? Are charges adjusted to meet your financial circumstances? Are you permitted to stretch out payments for major bills?

Very few physicians make house calls today, both because they are largely unnecessary and wasteful of a doctor's time and because a physician can generally give patients better treatment at the office, where medical records, equipment and staff are available. Nevertheless, it is worth asking if, in an emergency, the doctor will come to your home. What matters can be handled in telephone consultations, and what charge is made for them? Who covers for the doctor when he or she is not available? How does the physician feel about referring patients to specialists, or having them seek second opinions?

If you are satisfied with the doctor's answers and the way you are treated, you have found yourself a primary-care physician. But if you do not feel comfortable with the doctor's answers or manner, say good-bye and go on to the next physician on your list.

Dealing With Your Doctor. Once you have chosen a physician, make the most of your partnership by being an intelligent patient. Doctors estimate that patients could cut their bills for office visits virtually in half if they simply used common sense, plus a good do-it-yourself family medical book to help them recognize which symptoms require professional consultation and which do not, and when to administer home treatment for minor problems. If you are uncertain about whether to see your doctor, call and describe the problem; he or she can tell you if you need an appointment and what to do if you do not.

When you *do* bring a problem to your doctor, either in an office visit or on the telephone, make sure you tell the truth, the whole truth and nothing but the truth. Don't play guessing games, and don't hold anything back; even the most skilled doctor is not a mind reader. Describe any symptom in detail: its exact location, when it started, whether it comes and goes. Don't fail to mention any drugs you are taking or are allergic to, and don't be shy about revealing emotional crises, drinking problems or other factors that could be contributing to your illness. Few doctors are easily shocked by personal disclosures, and the doctor-patient relationship requires the physician to keep in confidence anything you reveal.

After a diagnosis is made, ask the doctor to explain it in simple, everyday terms: what you are required to do, how long before you are likely to see results, and any risks or precautions that may be involved. If necessary, ask the physician to put the information in writing or take notes yourself, and double check your understanding by repeating in your own words what you believe has been said. If a drug has been prescribed, be absolutely sure you know how much to take, at what intervals and for how long; what you should do if you miss a dosage; what other drugs, foods, beverages or activities you should avoid while on the medication; what side effects you can normally expect; and what reactions you should immediately report. An increasing number of doctors and pharmacists hand out printed instructions along with prescriptions, and the American Medical Association makes available to physicians a series of Patient Medication Instruction sheets on 40 of the most commonly used prescription drugs. To save money on expensive drugs, ask your doctor to prescribe your medication by the generic rather than the brand name, if he believes that one is just as good as the other (see Chapter 7 and "The Pharmacist," below).

Second Opinions. One of the most important rights a patient has in dealing with a doctor is to seek a second opinion from another physician when an important decision must be made. Not only is the practice sound, it is one that every conscientious physician will endorse. If your doctor treats a request for a second opinion as an insult or threat, you would be wise to look for someone else to care for your health.

There are a number of situations in which a second opinion is desirable and should be sought — and will be recommended by any ethical and competent physician. Among them are: if you are not getting relief from your symptoms after prolonged treatment; if you feel your doctor is not doing all that might be done; if the physician proposes what seems like overly complex and expensive therapy; if he or she diagnoses a potentially disabling or fatal disease; if nonemergency or elective surgery is recommended.

This last situation is probably the one that arises most frequently. A life-threatening emergency — acute appendicitis, severe injuries in an automobile accident — may not leave time for a second opinion before surgery, though it is reassuring if several doctors on a hospital staff agree. But the need for nonemergency surgery is often less clear-cut and, as medical knowledge advances, opinions on the subject are likely to change. Until the early 1960's, for example, tonsillectomies were routinely performed on children. Then it was discovered that the tonsils play a role in the body's immune response and should be saved if at all possible. Similarly, such elective operations as back and knee surgery, hysterectomy, and gall bladder and prostate gland removal are now coming under closer scrutiny.

Critics charge that as many as one out of five of the more than 20 million operations performed annually in the United States are unnecessary. But to label all surgeons as "knife-happy" is unfair. Often the need for surgery cannot be stated in absolute terms. Nevertheless, any time an operation is proposed, a second opinion is virtually a must. Many medical insurance plans will pay for it; some even insist on it as a preconditon to paying for an operation. Studies have shown that second opinions reduce the number of operations performed by 15, 30 and even 60 percent, depending on the type of surgery involved.

Before getting a second opinion, discuss the matter in detail with your primary-care physician: the benefits and risks of the proposed operation; alternative methods of treatment; estimated postoperative recovery period and what it involves; costs and how they can be paid. Ask him or her to recommend the best qualified specialist. Your doctor can help you set up an appointment, give the specialist the background information necessary to assure that he or she will not repeat procedures that have already been performed and arrange to get a report quickly, so that you can review the findings together.

Before getting a second opinon, be sure to discuss any proposed surgery with your primary-care physician.

Try to make sure that the second doctor's opinion will be truly independent — not simply that of a friend who will back up your physician and agree to do the operation. You can remove any suspicions you may have that the second doctor is acting exclusively out of a financial incentive by making it clear to him or her that you are only seeking an opinion and do not intend that the consultant perform any surgery that may be necessary. As added insurance, you can ask to be directed to a consultant whose hospital affiliation is not the same as your doctor's.

Prior to seeing the specialist, check his or her credentials, including board certification, in the *Directory of Medical Specialists*. The U.S. Department of Health and Human Services (HHS) has a list of second-opinion programs in various areas of the country. Specialists affiliated with these programs have agreed to serve as second-opinion consultants but not to perform surgery. To obtain a copy of the list, check with the local office of HHS (see directory, page 329).

Disagreements With Doctors. Patients become dissatisfied with their physicians for a variety of reasons: failure to spend enough time on problems; bills that seem out of proportion to services; treatments that do not alleviate or cure. Sometimes the doctor makes an error in diagnosis, or prescribes the wrong medication and the patient experiences unpleasant side effects.

Medicine is not an exact science and doctors, being human, do make mistakes. Moreover, they are often under unnecessary pressure from patients who, armed with their health insurance plans, rush to see physicians for every minor or imagined ill. In addition, many physicians and hospitals have too many patients to handle, and the effort to deal with all of them can sometimes lead to unsatisfactory results.

If you have a grievance against a doctor, there are several courses you can pursue. The first step, of course, is to talk to him or her. If the conversation does not clear things up and you still feel you have been badly used, complain to your local medical society or — if the problem is associated with your treatment during a hospital stay — to the hospital. Both undoubtedly have grievance committees which investigate and arbitrate complaints.

If you feel that the matter is serious enough to call for license suspension or revocation, complain to the state licensing board. Boards are generally reluctant to take such grave steps — after all, the physician's livelihood is at stake. Still, they cannot afford to ignore flagrant cases of, incompetence, negligence and alcohol or drug abuse by doctors and are increasingly cracking down on them. On the other hand, patients who want to bring charges before state boards need the help of a lawyer, preferably one who has considerable knowledge of both medical practice and negligence law. Ask your own attorney for suggestions, or contact the referral service of your local bar association for the names of lawyers experienced in this area.

You will also need a lawyer's help if you believe you have the basis of a malpractice suit. This is an enormously serious business, not to be undertaken lightly. In recent years the number of malpractice suits against doctors and hospitals has soared — as has the size of the awards in successful suits. Inevitably, the cost of malpractice insurance, particularly in such sensitive areas as neurosurgery and anesthesiology, has risen alarmingly. Individual practitioners are now paying upwards of $50,000 a year to protect themselves. Such costs are, of course, reflected in the bills sent to patients.

If a surgeon amputates the wrong leg or leaves a surgical sponge in a patient's abdomen, the malpractice is evident. It is equally blatant if a pediatrician gives a child a penicillin injection in full knowledge that the youngster is allergic, and the child dies.

Few cases are this clear-cut. Malpractice has been defined as "any deviation from the accepted standards of care in the delivery of health services by a doctor which results in injury to the patient." Broad as this definition sounds, it has clear limitations. "Pain and suffering" are not sufficient basis for a malpractice suit. To have this kind of case, the plaintiff must be able to prove that he or she suffered a concrete, definable injury, and that the injury was due to the doctor's negligence in commission or omission of treatment. If a doctor took all the standard precautions after an operation and a patient still developed a damaging or fatal infection, a court would be unlikely to sustain a malpractice suit, and would most likely find that the injury was due to chance. Finally, proof of malpractice requires the injury and the doctor's negligence to be linked by what the law calls "proximate cause." The injury must result from the specific act of negligence.

Packaged Health Care: The HMO Option

Over a period of several months, Judy S., a California secretary who is suffering from a malignant tumor, kept appointments with 27 doctors, spent five days in a hospital, received daily radiation treatments for six weeks, had ten sessions with a psychotherapist and worked with her physiotherapist three times a week for four months.

For all of this medical attention Judy paid exactly one bill: $10 for the rental of a hospital TV set.

Judy and her family belong to the Kaiser Foundation Health Plan, the nation's largest health maintenance organization (HMO), which currently has more than 4 million members.

For a fixed monthly fee, which is paid by her husband's employer, she and other members of the family can visit Kaiser physicians as often as necessary. They can be tested and treated for anything from a sprained ankle to a heart attack, can stay without charge in a Kaiser hospital and, if necessary, they can be referred to outside specialists — with Kaiser picking up the tab.

HMO's, which were pioneered on the West Coast half a century ago, have experienced explosive growth in the last decade or so. With encouragement from the federal government, they have increased in number from some 40 in 1971 to more than 269 today, and in membership to more than 12 million people.

Annual charges — which in a recent year ranged from $1,200 to $2,400 for an average family — are usually paid largely or wholly by employers under group benefit programs. There are also plans which permit eligible individuals to enroll with their own funds or with help from Medicare or Medicaid.

Because health maintenance organizations place emphasis upon preventive medicine and outpatient treatment whenever possible, their members are hospitalized less than half as much as are persons who make use of the more traditional fee-for-service medical care. Moreover, total costs are from 10 to 40 percent less than those associated with conventional health insurance plans.

Studies have shown that the quality of care members receive is at least as good as, and often superior to, that obtained in other programs.

The typical health maintenance organization is a prepaid group practice with its own clinical facilities and its own salaried physicians and staff. However, the same concept can occur in a somewhat different form. In some instances, for example, individual doctors have banded together to offer their own prepaid group plans. In these so-called Individual Practice Associations (IPA's), the physicians treat patients in their private offices, and contract with hospitals to provide services at fixed rates.

If there is a federally-approved HMO in your area and the company you work for has 25 or more employees and offers health insurance benefits, your employer is required to give you the option of joining the HMO.

Before you decide to become a member, check out the organization as you would any health-care service. Look into the extent of its clinic and hospital facilities; its physicians' specialties and credentials; its hours of emergency service; your rights in the event that you need medical services when you are out of town; the benefits for which you may have to pay — dental care, physical or mental therapy, prescription drugs — and compare overall costs and benefits with those available through conventional insurance plans.

You may request additional information about health maintenance organizations, as well as a list of HMO's in your vicinity, from the Group Health Association of America, 624 Ninth Street, NW, Washington, D.C. 20001.

Nor can a doctor easily be sued for malpractice or negligence in most cases where he or she renders emergency treatment, since most states have "Good Samaritan" laws which exempt physicians from all but criminal liability when they have rendered emergency help in good faith. A doctor who stops, for example, at the scene of an automobile accident is expected to render care only within the limits of the circumstances and his or her particular skills, and to make sure that another physician takes over when the first leaves.

Taking Charge of Your Health. Distressed by high costs and shortcomings in the medical system, a growing number of people in recent years have begun to take increasing responsibility for their own health. Some physicians disparage this self-care movement, but many welcome it as a help both to themselves and to patients. The purpose of the self-care movement is to give people enough accurate, up-to-date information to enable them to weigh alternatives and make rational decisions regarding the best course to follow in dealing with various medical problems.

There are many sources of such information: consumer health guides, medical encyclopedias, prescription and nonprescription drug guides and books of advice by doctors themselves. Local consumer agencies and such health organizations as the American Cancer Society and the American Heart Association make free pamphlets available on request. Many hospitals sponsor lectures or classes for people suffering from such chronic conditions as arthritis or high blood pressure. Hundreds of health agencies across the country offer free, 3- to 5-minute taped telephone messages on birth control, sexual problems, depression, heart disease, hearing loss and hundreds of other topics. Local numbers of the largest network, Tel-Med, can be obtained from area telephone directories or from Tel-Med, Inc., 952 South Mt. Vernon Avenue, P.O. Box 1500, Colton, California 92324. Information and aid for people suffering from a variety of ailments can also be obtained from the self-help groups listed in *Help: A Working Guide to Self-Help Groups*, by Alan Gartner and Frank Riessman.

Among a growing number of local sources for general medical information are such consumer bureaus as the nonprofit Center for Medical Consumers and Health Care Information in New York City, which maintains a free, walk-in library of books, periodicals and medical directories, clipping files and a phone-in service that will answer questions and play any one of some 200 telephone tape recordings on request. The most common complaint of clients, says Director Arthur Levin, is that they "don't get answers from their doctors," and so they come to the center to find out for themselves. The center publishes its own monthly newsletter, "Health Facts," which covers current findings on everything from hay fever and skin diseases to a patient's right to obtain his or her medical records. For information on subscriptions, published reports and other services write to the center at 237 Thompson Street, New York, New York 10012.

Monitoring the health-care scene from the nation's capital is the Public Citizen Health Research Group, founded more than a decade ago by consumer activist Ralph Nader and run by a staff of physicians, attorneys and researchers. The group publishes a host of books, pamphlets and hearing transcripts on drugs, food, psychotherapy, dental care, surgery, physicians' fees, medical devices, X rays, environmental health and other subjects. For a publications list, write to Public Citizen Health Research Group, Suite 708, 2000 P Street, NW, Washington, D.C. 20036.

Dental Care

Of all health problems, dental disease is the most prevalent. Tooth decay affects an estimated 95 percent of Americans. Well over 50 million teeth are extracted each year, and more than half of all adults have no teeth left by the time they are 65. Yet only about half the population visits a dentist as often as once a year, and half of these go only in an emergency. The rest stay away because they feel they are going to lose their teeth anyway, because of the cost or because of simple laziness and/or anxiety over anticipated pain.

The fact is, however, that modern dentistry, combined with sound preventive measures, can curtail most of the diseases that cause people to lose their teeth. Moreover, high-speed, water-cooled drills and advanced techniques of pain control — including everything from anesthesia through soft background music to hypnosis — assure that "no one should be uncomfortable in the dentist's chair," as the American Dental Association puts it. Nor is lack of money always a legitimate excuse. Dental costs have risen less than any other health-care costs and are increasingly covered by various benefit plans.

The Dentist's Training and Credentials. To become a dentist, a candidate must complete at least two years of predental college courses followed by four years of training at one of 60 accredited dental schools in the United States. Graduates receive a degree either as a doctor of dental surgery (D.D.S.) or of medical dentistry (D.M.D.) — the title depends entirely on the school's preference in terminology — and must pass state or regional board examinations, including both written and performance tests, to obtain a license to practice in the field.

The great majority of dentists are general practitioners in private practice (although group practice is becoming more common). General practitioners are capable of tending to most patients' needs and they are permitted by law to administer anesthesia, perform oral surgery, take X rays and prescribe drugs. An increasing number, however, now spend two or more years in specialized training in order to pass the rigid examination that qualifies them as board certified specialists (see box, page 303).

Choosing a Dentist. Although friends and acquaintances can be helpful in recommending a dentist, it is wise to have some professional advice as well. Your local dental society can give you the names of two or three of its members. It is, however, unlikely to give you an evaluation of their skills. If there is a school of dentistry in your area, or a nearby hospital with an accredited dental service, you may be able to get the names of faculty or staff members who are highly regarded practitioners; if they are unable to take you on as a patient, they may be able to recommend other top-notch dentists in the community.

Among more immediate sources are your family physician and a well-regarded dental specialist — an orthodontist, endodontist or periodontist, for example. Often, the specialist is the most astute judge: he or she actually sees, and has to deal with, the work of general practitioners when they refer patients to the specialist. If you want to check on the age, training and other credentials of a particular dentist, look in the current *American Dental Directory*, which is compiled by the American Dental Association and available in many public libraries.

On your first visit to a dentist, check carefully to see how thorough a professional he or she is. Are the waiting and treatment rooms orderly, uncrowded, pleasant? Do you have to wait more than 15 or 20 minutes beyond your appointment time without any explanation for the delay? Before your first treatment, does the dentist take down your complete medical and dental history to find out if you have any conditions that may require special precautions? Are you asked if you have allergies to any drugs, for example, if you are presently taking any medications, if you have ever been treated for problems such as diabetes, hemophilia, high blood pressure or heart disease?

Does the dentist make a complete examination of your mouth, using a probe to look under the gums around each tooth, checking the condition of the tongue, roof of the mouth and throat and examining your bite? Are you asked if you have dental records, including recent X rays, from your previous dentist? If your records are not available and your new dentist feels a full-mouth set of X rays is warranted before starting any treatment, does he or she use modern, properly shielded equipment and high-speed film with short exposures, and is a protective lead apron placed over you to minimize your exposure to radiation? Does the dentist recognize your right to your X rays and other dental records, and will you be given access to them should the need arise?

If a major problem is discovered, does the dentist clearly describe the proposed treatment, in terms of advantages, disadvantages and alternatives? (Under the doctrine of informed consent, discussed in detail on page 314, a patient who has not been fairly advised about the risks of treatment has not legally consented to it.)

Any dentist should be willing to discuss fees and payment plans in advance of treatment, and to give you a written, itemized estimate in advance of major dental work, as well as an itemized bill afterward. The dentist should have arrangements for emergency

Dental Specialists

Among the specialists who deal with various kinds of dental problems are:

Orthodontists. Specialize in straightening teeth and bringing teeth and jaws into alignment or occlusion to improve the health, function and appearance of a patient's mouth. Although some 15 to 20 percent of their patients are between the ages of 20 and 60, orthodontists work primarily with children.

Endodontists. Treat problems of the inner tooth pulp — extending from the tooth crown down through the tips of the roots into the jaw, and containing nerves, arteries, veins and lymph vessels. The most common is an infection, or dental abcess, resulting from a deep-seated cavity or fractured tooth. Treatment may require two or three visits and involves removing the pulp, cleaning and enlarging the canals that contain it so they can be filled. Root canal work is almost always preferable to extraction because it saves an infected but otherwise sound tooth.

Oral and maxillofacial surgeons. Specialize in extracting teeth and in reshaping mouth and jaw deformities, such as cleft lip and palate or mismatched jaws, which may occur either naturally or as the result of an accident.

Periodontists. Treat diseases of the gums — the tissues supporting and surrounding the teeth. Unchecked, such diseases — generally caused by bacterial plaque, the invisible film that forms on teeth — can result in destruction of bone and loss of teeth.

Prosthodontists. Concern themselves with the prosthetic devices used as substitutes for natural teeth: crowns, bridges and full or partial dentures of various kinds. They help determine whether teeth can be saved in order to support a partial denture, make impressions for proper fit, specify the making of dental devices by laboratory technicians and adjust the finished product to the patients' mouths.

Pedodontists. Specialize in the dental care of children from birth through adolescence. Also care for older patients with physical, mental or emotional problems.

Oral pathologists. Specialize in the diagnosis of tumors and other serious diseases of the mouth or teeth.

Dental public health specialists. Work in and with communities to encourage and organize efforts to prevent or control dental diseases and promote general dental health.

treatment, if the need for it should arise. If for some reason he or she cannot handle an emergency, is there a backup arrangement with another dentist or with an emergency referral service?

Any tooth should be removed only as a last resort, and a good dentist will do everything possible to save it. If your dentist *does* advise an extraction, you are entitled to a second opinion, and he or she should encourage you to seek it, sending your X rays and the results of your most recent examination to a consulting specialist.

A good dentist believes in preventive dentistry. He or she advises the patient on a dental routine to be followed between visits, discusses the importance of good diet and the avoidance of sugary foods that hasten decay, and sends periodic reminders of dates for checkups and cleanings.

Cutting Dental Costs. In recent years, dentistry has been increasingly included in health maintenance organizations (see box, page 300), and there has been a rise in the number of group practices and "walk-in" dental clinics at health centers, department stores and shopping malls. These clinics are sometimes disparaged by dentists in private practice who worry that they may divert people from ongoing personal care, including prevention. But the group frequently offers entirely adequate and quicker service, as well as lower fees that are often payable by credit card. You can make your own assessment of any such service in your area by applying the guidelines suggested above.

Another low cost source of dental care for consumers who do not have dental insurance is the hospital-based dental clinic or the student clinic at a dental school. Dental clinics which are run by hospitals are staffed by recent dental graduates and may charge one-third less than private practitioners. Dental school clinics which are manned by students working under close supervision during the third and fourth years of dental school may be even less expensive. But each visit usually takes a long time, since the students are working out their procedures on you. Those who cannot afford even these costs can call their local dental society or health department for information on programs for which they may qualify.

Problems With Dentists. If you are unhappy with your dentist, or feel you have been unfairly treated, be sure to let him or her know that a problem exists. Often grievances turn out to be merely matters of poor communication. But it can happen that even skilled treatment does not achieve the expected results; once a conscientious dentist realizes this, he or she will do the job over, try an alternate treatment or call in a consulting specialist.

In cases where a dispute cannot be readily resolved, ask your state dental society for an impartial review. You will first be instructed to put the details of the complaint in writing. Then, you and your dentist may be asked to meet with a member of the society's peer review or patient relations committee to see if your differences cannot be reconciled informally. If the problem is particularly difficult, it may be reviewed by the full committee, whose members may give you a dental examination and ask the dentist to submit the treatment records. The great majority of cases brought to such committees are successfully resolved, though the process is strictly voluntary: a dental society has no legal power to force either patient or dentist to accept its findings.

If you suspect that your dentist has violated professional dental practice laws enacted by your state, take the matter to your state board of dentistry or to your state attorney general's office. Violations include acts involving moral turpitude, allowing a dental hygienist to do work reserved for dentists, fee splitting and making misrepresentations or false promises to patients.

The Pharmacist

The pharmacist can play a more important role in health care than most of us realize. We use the services of our doctors and dentists only occasionally, but it is estimated that each week more than 200 million of us patronize the nation's 50,000-odd pharmacies, looking for everything from toothpastes and cold remedies to a fresh supply of tranquilizers or drugs for high blood pressure. Moreover, many of the drugs we use are complex and potentially dangerous and can interact badly with one another. Good pharmacists monitor the drugs their clients use and act as advisers to both patients and doctors. By keeping accurate records of all clients' medications, the pharmacist can spot possible adverse, even life-threatening reactions or interactions among drugs. In addition, the druggist can clarify instructions for using a medication, cut through the fog of advertising claims made for competing over-the-counter products, and save money for customers by substituting, with the doctor's permission, an equally effective generic prescription drug for the trade-name version of the medication.

Although pharmacists are not permitted to diagnose or prescribe for ailments, they can be a considerable help to the physician as well, calling attention, for example, to the fact that a drug the doctor has prescribed conflicts with another the patient is taking on the advice of a specialist, or to the fact that the patient has brought in several prescriptions for the same potent tranquilizer and thus may be involved in drug abuse.

To become a pharmacist, a candidate must attend one of the 72 accredited schools of pharmacy in the United States. There he or she studies not only pharmacology and chemistry but anatomy, pathology, immunology and the principles of disease, and also serves an internship in a hospital or community pharmacy. Most schools of pharmacy have five-year programs that lead to a bachelor of science in pharmacy, or B.S. Pharmacy, although a growing number offer six-year courses toward a doctor of pharmacy, or

Pharm. D. Before practicing, a graduate must pass an examination administered by a state pharmacy board, and in many states must take continuing education courses to remain licensed. State pharmacy boards monitor pharmacists in practice by sending out inspectors to scrutinize records, drugs and ways of working, keeping a special eye out for the handling of dangerous drugs under federal controlled substances laws.

Picking a Pharmacy. Given the important functions a pharmacist can perform, it is far wiser to find one good pharmacy and stick to it than to buy drugs — whether prescription or over-the-counter — in several different places. In looking for a pharmacy to patronize, ask the druggist whether it has and uses an effective system of "patient profiles" or "family medication histories." Such a system — maintained by a growing number of pharmacies, and required by law in an increasing number of states — is described in detail in the box on page 306.

Once you have checked out a pharmacy's record-keeping, determine if its hours fit your needs; if there is a registered pharmacist on duty at all times when the store is open; if one is available for emergencies when the store is closed; if the store will deliver a prescription to your home or office if you can't pick it up. Check prices for typical over-the-counter and prescription drugs against those of other pharmacies in the area (some states require that prices for commonly prescribed drugs be posted in each store), and inquire about methods of payment, including health insurance, charge accounts or credit cards.

Traditionally, pharmacies have established prices for drugs by adding a percentage markup to the wholesale price. Recently, the concept of charging a flat dispensing fee has been introduced. Many pharmacists are adopting this method because it more fairly reflects the cost of their time and skills than does the older method and because it removes any incentive to sell high-priced medicines instead of their less expensive equivalents. Remember, however, that the lower the price of a given drug, the higher the dispensing fee may *appear* to be: a $3 fee for dispensing a bottle of pills that costs $3 can seem considerably more shocking than that same fee added to the price of a $20 bottle.

In the final analysis, a pharmacy is only as good as the pharmacist. Is he or she willing to answer questions, make sure you understand what a given medicine is supposed to accomplish, and what you should do to get the desired results? Does the druggist suggest economies? Like any other health professional, a pharmacist should put the patient first.

Professional Care for the Eyes

Three separate and distinct kinds of professionals provide eye care. *Ophthalmologists* are physicians who put in three years of a post-graduate hospital residency devoted exclusively to diagnosing and treating disorders of the eye. In addition to performing eye surgery and prescribing drugs, they may also test eyes for vision, prescribe corrective lenses and sell glasses and contact lenses. Although many people reserve their dealings with ophthalmologists to problem situations, some prefer to entrust these medical specialists with their routine eye care as well.

Optometrists are nonmedical specialists in visual problems. Many hold the degree of doctor of optometry, or O.D., earned through a minimum of two years of college and four years of training at a college of optometry. They are licensed to examine eyes, to prescribe corrective lenses, to dispense eyeglasses and contact lenses and to suggest eye exercises to correct defects. Although they may not perform surgery or prescribe drugs, they *are* trained to detect eye diseases, for which they refer their clients to ophthalmologists or other physicians.

Opticians, who are generally state-licensed after four years of high school and two years of apprenticeship or training in an opticians' school, fill prescriptions written by ophthalmologists and optometrists and fit and adjust eyewear. They may not examine eyes or prescribe lenses.

Before the Federal Trade Commission stepped in with an "eyeglasses rule" in 1978, a professional who examined the eyes and prescribed corrective lenses was permitted to require clients to purchase glasses from him or her. Now, however, the prescriber must give clients their prescriptions at no extra charge, so that they can buy their glasses anywhere they want.

Contact lenses present a somewhat more complex problem. Before you can wear them,

Keeping Tabs on Drugs

To avoid medication errors and abuses, pharmacists should keep accurate records of the medicines they dispense. Some pharmacies rely on an ordinary card file, while others use sophisticated computers that enter and retrieve data and even type up prescription labels automatically. However such patient profiles are maintained, the American Pharmaceutical Association and the Academy of Pharmacy Practice strongly recommend that they include:

- Your name, address and telephone number.
- Your date of birth — needed to enable the pharmacist to make sure a specific drug or dosage is appropriate, particularly in the case of children and the elderly.
- Any allergies, special reactions or other adverse effects you may have experienced after taking any drug, as well as any medicines that have proved ineffective.
- Any health problems or diseases — diabetes, ulcers, high blood pressure — that preclude the use of certain drugs.
- Nonprescription medications that you or other family members use regularly, including any painkillers, antacids, vitamins, minerals or antihistamines, all of which can interact adversely with certain prescription drugs.
- The date and number of each prescription filled for you, including the name of the drug, dosage form and strength, quantity dispensed, directions for use, price charged, the name and address of the prescribing doctor and the initials of the pharmacist who filled the order.

To set up your profile properly, your pharmacist should first interview you and have you fill out a standard form. He or she should also record other pertinent information about you: special diets, drinking habits, problems with vision or hearing, the names of all doctors and dentists who may prescribe medications for you. When a prescription is filled or refilled, the pharmacist should check your record for potential dangers. If there is an inconsistency in a prescription, a suspect dosage or unclear notations, the pharmacist should call the doctor to clear things up.

you must have your eyes examined either by an ophthalmologist or an optometrist, not only to determine your prescription, but to discover whether you are a good candidate for contacts. Thereafter, you must have a fitting, to measure the curvature of your eyes and determine the kind of lens that is best for you. In all states, this fitting can be performed either by an ophthalmologist or an optometrist and in some states it can be carried out by an optician. The individual who fitted your lenses is *not* required to give you a copy of the lens-fitting prescription, though he or she may voluntarily do so. So if you want to shop around for contact lenses after you have your prescription, you may have to pay for a second lens-fitting examination.

Because it may take several tries before you find the right kind of lenses for your eyes, it is a good idea to use a practitioner who has a broad selection of different kinds of contacts. Make sure you know what the price includes. Are the eye examination, the lenses, fittings, adjustments, a lens-care kit and follow-up visits priced individually or sold as part of an overall package? It may take several visits and several adjustments to get a proper fit, so look for a reasonably priced package that includes unlimited visits. Also find out the seller's refund policy. Not everyone is able to adapt to contacts, and if you find later that you cannot tolerate them, you don't want to lose your entire investment. Remember, too, that it is easy to lose or damage a contact lens. In case you need a replacement, find out in advance how much you will be charged and how long you will have to wait.

Hearing Specialists

If you experience difficulty hearing, go first to your family physician or to a medical specialist in diseases of the ear: an otolaryngologist (ear and throat); an otorhinolaryngologist (ear, nose and throat); or an otologist (ear only). Such specialists can diagnose the cause, type and extent of your hearing loss, and determine how best to treat it — by medication, surgery and/or the use of a hearing aid.

In the event a hearing aid is required, the doctor may conduct the detailed hearing tests or refer you to an audiologist, a technician trained in evaluating and rehabilitating people with hearing problems. The professional organization to which most audiologists belong is the American Speech-Language-Hearing Association (ASLHA), which issues certificates of clinical competence to those of its members who meet specific standards.

The National Hearing Aid Society, the trade association of hearing aid dealers, which offers the designation "Certified Hearing Aid Audiologist," has as members about 2,000 of the nation's approximately 7,000 licensed hearing aid dealers. Most states now require all such dealers to show proof of competence before licensing, and have established penalties for those found to be incompetent or dishonest and provided methods for consumers to complain to licensing boards.

Under a 1977 rule of the Food and Drug Administration, which regulates such medical devices as hearing aids, a dealer in this field may not make a sale before obtaining a written statement from the client's physician that the doctor has evaluated the patient's hearing within the past six months and considers him or her a candidate for a hearing aid. Although a customer who is 18 or older may sign a written waiver of this requirement, the dealer must first warn the purchaser that it is not in the best interests of his or her health. The dealer must also advise any customer to consult a licensed physician, preferably an ear specialist, in the event that he or she detects any ear deformity, dizziness, pain, fluid drainage, rapid onset of hearing loss, significant accumulation of wax or a foreign body in the ear.

Under the rule, a dealer must give to and review with the customer an instructional brochure before any sale is completed. The brochure must not only stress the importance of medical evaluation but must provide information on how the hearing aid works and how to care for it. Warnings must be given that a hearing aid will not restore normal hearing, will not give full benefit if it is used infrequently and may have to be supplemented by special training in listening and lip reading.

Many different kinds of hearing aids are available, no single one of which is suitable for all types of hearing loss. Look for a dealer who will let you rent an aid for one or two months on a trial or purchase-option basis to make certain that it will actually improve your hearing and that you will be comfortable wearing it regularly at home and at work. You will have to purchase an ear mold to fit the aid to the precise shape of your ear and will have to pay a rental fee for the aid itself, but the expenditure can help considerably in finding out what kind of hearing aid is best for you. Make sure you shop not only for a high-quality device, but for a complete set of services: mechanical and electronic adjustments, counseling in the use of the aid, free maintenance through the guarantee period and repairs when they are needed afterward. You may need several visits to have the aid or the ear mold properly adjusted, so even though FTC regulations cover hearing aids purchased from door-to-door salesmen or through the mail (see Chapter 6), you may prefer to deal with a firm whose office is easily accessible to you.

In many areas, speech and hearing centers associated with hospitals or universities can provide help in ear examinations, hearing tests, counseling and selection of a proper hearing aid. Detailed information is given in a booklet, "Facts About Hearing and Hearing Aids," published by the National Bureau of Standards and the FDA, and available for $3.50 from the U.S. Government Printing Office, Washington, D.C. 20402.

The National Hearing Aid Society (NHAS), 20361 Middlebelt, Livonia, Michigan 48152, will answer questions and send the NHAS member directory and a Better Business Bureau booklet, "Facts About Hearing Aids."

The NHAS does not give medical advice, recommend specific products or quote prices, but it will investigate and attempt to resolve customer complaints. Complaints on sales practices can also be directed to the nearest FDA district office listed in the telephone directory; complaints on either sales or service can be made to your local state attorney general's office, consumer protection agency or state licensing board.

Foot Doctors

Physicians, including general practitioners and orthopedists, often treat foot problems, but the major providers of such care in the United States, accounting for an estimated two-thirds of patient visits, are podiatrists, specialists who concern themselves with the diagnosis, treatment and prevention of abnormal conditions of the human foot. Older practitioners, who may be known as chiropodists, hold the degree of doctor of surgical chiropody (D.S.C.) or doctor of podiatry (D.P.), but the standard of modern practice is a doctorate in podiatric medicine (D.P.M.). It takes at least three years of preprofessional college courses and four years of specialized training in a college of podiatric medicine to earn this degree. Most graduates also serve a postdoctoral residency of one or more years.

Today, podiatry has only about 9,000 practitioners in all the United States, but this number is expected to increase sharply in the years ahead as the number of elderly in the population increases and as more and more people participate in jogging and other strenuous exercises. Like other specialists, podiatrists tend to cluster in heavily populated urban areas where there is the greatest demand for their services. Most private and government health insurance plans provide coverage for at least some of their services, and in most states they are permitted to prescribe certain drugs and anesthetics, to perform foot surgery and to serve on hospital medical staffs. The American Podiatry Association recognizes two specialties in the field — podiatric orthopedics and podiatric surgery — and confers board certification on practitioners with demonstrated experience who have passed written and oral exams. Although some physicians still regard podiatrists primarily as trimmers of corns and calluses and prescribers of arch supports, many are more skilled in treating chronic foot disorders than their M.D. counterparts.

Chiropractors

Among the more controversial of health practitioners are the estimated 22,000 chiropractors, or doctors of chiropractic (D.C.'s). Chiropractic — from the Greek "done by hand" — holds that many disorders are caused or aggravated by misalignments of the vertebrae and other parts of the body's structure, and the consequent interference with the proper functioning of the nerves. Chiropractors do not prescribe drugs or practice surgery but rely instead on examination and, when deemed necessary, X rays and laboratory tests to diagnose the misalignments, which they subsequently treat by manipulations. In addition, many chiropractors recommend vitamins and special diets, and utilize physiotherapy, exercise programs, diathermy and ultrasound.

Chiropractors must be licensed to practice in all 50 states. To obtain a license, a candidate must have at least two years of prescribed college courses, four years of resident instruction at a chiropractic college, a D.C. degree, and must pass a state board examination. Thereafter, for relicensing, he or she must take continuing educational courses. Chiropractors' fees are widely covered under both government and private health insurance plans.

Mental Health Counselors

People with personal or emotional problems have a bewildering array of practitioners to choose from. But in this important area, it is not always easy to make a choice because even the minimum protection that licensing laws provide is not consistently available. Almost anyone can claim to be a counselor or psychotherapist because such terms are not clearly defined by law.

To find the right kind of help in this maze, probably the best bet is to talk first with your family physician, a local family services agency or a community mental health center (CMHC). All of these should be able to make appropriate referrals, keeping in mind both the nature of your problems and your ability to pay. The following are among the specialists to whom you may be referred:

Psychiatrists. These are physicians, licensed to practice medicine, who have completed at least three years of postgraduate training in psychiatry. The most reputable practitioners have also been certified by the American Board of Psychiatry and Neurology. As physicians, psychiatrists are the *only* mental health counselors legally permitted to prescribe drugs. Information on psychiatrists, including their credentials and their individual approaches to therapy, can be obtained from your local medical society, the department of psychiatry at a nearby hospital or medical school, the biographical directory of the American Psychiatric Association or the practitioners themselves.

Psychoanalysts. These practitioners are generally psychiatrists, although some have nonmedical backgrounds. They are trained in the use of the specific treatment techniques associated with psychoanalysis, and must themselves have undergone this therapy.

Psychologists. These men and women must hold a doctoral degree in their field, have two years of supervised clinical experience and pass an examination in order to practice in most states. Clinical psychologists work in the areas of personality assessment and the prevention or treatment of emotional and mental disorders. Others specialize in counseling, educational/school psychology or industrial/organizational psychology, and all obtain their certification from the American Board of Professional Psychology. Psychologists' fees are usually somewhat lower than those of psychiatrists and, like them, are covered under many insurance plans.

Certified clinic mental health counselors. Must have a master's degree, two years of counseling experience and have passed an examination administered by the National Association of Clinic Mental Health Counselors.

Clinical or psychiatric social workers. About half the states require licensing of these practitioners. They may also be certified by the Academy of Certified Social Workers (ACSW) after completing a master's or doctor's degree from a school of social work, two years of supervised postgraduate experience and the ACSW examination.

Marital and family counselors. They are licensed in only a handful of states. An indication of standards, however, is certification by the American Association of Marital and Family Counselors, which requires an appropriate master's or doctor's degree plus two years of supervised experience in the field.

Psychiatric-mental health nurses. These are registered nurses who have received advanced training at the master's degree level or above and are qualified to conduct individual, family and group therapy.

Health-care Institutions

As was mentioned at the beginning of this chapter, hospital care takes the biggest bite — 41 cents — out of every dollar Americans spend on health. Part of this cost reflects inflation and part the advances in medical technology. Still another part reflects the expanded functions and capacities of the modern hospital. We go to hospitals for diagnostic tests as well as surgery; for checkups as well as emergency treatment; for classes in natural childbirth as well as for the delivery of our babies. In some hospitals, families live in with their relative-patients while they are recovering from major surgery; in some, mothers live in with their children when the youngsters need hospital care. In one way or another, virtually every one of us uses a hospital at some time in our life. It is, therefore, especially important that we know something about the hospitals we deal with — both how to judge them and what rights we have as patients.

Similarly, we need to know about the other health-care institutions and facilities we may need — nursing homes, for example, and home health-care services. As our population ages, these are becoming increasingly necessary and important to many of us.

Hospitals. The hospital care available to you depends on two factors: where you live and who your doctor is. If you live in a rural area or a small town, there may be only one hospital in your immediate vicinity, and it may have only limited facilities — adequate for simple procedures, but not for more complex and difficult problems. In such circumstances, you would do well to find out if your physician has connections with a larger and better equipped hospital farther away — or, if not, connections with other doctors who do have privileges there.

If you live in a larger town or city and have chosen your primary-care physician wisely, he or she may have privileges at several nearby hospitals. In this case, you can — and should — do some advance comparison shopping on quality, services and rates so that, should the time come when you or a family member needs hospital treatment, you will be able to make an intelligent choice.

The first thing to ask is whether the hospital has been approved by the Joint Commission on Accreditation of Hospitals (JCAH), a nonprofit organization supported by the American College of Physicians, the American College of Surgeons, the American Hospital Association, the American Medical Association and the American Dental Association. All hospitals must be state-licensed in order to operate and JCAH accreditation is strictly voluntary. Nevertheless, it is a sign that the institution lives up to a fairly rigorous set of standards that is followed by two-thirds to three-quarters of the 7,000 general hospitals in the United States that have 25 beds or more. Such institutions usually display a JCAH certificate in the lobby or in some other prominent place.

JCAH survey teams visit nearly 3,000 hospitals yearly to see how well they live up to standards. JCAH accredited hospitals are required to have competent medical and nursing staffs and to review their performance periodically. They must also have programs that ensure safety, sanitation and infection control, and they are checked for their facilities, equipment, emergency and outpatient services and special care units, as well as their administration, medical records, hospital policies and regard for patients' rights. A hospital that is satisfactory in these respects is accredited for a two-year period; one that is not may have its accreditation revoked or may be put on a year's probation during which necessary changes must be made. All JCAH hospitals participate in the Medicare and Medicaid programs; those that do not have JCAH accreditation must pass specific tests set by the federal government if they are to participate. If you depend on either of these programs for your medical care, it is important to look into this matter.

The Joint Commission on Accreditation of Hospitals approves only institutions that meet high standards.

A general community hospital is adequate for most medical problems. Even a small one is likely to offer service in internal medicine, surgery, obstetrics and pediatrics; a larger one may cover such subspecialties as cardiology, gastroenterology and ophthalmology. Community hospitals are usually less expensive than large university or teaching hospitals, which must finance expensive equipment and research programs and serve affiliated medical schools. A routine appendectomy at a community hospital, for example, may cost considerably less than the same operation in a large teaching hospital, even if it is performed by the same surgeon. Although many teaching hospitals encourage the use of their facilities for such routine services, patients would do well to think twice — and check their hospital insurance coverage carefully — before making a decision on where to go for such procedures, especially since health agencies are increasingly urging the teaching hospitals to divert patients requiring routine care to less costly community hospitals and to concentrate, instead, on the sophisticated procedures that represent their special strengths.

For serious illness or major, specialized surgery, however, a patient is usually better off in a top-flight university or teaching hospital, where specialized skills and equipment are readily available, or in a specialty hospital or clinic devoted solely to the diagnosis and treatment of the particular problem involved. Such institutions generally have a high percentage of board-certified specialists and registered nurses on staff and a sizable support group of medical technologists to back them up. Every month they see hundreds of patients with similar problems, which gives them ample chance to sharpen their skills. Moreover, they are usually familiar with advances in their field. In surgery, particularly, quantity tends to breed quality — as the director of the prestigious Johns Hopkins Hospital in Baltimore puts it: "The more you do, the better you are" (see "Surgery," below).

If you are a veteran of the armed services, you may seek treatment at one of the Veterans Administration's nationwide network of hospitals, as well as at VA outpatient clinics, alcohol and drug treatment centers and nursing homes. First priority is given to veterans with illnesses or injuries incurred or aggravated in the course of their military service, and to those with service-connected disabilities who need treatment for unrelated ailments. Other veterans may be treated when professional help and beds are available, if they are financially unable to get the necessary care elsewhere. (In recent years some 70 percent of VA medical care has gone to veterans who do not have service-connected disabilities but who are 65 or older, have little or no

A Patient's Bill of Rights

"We do not check our human and legal rights at the hospital door," says George J. Annas, Chief of the Health Law Section at Boston University's School of Public Health. The words are worth remembering, particularly if it becomes necessary to enter a hospital. Member institutions of the American Hospital Association should subscribe to the "Patient's Bill of Rights" and should have a copy of that document prominently displayed.

The patient has the right:

1. to considerate and respectful care.

2. to obtain from his physician complete current information concerning his diagnosis, treatment and prognosis in terms the patient can be reasonably expected to understand. When it is not medically advisable to give such information to the patient, the information should be made available to an appropriate person in his behalf. He has the right to know, by name, the physician responsible for coordinating his care.

3. to receive from his physician information necessary to give informed consent prior to the start of any procedure and/or treatment. Except in emergencies, such information for informed consent should include but not necessarily be limited to the specific procedure and/or treatment, the medically significant risks involved and the probable duration of incapacitation. Where medically significant alternatives for care or treatment exist, or when the patient requests information concerning medical alternatives, the patient has the right to such information. The patient also has the right to know the name of the person responsible for the procedures and/or the treatment.

4. to refuse treatment to the extent permitted by law, and to be informed of the medical consequences of his action.

5. to every consideration of his privacy concerning his own medical care program. Case discussion, consultation, examination and treatment are confidential and should be conducted discreetly. Those not directly involved in his care must have the permission of the patient to be present.

6. to expect that all communications and records relating to his care will be treated as confidential.

7. to expect that within its capacity a hospital must make reasonable response to the request of a patient for service. The hospital must provide evaluation, service and/or referral as indicated by the urgency of the case. When medically permissible, a patient may be transferred to another facility only after he has received complete information and explanation concerning the needs for and alternatives to such a transfer. The institution to which the patient is to be transferred must first have accepted the patient for transfer.

8. to obtain information as to any relationship of his hospital to other health care and educational institutions insofar as his care is concerned. The patient has the right to obtain information as to the existence of any professional relationships among individuals, by name, who are treating him.

9. to be advised if the hospital proposes to engage in or perform human experimentation affecting his care or treatment. The patient has the right to refuse to participate in such research projects.

10. to expect reasonable continuity of care. He has the right to know in advance what appointment times and which physicians are available, and where. The patient has the right to expect that the hospital will provide a mechanism whereby he is informed by his physician or a delegate of the physician of the patient's continuing health-care requirements following discharge.

11. to examine and receive an explanation of his bill regardless of the source of payment.

12. to know what hospital rules and regulations apply to his conduct as a patient.

health insurance or cannot otherwise pay for the medical care they need.)

The children and wives (or husbands) of veterans who have been totally disabled or have died as a result of service-connected disabilities may also receive medical care, in hospital or out and generally at non-VA facilities, under a special VA program for civilians. For eligibility and details on all VA programs, call or write the nearest Veterans Administration Hospital or local VA office.

Finally, if you have no health insurance or for some other reason cannot afford to pay for hospital care, inquire whether there is a "Hill-Burton hospital" in the area. Under the Hill-Burton program of the U. S. Department of Health and Human Services (HHS), hospitals that have used federal funds for construction or modernization must provide a reasonable volume of free or low-cost services to needy patients in their region. The program covers only hospital costs, not private physicians' fees, and a hospital that has provided a given amount of free care during the year is not required to give any more. For more information and eligibility requirements, contact the nearest regional office of HHS (see directory, page 329).

A Hospital Checklist. In addition to checking the certification and accreditation of a hospital, and the range and quality of its services, there are several questions you should ask. Many of them can be answered by reading the hospital's annual report or others of its publications that describe its facilities, staff and services. Additional information can be obtained from the hospital administrator's office or its office of public information or community relations. Some hospitals will even arrange a tour of the facilities on request.

Find out if the medical staff consists mostly of primary-care physicians or if specialists are available around the clock. If the hospital is small and has only limited services and equipment, check whether it has affiliations or agreements with larger hospitals in the area to which you could be quickly transferred should the need arise.

Inquire how the hospital's credentials committee works and how it examines the competence of physicians before granting staff privileges. A good hospital will also have peer-review committees that periodically examine the work of staff physicians to see that they are competent and up-to-date, as well as a tissue-review committee that checks the analysis of tissues taken from patients during surgery to determine whether or not the diagnosis justified the surgery.

Check out the emergency room, its staff, facilities and hours. Some smaller hospitals have no emergency service; some close their emergency rooms after 10 or 11 P.M. or have only a minimum staff on hand and an experienced physician on call rather than on duty. Know ahead of time which hospital is best equipped to deal with children's illnesses, severe burns, automobile injuries and heart attacks.

To expedite matters in the event of an emergency, find out from the hospital you would be going to whether you can sign consent-for-treatment forms in advance. Many hospitals like to have such forms on file, especially if a child has to be brought to the emergency room when the parents are not available. Make sure you put down on the form the name of the physician you want the hospital to call, your health insurance coverage and policy number. In addition, fill out the sections that ask for pertinent medical information: blood type, allergies, past adverse drug reactions and any such conditions as diabetes or congenital defects that might affect treatment. It is a good idea to have this information on file at the hospital both for adult family members and children.

While checking out a hospital, find out about its prices for different kinds of rooms — private, semiprivate and ward — what latitude of choice you have, and whether the hospital will permit you to stay overnight with a sick child or other relative who may need you. Make sure that the hospital will accept whatever form of private or government health insurance you have.

Ask if the staff includes a patient representative, ombudsman or coordinator who can help you if questions or problems should arise. An increasing number of hospitals employ such professionals, whose job is to make the hospital less intimidating, to improve communications between staff and patients, to answer questions about hospital rules and procedures, to relay complaints about the food or other nonmedical aspects of hospital care, to explain charges on hospital bills and

CONSUMER ALERT

Drop-in Doctors

Enterprising physicians have recently discovered that the more convenient and affordable their services are, the more patients they will have, and they have therefore been establishing "same-day surgery" centers, "walk-in" medical clinics and house-call services for consumers in metropolitan areas.

The New York City area, for example, contains a score of small, privately owned medical treatment centers located in storefronts or shopping malls under such names as "Med-Stop," "Doctors Emergency Officenter" or "Walk-In Medical Treatment Office." Licensed nurses and physicians are on hand to take care of a wide range of complaints, from earaches to broken arms, and many patients say that they find the services quicker, less expensive and more pleasant than those available in a hospital emergency room. Minimum charge for a visit generally ranges from about \$20 to \$35, to which are added the costs of special treatments or diagnostic tests. The typical fee for examining a sore throat, for example, is \$25, with an additional \$10 for taking a culture; a sprained ankle might come to \$65 — \$25 for examination, \$35 for X rays and \$5 for an elastic bandage. Many centers accept major credit cards or evidence of membership in an insurance plan such as Blue Cross. Some doctors contend that such "supermarket medicine" is no substitute for ongoing care by a personal physician. Clinic spokesmen, on the other hand, point out that an estimated 25 percent of Americans do not have regular doctors and therefore *need* these services. Moreover, they insist they do not attempt to do more than they can, and that they refer patients with chronic or serious problems to the appropriate specialists.

For those who cannot or do not want to visit doctors in their offices, there are a growing number of services in metropolitan areas that are reviving the lost image of the friendly healer standing on the patient's doorstep with his little black bag. Listed in the "Physicians" section of the Yellow Pages under names like "House Calls" or "Doctors on Call," these services draw on pools of 20 to 100 or more physicians willing to make house calls at any hour of the day or night. A telephone call to a central number will summon an appropriate and available practitioner. Charges range from about \$40 to \$50 on weekdays to \$70 or more on weekends or during the wee hours of the morning. Many of the participating doctors, like those at walk-in medical clinics, are young physicians willing to practice their craft at almost any place and hour until they can become established with practices of their own.

help get any errors corrected. Some critics have charged that hospitals take on ombudsmen only for public relations reasons, and that they have no real authority to intervene on a patient's behalf. Try to find out ahead of time what the ombudsman at the hospital you are considering can and cannot do.

Finally, inquire if the hospital has a Patient's Bill of Rights, and read a copy to see specifically what it provides. This bill was adopted by the American Hospital Association in 1973 (see box, page 311), but different hospitals and state agencies have elaborated on the original to suit their own preferences. In essence, a good patient's bill should grant you the right to considerate and respectful care, to refuse treatment or change your mind about it, to privacy, to reasonable response to your requests for service, to obtain information about your condition, to be advised if you are to participate in any medical experimentation and to examine and receive an explanation of your bill. Some states also grant a patient the right to appoint his or her advocate, usually a relative or friend, who can make decisions on the patient's behalf. In such cases the bill of rights applies to the advocate, too.

You also have other basic rights, whether they are spelled out or not:

• To request that a person of your own sex be present while you are being examined.
• To refuse any visitor you don't want to see.
• To be transferred to another room if the behavior of someone in a semiprivate room or ward disturbs you.
• To leave the hospital against medical advice if you feel you are not getting your money's worth.

Informed Consent. The most important single right of any patient, in or out of a hospital, is the right to be informed about his or her condition and to determine what can and cannot be done under existing circumstances — a concept known as the "doctrine of informed consent." Specific legal requirements in connection with informed consent vary from state to state. In essence, however, the doctrine says that before treatment a physician must explain to the patient, in understandable language, his or her condition; the proposed treatment and any alternatives to it — including nontreatment; the benefits expected and the probability of success. Thereafter, the patient must give the physician "competent, voluntary and understanding" consent, generally in writing, if the case involves some risk. Only then can a course of therapy — whether surgical or medical, generally accepted or still in the investigative stage — be undertaken. In the case of a minor, the parent must give consent. But in every other case — unless the patient is mentally incompetent, or under the influence of a drug that impairs understanding, or unconscious and in need of emergency treatment — only the patient can give consent for treatment. Moreover, even after he or she gives consent, the patient can have a change of mind and revoke it.

Although the doctrine of informed consent has legal force, there is no comparable pressure on a doctor to give full information to a patient who is seriously ill. In this delicate situation, some physicians tend to fudge the issue or evade it, on the ground that it might upset the patient so much that he or she would refuse treatment and thereby increase the risk. And indeed, there are patients who, out of fear of the "gory details," prefer not to know what the doctor has to say.

On the other hand, as the American Medical Association points out, a presidential commission recently found that physicians who withhold full information from their patients are in fact practicing bad medicine. Studies show that patients are more likely to follow instructions and thus to heal faster when they are fully informed. And those who do not want to hear bad news will manage to block it from consciousness.

Diagnostic Tests. Patients who enter a hospital for surgery or other serious procedures are generally put through a battery of routine diagnostic tests, including chest X ray, electrocardiogram, urinalysis, blood chemistry and blood count. The doctor may not have any reason to believe the tests are necessary, but in the face of burgeoning malpractice claims, many physicians and hospitals practice so-called defensive medicine, not only for the sake of the patient, but to protect themselves in the event that they are ever sued.

Health authorities and health insurers have recently begun to crack down on this kind of indiscriminate testing, branding it not only unnecessary and expensive, but also potentially dangerous, and increasingly physicians are being required to specify that a test is actually needed before it is done.

Needless X rays have come under particular fire. Radiation exposure has been implicated in a wide range of problems, including genetic damage, cancer and heart disease, and it can be particularly harmful to women and their unborn children. According to the Bureau of Radiological Health of the Food and Drug Administration, 30 percent of all X rays are unnecessary, and others involve more radiation than is needed to yield a clear picture. At its annual meeting in 1982, the American College of Radiology recommended that routine chest X rays be discontinued for newly admitted hospital patients, pregnant women and those undergoing ordinary preemployment physical exams, and estimated that if these guidelines were adopted, the number of X rays taken in the United States each year would be cut by a third.

To minimize the risks of radiation exposure, never agree to an X ray until you have ascertained from the physician that it is truly necessary; always ask for X rays to be taken with low-dosage equipment or by a radiologist trained to protect patients from radiation hazards; avoid needless repetition of X rays

Nurses: Hands That Heal

Doctors are ultimately responsible for the diagnosis and treatment of disease. But of all health-care professionals, it is the nurses who have the most day-to-day contact with patients sick enough to be hospitalized or permanently confined to their homes. It is the nurse who monitors a patient's condition and progress, administers prescribed medicines and therapy, changes dressings and makes sure that the patient is comfortable and properly fed. Not least of all, a good nurse provides information, companionship, emotional support — the human touch that is often as important as physical treatment in helping a person get well.

Basically, there are three kinds of nursing personnel: professional or "registered" nurses, practical nurses and nurses' aides. To become a registered nurse, or R.N., an individual must be a high school graduate and must thereafter go on for more advanced training, at a two- or three-year hospital school of nursing, a two-year community or junior college or a four- or five-year college or university. A graduate of any of these programs, which include on-the-job hospital training in addition to classroom and laboratory courses, must pass an examination in order to be licensed, or registered, in the state in which he or she intends to work.

Most R.N.'s serve as general-duty nurses in hospitals and are paid by the hospitals for their work. (Some, however, prefer to be private-duty nurses, either in a hospital or at a patient's home; these are paid directly by their patients.) Others specialize as operating-room nurses, maternity nurses or psychiatric nurses, while still others take additional training in order to become nurse-midwives, anesthetists or public-health nurses. Included in this last group are visiting nurses, who care for patients just discharged from hospitals, instruct new mothers in baby care and teach people with chronic illnesses how to become as self-sufficient as possible.

Others serve as nurse practitioners and occupational health nurses, working in private clinics, doctors' offices or company health departments and giving physical examinations to patients, advising them on health problems and diagnosing and treating minor ailments — thus freeing physicians to devote their time to patients with more complex problems.

Practical nurses also work in hospitals and other health agencies, as well as nursing homes and private homes, providing care under the direction of registered nurses and physicians. They are usually high school graduates and must have completed an additonal nine to 18 months of classroom and firsthand experience in a practical nursing program. Thereafter, they take state examinations and, if they pass, are qualified as licensed practical nurses (L.P.N.'s) or, in California and Texas, licensed vocational nurses (L.V.N.'s). Practical nurses help patients with bathing, feeding and other routine tasks and may also perform more professional functions, such as taking blood pressures, administering drugs and helping with rehabilitative exercise.

Nurses' aides help out in hospitals and nursing homes, or as home health aides in patients' homes. They answer patients' calls, feed, bathe and walk them around, make their beds, keep their rooms in order and perhaps write a needed letter or read aloud from a book — thus freeing nurses to concentrate on problems requiring greater skills. Nurses' aides are often volunteers who have been given some instruction by the Red Cross. Many, however, are regular, paid employees and may be referred to as hospital attendants, ward helpers or, in the case of men, orderlies. Young people may choose to work as nurses' aides as a method of deciding whether or not to continue in the health field by going to nursing school.

Support for the Dying

Until recently, terminally ill patients usually spent their last months in the depressing and costly isolation of nursing homes or hospitals. Today, however, a growing number of hospice programs around the country help such patients live their remaining time in comfort and in cheerful and friendly surroundings. They are given medication to control pain; when they are pain-free, they are encouraged to engage in any activities they feel able to.

Hospice programs function both in patients' homes and in special institutional settings, providing patients and their families with the services of a backup team that includes not only physicians and nurses but, in many cases, physical therapists, pharmacists, psychiatrists, social workers, clergymen, financial advisers and trained volunteers. Patients who live at home are regularly visited by the health professionals on the team; these professionals are on call around the clock for emergency consultation. Volunteer team members take patients on outings or simply sit with them, thus freeing relatives to take naps, go on errands or just to have a little time to themselves.

Patients who are unable to stay at home or who need more intensive medical supervision may be moved to a special residential facility. The Connecticut Hospice, for example, has an attractive 44-bed homelike hospital in Branford; patients residing there can have visitors at virtually any hour.

Patients are generally admitted to hospice programs on the basis of need rather than ability to pay, and reimbursement is increasingly available under Medicare, Medicaid and private insurance plans.

Further information about hospice programs is available through your local community service agencies, visiting nurse associations, or write: National Hospice Organization, 1901 North Fort Myer Drive, Arlington, Virginia 22209.

by having your doctor send your X rays to another physician when necessary or by making duplicates for your own records.

You can minimize the costs associated with diagnosic tests done in a hospital by having them performed ahead of time in the doctor's office, at a laboratory he or she recommends or on an outpatient basis at the hospital. This simple step can cut a day off your hospital stay and save you hundreds of dollars.

Surgery. Scores of surgical procedures, including many that were in the past believed to require several days of hospital care, are routinely performed today under "same-day surgery" programs. Many hospitals now have outpatient clinics for minor surgery. A growing number of nonhospital settings are also being used for surgery — from surgeons' offices to independent "walk-in" centers designed solely for this purpose.

There are now more than a hundred of these "freestanding ambulatory surgical centers" in the United States. The prototype is Surgicenter of Phoenix, Arizona, which was founded by two anesthesiologists over a decade ago to provide a place where both patients and their surgeons could take advantage of modern operating and recovery facilities without all the delays, difficulties and high overhead associated with the typical hospital. Surgeons are carefully screened before they can use the facility, and only those who have operating privileges at an accredited hospital are accepted. As a protection for patients whose surgery results in unforeseen complications, Surgicenter has a transfer agreement with three Phoenix hospitals.

A number of common procedures can easily be performed on a same-day basis. Among them are certain kinds of biopsies and gynecological operations, tonsil and adenoid removal, hemorrhoid surgery, sterilization, dental surgery, uncomplicated plastic surgery, surgery for ear infections and simple cataract surgery. The average operation at Surgicenter takes about three-and-a-half hours from start to finish compared with seven hours in a hospital, with actual time in the operating room averaging between 30 minutes and an hour. A federally-sponsored study found that costs averaged 55 percent less than in a hospital and that the quality of care was at least as good. Moreover, patients like the idea of showing up in the morning, getting their operation out of the way and going home — or even back to work in the afternoon.

If an operation is serious enough to demand hospitalization, it is serious enough to require the best surgeon available. This means that the patient must do some investigating. It is important to find out how often the surgeon performs your particular operation in the course of a year. Some experts feel that a surgeon who does a common procedure 40 or 50 times annually is probably maintaining his or her skills, while one specializing in a complex procedure — a heart bypass, for example — would be better off doing 200 operations a year. Find out, also, what the surgeon's rate of success is. You may not be able to elicit precise statistics from the surgeon, but you can get a pretty good idea from talking to him or her and to other patients and doctors in a position to know. If the surgeon is reluctant to answer questions, find one who is not.

Inquire also who is to be your anesthesiologist. Whenever any anesthesia is used — particularly one that renders you unconscious — there are significant risks. You may have to trust the judgment of your surgeon to choose the best anesthesiologist, but that doesn't prevent you from sizing up the specialist yourself. He or she should visit you personally, usually the night before surgery, to ask about any allergies or previous adverse reactions to anesthetics, and to explain whether you have the option to choose local, spinal or general anesthesia, according to your wish to be awake or asleep. If you have a choice of anesthetic, ask about the pros and cons of each, which is most advisable and which may involve greater risk.

And, of course, ask about the fees — not only the surgeon's and the anesthesiologist's, but the assisting surgeon's and that of any other staff members who may be attached to the operating room.

Before undergoing your operation, you will be asked to sign a surgical consent form. Be sure the surgeon or any other physician who explains the surgery to you is mentioned by name, and if you have specified an anesthesiologist see that his or her name appears too. Make certain that the surgical procedure written on the form is precisely the one you agreed to. You have the right to ask for changes in the consent form, if you want them, and although the hospital is not obliged to make them, it will very often be willing to do so. For example, the form may contain language allowing surgeons to do anything they deem necessary once you have been opened up and the doctor has had a look. Permitting the surgeon to go ahead under these circumstances may save you money and protect you from the risks of a second operation, but it leaves you little recourse in the event that you subsequently disagree with what the surgeon has done. You may want to have such a clause deleted: if you do, don't sign the form unless your request is honored.

Long-term Care

For many people, particularly the elderly, long-term hospitalization is frequently undesirable. But who should take care of them, and how? The range of professional services available is broader than one might suspect.

Families faced with the problem of an ill or aging member they cannot take care of themselves often think first of a nursing home — a prospect they regard with some emotional and financial dread. There are many kinds of residential options, however, from foster homes that provide conveniences and congeniality to skilled nursing facilities for those who must have medical attention around the clock. Moreover, a host of services makes it increasingly possible for people to remain in the familiar surroundings of their own home, near family and friends. According to Representative Claude Pepper of Florida, longtime champion of aging Americans, "As many as 10 percent of hospital patients and 25 percent of nursing home residents could be cared for in their homes, where they could receive more compassionate, less costly care. They would be happier, which would promote their own health. Everybody should have the option of being treated at home."

Home Health Services. Many of the services necessary to maintain elderly or chronically ill persons at home — part-time skilled nursing, medical supplies and equipment, physical therapy — are reimbursable through Medicare, Medicaid and a growing number of private health insurance plans, as long as the therapy is prescribed by a physician and provided by a certified agency. Among these services are:

• Telephone reassurance. If you or a relative live alone, a volunteer will call every day at a predetermind time, ask if everything is all right and perhaps chat for a while. If all is not well, or if the stay-at-home doesn't answer the phone, a relative, neighbor or nearby police or fire station is asked to make an immediate check.
• Friendly visiting. A volunteer will drop by for an hour or so from one to several times a week. He or she may sit and chat, help write letters or provide escort service for a walk in the fresh air or a needed shopping trip.
• Meals on Wheels. Many local agencies deliver hot, nutritious lunches to persons unable to cook for themselves, and may also leave cold suppers to be eaten later on. Most programs deliver five days a week, though in some areas only a limited weekend service may be available. The fee is generally determined by an individual's finances.
• Transportation. An increasing number of communities provide transportation for the elderly or infirm to help them visit friends, doctors and local supermarkets and shops. Buses, specially-equipped vans or volunteers driving their own cars stop at or near homes to pick up and deliver their passengers.
• Day-care programs. Transportation may also be provided to an adult day-care or senior citizen center where people who would ordinarily stay at home all day can get minor medical treatment, eat a hot lunch, join in recreational programs and socialize with friends.
• Homemaker services. Persons unable to keep up with daily tasks can have a home health aide or homemaker come in to assist with meal preparation, laundry, shopping, bathing and grooming. Special help with lawn-mowing, home repairs and heavier work may be provided by teenagers or able-bodied older volunteers. Under "respite care" programs, paid staff or volunteers may take over light nursing care, meals and other chores, relieving family members during working hours, vacations or emergencies. Some respite programs have their own facilities where a person can choose to stay when the regular live-in family must be away.
• Visiting professionals. For those who have more serious disabilities or are recuperating from illnesses, licensed visiting nurses can see patients at home on a regular or short-term basis to check blood pressure, administer prescribed medicines, change dressings or give injections. Therapists may also come in to help with physical, speech or hearing disabilities. Social workers can help patients and their families adapt to illness and the resulting mental strain. Nutritionists often prepare menu plans for those needing special diets because of diabetes, high blood pressure or heart disease.

Nursing Homes. For those who cannot remain at home there are also several choices. Extended-care facilities, frequently attached to hospitals, provide for the needs of patients who require skilled convalescent care but not the full range of hospital services; a patient may be simply moved from his hospital bed to another wing where the cost is half as much. Rehabilitation centers, which may be used on either an inpatient or outpatient basis, have highly specialized staffs and facilities to help disabled people work to overcome their handicaps.

For those requiring longer or indefinite care, there are roughly 20,000 convalescent homes, rest homes and homes for the elderly in the United States. About three-quarters of them are privately owned and operated for profit. In recent years, as a result of scandals involving unsafe conditions and patient neglect and abuse, these institutions have come under increasing scrutiny and the regulations by which they are governed have been tightened. All nursing homes must be licensed by the states in which they operate, and must provide certain standards of care if they are to be reimbursed under Medicare, Medicaid or private insurance plans. Many of the better homes also voluntarily subject themselves to inspection and review by state nursing home associations affiliated with the American Health Care Association, and/or standards established by the Long-Term Council of the Joint Commission on Accreditation of Hospitals (JCAH). You should look for approval by these bodies when

The doctor should advise the patient on the level of nursing care that is needed for his or her condition.

shopping around for nursing home care.

Though nursing homes vary widely in amenities and costs, there are basically three kinds:

- *Skilled nursing facilities (SNF's)* are designed for persons needing fairly intensive care. Every such facility must have a medical director, a 24-hour nursing service with at least one registered nurse on duty, and physicians on call. It must also provide rehabilitation therapy and special diets if needed.
- *Intermediate care facilities (ICF's)* are for those persons who require less attention. ICF's offer basic nursing care with a licensed practical nurse on duty and at least one registered nurse as a part-time consultant. In addition, these institutions provide residents with some supervision and assistance in eating, dressing, walking and caring for various other personal needs.
- *Residential care facilities,* also known as *custodial* or *domiciliary facilities,* are for those who are in reasonably good physical condition but who either cannot, or do not want to, live completely on their own. Most such facilities provide meals, social programs and recreational therapy, as well as basic medical monitoring and the services of nurses or physicians on call. Increasingly popular variations on the theme, for those who can afford them, are life-care retirement homes in which residents pay large entry endowments plus monthly maintenance fees for their private apartments, meals and the privilege of nursing care if the need should arise. Residential care facilities must meet certain state standards to be licensed, but their regular, non-medical services do not qualify for reimbursement under health insurance plans.

In choosing a nursing home, first determine with the help of your doctor what level of care is needed. Names of several homes in the appropriate category can be obtained from the doctor and from the local health department, community and social service agencies, office of aging or your state health care or nursing home association. Narrow the list by making a few phone calls to find out if a given home provides the specific care you desire and at what cost. If you have Medicare, Medicaid or private insurance, ask if the home qualifies for reimbursement under the plan.

Make appointments to visit two or three of the most promising homes and have the administrators show you around. If you go there in the late morning, you will be able to observe, and perhaps join, the residents at the noon meal. This is one of the best ways to judge the spirit of the place as well as the quality of the food. A key to any nursing home is how the people who live there look and act — whether they are up and dressed, well-groomed and talking with one another, or whether they seem ill-cared for and listless, and sit around in nightgowns staring blankly out the windows or at the walls. Also make a note of how well the residents seem to get along with the staff.

Next, check the lobby, lounges, kitchen, therapy facilities, patients' rooms. Is the place clean, well lighted, as attractive and homelike as possible? Are hallways and bathrooms equipped with rails for the residents to hold onto as supports? Are bedrooms large enough to move around in, do they have comfortable easy chairs, personal decorations, adequate storage space? Is there a library or game room, a social program, access to religious services? Are special outings arranged for the residents? Are a dentist, barber and beautician on call? What are the visiting hours? What is included in the basic rate and what is extra? What medical help is available in emergencies, and does the home have arrangements to transfer a patient to a nearby hospital? Does the home have its own version of a "patient's bill of rights," and what does it guarantee? Is there a residents' council to help organize activities, make suggestions, work with the management to smooth out complaints? Look over the credentials of the home and its administrator, and scrutinize the contract carefully before you sign.

Once a member of your family has entered a nursing home, don't hesitate to bring up any complaints you may have with the administrator. If the problem remains unresolved, and is serious enough, it should be reported to the state department of health. All states have patient-care investigators, with laws to back them up, and can be tough when it comes to lack of safety or sanitation, patient mistreatment or neglect.

Legal Services

"Many people go to lawyers when they could help themselves or get help from someone else for less money," says Herbert S. Denenberg, attorney, author and consumer advocate. "But when they really need a lawyer, many people go too late."

Indeed, many problems can be resolved without an attorney: by consulting a good do-it-yourself family legal guide; by talking out a dispute and reaching a compromise; by seeking the advice of an appropriate third party, whether marriage counselor, banker or insurance agent; by taking the matter to a local Better Business Bureau, consumer protection agency or small claims court.

But on some occasions, you *need* an attorney — to deal with such problems as an accident involving personal injury or property damage, to help you establish a business, go through bankruptcy, buy or sell a home, make out a complex will, sign a substantial contract, resolve difficult estate or tax problems, settle terms of a contested divorce. In such cases, an hour's worth of advice at an early stage can save you trouble and expense later.

Shopping for Lawyers. There are about half a million lawyers in the United States — more per capita than anywhere else in the world. So if you need one, you should be able to find one — and not just any lawyer, but the one who will give you the best professional counsel at the fairest price. In this endeavor, there are several avenues you can pursue. Ask friends and neighbors about the lawyers they have used, and pay particular attention to what you hear from people who have been in a situation similar to yours and have had it resolved to their satisfaction. Check with professionals in other fields: accountants, bank officers or financial executives if your problem is financial; social workers, clergymen or marital counselors if you are seeking a divorce. Ask the legal department of the company you work for — or its outside law firm — for ideas and referrals. If you live or work near a law school, call the dean's office, ask for the names of faculty members who teach courses in the area of law that concerns you (domestic relations, tax law, probate, etc.), and get in touch with these individuals. They may not be able to take you as a client, but may be able to recommend others who can. Similarly, contact your city, county or state bar association and ask for the names of members associated with the committee that handles your area of concern; they, too, are apt to be highly regarded experts in their field. The bar association will probably have its own lawyer referral service as well, but since many such services simply offer the names of members on a rotating basis, it is wise to ask some questions. How are the names selected? What qualifications must the individuals have? Are they listed by the specialties in which they practice? What, if any, will the fee be for the first exploratory interview?

Once you have the names of several possible lawyers, look them up in the *Martindale-Hubbell Law Directory,* available in the reference sections of many public libraries. This publication, which charges a fee to those who are listed in it, will give you an idea of a lawyer's education, associations, publications, areas of expertise and often what clients he or she represents. It may also give a rating of the attorney's skills based on confidential recommendations by other lawyers and judges in the area. These ratings, however, do not reflect the clients' views nor are they published without the consent of the attorney involved. Some consumer groups have recently begun compiling their own local directories of attorneys for use by prospective clients; if there is an active consumer organization in your area, check to find out whether it has such a list. Finally, a 1977 Supreme Court ruling gave lawyers the right to advertise their services and fees. Though many still choose not to do so, you may be able to get a line on some of the more aggressive or lower-priced firms and their specialties by looking for ads in your local newspaper or in the Yellow Pages under "Attorneys" and "Legal Clinics" (see below).

Initial Interviews. Many lawyers will agree to a get-acquainted meeting without charge, as long as you make it clear that you do not expect free advice about the details of your case. Since your time with the lawyer will be limited, organize your thoughts and write down your questions in advance. Bring along copies of any relevant documents so that you can leave them in the event you decide to hire the lawyer. Here are some questions to ask:

• Do you handle cases like mine? If so, what were the outcomes of some of your recent cases, how long did they take, what were the fees and other costs and were any special difficulties involved? Most general-practice

CONSUMER ALERT

A Client's Bill of Rights

The requirements necessary to practice law vary from state to state. But most include graduation from an approved law school, passing a state bar examination, and having the character and moral fitness to practice law as an officer of the court. Lawyers must also abide by a strict code of ethics, established by custom and by law.

To ensure that these ethical requirements are met, some state bar associations have drawn up a bill of rights for their clients, to which all association members are asked to subscribe.

The document which follows has been drawn up for members of the New York Bar Association.

When I retain a lawyer, I am entitled to one who:

- Will be capable of handling my case.
- Will represent me zealously and seek any lawful means to present or defend my case.
- Will preserve my confidences, secrets or statements which I reveal in the course of our relationship.
- Will give me the right to make the ultimate decision on the objectives to be pursued in my case.
- Will charge me a reasonable fee and tell me, in advance of being hired and upon my request, the basis of that fee.
- Will show me courtesy and consideration at all times.
- Will exercise independent professional judgment in my behalf, free from compromising influences.
- Will inform me periodically about the status of my case and, at my request, give me copies of the documents prepared.
- Will exhibit the highest degree of ethical conduct.
- Will refer me to other legal counsel if he or she cannot properly represent me.

lawyers can handle contracts, uncontested divorces and other routine legal matters. But in more complex areas, legal practice has become increasingly specialized. Some bar associations certify their members in specific specialties. Specialists usually charge higher fees than general practitioners; on the other hand, they can often get a job done more efficiently and for less overall expense. If your case demands more knowledge and experience than a particular lawyer has, he or she should be frank enough to admit it and should refer you to an appropriate specialist.

- How much personal attention will I get? Will *you* do the work, or will it be turned over to someone else? It is common practice in law firms for experienced lawyers to interview prospective clients and then pass on the detailed work to junior associates or paralegal aides. This procedure can save a client money, since work done by juniors and paralegals is billed at a lower rate. But you should make sure the subordinates are properly supervised and should ask to meet any junior member of the firm who will actually be handling your case. Make sure also that the time each person puts into your case — partner, associate, paralegal, secretary — is separately entered on an itemized bill at the appropriate hourly rate. A lawyer who charges for all the work at his own rate, when in fact the bulk of it was performed by lower-paid employees, is to be avoided. If a firm makes efficient use of clerical help, standardized forms and automatic memory typewriters, at least part of the savings should be passed on to you in the form of lower costs.
- How long will it take to complete this matter, and can you give me a rough estimate of overall costs? A good lawyer should be willing to discuss fees openly and, if hired, furnish a written estimate of charges, services to be included and any likely extras, such as filing fees, depositions, documents, telephone expenses and court costs. He or she should talk to you in plain English, not legalese, and agree to inform you periodically, in writing, about the progress of your case.

Lawyers' Fees. In some cases, such as handling an estate or an uncontested divorce, the legal fee may be set by the court, which determines it by reviewing the attorney's application and considering the amount of work required. But on the whole, fees are set directly between clients and lawyers. To avoid unpleasant surprises, it is wise to get the matter right out on the table from the start. If you cannot afford the asking price, say so. Fees are negotiable, and you may be able to work out a lower price or a longer payment period. If you like the lawyer, these options are far better than the decision to work with someone in whom you have less confidence simply because his or her rates are lower.

Fees vary widely even for the same services, depending on a lawyer's experience, reputation, location, office overhead and the precise nature of the case. The most common is a straight *hourly fee,* under which the lawyer charges for his or her time at an agreed-on hourly rate, multiplied by the number of hours the lawyer actually works on a case. Per-hour charges can range from well under $50 for a rural attorney or a city lawyer just getting started as an independent practitioner to considerably more than $350 for the time of a senior partner in a prestigious Wall Street firm. Although they may not like to do it, lawyers can usually predict how much time they are likely to spend on a given case. You should ask for such an estimate when you retain your counsel, and ask for periodic revisions as the case progresses, so that you know where you stand. Most attorneys charge for their time to the nearest tenth, sixth or quarter of an hour, and they are not in the habit of

Before hiring any lawyer, be sure to discuss his or her fees and charges.

giving free advice. If you telephone your lawyer for information or an opinion, even if you spend only five minutes on the call, don't be surprised if you are billed for it at some fraction of the hourly rate.

A lawyer working at an hourly rate may ask for a retainer — a down payment against whatever the total fee turns out to be. If he or she spends more time than the retainer covers, you will be billed for additional hours; if the attorney spends less, you should get a refund. Make sure any retainer is reasonable, get a receipt for it and have the lawyer specify in writing that he or she will bill you periodically and will return any money you have paid in excess of the actual bill for time. You may want to ask your lawyer for an itemized bill — not simply a statement of the total you owe. Some lawyers resist this, and even charge for the time it takes them to make up the bill, but others will cooperate.

For common legal matters whose time and costs are predictable — such as simple wills, title searches and transfers of property — an attorney may quote you a *flat* or *fixed fee.* Like hourly rates, fixed fees can vary widely. However, they are the easiest to compare. Call several lawyers and ask what they would charge for the service you have in mind, and whether there are any additional costs not quoted in the price. According to a 1975 Supreme Court decision, local bar associations can no longer set minimum fee schedules for particular jobs. In cases that involve such matters as the amount of an estate or the selling price of a house, try to avoid lawyers who base their fees on a percentage of total value. A fairer basis is an hourly rate for the actual work involved.

On the other hand, if you are seeking damages for personal injury stemming from negligence or an accident, a lawyer may take your case for a *contingent fee,* that is, a percentage of the money you are awarded. If you lose, the attorney gets no fee. Win or lose, however, the lawyer is entitled to bill you for expenses and court costs, which can mount up. Although in some cases contingent-fee agreements can give the lawyer as much as 60 percent of the amount awarded, most commonly the fee runs one-third, and the larger the potential recovery, the lower the percentage should be. A common practice is for lawyer and client to agree in advance on a sliding scale, determined by whether or not the case is settled out of court, as most negligence cases are. For example, a wise client might guarantee the attorney as little as 15 percent if a settlement is negotiated before the case is filed in court; 25 percent if it is settled before the trial starts; 35 percent if it is settled after the start of the trial but before a decision by the court; and 35 percent if the case goes to appeal. Critics of contingent fees have described them as devices for lawyers to drum up business and make excessive profits. On the other hand, they *do* encourage attorneys to seek just recoveries for clients who might not otherwise be able to afford to hire a lawyer and go to court. If you enter into a contingency arrangement, try to make sure that your lawyer's expenses will be deducted from the total recovery *before* his or her percentage is figured on the remaining amount; this could save you a fair amount of money. The types of cases subject to contingency fees, and the maximum percentages permitted on amounts of awards, are regulated by law in many states. If you have any question about the legality of a contingency fee requested by your lawyer, check with your state's attorney general's office (see directory, page 48).

Dealing With Your Lawyer. When you have decided on a lawyer and agreed on services and fees, have him or her put all the particulars of your arrangement in writing: a clear description of the legal matter; the services to be rendered; the fee basis and total estimated fee (including the hourly rates at which the services of the lawyer, associates, paralegals and secretaries will be billed, the details of any retainer or other specifics if it is to be a fixed or contingent fee); an estimate of additional costs and expenses; a promise that the lawyer will send you itemized billing statements either monthly or on some other regular basis; a statement that you will be provided with periodic status reports at specified intervals, including copies of any pertinent correspondence and documents that have been prepared or received. You should both sign the agreement, and each of you should have a signed copy.

To keep up your end of the bargain, you should be prepared to tell your lawyer *all* the facts of the case, good and bad, whether they reflect well on you or not. An attorney is bound both by custom and law to hold them in the strictest confidence. Be sure to keep him or her informed of any new developments that might affect the case, but avoid unnecessary phone calls just to "see how the case is coming along." Be skeptical of promises of sure-fire results; rather, ask to be kept posted on both the positive and negative aspects of your case.

If You're Not Satisfied. Should you feel at any point that your lawyer is not working diligently for you, or that he or she is engaging in questionable practices, there are several steps you can take. First, bring your dissatisfaction to the attorney's attention. A good way to secure that attention, and to go on record, is to write him or her a letter outlining your complaint, asking pertinent questions and requesting a meeting to sort things out. If that doesn't bring results, remember that a client has the legal right, at any time, to discharge an attorney, with or without cause, although if you have no valid cause — misconduct, for example — you will have to pay for services rendered up to that date.

Before firing your lawyer, however, it is prudent to consult with another lawyer who can and will take over, so that your case will not be hurt in the switch. If you have paid the first lawyer for the services thus far rendered, he or she is obligated to turn over your files. If you believe the lawyer has acted incompetently or dishonestly, you can file a formal complaint with the local bar association, or ask the association if you should direct your complaint to a special agency set up by the state's highest court. Although state disciplinary boards have traditionally been made up of lawyers, who may be reluctant to act against their fellows, in recent years the American Bar Association has promoted the inclusion of nonlawyers in these groups.

Some disciplinary boards will arbitrate fee disputes, but generally consider disciplining their members only in cases where ethical misconduct is shown. If an investigation does not reveal any convincing evidence of such misconduct, the charges will be dismissed. A minor infraction may bring a private reprimand, disclosed only to the lawyer and the client. A more serious one will merit a public reprimand, which will soon get around in legal circles. A still graver one can result in suspension of a lawyer's right to practice for a specified period ranging from a few days to a year or more, or for an indefinite period until he or she can prove ethical fitness. The severest penalty, disbarment from practice, is invoked only for such serious misconduct as a criminal act or severe neglect of clients' interests — caused, for example, by alcoholism.

Other Sources of Help. If you are not sure you need, or can afford, the services of a personal attorney, there are other sources you can turn to for aid. An increasing number of legal clinics are sprouting up in major cities to practice "supermarket law," handling routine matters quickly at a fraction of the normal fees. Often located in storefronts and open at convenient hours, they process simple wills, trusts, bankruptcies, uncontested divorces, adoptions, name changes and other standardized procedures. Costs are kept down by using lower-rent space, paralegal assistants, standard forms and computers, as well as by advertising to bring in a high volume of legal business.

If you want to have a will made out, for example, you may be interviewed first by an assistant, who will mark down code numbers that indicate the provisions he or she thinks you need. Then an attorney, who may be the clinic's specialist in wills, will review the provisions with you and, if everything is satisfactory, ask you to have a seat while your will is typed up. A secretary will enter the codes into a programmed word processor, which prints the finished product in minutes. You sign it, pay at the desk and walk out the door.

For some matters you may not need a lawyer at all. Depending on the state, minor disputes, involving sums from hundreds to thousands of dollars in damages, can often be settled by the parties directly in a small claims court. Family quarrels and business disputes can be resolved, usually sooner and at less cost than going to court, by mediation or arbitration services offered by the American Arbitration Association, the Better Business Bureau or some other organization in your area. If your income is below a certain level, you should be able to get free legal services from legal aid societies, and anyone can seek redress through various government and private agencies for unfair practices in retailing, housing, employment and civil rights. For further information, call or write your local bar association or consumer affairs organization, and see Chapters 13 and 14 of this book.

Accountants and Tax Preparers

Many people turn to professionals for help with such financial matters as tax advice and aid in the preparation of tax returns. They may need accountants and auditors for their business or personal finances or assistance in financial management or applications for business loans. Since the qualifications, services and fees of advisers vary widely, it is prudent to examine them closely before choosing one to handle your affairs.

Some three out of five American taxpayers still prepare and file their federal, state and local income tax forms themselves, using the instructions that come with the forms, the plethora of free pamphlets available from the Internal Revenue Service and, perhaps, one or more of the numerous books available. The IRS also offers toll-free telephone lines to answer questions, and assists people who visit its many offices scattered around the country. If your tax situation is simple enough to use one of the "short forms," the IRS will even complete most of the form and compute your taxes without charge. Persons 60 or older can also get free tax assistance through the National Retired Teachers Association, 1909 K Street, NW, Washington, D.C. 20006, which maintains a network of counselors in many communities from about February 1 to April 15.

For the other two out of five — whether because they cannot cope or because their finances are somewhat more complex — there are many services that will prepare taxes for a fee. Perhaps a quarter-million or more individuals hang out signs as "tax consultants," many of them operating out of rented storefronts during the tax season and vanishing after April 15. While many do a competent job, IRS statistics show an appreciable percentage of incorrectly prepared returns from such sources — and a greater chance that such returns will be audited with possible embarrassing results.

On the other hand, the services that do business nationwide — high volume, low-fee operations that churn out millions of returns each year — are usually more reliable. But although they can process routine forms, they may not be equipped to deal with more complicated returns. Even if they promise to accompany a taxpayer to an IRS office in the event of an audit, they may not be qualified to represent the taxpayer in higher-level proceedings with the IRS.

A step up from tax preparation services is the so-called enrolled agent, who is certified by the IRS after working for five years as an IRS auditor or after passing a stiff Treasury Department examination. Enrolled agents can prepare returns, argue points of tax law, negotiate settlements and otherwise represent clients through the appeals process of the IRS. You may be able to locate one through a local IRS office or in the Yellow Pages under "Accountants" or "Bookkeepers" with the added legend "Enrolled to Practice Before the IRS."

In choosing any tax service, remember that it is *you*, not the tax preparer, who is legally responsible for the accuracy of your return. Some states and municipalities have laws to protect consumers against shoddy practices. New York City, for example, requires that all tax preparers post signs describing their qualifications, giving their year-round addresses and telephone numbers, and notifying taxpayers if they cannot provide representation at audits. The signs must also state how fees — which cannot be based on the amount of tax paid or the amount of refund due — are calculated and must list minimum charges.

Public Accountants. For more sophisticated help with taxes and other financial matters, you may want to consider a public accountant — either certified or not.

Public accountants, who are not eligible to represent clients before the IRS unless they are also lawyers, generally serve small businessmen and individuals of moderate income, and some of them do a good job at a moderate price. Most states do not require them to be licensed, nor do these states impose any educational standards or tests before permitting them to practice.

Certified public accountants (CPA's), on the other hand, must complete an accounting curriculum at college, pass a rigorous two-and-a-half-day examination and be certified by the state in which they practice; in many states they must also meet requirements of experience and/or continuing study to retain their licenses. Close to 200,000 CPA's belong to the American Institute of Certified Public Accountants, which accepts only those in good standing who agree to abide by the institute's code of professional ethics.

A CPA who has been given the power of attorney by a client is automatically authorized to represent that client before the IRS. You might want the services of a CPA if your finances are somewhat more complicated than average — if, say, you have income from investments, royalties, trust funds or from the sale of a home; if you use your home or car partly for business; if you suffer a casualty loss or face financial and tax changes because of marriage, divorce, retirement or family death. A CPA can assist you with long-range personal or business planning and annual balance sheets, do your accounting or audit it for you and also offer advice on the planning of estates and trusts — although trust planning will in all probability require the services of a lawyer as well.

Smaller CPA firms and individual practitioners are usually the best choice for individuals and smaller businesses, not only because they can give their clients close attention, but because they charge less than the giant accounting organizations. On the other hand, some larger firms, although they concentrate on major corporate clients, may have special departments that suit your needs. The important questions for you to investigate before choosing a CPA are: who will be handling your financial matters, and what his or her particular skills are.

The small accounting firm is often able to offer personal service at a moderate cost.

The best way to begin looking for an accountant is to ask friends or business colleagues whose situation, income or type of work is similar to yours. Bankers are often an excellent source of names, as they deal regularly with audited financial statements prepared by various accountants. Lawyers are often knowledgeable too, especially about accountants adept in estate and trust work or in negotiating with the IRS. Indeed, some lawyers are also expert accountants.

In sizing up any accountant, find out if he or she has clients with problems similar to yours, has the time and expertise to handle your affairs and how long it takes to render various services. Compare his or her hourly fees with those of other accountants, and determine whether the accountant differentiates between his or her personal time and that of associates when bills are submitted. If you decide to hire the individual, get all the particulars — services, deadlines, limitations, hourly fees and terms of payment — in a letter of agreement.

In the event a serious dispute arises between you and your Certified Public Accountant, you can file a complaint with the national office of the American Institute of Certified Public Accountants, 1211 Avenue of the Americas, New York, New York 10036. It will either refer you to its office in your state or, if no office exists, will itself investigate the charge and, if warranted, initiate disciplinary action. Or you may complain directly to the state board of accountancy, which can hold hearings and, if necessary, suspend or revoke the license of your CPA.

Funerals: The Last Service

Few consumers would ordinarily admit to spending $5,000 or more on something that they knew little or nothing about. Yet every day thousands of Americans do just that when a family member dies. On short notice, with their judgment often clouded by grief or guilt, they turn to the nearest funeral director to tell them what to do.

There is the agonizing choice of the casket, of course, which can range from a few hundred dollars for a plain box to several thousand and up for a top-of-the-line model with ornate appointments, guaranteed to remain air- and water-tight for "eternity." And there are other expenses: for embalming and "cosmetizing" the body for public viewing; for burial clothes, pallbearers, flowers, music, newspaper notices, death certificates, chapel and clergy fees, purchase of a cemetery plot, transportation to graveside, labor for opening, closing and maintaining the grave. Among the typical expenditures of the average American, a funeral ranks in third place. Only a home and an automobile cost more.

There is no question that funeral directors — members of an industry now approaching a volume of $7 billion a year — perform a vital function and that many of them show genuine consideration and good taste. But the economic constraints they operate under often press them to urge their customers to spend much more than they can realistically afford. At present, there are some 22,000 funeral homes in the United States and, since roughly 2 million people die annually, the average number of deaths per funeral home is less than 100 a year. To maintain an attractive, well-staffed facility, with new hearses and limousines, nearly half the funeral directors in America have to make ends meet on a single sale a week.

But expensive funeral services are not the only ones available. In recent years an increasing number of people have found alternative arrangements that they consider of equal dignity, and that cost only a fraction of the usual price. To take advantage of them, however, a family should look into each one, choose the most appropriate for its purposes and make the necessary arrangements well ahead of need.

Shopping Around. While few people are comfortable about discussing funerals in advance, it is really a very poor idea to decide on arrangements under the pressures of time and emotional stress. The best way to avoid unnecessary problems and expenses later is simply to visit several funeral homes in your area, compare services and prices and make out a tentative list of exactly what you want.

Some funeral homes display their best caskets in a front room, dividing them into low, medium and high prices, and keep their least expensive caskets in the back, making them difficult to find or embarrassing to buy. But if you do not want a fancy casket, you should not hesitate to say so and to ask if a cheaper one is available.

The caskets that are least expensive are often kept in the back and may be difficult to find.

Because the casket is usually the most profitable part of the package, a funeral parlor employee, like a car salesman, may try to "trade up" a customer to a higher-priced model by claiming it is more "protective" or will "last forever." While a "sealer" casket, made from heavy metal with a rubber gasket around the outside edge of the lid, may prevent water from seeping in, it cannot preserve the remains. No casket can do this regardless of any guarantees the salesman or manufacturer may make. Nor, indeed, does the law require the use of a casket if the body is to be cremated. On the other hand, a crematory may not accept the remains unless they are in a "suitable" container of some kind.

Many funeral directors automatically embalm a body entrusted to them, whether requested to or not, and some may imply that this is required by law or is necessary for the long-term preservation of the remains. Embalming, which involves the substitution of chemicals for blood, is not required by law in any state except for public health reasons — if for example, the individual has died of a certain contagious disease; if the remains are not disposed of within a specified period, which ranges from 24 to 72 hours; or if the body is to be shipped across state lines. Moreover, embalming is only a short-term measure. It may be desirable if the body is to be held a day or two for viewing in an open casket. On the other hand, refrigeration can often accomplish the same result. If you do not want embalming, and its attendant costs (which can run as high as $250 or more), you should make your wishes clear at the start.

In a study of the funeral industry, the Federal Trade Commission concluded that the major problem is the widespread use of "package pricing," which requires customers to pay for casket, embalming and a spectrum of other goods and services whether they want them or not. An FTC rule requires that all funeral homes provide consumers with prices for individual items before selection — over the telephone if requested. The rule also prohibits funeral directors from misstating facts about legal or cemetery requirements; claiming that embalming or a casket can preserve a body for extended periods; requiring a casket for direct cremation; or conditioning the purchase of any item on the purchase of another.

Alternatives. While many Americans cling to the traditional funeral, complete with everything from open-casket viewing to a cemetery procession, an increasing number of people are turning to alternatives that cost less and are acceptable, emotionally, to those who decide to use them.

Cremation, extensively practiced in England and Japan, has been growing in acceptance in the United States. The ratio of cremations to deaths has risen to a national average of 11 percent in recent years, and more than 30 percent in the West Coast states. In carrying out this process, the body is often transported immediately to a crematory where, in a simple wooden box or corrugated-board container, it is reduced to ashes by intense heat or flame. The survivors have several options: asking the crematory to dispose of the ashes; placing them in an urn that can be displayed with other urns in the crematory's "columbarium;" taking them home to be kept in the house, on private property or in a cemetery; or scattering them in some place that had a special meaning to the deceased.

Advocates of cremation point out that it is not only simple, dignified and less expensive than earth burial, but that it also reduces the growing need for extensive cemeteries, since some cities are already short of needed open space. More than one family has taken the difference in cost between cremation and burial and either given it to the deceased's favorite charity or used it to start a scholarship or other "living memorial" fund.

Cremation, like immediate burial without a funeral, also permits the survivors to hold a memorial service at any time and place, without having the body present. This procedure is not only less expensive, but may be more comfortable for families and other mourners. Alternatively, a simple committal service, either public or private, can be held at the graveside immediately before burial or in the crematory chapel prior to cremation. Obviously, however, cremation is not an answer when religious or personal beliefs forbid the practice.

In addition to funeral homes and crematories, some areas have so-called direct disposition companies that often advertise on the obituary pages of newspapers. For a few hundred dollars they will pick up and deliver a body to a crematory or cemetery, arrange for the appropriate disposition and complete the necessary paperwork. The family generally makes its own arrangements for a memorial or graveside service.

For those who wish to benefit the living when they die by bequeathing their bodies or specific organs to medical science, procedures have been approved in all states under the Uniform Anatomical Gift Act. Among needed gifts are corneas for eye transplants; kidneys to free patients from dependence on dialysis machines; pituitary glands to help children suffering from growth disorders; human skin for grafting on victims of serious burns. Some medical schools have specific needs for bodies to be used in medical education or research. Since not all bodies or organs may be suitable, and some organs must be removed swiftly after death to be of use, any such arrangements should be made in detail and well in advance. Many states issue donor forms in connection with drivers' licenses. A Uniform Donor Card and further information can be obtained from such organizations as the Continental Association of Funeral and Memorial Societies, 1146 19th Street, NW, Washington, D.C. 20036, or the Living Bank, P.O. Box 6725, Houston, Texas 77265.

Paying for a Funeral. Before committing yourself to payment, ask any funeral home, cemetery, crematory or other provider for a written, itemized cost list of the goods and services you have selected, and find out what amount, if any, is due before the services will be provided. Look over carefully any "preneed" or prepayment plan that may be offered. It may lock you into using the services of a particular funeral home at uncertain future prices, and if you move away or the home goes out of business, you may have trouble getting your money back. Reject any such plan unless the home has a sound reputation, the price is guaranteed in writing, the funds are placed in trust, earning interest, and you can get a full refund if you decide to cancel. A better idea may be to put money aside in a special savings account or insurance policy of your own, under your control, with the proceeds

Funeral instructions should be notarized and entrusted to a lawyer, not included in a will.

earmarked for your survivors to pay for funeral expenses at your death, or to a specified funeral home as beneficiary if you have no one else.

If you are thinking of buying a cemetery plot in advance, check it out just as thoroughly. How big a plot do you need? What type of marker do you want? Are there any options for reselling the plot if you decide not to keep it or have to move away? Does the price of the plot include interment and maintenance? Beware of phone calls or promotions claiming that you have just "won" a "free" cemetery plot. They may be simple bait-and-switch schemes to get you to buy a regular — and high-priced — place to lay your remains.

Remember that you or your survivors may be eligible for benefits to help cover funeral expenses after death. If you have Social Security, ask your local Social Security office for details of its lump-sum benefit; if you are a veteran, inquire of the nearest Veterans Administration branch whether you qualify for one of its various funeral benefits. Death benefits are also paid to civil servants, employees of certain companies and members of some unions and fraternal groups.

Never include instructions for your funeral arrangements in your will, which is generally read only *after* burial or cremation. Prepare a separate statement, have it notarized and be sure to tell family members, your attorney or a trusted friend what the statement contains and where it is located. Do *not* put it in a safe deposit box, which may automatically be sealed after your death until the process of probating your will can begin.

Memorial Societies. For help with funeral decisions, and funerals themselves, a growing number of people are relying on memorial or funeral societies, of which there are more than 200 around the United States and Canada. These nonprofit organizations — typically affiliated with churches, consumer cooperatives, labor unions or civic groups, and run largely by volunteers — stress dignity, simplicity and economy in funerals to reduce both emotional suffering and expense at the time of death. A memorial society (so named because members commonly choose simple memorial services rather than elaborate funerals) does not provide any goods or services directly, but generally has either contracts or cooperative arrangements with funeral directors to take care of its members' needs at predetermined prices, frequently saving 50 or even 75 percent of usual funeral costs.

Anyone can join a memorial or funeral society for a modest, one-time fee that rarely exceeds $25. Societies encourage planning and frank discussion among family members well in advance of need, but do not require advance payment of funeral costs and allow individual plans to be changed or canceled at any time. Members who move to a new area can usually arrange to transfer their memberships to the nearest local society at little or no cost; if death occurs away from home, the nearest society can be contacted for help. The majority of memorial society members choose cremation and/or donation of their bodies to medical science, matters on which the societ-

Offices of the Department of Health and Human Services

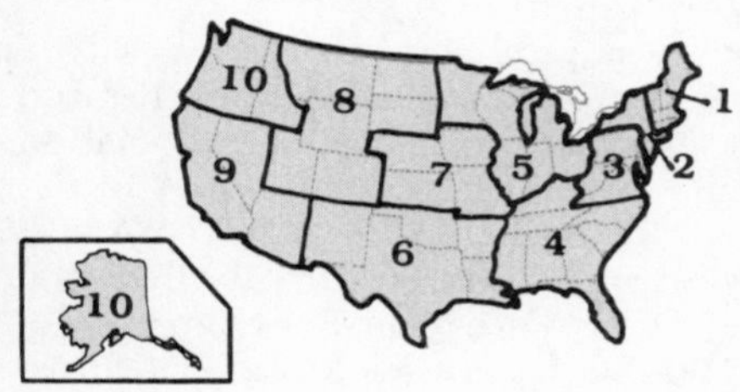

Main Office **401 M Street, SW, Washington, DC 20460**

Region 1 **Connecticut, Maine, Massachusetts, New Hampshire, Rhode Island, Vermont**
John F. Kennedy Federal Building, Boston, MA 02203

Region 2 **New Jersey, New York, Puerto Rico, Virgin Islands**
26 Federal Plaza, New York, NY 10007

Region 3 **Delaware, District of Columbia, Maryland, Pennsylvania, Virginia, West Virginia**
3535 Market Street, Philadelphia, PA 19101

Region 4 **Alabama, Florida, Georgia, Kentucky, Mississippi, North Carolina, South Carolina, Tennessee**
101 Marietta Towers NE, Atlanta, GA 30323

Region 5 **Illinois, Indiana, Michigan, Minnesota, Ohio, Wisconsin**
300 South Wacker Drive, Chicago, IL 60606

Region 6 **Arkansas, Louisiana, New Mexico, Oklahoma, Texas**
1200 Main Tower Building, Dallas TX 75202

Region 7 **Iowa, Kansas, Missouri, Nebraska**
601 East 12th Street, Kansas City, MO 64106

Region 8 **Colorado, Montana, North Dakota, South Dakota, Utah, Wyoming**
1961 Stout Street, Denver, CO 80294

Region 9 **Arizona, California, Hawaii, Nevada,**
50 United Nations Plaza, San Francisco, CA 94102

Region 10 **Alaska, Idaho, Oregon, Washington**
1321 Second Avenue, Seattle, WA 98101

ies can supply information and assistance. Many societies, however, offer members a choice of simple traditional funerals at prenegotiated prices.

Since some funeral businesses use the words "memorial" or "society" in their names, and some charge a high "membership" fee in addition to trying to sell expensive goods and services in advance, it is important to be sure you are dealing with a genuine memorial society. Nearly all belong to the Continental Association of Funeral and Memorial Societies, Inc. (CAFMS).

The organization publishes many useful pamphlets, forms and books, including *A Manual of Death Education and Simple Burial*, and *Smoothing the Way: A Guide to Funeral Planning*.

CAFMS offers a geographical directory of member societies in addition to a complete publications list. Both are available upon written request to CAFMS, 1146 19th Street, NW, Washington, D.C. 20036.

State and city consumer agencies are good sources of information and literature about funerals and local regulations. Consult them.

A comprehensive guide to planning a funeral is *It's Your Choice* by Thomas C. Nelson, which was published in 1982 as a consumer action project of the National Retired Teachers Association/American Association of Retired Persons. Individual copies of the book, at $4.95 each ($3.50 to NRTA/AARP members), can be ordered directly from the publisher, Scott, Foresman & Company, located at 400 South Edward Street, Mt. Prospect, Illinois 60056.

Information and pamphlets regarding various aspects of death, burial and cremation can be obtained from local funeral homes or by writing to the National Funeral Directors Association, 135 West Wells Street, Milwaukee, Wisconsin 53203.

The association also sponsors Thana-CAP, a consumer action panel that investigates complaints against funeral practitioners. ThanaCAP is discussed further in Chapter 13, The Compleat Complainer.

The Compleat Complainer: How to Complain and Get Results

On any given day, numerous Americans have reason to complain about the goods and services for which they have spent their money. Hair dryers and automobiles fail to perform properly. Packaged and frozen goods are defective in some way. A new knit suit shrinks to an unwearable size after the first dry cleaning. The roof on a new house leaks and the builder refuses to honor the contract which requires him to repair it. An appliance or heating system, purchased at great expense, proves downright hazardous to life and limb. The list of difficulties caused by faulty products or inadequate service is a long one, and most consumers can add to it without too much trouble.

But defective merchandise and unsatisfactory service, widespread as they may be, are not the only problems plaguing consumers. Advertisers or salesmen may make deceptive claims, thereby encouraging the purchase of items that are a total waste of money. Credit may illegally be denied to individuals who qualify for it. Goods bought through mail order may simply fail to arrive.

Other infuriating consumer problems concern billing. People are billed for items they never bought; they are badgered for payments they have already made; they are reported to credit bureaus as bad risks when they are not at fault. Most large companies have given computers the job of sending out bills. But computers sometimes malfunction, and are sometimes given the wrong information and when these things happen, the errors can be very difficult to correct.

Yet in the face of all these difficulties, too many consumers seem to be content to swallow their irritation and absorb whatever financial loss they may have suffered. Why do they remain silent? Some apparently feel that the game is not worth the candle — that they will have to pay such a high price in time, trouble and emotional wear and tear that it is easier to cut their losses than to enter the battleground. Others fear that they have been beaten even before they begin — that the cards are so heavily stacked against them that they cannot possibly win. So they, too, back out of the fight, retreating into sullen resentment against retail stores and auto dealers, insurance agents and doctors, and manufacturers of everything from breakfast cereal to refrigerators.

These defeatist views are — to put it simply — all wrong. As growing numbers of American consumers have learned, they have both rights and economic leverage whether their cases involve 10 cents or $10,000, and when they exert their rights and their leverage, they can obtain results. They have learned also that they have allies — in government agencies, the media, business and consumer groups and in the judicial system — and do not have to battle alone. Moreover, they have learned the importance of asserting their rights and their leverage — not only for their own sakes as individuals, but for all consumers. Every time a consumer wins a just fight, it is an incentive for reputable businessmen to maintain high standards of manufacture and service and, at the same time, a deterrent to those who are less than scrupulous. If every shady practice leads to a consumer battle and a consumer victory, that practice may begin to seem unprofitable.

On the other hand, not every consumer quarrel is just. We have rights as purchasers, but we also have obligations. If you buy an item which is plainly labeled "Damaged," you have forfeited your right to complain when you discover it is less than perfect. If you neglect to read the warranty that comes with your television set or gas stove (see Chapter 7 for a discussion of warranties and the protections offered by the Magnuson-Moss Act) and violate its terms by failing to perform the periodic maintenance or by taking it to an unauthorized dealer for repair, you will have no further claim on the warrantor. If you throw away important documents — receipts, warranties, contracts, repair orders, cancelled checks — you will leave yourself with little evidence on which to base a claim if a purchase turns out to be unsatisfactory. Both the law and good business practice offer us protection against shoddy merchandise and unethical methods of doing business. But it is our responsibility to make sure, when we have complaints, that they are legitimate — and that we present them clearly and act as quickly and effectively as possible.

Results, not bickering, are what consumers are after. At the same time, they are reluctant to engage in long, costly legal battles, and on the whole they would prefer not to have to submit to binding arbitration by third parties. These routes are sometimes necessary, and they will be discussed in detail in the chapter that follows. But in the overwhelming majority of instances, it is not necessary for consumers to put their cases before judges or arbitrators. In this chapter we will discuss the various dispute resolution mechanisms, short of court action, that are available to consumers. Throughout this book, we have been touching on some of them briefly in connection with the specific kinds of merchandise or services to which they apply; in this chapter, we describe them more fully.

We will talk about the most effective way of dealing with the institution with which you have your problem; about the best way of dealing with a computer; of using the federal protections that cover such specific purchases as those made with credit cards and through door-to-door salespersons; of writing letters of complaint. We will describe the various mediation procedures that have been set up by professional, business and industry organizations to resolve consumer complaints; we will talk about the role of government agencies, the media and consumer groups in working out consumer difficulties. In short, we will tell you what you need to know in order to resolve your consumer problems with a minimum of time, trouble and expense — and with the greatest assurance of success.

The Internal Solution

The solution to many consumer problems can often be found inside the organizations that created them — whether stores, dealerships or manufacturing businesses. This so-called internal solution is the first one that any aggrieved consumer should try. Indeed, until you have tried it, there is no point in trying anything else.

Returning Purchases. Returning merchandise is a privilege rather than a right. Unless a store has sold you something fraudulently or with deception, or has saddled you with defective merchandise, it is not legally compelled to permit you to return any item you have purchased. But most responsible business establishments *do* have a policy that covers goods returned in the same condition as at the time of purchase and within a specified period of time. In some states, it is required by law that the policy — whatever it is — be posted in some prominent place on the premises, but since this requirement does not obtain in all states, it is best to inquire about the policy before you buy. Discount and warehouse stores often have "final sale" or "no return" policies. If, however, returns are permitted, the policy usually involves one of the following steps:

- Exchange. Merchandise may be returned and another item of the same type — in a smaller or larger size or a different color — may be substituted.
- Credit. Customers returning merchandise are given a credit slip, which can be used against the purchase price of any other item in the store.
- Refund. This is the most liberal returns policy, and amounts to a guarantee of customer satisfaction. Under it, the customer returns the goods and is given back the purchase price, either in cash or as credit on the card through which the article was bought.

Most supermarkets have liberal refund policies on groceries. Supermarkets are highly competitive, and no store manager wants to lose a customer who may spend as much as $1,000 a year for the sake of a mere $10-

CONSUMER ALERT

How to Complain by Mail

The U.S. Office of Consumer Affairs (see page 16) offers the following model for the letter of complaint that consumers should send when faced with problems associated with unsatisfactory purchases or repairs:

Your Address
Your City, State,
Zip Code
Date

Appropriate Person
Company Name
Street Address
City, State, Zip Code

Dear (Appropriate Name):

[State Your Purchase] Last week I purchased (or had repaired) [Name Product and Serial or Model Number or Service] a (name of product with serial or model number or service performed). I made this [Include Date and Location of Purchase: Other Details] purchase at (location, date and other important details of the transaction).

[State Problem] Unfortunately, your product (or service) has not performed satisfactorily (or the [Give History of the Problem] service was inadequate) because ———. [Ask for Satisfaction] Therefore, to solve the problem, I would appreciate your (here state the specific action you want). [Enclose Copies of All Documents] Enclosed are copies (copies—**not** originals) of my records (receipts, guarantees, warranties, cancelled checks, contracts, model and serial numbers and any other documents).

I am looking forward to your reply and [Ask for Action Within Reasonable Time] resolution of my problem, and will wait three weeks before seeking third-party assistance. [Include Your Address, Work and Home Phone Numbers] Contact me at the above address or by phone at (home and office numbers here).

Sincerely,

Your Name

refund. Moreover, when customers return packaged products that are spoiled or otherwise defective, the supermarket is fully compensated by the distributor. Therefore, the store can afford to accommodate customers who have legitimate reasons for bringing back groceries. On the other hand, this is not a license for consumers to attempt sharp practices. If you try to return an empty jar of peanut butter, claiming that it was bug-infested, you are not likely to get very far. To prove that there is something wrong with the product, bring it back before it has been used up. An empty jar or carton is not likely to be persuasive.

You can return merchandise to most supermarkets even if there is nothing wrong with it. If, when you get home, you realize that you overspent your budget or bought some items you already had in stock, you should not hesitate to take back the unopened cans and packages and explain your situation to the manager. Describe the problem in a straightforward way and ask for a refund. It's unlikely that you will have any trouble and your money will probably be returned.

Some stores present a more difficult problem. The business sections of many large cities abound in questionable retail establishments — so-called tourist traps that depend entirely on transient business and therefore have no particular need to keep themselves in their customers' good graces. One popular tourist city — New York — has a special consumer protection unit to deal with just such problems; it is described later in this chapter. In other cities, however, you may be in for a hassle in trying to deal with stores like these. But if you deal with reputable establishments, you should have no serious problems.

The first step in returning goods is to phone, write or go directly either to the individual who sold you the product or service involved or to the returns department, if there is one, of the establishment. The chances are that if you have a good case, explain your problem calmly and show whatever documents you have, your difficulty will be resolved then and there. If it is not, ask for the supervisor of the department, the manager of the store or — if necessary — the owner of the establishment. Never hesitate to take your case to the top — not only because that is where the authority resides, but because the people closest to the top are the ones most aware of the importance of good customer relations and most eager to satisfy consumer complaints. Still, it is always possible that even here your complaint will not be satisfied. Fortunately, you can go farther, as you will find later in this chapter.

Battling the Computer. It is the fortunate consumer who has never done battle with a computer, and the even more fortunate one who *has* done battle and has emerged with blood pressure levels and temper intact. Most of the struggles concern bills, and in virtually no case does the computer admit it could ever be in error.

In some cases, consumers have been pushed to extreme actions — and have eventually triumphed. Take the case of the California woman whose credit card was stolen. Even though she reported the theft promptly, as required by law, someone subsequently ran up unauthorized charges on her card, and these got into the computer and onto her bills. She refused to pay them — as was her right — but the credit card company continued to bill her for them. For some reason, officials at the company were unable to get the computer to stop spewing out the erroneous bills.

To make things worse, after a specified period of time, the computerized system, in accordance with the program under which it was operating, informed credit bureaus all over the state that the woman was a bad credit risk. Her repeated complaints were unavailing, and she was finally driven to sue. She won her case. Citing "computer-hearted insensitivity," the court awarded her damages in six figures.

Take unresolved complaints to top management. They are most aware of the need for good public relations.

Then there was the Boston journalist who engaged in a long duel with a credit card company over a charge of several hundred dollars. He had paid the bill but, for reasons unknown, the payment had not been registered by the computer. The journalist wrote and phoned, and on several occasions was informed by officials of the card company that they would look into the matter and straighten it out. Still the computer kept sending notices of overdue charges and turning out nasty notes threatening to damage the journalist's credit rating.

Finally, in desperation, the journalist, accompanied by his lawyer, flew to New York City, went to the national headquarters of the company and marched into the office of the president. He was not there, so the two scoured the corridors until they found the office of the company's general counsel. The lawyer informed him that a suit for a sizable sum would be brought against the company if it did not get its computer to stop making threats about the journalist's credit rating. That statement finally pounded the message through. The general counsel promised that the error would be corrected, that he personally would inspect all bills sent to the journalist until the computer was put straight. He also agreed that the company would pay all expenses for the round-trip protest visit. The computer quickly got its proper instructions and the matter was cleared up.

Unlike these two redoubtable consumers, many victims of computer error either do not notice mistakes in billing or resign themselves to losing the jousting match with the supposedly infallible machines. It really is not necessary to do so. Computers *can* make mistakes, and when they do, the mistakes *can* be straightened out without recourse to threats or lawsuits. But it is important for consumers to read their computerized bills carefully, to check the addition and *not* to assume that the computer is always right. Computers sometimes misread account numbers, and will see an eight instead of a three or a five instead of a six. When that happens, a consumer can be charged for merchandise someone else has bought.

Nor is the computer itself always the villain. Sometimes inaccurate information is fed into it, either accidentally or deliberately. One leading credit card company cites the following examples:

- You and your family dine in a restaurant. The food is poor and badly served. You pay the $50 bill with your card and leave a dollar tip to express your dissatisfaction. After you leave, the waiter changes the one to an 11, and the charge is sent to the credit card company and fed into the computer.
- A store sends two charges for one purchase to the credit card company. Such charges are usually weeded out, but occasionally they are not, and find their way into the computer and onto your bill.
- Someone orders something over the telephone using a credit card, and the person taking the order writes down the wrong number. As a result, you are charged for a bottle of perfume or a record album that you neither wanted nor received.
- The payment checks that card holders send in are encoded manually, and this in itself can create mistakes. A $100 payment, for example, may be entered in the computer as $10, thus making it appear that the card holder is behind in paying bills.

All such mistakes can be dealt with. But you must act properly. It does not help to put a note of complaint on your bill when you pay your account. It will only be fed into the computer and vanish. Nor does it help to fold, spindle or mutilate the card, no matter how emotionally satisfying the action may be. It may upset the computer, but it will not solve the problem.

You may, if you choose, call the company's complaint, consumer affairs or billing department (the appropriate department and its address and telephone number will be found on your bill) as soon as you discover the error. Describe it; get the name of the person you speak to and the name of his or her supervisor; and say you are sending a letter confirming your conversation to both of them. Even if you do not call, be sure to send a letter, with your name, account number, if any, and a precise statement of why you believe the bill is wrong. Pay the undisputed portion of your bill just as you would normally, but do not pay the portion under dispute. And, of course, keep a copy of the letter you send.

When you do this, you are exercising your rights under the Fair Credit Billing Act, passed by Congress in 1974 to help consumers beset by computer-generated billing problems. This legislation requires all credit card companies, retailers offering charge accounts and others who send out bills on a regular basis to take a series of specific actions

When a billing error occurs, pay the undisputed amount and notify the company about the questioned item.

when consumers report billing errors. When you inform a creditor *in writing* about a mistake on your bill, the creditor is required by law to investigate the problem and notify you of the findings within 90 days.

If the creditor finds that you are correct, the erroneous charge and the finance charges on it must be taken off your bill. If the creditor concludes that the charge is valid, you must be given an explanation. If the explanation does not satisfy you, the law gives you the right to send the creditor another letter within 10 days of receiving his. This will not prevent him from informing credit bureaus that you have been delinquent, but the law requires him to inform them that the charge is under dispute; the law further requires that you be

CONSUMER ALERT

The Three-Day Cooling-Off Rule: Cancelling Purchases

A letter similar to this model should be supplied by door-to-door sellers. If it is not, refuse to sign any orders or make any payment until you receive the document.

NOTICE OF CANCELLATION

Date of Transaction

You may cancel this transaction, without any penalty or obligation, within three business days from the above date.

If you cancel, any property traded in, any payments made by you under the contract or sale, and any negotiable instrument executed by you will be returned within 10 business days following receipt by the seller of your cancellation notice, and any security interest arising out of the transaction will be cancelled.

If you cancel, you must make available to the seller at your residence, in substantially as good condition as when received, any goods delivered to you under this contract or sale; or you may, if you wish, comply with the instructions of the seller regarding the return shipment of the goods at the seller's expense and risk.

If you do make the goods available to the seller and the seller does not pick them up within 20 days of the date of your notice of cancellation, you may retain or dispose of the goods without any further obligation. If you fail to make the goods available to the seller, or if you agree to return the goods to the seller and fail to do so, then you remain liable for performance of all obligations under the contract.

To cancel this transaction, mail or deliver a signed and dated copy of this cancellation notice or any other written notice, or send a telegram, to (name of seller), at (address of seller's place of business), not later than midnight of (date):

I hereby cancel this transaction

Date:

(Your signature)

Make certain you retain a copy of the cancellation form and keep it with your records of the transaction. As a precaution send it with a return receipt requested or, if you deliver it by hand, be sure you get a receipt.

informed which credit bureaus have received the potentially damaging information.

The Fair Credit Billing Act does not guarantee that your billing problem will automatically be resolved to your satisfaction. But it does compel a creditor to read your letter, investigate the problem and give you an explanation of the determination that has been made. During the investigation, the creditor cannot bring a lawsuit against you or try to collect the money from you. If he fails to follow these procedures, the law releases you from paying the disputed amount — up to \$50 — even if the creditor turns out to have been correct.

Cancelling Door-to-Door Purchases. A wide variety of products and services are sold from door to door (see Chapter 6) — from encyclopedias, carpets, cookware, cosmetics, magazine subscriptions and vacuum cleaners to family photographs. These sales create a large volume of consumer complaints.

If you have a problem with a door-to-door purchase and cannot resolve it by discussion with the salesperson, your next step should take you to the consumer affairs officer of the manufacturer of the product. If that fails, the Direct Selling Association may be able to help; its program is discussed later in this chapter.

But many of the consumer problems associated with door-to-door sales stem from second thoughts — and a simple remedy is available for all such problems. The men and women who sell door-to-door work on commission and are, therefore, eager to sell you as much as they possibly can. They can be persuasive, and many a consumer — after contracting to buy hundreds or even thousands of dollars worth of merchandise or service — has experienced profound regret the moment the salesperson leaves the house. Those second thoughts can save you from making an unwanted purchase — if you move quickly.

A Federal Trade Commission regulation issued in 1974 establishes a three-day "cooling-off" period on all door-to-door sales. It applies to all sales of $25 or more that are made in your home or anywhere other than the seller's normal place of business — a hotel or a neighbor's living room, for example. According to this regulation, which is discussed in more detail in Chapter 6, the buyer may cancel any such transaction without penalty within three business days of the sale.

The FTC ruling requires the salesperson to furnish customers with a fully completed receipt or contract in whatever language was used in the transaction. This document must contain the exact date of the transaction, the name and address of the seller and the following statement in prominent type: "You, the buyer, may cancel this transaction at any time prior to midnight of the third business day after the date of this transaction. See the attached notice of cancellation form for an explanation." (See box on page 336 for a copy of this cancellation form.) In addition, the regulation requires the salesperson to tell the buyer orally about the right to cancel.

In some states, even longer cooling-off periods have been established by law and in some, telephone solicitation sales are also subject to rules requiring written agreements and notice of cancellation rights. You can find out if you are covered by such local legislation by calling your state attorney general's office (see directory, page 48).

To safeguard your rights under this regulation, make certain the receipt or contract is properly dated and signed and be sure that it accurately describes the transaction — what you are buying, the price and the installment payments. If you decide to cancel your order, send the cancellation notice by registered mail or convey the message in a telegram so that you will have proof that you acted by the required date.

Going up the Ladder. Studies have shown that few people — of the minority that complains at all — pursue their problems beyond the lower levels. But if you have a legitimate complaint and cannot get satisfaction at the lower levels, do not give up. Escalate quickly and be persistent. Go to the higher echelons with your complaint.

The best people to complain to are those with power: they are able to resolve the dispute and are deeply concerned about their company's image. Focus on the president of the company, the vice president in charge of operations or the consumer affairs officer. You can get their names from the dealer who sold you the goods or services in question or by telephoning the national office of the company; if they are not available through this method, visit your local library and consult such reference books as Standard & Poor's *Register of Corporations, Directors and Executives* and Moody's *Industrial Manual.* If you know the name of the product but not the name of the manufacturer, consult the *Thomas Registry*. A very useful booklet published by the U.S. Office of Consumer Affairs is the *Consumer's Resource Handbook*. It contains the names and addresses of the heads of consumer relations departments in hundreds of American companies. You can obtain a free copy by writing to Handbook, Consumer Information Center, Pueblo, Colorado 81009.

Once you have the name of the appropriate official, you are ready to send a letter of complaint. But be sure it is properly written:

- Make certain it is businesslike, legibly written or neatly typed, and to the point.
- Keep it calm in tone, not angry, and state the nature of your complaint, giving details about the time and place of purchase and the steps you have taken to resolve the problem.
- Include copies (not originals) of cancelled checks, receipts, warranties, advertisements and any previous correspondence that might have some bearing on your complaint.
- Be precise — say what you want done and within what time period.
- Send copies of your letter to the company's legal department and public relations department, and, of course, keep copies of all your correspondence.

Obviously, there is no single form for such a letter, and the details will vary with the problem involved. But the one suggested by the U.S. Office of Consumer Affairs and shown in the box on page 333 provides a good model to follow.

If things work out well, such a letter will get results. But if you do not hear from the company, or if you get a politely worded brush-off, send another letter to the same person, referring to the first and to the fact that you have had either no response or an unsatisfactory one. Then state that you are pursuing the matter with a third party — either within the industry, with the Better Business Bureau, with a particular consumer action group, with the media or with the government. Some consumer advocates recommend trying all these methods at once. Others think it a bad idea which makes it appear that you are groping. The course you choose is up to you, as long as you make it clear that your complaint is still alive and that you mean business.

Before you take your complaint outside the company, be aware that some major companies have in-house appeals procedures. If your complaint involves a substantial amount of money, you might want to find out from the consumer affairs officer whether such an appeals mechanism is available.

The Ford Motor Company, for example, has a Consumer Appeals Board that allows any owner of a Ford car who has a service complaint about his vehicle to request a board review of the problem, provided that the dealer from whom the car was bought is in a state where such a board exists. Each board consists of five members: three consumer representatives and two representatives of the company. Presentations are usually made in writing. The automobile company and its dealers are bound by the decisions of the board. Consumers are not, however, and are free to take their cases to the courts if they are dissatisfied wih the decision.

Some consumer advocates view in-house appeals procedures with suspicion, on the grounds that any body established by a company will be dominated by company interests. It is difficult to assess the merit of the criticism. But if you have a complaint against a company that has such an appeals mechanism, why not use it? You are not bound by the decision and can go on to the next step in the complaint process. Incidentally, a number of other automobile makers, domestic and foreign, have agreed to go beyond in-house procedures and accept third-party binding arbitration of consumer complaints by the Better Business Bureau. In Chapter 14 you will find a discussion of this process.

Private Sector Forums

If you are unable to obtain satisfaction through the complaint procedures of an individual company, you may want to try one of the many consumer complaint mechanisms that have been established within various industries. The effectiveness of these mechanisms and their determination to be fair to the consumer varies from industry to industry and there is no guarantee that you will be successful if you take your case to any one of them. On the other hand, if you are persistent and your case is strong, you may be able to resolve your problem and save yourself considerable money and distress.

Consumer Action and Advisory Panels (CAP's). These are special organizations which have been established by a number of major industries to help resolve problems between consumer and industry members. The various panels differ among themselves in the details of their organization, but all have some things in common:

All make it clear that a consumer with a complaint should contact them only after having registered the complaint with a retailer, dealer or manufacturer without a satisfactory result.

All want complaints filed in writing. By the time a complaint gets to the point where a CAP is willing to act on it, it has probably grown quite complex and involves a considerable sum of money. Consumers who are able to explain their position clearly and concisely may therefore have an advantage.

Basically, the CAP's will do two things for a consumer: ask the manufacturer to reinvestigate the case and notify the CAP of any action taken; and — if the action does not resolve the case — refer it to a so-called Action Panel, which usually includes representatives both of industry and the consumers. After hearing the case, the panel will recommend an action to the manufacturer or dealer.

CAP's differ, however, not only with respect to specific techniques and in the composition of their panels, but also in the zeal with which they do their jobs.

Major Appliance Consumer Action Panel (MACAP). Established in 1970 after an avalanche of consumer complaints about faulty appliances and poor service — and a critical federal government report — MACAP was the first consumer action panel formed. It is one of the busiest, hearing complaints on refrigerators, washers, dryers, dishwashers, gas and electric ranges, room air conditioners, garbage disposals, trash compactors, water heaters, humidifiers, dehumidifiers and gas incinerators. The panel is composed entirely of non-industry representatives, usually academics, lawyers, consumer advocates and technicians.

MACAP does not hear all the cases that are presented to it. A good many are dismissed, especially when warranties have run out or documentation is lacking — a fact that points up the importance of a MACAP recommendation to consumers: keep file folders on major appliances as a depository for receipts, warranties, correspondence and the like. Although the board's decisions are binding neither on the consumer nor the manufacturer, MACAP claims that of the cases it agrees to hear, approximately 80 percent are resolved to the consumer's "full or partial satisfaction." In one instance, for example, a woman had to have her refrigerator repaired three times in the first year after its purchase. On the basis of the MACAP recommendation, the manufacturer refunded her the purchase price. In another, a consumer complained that her dishwasher had suffered repeated parts failures and had been repaired four times in two years by an authorized dealer — three times within the warranty period and once after the warranty had run out. In this case, the panel recommended a refund of the money she had paid for the post-warranty repair, on the grounds that the machine had not been properly serviced by the dealer during the three "in-warranty" repair jobs.

If you have a complaint about a major appliance that you have been unable to resolve through normal channels, write to MACAP. Include your name, address and telephone number; the brand, model, serial number and type of appliance; the name and address of the dealer from whom you bought it and of the service agent; give a clear description of your problem, what you have done to resolve it, and the remedy you seek. Major Appliance Consumer Action Panel is located at: 20 North Wacker Drive, Chicago, Illinois 60606.

Automobile Consumer Action Panel (AUTOCAP). Automobiles are one of the major sources of consumer complaints throughout the country. In small towns and large cities automobile owners struggle with warranty disputes and cars that simply do not run as well as they should. Many car-buyers have the feeling that dealers are simply not interested in them once customers have concluded their purchase and left the showroom.

As a result, automobile dealers in various parts of the country gradually realized the necessity of polishing their tarnished image by offering greater help to car buyers with persistent, unresolved complaints. They gradually set up a loose network of state and local complaint boards called AUTOCAP's. At first, the AUTOCAP's were not organized on a national basis, and procedures varied widely from one community to the next. In some places, for example, panels mediated disputes, while in others they did not. This problem was remedied in 1979 when the National Automobile Dealers Association (NADA) adopted uniform national standards and set up a Division of Consumer Affairs to ensure that all dealers complied with these standards. As AUTOCAP expanded, it broadened its industry representation to include manufacturers as well as dealers. Although Ford, Chrysler and General Motors maintain their own complaint resolution services, American Motors and virtually all foreign car manufacturers have agreed to accept AUTOCAP as their "court of last resort" for product and warranty performance problems and to honor its decisions in cases where the manufacturer and the consumer cannot agree.

Complaint-resolution services are offered by almost all domestic and foreign automobile manufacturers.

Contact with an AUTOCAP is usually made through a local or regional Automobile Dealers Association, although it can be made directly. Complaints can sometimes be resolved over the telephone, but in most cases, the consumer must describe the problem in writing. The AUTOCAP manager will then attempt to mediate a solution in an informal manner and — according to NADA — will succeed in about 88 percent of all cases. The 12 percent that are not resolved at this stage are then referred to an AUTOCAP panel.

Most AUTOCAP panels consist of about

The Power of the Press

Among the most powerful allies consumers have are the consumer affairs columnists in the newspapers. Complaints that often go unanswered when ordinary citizens make them become the objects of serious attention when journalists get into the act. Consider the two examples that follow:

Action Line, one of the busiest consumer affairs columns in the western states, and a regular feature of Denver's *Rocky Mountain News*, received a letter from a woman who had moved to Colorado Springs from Albany, New York. Before the move, she wrote, she had left an electric blanket for repair in a large Albany store, with instructions that it be shipped to her in Colorado when the repair was made. "We never got it," the consumer wrote. "When we complained, the store officials said they would trace the shipment through the delivery service. However, we have heard nothing in a year."

The Rocky Mountain News was interested and investigated her complaint. As the Action Line column told the woman: "Both the store and the delivery service made a mistake — and both offered to make good. Yes, the delivery service took the parcel to the wrong house, its consumer service officer told us. But even when a delivery service is at fault for a lost parcel, as it is in this case, it is legally responsible to pay for it only if the shipper filed a lost-package claim within nine months — which the Albany store failed to do. . . . "

Still, the problem would not remain unsolved: "A representative of the Albany store called to tell you to buy a new electric blanket and send them the bill. But if for some reason the store fails to take care of it, the delivery company said that it will pay your bill."

The Record, New Jersey's largest evening newspaper, described a problem it solved for a reader who, unable to write by hand because of painful arthritis, owned two typewriters, both of the same manufacture and both over five years old. When they broke down, the owner tried to get them repaired through the offices of the manufacturer, first in one New Jersey city and then in a second. But neither was prepared to do repairs, and even stated that there was no way the machines could be fixed, since the needed parts were no longer available. When a call was placed to the manufacturer's office in Connecticut, the consumer still was not able to get any help.

At this point, the exasperated consumer contacted the Action Line column at *The Record.* Staffers took on the case and soon were able to report: "After Action Line wrote to the manufacturer's office in New Jersey, the customer relations manager called to apologize. The Connecticut office offered to fix your seven-year old machine and reimburse you for the postage. The New Jersey office, however, sent you a four-year old rebuilt model, free of charge."

eight members, all serving on a voluntary basis. At least half must be consumer representatives; the others are dealer representatives. The consumers are usually associated with state and local agencies, with the media or with education. At least one consumer with technical knowledge is sought for each panel. Once the panel has weighed the testimony in the case, it arrives at a consensus regarding an equitable solution. The consumer who gets a favorable AUTOCAP decision is in an excellent position since the decision is binding on any dealer who belongs to the local association sponsoring the AUTOCAP. But no decision is binding on the consumer. This means that any car owner who does not like a determination is free to pursue other means of redress.

To locate the AUTOCAP nearest you, call your local Chamber of Commerce or Better

Business Bureau or write to: National Automobile Dealers Association, 8400 West Park Drive, McLean, Virginia 22102.

Furniture Industry Consumer Advisory Panel (FICAP). Sponsored by the Southern Furniture Manufacturers Association, whose members manufacture almost half of all furniture sold in the United States, FICAP handles disputes involving both problems of manufacture — couches that collapse, poorly made kitchen sets and other physical aspects of furniture that do not live up to promise — and difficulties with service — failure of manufacturers to make repairs or restitution in these situations. Its panel, composed of furniture industry representatives, consumer advocates and independent experts, cannot impose its decisions on either party to the dispute. From the consumer's point of view, therefore, FICAP has limitations. Nevertheless, it can be an avenue worth exploring. If you wish to pursue a furniture complaint, write to: Furniture Industry Consumer Advisory Panel, Director of Consumer Affairs, Box 951, High Point, North Carolina 27261.

Funeral Industry Consumer Action Panel (ThanaCAP). The funeral industry has been the target of criticism from both private and government sources. The critics point to the high cost of funerals in the United States and the inclusion in that cost of such possibly unnecessary extras as floral arrangements, limousines, embalming, organists, death announcements and hair styling and makeup for the deceased, and also to the fact that families using the services of funeral directors are, by reason of their grief, less likely than they would ordinarily be to make wise financial decisions.

In response to this criticism, the National Funeral Directors Association in 1981 established ThanaCAP (from the Greek word *thanatos*, which means death, and CAP for consumer action panel). Consumers with complaints about treatment at the hands of funeral directors should write to ThanaCAP for a complaint form, which they can fill out and return. The complaint will be turned over to the National Funeral Directors Association, which will attempt to mediate the dispute informally. If the mediation is not successful within 30 days, ThanaCAP will ask both parties to accept arbitration by a panel made up of two consumer representatives and one funeral director. Their decision is binding.

ThanaCAP has found that many of the complaints it receives do not concern funeral directors, but involve cemeteries or monument companies. When it receives such complaints, ThanaCAP either directs the consumer to the correct individual or firm or passes the complaint along to the appropriate trade organization. If you wish to file a complaint about a funeral director, write: ThanaCAP, 135 West Wells Street, Milwaukee, Wisconsin 53203.

Trade Associations

Most American industries have trade associations whose major function is to help the industry as a whole, through such activities as education, training, a publications program and, sometimes, legislative lobbying. In addition, these associations sometimes receive complaints from consumers, and some have set up consumer affairs departments at their national headquarters. Like the CAP's, these trade association consumer departments vary in their policies and procedures. Some may file your complaint in the wastebasket. But most make an honest effort to handle consumer complaints with seriousness and courtesy, if only to protect the good name of their respective industries.

As there are some 40,000 trade associations in the United States, it is impossible to discuss all their consumer programs within the compass of one book. We have therefore limited ourselves to describing those that cover major industries and services and that have reasonably good records in dealing with consumer complaints. If your problem concerns goods or services not discussed in the following section, you may want to get in touch with the appropriate trade association anyway, and inquire if it handles consumer complaints. Your local library should have a copy of the directory, *National Trade-Professional Associations of the U.S. and Canada*. It lists these groups by name and address.

American Movers Conference (AMC). Although the American Movers Conference has a Consumer Assistance Office, it has no active mediation program. Many members of the Conference have agreed to offer customers binding arbitration through a program administered by the American Arbitration Association (see Chapter 14). These movers are required to inform consumers of the program prior to a move, and to give them a brochure about it. Write to: American Movers Conference, 400 Army-Navy Drive, Arlington, Virginia 22202 for further information.

Another industry organization, the Movers' & Warehousemen's Association of America, also has a binding arbitration program administered by the American Arbitration Association. Write to the organization at: 1001 North Highland Street, Arlington, Virginia 22201.

American Society of Travel Agents (ASTA). Disputes with travel agents are not uncommon. You may find yourself booked into a hotel far from the beach, ski slope or music festival you were hoping to enjoy, or on a charter flight that never takes off. You may be saddled with accommodations that do not begin to merit the prices that are charged. If you cannot resolve your problem directly with the travel agent involved, ASTA will attempt to mediate the dispute. Your letter to the organization should include copies of all relevant documents — not only receipts and copies of cancelled checks, but, where possible, advertisements placed by the travel agency. On receipt of this material, ASTA will write to the agent, advising of the complaint and asking for a reply. After hearing both sides of the problem, it will attempt to mediate the dispute. If mediation fails, the society takes no further steps, but claims that most agents will try to accommodate the consumer. Write to: American Society of Travel Agents, 4400 MacArthur Boulevard, NW, Washington, D.C. 20007.

Direct Marketing Association (DMA). The Direct Marketing Association (formerly the Direct Mail/Marketing Association) is the world's oldest and largest international organization of mail order businesses. Its approximately 3,000 members represent most of the legitimate firms in this enormous industry. To deal with the problems of dissatisfied customers, the DMA has established the Mail Order Action Line (MOAL), which annually receives about 25,000 complaints regarding goods ordered by mail and by telephone. The majority of complaints cover such problems as damaged shipments, failure to deliver or make refunds on goods, faulty billing and misrepresentation in advertising.

MOAL acknowledges every complaint it receives, and requests the consumer to write again if its intercession does not produce a satisfactory solution to the problem within approximately 30 days. It also sends a copy of the complaint to the company in question, along with a letter asking the firm to look into the matter and inform it of any action taken. If this does not solve the problem and the consumer writes to say so, MOAL will write the company a second and even a third time.

MOAL keeps files on all the firms about which it has received complaints, and the failure of a firm to respond may lead to an investigation by the DMA's Ethics and Consumer Affairs Department. If illegal practice is suspected, the DMA will turn over all relevant information to the Federal Trade Commission or to the U.S. Postal Inspection Service, which has jurisdiction over mail order fraud.

While it has no power to force any company to act, MOAL's record of success is high, not only with DMA member companies, but with others as well, and its files are crammed with letters of thanks from consumers all around the country.

Complaints to MOAL must be sent in writing, with copies (never send originals) of cancelled checks or credit card statements. Complaints should include the consumer's name and address, the name and address of the company involved, the gist of the problem and the solution that is being sought. Write to: Direct Marketing Association, Mail Order Action Line, 6 East 43rd Street, New York, New York 10017.

Direct Selling Association (DSA). In Chapter 6 we discussed the way to cancel deals made with door-to-door salespersons. But if you have a stubborn problem about a door-to-door sale — whether it involves cancellation, nondelivery of goods for which full or partial payment has already been made, or any similar difficulty — the DSA is where you should go to complain. The association claims that it resolves 95 percent of the disputes it hears about, although its procedures are entirely informal. Write to: Direct Selling Association, Director of Consumer Affairs, 1730 M Street, NW, Washington, D.C. 20036.

Electronic Industries Association (EIA). This trade association represents thousands of manufacturers and sellers of television sets, radios, stereo equipment, tape recorders, hand calculators and home computers. It does not handle consumer complaints unless prior efforts to resolve them through the dealer or manufacturer have been to no avail. Nor is it prepared to deal with all the problems consumers bring to it. If, after 10 years of faithful service, your air conditioner fails to function properly, the EIA will not be sympathetic, if only because your warranty expired a long time ago.

On the other hand, if your complaint is considered legitimate, the EIA will intervene, even if the firm with which you are having trouble is not a member of the association. In your letter state your complaint; give the name of the dealer from whom you bought the product and its brand, model and serial number, and indicate the remedy you are seeking. Include copies of all pertinent correspondence, receipts and other documents. On receipt of your letter, EIA's Consumer Division will call or write the appropriate person in the company involved. Thereafter, it will follow up to determine what action the company has taken and, if necessary, suggest a solution.

In one case, for example, a consumer complained about a television set that apparently had a defective transistor. It had twice been replaced free of charge by the manufacturer, acting on a request from the dealer. But when it failed a third time, the manufacturer refused to perform this service on the grounds that it was now time for the set owner to absorb the charge. When EIA's Consumer Division asked the manufacturer why, in its view, the transistor had failed so often, the manufacturer assigned the Regional Service Manager to examine the set. This highly-skilled technician discovered something that had previously been overlooked: a defect in the manufacture of the set itself that was causing the transistor to fail. Given this new information, the manufacturer agreed to repair the defect *and* to replace the transistor at no cost to the consumer for parts, labor or delivery.

The EIA can be reached through a letter to: Consumer Division, Electronics Industries Association, 2001 Eye Street, NW, Washington, D.C. 20006.

Home Owners Warranty Corporation (HOW). This organization, founded in 1974 by the National Association of Home Builders, is not strictly a trade association, but an independent company owned by its more than 11,000 home-builder members. If you have bought a home from a builder who is not a member of the HOW Corporation, there is nothing this group can do for you. But if your builder *is* a member, and if you have agreed to purchase the HOW Corporation's insured warranty program, it is likely that your complaint will be dealt with to your satisfaction.

Whether the purchase involves a house, a town house or a condominium, HOW offers new home buyers a solid two-year warranty from the builder. During the first year, the builder is responsible for correcting problems caused by faulty workmanship and defective materials and for correcting any major structural defects. The warranty for major structural defects continues during the second year, and the house is also warranteed against defects in the wiring, piping and duct work of the mechanical and electrical systems. From the third through the 10th year of the warranty, the home owner is protected against major structural defects through insurance coverage arranged by the HOW Corporation and requiring the payment of a one-time deductible of $250. If, for any reason, the builder cannot meet his warranty responsibilities during the first two years, the HOW Corporation will assume them — again, subject to a one-time $250 deductible paid by the home owner.

Even under such a warranty program difficulties may, of course, arise, and procedures have been established to deal with them. The home owner sends the builder a letter spelling out specific grievances in detail, and sends a copy to the HOW Corporation. If the letter produces no response from the builder — or if the builder feels the complaint is unjustified — the next step is for the aggrieved party to contact the local or regional HOW Corporation office and ask for assistance in settling the dispute. A neutral third party is then chosen to mediate or, if this informal process holds no promise of success, to arbitrate, with the understanding that the decision of the arbitrator will be binding on the builder but not the home owner, who may choose to pursue other remedies.

CONSUMER ALERT

Telephone Tips

In many communities, excellent free advice on consumer complaints is only a telephone call away. Whether the problem has to do with a car, home improvements, offensive mail or any one of a number of other things, all the consumer has to do is dial the appropriate number, describe the difficulty and wait for the tape recorded message of instructions and information.

There are hundreds of these tape information services across the United States, at no cost to the consumer save that of the telephone call.

Some of these services are operated by Better Business Bureau branches; they are called Tel-Tips. Others are sponsored by county or municipal consumer affairs agencies; these may be called Tel-Consumer or something similar. Either the BBB or your consumer affairs office (see directories on pages 32 and 16) can give you the telephone number to call in your area and a list of the consumer tapes it contains.

When you make your call, be sure to have pencil and paper handy, since some of the messages are detailed and you will probably want to take notes. But don't worry if you miss something. You can always dial the number again.

HOW also has a warranty program that covers remodeling. It runs for five years, and HOW members are obliged to offer it to consumers in connection with all jobs costing over $5,000. During the first year, the contractor is responsible for correcting all major structural defects and defects in workmanship and material. During the second, the wiring, piping and duct work of the mechanical and electrical systems are insured against defects and the warranty on major structural defects continues. From the third to the fifth year, the remodeled portion of the house is insured against major structural defects over and above a $100 deductible. The complaint procedure in the case of the remodeling warranty is the same as for a new home.

The HOW program is generally considered among the most successful attempts by an industry to regulate itself and its members. If you are buying a home — or planning to have your home remodeled — ask whether the builder or contractor is a member of the Home Owners Warranty Corporation. For further information on the various HOW programs, get in touch with your state or local home builder's and remodeler's associations or write: Home Owners Warranty Corporation, 2000 L Street, NW, Washington, D.C. 20036.

Magazine Action Line (MAL). Publisher's Clearing House, a company that sells magazines at cut-rate subscription prices, has established this consumer complaint mechanism both to keep consumers happy and to weed out that minority of dishonest salespersons who take money for magazine subscriptions they have no intention of delivering. MAL is prepared to act on all complaints in this area, no matter what individual or organization sold the subscription. If you write to MAL with the details of your transaction, it will follow through and may be able to get you a refund — whether from a subscription seller who took your money but did not deliver the magazine or from one who pressured you into buying more than you intended. Write to: Magazine Action Line, 382 Channel Drive, Port Washington, New York 11050.

Better Business Bureau (BBB)

The Better Business Bureaus, to which we have referred a number of times in this book, are business-sponsored nonprofit organizations. Approximately 150 local branches now exist across the country. Originally organized in the early years of the century to monitor advertisements for honesty — a function it still performs — the BBB has expanded its scope considerably over the years. Many of its branches are both active and effective as consumer allies.

BBB branches keep files on firms in their communities, registering any complaints that may be raised against them by consumers. If you check with your local BBB office before making a substantial purchase at any establishment with which you are unfamiliar, you will be able to discover what, if any, problems other consumers may have had in dealing with it. The BBB will not recommend a course of action but it will give you the information necessary to make a decision.

Some BBB branches send their own shoppers to size up firms in which a pattern of questionable dealing is suspected. One BBB in Texas, for example, received numerous consumer complaints about a television repair service. Set owners accused the firm of misrepresenting the repairs they made, making repairs that were not authorized and others that did not work, and failing to make promised refunds. The BBB checked out the service by placing one defective $12 tube in an otherwise working set and marking all the other parts with a special chemical, visible only under a certain kind of light. The set was then installed in the home of a cooperative consumer. When the TV repair service was called to the house, its representative announced that the transformer was burned out and that it would cost $92 to replace it. The consumer agreed, and the set was, indeed, restored to working order. But, as subsequent examination made clear, the only change was replacement of the defective tube. Armed with this evidence, the BBB referred the case to the Consumer Protection Division of the state attorney general's office, which brought suit against the company.

A BBB branch in Tennessee reported another example: "A local carpet company had racked up 15 complaints in a little over two years, a record unmatched by any other company in our area. We charted the complaints, identifying the date, complainant, cause for complaint, company response and name of company person. It soon became clear that the company made promises it was not keeping, had installation problems, and though we had the name of the owner, it was difficult to identify who was 'in charge.'

"We wrote to the owner, telling him of the concerns we had, asked him to examine our report and talk to us about the information. Within one month's time, the company had re-made appointments with four of the listed customers, solved year-old problems and fired the salesman who was clearly one source of their problems."

Often, BBB branches intercede on behalf of individual consumers who have had difficulties with businesses that behave irresponsibly. If an appliance dealer refuses to help you get repairs done on your dishwasher, even though the equipment is still under warranty, your local BBB may be willing to send a letter to the store, spelling out your complaint and asking for a response. A small number of firms so contacted will ignore the BBB letter, and others will stick to their guns and insist the consumer is wrong. But the largest number will make an effort to resolve the dispute to the consumer's satisfaction. No reputable firm wants to get a black mark on its record in the BBB files.

A BBB in Pennsylvania received a letter from a couple complaining that two of the chairs in an expensive dining room set started falling apart only weeks after they arrived and that the furniture store refused to do anything about the matter, on the ground that the furniture did not come with a guarantee. When the BBB contacted the store, reminding it of the importance of customer goodwill and of the fact that the manufacturer would probably want to know about defective merchandise, the store reversed its position and gave the couple two new chairs.

Although the BBB has no enforcement power in situations like the one described above, its record of success is good. The organization is also active in the field of arbitration of consumer complaints, especially in connection with automobiles. This program is discussed in Chapter 14.

On page 32, you will find a directory of the BBB's state offices, through which you can find the address of the branch nearest you. If you feel you need the attention of the BBB's national office, write: Council of Better Business Bureaus, Inc., 1515 Wilson Boulevard, Arlington, Virginia 22209.

Professional Services

Some of the most serious consumer complaints — both in connection with costs and with services — are those against individuals and agencies rendering professional services. Doctors, dentists, lawyers, hospitals, medical insurance — all create their share of difficulties. The problems are seldom easy to solve, but steps that hold significant hope of success can and *should* be taken.

Physicians. The great majority of physicians are competent, ethical and honest. But there are exceptions, as in any profession. When you have a legitimate grievance against a doctor, do not hesitate to complain. Until recently, the medical profession was highly protective of its members. But the skyrocketing cost of malpractice insurance, together with growth in patient education and awareness, has encouraged doctors to adopt improved methods of self-policing. Today, the profession is much more willing than it was in the past to warn, penalize and — if necessary — get rid of the bad apples in its midst.

If you have a complaint about a doctor and have been unable to resolve it by direct discussion, get in touch with your county medical society. The listings are not always easy to find in the telephone book. Some groups begin their names with the name of the county in which they are located; others list themselves as "Medical Society of . . ." You may have to ask the directory assistance operator for the name and address.

The groups also differ in the ways in which they deal with patient complaints. But most societies have grievance committees and, although the committees are generally made up of doctors and in some cases have a built-in bias in favor of their colleagues, most try to be impartial. If you are not satisfied at this level, the next step is to go to the state board that licenses physicians.

If, however, you have reason to suspect that the doctor is engaged in fraud — inflating bills that will be paid by an insurance company or by the government, for example — notify both your state attorney general (see directory, page 48) and the insurance company or government office involved. If you think you have grounds for a malpractice suit, consult a lawyer. The procedure to be followed thereafter is discussed in Chapter 14.

Hospital Bills. Even the best medical coverage is unlikely to include all the expenses of a hospital stay. It is therefore important to check your bill carefully — before leaving the hospital, if possible, or as soon as you have arrived at home.

The process will probably not be easy. Hospital bills are often almost indecipherable, especially those prepared by computer. Moreover, it is difficult for a layman to assess the fairness of charges for drugs and special therapies. Still, you can make certain that you have been charged for the correct number of days and at the correct rate, and you should be able to spot such errors as charges for costly extras that you never received.

If you find a charge that you know to be in error, do not pay that part of the bill until it is straightened out. Some hospitals say that they will give you a refund if your claim is verified after you have paid in full. But even when they have been proved wrong in their billing, they may be slow to make a refund — if only because they cannot get their computers to digest the idea. So it is important for you *not* to pay erroneous charges and to notify your insurance company both of the mistake and of your action.

Blue Cross and Blue Shield. The national office of Blue Cross/Blue Shield has established a division of Consumer Affairs to which subscribers can refer complaints about actions taken by state or local branches of the organization, whether with regard to medical bills or payments of premiums. The national office cannot dictate to the local branches, but it can bring considerable pressure to bear if you have a solid case against a branch. Make sure your letter is complete and detailed; if you have been denied payment on a claim, for example, you will have to indicate the reason given by the local office for its denial. Address: Blue Cross/Blue Shield, Office of Consumer Affairs, 1709 New York Avenue NW, Washington, D.C. 20006.

Dentists. If you have a complaint about a dentist that you have been unable to resolve in talks with him or her, take your case to the grievance committee of the county dental society. The procedures established by these committees vary from locality to locality, but usually they require the patient to submit a concise written statement of the complaint, indicating what type of work was done and why it is unsatisfactory. The dentist is also asked to present his or her side of the case. Thereafter, the grievance committee — made up of practicing dentists — may want to examine the patient's mouth and check the quality of the work. It will then render its decision. A dentist who refuses to accept a negative decision by the grievance committee could be in for serious trouble, and, in an extreme case, charged with a violation of the society's code of ethics and expelled.

A consumer who is not satisfied with the

grievance committee's decision can appeal to the state dental society. If the case involves gross negligence, it should be taken to the state board of medical examiners, which licenses dentists as well as physicians.

Lawyers. Lawyers sometimes seem intimidating to their clients, who suffer in silence as the fees mount up and the legal matter drags on interminably — a problem made even worse by the client's uncomfortable suspicion that the attorney really is not interested in his or her case. As a result, problems frequently fester, and matters grow worse.

The first step, obviously, is to prevent this from happening. If you have any difficulty with your lawyer, insist that the two of you discuss it openly. If this does not resolve the problem, the next step is the state bar association's grievance committee. It will ask you to submit your complaint in writing, stating the attorney's name and address; what work you expected to have performed what transpired during the course of your relationship; what you think the lawyer did that was wrong; what you have done to try to resolve the dispute; and what remedy you want.

The specific procedures followed by grievance committees vary from state to state, but generally they read the complaint, acknowledge it and send a copy to the attorney, asking for a response within a certain period of time. The attorney almost always will respond, and a copy of the response will be sent to you, with a request that you reply to it via the committee. With all these letters in hand, the committee will try to resolve the matter informally, and often will succeed.

If the complaint is not resolved, the case may be brought before a hearing panel composed of lawyers and laymen. These hearings can be quite formal; you and the attorney may be asked to testify and submit to questions in private. If the panel decides your complaint has no merit, your next step is to go to the state licensing board.

But if the panel finds merit in your complaint, its action will be based on the seriousness of the lawyer's breach of legal ethics and his or her past record. The punishment may be no more than a slap on the wrist — some sort of private admonition. It may be a simple reprimand. Or the reprimand may be accompanied by a referral to the court and a recommendation for such sanctions as temporary suspension from the bar or even disbarment. Usually, the court accepts the panel's recommendation, but it is free to deliver a softer or tougher judgment than that proposed.

What good does this do the client, other than the satisfaction derived from seeing the lawyer punished in some way? It may produce some financial reward as well. A number of states have "client protection funds" or "client security funds," usually supported by members of the state bar. In some cases, this fund will compensate the client for expenses incurred while pursuing the complaint and even for part of the money that may have been in dispute in the first place. You can find out if such a fund exists in your state by inquiring of your state bar association.

Consumer Action Groups

Scattered throughout the country is a network of private and voluntary consumer action organizations. Some are large and some small; some focus their attention on one particular kind of consumer problem — landlord-tenant relations, for example, or dealings with utilities — while others deal with a whole range of consumer issues. Some, formed for the purpose of coping with a one-time difficulty or emergency, stay in existence for no more than a few months; others are permanent. Some may be offshoots of other organizations — churches, unions, public interest groups, professional associations, student groups — while others spring up independently at the grass-roots level. Moreover, they go about their work in many different ways. Some concentrate on taking surveys that relate to consumer problems — the pricing practices of local businesses, the quality of their goods or services, the cleanliness of their establishments, the degree of their compliance with consumer laws, for example — and then publicize the findings through fliers, booklets and media coverage, in order to effect changes in the policies of establishments that do not live up to standard. Other groups address themselves to public policy questions; their activities include petitioning and testifying before government agencies, lobbying for legislation, initiating consumer-interest lawsuits, publishing, teaching and launching voter registration or media drives.

Some groups will also assist consumers

with individual complaints. The Consumers Education and Protective Association (CEPA) of Philadelphia, for example, which was founded in 1966 by a group of frustrated consumers in that Pennsylvania city, is dedicated entirely to resolving individual complaints brought to it by community members. Its newsletter regularly records the victories: "Builder Refunds $2,000" . . . "Dentist Refunds $400."

CEPA operates in an orderly, determined way, using methods it sums up in three words: Investigate, Negotiate and Demonstrate. Consumers are invited to bring complaints to a CEPA weekly branch meeting and the members then question the complainant to determine whether the protest has merit. If they believe it does, a grievance committee investigates the matter more thoroughly, examining relevant documents and consulting experts if necessary. A letter is then written to the merchant or business against which the complaint has been made, explaining the problem and asking for the other side of the case. If the difficulty cannot be resolved at this level, the merchant is asked to meet with the consumer and representatives of CEPA in order to negotiate a fair settlement. In most cases, the negotiations succeed. But if the merchant refuses to budge, CEPA acts decisively, setting up a picket line outside his or her place of business. A vast majority of the complaints that reach this stage are settled shortly after the picketing begins.

CEPA asks only one thing of consumers for whom it acts: that they join the organization and picket for other consumers when called upon to do so.

Even in areas where there is no such consumer activist group, it may be possible to employ the CEPA tactic. But before you paint yourself a sign and march out to demonstrate, you would be well advised to consult with an attorney to make sure that the action you plan to take is within the law in your community.

If you are interested in finding out about a consumer action group in your area, check with your local Consumer Affairs Department (see directory, page 16). Further information is available in *HELP: The Useful Almanac*, and the Consumer Federation of America's *Directory of State and Local Consumer Groups*. Both should be available at your local library.

The Media Route

All business owners — small local merchants or presidents of giant corporations — fear bad publicity. They do not want consumer complaints aired in public. So if you have been unable to get your complaint heard and resolved through other mechanisms, you may want to try your luck with the news media.

More than 100 newspapers and at least 50 radio stations in the United States have "Action" or "Hotline" services to help consumers with problems. Locate them through your local newspapers, radio and television stations, or consult *HELP: The Useful Almanac*.

Newspapers. In 1961, the Houston *Chronicle* began publishing "Watchem," the nation's first media dispute-resolution column. Newspapers across the country have since established their own consumer action columns — called "Action Line," "Action Please" or something similar. To a floundering consumer, they can sometimes prove a godsend.

In larger cities, the columns receive so many complaints that it is not always possible for the staff to handle all of them. But in smaller localities, an attempt is made to deal with every problem that appears to have some merit. Not all complaints are published in the columns, but they are acted on, nevertheless. Usually, an action column staffer phones or writes the merchant or dealer in question, asking for a response by a certain time. If it is not forthcoming, the newspaper will follow up, this time getting in touch with the highest level of management.

Sometimes it develops that the problem has been created by a failure of communication between buyer and seller; sometimes the problem is the result of laziness or reluctance on the seller's part. In such cases, fear of bad publicity, once the newspaper has become interested, is likely to galvanize action. When problems have been created by lower-level employees, company executives or owners are often glad to have the difficulties called to their attention so that they can be remedied.

As is to be expected, the consumer complaints that newspapers receive come in every size and shape. Mail-order services seem to present the most common problem. Next come problems with automobiles and other major purchases, followed by credit and billing, chiefly in connection with utilities.

Most action columnists ask consumers to submit their complaints in writing, together with copies of all relevant documents. And be sure, when you write, to include your name and address. In the words of the consumer columnist of the Idaho *Statesman*, headquartered in Boise: "We try to work with every letter, provided that the reader has given us a name and address to contact in case we need further information. You'd be surprised how many people write to say that they've sent away for such-and-such and never received it . . . and then fail to sign their names."

Radio and Television. Radio and television stations in most parts of the country have consumer action broadcasters whose influence is enormous. As one might expect, these men and women are deluged with calls from indignant consumers and so have to be quite selective in choosing the cases with which to deal. They seldom have enough air time to pursue individual cases and usually emphasize types of complaints — about autos, appliances, mail-order merchandise, prices, safety, fraud and the like — or unusual cases, which have a broad appeal because they are so strange. You stand little chance of obtaining help from them if you have a quarrel with a local dry cleaner. But if you buy a well-known brand of baby crib and find that the spaces between the slats are so wide that the infant can be harmed, or if you fall prey to some new confidence game, your local broadcasters would be interested in hearing about it.

A particularly useful forum for consumer complaints is Call For Action (CFA), a nonprofit organization financed by corporate gifts, foundation grants and the dues paid by the approximately 30 radio and television stations throughout the country that belong to it. CFA provides free, confidential assistance to a quarter of a million people yearly: its teams of trained volunteers and staffers either give consumers advice on where to go to solve specific problems or act directly on behalf of the consumers who call them. Almost all of its work is done off-camera and off-microphone, although occasionally its broadcasters may feature Call For Action cases in news or editorial segments.

Everyone who contacts Call For Action receives individual attention, and CFA volunteers stay on every case until it is resolved. As it is a national network, CFA can deal effectively with complaints involving more than one state. If a CFA station in Boston receives a consumer complaint against a merchant in Chicago, it works through the Chicago CFA station to track down the merchant and deal with the problem.

CFA and its affiliates report many successful interventions. In a single week, the San Francisco affiliate got hundreds of dollars in refunds for Bay Area residents — not only from Bay Area merchants. The checks included $113 from a sewing-machine company in New York, $57 from a Miami truck-rental company and $500 from a major airline.

The CFA affiliate located in Kansas City, Missouri, recovered nearly $150,000 for consumers over a period of five years. Refunds came from local merchants, national concerns and even from the IRS. "In one case," the station reports, "a honeymooning couple missed plane connections and their ocean liner left Miami without them. They flew to Nassau to meet the ship there, but it couldn't get there because of bad weather. They missed the entire cruise and they couldn't get a refund until we talked to all parties concerned . . . In another case, a family's furnace stopped working in the middle of winter and even though they had a service contract, the company did not respond for two weeks. We called the company and they fixed the furnace the next day."

Denver's CFA affiliate helped a rural Colorado woman whose new septic tank had been improperly installed and was attracting rats and becoming a health hazard. She had tried for eight months to get the contractor and the county to act on the problem. The day after she finally got in touch with CFA, a new septic tank was delivered and the area around it was cleaned up. All it took was one telephone call to an official in the county health department from the CFA volunteer.

In addition to handling individual consumer problems, Call For Action also offers expert information and advice. At specified times lawyers, doctors, tax accountants, family budget counselors and legislators make themselves available to answer questions telephoned in by consumers.

To find out about the CFA affiliate nearest you, write: Call For Action, 575 Lexington Avenue, New York, New York 10022.

The Government

Government agencies are not the cure-all for every consumer complaint nor the referee of all consumer disputes. But certain kinds of problems properly belong in the hands of the government for resolution, and sometimes it may even be your duty as a citizen to take your complaint to the authorities.

Community Remedies. The most appropriate level of government to approach with an individual consumer complaint is the city or county. Many parts of the country have local consumer affairs offices. Some are separate agencies; others are part of the justice system. If you do not know what government office handles consumer affairs in your immediate area, you can find out through your state consumer affairs division (addresses are listed in the directory on page 16).

Not all local consumer affairs offices are equally active. Some have considerable power — not only to investigate consumer complaints but to prosecute offending businesses. Others have far less leverage, and do not even act as mediators: they may be able to do no more than advise you of the steps you should take on your own.

Not surprisingly, one of the most active and effective local consumer affairs offices in the country is the one in New York City. The city's huge population, its wide variety of businesses and its position as a tourist Mecca — all ensure an extraordinarily high number of consumer complaints: its Department of Consumer Affairs receives nearly 13,000 a year, and pursues every one that it deems legitimate. Sometimes the department acts as an adviser to the complainant, suggesting further ways of resolving the problem directly with the merchant involved, or referring the matter to another government agency that may be better qualified to handle it. But often, the department investigates the complaint and then acts as mediator between the consumer and the seller. Most of the disputes the department handles are resolved at this mediation stage — as they are in consumer affairs offices across the country.

Over the years, the New York City Department of Consumer Affairs has gained millions of dollars worth of refunds and debt cancellations for consumers. Most of the cases involve small sums, but it is not unusual for the department to get a building contractor to refund several thousand dollars for work improperly done on a house.

The department is also active in protecting visitors to the city, who sometimes find themselves cheated by unscrupulous merchants in the midtown area, where tourists are most likely to be. These so-called tourist traps frequently mark the merchandise they sell — cameras, radio and television sets, audio equipment, calculators, watches, home computers — as "sale" priced when in fact the price is far above the manufacturer's list. Complaints to the department about such establishments get prompt attention, especially when they come from callers who identify themselves as visitors to the city, and usually produce refunds. Many of the stores involved are licensed by the city and therefore fearful that government action may force them to close down.

Other programs sponsored by the Department of Consumer Affairs in New York include the publication of a wide range of consumer pamphlets on such topics as furniture purchases, mail order and other areas in which consumers may experience difficulty; and a telephone service, Tel-Consumer/Tel-Law, which plays tapes on a variety of consumer subjects from store refund policies to erroneous billing charges.

The consumer affairs department in your community may not be this active. Still, it is a proper place to take complaints.

Dispute Centers. Many communities do have specific centers that can be useful to consumers who have disputes with local merchants. The centers have different names in different communities: "Citizen Dispute Settlement Center," "Neighborhood Justice Center," "Community Mediation Center," "Community Board Program," "Night Prosecutor Program," "Urban Court Project" are just a few examples.

These centers, which are sponsored both by private organizations and by local governments, courts or district attorneys, handle a wide range of problems, from arguments between neighbors to vandalism and other petty crimes. But they also handle consumer problems and can be very helpful in resolving difficulties without the necessity of taking them to court.

Turning the Tables

Although merchandise is sometimes sent to the wrong address by error, the shipment of unordered goods to businesses and other institutions is often the work of con artists who hope that no one will verify whether a purchase was made and that, therefore, the accompanying bill will be paid automatically. The con is often successful. Most recipients return the merchandise, but the number who send checks is generally large enough to assure that the scam pays off handsomely.

Con men can, however, be given their comeuppance, as they were by the administrators of a small church that had been receiving unwanted packages and dutifully returning them at considerable cost. When a large shipment of unordered light bulbs arrived, along with a bill for $207.79, the administrators realized what was happening. They returned the bill to the offending company with the following note:

"We received a shipment of light bulbs from your company for which we had made no order. Please use this letter as a statement of your contribution to our church, and remember that your contribution is tax deductible. A record of your contribution will be kept in our office. May the Lord bless you."

If you receive unordered merchandise of any sort — whether it is sent to your business or your home and whether it is sent by a charity or a firm representing itself as a supplier, you are absolutely under no obligation to return it or pay for it. If you believe the material was sent in error, you should, of course, inform the sender, at the same time requesting sufficient money to cover the cost of shipping it back. But if you have any reason to suspect attempted fraud, you should report it to the attorney general's office of the state from which the merchandise was shipped (see directory, page 48) or — if the shipment was made through the mail — to your local office of the U.S. Postal Inspection Service (see directory, page 175).

The hearings at dispute resolution centers are informal. They are not conducted by judges or other officials, but by ordinary citizens with training in dispute-solving techniques. The specific procedures followed vary from one area to another, but usually they involve a face-to-face meeting between the disputants under the guidance of a mediator, whose job it is to help the parties arrive at a mutually satisfactory solution of their difficulty. (This procedure is significantly different from arbitration, in which the third party — the arbitrator — makes the decision.) When agreement is reached, both parties may be asked to sign a written document summing up its terms, and in some cases, that document may be enforceable in court.

To locate the dispute resolution center that may serve your community, check at your local city hall, municipal or county court or district attorney's office.

The State Level. If you cannot find help on the local government level, the next step is to take your case to the state government. Some states have a separate Department of Consumer Affairs; others have an Office of Consumer Affairs as part of the attorney general's office; the directory on page 48 will give you the name and address of the office in your state. Remember that — except in the case of mail order purchases — these offices can act only on transactions that take place *within* the state: if your complaint involves a product you bought in another state, you will have to get in touch with that state's consumer affairs office. Nor will all state offices act on individual problems. Nevertheless, it is worth getting in touch with them.

Should your complaint involve any individuals or firms licensed by the state — such as doctors, dentists, nurses, pharmacists, insurance agents, accountants, funeral directors, plumbers, electricians, auto repair companies, employment agencies, collection agencies and electronic repair shops — you may be able to get help from the appropriate state licensing board, which sets standards for the issuance of licenses and usually listens carefully to consumer complaints about licensees.

If you go to a state licensing board for help with a legitimate complaint, it will bring the problem to the attention of the licensee and seek a satisfactory resolution. The board will conduct an investigation, if necessary, and if it is shown that the licensee was wrong and still refuses to act, the board has the power to take disciplinary action against the offender in the form of probation, license suspension or even revocation. To find out how to get in touch with the correct licensing board, consult your state office of consumer affairs.

Every state has its own public utility laws and regulations. Complaints about utilities should be taken to your state's Public Utilities (or Service) Commission: you will find the address in the directory on page 98.

Federal Assistance. Many people are reluctant to take their complaints to federal agencies because — with some reason — they suspect that their grievances will not be dealt with swiftly and decisively. It is true that the mills of the federal bureaucracy often do grind slowly, and it is equally true that federal agencies, on the whole, are not geared to deal with individual complaints.

Even so, the federal government plays an important role in consumer affairs, both in the enactment of consumer protection legislation and in the enforcement of federal regulations and rules that affect consumers. Your complaint about a defective car or an over-the-counter drug, for example, can be of great service to your fellow-consumers. Federal agencies keep records of consumer complaints about goods and services, and they will act if they receive a sufficient number of protests to warrant an investigation.

Moreover, complaining to federal agencies may have a direct payoff for the aggrieved consumer. Merely by sending a complaint to the government and mailing a copy of it to the seller you sometimes can induce the offender to soften his or her position in a dispute.

Listed below are the federal agencies that consumers are most likely to want to contact, together with a description of the problems these agencies handle. Except in the case of the Department of Agriculture, it is best to get in touch with the regional office nearest you.

- Consumer Product Safety Commission. All complaints about the safety of household or recreational products should be directed to the CPSC (see directory, page 201).
- Federal Trade Commission. Complaints about unfair trade practices, false and deceptive advertising, and lending and credit practices belong here (see directory, page 199).
- Food and Drug Administration. Any complaints about the marketing of foods, drugs, cosmetics and medical devices should go to this agency (see directory, page 200).
- National Highway Traffic Safety Commission. This is the agency that deals with safety-related problems of motor vehicles and tires (see directory, page 153).
- Securities and Exchange Commission. This agency handles inquiries on the promotion and sale of securities.
- U.S. Department of Agriculture. This department inspects food products for safety. It is located at 14th Street and Independence Avenue, SW, Washington, D.C. 20250.
- U.S. Postal Inspection Service. This law enforcement agency handles all cases of mail fraud. If you believe you have been cheated or deceived in a transaction that involves the use of the mails, this is the agency to approach (see directory, page 175).

If you want to complain to a federal agency and are not sure which is the appropriate one to address, call the Federal Information Center nearest you. This little-known free service, which is available to everyone, is listed in your local telephone book, either under its own name or under the U.S. Government listings. When you call, a staff member will help you find a government expert or agency equipped to deal with your problem.

Very few people enjoy complaining about their misadventures in the marketplace. Many complaints, unfortunately, are never voiced at all. This is a pity, since complaining really does pay off in most cases. What is more, although it may take time and trouble to solve your problem, you can usually achieve results without the expense or delay that a court case involves. If you are persistent, calm and orderly, and if you pursue your problem from one level to the next, you will get results.

Chapter 14

Remedies, In and Out of Court

The great American pastime, say some observers, is neither baseball nor football, but taking people to court. Estimates of the number of lawsuits filed in state and local courts range as high as 12 million a year. Several hundred thousand more are started in federal courts. According to Chief Justice Warren E. Burger of the U.S. Supreme Court, the country is plagued "with an almost irrational focus — virtually a mania — on litigation as a way to solve all problems."

As consumers, we certainly need the courts. We depend on the government to use them on our behalf when business or industry fail in their responsibilities. The pressure of consumer lawsuits plays a major role in keeping those who sell us goods and services accountable for the quality and reliability of their work. And lawsuits provide us as individuals with a way of obtaining recompense for losses — either physical or economic — that we are otherwise unable to redress.

But the courts are not always the best mechanisms for the solution of serious consumer problems. When lawsuits *are* brought, they are usually settled out of court. What's more, insurance industry statistics indicate that 75 percent of defective products cases that go to a jury are won by the manufacturer and one study shows that in those cases where consumers win, the average product liability award is less than $4,000. Even when, out of a sense of outrage at particularly irresponsible business practices, juries award consumers spectacular sums in punitive damages — $2.1 million to a Virginia woman who bought a demonstrator car and was not informed by the dealer that the vehicle had been involved in an accident and then repaired; $125 million to a California teenager who was horribly burned and disabled when his car's gas tank caught fire in an accident — the amounts are generally drastically reduced by a judge, or on the defendant's appeal to a higher court.

Moreover, exclusive reliance on the courts generates unwanted byproducts of its own. Lawsuits breed more lawsuits: court calendars become so crowded that, in some instances, cases are not heard for years and when they finally come up, the rush to handle them puts a severe strain on the quality of the justice that is meted out. In addition, liability insurance rates become almost prohibitively high: to pay them and to guarantee safer products, companies raise the prices of their goods. Last, but far from least, it is an expensive business for a consumer to go to court. Often, it costs far more than the matter is worth. Even when punitive damages are awarded, the price of getting them — lawyers' fees, witnesses and myriad other costs — can turn out to be higher than the sum originally lost. And if the loser in a suit for money damages has inadequate insurance coverage and insufficient assets with which to pay, the winner will not be able to collect his or her award, whether it is large or small.

Fortunately, there are procedures other than court action that consumers can follow to resolve problems. In the best of circumstances, the simplest is the only one required: politely but firmly discussing the difficulty with the other party and finding a solution acceptable to both sides. If this does not work, there are the so-called "alternative dispute resolution" procedures — those that do not involve going to court.

There is mediation: the two sides, with the help and advice of a third person knowledgeable in the type of matter involved, try to work out a mutually satisfactory solution. There is arbitration, in which a trained and experienced arbitrator chosen by both parties has the final say. Mediation and arbitration are

Negotiating a Large Settlement

Many people who have been severely hurt or lost a relative in an accident, and thus have a substantial claim, are choosing to accept a so-called structured claims settlement rather than a single lump sum of money. A structured claims settlement is a combination of an immediate payment with additional sums paid periodically over a number of years.

Suppose, for example, a 42-year-old well-paid executive of a large corporation is killed in an accident which also badly injures his 10-year-old son. Liability for the accident is clearly established. The victims were in their car, which had stopped at a traffic light, when a large van belonging to an international delivery service went out of control and smashed into the vehicle. The widowed mother is suing the delivery service and its insurance company for $1.5 million.

Rather than fighting the case in court, the insurance company decides to settle and, with the widow's lawyers, works out a structured claims settlement. The insurance company pays an initial settlement of $300,000 for the widow's past and future pain and suffering, and her legal fees. In addition, it provides two annuities — the first to make up for the husband's lost earnings and the second to make up for the earnings the wife has lost because her son's injuries have forced her to stop work. These annuities are to be paid to the widow for her lifetime. If the woman is 39 years old at the time of the accident, the annuities have a total expected payment of $2.3 million.

The settlement also includes additional payments for the son: $50,000 in deferred surgical payments, $60,000 for college education and $250,000 in a deferred lump sum payment. The maximum payout of the settlement is about $3 million, and the guaranteed minimum payout is $1.6 million.

Since the payments will be largely deferred, however, and will be funded by annuities purchased by the insurance company from an unrelated life insurance company, the cost to the insurer for the settlement is approximately $878,000.

The advantages to the insurance company of this kind of settlement in a serious accident case is obvious. It costs considerably less than would a lump sum payment. For the injured or their survivors, it provides cash for medical and legal fees while at the same time assuring them of additional income over many years. In addition, the structured claims settlement can be a hedge against poor investments on their part, and against other ways of dissipating large sums of money. Such a settlement, however, should be negotiated by an attorney and should not be entered into casually without competent legal and financial advice.

voluntary processes, in which both sides must agree to participate. Indeed, except in some rare cases which will be discussed later, a dispute cannot go to arbitration until the parties have consented, in writing, to use this mechanism to solve their problems.

Court procedures, on the other hand, do not require such mutual consent. The party that feels aggrieved brings suit, and the other is required to appear. Many consumer complaints can be settled in the small claims courts, which have been expressly designed to deal with problems involving sums of money that, depending on the state, may range up to several thousand dollars, but not involving personal injury or damage claims beyond the cost of the goods or services in dispute. And, as a last resort, there is always a full-dress trial with all its trappings and expenses, in a regular civil court. In this chapter we will discuss these processes — both the alternative dispute resolution mechanisms and the courts.

Mediation

Mediation is a diplomatic process in which both parties in a dispute try to work out a voluntary agreement with the help of a qualified, impartial mediator. The mediator has no power to impose a solution: his or her job is to help the disputants arrive at a compromise. The process is non-binding: the parties are free to modify or reject the mediator's suggestions and solutions. Mediation is frequently used to solve labor-management conflicts and landlord-tenant disagreements. In addition, it plays a major role in the solution of consumer-business disputes. Many of the processes discussed in Chapter 13, from those used by trade associations to those used by Consumer Action Lines, involve mediation at some point along the way.

But mediation may not succeed or the parties involved may have difficulty keeping the agreements they have made. In such cases, they may want to try arbitration.

Arbitration

Arbitration, a time-honored method of solving commercial as well as labor-management disputes, has only recently come into wide use as a way of dealing with consumer problems. Unlike mediation, it does not involve negotiation and compromise: the decision, which is made by one or more impartial, trained arbitrators, who often have special expertise in the area of the dispute, is based strictly on the merits of the case. The arbitrator — or panel of arbitrators — must be acceptable to both sides, and both must agree formally in advance on whether or not they will be bound by the decision.

In this respect, they have three choices. In very rare cases, the arbitration is non-binding, and neither party is required to accept the decision. Most commonly, it is binding, in which case both parties must accept the decision and it is enforceable in court. By agreeing in advance to go to arbitration and accept the arbitrator's decision, the two parties have made a contract, which the courts will honor. There are only a few grounds for an appeal to the courts in a binding arbitration, among them that the arbitrator demonstrated bias or overstepped his or her powers or that the award was obtained by fraud.

The third option is one-way binding arbitration: one party agrees to accept the decision, but the other makes no such commitment. When this last procedure — a relatively new one — is used in consumer complaints, as it is by AUTOCAP, the automobile industry panel (see Chapter 13), the business or industy concerned generally binds itself to accept the arbitrator's decision, but the consumer does not.

At first sight, such one-way binding arbitration would seem to give consumers every possible advantage. If they win, they are assured of satisfaction, since the arbitrator's decision is legally enforceable against the business or industry concerned. If they lose, they can always pursue the case further, in court. But there are some problems. If the case *does* go to court, the arbitrator's decision can be entered as evidence, and although the court is not required to give it any weight, it generally has an influence. This fact in itself tends to discourage consumers from pursuing cases beyond the arbitration stage. An AUTOCAP survey has found that the vast majority simply accept negative decisions and do not proceed further.

Another problem lies in a stipulation some businesses make that considerably reduces the consumer's freedom of action. Suppose, for example, that the arbitrator makes an award to the consumer, but the consumer does not consider it adequate. In such a case, these businesses say, they will be bound by the decision only if the consumer agrees to accept the arbitrator's award as full compensation, and not to look for further redress in the courts. This gives the consumer a choice between two equally undesirable alternatives: accepting the half a loaf awarded by the arbitrator or starting an entirely new proceeding in the courts.

Why Arbitrate? There are two major reasons for choosing arbitration rather than a lawsuit: time and expense. American business has been spending more than $24 billion a year on legal services, and a good part of this is the cost of extensive litigation. Comparable figures for individuals are unavailable, but as anyone knows who has gone to court, the costs can be enormous.

In comparison, the cost of arbitration is low. Most arbitrators are volunteers who donate their time and talent and neither side is likely to need a lawyer; if only for these reasons, some court expenses are eliminated. The American Arbitration Association (AAA) charges as little as $150 for a relatively simple case, and although the fee generally increases in proportion to the settlement demands and the complexity of the problem, it is unlikely ever to reach the often staggering costs of litigation. Generally, the fee is paid by the person who brings the action, but the arbitrator may later assign a portion of it to the other party if he or she deems it appropriate. In many consumer-business conflicts, the company routinely pays the fee as an act of goodwill toward its customers. In such cases, the cost to the consumer is only the expense of getting the necessary information together and taking the time to appear at the hearing.

Not only is arbitration less costly, but it is generally much faster than a courtroom trial. The backlog is seldom heavy, as it is in many courts; as a result, proceedings can be scheduled promptly. And because most arbitrations turn on questions of fact or practice, rather than complex legal matters, procedures are simple. Some arbitrations are handled as "desk" decisions, in which the parties submit all their evidence in writing and do not actually appear in person. But most require both parties to present their sides of the case personally. Hearings — which may be held almost anywhere: in a convenient office, in someone's home, even at the site of the dispute — are usually limited to questioning witnesses, examining exhibits and making opening and closing statements, and often take less than half a day. Because arbitrators come from all walks of life and often bring years of experience to the particular kind of case on which they sit — a jeweler, for example, may be called in to arbitrate a dispute concerning a diamond ring; a furrier to settle a dispute over the reconditioning of a fur coat — it is seldom necessary to spend valuable time educating them in specialized areas, as is often required in a courtroom trial. Moreover, unlike the verdict of a court, which may be a long time in coming, an arbitrator's decision is generally handed down within a matter of days. Ordinarily there is a set time limit within which a decision must be made: 40 days for arbitrations conducted under FTC guidelines, 30 days for those held under the auspices of the American Arbitration Association, 10 days in arbitrations sponsored by Better Business Bureaus. Most decisions are made well within the time limit.

Unlike court trials, arbitration hearings are open only to the people involved, and to invited outsiders who may appear as witnesses. Arbitrators are not required to base their decisions on legal precedents or to conduct their proceedings in conformity with the legal rules of evidence. They may be willing to accept material — hearsay, for example — that would be inadmissable as evidence in a court of law.

While many business-consumer conflicts can be handled very effectively by arbitration, some fall outside its scope. Cases in which consumers demand punitive damages — as for example, those that arise when a health insurance company fails to pay a claim within a timely period — must be heard in the courts and cannot be brought to arbitration. Some arbitrations operate on ground rules that prohibit claims for what the law

CONSUMER ALERT

A Standard Arbitration Agreement Form

No dispute can go to arbitration without the written consent of both parties. That consent can be given at any time —even after a dispute between them has developed. But it is preferable to make the arrangement beforehand. Once there *is* a problem, positions are likely to harden, and people become stubborn. For this reason, it is fairly common for commercial contracts to contain a future disputes arbitration clause — an agreement to use arbitration in the event that difficulties arise. Such a clause can also form a part of consumer-business documents — not only contracts, but bills of sale and service agreements. The American Arbitration Association (AAA) has prepared a standard wording, which can be used without applying for permission, and inserted in any appropriate document:

"Any controversy or claim arising out of or relating to this contract, or the breach thereof, shall be settled by arbitration in accordance with the Rules of the American Arbitration Association, and judgment upon the award rendered by the arbitrator(s) may be entered in any court having jurisdiction thereof."

calls consequential damages, such as compensation for a business loss or physical injury that developed as a result of a defective product or service. An arbitrator operating under such ground rules could award a consumer the cost of repair and replacement of a broken automobile crankshaft. But if the damaged crankshaft caused the car owner to miss work, and this in turn led to a loss of income, the consumer's demand for additional compensation would be outside the arbitrator's jurisdiction and could be heard only in a court of law. Claims involving personal injury, property damage and allegations of fraud may similarly be excluded from a particular system of arbitration.

Arbitration Programs. A variety of industries and non-profit organizations administer arbitration programs. The two largest are the American Arbitration Association and the Better Business Bureau. In addition, some industries have established their own arbitration programs to handle consumer complaints; these are discussed in Chapter 13.

How the AAA Operates. The American Arbitration Association (AAA) is a private, nonprofit organization with headquarters in New York City and 25 regional offices around the country. (See directory, page 373). The AAA, which was founded in 1926, is the oldest organization in its field in the United States, and currently it handles more than 40,000 arbitrations a year. In addition to its dispute-resolution services, the AAA acts as a center for training and research and issues special publications concerning a range of alternative dispute-settlement procedures.

Traditionally, the organization's efforts have been directed toward resolving commercial and labor-management disputes, but since the early 1950's the AAA has expanded into the field of consumer-business arbitration. It administers the arbitration programs available through the American Movers Conference and the Movers and Warehousemen's Association of America and those available under various homeowner warranty programs, all of which are discussed in Chapter 13. In addition, it handles the arbitration proceedings that may be called for under the terms of some automobile insurance policies. If, as an insured driver, you or your passengers are injured by an uninsured motorist and you are unable to settle the matter satisfactorily with your insurance company, either party may demand arbitration under AAA auspices. AAA also administers the arbitration of disputes arising under the state no-fault insurance laws of Hawaii, Minnesota, New York and Oregon.

More than 60,000 arbitrators from a wide variety of professions are listed with the AAA. Their names, along with their biographies, are cross-filed on computers by their fields of expertise and their geographic location. Most of the proceedings the AAA conducts demand the presence of both parties involved, who present their cases orally. Although routine AAA arbitrations seldom require the services of attorneys, the disputants often *do* use lawyers in more complex cases or those involving large sums of money. The arbitrations the AAA conducts under homeowners' warranties are not binding on the consumer, but all other AAA arbitrations are legally binding on both parties.

How the BBB Operates. The National Council of Better Business Bureaus (BBB) has the largest nationwide system for settling consumer disputes of any organization in the country. Through its local bureaus, the BBB handles over a million and a half consumer complaints each year, using not only mediation and conciliation to resolve conflicts, but two-way and one-way binding arbitration as well. The Bureau deals with many different kinds of businesses and industries, from such local establishments as appliance stores, carpet merchants, electrical contractors, lawn-care services, cabinet-makers, roofing and insulation companies and air conditioner repair firms to such nationwide businesses as automobile companies.

Most BBB arbitration cases are presented in person by the parties involved at hearings which, according to Dean W. Determan, Vice President of the Bureau's Mediation/Arbitration Division, can be held almost anywhere, depending on the nature of the case. The BBB's volunteer arbitrators have held hearings on rooftops, in car washes, even in a cemetery. They are drawn from a community pool, which also includes other volunteers with specialized expertise who can be called on for assistance and advice.

BBB arbitration programs are funded through local members' dues and are free to consumers. The BBB will not handle claims for lost wages, personal injury or any other consequential damages; it will not, in other words, arbitrate disputes in which anything other than actual loss of money or services is involved. Moreover, some local branches will only hear cases in which at least $100 in money or services is claimed.

A special BBB arbitration program has been set up to cover the dry cleaning industry. In New York City, more than 50 dry cleaners have joined this program, agreeing to submit their consumer problems to a panel of five arbitrators — a representative of the Neighborhood Cleaners Association, a textile manufacturer, a textile retailer, a home economist and a consumer advocate, who examine the item at issue. Unlike most other BBB arbitration panels, this one issues desk decisions, based on written statements submitted by both parties. If necessary, the panel has items in question examined by an independent laboratory at BBB expense.

On a national level, the BBB now offers arbitration services to all U.S. and Canadian owners of General Motors, Volkswagen, Porsche, Audi and Datsun cars.

Government Sponsored Arbitration Programs

Some — although not all — local Consumer Affairs Offices offer arbitration services and some states offer court-annexed arbitration as an alternative to a full-scale trial. In the city of Philadelphia, for instance, such arbitration is mandated as the procedure to be followed in all cases involving relatively small sums of money. A panel of three attorneys, acting as arbitrators, hears the complaint, and the award granted by this panel becomes the judgment of the court unless either party demands a full trial in a regular civil court.

To discover whether any government-sponsored arbitration programs are available in your locality, check with your state's Consumer Affairs or attorney general's office. (See directories, pages 16 and 48 respectively.)

The Arbitration Process. To enter into arbitration, the parties must first agree in wanting to do so — except, of course, in those few places where the procedure is mandated by the courts. They then file a demand for arbitration with the organization that will administer it — whether the American Arbitration Association, the Better Business Bureau, the appropriate consumer action panel, a local court system or any other entity that provides such a service. All parties named in the demand are notified by the administering agency that it has been filed, and they, in turn, must respond in writing. The disputants are then offered a list of suitable arbitrators, together with a brief biographical sketch of each, from which to choose the person. Each party to the dispute crosses off unacceptable names and assigns priorities — one, two, or three — to those that remain. The person with the highest common priority becomes the arbitrator.

If the choices do not overlap, the arrangement may call for each party to select an arbitrator and for these two in turn to appoint a third. If the chosen arbitrator is not expert in the particular field the dispute involves, an impartial expert is appointed to provide inspections or technical advice.

A convenient hearing time and place is set up through the administering authority. Onsite locations may be chosen so that the actual product or service in question can be examined. In cases where people have to travel great distances or are unable to agree on meeting times, arbitration can be carried out over the telephone or in writing.

During a typical hearing, both sides submit testimony and evidence to the arbitrator and may question and cross-examine witnesses. After considering all the facts, the arbitrator issues a written decision, and award, on each claim submitted.

Preparing for Arbitration

If you enter into binding arbitration, you have, in effect, chosen not to go to court. First you must submit a written statement of the dispute and the settlement you demand, often by filling out a standard form. You will then receive in the mail the arbitration agency's summary of the case. You should read this carefully, and contact the administering agency about anything that is incorrect. Do not sign the document until you are sure that it presents an accurate statement both of the dispute and your demands for settlement.

At the arbitration hearing, you may represent yourself or be represented by a friend or relative you believe to be better able than you to state your case. You also have the right to appear with an attorney if you choose, but in this case, you must notify the other party of the fact immediately.

None of the people involved in an arbitration, or their representatives, may have any dealings with the arbitrator at any time unless the other party is present. All correspondence must be directed to the administering agency, which will provide copies to any individuals who should receive them.

The intent of an arbitration hearing is to get a full, accurate picture of the dispute. For this reason, most people find it is to their advantage to attend the hearing and make an oral presentation. Write a detailed outline of the events in your case, so that you or your representative will be able to recount all the relevant information at the presentation.

The other party, and perhaps the arbitrator, will question you; in turn, you will have the opportunity to question the other party and any witnesses brought in. Be sure to prepare a list of questions you want to ask. At the hearing itself, listen carefully to the statements of the other party and the witnesses and write down any new questions that occur to you.

After each side has presented its case, you will be given an opportunity to respond to the other side's statement and summarize your own position. Again, be sure that you have prepared a clear outline of your position and your demands. Clear up any questions that have not been answered and tell the arbitrator exactly what you want and why.

The Better Business Bureau has prepared a list of questions that may help a consumer to prepare his or her case. Whether you present your case in person or in writing, you should be able to answer them:

1. Can you clearly state what the problem is, and why you think the company is responsible for it?
2. To whom at the company did you speak?
3. When did the conversation occur?
4. What did the seller tell you, and/or what action was taken?
5. Were other business/service persons involved? Who? When? Why?
6. What did they tell you and/or what action did they take? (Their written statements, or their presence as witnesses, are preferable to your statements in presenting your case.)

Things to Bring

Documents. Bring all available written information: bills of sale, contracts, warranties, guarantees, correspondence between parties, advertisements of services or sales, delivery receipts. Bring original documents whenever possible, plus copies for both the arbitrator and the other party. If you are submitting your case in writing, send copies of the documents, not the originals.

Witnesses or Statements of Witnesses. You are responsible for the submission of evidence from your witnesses. If they cannot appear in person, be sure to obtain written statements from them. If they can appear, keep them informed as the schedule of the hearing develops.

Your Outline of the Dispute. List in chronological sequence the events that have occurred in your attempts to solve the problem. Such an outline is essential whether you appear in person or submit your case in writing.

Small Claims Courts

In addition to mediation and arbitration, there is another way a consumer can seek justice without resorting to a full-scale trial. If you think that you have reason to sue somebody, but are not seeking punitive damages or restitution for an injury, the legal system provides an inexpensive way to get a hearing: the small claims court.

These courts have been set up in all states specifically to handle claims that do not exceed a certain dollar amount. The maximum varies widely from state to state: in Arkansas it is $300, the lowest in the country; in Florida, Tennessee and Virginia it is $5,000, the highest in the United States; in most states it ranges between $500 and $1,000.

The first small claims courts were opened in the early years of this century to simplify regular court proceedings and to reduce both court expenses and delays. Basically, a small claims court functions in the same way as any other civil court: it is not a mediation or conciliation service, but an adversary proceeding, in which a plaintiff sues a defendant to win a judgment. But in a small claims court, the services of a lawyer are not required. In fact, small claims courts in eight states (California, Colorado, Idaho, Kansas, Michigan, Nebraska, Oregon, and Washington) do not permit lawyers to participate at all. The judge

— or, in some courts, the referee — does not act as an impartial observer, but plays an active role, helping both sides to bring out the facts and understand the issues. The trial procedures are usually informal and rules of evidence are relaxed.

Disputes that can be handled through a small claims court include all kinds of everyday problems. For example:

- You take your ailing television set to a repair shop. The owner says that he guarantees his work for 30 days. When you get the set back, it works for two weeks and then goes blank. You call the television repair shop and the owner refuses to honor the guarantee. He will fix the set again, but you will have to pay.
- A new coat you just bought for $300 is lost at the dry cleaner's. The cleaner offers you $50.
- The bubble skylight you had installed in your living room is leaking. The installer says that he did a good job, that if anyone is at fault it is the manufacturer and that you will have to collect from the company.
- You take a plane trip and the airline loses your luggage. Your vacation is ruined. You have also lost hundreds of dollars worth of clothing and an expensive new camera, for which you have a receipt. The airline's settlement offer is far less than the value of the lost property. You try to negotiate, but cannot reach agreement.

All these cases can be settled in a small claims court. But remember: you cannot sue for more than the actual cost of property or services lost. For example, if you were to sue the airline that lost your luggage in a regular civil court, you might be able to ask for damages because of your ruined vacation. In a small claims court, however, you can sue only for the cost of your baggage and its contents. Moreover, if you sue in small claims court, you have to be ready to go to court whenever your case comes up, and you cannot recover damages for the time you lose in court appearances. Finally, small claims courts generally have limited jurisdiction. If your dispute is with someone who lives or does business in another state, it may not be possible to get the defendant to court or to collect an award.

Preparing Your Case

If you decide to take a case to small claims court, you first have to find the local court. There is no rule of thumb for doing this, since you will not always find it listed in the telephone directory. In Bridgeport, Connecticut, for example, you have to go to the Court of Common Pleas and then to the Small Claims Clerk. Similarly, in most other places you will have to inquire at the regular courts.

Small claims courts usually offer the fastest, least expensive way of settling minor financial disputes.

The clerk of the court will help you with the procedures necessary to get your case underway. First you will have to file a complaint. In many states, this can be done simply by filling out a standard form. You can do this on the spot or take it home to complete and then mail it in. You will also have to pay a filing fee, which varies from state to state, but generally runs between $5 and $20. (In some states, this fee is added to the judgment against the defendant if the plaintiff wins the case.) In many courts you must also pay a modest sum for the clerical work involved in notifying the defendant that a lawsuit has been filed against him or her; in others, you will have to arrange to serve the papers yourself.

The Complaint

Your written complaint should be simple, brief and clear. Make sure you describe the dispute concisely and stick to the issue.

If you are suing an individual who works for a company that may also have legal responsibility for your loss, include the names of the individual and the company in your complaint: both will be defendants in the case. If anyone in addition to yourself — a friend or relative, for example — has also sustained losses as a consequence of the problem, it will probably be to your advantage to include that person (with his or her permission) as another plaintiff in your suit.

In making out your complaint, be sure to get the defendant's correct *legal* name and address. It may not be the one commonly used. The sign outside a store may, for example, read "Ralph's Discount TV," while the legal name of the business may be "Ralph Roberts Television Outlets, Inc." To find the firm's legal name, check business directories in your local library or inquire of an appropriate agency: your state or city licensing agency, the office of the secretary of state for your state, the state or local corporation commission or the Better Business Bureau.

The court can only have jurisdiction over a case if the defendant has some type of presence in the area the court serves. This presence may be a store, a residence or an agent registered to receive court papers. If your complaint is against a corporation which does not have a store or office in your area, you can find the name of its registered agent through the office of your state's secretary of state.

The clerk of the small claims court will notify the defendant of your suit and the trial date, usually by registered mail. If the defendant cannot be reached by this means, you may have to get the notice delivered yourself. You can do this through a paid process server; ask the clerk how to find one. The server must sign a notarized statement that the notice was actually served on the defendant.

Defendant's Moves

The defendant may ask for a change in the trial date. If there is a good reason, the request will ordinarily be granted and you will be notified of the new date. The defendant may also file a counterclaim against you; in that case, the clerk will notify you. If the defendant thinks that you have the wrong culprit and knows who the right one is, he or she may, in some courts, file an "impleader" to bring that person into the lawsuit. Finally, in many courts the defendant may request a full jury trial. Once you have filed in small claims court, you forego the right to make that request. The defendant does not, however, and in many jurisdictions can have the dispute transferred to a regular civil court, where you will both be required to have lawyers.

Before the Trial

Well before the trial date, gather all the evidence concerning your case — estimates, contracts, letters, paid bills, receipts, pertinent photographs, and so forth — and place them neatly in a file folder to be presented at court. If you know of documents that would help your case but are in the possession of the defendant or someone else, you may be able to subpoena them. Check with the clerk of the small claims court before the trial date to find out how you can get a *subpoena duces tecum.* You may also subpoena witnesses for your case if they will not come voluntarily. But check first to find out whether the court permits witnesses, or limits the number that may be called; some courts have restrictions in this area. And be careful not to subpoena unnecessary documents or people; you will have to pay the court for that service.

Remember that a witness' written statement, even if it is sworn, is never considered as persuasive as testimony given in person. If the court permits you to have witnesses, try to persuade any friends or relatives who can back up your side of the story to come to court with you.

Your case may require the presence of an expert, impartial witness who can testify to the technical or monetary extent of damages. Since, in many jurisdictions, such witnesses cannot be subpoenaed for small claims court cases, but must appear voluntarily, you will have to find one who will agree to testify for a reasonable fee.

Consulting a Lawyer

While you may not want or be permitted to have a lawyer with you at small claims court, you may want to consult one about the merits and strategy of your case. An attorney can generally tell you whether the evidence you have is sufficient to gain a favorable verdict. This is important, because small claims judges generally do not award damages unless a plaintiff has clearly established the liability of the defendant.

A good lawyer can also tell you the best way to organize and present your case. Such advice can be well worth a fee of $25, $50 or even $100 for a brief consultation, particularly if it helps you to win a judgment of $500, $1,000 or more.

Adjournments

If you find that you cannot appear at the trial once it has been scheduled, call the clerk's office to find out what the proper procedure is for requesting a "continuance," in effect a postponement. You will probably be required to file a paper explaining why you cannot be present and indicating the earliest date you can appear. If your excuse does not seem adequate to the judge, he or she may deny your request and require you to appear or may dismiss the case.

Settlement Offers

Rather than undergo the embarrassment and expense or burden of appearing in small claims court, the defendant may offer to settle the dispute to your satisfaction out of court. If the two of you agree on the terms before the case comes to trial, and you have already received the settlement money, inform the clerk of this fact and the trial will be canceled. If you have not yet received the money, it is imperative that you go to court. If you do not, the case will be dismissed. Tell the judge that a settlement offer has been made, but you have not yet received the money. In many cases, the judge will reschedule the case for a future date with the stipulation "subject to settlement." If you receive the money before the new trial date, notify the court clerk so the trial can be removed from the calendar.

The Trial

A trial in a small claims court is not complicated. The judge knows that the participants are not lawyers and is not likely to bother with the formalities of legal procedure.

Nevertheless, if only to enable you to know more about the proceedings and feel more comfortable in court, it is a good idea to visit the small claims court in your community and watch a case or two being tried before your own lawsuit comes up.

Be sure to arrive on time for your case. You may have to wait, but if you are not present when your case is called, it may be dismissed. In most courts each case is allotted only so much time and there is pressure to move things along.

Because the judge will have read the complaint before the trial starts, he or she already knows something about your case. When you tell your story, be sure to get in all the key facts, but be as brief as possible. You will speak first, and the judge will probably ask you specific questions about your claim. Be concise and factual in your answers. You can present your evidence and introduce any witnesses at this point. The judge may question your witnesses and ask to examine any evidence you present.

Then the defendant, calling on his or her own witnesses, will have a chance before the judge, who may ask questions once again.

If the defendant does not show up at the trial, you will not automatically receive a judgment by default. You will still have to prove your case before the judge. In some small claims courts you may be awarded a judgment but the defendant may have the right to reopen the proceedings at a later date if he or she can show good cause for not appearing — as, for example, failure to receive proper notice.

In some small claims courts, such as those in New York State, you may be given the choice of having your case heard by a judge or by an arbitrator — a lawyer who has volunteered his or her time to help the small claims process. Generally, if you choose to put your case before an arbitrator, you will have a shorter wait before the case comes up. But most people prefer to go before a judge, and the judges' calendars are, therefore, more crowded. On the other hand, the arbitration is binding: you can make no appeal from the arbitrator's decision.

Whether your case is heard by an arbitrator or a judge, the decision will be announced either immediately after the hearing or, if more time is needed to decide, will be mailed to you.

Appealing a Decision

If you lose your case or are dissatisfied with the judge's decision, you may appeal in most states. Because small claims court proceedings are informal, appeals courts do not usually consider technical errors that may have been made during the trial. You may, for example, think that the judge relied heavily on hearsay evidence — what one person reports another to have said — which is not admissible in a regular court of law. But the court may deem that insufficient basis for an appeal. Its primary concern is whether the small claims court decision was fair.

If you decide to appeal, you will need a lawyer to draw up and file the papers. You will also need a transcript of the trial proceedings, which you may buy from the court stenographer. If no court stenographer was present, you must get a general statement of the proceedings from the judge or the court clerk.

A dissatisfied defendant is also entitled to appeal the decision of a small claims court. In that case, he or she is not required to pay any judgment that may have been awarded unless and until the appellate court upholds the lower court decision.

Collecting a Judgment

"Winning a judgment in small claims court is only half the battle," says one expert. In a substantial number of cases a defendant who loses simply refuses to pay. In order to collect, some plaintiffs have had to locate and put a lien on a defendant's assets — a difficult problem at best. "You can try to get the information by hiring a private detective," one chief clerk observed, "but in many cases it's not worth the expense."

Still, consumers who refuse to be cheated can often find a way. One woman, for example, gave her nearly-new color television set to a neighborhood repair shop to be fixed. After she had heard nothing for two weeks she went to the shop to ask where her TV was. "It's out on rental," the clerk replied, "but it will be back in a couple of weeks." "How could you rent my television set to somebody?" she demanded. "Don't ask me," he said, "I only work here." The woman tried to reach the owner, but repeatedly failed. Three weeks went by. She filed suit in small claims court for the value of her television set, about $400, and won her case.

When she took the judgment to the store, however, the owner refused to pay. Her set was back in the store, he said, and she could have it if she paid for the repairs. The woman went to a city marshal, paid a fee of $20 to have the store owner served with the judgment, and accompanied the marshal to the store, only to be told that the owner was not there. The woman spotted the owner in the back of the store, and told the marshal so. "I went as far as my authority lets me," he replied, and suggested that she forget about the whole thing.

She refused to forget about it and complained to the licensing commission. After some correspondence and a hearing, the commission suspended the owner's license to do business. But by this time, the woman was fed up, and unwilling to wait for the commission to enforce its edict. She went straight to a local television station, which interviewed her on a news show. The negative publicity finally convinced the store owner of the error of his ways and she got the money the court had awarded her.

The consumer affairs department in New York City has recently adopted a program designed to help individuals who are having difficulty collecting judgments awarded them in small claims courts. Under this program, which could serve as a model for other consumer affairs offices, the department will issue subpoenas to banks, compelling them to reveal the assets of a depositor against whom a judgment has been issued.

Defending a Small-Claims Suit

If you become a defendant in a small claims suit, you should observe the same rules and precautions as you do when you are the plaintiff. Prepare your defense well ahead of time. Familiarize yourself with the court procedure; know what you are going to say and make it brief and to the point. If you have any written evidence or photographic exhibits, have them in proper order and bring along whatever witnesses the court permits to help your case.

In several states, collection agencies and business creditors use the small claims courts to collect past-due debts. The practice is not permitted everywhere, and in some states, there is a separate court for such "mass filers." If you are being sued for an unpaid bill in a small claims court, you will be notified by mail of the claim and the trial date.

If you do in fact owe the money, you should make every effort to discharge the debt before the trial date, especially since installment terms can usually be arranged. If you and your creditor reach an agreement, get a statement to that effect in writing from him or her.

If, on the other hand, you do not think that you owe the money, or if you feel you should not be forced to pay, prepare your case carefully and go to court on the trial date. Do *not* ignore the summons: if you fail to appear, a default judgment will probably be entered against you. This can result in a lien against your property or, if a garnishment action is brought, in forced deductions from your salary. Your credit rating may also be affected.

If for any reason you cannot appear in court on the trial date, notify the court clerk and ask for a postponement. You must have a good excuse, however; most judges will not reschedule hearings for trivial reasons.

Civil Courts

If you have been unable to resolve a consumer problem through any of the mechanisms previously described in this book, and if your case involves punitive damages, restitution for an injury or a sum too large for small claims court, you will have to take the matter to a civil court. This is not a step to be undertaken lightly. The costs of litigation are high, both in time and money, and although anyone can sue for any reason, no suit stands any chance of success unless it is founded on solid legal ground. Obviously, you will want the advice, as well as the assistance, of a lawyer — preferably one with special skill and experience in the area of your particular concern. (See Chapter 12 for a discussion on how to select a lawyer.) But even before consulting with a lawyer, you should feel reasonably certain that your claim has legal validity.

The law provides several bases on which consumers can take court action if they feel they have been wrongly used. A case may rely on contract-law theory or tort-law theory, or it may be based on a right created by statute.

Contract Law Theory. If your case is to be based on contract law theory, you must be able to prove both that you had a valid contract and that the other party breached it. The validity of a contract depends upon several factors. First, one party must make an offer which the other party accepts. As the law puts it, there must be a "meeting of the minds" between them: they must agree both as to the content of the contract and its terms. For example, if, in response to a magazine advertisement for a wristwatch that costs $19.95, you fill out the order form and mail it along with a check for $19.95, the law considers that a contract has been formed between you and the advertiser. If your check is for $15.75, however, there is no contract. Your acceptance has been made on terms different from those of the offer and there is, therefore, no "meeting of the minds."

There is another requirement for a valid contract. Each of the parties must promise or agree to do something — one, for example, to provide goods or services; the other to pay a specified amount of money. Without this so-called "consideration," the contract would be one-sided, and therefore invalid.

In determining whether or not a contract has been breached, the courts have some latitude. They will doubtless rule that a violation has occurred if one party fails to fulfill the contract terms through negligence. But if some mitigating circumstance makes it nearly or totally impossible for that party, despite its best efforts, to carry out every single detail of the contract terms, the court will probably consider that no breach has occurred. As long as there has been what the law calls "substantial performance," the courts are likely to rule that the contract has been honored.

This "substantial performance" factor is important to keep in mind. It frequently plays a part in consumer cases, as, for example, those that involve construction contracts. If you want a brown tile roof and the contractor uses blue tiles because no brown ones are available, you will have a difficult time recovering damages for breach of contract. Only if you can show that the substitution made a difference in your use or enjoyment of your home — that the blue tile turned your house into an eyesore, for example, because it clashed with the other colors on the exterior — are you likely to win an award. In general, as long as a substituted product functions well, you will have a difficult time collecting damages for this kind of breach. It is, therefore, important to specify particular requirements in as much detail as possible when entering into contracts for construction or

Courts often rule that "substantial performance" honors a contract even if your requirements are not met.

similar work. If you want a certain brand of product used, or a particular style, be sure to say so clearly in the contract, so that it can form a basis of the bargain.

If you are successful in a suit for breach of contract, the court may either award you damages or order that the contract be enforced. If the object of a contract is unique, or cannot be duplicated — if, for example, the sale of land or real estate is involved — the courts will often order enforcement. But in most cases, there will be an award for damages. The size of the award will be based not only on the damage you have suffered but, to some extent, on your conduct: the court considers it your responsibility to try to minimize the damages caused by the contract breach. Suppose, for example, that an automobile mechanic botches a repair job on your car. If your continued use of the vehicle harms it even further, you have an obligation to stop driving it, even if that means additional expense for you in the form of fares. If you win your suit against the mechanic, the court will usually reimburse you for that expense by awarding you so-called "incidental" damages.

One last point. A contract does not have to be written in order to be valid and enforceable. It may be oral, as well, and the breach of an oral contract is also grounds for a suit. But its terms are likely to be more difficult to prove than those of a written document. If you plan to bring suit over an oral contract you would do well to have a witness who can attest to its terms. Without one, your chances of success are not very good.

Closely related to the oral contract are two kinds of warranties — express and implied. As was pointed out in Chapter 7, every product carries an implied warranty — an assurance to the buyer that it will perform the function for which it was made. Some products carry written warranties, as well. Indeed, a written warranty is one form of an express warranty, which the law defines as a statement made by a seller to a buyer about the character and quality of what is being sold. The seller makes the statement in order to persuade the buyer to buy and the buyer generally relies on it as fact.

Most warranties are governed by the provisions of the Magnuson-Moss Act, (see Chapter 7) and the law concerning them is also covered in the Uniform Commercial Code, in force in every state of the union save Louisiana. This law gives you the right to sue for breach of contract if you make a purchase based on an express warranty that turns out to be false. But you must be sure that there was, in fact, an express warranty. If, for example, you buy a particular lawnmower on the basis of your hardware dealer's statement that it is the best that money can buy, you have no grounds for a suit against him if your neighbor comes home the next day with a mower you think superior. The hardware dealer's statement was only an opinion, not a legal warranty. If, on the other hand, you buy a ring on the basis of a jeweler's statement that its stone is a three-carat emerald and it turns out to be only two carats, you *do* have the basis of a suit. The jeweler's statement was an express warranty.

You may also have the basis of a suit if an implied warranty is violated. For example, there is an implied warranty throughout the United States that the food served in restaurants will be wholesome and edible. If it contains harmful bacteria or some other foreign substance, you may be able to sue the restaurant owner. But the law makes fine distinctions in this area.

For example, a customer who broke a tooth on a pit in a cherry pie he was eating in an Oregon restaurant was unable to recover damages when he went to court: the Oregon court did not consider that a cherry pit in a cherry pie was a "foreign" substance. But if he had broken his tooth on a piece of bone in a hamburger, he *would* have had a claim. Hamburger is not supposed to contain bone.

Tort Law Theory. To bring suit successfully under tort law theory, you must be able to prove that there was a duty owed you by the party you are suing; that the duty was breached; and that you suffered an injury as a direct result of that breach. There must, in other words, be a recognized legal relationship between the injured party and the party that caused the damage.

Tort law theory has its place in consumer litigation because companies that sell products to consumers have a legal duty to ensure that the products they market are safe and useable for the purpose for which they are sold. If you purchase a stepladder that collapses the first time you attempt to use it, and thus injures you, you would have sound grounds for alleging that your injury was the result of a defect in the product, and you might well be able to collect damages in court. You would have no such grounds, however, if the ladder collapsed — with you on it — because you had placed it on top of a rickety table.

In recent years, the courts have been increasingly inclined to hold manufacturers and sellers liable for injuries caused by products they make or sell. Under the theory of "strict liability," a court will examine what the company actually did to ensure the safety or reliability of its product and will compare that with what the company *should* have done to make sure the product is safe. Moreover, the courts have applied the strict liability theory not only to products that cause immediate damage, but to those with hidden de-

Handling an Accident Claim

If you are in an automobile accident, or are the victim of someone's negligence, you may become involved in a lawsuit. At the very least, you will probably have some discussion with lawyers from an insurance company. You can, if you choose, turn the matter over to a lawyer to handle for you, or you can negotiate for yourself.

If the accident is serious, with severe injuries and extensive property damage, it is best to consult a lawyer. But if the accident is relatively minor, with no personal injury and little damage to property, you may be able to deal with it alone.

There are a number of steps you should follow after the accident if you possibly can:

1. Do not leave the scene until you have identified yourself, gotten all pertinent information (name, address, license number, insurance company) from the other party and made sure that no one is hurt.

2. If a police officer appears to investigate, get his or her name and badge number. Cooperate with the officer, but make as few statements about how the accident occurred as possible. If you can avoid it, do not sign any statements. You are not required to do so. But be sure to ask for a copy of the accident report, if any.

3. Get the names and addresses of any witnesses whose story might be favorable — or adverse — to you.

4. As soon as possible inform your insurance company about the accident. It will advise you on how to proceed. If you are at fault, it will usually help you defend any lawsuit that is filed.

5. Write down your recollection of the events as soon as possible, recalling as many details of the scene — signs, lights, directions — as you can.

6. Try to take photographs of the scene or have them taken, including any skid marks and, if possible, the automobiles involved.

7. If you are taken to a hospital, write down its name and get the names and addresses of any doctors who treat you, as well as their medical diagnoses.

8. Get estimates of how much repairs will cost from two or three mechanics or body shops in your area.

9. If you have a new car or one that was just repaired, and you think that the accident might have been the result of a mechanical defect or faulty repair work, do not get the car fixed until you have an expert examine it and give you an opinion. You may have cause for an action against the manufacturer.

10. If the other person is definitely at fault and offers to pay, do not accept any money until you are sure there are no injuries and the amount offered is adequate to repair any damage to your car.

Similar precautions should be observed in the case of any other kind of accident that may lead to legal action. If, for example, you are shopping in the supermarket, trip over a case of canned peaches left in an aisle, and fall and

fects, or flaws that are not discovered until several years have passed. A person who develops a long-term health problem — cancer, for example — as a result of inhaling a chemical used in a building material produced by a firm that did not apply proper care in making that chemical, may well be able to recover damages. However, cases of this type can be extremely complex and litigation can go on for many years. Therefore, before bringing suit, you should feel very confident of your ability to prove that your injuries were the direct result of the product concerned.

Statutory Rights. In recent years, Congress has provided consumers with some new tools in seeking redress for legal wrongs. Under the so-called "private right of action," a few federal laws give consumers a statutory right to go to court to recover damages in cases where they have been denied something specifically due them. Examples of cases that can be brought under the private right of action include the following:

- You have been injured by a consumer product which the manufacturer knowingly produced in non-compliance with a standard set wrench your back, you may have grounds for legal action. Even if the manager of the store is called over to where you are, apologizes profusely, takes your name and address, and offers to have someone drive you home, you should still get as much of the information suggested above as your condition permits.

If you retain an attorney for any personal injury case, you should let him or her do all of the negotiating and the collection of a settlement. But remember that lawyer's fees can be high: usually about 40 percent of the amount received and somewhat less if the case is settled out of court.

If you negotiate directly with the other person's insurance company, you will save the lawyer's percentage of the settlement. If the case is simple, and there are neither permanent injuries nor residual effects, that saving may more than make up for the increase in the settlement amount that a lawyer might be able to get for you.

If you decide to handle your own accident case, the first thing to do is write to the defendant or the defendant's insurance company, briefly stating what happened, and explaining that you have been hurt as a result of the defendant's negligence. Insurance companies are generally eager to settle small claims, and the company will probably contact you within a week or two with some kind of offer. If you hear nothing in three weeks, write follow-up letters. If you still hear nothing after a couple of months, consult your lawyer.

There are a number of factors that affect the amount you may be awarded in a personal injury case. First, if you have a history of filing claims for personal injury, the insurance company may regard you as a chronic complainer and it may be difficult for you to collect. If you have no such history, however, there are other factors they will consider:

1. Your job. People with positions of responsibility, with good pay and/or a bright future, are usually better able to negotiate settlements than those less favorably situated.

2. Where you live. You will generally get more if you live in a city than in a rural area.

3. The obviousness of any negligence involved. You will get more if the defendant is clearly at fault — except, of course, in states with no-fault insurance laws.

For most people handling their own accident cases, a major question is: "How much money should I ask for?" As a rule of thumb, according to attorney and author Samuel G. Kling, you should ask for three to four times the total of your actual damages and expenses. Thus, if your medical expenses, loss of wages and other costs total $1,000, you can reasonably ask for $3,000 to $4,000 in an ordinary case where there is no possibility of lingering injury or pain.

You should never settle a case until you have been completely discharged by a physician and are assured that your injury will leave no lasting residual effects. Once you have signed a release on a claim in a personal injury case, you can collect no further damages on that claim — even if the problem connected with the injury should crop up again many years later. So be sure before you sign.

by the Consumer Products Safety Commission. In this case, the Consumer Product Safety Act allows you to recover your damages in federal court, including attorney fees.

• You have been defrauded or deceived in the purchase or sale of a security regulated by the Securities and Exchange Commission. In this case, you may be able to recover your losses under the Securities Exchange Act of 1934.

• You have been damaged by the failure of a bank to make a timely electronic funds transfer when you authorized it to do so and even though there were sufficient funds in your account. Under these circumstances, the Electronic Funds Transfer Act allows you to recover your losses from the bank.

The Summons. Once you have determined that you *do* have grounds for a lawsuit, and have enlisted the services of a competent attorney, the wheels can be set in motion. The first requirement if you bring a lawsuit is that you notify of the other side, so that it can prepare its defense. A summons is issued, usually by the court, which is then delivered to the defendant by a sheriff. Ordinarily, the summons must be presented to the defendant personally, although in some cases it may be sent by registered mail. Included with the summons is a declaration of the complaint that you as the plaintiff have against the defendant. This complaint, which should be drawn up by your lawyer, contains the nature and charges of your suit as well as the amount of money damages that you demand.

Pleadings. If the defendant decides to fight the lawsuit rather than settle out of court immediately, he or she must file an answer to the complaint within a specified number of days. The answer can contain a counterclaim that the defendant may have against the plaintiff, and the defendant may bring in other parties who could also be liable to the plaintiff. All these documents are called the "pleadings" and they are intended to clarify the issues that will be heard at trial. Even if the defendant plans to settle out of court, he or she will file an answer unless the settlement is made quickly: otherwise, the plaintiff may receive a "default judgment."

Summary Judgment. If the defendant's lawyer thinks that you have a very weak case, he or she may file a "Motion for Summary Judgment" with the court. If the judge agrees that your lawyer has failed to state a valid claim, the court may simply refuse to hear the case. Or the judge may allow your lawyer to change the complaint, so that your case has a sounder basis in law.

If it appears that the lawsuit will proceed to trial, the next stage of the process is known as "discovery." Your lawyer and the defendant's lawyer take and record statements of witnesses (known as "depositions"), file interrogatories requiring written responses from the opposing side, obtain subpoenas for important documents and the like. The purpose of discovery is to allow each party to learn all the evidence that will be presented during the trial, for both the plaintiff and the defendant. Often, when discovery is completed and the evidence is clearly spelled out, one or both of the parties will want to try to settle the case before it goes to trial.

Trial. A civil trial can be held before a judge alone, although if either side wants a jury trial, it has the right to request one. The jury in a civil case generally consists of six persons, although the number is different in some states, and it is selected from a larger panel by the lawyers for the two sides. Each lawyer asks each prospective juror a number of questions; this so-called *voir dire* is designed to enable the attorneys to discover any possible prejudices on any juror's part, and each attorney is permitted to dismiss a small number of prospective jurors without cause merely because the *voir dire* has led the lawyer to believe that they may be unsympathetic to his or her client. Each lawyer can also challenge any number of jurors for cause — good reason — by showing that they are openly opposed to his or her client.

Once a jury has been selected, your lawyer makes an opening statement, telling the jurors what the facts of the case are from your side, why you decided to sue and the amount of the damages demanded. The defendant's lawyer can then also make an opening statement, either denying the charges or offering a defense to them. After these statements have been made, your lawyer may call witnesses to substantiate your claim and the defendant's lawyer may then cross-examine them. The defendant can then call his or her own witnesses, who will be questioned first by the defense lawyer and then cross-examined by your attorney. Thereafter, your lawyer may be permitted to call witnesses who can rebut what the defendant's witnesses have said.

At various points during the trial, one or another of the lawyers may ask for a "directed verdict" — that is, a decision, by the judge alone, in favor of his or her client, on the ground that the other side has not even come close to proving its case. If the case has gone a long way when this request is made, most judges tend to deny it.

In the final portion of the trial, your lawyer may address the jury, summing up your case in a closing argument, after which the defendant's lawyer also makes a summation. Some states allow the plaintiff's lawyer one more turn, or a rebuttal, to answer the defense lawyer's closing argument.

Charging the Jury. In all court cases, the judge is the expert on the law and the jurors are the "triers of fact." In the charge to the jurors, the judge instructs them about the law involved in the case, and reminds them that it is their

(continued on page 374)

Small Claims Courts

State	Court	Maximum Claim	Filing Fee	Lawyers Allowed	Appeals Allowed	Contact[2]
Alabama	Small Claims Division of District Court	$500	$5-10	Yes	Yes	Administrative Office of Courts Montgomery, AL 36130
Alaska	Small Claims Court of District Court	$2,000	$5-10	Yes	Yes	Attorney General's Office, Anchorage, AK 99501
Arizona	Justice of Peace Court	$1,000	$5-10	Yes	Yes	Attorney General's Office, Phoenix, AZ 85007
Arkansas	Small Claims Division of Municipal Court	$300	$5-10	Yes	Yes	Attorney General's Office, Little Rock, AR 72201
California	Small Claims Division of Municipal or Justice Court	$750	$0-5	No	Defendant only	State Consumer Affairs Dept., Sacramento, CA 95802
Colorado	Small Claims Division of County Court	$500	$5-10	No	Yes	Attorney General's Office, Denver CO 80203
Connecticut	Small Claims Division of Superior Court	$750	$5-10	Yes	No	State Consumer Protection Dept., Hartford, CT 06115
Delaware	Justice of Peace Court	$1,500	$16-20	Yes	Yes	State Consumer Affairs Division, Wilmington, DE 19801
District Of Columbia	Small Claims Branch of D.C.	$750	$0-5	Yes	Yes	D.C. Superior Superior Court Court Clerk, Disrict of Columbia, 20001
Florida	Summary Claims Division of County Court	$5,000	$5-20	Yes	Yes	State Consumer Services Division, Tallahassee, FL 32301
Georgia	Small Claims Court [3]			Yes	Yes	State Consumer Affairs Office, Atlanta, GA 30303
Hawaii	Small Claims Division of District Court	$1,000	$5-10	Yes	No	State Consumer Protection Office, Honolulu, HI 96812

[1] This chart contains early 1980 data; changes are frequently made by state legislatures.

[2] Contacts: A central contact point for each state is given; however, it is recommended that individuals first call their nearest court or local consumer affairs office.

State	Court	Maximum Claim	Filing Fee	Lawyers Allowed	Appeals Allowed	Contact:[2]
Idaho	Small Claims Department of District Court	$1,000	$20+	No	Yes	Attorney General's Office, Boise, ID 83720
Illinois	Small Claims Court or Pro Se Court (Cook County)[4]			Yes	Yes	Consumer Advocate, Office of Governor, Chicago, IL 60601
Indiana	Small Claims Court	$3,000	$15-20	Yes	Yes	Attorney General's Office, Indianapolis, IN 46204
Iowa	Small Claims Division of District Court	$1,000	$5-10	Yes	Yes	Attorney General's Office, Des Moines, IA 50319
Kansas	Small Claims Court	$500	$5-10	No	Yes	Attorney General's Office, Topeka, KS 66612
Kentucky	Small Claims Division of District Court	$1,000	$11-16	Yes	Yes	Attorney General's Office, Frankfort, Ky 40601
Louisiana	Small Claims Division of City Court, or Justice of Peace Court	$750	$11-16	Yes	No	State Consumer Protection Office, Baton Rouge, LA 70804
Maine	Small Claims Division of District Court	$800	$5-10	Yes	Yes	Attorney General's Office, Augusta, Me 04333
Maryland	Small Claims Division of District Court	$500	$5-10	Yes	Defendant Only	Attorney General's Office, Baltimore, MD 21202
Massachusetts	Small Claims Division of District Court or Municipal Court	$750	$0-5	Yes	Yes	State Consumer's Council, Boston, MA 02202
Michigan	Small Claims Division of District Court[5]	$600	$5-10	No	No	State Consumer's Council, Lansing, MI 48933
Minnesota	Conciliation Court	$1,000	$0-5	No	Yes	Attorney General's Office, St. Paul, MN 55155
Mississippi	Justice of the Peace	$500	$5-10	Yes	Yes	Attorney General's Office, Jackson, MS 39205

[3] Georgia has no statewide system; many counties have small claims courts with varying claim limits, fees and procedures; first contact should be with County Clerk.

[4] Illinois fees and procedures vary from circuit to circuit; first contact should be with Circuit Clerk of County. The general small claims limit throughout the state is $1,000 but in Cook County there is a special court called Pro Se Court of Circuit Court in which the claim limit is $500.

State	Court	Maximum Claim	Filing Fee	Lawyers Allowed	Appeals Allowed	Contact:[2]
Missouri	Small Claims Court of Circuit Court	$500	$5-10	Yes	Yes	State Court Administrator's Office, Jefferson City, MO 65101
Montana	Small Claims Division of Justice of Peace Court	$750	$5-10	Yes	Yes	State Consumer Affairs Division, Helena, MT 59601
Nebraska	Small Claims Division of Municipal or County Court	$1,000	$0-5	No	Yes	Attorney General's Office, Lincoln, NE 68509
Nevada	Justice Court	$750	$5-10	Yes	Yes	Attorney General's Office, Las Vegas, NV 89158
New Hampshire	Small Claims Court of Municipal or District Court	$500	$5-10	Yes	Limited	Attorney General's Office, Concord, NH 03301
New Jersey	Small Claims Court of County District Court	$500	$5-10	Yes	Yes	State Consumer Affairs Division, Newark, NJ 07102
New Mexico	Small Claims Court (Bernalillo County only)	$2,000	$5-10	Yes	Yes—Limited	County Small Claims Court, Albuquerque, NM 87102
New York	Small Claims Court	$1,000	$0-5	Yes	Limited	State Office of Court Administration, New York, NY 10007
North Carolina	Small Claims Court of Magistrate's Court	$800	$11-15	Yes	Yes	Attorney General's Office, Raleigh, NC 27602
North Dakota	Small Claims Court of Justice[6] or County Court		$0-5	Yes	No	Attorney General's Office, Bismarck, ND 58505
Ohio	Small Claims Court	$500	$5-10	Yes	Yes	Attorney General's Office, Columbus, OH 43215
Oklahoma	Small Claims Division of District Court	$600	$5-10	Yes	Yes	Attorney General's Office, Oklahoma City, OK 73105
Oregon	Small Claims Division of District Court	$700	$16-20	No	No	Consumer Services Division, Salem, OR 97310

[5] Michigan has 28 cities with municipal small claims courts rather than district courts. In these municipal courts, the maximum claim is $1,500 and the procedures are more complex.

State	Court	Maximum Claim	Filing Fee	Lawyers Allowed	Appeals Allowed	Contact:[2]
Pennsylvania	District Justice Court Municipal Court (Philadelphia)	$2,000 $1,000	$0- $20 +	Yes	Yes	State Consumer Protection Bureau, Harrisburg, PA 17120
Puerto Rico	Department of Consumer Affairs[7]					Departamento de Asuntos del Consumidor, Santurce, PR 00940
Rhode Island	Small Claims Division of District Court	$500	$0-5	Yes	Defendant only	Attorney General's Department, Providence, RI 02903
South Carolina	Magistrate's Court	$1,000	$11-15	Yes	Yes	State Consumer Affairs Department, Columbia, SC 29250
South Dakota	Small Claims Division of Magistrate's Court	$2,000	$0-5	Yes	No	Attorney General's Office, Pierre, SD 57501
Tennessee	General Sessions Court	$5,000	$16-20	Yes	Yes	State Consumer Affairs Division, Nashville, TN 37204
Texas	Small Claims Court of Justice of Peace Court	$500	$16-20	Yes	Yes	Attorney General's Office, Austin, TX 78711
Utah	Small Claims Court of Circuit or Justice Court	$400	$0-5	Yes	Defendant only	Consumer Affairs Division, Salt Lake City, UT 84111
Vermont	Small Claims Division of District Court	$500	$5-10	Yes	Yes	Attorney General's Office, Montpelier, VT 05602
Virginia	General District Court[8]	$5,000	$5-10	Yes	Yes	State Consumer Affairs Office, Richmond, VA 23209
Virgin Islands	Small Claims Division of Territorial Court	$750	$0-50			Consumer Service Administration, Christiansted, VI 00820
Washington	Small Claims Court	$500	$5-10	No	Defendant only	Attorney General's Office, Seattle, WA 98104
West Virginia	Magistrate's Court	$1,500	$11-15	Yes	Yes	Attorney General's Office, Charleston, WV 25305

[6] Some North Dakota counties have County Justice Courts in which the maximum claim is $500. Seventeen other counties have County Courts of Increased Jurisdiction in which the maximum is $1,000.

State	Court	Maximum Claim	Filing Fee	Lawyers Allowed	Appeals Allowed	Contact:[2]
Wisconsin	Small Claims Court of Circuit Court	$1,000	$5-10	Yes	Yes	State Justice Department, Madison, WI 53702
Wyoming	Justice of Peace Court	$750	$11-15	Yes	Yes	Attorney General's Office, Cheynne, WY 82002

[7] While Puerto Rico has no small claims court system, as such, the Department of Consumer Affairs performs certain adjudicative functions similar in concept to small claims proceedings.

[8] In Virginia, if the amount involved is greater than $1,000 and the defendant files an affidavit with the court indicating a substantial defense, and pays accrued court costs, the case will be transferred to the regular civil court, the Circuit Court.

Regional Offices of the American Arbitration Association

Arizona
77 East Columbus
Phoenix, AZ 85012

California
443 Shatto Place
Los Angeles, CA 90020

530 Broadway
San Diego, CA 92101

445 Bush Street
San Francisco, CA

Connecticut
2 Hartford Square West
Hartford, CT 06106

Colorado
789 Sherman Street
Denver, CO 80203

District of Columbia
1730 Rhode Island Avenue, NW
Washington, DC 20036

Florida
2250 SW 3rd Avenue
Miami, FL 33129

Georgia
1197 Peachtree Street, NE
Atlanta, GA 30361

Illinois
205 West Wacker Drive
Chicago, IL 60606

Massachusetts
60 Staniford Street
Boston, MA 02114

Michigan
615 Griswold Street
Detroit, MI 48226

Minnesota
510 Foshay Tower
Minneapolis, MN 55402

New Jersey
1 Executive Drive
Somerset, NJ 08873

New York
585 Stewart Avenue
Garden City, NY 11530

140 West 51 Street
New York, NY 10020

720 State Tower Building
Syracuse, NY 13202

34 South Broadway
White Plains, NY 10601

North Carolina
3717 Latrobe Drive
P.O. Box 220565
Charlotte, NC 28222

Ohio
2308 Carew Tower
Cincinnati, OH 45202

1127 Euclid Avenue
Cleveland, OH 44115

Pennsylvania
1520 Locust Street
Philadelphia, PA 19102

221 Gateway Four
Pittsburgh, PA 15222

Texas
1607 Main Street
Dallas TX 75201

Washington
811 First Avenue
Seattle, WA 98104

job to reach a verdict based only on the facts and not on sympathy for one side or the other.

The Verdict. Once the jurors have reached a decision, they return to the court from the jury room, and their decision is announced by the foreman, who is usually selected by the jurors themselves. If the jury decides for the defendant, you have lost the case. If it decides in your favor, it will, in most jurisdictions, also decide the amount of the damages to be awarded you. In some jurisdictions, however, damages are not determined at this point, but in a separate trial. If you win, the defendant's attorney may ask the judge for a "judgment notwithstanding the verdict:" a request that the court dismiss the jury's verdict on the grounds that there was no evidence to warrant it. If you lose, your attorney is entitled to make the same request.

The Judgment. If you win, and the judge denies a defense motion to set aside the jury's verdict, the judgment is entered in the amount the jury awarded you. However, the defendant's lawyer can still make a motion for a new trial on grounds that a "reversible error" — prejudice on the part of the jury, for example — was committed during the course of the trial. If the judge grants the motion, a new trial will be held.

If a new trial is not granted, the loser can appeal to the next higher court on the ground that the trial court committed an error of law. But the appeals court will not retry the facts of the case. If the court agrees to hear the legal issues that have been raised, the lawyers will then have to appear before an appellate court judge — or panel of judges — to present their arguments. The written decision of the appeals court is usually sent to the lawyers some time later.

Awards and Fees. Let us say that the jury awarded you damages of $100,000, the defendant appealed, and the decision in your favor was upheld in the appellate court. Now you would like to get your money. If your lawyer handled the case on a contingent-fee basis (see Chapter 12), he or she would like the money, too. If the firm that owes the money is solvent and responsible, your lawyer will ordinarily be able to collect the amount of the judgment with little or no difficulty, and will pay you your share after deducting his or her fee. If, however, the defendant refuses to pay the judgment, you may have to resort to further legal action, such as seizing the defendant's assets and if necessary selling them to obtain the amount of the award.

The cost of proving a case in civil courts can be high. Expert witnesses may have to be paid as much as $1,000 a day to testify in court; transcript fees, too, can be painfully expensive. One specialist in negligence law estimates that the average automobile accident case costs between $10,000 and $20,000 simply to prepare for trial. And that estimate does not include a lawyer's time which, if it were billed by the hour, could be many thousands of dollars. Negligence lawyers, as a result, are not apt to take a case unless it is likely to yield at least $50,000 in an award or out-of-court settlement. Many lawyers try to avoid cases that might be difficult to prove: if the decision goes against them they will have wound up spending considerable time and money and getting nothing in return.

If only for this reason, a full-dress suit in civil court is probably not the best route for the average consumer seeking redress in cases involving only moderate sums. Costs are high, much time must be devoted to preparation of the suit and, because of overcrowded court dockets, years may pass before a judgment is rendered.

One or more of the many alternatives discussed here and in Chapter 13 are usually the better way to fight back against a seller of goods or purveyor of services who has behaved irresponsibly or attempted to bilk you. But whatever course you choose, judicial or non-judicial, it is important to *take action* when you have been wronged.

Aggrieved consumers now have an arsenal of weapons at their disposal. State and federal laws, mediation and arbitration services, hearings before various industry and consumer-industry panels, newspaper, radio and television Action Lines are only some of those available.

We have come a long way since the days when "Let the buyer beware" was the only truly effective rule of the marketplace. Consumers now have power — real power — on their side, which should be vigorously used when rights are trampled on or ignored.

Chapter 15

In Over Your Head

For most Americans the enticements to borrow are constant and omnipresent. Ads on radio and on television screens, in newspapers and magazines, letters in the mail, all offer the average citizen thousands of dollars of credit. The message is the same: "Buy now, pay later." A wide variety of credit cards is readily available. Banks trumpet their installment loans and lines of credit linked to checking accounts; department stores, oil companies and other business institutions virtually plead with customers to take out charge cards; financial institutions dispatch thousands of mailings per month offering high-salaried executives and professionals generous lines of credit that can be secured by nothing more than a signature.

In the space of a few generations, we have transformed ourselves from a society in which the use of credit to finance purchases bore a slight taint of irresponsibility to one in which the use of cash — or even a personal check — to pay for a relatively expensive item carries the stigma that, perhaps, the buyer may not be credit-worthy. The popular song lyric of two decades ago that declared, "Money makes the world go around," might well be updated to read "Credit makes the world go around."

But if credit is indeed the motive force of commerce, it can also be a terrifying trap for the individual and the family. It is the easiest thing in the world for families from every walk of life and every income group to find themselves badly over-extended. The siren song that promises instant gratification for a few dollars down and a few dollars a month quickly becomes a chorus of panic when payments must be made, not on just a few purchases, but on dozens. And if this situation is aggravated by the sudden loss of a job, large, unexpected medical expenses or any other major financial drain, the burden that time payments impose on a family may become impossible to bear.

In the early 1980's, the load of consumer debt in the United States amounted to about $1.5 *trillion*, an amount considerably larger than the national debt. Estimates vary on the number of people who are having difficulty — to one degree or another — meeting their obligations to creditors, but a telling indication of how this credit burden is affecting Americans can be seen in the sharp rise in personal bankruptcies.

In 1978 there were 179,194 such cases recorded. Only three years later this figure had risen to 456,919. And bankruptcies take into account only the most extreme cases. They tell nothing about the millions of families whose debts have forced them to defer college educations for their children, put off necessary medical treatments, delay the purchases of new homes or much-needed automobiles, or even scrimp on the weekly groceries as they struggle against enormous odds to pay off their obligations and avoid the bankruptcy courts.

The excessive burden of personal debt also hinders the economy as a whole. Families struggling to meet current obligations are in no position to take on new ones. Housing developers, manufacturers of every type of product, people in service industries are all forced to cut back — or even, in some cases, to close down — as markets for their goods shrivel and die.

Falling into the Trap

Superficially, it seems simple to avoid falling into the debt trap. Though most people may not be able to tell you exactly what they owe, just about everyone knows what he or she earns. A short session with a paper and pencil or a hand calculator can quickly reveal disposable income after the necessities are taken care of. So much for the mortgage or rent, for utilities, for food, for insurance, for transportation and other fixed expenses. Subtract the total from your family's take-home pay and the remainder will be your disposable income, a portion of which may be put aside for savings and the rest spent to buy the things you want.

Unfortunately, things seldom work that neatly. With everything from automobiles to baby clothes offered on credit in one form or another, and with each purchase being paid for just a little each month, it takes a strong will to resist the attractions of borrowing and getting what you want immediately. To take a typical example of how the trap can entice and then close, let's look at the case of a couple we shall call Bob and Joan.

Back in 1976, when Bob and Joan were newlyweds, they had a combined income of $35,000 a year, a fairly substantial amount for a couple in their mid-twenties. Believing themselves to be financially secure and desiring to begin married life with a home of their own, they purchased a house for $62,000. Thanks to savings they already had, and to gifts from their parents, the young people were able to put down 40 percent on the house, thus taking advantage of the lowest mortgage rate then available in their town, 8 percent. In all, the carrying charges on their mortgage came to only $250 per month, hardly a great amount for a couple earning almost $3,000 per month. In fact, the outlay seemed downright modest.

But there was a catch. The New Jersey suburb they chose to settle in had a high real estate tax. Each month the couple had to send an additional $200 to the bank for their escrow account. In the years to come, though their mortgage rate remained stable, their real estate taxes did not. By early 1983 this tax was up to nearly $400 per month. Another factor that Bob and Joan had not counted on was the rise in utility rates. When they first moved into their house, the cost of gas and electricity was well under $200 per month even in the coldest winter months. By the winter of 1983, they were paying nearly $400 per month just to keep their house warm, the water hot and the appliances running.

But even if Bob and Joan had been apprised of these future expenses back in 1976, they probably would not have worried. After all, Bob's salary was $22,000 per year and Joan's was $13,000, and there was every indication that their joint income would rise and more than keep pace with inflation. And for a while this proved to be the case. In 1977 Bob took a new job as an electrical engineer with a computer firm, and in 1978, Joan left her secretarial job to become a real estate agent. In 1980 they earned $58,000, and it was in that year that they laid the foundation for financial troubles to come.

It was all so easy. Until then, Bob and Joan had been getting by with furniture from the apartments they had had when both were single. Now, with their income suddenly much higher, they decided to splurge a little. Having had little time to put aside substantial funds in a joint savings account, they could only finance major purchases by borrowing. Given the size of their income, banks, department stores, credit card and finance companies were eager to extend all of the credit the couple wanted. Within a few months, Bob and Joan had bought a new dining room set, beds and bureaus, living room chairs and a sofa, a few paintings, a stereo and a new color television set.

Individually, each of the payments they made hardly amounted to much: about $50 a month for the dining room furniture, $35 for the bedroom set, $22 for the stereo and television sets, and $18 for the paintings — all told, $125 per month. Given their income, this was hardly excessive. In early 1981, however, Joan came to realize that her work required her to have a car of her own, and this meant another monthly expenditure of $259 to meet the payments on the auto loan they now took out. This too occasioned little worry, for 1980 had been a banner year for her real estate agency, and Joan, though new in the field, had done exceedingly well — so well that in the summer of that year Bob suggested a vacation trip to Europe. After all, they were both working very hard and, as the saying goes, "they owed it to themselves." The European jaunt was financed with an additional $4,500 loan from the bank. Monthly payments on this loan came to $149.

The year 1981 opened with a sudden drop in the real estate market and, at the same time, Bob's company found itself in financial difficulties. First, all raises were cancelled — and Bob had been depending on a promised salary increase of $3,000. Then his organization announced that all professional employees would be required to take a 10 percent cut in salary, and Bob's income, instead of rising,

A Dozen Ways of Cutting Back

In the typical family, a large proportion of discretionary income is likely to be dribbled away in expenditures that are both unnecessary and unrewarding.

Here are a dozen suggestions that may enable you to reduce your expenses without making any great sacrifice in your standard of living. Probably not all of these hints will apply to your situation, but perhaps enough of them will to make a substantial difference in your financial outlay.

- Reduce or even eliminate all credit purchases until you have made significant reductions in your credit bills.
- If you are paying high credit card interest rates on several accounts, consider getting a lower interest rate loan from a bank to pay off these debts. Shop around from bank to bank to secure the lowest possible rate. Do not, however, secure the loan from a finance company that may charge you rates higher than the ones you are now paying.
- If your family needs a second car, but only on occasion, consider renting one when the need arises rather than buying.
- In the supermarket, always buy from a list that you have prepared beforehand. It will be much easier to refrain from impulse buying.
- Check on sales in every kind of store. Clothing stores regularly run end-of-season sales. For example, many stores sell their winter apparel at greatly reduced prices shortly after Christmas, while summer sales are often held after Independence Day (see Chapter 7). Coupons issued by manufacturers or supermarkets can save you large sums on your purchases — but only if you intend to buy the product anyway, and only if the coupon makes the cost of the purchased item less than that of a similar and equally satisfactory product.
- Be particularly wary of mail-order brochures that are inserted in the envelopes of your monthly credit card bills. By ordering the goods advertised through your credit card account you will only be increasing your outstanding debt.
- When you receive a bill for a charged purchase, or for that matter your telephone bill, always check it very carefully. Computers — or the people who operate them — can sometimes make mistakes.
- Watch the cost of heating and air conditioning very closely. By turning off radiators, heating outlets and air conditioners in rooms not being used you can sharply reduce your utility bills. Also, when buying appliances, always check their energy efficiency ratings (EER) cards. The higher the number shown on the EER card, the more energy efficient the appliance. Remember, an inexpensive air conditioner or refrigerator with a low EER may be a poor investment compared to a somewhat higher priced model with a higher rating.
- Consider forming co-ops with friends and neighbors. A food co-op, for example, can save you substantial amounts in routine produce purchases, and a baby sitting co-op can help to lessen the cost of a night on the town.
- Buy second-hand goods when it seems appropriate. Thrift shops, flea markets and garage or estate sales can often be inexpensive sources for things you need or want. Check classified ads for those items you expect to use for a relatively short period of time. For example, if your son is taking up ice hockey, you probably will be able to find excellent equipment being sold by parents of a boy who has outgrown his ice skates or padding.
- Do your own routine maintenance on your automobile. There are many books on the market that will tell you how to perform relatively simple tasks.
- Keep a file of all receipts, credit card payments and interest payments. At tax time these may be invaluable, both as reminders of deductions to which you are entitled and as records of expenditure should the IRS audit your return.

dropped. Meanwhile, inflation, though falling off slightly, was still an inescapable fact of life. Gasoline costs, utility expenses, real estate taxes, and food and clothing prices seemed to rise higher every month. As for Joan, her income dropped drastically. Because of soaring interest rates, real estate sales plummeted. From January to June of 1981 she did not sell a single house; from June through December, she sold only one.

By the end of 1981, Bob's salary cut had brought his earnings down to $27,000 before income taxes and Joan's earnings for the year were only $3,000. Their monthly income after taxes was only about $2,000. But their fixed monthly expenses, including payments on their loans, now came to almost $1,500 per month, leaving barely $500 for food, clothing, transportation, insurance and other necessities, to say nothing of an occasional movie or dinner in a restaurant. Bob and Joan were now skating on very thin ice. Just another modest rise in heating costs or commuting expenses could push them over the edge.

That is exactly what happened. In early 1982 their utility bills went up again, and commuting costs rose by 15 percent. Now Joan and Bob were really in trouble. Like many people caught in similar situations, they steadfastly refused to recognize reality. Instead of taking stock of their situation and trying to find where they could cut down, they began using their bank credit cards for all sorts of ordinary, day-to-day purchases that they would normally have paid for in cash. Things like drugs and shoes they now charged against their bank credit cards, and they began running up monthly bills with the neighborhood grocer and butcher. For a while they maintained payments on all of their accounts, but on their bank cards they made minimum payments, so small that they were not even keeping pace with the interest charges. Then they started to delay payments, paying the minimum on one card this month, the minimum on another the next. Twice they were unable to pay the installment loans they had taken out for the vacation of two years before and for Joan's auto, and they allowed their bills at the grocery store and butcher shop to go unpaid for months at a time. And when they did clear these accounts, they did so by taking out a new bank credit card and borrowing cash against their credit line.

By the summer of 1982, Bob's and Joan's financial life was in a state of collapse. They could no longer meet their creditors' demands. Each day's mail brought a new load of dunning letters, and neither could bear to answer the telephone for fear that it might be a creditor demanding payment. Their conversations now almost always revolved around money — how to get more of it, how to meet payments, and which of them bore responsibility for the difficulties they were in. They had come to the point where they were thinking of declaring personal bankruptcy. Though they knew that this would destroy their credit ratings for years to come, they saw no other way out of their dilemma.

Finally, however, they went to a local nonprofit credit counseling service, which functioned on the principles described later in this chapter, and which was able to give them the help they needed to put them back on the road to financial solvency.

The story of Bob and Joan is hardly unusual. In fact, they were extremely lucky. Through all of their difficulties, neither became unemployed — indeed with the recovery of the real estate market in early 1983, Joan actually began selling houses again. There was no medical emergency to eat away at their income. And as they had no children, their financial resources could be stretched further than might otherwise have been the case. Yet the dream of a good life had turned into a nightmare, and in their story may be found most of the standard reasons why people get into debt over their heads.

The Reasons Why

Bob and Joan are typical children of American affluence and its concommitant, easy credit. The reasons why they fell into the credit trap are readily understandable.

Instant Gratification. Throughout their childhoods Bob and Joan had been living in secure, comfortable environments — pleasant, well-furnished houses, yearly vacation trips, late model cars, all of the other amenities of a solid middle-class life. By the time they reached adulthood, began working and were married, all of these things seemed natural parts of living. Given the size of their joint income, it never even occurred to them that they should delay having almost everything

The High Cost of Borrowing

The actual cost of taking out loans varies widely according to the type of loan and the source of the money. In addition, interest rates over the past decade have gone up and down like a roller coaster. In the table below different types of loans are listed in order of their cost to consumers, an order that tends to remain stable. Study them carefully to see what sources of low-cost credit are available to you. Obviously, high-cost loans should be avoided if possible.

Low-Cost Loans — In Order of Cost

- From employers, friends and relatives
- On insurance policies
- Secured loans such as passbook loans from banks
- Federal and state-subsidized education loans
- Personal loans from banks
- Unsecured personal loans from credit unions
- First mortgage loans from savings institutions
- Loans for new cars from thrift institutions
- Unsecured personal loans from thrift institutions
- Second mortgage loans from bank holding original mortgage

Moderate-Cost Loans — In Order of Cost

- Subsidized education loans to parents from banks
- Second mortgage loans from bank not holding original mortgage
- Second mortgage loans from finance companies
- Bank charge cards and credit lines

High-Cost Loans — In Order of Cost

- Unsecured personal loans from finance companies
- Loans on used cars from banks, finance companies or automobile dealers
- Pawnbrokers' loans
- Loan sharks

they had enjoyed when they were children — certainly not when credit was so easy to obtain and individual monthly payments so seemingly insignificant.

Inflationary Thinking. Through the late 1970's and early 1980's, inflation in the United States became a way of life. People adjusted their thinking to reflect this economic reality, and the implicit notion that it was better to buy something you wanted or needed now, rather than wait, because the price would certainly go up. If you didn't have the cash to buy it, borrow, for undoubtedly your income would rise with inflation and you would be paying back your loans with inflated currency. It seemed to make good economic sense to buy now and pay later. Very few people actually took into consideration the possibility that inflation would continue while the overall economy declined. The idea that your income would actually drop — or that you might be out of a job — seemed too remote to contemplate seriously.

Unwarranted Optimism. Hand-in-hand with inflationary thinking went unwarranted optimism. For Americans of the post-World War II generations brought up in boom times, it seemed unthinkable that there would not be new and continuing financial opportunities. Incomes, it was thought, would not only keep pace with inflation, but would outstrip it. For young professionals and business people in particular, optimism became almost a disease. If your job at Consolidated Everything paid too little, there was an excellent chance that the competition, United Everything, would pay you a much higher salary. So why worry about rapidly accumulating debts when you only had to find an easily obtainable new position to get the money to meet your obligations?

"It's All Deductible." While government officials regularly bemoan excessive consumer credit, they underwrite the credit economy by making interest payments tax deductible. When Joan and Bob were earning $58,000 per year, which put them in the 50 percent bracket, they told each other that their interest payments were not nearly as large as they seemed because half could be deducted from their income tax. They never considered the fact that if their income fell, so too would the tax saving on their interest payments. If you are in the 20 percent bracket, your income tax savings on interest payments amount to only 20 percent.

Inadequate Record Keeping. It is very easy for debts to accumulate without the debtor being aware of what is happening. Everybody remembers when he or she borrows $10,000 for an automobile or signs an $80,000 mortgage on a house. Few people, however, keep track of the many small debts that can build up day by day, month in and month out. The three shirts charged on a bank card, the toaster bought on credit from a department store, the meals paid for with plastic, and the concert tickets bought with an overdraft check — all of these easily forgettable costs can add up very rapidly, resulting in enormous monthly bills and high interest charges.

Confusion of Priorities. In a world of full employment and rising salaries, it is very easy to confuse luxuries with necessities. Bob and Joan did so regularly. For example, they told themselves that they had earned their European vacation, but in fact they could ill afford it. And while Joan really did need her own car to carry on as a real estate saleswoman, a late model used car might have done as well as a new one.

Psychological Factors. Consumer counselors generally agree that psychology plays an important part in the accumulation of excessive debt. People who try to buy their family's love with expensive presents, or their colleagues' respect by always picking up the lunch checks, have insecurities that will probably result in financial troubles.

The Warning Signals of Financial Disaster

If Bob and Joan had been paying attention to their financial condition instead of concentrating on the accumulation of goods, they might have been aware of several distinct signals warning them that they were getting into debt over their heads. These signals are not necessarily hard and fast, but if two or three are going off simultaneously, it's a pretty good bet that the time has come to slow down and take stock.

- You are spending more than 20 percent of

A Simple Budget Form for Householders

Item	Av. Mo. Expense	Budgeted Amount
SHELTER		
Rent or mortgage payment	______	______
Property taxes	______	______
Property insurance	______	______
Maintenance	______	______
Gas, oil, electricity	______	______
Telephone	______	______
Water and sewer	______	______
Other	______	______
FOOD		
Groceries	______	______
Meals away from home	______	______
Tobacco products/ alcohol	______	______
Other	______	______
TRANSPORTATION		
Car payments	______	______
Gasoline, oil, etc.	______	______
Maintenance, repair	______	______
Auto insurance	______	______
Public transportation	______	______
Car-pool costs	______	______
Taxes and fees	______	______
Other	______	______
CLOTHING		
New purchases	______	______
Dry cleaning, laundry	______	______
Mending, repair	______	______
Other	______	______

ere is a budget form, prepared by the American Financial Services Association, that can be filled it in a relatively short period of time. Some of the listed items may not apply to your situation, in hich case you can just skip or replace them with categories that do apply but are not on the form.

em	Av. Mo. Expense	Budgeted Amount
EALTH CARE		
ıysicians, dentists		
rugs (inc. non-prescription)		
ealth/hospital insurance		
ospital costs		
ther		
ERSONAL CARE		
air care		
oiletries		
ersonal care appliances		
ocket money allowances		
ther		
ECREATION		
acations		
ecreational equipment		
ecreational activities		
lovies, theater		
arties hosted in home		
lewspapers, books, etc.		
lub dues		
)ther		
IFTS & CONTRIBUTIONS		
eligious and charities		
olitical causes		
amily gifts		
on-family gifts		
hristmas gifts		
)ther		

Item	Av. Mo. Expense	Budgeted Amount
SAVINGS		
Savings accounts		
Life insurance		
Disability insurance		
Investments		
Retirement contributions		
Other		
OBLIGATIONS		
Alimony/child support		
Child care		
Credit card payments		
Other debt payments		
EDUCATION		
Education/training expenses		
TOTAL EXPENDITURES		

INCOME	Monthly	Yearly
All salaries and wages		
Average commission income		
Average part-time work		
Alimony/child support		
Dividends/interest		
Pension/Social Security		
Other		
TOTAL INCOME		
TOTAL EXPENDITURES		
BALANCE		

your take-home pay to service your credit account debts. This is the figure cited most often by credit counselors, but they make exceptions. A family with $10,000 per year income, two young children and a mortgage, probably cannot afford anything like the 20-percent figure. If that same family was earning $50,000, however, it might be able to afford 25 or even 30 percent.

- You are spending more than one-third of your discretionary income on credit account debts. This is probably a more useful indicator of trouble ahead. Here too, however, those with very high incomes may be able to afford a somewhat higher percentage in credit account debts; those with very low incomes, a lower percentage.
- You are using bank or credit cards to pay for relatively small, routine bills. If you regularly don't have enough cash for such purchases, it is an almost sure sign that you are in debt over your head.
- You are letting some credit account bills accumulate while paying off others, or are paying one bank card this month and another bank card the next. If your income is not large enough to meet all of your credit accounts on time, there is little doubt that you are in financial difficulty.
- You regularly make only the minimum payment on each of your credit card accounts. If you do this while continuing to charge purchases on these cards, you probably are not even paying the full interest charges, and your debt can only mount higher.
- You are regularly borrowing small amounts from friends to tide you over from payday to payday. Even when interest is not charged, such borrowing indicates that you are accumulating more debts than you can afford.
- You are dipping into savings to service your monthly credit accounts. The result of this over an extended period is, of course, no savings and, if you continue to buy on credit at the same rate as before, no lessening of debt.
- You are relying on overtime pay to discharge your debts and finance new credit purchases. This may be of short-term assistance, but hardly a dependable answer; the slightest downturn in your employer's business could wipe out overtime earnings. Money earned through overtime should really be set aside in savings rather than used to finance credit purchases.

Staying Out of Trouble

For most people, keeping ahead of one's creditors and maintaining a reasonable balance between income and expenditures is a relatively simple matter. If you know what your income is, and where your money is spent, you should be able to figure out how much discretionary income you have left over and how much credit you can reasonably employ. The problem is that very few Americans actually have an idea of how they spend their money. The first step toward finding out is to keep an expenditure diary for a period of at least two months.

The Diary of Expenses. A day-by-day accounting of expenses need not be elaborate. But if it is to be useful, it must be complete. All you need in the way of supplies is a small notebook and a pencil. At the top of each page, write down the date. Then list every purchase you make — no matter how large or how small — and the amount of every bill you pay. Do not forget a thing, not even a candy bar, a pack of cigarettes or a bus token. Also, be sure to include any checks you write — your mortgage payment, rent, charge account payments — everything! Any omissions will seriously affect your bookkeeping.

At the end of the two-month period sit down and tally up the large payments, such as insurance premiums or tuition, that you ordinarily make on an annual, semiannual or quarterly basis. Then prorate these expenses on a monthly basis. If, for instance, tuition amounts to $1,200 a year, enter $200 in your two-month accounting. (If the tuition payment falls due during the period you are keeping the account, put it down as only $200 rather than the full amount.) Remember, your accounting is on a monthly basis.

There may be other one-time payments that should be included in your accounting. For example, suppose you recently had an appendectomy that cost $1,800. This, too, should be distributed on a 12-month basis — or $150 per month.

Once you have completed the two-month accounting you will have the information you need to draw up a budget, a document that will not only help you manage your family's finances on a sound basis, but may be invaluable to you in setting your priorities and achieving your goals.

Family Balance Sheet

Assets. Liquid

Cash	$______
Bank Balances	
Savings	______
Checking	______
Other	______
Money owed you	______
Stocks	______
Bonds	______
Cash value of insurance	______
Other liquid assets	______

Assets. Fixed

Real estate	$______
Automobiles	______
Long-term investments	______
Retirement funds	______
Furniture & other house items	______
Business interests	______
Other	______
TOTAL ASSETS (liquid & fixed)	______

Liabilities. Short Term

Credit card balances	$______
Tax arrears	______
Other	______

Liabilities. Long Term

Mortgage outstanding	$______
Secured loans, outstanding	______
Unsecured loans, outstanding	______
Margin due on stocks	______
Other	______
TOTAL LIABILITIES (long term & short term)	______

Budgeting Yourself and Your Family. The secret of successful budgeting is absolute honesty. You must include what your actual income is and, just as important, you must write down every item of expenditure. This, of course, is where that diary comes in handy. You must also deal with current reality, not hope. You may have every reason to anticipate that in six months you will be getting a 10 percent raise, or that tomorrow you may be giving up cigarettes for good. But until such hopes and intentions become reality, they should have no place in your family's budget. You can always adjust the budget later — when and if the raise has come through and you have actually smoked your last cigarette. In short, erring on the side of caution can only be beneficial, while erring on the side of optimism may do you great harm.

A budget is a family affair. If you are married and have no children, draw up the budget with your spouse. If you have teenage children, at least consider bringing them into the budgetary process. After all, the way you spend money affects them. And by listening to their views on how the family's money should be spent, you may become better acquainted with their needs and desires. More important, they will learn vital lessons in family finance if they are consulted.

Although there are undoubtedly some people who enjoy drawing up budgets, for most of us the process of listing income and expenditures and then trying to cut back can be a tension-producing experience. When everything is listed in black and white, recriminations between husbands and wives and parents and children are hardly uncommon. Charges and counter-charges of "you spend too much on lunches," and "you spend too much on clothes" can poison the atmosphere. But if you all go into budget-making with a positive point of view — such as "this exercise will help us plan for a new house or a vacation abroad" — you will probably find that tensions can be greatly eased.

The Budget Form

Budgets can take any of a number of forms, but they all have two things in common: they include a family's income and its expenditures. On page 381 is a budget form adapted from one prepared by the American Financial Services Association. Note that for ease of

First-in, First-out Rule

In some circumstances, disputes may arise between debtors and creditors as to what a secured loan is. For example, if you go to a department store and use your charge account to buy a sofa, then return the next day and charge a refrigerator, both of those purchases may be considered loans and be subject to repossession if you should fail to pay off the debt.

Let us suppose that the sofa cost $500 and the refrigerator $600, and for several months you have been making payments on these purchases. In all, you have paid $900 of the $1,100 (plus interest) owed. At this point you can no longer afford to continue payments, and the store threatens to repossess both items. In many states the store cannot do this. Because you have paid off more than the amount owed on the first purchase — the sofa — it cannot be considered security for the loan. Only the refrigerator remains as security.

This is known as the first-in, first-out rule, which holds that when more than one purchase is made in this manner, all payments must be applied to the first purchase until that obligation is liquidated. Only then may payments be applied to the second purchase. Thus, when you have finished paying the amount owed for the sofa, it is yours free and clear. Additional payments go toward the refrigerator, which remains as security for the loan until it has been paid for.

If, however, you had bought both of these items using a bank credit card instead of the store's charge plate, then neither item could be considered security. The store would have received payment from the bank that had issued the card. The bank itself, having demanded no security for the use of its card, could not take possession of the items you bought.

Although the merchandise could not be taken from you under this circumstance, the interest on the remaining debt will, of course, continue, and the amount you owe will increase substantially.

reading, expenditures are divided into several major categories with a number of subheadings below. When filling in the boxes, first deal with those marked by an asterisk. These are major recurring and fixed expenses, difficult, though in some cases not impossible, to cut. Then proceed to the rest, bearing in mind that some of them — public transportation, car-pool costs, physicians' and dentists' fees, for example — may also be hard to reduce.

When you finish listing all of your expenses, you may be astounded to find that you are spending a substantial amount of money on goods, services and activities that are relatively unimportant to you. For example, under meals away from home, you may be providing two teenagers with $2 per school day for lunches — money they usually spend on pizza or hot dogs. If each child attends school 180 days a year, you will be spending $720 for their lunches. For a fraction of that cost, you can prepare bag lunches for them at home.

If you live in the suburbs and ordinarily drive to work every day, you may be able to save a lot of money on transportation by joining or forming a car pool with your neighbors. A few do-it-yourself books in your library can show how to reduce expenditures enormously for routine repairs and maintenance in your home. Women who learn how to do their own hair can cut down on visits to the beauty parlor. Such a list can be almost endless.

Altering the Budget

A budget is not engraved in stone. Certainly when you and your family plan expenses based upon income and needs, you should try to be as realistic as possible. But you will undoubtedly find that in some areas you have underestimated your needs and in others you have, perhaps, overestimated them. You may, for example, discover that the car pool to work is just not possible if you are to get to your job on time. But do not ignore the budget you and your family have drawn up merely because some ideas don't work. Talk to other family members and search for a substitute cut in expenditures. Whenever a change must be made, account for it in the written budget.

This is particularly important when you receive additional income. The tendency at such times is to abandon the budget happily or, perhaps, just let it lapse. Yet it is as important to budget in new income as it was to keep a wary eye on expenditures before you received that raise or before your previously non-working spouse got a job. In fact, a sudden increase in family income can be almost as great a trap as a sudden decline. The impulse to go off on a spending spree, particularly if it is financed by charge cards, is a highly dangerous one. By all means, upgrade your standard of living modestly if that is what you want to do. And feel free to use those charge cards a bit more often than you used them in the past. But do so within the context of a revised budget. Otherwise expenditures are very likely to get out of hand again, and you may find yourself in even more difficulties than you were before.

Getting Out of Trouble

Unfortunately, too many people do not begin the budget-making process until they are already in desperate financial difficulties. The day comes when it is abundantly clear that the gap between outgo and income is far too great to be bridged by ordinary means. Suddenly bills are out of hand. You have no reserve funds and you have borrowed to the limit against your credit cards and from local banks. Your financial situation has deteriorated almost to the point of no return. Now truly drastic action must be taken. The first step is to make an inventory of your debts and assets.

Your Financial Balance Sheet. Such an inventory is absolutely essential, for unless you know in exact terms how much you owe and how much you own, you cannot make an honest appraisal of your financial situation.

There are two basic types of assets. One consists of cash and of stocks, bonds and the like that are easily converted into cash. These are generally called liquid or current assets. Then there are fixed assets, which can be converted into cash but only with some difficulty and over a period of time. Real estate, automobiles, furniture, interest in a business, a boat or long-term investments generally fall into this category. You may need the assistance of experts in figuring the worth of some of your fixed assets. If you wonder what your foreign sports car will bring on the open market, take it to a car dealer and see what he would be willing to pay you. Then go to your library or to your local bank and check on the worth of your car in the auto dealers' *Blue Book*. Similarly, if you don't know how much your house has appreciated or gone down in value since you purchased it, a real estate broker in your area will be happy to provide a realistic figure.

Debits, or liabilities, are your obligations, and they too may be divided into two types: long-term and short-term. The bill you owe your physician, your credit card balances, the taxes you haven't paid are all short-term liabilities. Long-term liabilities are such items as your mortgage and other loans that extend over several months or years.

Although there are many different ways of drawing up a financial balance sheet, the one appearing on page 383 is perhaps the easiest to deal with.

A financial balance sheet like this one should give you a good idea of what you might sell off in order to pay your most pressing obligations. You may well find, however, that you have very little of value that can easily and quickly be turned into ready money. Or you may decide that the last thing you want to do is sell your house or automobile. Fortunately, there are usually other options far less draconian in nature.

A Self-Help Plan

In most instances, creditors are the last people on earth who want to see you go broke. Not only are they likely to lose money immediately, they may want your business in the future. If your financial problems show any possibility of solution, most will be willing to help. But if they are to do so, they have to know that you *are* in serious difficulty. If you owe money to local merchants, department stores and thrift institutions, go to each of them and attempt to work out a new, easier payment schedule. You must be totally honest about your current financial condition and your future prospects. If you have been laid off from work, by all means say so. If you have had unusual medical expenses, tell them that as well. Even bank credit card companies will usually be willing to work with you to determine a new schedule of payments.

Your creditors would, of course, be happier if you could pay off your debts on time. But a new schedule of payment may somewhat mitigate their concern: you will, after all, be paying more in interest than if you had met your obligations when they were due. In addition, they have a selfish interest in saving you from bankruptcy, for then they would probably get only a fraction of the amount that you owe them.

The Role of Your Bank. The key to paying off your creditors will probably be the bank with which you had regular dealings. Probably that institution will be one of the largest, if not *the* largest, of all of your creditors. When approaching your bank for help, do not just walk in off the street. Call in advance and ask for an appointment with one of the officers. Bring with you all relevant papers concerning the amounts you owe and to whom you owe them. Take along the budget you have made out and your financial balance sheet. Naturally, your bank will be most interested in the money you owe it, and your banker's advice may be keyed primarily to liquidating that obligation quickly.

However, like all your other creditors, your banker has no interest in seeing you go broke. If you make your position clear, chances are good that he will help you work out a program of repayment you can live with. The banker may also suggest that you take out a consolidation loan. Whether this is a good or bad idea depends on your individual circumstances. If, for example, you owe large amounts in high-interest loans to finance companies or credit card organizations, a consolidation loan from a bank may save you money because the bank interest rate may be lower than the rates you are charged on these other accounts. Moreover, a consolidation loan will permit you to pay off all your other current obligations immediately while spreading out payments on the new loan over several years.

You should, however, be wary about taking out a consolidation loan, even on very good terms. First there is the temptation not to use all the proceeds of your new loan to pay off your other outstanding debts, but instead to splurge on something you want. Even if you resist this temptation, the fact that you used this money to wipe out old obligations may bring a flood of offers from credit card companies for new lines of credit. If you accept and resume your old spending habits, you will be far worse off than you were before you took out the loan.

If you agree to a consolidation loan from your bank, the banker may insist that this new obligation be secured, possibly by your house or other assets. This is not necessarily a bad thing, since a secured loan generally carries a smaller interest rate than one that is unsecured. If the security is your house, on which you are already carrying a mortgage, you will have gotten what is known as an equity loan. This is based upon the fact that your home has increased in value since you bought it and upon the fact that over the years you have reduced the principal of the original mortgage loan.

If at all possible, arrange a consolidation loan with a bank or savings and loan institution rather than with a finance company. The latter may offer you more money, but usually the interest charged will be much higher.

The Uncooperative Creditor. If you find that you cannot get, or do not want, a consolidation loan and wish instead to reschedule your debts, you will have to deal with each creditor individually. Most will probably be willing to help, but there may be one or two who will decline a rescheduling. In that case, try to arrange the rescheduling with your other creditors in a way that will enable you to concentrate on paying off the uncooperative ones first. If this cannot be done, your next move should be to consult a professional credit counselor.

The Collection Agency

If one or more of your loans is past due by several months and you have not made arrangements for rescheduling, you are likely to begin receiving letters announcing that the debts have been turned over to a collection agency. A lender has the right to do this with a past due loan. Because the agency's fee is a percentage of the amount it collects from you, its employees will be extremely diligent in trying to get you to pay off the obligation. In the past, there were few restrictions on the tactics used by collection agencies, and many debtors were harassed by phone calls at 3 A.M., or embarrassed to discover that their friends and relatives had been told of the unpaid debts. Today, most such harassing practices are illegal. For a discussion of the limits on collection agencies, see Chapter 9.

The Professional Debt Counselor

Throughout the United States there are organizations to assist people when they discover

CONSUMER ALERT

Credit Counseling for Profit

Perhaps you have seen the ads in your local newspaper, or heard them on a radio station. They promise to show you how to rid yourself of your debts without pain or sacrifice, and invite you to a seminar, usually held in a nearby hotel. Unfortunately, many organizations of this type thrive on bilking people who are already deeply in debt and frantic to find a way out. The "small fee," promised in the ad, may very well amount to a considerable sum, and the advice given often is nothing more than information on consolidation loans or bankruptcy procedures. In addition, it is not unusual for such organizations to have informal agreements with unscrupulous local lawyers. They refer their clients to these attorneys who then advise bankruptcy actions, often in cases when there are several alternatives to this drastic procedure.

In view of the fact that there are numerous nonprofit debt counseling services that charge virtually nothing for their advice and help, there seems little reason to pay a high fee to a profit-making company. But if you feel such an organization might help you, at least check its record with your local Better Business Bureau, the Chamber of Commerce, your state attorney general's office (addresses on page 48) or your state consumer protection agency (addresses on page 16.)

that their burden of debt is too much for them to handle. Some of these are purely local. Your banker will probably know whether there is such an agency in or near your community. Others are connected with the National Foundation for Consumer Credit, which has about 200 affiliates in 47 of the 50 states and the District of Columbia (see directory, page 397). These groups are generally known as Consumer Credit Counseling Services (CCCS).

These non profit services are funded by such organizations as banks, retailers and finance companies, by foundations and by a variety of businesses and community service agencies. Their primary purpose is to help people manage their finances realistically, so that they can handle their debts without resorting to the bankruptcy courts. In general, Consumer Credit Counseling Services do not charge for their work, though occasionally they may levy a small fee or ask for a contribution to help offset their direct expenses.

Most people who seek help from a CCCS need little more than the backing of the agency in a rescheduling of debt, and a plan for paying off old obligations without incurring new ones. If clients need more help, the CCCS will usually provide it by taking over some aspects of a family's financial life until all outstanding consumer debts are paid and the family can once more stand on its own. A small minority of clients are so deeply in debt that the CCCS can do little except give them advice on filing for bankruptcy.

The procedures of the CCCS vary slightly from region to region and state to state, but in general these steps are followed:

- A prospective client calls and asks for an appointment. Before scheduling it, the CCCS sends the client several papers to fill out. These usually include budget forms, financial balance sheets and a complete listing of creditors.
- After the completed forms are mailed back, a CCCS representative calls to set up an appointment. If the client is married, both husband and wife are expected to appear.
- At the first counseling session, the clients are expected to produce papers confirming their employment and salaries, and others relating to their financial status, such as mortgage payments, credit bills and the like.
- Using the budget forms already submitted and the information elicited during the interview, counselor and client together draw up a new financial information form that accurately lists all the clients' obligations and assets. This is the basic material that the counselor uses to help the clients achieve a rational debt management program.
- By the end of the first session, the clients will know what alternatives they have. There may be additional counseling sessions, or one may be enough to start the rehabilitation of the financial structure.

Depending upon a number of factors, including the extent to which the clients are in debt, their assets and income, their attitudes towards paying off their creditors and their past records in this regard, the counselor may offer one of two basic programs.

If the clients' debt is relatively easily managed, and their income is large enough to cover the necessities of life and to permit them to pay off obligations, it is often sufficient to show the debtors just how their finances can be rearranged so that their liabilities will be covered.

The Debt Management Program. There are, however, many cases in which more than this is required, in these instances, the CCCS counselor will recommend its debt management program. For example, the client's emotional state may make it impossible for him or her to handle all obligations personally. The imbalance between income and debts may be so large that continuing professional help is deemed necessary. In such cases, and with the client's approval, the CCCS takes over a part of the individual's financial affairs. Generally, the client continues to handle as much of his or her financial life as possible, while the CCCS deals with creditors whose bills are already in arrears.

While there will always be variations from one case to the next, the debt management program generally works as follows:

- When client and counselor agree that the program should be instituted, the CCCS immediately gets in touch with all creditors and asks them to participate by rescheduling the debts. A creditor who has turned a deaf ear to a debtor's personal plea for a rescheduling is more likely to agree once the CCCS has become involved.
- The client agrees to turn over a portion of his or her paycheck each week or month to the CCCS. The organization uses this money to pay off outstanding debts according to the new scheduling arrangement.
- To diminish the burden on the debtor, the CCCS generally attempts to convince creditors to waive or reduce interest or service charges. The agency cannot, of course, guarantee that all or even any of the creditors will be willing to comply.
- The client agrees to inform the CCCS as far in advance as possible if a payment to the agency is delayed because of a financial emergency, such as the loss of a job, necessary repairs on a car or a major medical problem.
- As much money as possible is left in the client's hands. If the client has been paying on a regular and up-to-date basis such bills as the mortgage and the utilities, he or she will be expected to continue meeting these obligations. Normally the CCCS deals only with debts that are in arrears.
- During the period that the debt management program is in effect, the client is expected to attend counseling sessions on such matters as budgeting and the proper use of credit. While the CCCS does not absolutely forbid the use of credit during the debt management period, it does hold the client's credit cards and will release them only for a specific purpose approved by the debt counselor.

If there is a medical emergency, for example, the counselor will first attempt to get the physicians involved to accept payments under the terms of the debt management program. If the doctors agree, it may not be necessary for the client to borrow against credit cards. If the physicians refuse to cooperate, the cards may then be turned over to the client for the express purpose of charging the medical expenses.

When a large, new expenditure — such as a medical emergency or the breakdown of a major appliance — adversely affects the client's financial condition, he or she sends those bills to the CCCS and the agency tries to persuade existing creditors to agree to a revised payment plan that takes the changed circumstances into account.

- Just before the completion of the debt management program — which usually lasts 36 months or less — there is a final counseling session, at which time a new budget is drawn up and new goals are set.

The Educational Effort

The National Foundation for Consumer Credit, its Consumer Credit Counseling Service affiliates, banks and other thrift institutions and various service organizations have all launched educational programs designed to help people deal with credit. Some banks offer seminars; speakers from community service groups often address school audiences; and many organizations publish a wide variety of pamphlets on the subject. For more information on available educational pro-

Debtors Anonymous: A Support Group

A few years ago a group of women who were in the habit of discussing their problems together noticed a common thread throughout their informal get-togethers: most of them had problems meeting the payments on their debts. Out of their discussions a new organization came into being, Debtors Anonymous, a support, self-help and information group that within a very short time had chapters in 10 states. The number of members is still growing rapidly.

Debtors Anonymous is an informal organization. There are no membership rolls, dues or officers. People interested in getting and staying out of debt simply show up at meetings. They discuss their own credit problems and listen to those of others. Sometimes there are discussions of the psychological aspects of overspending; on other occasions the meetings concentrate on making up budgets. Frequently there will be tips on how to apply for credit, where interest rates are lowest, and what protections consumers have through federal and state credit laws. Members also share experiences on a one-to-one basis — an individual who is deeply in debt may be helped by talking with another member whose situation was once similar but who has managed to become solvent once more.

Debtors Anonymous has four important goals:

- To help members create and maintain budgets that are realistic. During meetings members report how well they are adhering to budgets.
- To pair off members, with each person in the pair working to help the other resist the temptations of overspending and credit abuse.
- To educate debtors in all aspects of personal finances so that they can become knowledgeable about credit laws, credit rates and even about where to obtain all kinds of goods at the most advantageous prices.
- To help members decide what their long-term financial goals really are and how to attain them.

For further information about the organization, write to: Debtors Anonymous, Women's Center for Education and Career Advancement, 198 Broadway, Suite 200, New York, New York, 10038.

grams write: National Foundation for Consumer Credit, Suite 601, 8701 Georgia Avenue, Silver Springs, Maryland 20910.

Alternatives to Bankruptcy

Any credit counselor will tell you that declaring personal bankruptcy is a very serious step and should only be undertaken as a last resort. For many who are besieged by debt and harassed by creditors, there may yet be a few alternatives to outright bankruptcy. One may be an extension or lowering of debts arranged through a lawyer. This is the sort of service that a credit counseling agency often performs, but if the agency lacks sufficient status among creditors to secure their voluntary cooperation, it may be helpful to secure the services of a lawyer. An attorney who is well versed in credit and bankruptcy can approach creditors with an implied warning: that the debtor will seek relief through the bankruptcy courts. If, as a debtor, you have been unable to obtain help from a qualified credit counselor, ask the service for advice in finding an attorney with experience in representing clients in their dealings with creditors.

If an attorney cannot work out an agreeable arrangement for the extension or lowering of debt, your next step is the bankruptcy court. Here too, you have a choice between declaring a straight bankruptcy — Chapter 7 of the Bankruptcy Act of 1978 — or seeking the kind of arrangement that neither the credit counselor nor the attorney were able to work out: a lengthening of the period of repayment and, perhaps, a lowering of the debts — a procedure possible under Chapter 13 of the Bankruptcy Act.

Chapter 13: An Alternative to Straight Bankruptcy

For anybody who can possibly deal with it, a Chapter 13 procedure is generally preferable to a Chapter 7 straight personal bankruptcy. The primary difference between the two procedures is that a Chapter 13 permits the debtor to retain his or her assets and pay off creditors out of current assets or future income, whereas under Chapter 7 the debtor's non-exempt and unsecured assets must be sold to pay off creditors and discharge the debt. The debtor's future income is not affected in any way.

In a Chapter 13, the debtor proposes a plan to repay creditors over a certain time. This plan can be approved by the court even if all creditors do not agree to its terms. The law simply requires the debtor to make a "good faith" effort to repay his or her debts, so that each creditor receives as much under the plan as he or she would in a Chapter 7 bankruptcy.

Who May Apply for a Chapter 13? The primary qualification for applying is that the applicant have a regular income. Not too long ago, this was meant that the debtor be a regularly employed wage earner. In fact, this kind of relief from indebtedness used to be known as the Wage Earner's Plan. Today, the qualifications are somewhat looser, and an applicant who shows a continuing income from nearly any source — a small business, some other type of self-employment and the like — is apt to qualify.

Beginning a Chapter 13 Procedure. The debtor must first file the proper papers with the bankruptcy division of the nearest United States District Court. These forms, Set Number S3013, are essentially self-explanatory, and you can generally buy them at a large stationery store or secure them through the clerk of the court. At this point the debtor should probably decide whether or not to hire an attorney. Chapter 13 procedures tend to be less complex than those involved in Chapter 7, and it is often quite possible to complete the process without a lawyer's assistance. If the debtor has any problem filling out the forms, the clerk of the court will usually help. The local Chapter 13 trustee, whose name can be obtained from the bankruptcy court clerk, may also be of assistance.

From the time that the Chapter 13 papers are filed with the court, creditors are prohibited from acting to collect their debts. This "automatic stay" is designed to give the debtor a period of time to get his or her financial affairs in order and to develop a plan for repayment of debts.

Plan of Repayment. Perhaps the most important paper to be filed is the Debtor's Plan. This is essentially a household budget that lists income, general household expenses and the debtor's own assessment of how much is left over to pay off obligations on a month-by-month basis. It would probably be wise for the applicant to construct this plan with the aid of either a lawyer or a consumer credit counselor. The plan should be a totally honest and straightforward account of the debtor's income and expenses, though it need not include a breakdown of all debts. Remember, the latter is a court proceeding and any effort to hide income could result in the court's refusal to discharge the debtor's obligations.

Here is an example of such a budget.

Estimated Monthly Income

Husband's pay after taxes and other deductions	$700
Wife's pay after taxes and other deductions	250
Other income	70
TOTAL INCOME	$1,020

Estimated Monthly Expenses

(Debts, except for mortgage, not included)

Mortgage and real estate taxes	$400
Utilities	125
Clothing	18
Food	200
Insurance (amounts not deducted from salaries)	20
Commuting costs (not including car payments)	40
Uninsured medical	35
Union dues (if not deducted)	00
Nondeducted taxes	30

Support for nonresident dependent (child in college, for example) 00

Other necessary expenses (be specific) . 00

- TOTAL EXPENSES .... (estimate) $868
- Excess of income over expenses ... $152
- Total suggested monthly payments under plan $125

Working Out the Plan. After the debtor submits the budget and other necessary papers to the bankruptcy court, it arranges a meeting of all creditors, the Chapter 13 trustee who will administer the repayment plan, the debtor and the debtor's counsel, if there is one. At this hearing, sometimes called a confirmation hearing, creditors can object to the terms of the plan.

In bankruptcy, there are two general classifications of creditors — secured and unsecured. A secured creditor holds some type of security for repayment of the debt. For example, a bank that has loaned money to the debtor to purchase an automobile, and holds title to the auto as security, is a secured creditor. Unsecured creditors do not have any specific security for their debts. A debt is considered to be secured up to the value of the collateral on the day the debtor files a petition with the bankruptcy court. Any excess debt is considered unsecured. For example, a debtor may owe $4,000 on a car valued at $3,200. On the date of filing, the bank has an unsecured claim for $800. The debtor's Chapter 13 plan must provide for payments to each individual creditor, and all creditors of the same class must be treated alike. For example, the debtor can propose to pay all unsecured creditors 80 cents on the dollar over the length of a plan, but cannot propose to pay one unsecured creditor 40 cents on the dollar and another unsecured creditor 90 cents on the dollar.

During the meeting your creditors may ask you questions about your budget report and any other aspects of your financial life. Your plan for repayment will be inspected by the creditors, probably prior to the meeting. As the law stood in the past, all creditors had to vote in favor of the Chapter 13 plan. However, under current law, creditors may only object to the court approving a plan if it is not a "good faith" effort to repay debts, or if secured creditors will not receive, over the length of the plan, an amount equal to the value of their collateral on the date the debtor initially filed a petition with the court. If the court determines that these conditions are satisfied, it may approve the plan despite the objections of the creditors.

Final Actions. When the debtor and creditors have all agreed on a plan for extension, composition or a combination of both, or the court has approved a debtor's plan despite creditors' objections, the judge refers the plan to the local Chapter 13 trustee who administers the agreement. During the period the plan is in operation (usually 36 months, though it can be up to 60 months), the trustee receives a set amount each month from the debtor, deducts administrative expenses and disperses the rest to the creditors according to the agreed upon schedule.

Advantages of a Court-administered Debt Repayment Plan (Chapter 13)

If a debt repayment plan is at all workable, it offers several major advantages over a straight bankruptcy. The most important of these are as follows:

- The debtor avoids the taint of straight bankruptcy by acknowledging his or her obligation to repay debts, either in full or in part under a plan approved by the court.
- In most instances, creditors receive more through this option than through a straight personal bankruptcy.
- As with a Chapter 7 bankruptcy, creditors must cease all efforts to collect on outstanding loans as soon as the debtor files a debt repayment plan.
- The debtor retains ownership of current assets while paying off debts from future income.
- The debtor's credit rating is not nearly so adversely affected through this plan as through straight bankruptcy. Though a notation of participation in a court-administered repayment plan is made for 10 years on the debtor's credit report, reputable lending agencies may still find it in their interest to provide loans: after all, the debtor has acknowledged his or her obligations and is making an honest effort to pay them off.
- If the debtor, because of unforeseen financial reverses, cannot continue with the plan,

the court may declare all debts discharged so long as the creditors have received as much as they would have in a straight bankruptcy petition. Alternatively, the debtor, after making payments for some months, may then declare personal bankruptcy, if it seems advantageous to do so. Or the court may reassess the plan itself and order new terms that will more closely conform with the debtor's changed circumstances.
• Even when the debtor hires an attorney to help with the plan, legal costs are usually considerably less than with a Chapter 7 straight bankruptcy.
• Through participation in a court-administered repayment plan, debtors may become more capable of handling their finances and more realistic about incurring obligations.

Disadvantages of a Chapter 13

A court-administered repayment plan does have some drawbacks that a debtor should consider. Among these are:
• Debt-repayment obligations continue, though they may be extended in time and reduced in amount.
• Historically, 50 to 60 percent of debt repayment plans are not fulfilled, forcing the debtor into bankruptcy. In the end this can be considerably more expensive than if the debtor had originally opted for straight bankruptcy. However, under the Bankruptcy Reform Act of 1978, if circumstances change, judges are given wide discretionary power to alter repayment plans after they have gone into effect. The likelihood is that this will make it easier for debtors to fulfill their obligations under the plans.
• Though the stigma attached to court-administered debt repayment plans is not as great as with straight bankruptcy, a Chapter 13 does carry a financial taint.
• Because credit may be relatively easy to obtain, the debtor could be tempted to continue on his or her wayward course, leading once again to debt.

Straight Bankruptcy: Chapter 7

If as a debtor, you have concluded that a Chapter 13 procedure is not for you, and you have no other means of paying off your obligations, you may find youself in a position where a straight bankruptcy is your only out. Known as Chapter 7, from its place in the Bankruptcy Reform Act of 1978, this procedure differs in many important respects from a Chapter 13 action.
• In a straight bankruptcy, as in a Chapter 13 proceeding, once the petition is filed, all creditors (with certain rare exceptions) must immediately cease their efforts to collect. At some point during the proceeding, some or all of your debts will be discharged. (Exceptions from discharge are discussed below.) In a Chapter 7 proceeding, no effort is made to force the debtor to pay off his or her obligations in whole or in part through future earnings. Instead, a court-appointed trustee takes control of and sells whatever assets the debtor owned at the time the bankruptcy petition was filed, again with certain exceptions discussed below. A portion of the money derived from the sale is used to satisfy creditors after administrative, legal and other expenses have been paid.
• A notation will be made on your credit reports that you have gone bankrupt and will remain on these reports for 10 years — in some cases, even longer. This will make it extremely difficult, if not impossible, for you to secure normal credit during this period. (An exception: because you may not declare bankruptcy again for six years, certain lenders, particularly those who charge extremely high interest rates, may be ready to advance credit. Most creditors, however, will not deal with you.)
• Because creditors are satisfied out of the assets owned on the date the bankruptcy petition is filed, the trustee may not use your future earnings to pay the creditor in the bankruptcy proceeding.

Debts NOT Affected by Bankruptcy Proceedings

Although most debts are discharged through bankruptcy, not all are. Among the debts that are unaffected are the following:
• Back taxes owed federal, state, county or municipal governments, provided these taxes are less than three years old. Taxes overdue by more than three years may be discharged under a Chapter 7 bankruptcy.
• Obligations incurred by making false statements. Suppose, for example, that you secured a loan but on the application form you failed to list all of your debts. If a creditor can prove that the loan was given as a result of

Debt Insurance: A Hedge Against the Future

One of the major reasons people get into debt over their heads is because they contract credit obligations when times are good only to find themselves unemployed at some later time and thus unable to continue payments. Debt insurance — only rarely offered until recently — is now a fast-growing business that grants some protection to the debtor who is caught in that unfortunate situation.

Unlike credit insurance (routinely offered by banks with their loans) that discharges a debt only when the borrower dies or becomes disabled, debt insurance is specifically aimed at protecting the debtor in the event of job loss. Usually the term "job loss" includes not only outright dismissals but layoffs, strikes and lockouts. In order to qualify for most debt insurance policies, the buyer must have been employed for at least a year before making application. To receive benefits, the policyholder must usually have been jobless for a month, must be receiving unemployment benefits and must be able to show that he or she is actively searching for employment.

Debt insurance is not intended to pay off all of the policyholder's obligations. Rather, it usually offers payments only for a specified period of time or sum of money. If, for example, the policyholder has a bank loan that requires 24 monthly payments, most policies will pay the installments for six months. On revolving credit card accounts, a policy usually offers a minimum payment.

Premiums for debt insurance generally amount to about 3.5 percent of the loan or loans being covered. If, for example, you have a bank loan of $4,000, the premium will be $140. A number of insurance companies are now offering these policies, and they are available in several states. To find out more about these contracts, check with a local insurance agent. Be sure to read the terms of the policy carefully. If a particular policy states that it will cover you only if you have been dismissed from your job "without cause," make certain that this phrase does not mean that you will not be covered if you are fired because of an honest disagreement between you and your employer or because of economic circumstances over which you have no control.

your fraudulent statement, the debt will not be discharged. To protect yourself from such eventualities, it is wise when applying for credit to exaggerate by a bit the amount you actually owe. After you have answered questions on the application form concerning debts to banks, finance companies, department stores and credit card concerns, write in an item called "miscellaneous debts" and put down a figure you consider reasonable.

- Alimony and child support obligations.
- Debts that the applicant failed to list on his or her debt schedule when the bankruptcy petition was filed. If, for example, you filed for bankruptcy, but neglected to list a particular loan among your obligations, your debt to that lender will not be discharged.
- Certain types of education loans.
- Debts incurred from injuries to people or property that were held to be the result of malicious intent on the debtor's part. For example, if you tore down your neighbor's fence in a fit of pique, and were held legally liable for making financial restitution, your debt would not be cancelled by the bankruptcy procedure.

Secured Debts: A Special Category

A secured debt is one in which the lender holds a special type of interest known as a "security interest" in certain of the debtor's property until the obligation is paid off. Property that is subject to a security interest is called "collateral." Most automobile loans, for example, fall into this category. Though the borrower has the use of the car during the period he or she is paying for it, the lender holds a security interest and may repossess the vehicle if the buyer fails to live up to the terms of the loan. Similarly, a debt that is secured by household furnishings is a secured loan, and in the event the borrower defaults on the payments the furnishings may be seized by the lender.

After a debtor files a bankruptcy petition, the holder of a secured claim may seek court permission to repossess his or her collateral. If the value of the collateral is less than the amount outstanding on the loan, the court will probably either allow the creditor to repossess it or require the debtor to make monthly payments to offset the the depreciation on the collateral. If, on the other hand, the value of the property exceeds the amount outstanding on the loan, the property will go into the assets pool to be sold by the trustee. The secured creditor will be paid in full and any excess proceeds from the collateral will go to unsecured creditors. In general, it is unsecured creditors who lose the most in bankruptcy proceedings.

Other Assets Usually Not Taken to Satisfy Creditors

The Bankruptcy Reform Act of 1978 specifies certain assets that ordinarily are not taken to satisfy creditors. The states, however, are granted the power to substitute their own list of exempt property for the list contained in the Bankruptcy Code (see below). Included in this federal list of exempt property are the following:

- The major item that the debtor may retain is up to $7,500 worth of equity in his or her primary residence. This is known as the homestead exemption. In some states, in order to qualify the owner must file a homestead form with the county clerk or county recorder before filing for bankruptcy.
- Up to $1,200 equity in an automobile.
- Any item of household goods or furniture that has a value of not more than $200. If, for example, you have a sofa, two chairs and a coffee table in your living room and each is worth $180, none of these pieces can be seized to satisfy creditors. If the sofa is worth $250 and other items are worth less than $200, only the sofa may be claimed by the trustee.
- Personal jewelry valued at less than $500.
- Tools, valued at less than $750, that are necessary for your employment.
- Medically necessary devices, such as hearing aids, eyeglasses and wheelchairs, used by the debtor or his or her dependents.

States' Powers Over Exemptions

There is a major exception in federally exempt items. As was mentioned above, the federal Bankruptcy Reform Act of 1978 permits each state to specify its own exemptions, and a number of states have exercised this right. In such states, the debtor usually must use the state list rather than the federal one. To find out if your state has adopted its own exemption schedule, check with the clerk at the nearest U.S. district court.

In many instances, the state-permitted exemptions are considerably less generous to the debtor than the federal exemptions. But in a few states, particularly those in the Far West, the exemptions are more liberal than the federal law allows. For example, under certain circumstances, Californians may be permitted an exemption of up to $45,000 (in some cases $30,000) equity in a primary home. Some states permit more in one type of exemption and less in another than does the federal statute. In those instances — if you are not barred by state law from taking advantage of the federal list — you may choose between them. However, you must choose one *entire* list or the other. You cannot pick and choose from among items on the state and federal exemptions.

Bankruptcy Procedures

As is already apparent, going into personal bankruptcy can be a complicated business. Although it is possible to complete the procedures without professional help, anyone considering bankruptcy who has substantial assets would be well advised to consult an attorney.

To file for bankruptcy, you must complete a number of forms. Theoretically, there could be as many as 30, but not all of them are applicable to every case and you will probably have to complete only seven or eight. If you have a lawyer, he or she will know what is necessary and will help you complete these forms. If not, the clerk at your nearest federal district court may be willing to offer advice on the completion of the forms although he or she cannot offer legal aid or counsel.

Once the forms are complete and filed (they can be mailed to the court or you can deliver them in person) and a required small fee is paid, the debtor is immediately relieved of the necessity of fending off importunate creditors. They can no longer phone you or write to you demanding payment. In effect, you have turned over the question of debt repayment to the bankruptcy court system and from here on in, your creditors must deal with the bankruptcy trustee and not with you. (An exception to the rule: *secured* creditors, under certain circumstances, some of which are described above, may obtain court permission to repossess their collateral.)

Within two or three weeks of filing, you will receive notice of the first meeting of creditors. You *must* attend this meeting or your petition for bankruptcy will be denied. Appear with all of your financial records and be prepared to answer questions about your credit practices. Your creditors or their attorneys may question you concerning your financial affairs. Many of them, however, will not even bother to appear at the meeting. Unless you have significant assets it will probably not be worth their time and effort.

A creditor's failure to appear at this first meeting does not affect his or her right to file a claim in your bankruptcy. The deadline by which creditors must file their claims is set by either the Bankruptcy Code or the court. A creditor may seek to have his or her own debt declared non-dischargeable or may move to have your bankruptcy petition dismissed completely if you have somehow misled the court or otherwise shown bad faith. Motions to dismiss the entire proceeding are quite rare, however.

The trustee oversees the sale of your nonexempt assets and the funds derived from them are used to pay debts. First, all administrative expenses are paid. The next claimants to be satisfied are any people to whom you owe wages that were earned in the three months before you filed. The third, in order of preference, are the various levels of government to which taxes are owed. (Remember that in most instances, if these taxes are not paid in full from the sale of your assets, you remain liable for the remainder.) Finally, if there is any money left over — and often there is not — your creditors receive a percentage of what is due them.

At some point in the proceeding, the debtor is discharged by the court. He or she is no longer liable for the debts incurred prior to the filing of the bankruptcy petition (except for the debts cited above). The debtor is thus able to make a new start in life without a crushing burden of debts incurred earlier. However, he or she may not file a new bankruptcy petition for at least six years. A person who has gone bankrupt may seek new relief at any time, however, by filing a petition for a Chapter 13.

A Strategy for Bankruptcy

If you have determined that you cannot pay your debts and must declare bankruptcy, you will probably want to conserve as many of your assets as possible. In large measure, the way in which you proceed will depend upon the law in your state. If the federal exempt property list is operative in your state and the state list is less generous, you will, of course, file under the federal list. If the state list is more generous or meets your needs more closely than does the federal, you can choose the state list. However, you may live in a state in which the federal list is not available, in which case you will have no choice but to use the state listing of exempt property. Even so, you will probably have some room in which to maneuver.

Your primary goal, *before* formally filing a petition, will be to transfer as much property as possible to the exempt list. For example, you will want to take full advantage of the homestead exemption. Therefore you will try to increase your equity in your home to the maximum allowed by law. Remember to consult the state list of exempt properties as well as the federal, for in states where either can apply the state exemption on a homestead may be larger. As this is usually the most valuable item in a state's exempt property list, it pays to take full advantage of it. Keep in mind that such transfers of property must be made before filing for bankruptcy because after filing, the trustee, not the debtor, has control of your property.

One thing you may *not* do is transfer property to others to avoid having your assets taken by a bankruptcy trustee. You may not, for example, transfer your house to someone else unless the transfer was made at least 90 days before you filed for bankruptcy (one year if the person to whom it was transferred is in some way related to you). Similarly, you must

Glossary of Terms Used in Bankruptcy Proceedings

Attachment: A creditor's act of seizing property to be used to satisfy a claim.

Chapter 7: A straight bankruptcy proceeding under the Bankruptcy Code in which creditors are satisfied through the sale of the assets owned by the debtor on the day the bankruptcy was filed.

Chapter 13: A repayment plan under the Bankruptcy Code that permits a debtor to discharge his or her obligations out of future income as well as current assets. The plan usually includes an extension of the repayment periods and/or a reduction in the overall amount of the debt.

Discharge: The relief accorded a debtor from continued legal obligations to repay past debts.

Exempt assets: Property owned by the debtor on the date the bankruptcy is filed, which the trustee may not sell to pay the claims of creditors.

Homestead: Land or a dwelling which the debtor uses as his or her residence. A portion of this may be exempt from creditors' claims.

Lien: A legal interest in property to secure the payment of a debt or performance of an obligation.

Mechanic's lien: A lien created by law against certain property to secure payment for services rendered in erecting, repairing or otherwise improving that property. This particular type of lien has priority over most other liens.

Note: The written promise by a debtor to pay money at a specific rate over a specified period of time.

Priority: The order in which claims in a bankruptcy are paid.

Replevin: Legal action by a creditor to obtain possession of property to which he or she is entitled.

Secured debt: A debt whose repayment is backed by a security interest in certain of the debtor's property.

Security interest: An interest that a creditor may hold in certain property of the debtor. Entitles the creditor to repossess that property upon the debtor's default and gives the creditor priority to the property over creditors who do not hold a security interest.

Trustee: The person appointed by the court to take charge of the debtor's assets and arrange for their sale or to oversee a repayment plan to satisfy outstanding debts.

Unliquidated claim: A debt whose exact amount cannot be determined.

Unsecured debts: A debt whose repayment is not secured by a lien or a security interest in the debtor's property.

Wage earner plan: Another name used to describe a Chapter 13 bankruptcy repayment plan.

not hide any financial records from the court or make any kind of false or misleading statement either in your bankruptcy petition or when answering questions at a hearing. If you hide any asset or misrepresent your financial situation, the bankruptcy petition may be dismissed and you may be subject to criminal charges. In considering your financial tactics when preparing for bankruptcy, the wisest course is to consult an attorney, if it is at all possible.

Advantages of a Chapter 7 Petition

Given the complexities of a Chapter 7 (see page 405) personal bankruptcy, it may help to recapitulate some of its positive features from the viewpoint of the debtor.

- Once the petition is filed, creditors must cease all efforts to secure payment.
- When the debts have been discharged, the debtor is permanently relieved of most of his or her obligations.
- Payments to creditors come out of the debt-

(Continued on page 405)

Representative Offices of the Consumer Credit Counseling Service

Alabama
Consumer Credit Counseling Service of Alabama, Inc.
Executive Building, Suite 617
Montgomery, AL 36104

Alaska
Alaska Consumer Credit Counseling Service
P.O. Box 41996
Anchorage, AK 99509

Arizona
Money Management Counseling and Service
3056 North 33rd Avenue
Phoenix, AZ 85017

Tucson Family Debt Counselors
5834 Speedway
Tucson, AZ 85712

Arkansas
Crawford-Sebastian Community Development Council, Inc.
CCC Division
4831 Armour
Fort Smith, AR 72914

California
Consumer Credit Counselors of California
(State Administrative Office)
1429 Market Street
San Francisco, CA 94103

Consumer Credit Counselors of Kern County
1706 Chester Avenue
Bakersfield, CA 93301

Consumer Credit Counselors of Fresno, Inc.
2135 Fresno Street
Fresno, CA 93721

Consumer Credit Counselors of Los Angeles
650 South Spring Street
Los Angeles, CA 90014

Consumer Credit Counselors, Twin Cities
720 "D" Street
Marysville, CA 95901

Consumer Credit Counselors of East Bay (Oakland)
1212 Broadway
Oakland, CA 94612

Consumer Credit Counselors of the North Valley
P.O. Box 4044
Redding, CA 96099

Consumer Credit Counselors of Inland Empire
3679 Arlington Avenue
Riverside, CA 92506

Consumer Credit Counselors of Sacramento, Inc.
1815 "J" Street
Sacramento, CA 95814

Consumer Credit Counselors of San Diego
861 Sixth Avenue
P.O. Box 2131
San Diego, CA 92109

Consumer Credit Counselors of Orange County, Inc.
1616 East Fourth Street
Santa Ana, CA 92701

Consumer Credit Counselors of Stockton
242 North Sutter Street
Stockton, CA 95202

Consumer Credit Counselors of Ventura County
3445 Telegraph Road
Ventura, CA 93003

Colorado
Consumer Credit Counseling Service of Greater Denver, Inc.
311 Steele Street
Denver, CO 80206

Connecticut
Consumer Credit Counseling Service of Connecticut
36 Woodland Street
Hartford, CT 06105

Delaware
(See Financial Advisory Services of Eastern Pennsylvania)

District of Columbia
Consumer Credit Counseling and Educational Service of Greater Washington, Inc.
1012 14th Street, NW
Washington, DC 20004

Florida
Consumer Credit Counseling Service of North Florida, Inc.
2203 Art Museum Drive
Jacksonville, FL 32207

Consumer Credit Counseling Service of Pinellas County, Inc.
801 West Bay Drive
SE Bank Building
Largo, FL 33540

Consumer Credit Counseling Service of Central Florida, Inc.
710 East Colonial Drive
Orlando, FL 32803

Consumer Credit Counseling Service of West Florida, Inc.
Cary Building
2 North Palofox Street
P.O. Box 943
Pensacola, FL 32594

Consumer Credit Counseling Service of the Tampa Bay Area, Inc.
730 South Sterling Avenue
Tampa, FL 33609

Georgia
Consumer Credit Counseling Service of Greater Atlanta, Inc.
100 Edgewood Avenue, NE
Atlanta, GA 30303

Consumer Credit Counseling Service of Middle Georgia, Inc.
206 Fulton Federal Building
P.O. Box 31
Macon, GA 31202

Consumer Credit Counseling
Service of the Savannah
Area, Inc.
400 Mall Boulevard
Savannah, GA 31499

Hawaii
Consumer Credit Counseling
Service of Hawaii
1125 North King Street
Honolulu, HI 96817

Idaho
Consumer Credit Counseling
Service of Idaho, Inc.
P.O. Box 9264
Boise, ID 83707

Consumer Credit Counseling
Service of Northern
Idaho, Inc.
307 Weisburger Building
Lewiston, ID 83501

Consumer Credit Counseling
Service of Southeastern
Idaho, Inc.
P.O. Box 112
343 West Lewis
Pocatello, ID 83204

Illinois
Family Counseling Service
411 West Galena Boulevard.
Aurora, IL 60506

Family Counseling Center
201 East Grove
Bloomington, IL 61701

Family Service Association of
Greater Elgin Area
Financial Counseling Service
164 Division Street
Elgin, IL 60120

Central Illinois Credit
Counseling Service, Inc.
505 First National Bank Building
Peoria, IL 61602

Consumer Credit Counseling
Service of Springfield
1021 South Fourth Street
Springfield, IL 62703

Family Service Association of
DuPage County-Budget
Counseling/Debt
Management
402 West Liberty Drive
Wheaton, IL 60187

Indiana
Consumer Credit Counseling
Service of Tri-State, Inc.
1020 Southern Securities
Building
P.O. Box 883
Evansville, IN 47706

Consumer Credit Counseling
Service, Inc. of Allen County
345 West Wayne Street
P.O. Box 11403
Fort Wayne, IN 46858

Consumer Credit Counseling
Service of Northwest
Indiana, Inc.
2504 West Ridge Road.
Gary, IN 46408

Consumer Credit Counseling
Service of Central Indiana
615 North Alabama Street
Indianapolis, IN 46204

Family & Children's
Center, Inc.
CCCS Division
1411 Lincoln Way West
Mishawaka, IN 46544

Iowa
Consumer Credit Counseling
Service
A.I.D. Center
406 Fifth Street
Sioux City, IA 51101

Consumer Credit Counseling
Service of Eastern Iowa, Inc.
415 Maple Drive
Walford, IA 52351

Kansas
Consumer Credit Counseling
Service of Greater Kansas
City, Inc.
(See CCCS of Greater Kansas
City, Mo.)
Service available in both Kansas
and Missouri

Community Credit Counseling
Service of South Central
Kansas, Inc.
1404 "B" North Severance
P. O. Box 2361
Hutchinson, KS 67501

Consumer Credit Counseling
Service of Salina
Credit Bureau Building
125 South Seventh Street
P.O. Box 307
Salina, KS 67401

Consumer Credit Counseling
Service of Greater
Wichita, Inc.
Kaufman Building
212 South Market
Wichita, KS 67202

Louisiana
Consumer Credit Counseling
Service of Greater New
Orleans, Inc.
1539 Jackson Avenue
New Orleans, LA 70130

Maine
Credit Counseling Centers, Inc.
P.O. Box 1021
175 Lancaster Street
Portland, ME 04101

Maryland
Consumer Credit Counseling
Service of Maryland, Inc.
Bradford Federal Building
Fayette Street & Luzerne
Avenue
Baltimore, MD 21224

CCCS & Educational Service of
Montgomery County,
Maryland
10400 Connecticut Avenue
Kensington, MD 20795

Consumer Credit Counseling
Service of Southeast
Maryland, Inc.
Weber Professional Building
9418 Annapolis Road
Lanham, MD 20706

Massachusetts
Consumer Credit Counseling
Service of Eastern
Massachusetts, Inc.
8 Winter Street
Boston, MA 02108

Pioneer Valley Consumer Credit Counseling Service, Inc.
293 Bridge Street
P.O. Box 171
Springfield, MA 01101

Michigan
No affiliate reported

Minnesota

Consumer Credit Counseling Service of Minnesota, Inc.
924 Plymouth Building
Minneapolis, MN 55402

Family Service of Duluth, Inc.
600 Ordean Building
424 West Superior Street
Duluth, MN 55802

Mississippi
No affiliate reported

Missouri
Consumer Credit Counseling Service of Greater Kansas City, Inc.
3435 Broadway
Kansas City, MO 64111

Consumer Credit Counseling Service of Metropolitan St. Louis, Inc.
906 Olive Street
St. Louis, MO 63101

Springfield Area Family Debt Counselors
950 St. Louis Street
Springfield, MO 65806

Montana
Consumer Credit Counseling Service of Billings, Montana
2106 Central
Billings, MT 59102

Consumer Credit Counseling Service of Gallatin Valley, Inc.
2304 West Main
Bozeman, MT 59715

Consumer Credit Counseling Service of Cascade County
1125 Second Avenue, North
P.O. Box 2343
Great Falls, MT 59403

Consumer Credit Counseling Service of Western Montana, Inc.
P.O. Box 7521
Missoula, MT 59807

Nebraska
Consumer Credit Counseling Service of Nebraska, Inc.
P.O. Box 31002
Omaha, NE 68131

Nevada
Clark County Community Debt Counseling Service
2700 State Street
Las Vegas, NV 89101

New Hampshire
Family Financial Counseling Service Administrative Office
8 Union Street
P.O. Box 676
Concord, NH 03301

New England Center for Christian Financial Management
CCCS Division
P.O. Box 122
North Salem, NH 03073

New Jersey
Consumer Credit Counseling Service of New Jersey, Inc.
P.O. Box 97C
Convent Station, NJ 07961

Family & Children's Service of Monmouth County
191 Bath Avenue
Long Branch, NJ 07740

New Mexico
Consumer Credit Counseling Service of Albuquerque, Inc.
5318 Menaul, NE
Albuquerque, NM 87110

New York
Consumer Credit Counseling Services of the Capital Region, Inc.
11A Vatrano Road.
Albany, NY 12205

Consumer Credit Counseling Service of Buffalo, Inc.
43 Court Street
Buffalo, NY 14202

Family Service Association of Nassau County
129 Jackson Street
Hempstead, NY 11550

Consumer Credit Counseling Service of Rochester, Inc.
50 Chestnut Plaza
Rochester, NY 14604

Consumer Credit Counseling Service of Central New York, Inc.
114 South Warren Street
404 Larned Building
Syracuse, NY 13202

North Carolina
Consumer Credit Counseling Service of Western North Carolina, Inc.
331 College Street
P.O. Box 2192
Asheville, NC 28802

Consumer Credit Counseling Service
(A division of United Family Services)
301 South Brevard Street
Charlotte, NC 28202

Consumer Credit Counseling Service of Fayetteville
118 Gillespie Street,
P.O. Box 272
Fayetteville, NC 28302

Family Counseling Service, Inc. of Gaston County
318 South Street
Gastonia, NC 28052

Consumer Credit Counseling Service
(A division of Family and Childrens Services of Greater Greensboro, Inc.)
1301 North Elm Street
Greensboro, NC 27401

Consumer Credit Counseling Service
No. 17 Highway 64-70 SE
Hickory, NC 28601

Consumer Credit Counseling
(A division of Family Services of Wake County, Inc.)
3803 Computer Drive
Raleigh, NC 27609

Consumer Credit Counseling Service
Family Service/Travelers Aid
208 First Union National Bank Building
P.O. Box 944
Wilmington, NC 28402

Consumer Credit Counseling Service of Forsyth County, Inc.
440 First Union National Bank Building
Winston-Salem, NC 27101

North Dakota

The Village Family Service Center
1721 South University Drive
Fargo, ND 58103

Ohio

Family Services of Summit County
CCCS Division
212 East Exchange Street
Akron, OH 44304

Consumer Credit Counseling Service
618 Second Street, NW
Canton, OH 44703

Consumer Credit Counseling Service of Northeastern Ohio
423 Euclid Avenue
Cleveland, OH 44114

Consumer Credit Counseling Service of Central Ohio, Inc.
620 East Broad Street
Columbus, OH 43215

Lutheran Social Service of the Miami Valley
CCCS Department
573 Superior Avenue
Dayton, OH 45407

Family Service of Butler County
CCCS Division
111 Buckeye Street
Hamilton, OH 45011

Consumer Credit Counseling Service of Portage County
302 North Depeyster
Kent, OH 44240

Consumer Credit Counseling Service of Columbiana County
964 North Market Street
P.O. Box 213
Lisbon, OH 44432

Consumer Credit Counseling Service
Family Counseling Service
122 West Church Street
Newark, OH 43044

Consumer Credit Counseling Program
1704 North Road, SE
Heaton Square
Warren, OH 44484

Children's & Family Service
CCCS Division
535 Marmion Avenue
Youngstown, OH 44502

Oklahoma

Consumer Credit Counseling Service of Central Oklahoma, Inc.
2519 Northwest 23rd,
P.O. Box 75405
Oklahoma City, OK 73147

Credit Counseling Centers of Oklahoma, Inc.
2140 South Harvard
P.O. Box 4450
Tulsa, OK 74104

Oregon

Consumer Credit Counseling Service of Linn-Benton, Inc.
201 West First
P.O. Box 1006
Albany, OR 97321

Consumer Credit Counseling Service of Central Oregon, Inc.
2115 NE First Street
Bend, OR 97701

Consumer Credit Counseling Service of Lane County, Inc.
110 East 16th
Eugene, OR 97401

Consumer Credit Counseling Service of Southern Oregon, Inc.
10 North Central
Medford, OR 97501

Coos-Curry Consumer Credit Counseling Service
Pony Village
North Bend, OR 97459

Consumer Credit Counseling Service of Oregon, Inc.
3420 SE Powell Boulevard
P.O. Box 42155
Portland, OR 97242

Consumer Credit Counseling Service of Roseburg, Inc.
P.O. Box 1011
Roseburg, OR 97470

Consumer Credit Counseling Service of Mid-Williamette Valley, Inc.
665 Cottage, NE
Salem, OR 97301

Pennsylvania

Consumer Credit Counseling Service of Lehigh Valley, Inc.
411 Walnut Street
Allentown, PA 18101

Financial Advisory Services of Eastern Pennsylvania
Constitution Building
1950 Street Road
Cornwells Heights, PA 19020

Consumer Credit Counseling Service
110 West 10th Street
Erie, PA 16501

Consumer Credit Counseling Service of Delaware Valley
(also serving southern New Jersey)
1211 Chestnut Street
Philadelphia, PA 19107

Consumer Credit Counseling Service of Western Pennsylvania, Inc.
The Bank Tower
307 Fourth Avenue
Pittsburgh, PA 15222

Consumer Credit Counseling Service of Northeastern Pennsylvania, Inc.
402 Connell Building
North Washington Street
Scranton, PA 18503

Rhode Island

Consumer Credit Counseling Division
Rhode Island Consumers' Council
365 Broadway
Providence, RI 02909

South Carolina

Consumer Credit Counseling Service of Greater Charleston, S.C.
3005 West Montague
Charleston, SC 29405

Family Service Center
1800 Main Street
P.O. Box 7876
Columbia, SC 29201

Family Counseling Service-Travelers Aid for Greenville County, Inc.
300 University Ridge
P.O. Box 10306
Federal Station
Greenville, SC 29603

South Dakota
Consumer Credit Counseling Service of the Black Hills
P.O. Box 14
Seventh and Kansas City Streets
Rapid City, SD 57701

Tennessee
Family & Children's Services of Chattanooga
CCCS Division
317 Oak Street
Chattanooga, TN 37403

Consumer Credit Counseling Service of Greater Knoxville, Inc.
705 Broadway
P.O. Box 3343
Knoxville, TN 37917

Credit Counseling Service of Memphis-Shelby County
81 Madison
Memphis, TN 38103

Consumer Credit Counseling Service of Metropolitan Nashville
109 Third Avenue, North
Nashville, TN 37201

Texas
Child and Family Service
CCCS Division
2001 Chicon Street
Austin, TX 78722

Money Management Counseling & Services
3210 Reid Drive
Corpus Christi, TX 78404

Consumer Credit Counseling Service of Greater Dallas, Inc.
5415 Maple Avenue
Dallas, TX 75235-7490

Consumer Credit Counseling Service of Greater Fort Worth
807 Texas Street
Fort Worth, TX 76102

Consumer Credit Counseling Service of Houston & the Gulf Coast Area, Inc.
3215 Fannin Street
Houston, TX 77004

Consumer Credit Counseling of North Central Texas, Inc.
203-A West Louisiana Street
McKinney, TX 75069

Utah
Community Consumer Credit Counseling Service of Northern Utah, Inc.
295 30th Street,
P.O. Box 547
Ogden, UT 84403

Consumer Credit Counseling Service of Utah, Inc.
220 East, 3900 South
Salt Lake City, UT 84107

Vermont
(See New Hampshire)

Virginia
Consumer Credit Counseling and Educational Service of Northern Virginia
6911 Richmond Highway
Alexandria, VA 22306

Consumer Credit Counseling and Educational Service of Northern Virginia
3541 Chain Bridge Road
Fairfax, VA 22030

Peninsula Family Service and Travelers Aid, Inc.
CCCS Division
1520 Aberdeen Road
P.O. Box 7315
Hampton, VA 23666

Consumer Credit Counseling Service of Tidewater (Division of Family Service/ Travelers Aid)
222 Nineteenth Street, West
Norfolk, VA 23517

Consumer Credit Counseling Service of Virginia, Inc.
6 North Sixth Street
Richmond, VA 23219

Consumer Credit Counseling Service of Roanoke Valley, Inc.
State and City Building
104 West Campbell Avenue
Roanoke, VA 24011

Washington
Consumer Credit Counseling Service of the Tri-Cities
113 West Kennewick Avenue
P.O. Box 6551
Kennewick, WA 99336

Consumer Credit Counseling Service of Seattle
2316 Sixth Avenue
Seattle, WA 98121

Consumer Credit Counseling Service of Tacoma-Pierce
11300 Bridgeport Way, SW
Tacoma, WA 98499

Consumer Credit Counseling Service of Yakima Valley
1218 West Lincoln
Yakima, WA 98902

West Virginia
Consumer Credit Counseling Service of the Kanawha Valley
503 Terminal Building
8 Capitol Street
Charleston, WV 25301

Consumer Credit Counseling of Family Service, Inc.
1007 Fifth Avenue
Huntington, WV 25701

Consumer Credit Counseling Service of the Mid-Ohio Valley, Inc.
410½ Market Street
P.O. Box 454
Parkersburg, WV 26101

Children and Family Service Association
CCCS of the Upper Ohio Valley
11th and Chaplin Streets
Wheeling, WV 26003

Wiconsin
Madison Consumer Credit Counseling Service Division of Family Service
214 North Hamilton Street
Madison, WI 53703

Wyoming
Consumer Credit Counseling Service of Wyoming, Inc.
145 West 9th
P.O. Box 215
Casper, WY 82601

United States Bankruptcy Courts

Alabama
Northern District
500 South 22nd Street
Birmingham, AL 35233

Middle District
One Court Square
Lee Street
P.O. Box 1248
Montgomery, AL 36192

Southern District
106 U.S. Courthouse
P.O. Box 2865
Mobile, AL 36602

Alaska
Federal Building
701 C Street
P.O. Box 47
Anchorage, AK 99513

Arizona
U.S. Courthouse
230 North First Avenue
Phoenix, AZ 85025

Arkansas
600 West Capitol
P.O. Drawer 2381
Little Rock, AR 72203

California
Northern District
450 Golden Gate Avenue
P.O. Box 36053
San Francisco, CA 94102

Eastern District
8038 U.S. Courthouse
650 Capitol Mall
Sacramento, CA 95814

Central District
U.S. Courthouse
312 North Spring Street
Los Angeles, CA 90012

Southern District
U.S. Courthouse
San Diego, CA 92189

Colorado
400 Columbine Building
1845 Sherman Street
Denver, CO 80203

Connecticut
U.S. Courthouse
450 Main Street
Hartford, CT 06103

Delaware
U.S. Courthouse
844 King Street
Wilmington, DE 19801

District of Columbia
U.S. Courthouse
3rd and Constitution
Avenue, NW
Washington, DC 20001

Florida
Northern District
110 East Park Avenue
Tallahassee, FL 32301

Middle District
700 Twiggs Street
Tampa, FL 33602

Southern District
1401 Federal Building
51 SW First Avenue
Miami, FL 33130

Georgia
Northern District
Richard B. Russell Building
75 Spring Street, SW
Atlanta, GA 30303

Middle District
126 U.S. Courthouse
P.O. Box 90
Mulberry and Third Streets
Macon, GA 31202

Southern District
213 U.S. Courthouse
P.O. Box 8347
Savannah, GA 31412

Guam
P.O. Box D C
Agana, GU 96910

Hawaii
New Federal Building
P.O. Box 50121
Honolulu, HI 96850

Idaho
Eighth and Bannock Streets
P.O. Box 1278
Boise, ID 83701

Illinois
Northern District
U.S. Courthouse
219 South Dearborn Street
Chicago, IL 60604

Central District
327 U.S. Courthouse
P.O. Box 2438
600 East Monroe Street
Springfield, IL 62705

Southern District
Post Office Building
750 Missouri Avenue
East St. Louis, IL 62202

Indiana
Northern District
152 U.S. Courthouse
204 South Main Street
South Bend, IN 46601

Southern District
107 U.S. Courthouse
46 East Ohio Street
Indianapolis, IN 46204

Iowa
Northern District
Federal Building and
U.S. Courthouse
P.O. Box 4371
Cedar Rapids, IA 52407

Southern District
318 U.S. Courthouse
East First and Walnut Streets
Des Moines, IA 50309

Kansas
303 U.S. Courthouse
401 North Market Street
Wichita, KS 67202

Kentucky
Eastern District
434 Federal Building
P.O. Box 1050
Lexington, KY 40588

Western District
414 U.S. Courthouse
601 West Broadway
Louisville, KY 40202

Louisiana
Eastern District
U.S. Courthouse
500 Camp Street
New Orleans, LA 70130

Middle District
352 U.S. Courthouse
Baton Rouge, LA 70801-1770

Western District
3A10 Federal Building
500 Fannin Street
Shreveport, LA 71101

Maine
U.S. Courthouse
156 Federal Street
Portland, ME 04101

Maryland
201 U.S. Courthouse
101 West Lombard Street
Baltimore, MD 21201

Massachusetts
212 John W. McCormack
Post Office and Courthouse
Boston, MA 02109

Michigan
Eastern District
231 West Lafayette
Detroit, MI 48226

Western District
746 Federal Building
110 Michigan Street, NW
Grand Rapids, MI 49503

Minnesota
600 Galaxy Boulevard
330 Second Avenue, South
Minneapolis, MN 55401

Mississippi
Northern District
344 May Building
P.O. Box 1558
618 Washington Avenue
Greenville, MS 38701

Southern District
1619 Deposit Guaranty Bank Building (Old)
P.O. Drawer 2448
Jackson, MS 39201

Missouri
Eastern District
730 U.S. Courthouse
1114 Market Street
St. Louis, MO 63101

Western District
913 U.S. Courthouse
811 Grand Avenue
Kansas City, MO 64106

Montana
432 Northwestern Bank Building
21 Third Street, North
Great Falls, MT 59401

Nebraska
8419 New Federal Building
P.O. Box 428
Downtown Station
Omaha, NE 68101

Nevada
U.S. Courthouse
300 Las Vegas Boulevard, South
Las Vegas, NV 89101

New Hampshire
North Cotton Federal Building
275 Chestnut Street
Manchester, NH 03103

New Jersey
U.S. Post Office and Courthouse
402 East State Street
Trenton, NJ 08608

New Mexico
11006 Federal Building and U.S. Courthouse
500 Gold Avenue
P.O. Box 546
Albuquerque, NM 87102

New York
Northern District
311 U.S. Courthouse
Utica, NY 13503

Southern District
U.S. Courthouse
40 Foley Square
New York, NY 10007

Eastern District
1635 Privado Road
Westbury, NY 11590

Western District
312 U.S. Courthouse
68 Court Street
Buffalo, NY 14202

North Carolina
Eastern District
P.O. Drawer 2807
Wilson, NC 27893

Middle District
418 U.S. Post Office and Courthouse
324 Market Street
P.O. Drawer C-2
Greensboro, NC 27402

Western District
209 Post Office Building
401 West Trade Street
P.O. Box 32397
Charlotte, NC 28232

North Dakota
P.O. Box 1110
Court and Federal Building
655 First Avenue, North
Fargo, ND 58108

Ohio
Northern District
421 U.S. Courthouse
Public Square
Cleveland, OH 44114

Southern District
149 U.S. Courthouse
85 Marconi Boulevard
Columbus, OH 43215

Oklahoma
Northern District
4-540 U.S. Courthouse
333 West 4th
Tulsa, OK 74103

Eastern District
520 McCulloch Building
P.O. Box 130
Okmulgee, OK 74447

Western District
Post Ofice Building
201 Dean A. McGee Avenue
Oklahoma City, OK 73102

Oregon
900 Orbanco Building
1001 SW Fifth Avenue
Portland, OR 97204

Pennsylvania
Eastern District
3726 U.S. Courthouse
601 Market Street
Philadelphia, PA 19106

Middle District
217 Federal Building
197 South Main Street
Wilkes-Barre, PA 18701

Western District
1602 Federal Building
1000 Liberty Avenue
Pittsburgh, PA 15222

Puerto Rico
Federal Building and
U.S. Courthouse
Ch. 105D
Chardon Street
Hato Rey, PR 00918

Rhode Island
409 U.S. Courthouse
Exchange Street
Providence, RI 02903

South Carolina
316 U.S. Courthouse
1100 Laurel Street
P.O. Box 1448
Columbia, SC 29202

South Dakota
Federal Building and
Courthouse
400 South Phillips Avenue
Sioux Falls, SD 57102

Tennessee
Eastern District
343 Federal Building
P.O. Box 1189
Chattanooga, TN 37401

Middle District
750 U.S. Courthouse
Eighth Avenue and Broadway
Nashville, TN 37203

Western District
1160 Federal Building
167 North Main Street
Memphis, TN 38103

Texas
Northern District
U.S. Courthouse
1100 Commerce Street
Dallas, TX 75242

Southern District
U.S. Courthouse
515 Rusk Street
Houston, TX 77002

Eastern District
300 U.S. Post Office and
Courthouse
214 West Ferguson Street
P.O. Box 117
Tyler, TX 75710

Western District
Post Office Building
Alamo Plaza
1615 East Houston Street
P.O. Box 1439
San Antonio, TX 78295

Utah
361 U.S. Courthouse
350 South Main Street
Salt Lake City, UT 84101

Vermont
Gryphon Building
P.O. Box 865
Rutland, VT 05701

Virgin Islands
P.O. Box 720
Charlotte Amalie
St. Thomas, VI 00801

Virginia
Eastern District
1100 East Main Street
P.O. Box 676
Richmond, VA 23206

WesternDistrict
New Federal Building
2nd Street and Franklin
Road, SW
P.O. Box 2390
Roanoke, VA 24010

Washington
Eastern District
304 U.S. Post Office Building
904 West Riverside Avenue
P.O. Box 2164
Spokane, WA 99201

Western District
220 U.S. Courthouse
1010 Fifth Avenue
Seattle, WA 98104

West Virginia
Northern District
332 Federal Buiding and
U.S. Courthouse
12th and Chapline Streets
P.O. Box 70
Wheeling, WV 26004

Southern District
P.O. Box 3924
Charleston, WV 25339

Wisconsin
Eastern District
333 Federal Building
517 East Wisconsin Avenue
Milwaukee, WI 53202

Western District
44 East Mifflin Street
P.O. Box 548
Madison, WI 53701

Wyoming
New Post Office and Courthouse
2120 Capitol Avenue
P.O. Box 1107
Cheyenne, WY 82001

or's assets at the time the bankruptcy petition is filed rather than from assets acquired later, such as future earnings.

• Some assets are exempt from seizure, thus leaving the debtor with a financial base on which to build a new life.

Disadvantages of a Chapter 7 Bankruptcy

Though a straight bankruptcy procedure offers a relatively simple method of relieving the burden of debt, it has numerous disadvantages. Here, too, a recapitulation is in order.

• Considerable stigma is still attached to bankruptcy, although this varies from place to place and from time to time. In periods of recession or depression when many people are having severe financial difficulties, those declaring personal bankruptcy are generally treated with more sympathy than they would be in prosperous times.

• A notation of bankruptcy appears on credit reports for at least 10 years and, in many cases, for an even longer period. This may make credit extremely difficult to get except on the most onerous terms. Worse yet, in some situations a credit-reporting firm may continue to state that you have gone bankrupt even decades after the event. For example, if you apply for a well-paying job and your prospective employer asks for a credit report stipulating that it is for purposes of employment, the reporting agency is within its rights to note that you declared personal bankruptcy even 25 or more years ago.

• If the debtor's assets are large, he or she is likely to lose many expensive possessions.

• Personal bankruptcy can be declared only once every six years. If new financial difficulties are encountered, the bankruptcy route is foreclosed unless the required period has elapsed.

Getting in over your head financially is, at the very least, a humiliating, emotionally painful experience. It can also have a disastrous effect on family relationships and, if serious enough, can wreck careers and even lives. Often an individual or family arrives at this crisis state through a series of unfortunate circumstances — a prolonged period of unemployment, huge medical bills, a severe economic slump that wrecks a small business — that are beyond anyone's control. But probably the majority of people simply drift into deep financial waters like careless swimmers who suddenly realize they have let themselves get dangerously far from shore.

Oscar Wilde once observed that he could resist everything but temptation. As consumers, many of us are in that category. We are exposed daily to seductive advertising for everything from exciting new automobiles to wondrous trips to Zanzibar, all on a buy-now, pay-later basis. Charge accounts and credit cards can convert desires into reality immediately and, at least for the moment, painlessly — no reaching into the wallet or purse for real money, not even the writing of a check on the scene and deducting the amount from our bank balance. No wonder the legendary fiddler, who eventually must be paid in hard cash, seems a remote figure.

"Know thyself" should be a primary commandment for every consumer. It is mandatory for those who want to stay out of serious financial trouble but, like Oscar Wilde, find temptation irresistible. People who really want to lose or control weight but know that self-discipline is not their strong suit, banish calorie-rich snacks from their homes. It's all too easy to tell oneself that a few pieces of candy or a handful of salted nuts are not important.

Credit can be an enormously helpful and convenient financial aid for those who can handle it sensibly. It can be as dangerous as an addictive drug for those who cannot. For such consumers, credit cards and charge accounts belong in a locked dresser drawer, not readily available in a wallet or purse. Signing of an agreement to buy something on time payments must be viewed as a most serious pledge, to be made only after a thoughtful assessment of the need for the item.

This does not mean eliminating all uses of credit from your economic life. It does mean seeing each new obligation you assume in perspective, as an addition to the debts you have already incurred. Most of all, it means taking an honest, realistic look at your current economic situation and asking yourself whether you are being a shrewd manager of your money or simply an indulgent one.

Acknowledgments

Among the many organizations and individuals helpful in the preparation of this volume, the following gave especially generously of their time and expert knowledge:

- Advertising Research Foundation
- Better Business Bureaus throughout the country and Karl Lauby of the Metropolitan NY Better Business Bureau in particular
- Consumer Federation of America
- Consumers Union
- Direct Mail Association
- Consumer Frauds and Investment Frauds Divisions, NY State Attorney General's Office
- Clarence Ditlow, Center for Auto Safety
- Jane Downey, American Movers Conference
- Richard E. Lerner, American Arbitration Association
- Penelope Longbottom, National Automobile Dealers Association
- Peggy Penecost, Automotive Information Council
- Sam Schiff, Insurance Information Institute
- Jane Moss Snow, Home Owners Warranty Corporation
- Lea Thompson, WRC-TV, Washington, D.C.
- Robert Waldron, American Council of Life Insurance
- Allan Wilbur, American Automobile Association

Contributors

Oliver Allen

Peter M. Chaitin

Raymond Carroll

Neil Felshman

Nancy E. Gross

Lynne Rogers

Ogden Tanner

Bernard A. Weisberger

Josleen Wilson

Index

A

B

C

D

E

F

G

H

I

J

K

L

M

N

O

P, Q

R